Peter Kenney SJ, 1779–1841

Peter Kenney SJ

1779–1841

The Restoration of the Jesuits in Ireland, England, Sicily, and North America

Thomas Morrissey SJ

With a Foreword by
Professor Emmet Larkin

THE CATHOLIC UNIVERSITY OF AMERICA PRESS

Set in 10.5 on 12.5 Ehrhardt
by Verbatim Typesetting & Design for
THE CATHOLIC UNIVERSITY OF AMERICA PRESS
620 Michigan Avenue N.E., Washington, D.C. 20064

Library of Congress Cataloging-in-Publication Data

Morrissey, Thomas J.
    As one Sent: Peter Kenney SJ, 1779-1841: The restoration of the Jesuits in Ire-
land, England, Sicily, and North America.
        p.   cm.
    Includes bibliographical references and index.
    ISBN 978-0-8132-2713-9
    I. Title
    BX4705-K386M67   1996
    271'.5302—dc20   96-32317
    [B]   CIP

FOREWORD

The Roman Catholic Church in pre-Famine Ireland (1780-1850) was extraordinarily rich in significant personalities. Among these makers of the modern Irish Church must be included John Thomas Troy and Daniel Murray, successively archbishops of Dublin, Patrick Joseph Plunkett, bishop of Meath, Francis Moylan, bishop of Kerry and then Cork, James Warren Doyle, bishop of Kildare and Leighlin, John MacHale, archbishop of Tuam, Peter Kenney, first superior of the restored Society of Jesus in Ireland, Theobald Mathew, the celebrated Capuchin Temperance priest, Nano Nagle, Mary Aikenhead, and Catherine McAuley, founders respectively of the Presentation Sisters, the Sisters of Charity, and the Sisters of Mercy, Ignatius Rice, founder of the Irish Christian Brothers, and finally Daniel O'Connell, the greatest of all Irish-Catholic laymen before or since. What is most remarkable about this galaxy is that none of the stars, except Daniel O'Connell, and now Peter Kenney, have, as yet, received a modern biography worthy of their historical importance. In that sense this very fine biography by Thomas Morrissey is a pioneering work which sets a very high standard for what yet remains to be done.

Father Morrissey's vantage ground has been enhanced by the fact that Peter Kenney's achievements, by any standard or measure, were remarkable. In the thirty years after he returned to Ireland in 1811 at the age of thirty-two, until his death in 1841, Kenney was the key figure in the reorganisation of the restored Society of Jesus in both Ireland and the United States. In the great tradition of the Society he strove for wholeness and holiness in his ministries as pastor, educator, and administrator. As a pastor, he had a deep and abiding concern for the cure of souls, which he fulfilled by becoming the pre-eminent Catholic preacher of his day in the English-speaking world, as well as a most influential spiritual director, confessor, and retreat master. He was also intimately involved in the founding of the Loreto Sisters and the Sisters of Charity in Dublin as well as in the affairs of the Irish Christian Brothers for twenty years. As an educator, Kenney made an equally profound contribution in Ireland and America. Shortly after his return to Ireland, he was requested by the Irish bishops to assume the vice-presidency of St Patrick's College at Maynooth, the national seminary, and he quickly helped to bring order and stability to that much troubled institution. Several years later he founded in rapid succession the two most prestigious Jesuit colleges in Ireland, Clongowes and Belvedere, and as Visitor and superior to the American mission he later reformed and reorganised both Georgetown and Saint Louis Universities, thus ensuring at very critical moments in their history their survival. Finally, as an administrator, Kenney displayed extraordinary talent and energy both in Ireland and America. In Ireland, he early established the independence of the

Jesuit mission from the English Jesuit province, and eventually had the satisfaction of successfully recommending that the Irish mission be raised to the
status of a vice-province. In America, Kenney was instrumental in reforming
the Maryland mission, and then having it erected into a full province of the
Society, while at the same time preserving the independence of the Missouri
mission of the Maryland province, thus laying the foundation for the growth
and rapid expansion of the Society in the United States. In all of his endeavours, pastoral, educational, and administrative, in Ireland and the United
States, moreover, Kenney was scrupulous in cultivating the support of the
bishops, whose good will was crucial to the long-term success of the Society's
mission in those two countries.

In his rendering of Kenney's spectacular career on two continents, however, Father Morrissey has not only given point to all the achievements in an
exquisitely detailed narrative that supplies this biography with its marvellous
texture and underpins its authority as a presentation, but he has also at the
same time answered the question fundamental to all biography by explaining
what indeed made Kenney go. Father Morrissey makes it clear that Kenney
was driven by his duty to God and man and governed in that duty by obedience. Kenney was, moreover, like all men, in Pascal's phrase, "a weak reed",
and his frailties and faults are as compelling in this presentation as his gifts
and abilities are admirable. In pursuing his duty to God and man Kenney was
also a compassionate man, whose moral indignation bristled at injustice and
man's inhumanity to man. In a word, this is the compelling story of a rare and
good man and a great human being.

Emmet Larkin
The University of Chicago

August 12, 1996

CONTENTS

LIST OF ILLUSTRATIONS

CREDITS

5 Tourism Association of Milazzo, Sicily; 7 the Archivist and Professor P.J. Corish, Maynooth College; 8, 26, 27 the parish priest of Gardiner Street church, Dublin; 9, 11, 12 the Archivist, Irish Christian Brothers, Irish Sisters of Charity and the Sisters of Loreto respectively; 15, 16, 17 Special Collections, Lavinger Library, Georgetown University; 18, 19, 22 Jesuit Missouri Province Archives.

On the occasion of the bicentenary of the Restoration of the Society of Jesus, 2014-2015, it seemed appropriate to re-issue under a new title the much acclaimed *As One Sent. Peter Kenney, S.J., 1779-1841. His Mission in Ireland and North America*; for Kenney grew up, was educated, and ordained while the general body of the Jesuits remained suppressed, and then became a major figure in the years following the Restoration.

The brief of suppression of the Society of Jesus was issued by Pope Clement XIV in 1773 as a result of intensive and persistent pressure from the Bourbon monarchs of France, Spain, Naples, and Parma. The brief required that it be promulgated by the bishop in each diocese. Catherine the Great of Russia refused to permit promulgation in her dominions. The Jesuits continued there. In time, other Popes approved *sotto voce* of their continuance. Their presence was formally recognised by papal brief in 1801. In England, meanwhile, former Jesuits lived in community at Stonyhurst College and claimed affiliation with the Society in Russia.

The French Revolution changed the world of the Bourbon monarchs. Thus, in 1804, the Bourbon Ferdinand IV of the Kingdom of Naples and Sicily petitioned Pope Pius VII to have the Society of Jesus restored in his kingdom. The Pope agreed. Jesuits came from Russia to effect the restoration. While this was proceeding, Kenney and some other young men of slender means were educated by former Jesuits in Dublin. They came to share their mentors' belief that the Society would be restored some day, and they prepared themselves to join that body. Following the papal approval of the Jesuits in Naples and Sicily, Irish former Jesuits paid for Kenney and his companions to go to Stonyhurst for their novitiate, and subsequently to Sicily for further studies leading to ordination.

Thus, Kenney was prepared for his career in three countries. His time in Italy, however, was of particular importance. In Sicily he developed a deep appreciation of classical culture and studies, a feeling for the Society of Jesus as an international body, for its history, and its commitment to spirituality and education. He continued his studies there with distinction and was ordained. Sicily, at this period, was an outpost of defiance in a Europe dominated by Napoleon. It was defended by the British army and navy. Kenney acted as chaplain to Irish soldiers in the army, and was also involved in an abortive attempt to rescue the Pope from the control of Napoleon.

On his return to Ireland, Kenney founded Clongowes Wood College in 1814, the year of the general Restoration of the Society of Jesus by Pope Pius VII. Under his leadership, a novitiate was opened, and the Church of St Francis Xavier, Gardiner Street, Dublin and Belvedere College were established. He served as vice-rector of Maynooth College, the national seminary, and had a profound influence on generations of diocesan priests. He was sought throughout much of Ireland as a preacher and retreat director. A friend and confidant of Archbishop Murray of Dublin, he played a significant role in assisting the newly formed Irish Sisters of Charity, and the Irish Loreto Sisters, and in supporting Edmund Rice, founder of the Irish Christian Brothers. Kenney served as superior of the Irish Jesuit Mission and later as provincial of the Irish vice-province. His pastoral work and his concern for the poor led to his being termed 'the apostle of Dublin'. His most far-reaching influence, however, was most probably in North America.

He was twice appointed by Jesuit Generals as official visitor to the Jesuits in the United States of America. In 1820 his task was to report on and cope with serious divisions between "native" American Jesuits and foreign Jesuits, with the disorder and debt in the farms which helped to finance the Society, and with the very depressed condition of the University of Georgetown. During his second visitation, 1830-1834, he was overall superior of the Jesuit mission in Maryland and Missouri. Having dealt again with problems in Maryland, he moved on to Missouri. There he strengthened the foundations of St. Louis University, brought order into the finances, set down rules for the running of farms, the treatment of the slaves, and renewed the commitment of the Missouri mission to the Indians. His impact not only among Jesuits but also among other churchmen was such that a number of prelates put forward his name for the bishoprics of Cincinnati, New York, and Philadelphia. In Ireland, similarly, his name was put forward for the diocese of Kerry and the archdiocese of Armagh. Peter Kenney was viewed as a man of the universal church. His life earned widespread respect for the restored Society of Jesus.

He played a prominent role in the 21st General Congregation of the Society, the first after the Restoration. Towards the end of his life, he was elected to the Jesuit Procurators' Congregation in Rome. Despite being crippled with asthma, he travelled through floods and storms to attend the sessions. He died while there, attended in his final hours by the Jesuit General and members of the Congregation. He was buried in the church of the Gesu in Rome, where many Jesuit Generals of the order were interred. He was, in the words of Archbishop Rosati of St. Louis, 'a man of no ordinary mark'. That, too, it is to be hoped, will be the verdict of the readers of this book.

It remains to add to the former acknowledgements, some of whom have gone to join Fr. Kenney, my thanks to the Centenary Committee, chaired by Rev. Noel Barber, S.J., which approved this publication, and to Trevor Lipscombe of CUA Press who has been a mentor and guide to this venture.

PART I

Years of formation, and of new beginnings in old countries and the new world, 1779–1821

With glad endeavour we begin the quest
That destiny commands, though where we go,
Or guided by what star, no man doth know.

Uncharted is our course, our hearts untried,
And we may weary ere we take the tide,
Or make fair haven from the moaning sea.

James Stephens, "Joy Be with Us"

Growing up in Dublin, 1779–1801:
Connivance, freedom and high horizons

> The Irish are in a most unnatural state, for we see there
> the minority prevailing over the majority.
>
> Dr Johnson

Into a changeful era

Peter Kenney was born into a decade of major, seemingly disparate, events. In 1772 Poland was partitioned by the rulers of Russia, Prussia, and Austria. The following year, the papacy suppressed the Society of Jesus. On 4 July 1776, the colonists in part of North America declared independence, and a year later received the surrender of a large British force at Saratoga. The following year, the *Hibernian Journal* in Dublin published a letter in the name of Benjamin Franklin explaining that the cause of America was that of Ireland. That same year, the demands of the war on British manpower and the need to pacify the majority population in Ireland led to the first formal relaxation of the penal laws against Irish Catholics. Three years prior to 1778 was born the quintessential Irishman of the nineteenth century, Daniel O'Connell, future orchestrator of the successful campaign for Catholic emancipation. "History has many cunning passages, contrived corridors and issues."[1] These diverse occurrences were to be inter-related in Peter Kenney's career and were to contribute in various ways to the era of dramatic change in which he spent his boyhood and as a result of which the despised majority population would emerge from passivity to become "makers of history", seeking the cultural, religious, and political equality for which they had long yearned yet scarcely dared to hope. Kenney, in a modest way, was to be both a product and a moulder of that new emerging Ireland and was also to contribute to the religious and educational development of the vernal, vibrant North American republic.

He was born on 7 July 1779, probably at 28 Drogheda Street, which disappeared a few years later with the extension of the city's main thoroughfare, Sackville Street.[2] He was baptised at St Catherine's church, Meath Street, on the south side of the River Liffey – an indication that his mother, Ellen Molloy, came from that parish.[3] Her husband, also Peter, appears to have been much older and to have been a native of the city of Waterford. It is not clear what occupation he followed, but a letter almost thirty years after Peter junior's birth mentioned a business, then in difficulties, for which Mrs Kenney had assumed responsibility, her husband being "languid from age and weakly credulous".[4] The latter may have married twice. Apart from Peter, and a sister, Anne Mary, who entered the convent of the Sisters of St Clare at Harold's Cross, Dublin,[5] there was a much older brother, or half-brother, Michael, who obtained a qualification to set up a medical hall or apothecary shop as early as 1792,[6] and several years later was described as "for many years at the head of one of the most respectable medical establishments in the south" and as a brother of "the late Dr Peter Kenney SJ, whose family resided in Waterford".[7] That Peter, himself, lived for a while in Waterford, or visited there for periods of time, was indicated by a letter of his from Sicily in 1808, which mentioned that he was "for some time acquainted at Waterford" with its bishop.[8]

Whatever about sojourns at Waterford, it is unlikely that for the first twenty-two years of his existence he moved much out of Dublin. And although there is little direct information concerning his life during those years, he was inevitably affected by the city's social and political history, and the religious faith of, and constraints on, the Catholic population. The fact that the leading local clergy were former Jesuits was also to be a key factor in his spiritual and educational development and in his eventual choice of career.

Capital city, Protestant ascendancy, and resurgent papists

The year before Peter's birth in 1779, the widespread withdrawal of British troops from Ireland for the war against France and the American colonists provided the Irish Protestant ascendancy with the opportunity to wrest an independent parliament and free trade from a beleaguered British government. During the next twenty years native industries were promoted, and the impact of the industrial and technological revolution was manifested in better roads, the development of canals, and generally improved communications. By the end of the century, the city was characterised to a notable degree by wide streets, and by a collection of public buildings which, in Macauley's estimation, would have been thought magnificent even in Paris.[9] Other visitors commented on the great number and variety of horse-drawn carriages, on the practice of lavish hospitality, and on the interminable discussion about politics and the admiration accorded those who, like Henry Grattan, could dress ideas "in a rich wardrobe of words".[10] Not surprisingly in this setting, Peter's parents apprenticed him to the trade of coach-making, and he himself acquired a regard for gracious hospitality and a determination to develop his natural talent for public speaking.

Reminders of the reverse side to that gilded, progressive world, however, were all about him. The contrast was unavoidable, the English traveller, the Revd John Milner, remarked, between the magnificence of the public buildings "and the circumstances of the people at whose expense they have been erected".[11] These lived in over-crowded tenements in filth-laden streets, and among them epidemics of fever and plague were frequent. Even among the well-to-do, in that Georgian era of insensitivity to sanitary arrangements, the contagion of fever made its way, and attacks of asthma and tuberculosis were all too common. Peter became an asthma victim, notwithstanding a sturdy and energetic physique and, it would seem, relatively comfortable circumstances. The Kenneys, in a small way, appear to have been among the increasing number of relatively prosperous Catholic merchants who advanced materially in the second half of the eighteenth century by availing of loopholes in the penal legislation, and the government's connivance at its non-application. Resentment at the legislation, nevertheless, grew with increased freedom, and middle class Catholics relished Edmund Burke's reminder to the House of Commons, recently highlighted in Arthur Young's *Tour of Ireland* (1780), "Connivance is the relaxation of slavery, not the definition of liberty."[12]

Peter, then, grew up in a climate of improved opportunities for Catholics and an increased demand for equality from Catholics. The success of the North American colonists, and the concurrence of their proclamation of "self-evident truths" with the prevailing ethos of the Enlightenment among many in the Irish parliament, prompted a further Catholic Relief Act in 1782. There remained, nevertheless, the absence of the franchise, the exclusion from certain professions, the barring of Catholic colleges, and a number of minor restraints, all of which marked Catholics off as clearly inferior. As he entered his teenage years, the French Revolution of 1789 radically changed the character of Irish politics. The cry of "Liberty, Equality, Fraternity" stirred the blood of many middle class and working class Catholics and Presbyterians. Seven editions of Thomas Paine's *Rights of Man* appeared in Dublin between 1791 and 1792;[13] and some of the Dublin clergy were said to "canonise ... with unqualified praise, the whole proceedings of the late National Assembly of France".[14] In 1792, further concessions were granted. University education was made available, the establishment of Catholic colleges was permitted and entry to the legal profession. This measure paved the way for the founding of Carlow College and Peter's education there, and for Daniel O'Connell's emergence as a lawyer. The following year, the British government, facing war with France, obliged the Irish parliament to pass a further concessionary act, which extended parliamentary franchise to Catholics, enabled them hold civil and military offices, apart from some specific exceptions, and removed the statutory bar to university degrees. It is not unreasonable to assume that Peter's later rapport with, and appreciation of the political system and the spirit of liberty in the United States was influenced by the enthusiasm and achievement of these years, and also by their sad aftermath.

The extension of the franchise to the majority Catholic population threatened the ascendancy's position. From 1795, the Lord Chancellor of Ireland, John Fitzgibbon, determined to safeguard the Protestant ascendancy for all time by bringing about a parliamentary union with Britain. Fear of French invasion provided scope for playing the sectarian card and provoking premature rebellion. Catholics were represented as of suspected loyalty to the crown. During 1797–8 government forces exhibited unbridled violence; an uprising was provoked in Wexford; and in Dublin martial law was proclaimed. "Troops continually searched for arms. Those suspected ... were tortured or flogged. Those convicted were hanged ... Each day the bodies of rebels killed in the surrounding countryside were brought into the city in carts, and heaped up in the Castle yard."[15] Peter's nineteenth year, 1798, was marked, as a result, by "probably the most concentrated episode of violence in Irish history". By the end of the summer the death-rate on both sides, from various causes, was estimated at 30,000.[16] Atrocities and achievements became entrenched in folk memory. In 1800 the Act of Union was passed. Henceforth, the majority population were confined to a small minority representation in the British parliament. The former Irish parliament took on a romantic glow, and its restoration became their objective and panacea throughout the new century.

During the turmoil and excitement of the 1790s, there is no evidence of political involvement on the part of the Kenney family, nor of they experiencing any *direct* military harassment. Peter, in fact, was likely to have been discouraged from any militant inclinations by the influence of his mentor and friend, the much respected, elderly ex-Jesuit, Dr Thomas Betagh, Vicar-General of the diocese, who, in accordance with the policy of his Dominican archbishop, Dr John Troy, sought to inculcate solid religious teaching, and to promote a peaceable demeanour towards "the constituted authorities", [17] even though neither he nor Troy had much regard for government policy. Following the fall of Rome to the French and the arrest of Pope Pius VI in February 1798, he was reported to have given from the pulpit of the parish church of St Michael "a powerful course of lectures against the pernicious doctrines of Tom Paine to overflowing audiences with great effect".[18] He became adviser, teacher, and friend to Peter Kenney when he (Peter) was relatively young, and proved, perhaps, the biggest single influence in preparing his future. He raised his vision towards high horizons. His influence and that of a fellow ex-Jesuit, Richard Callaghan, was to direct Peter's steps towards the Society of Jesus and effectively map the course of the restored order in Ireland.

Kenney, Betagh, Callaghan, and the Jesuits of the suppression

Thomas Betagh, born in 1738 in Kells, Co. Meath, received a classical education at a school run by a Jesuit priest, John Austin, in Cook Street, Dublin. Betagh entered the Society of Jesus in France in 1754 and after ordination returned to Dublin where he enabled Austin to expand his school work. A boarding school was set up which became, in effect, a seminary for the dioceses of Meath and Dublin.[19] In addition, Betagh developed a variety of schools, providing basic free education for poorer children[20] and evening classes for young apprentices and labourers.[21] At his funeral, the preacher, Dr Michael Blake, told of his teaching children night after night in cold cellars when he was already past seventy years of age, and of his clothing forty of the most destitute each year at his own expense. In Blake's estimation, he educated more than 3,000 boys.[22]

Kenney is said to have attended two of Betagh's schools: at Saul's Court, off Fishamble Street, and at Skinner's Row; one of them during his apprenticeship. Few names of students from these and other of Betagh's establishments have been recorded and those that have are mainly of clergymen. They include eight future priests of the Dublin archdiocese; two vicars-general, William Yore and Patrick Coleman; Daniel Murray and Michael Blake, destined to be archbishop of Dublin and bishop of Dromore respectively; Charles Stuart, provincial of the Augustinians; and eleven young men who were to be involved in re-establishing the Jesuit order in Ireland.[23] Among his many pupils, Betagh appears to have had a particular regard for Peter Kenney.

Apprenticeship, schooling, and development

Probably in the years 1793-4, when he was thirteen to fourteen, Peter began his apprenticeship to a coachmaker. No information on this part of his life has survived, except for a story, with various modifications, relating to his dismissal and to his close friendship with Betagh.

According to the story he was in the habit of preaching to his fellow apprentices on the subject of the sermon he had heard on the Sunday, and the master had arrived during one of these performances and dismissed him. Ashamed, he dropped out of his evening classes. After some weeks, Betagh sent for him, enquired the reasons for his absence, and, on being told, got him to stand up and give a sample sermon. When this was done, he warned him not to miss class again. Thereafter, according to a near contemporary account, "Peter Kenney had a fast friend in Dr Betagh".[24] Subsequently, to judge from remarks of his later friend, John McElroy, celebrated American missioner and founder of Boston College, he attended school by day, and soon graduated to a Latin school. In his spare time, he earned some money by cleaning knives and blacking boots.[25]

By then, Peter appears to have become virtual assistant to Betagh. He taught catechism to children in Rosemary Lane chapel.[26] He assisted in a school for poor boys in Derby Square, and used to bring some of the more senior ones to Rosemary Lane to recite vespers.[27] From this there developed in 1799 the first young men's evening confraternity in Dublin (at St Michael's Chapel, Rosemary Lane), of which Peter was the recognised founder.[28] Subsequently, similar confraternities were set up in different parts of the city, in suburban parishes, and, at times, in rural towns. In the *Limerick Reporter and Tipperary Vindicator*, on 16 August 1869, Maurice Lenihan, in his informative series of articles on "Father Peter Kenney, SJ", added that Fr Betagh "usually employed" him "to address an instruction to the Young Men's Confraternity when they met on Sundays", and he recalled the impression made on one of the congregation:

> Mr James Charles Bacon, a most respectable Catholic merchant, and a most confidential friend of Fr Betagh, was often heard to say that he was frequently present at young Kenney's instructions, and that he was even at that time as eloquent and as impressive a sacred orator as he was afterwards when so admired as the great preacher of his time.

It can have come as little surprise to contemporaries, therefore, when he and three other former students of Betagh – Paul Ferley, Joseph Kavanagh, and William Yore – entered St Patrick's College, Carlow, on 6 June 1801, to study for the priesthood.[29] Eighteen in all went to Carlow from Betagh's schools between 1801–4;[30] and a number of them had been members of the Young Men's Confraternity. That body appears to have been, in effect, a resource for vocations to the priesthood. A registry of past members who became priests, carried out in 1833, showed that in the thirty-four years of its existence thirty-one young men became secular or regular clergy.[31] Those who attended Carlow between 1801–4, however, were distinctive in that they promised in writing to join the Society of Jesus. On this understanding, the fees of almost all were paid by Fr Richard Callaghan, as administrator of the Irish Jesuit mission fund – money which accrued to the former Irish Jesuits from the proceeds of the Irish property of the order and which was carefully husbanded against the day when the Society would be restored. Many of the aspirants, for various reasons, did not become Jesuits;[32] but the remarkable thing, in the circumstances, was that they wished to become such.

"Remarkable" in that the Jesuit order had been suppressed before they were born. They had grown up in a world where Jesuits as a body were a thing of the past. Their wish to become Jesuits was undoubtedly a tribute to the men they knew as former Jesuits in their parishes and their schools. They had imbibed from them something of the spirituality of the order's founder, St Ignatius Loyola, their pride in the Society's history, and above all, perhaps, their remarkable faith in the eventual restoration of the order – a faith and hope which rested, in part, on the preservation of the body in White Russia, and which had recently been confirmed by the papal recognition of the order there. The future, however, was still very uncertain; and the young candidates cannot but have been aware of the harshness of the suppression, and of the likelihood of intense opposition to a full restoration, as well from within the Church as from outside. Kenney, because of his interest in history and his

closeness to Betagh, was probably the best informed of the group with respect
to the past story and more immediate problems.

Jesuit suppression and gradual restoration

Hostility to the order had been fanned to a fierce blaze in the second half of
the eighteenth century. It was the age of the "enlightened despots", when all
power and control was sought by the monarch. The influence in his dominions
of an outside ruler was unacceptable. The fact that the pope claimed only *spiritual* dominion was clouded by his position, and allegiances, as a temporal
ruler. He was in Burke's descriptive phrase, "that mixed person of politics and
religion".[33] The Jesuits, as the zealous defenders of "that mixed person", and
themselves under a centralised government in Rome, became the focus of
much of the anti-papal feeling. They were also the focus of the hostility of the
Catholic puritans, the Jansenists, who were influential in the Roman curia and
in the Congregation of Propaganda Fide, and who accused them of moral
laxity. And there were a number of prominent churchmen and heads of religious orders who resented the Society's influence and privileges, and the corporate pride displayed by some of its members. During the 1760s, the Society
was expelled from Portugal, and then, by family compact, from the Bourbon
kingdoms of Spain, France, Naples and Parma. Bourbon demands for the general suppression of the order were eventually conceded by the beleaguered
Giovanni Ganganelli, Clement XIV, in order to secure peace for the papacy and
the Church. He was too harassed to perceive, as Von Ranke observed, that
once "the outworks had been taken, a more vigorous assault of the victorious
opinion on the central stronghold would inevitably follow".[34]

   Clement, without any judicial process, suppressed the Society by the brief
Dominus ac Redemptor, which was published on 18 August 1773. With it, there
was sacrificed a network of schools across much of the world and far-flung
missionary initiatives from the Americas to the Indies. The order, however,
was not entirely destroyed. The pope decided on a method of local announcement for the execution of the brief, a method similar to that chosen at the
Council of Trent with regard to the decree on clandestine marriages.[35] This
meant that the regulations of the Brief of Suppression "did not come into
force until they had been officially announced by the bishop or his plenipoten-
tiaries in the Society's establishments that lay in his diocese". No such official
publication took place for some time in the Jesuit establishments in Prussia,
and never occurred in the territories of Catherine the Great. Indeed, in 1774,
when Frederick II of Prussia, anxious to preserve the Jesuit schools in his territories, appealed for the preservation of the order, the new pope, Pius VI, gave
him the not unsympathetic response "that he feared the anger of the Bourbon
courts too much to dare give his express approval to the continued existence
of the Jesuits; but if the king could find ways and means of preserving them

he would not object nor would he pass sentence of irregularity on them".[36]
Frederick changed his policy; but the Society continued under Catherine the
Great; and the *viva voce* approval of the papacy became bolder with the passage of time and of Bourbon opposition, until eventually formal approval was
granted to the order in Russia with a papal brief, *Catholicae Fidei*, 7 March
1801. It was the signal for which Fr Richard Callaghan had eagerly awaited;
and buoyed up by it, he decided, as mentioned, to send his young men to
Carlow College.

Although the suppression had been carried out with much uprooting and
inhumanity in many countries and regions, the process in Ireland went quietly
and smoothly. There was only a small number of Jesuits. They were mainly
involved in parish work, and their relations with the bishops had always been
good. In accordance with the papal brief, they conveyed their acceptance to
the local bishop and expressed their readiness to serve obediently as secular
clergy. They were readily absorbed into different dioceses during 1774. Eleven
of the seventeen were in Dublin.[37]

A number of these men became known to Kenney during his boyhood, and
he would have learnt something of their education and background. What he
did not know for many years, however, was their special and concerted effort
to prepare for the day when the Society would be restored by pooling and preserving the funds of the Irish Jesuit mission. Their financial husbandry would
enable him many years later to reopen an Irish Jesuit mission.

Funding for survival – Suspicions – Limited restoration

The superior of the Irish mission at the time of the suppression entrusted the
care of the mission property to Fr John Fullam. The latter bound all members
to secrecy with regard to possessions, and drew up an agreement requiring
that the capital be not touched, and that, should their number "be reduced to
three without any immediate prospect of a restoration" of the Society, they
would lay out the funds in such "pious foundations" as seemed most to God's
glory "and the spiritual advantage of the mission".[38] If the order were restored,
the capital was to be placed at the disposal of the General. During his eighteen
years of stewardship, Fullam diligently sought news of the Jesuits in White
Russia, of the English ex-Jesuits living in community and running a college at
Liege with papal approval, and of every favourable sign of the future restoration for which he was preserving and augmenting capital.

Informally, like his more prominent English counterpart, Fr William
Strickland, he came to occupy a controlling role, and this was carried forward
by his enthusiastic successor, Richard Callaghan. The danger was that a man
in such a position would come to identify himself and his plans with the
Society and view opposition as betrayal. Something of this occurred in
Fullam's and Callaghan's relations with Thomas Betagh. Fullam, indeed, who

had watched the funds grow considerably by means of bequests, carried his mistrust of colleagues to the point of bequeathing a large section of the property to his sister, with the instruction that the great part of it was to go to the Society of Jesus if restored within twenty years of his death.

At his death in 1793 there remained but five of the former Jesuits. The prospects for the restoration of the order never seemed blacker. The anarchy of the French Revolution was spreading across Europe. The five, still unaware of the extent of the wealth in Miss Fullam's hands, made a new agreement destined to have considerable repercussions: namely, that when reduced to three, they would disclose their financial situation to such of the Irish bishops as had the greater good of the Jesuit mission at heart, and discuss with them how the property might be used to endow "some school or college for the education of secular priests to serve on the mission".[39] The presumption, however, was that the capital could not be appropriated until it devolved on the last survivor, and not then if the Society were re-established by the Holy See. Callaghan would seem to have had some communication with the archbishop of Dublin, and some other bishops, then, or earlier, but they exhibited no special interest at this stage as the overall sum, so far as Callaghan was aware, came only to £8,650.[40]

In 1796 Miss Fullam died, and Callaghan found he had a very considerable amount of money at his disposal. He called a meeting of the remaining four. They broke up without agreement. External events discouraged planning ahead. Ireland was convulsed by dissension; and French forces had occupied a good part of the Papal States. The success of French arms in the Low Countries, moreover, had obliged the English ex-Jesuits and their pupils to leave Liege. They took up residence at Stonyhurst, near Clitheroe, in Lancashire, an estate presented to them by their former student, Thomas Weld of Lulworth Castle, Dorset; and there they continued to run their academy as at Liege – a pontifical seminary for the education of secular clergy, and a house of education for young lay people. The change permitted Callaghan communicate more frequently with his English counterpart, Strickland, and was to provide a new option for the education of his Irish students.

The dark scene changed dramatically, however, in 1801 when the pope granted formal acknowledgement of the existence of the Jesuits in Russian territories and recognised their superior, Gabriel Gruber, as Vicar-General. The acknowledgement seemed to the new Vicar-General and his advisers to permit the incorporation of former Jesuits from other regions. The Jesuits at Stonyhurst applied and were accepted by Gruber, who re-established an English Jesuit province, with Marmaduke Stone as provincial. Callaghan now spoke of visiting Stonyhurst and sending his students there for education, and, almost immediately afterwards, wondered about sending them to a noviceship in White Russia where they would be truly formed as Jesuits.[41] At this stage, he expressed to Strickland on 17 December 1802, his belief that Betagh was not interested in the restoration of the Society but had designs on the mission's funds; and in a postscript he disclosed that he now possessed "at least £35,000 Irish", which he wished to see used for the establishment of a college in Ireland.[42] In the context of the times, it must have seemed a visionary and unrealistic goal, but it was to become an inspiration and target for the young Irish Jesuits of the restored Society.

Callaghan's excitement at the papal approval of the order in Russia, and his quoting of Strickland to the effect that Fr Gruber's jurisdiction extended beyond Russia, led to Archbishop Troy seeking the grounds for Fr Strickland's communication.[43] Strickland informed him on 18 April 1803, that His Holiness, through Cardinal Consalvi, had communicated to Fr Gruber that Jesuits in other countries might be aggregated to the Society in Russia, and a request to that end from the English Jesuits had been approved. He added, however, that such authority from the pope could not "be pleaded in *foro externo*".[44]

The archbishop, not surprisingly, sought to have matters clearly established in the external forum. He had been assured already by a member of the Sacred Congregation that there was no change in the legal position of the Society outside Russia.[45] The English vicars-apostolic who, apart from Bishop Milner, were far less well disposed than Dr Troy, also received negative responses from Propaganda. Many former Jesuits were also hesitant.[46] Meantime, the French Revolution had wrought a change in Bourbon attitudes. In 1804 the Bourbon monarch of the Kingdom of the Two Sicilies obtained the approval of Pope Pius VII to have the Society restored fully in his dominions.[46] On 30 July, that year, the pope, in a formal brief, placed any Jesuit houses opened in that kingdom under the jurisdiction of Fr Gabriel Gruber.[47] Even after that, nevertheless, Cardinal Borgia and other heads of Propaganda notified Dr Troy that there was no legal change in the Society's status![48]

Meantime, Gruber had sent to Rome at the pope's request a Fr Angiolini, as procurator-general of the order. (Angiolini would later be a staunch friend to Peter Kenney in Sicily.) His account of his kindly reception by the pope took away, in Strickland's view, "all reasonable doubt".[49] It did not, however, for Betagh, nor for his friend and colleague, Bishop Carroll of Baltimore. They wished to see "a firmer foundation".[50] The shock of the original dissolution left them requiring indubitable assurance.

Callaghan's position, of course, was very different. He formally pronounced his vows in the Society during a visit to England, [51] and made a will entrusting the Irish funds to the English provincial, Fr Stone, to be preserved for the use of the Irish mission. The setting up of the English province by Gruber also gave a new impetus to his deliberations about sending his élèves, or students, to a noviceship. The young men seemed to be as enthusiastic as he. "I am concerned for my 18 élèves of Carlow", he wrote on 30 December 1803, "who are as anxious as I for the noviceship. They are as much united in brotherly love as if they had been reared in the Society."[52] Time would show that his picture of their unity owed more to his optimistic nature than to reality. Shortly before his letter, a noviceship had been opened at Stonyhurst.[53] A year later, he sent his first Irish novices there; and shortly afterwards, in July 1804, as noted, the restoration of the order took place in the Kingdom of the Two Sicilies.

Thus, the stage was set for the Society of Jesus to emerge from the obscurity of virtual dissolution; and with that, all was in place for Peter Kenney's departure from the practical anonymity of his early years to undertake better documented, more visible roles – first at Carlow, then Stonyhurst, and subsequently, during critical years of war, in unlikely foreign destinations, before returning home to fulfil Richard Callaghan's vision.

The next instalment of the story, therefore, moves from the general introduction to the Ireland of Kenney's youth, the gradual revival of the Society of Jesus, and the beginnings of a new generation of Irish Jesuits, to a more immediate consideration of the time and training of Peter and his companions at Carlow and Stonyhurst, and how the funds protected and developed by Fullam and Callaghan continued to provide occasions of covetousness and anxiety as well as of opportunity.

II

Towards an uncertain future: Carlow – Stonyhurst – Dissensions, and "the glare of gold"

THE PROVING GROUND – ACADEMIC AND RELIGIOUS PREPARATION

On 6 June 1801, Peter Kenney, Paul Ferley, Joseph Kavanagh, and William Yore entered St Patrick's College, Carlow.[1] Sent and paid for by Fr Callaghan, with the approval of Dr Betagh, their lives would continue to be directly influenced by both men for some years.

It was a pivotal year in Irish history. In January, the parliamentary union of Ireland and Great Britain had been effected. The prospect of Catholic Emancipation, held out as an inducement to the bishops and lay leaders of the majority population in return for their support of the union, quickly faded before the opposition of George III. William Pitt's announcement of his resignation as prime minister on 3 February, because of the king's intransigence, did little to win credibility for the government. The stage was set for a long struggle.

The college to which Betagh's students came had been opened eight years earlier, 1793, for the training and education of clergy in the face of the rapidly expanding Catholic population, which would reach 6,540,000 by the year 1840, and the virtual closure of the continental colleges to Irish clergy because of the French Revolution and the war. The college was a four-storey building near the town, on a 4½-acre site enclosed by a ten-foot wall.[2]

The town itself, which became so familiar to Kenney and his companions, was a garrison centre situated on the River Barrow, which the contemporary English traveller, Edward Wakefield, described as "a very neat place" with many inns.[3] When they arrived at the college, Canon Henry Staunton was president. The professors of theology, philosophy, and *belles lettres* in 1801 were three French emigrant priests. Also in the college, as professor of classics, was the colourful and popular Dominican, Andrew Fitzgerald, who had studied at Louvain and then professed philosophy at Lisbon. In 1803, Fr Kyran Marum came as professor of philosophy. He was to be appointed bishop of Ossory eleven years later.[4]

From the few available references to his studies, Kenney appears to have done well at logic, metaphysics, and ethics. Subsequently, he was considered sufficiently competent in these to be recommended for immediate movement to the theology course at Stonyhurst.[5] In the classical languages, to which he had been introduced by Betagh, he also seems to have done well. Charles Plowden, his future novice master and an exacting critic, commented in 1806 that he was "well grounded in classical studies".[6] In this, he had no doubt been greatly assisted by the talented Fr Fitzgerald, whose vigorous hostility to the restored Society of Jesus in Ireland – arising perhaps from his time in Portugal – would later take him aback. "He attacks us everywhere he goes," Kenney complained in 1814. In fact, "he said such extravagant things against us at the professors' table at Maynooth, that Dr Delahogue was obliged to interrupt him".[7]

Despite the shortage of information on Kenney's work and experiences at the college, it is clear that the abiding influences from those years included friendships made and links established with other ecclesiastics. Among future diocesan clergy, he was closest to William Yore, whose plans to join the order were to be upset by ill health, and who became a much esteemed Vicar-General in the Dublin archdiocese.[8] An acquaintance, and future correspondent, if not close friend, was a Cork student, John England, who entered in September 1803. After twelve years of active work as a priest, he was to depart Ireland in 1820 to become bishop of Charleston in the United States of America, where Kenney would meet him again. Others of note, not from his own time but sharing the college as a common link, were Michael Slattery, who entered Carlow in 1805, became professor there, and in 1833 was consecrated archbishop of Cashel; and Slattery's close friend and fellow professor, the redoubtable Dr James Doyle, who was appointed bishop of Kildare and Leighlin in 1819. The at times uneasy relationship between the brilliant but domineering bishop and the Jesuits at Clongowes was eased by the fact that Kenney and some other members of the community were alumni of the bishop's college.

Dr Doyle was concerned with improving the performance of pastoral and liturgical duties among his clergy. The Catholic Church in Ireland, as it emerged from its partly unstructured and underground existence in penal times, suffered from a laxity of discipline among its priests. In addition to other abuses, there was said to be inadequate attention to preaching, catechising, and the performance of religious services.[9] Against such a background, it is not surprising that the sole chronicled memory of Peter Kenney at Carlow relates to a sermon on "The Dignity of the Priesthood". It was customary for each student to preach in turn before the professors and fellow students. Peter is said to have so gripped his audience with the theme entrusted to him that, at the end of the sermon, all, including the president, greeted him with rounds of applause.[10]

Their time at Carlow, however, held one particularly sad memory for Peter and his companions: namely, the tragic death of Robert Holmes, a fellow student from one of Dr Betagh's schools, who entered St Patrick's College in February 1802, and lost his life in the River Barrow on 8 August 1803, in a fruitless effort to rescue another student. The impact of his personality and generous action was recognised by a special monument, erected by Canon Staunton, in the college cemetery, with a tablet carrying a long inscription in his praise.[11]

Outside pressures and unease – Opting for Stonyhurst

The tragic loss of one of his students by drowning added to Fr Callaghan's fears of other losses. He complained to the English provincial, Marmaduke Stone, in the spring of 1804, that there were "tempters" at Carlow seeking to persuade his young men to become secular priests, and that some of the bishops sought the same and one, indeed, had called to the college with an "authentic" account from Rome that all hopes of the restoration of the Society were destroyed.[12] Subsequently, Callaghan complained of his brighter students being employed in teaching "the underclass of the college" instead of being applied to philosophy.[13] For all these reasons, he planned to withdraw his élèves, as he called them, from Carlow.

On these, and related matters, however, his judgement was far from calm and objective at this time. He began to talk again of sending his young men to Russia; disturbed, it would seem, both by Fr Stone's dilitariness in responding to his earlier expressed intention to send his élèves to Stonyhurst, and by a communication from Cardinal Borgia, prefect of Propaganda, which Dr Troy had sent him, and to which the bishop at Carlow was presumably referring, which stated that "the Holy Father did not recognise the Jesuits outside Russia" and "that those who called themselves Jesuits" (in Ireland and England) were simply to be "numbered among the secular clergy subject to the ordinary in everything like other priests".[14]

The letter from Borgia was the beginning of a protracted campaign by Propaganda, prompted by Dr Troy, to obtain control of the ex-Jesuit property in Ireland. Callaghan's trusted informant, Peter Plunkett, the former Irish Jesuit who had been accredited to the Roman province, provided assurance and a hard-headed perspective for future dealings with Propaganda. Writing from Leghorn, in Tuscany, on 19 October 1804, in response to a communication from Callaghan concerning letters "written by Borgia and other heads of Propaganda" to Archbishop Troy, he remarked that he was not in the least surprised "since these gentlemen pretend that, with regard to missions and heterodox communities, nothing is legal that does not pass through their channels". Consequently, he continued, it was no wonder "they act with your country as if (Cardinal) Consalvi had never written to Fr Gruber authorising him, in the name of his Holiness, to take under his direction and obedience all the ex-Jesuits and others both in Catholic and non-Catholic countries that desired to be aggregated to him."[15]

The English Jesuits, with recollections of Roman curial involvement in the suppression and how the pope's name could be invoked to give credence to a purely curial strategy, were similarly unimpressed. Stone, who had already suggested to Callaghan that the four or five senior members of Callaghan's eighteen or so élèves might be sent to the noviceship, and the remainder to Stonyhurst to study humanities,[16] endeavoured, together with Strickland, during June and August 1804, to provide him with assurances regarding the pope's favourable attitude and his Holiness's disposition to openly restore the order wherever requested by Catholic princes; and they emphasised that the king of Naples had already made such a request.[17] This finally banished Callaghan's Russian deliberations. And Strickland raised his spirits even higher by the news that Bishop Moylan sought a college of the Jesuits for Cork when men were available.[18]

Callaghan's protective vigilance towards his proteges, however, was not confined to Carlow and Ireland. He had also recommended a considerable reformation in the discipline at Stonyhurst.[19] Stone and Strickland received his comments well. Quite apart from the high fee of 45 guineas arranged to be paid for each student, [20] they had a genuine affection for the old man who seemed to be managing single-handed to keep the Society alive in Ireland, and who in his seventy-sixth year was growing very forgetful and very deaf[21] and prone to see "vile and sinister schemes" operating against his plans.[22] He changed his mind three times between June and August with regard to sending his young men to Stonyhurst.[23]

On 11 September, however, he wrote to Stone that he had sent his fifteen charges to England in groups of three, in different ships, and by different routes; and he concluded with the news: "I have just received an account of Peter Kenney's and his two companions safe arrival in Liverpool by a letter from him, and of the safe arrival of the other ternary that sailed at the same time but got to Liverpool a day before him".[24] Stonyhurst, however, was not to be a haven out of the swell of the sea. The distinctive background and ethos of the college, the hotch-potch of lifestyles and disciplines prevailing there, and the intrusive influence of Fr Betagh were to test the vocations of the Irish élèves as never before.

Stonyhurst traditions and personalities

For two centuries English Jesuits had found shelter from persecution in France and Flanders. Now they had been obliged to seek a haven in their homeland from persecution in Europe. But they lived a muted existence, and necessarily so. The Irish Catholics might be discriminated against by law, but they were the majority population in their country. They practised their religion with increasing openness and assertiveness. Their bishops and people supported religious orders, and there was no particular animus against Jesuits. English Catholics had a greater sense of oppression in many ways. They were a small minority in an anti-Catholic country, where the general population had no understanding of religious orders. And they were frequently accused of being unpatriotic. As a result, they became markedly defensive and circumspect. The Jesuits had further reason to be so in that they had passed into legend in Britain as conniving men, disturbers of the public peace; and now they also found their reappearance unwelcome to most of the hierarchy and many of the clergy. Talk of the restoration of the order had set off alarm bells for many of the bishops. It stirred up old resentments about the privileges and exemptions claimed by religious orders; and the fact that the "Gentlemen of Stonyhurst", though essentially diocesan priests, acted as quasi-religious and were still empowered by papal brief to run a pontifical academy, fanned the coals of resentment and evoked concern lest their restoration provide the government with excuses for making life more difficult for ordinary Catholics and for deferring indefinitely the granting of Emancipation.

The Jesuits at Stonyhurst, when the Irish arrived there, had become almost obsessive about caution and secrecy. The very mixture of the population in the college generated tension. There were lay pupils, seminary students, secret Jesuits who sought the return of the strict regime of the continental colleges, ex-Jesuits no longer bound by religious vows of poverty and obedience, and a number of secular clergy some of whom taught in the school. There were different views, as a result, about the possibility, and desirability, of the restoration of the Society. A spirit of union, confidentiality, and discipline, was lacking. Fr Callaghan had good grounds for questioning the suitability of Stonyhurst as a location for the spiritual formation of his young élèves!

The man who held the diverse parties in some form of liveable union was the rector, Fr Marmaduke Stone. "In face and figure corpulent and cherubic", he was a mild man of unaffected piety, who had great difficulty in making a decision and even more in answering letters,[25] and yet he disarmed criticism by his genuine humility and good will. In 1803, this most unlikely of appointees was made provincial. He was to govern the English province for fourteen years. For a time he acted as provincial for Ireland, as well as for England and Scotland, and was entrusted by the newly appointed Vicar-General, Fr Gabriel Gruber, with authority to accept novices.

The Jesuit chosen as master of novices was to play a key role in the future of the Society both in Britain and Ireland. He was Fr Charles Plowden: one of three colourful brothers, all of them authors, all forthright and fearless, all independent minded, and disputatious. He was educated on the continent, and, following ordination at Rome, taught at Bruges where he experienced the full rigour of the suppression – spending eight months in prison. Subsequently, as a secular priest, he lived in comfort in the role of chaplain to his close friend, Thomas Weld, and enjoyed a life of social and literary distinction. He published a vigorous *Account of the Preservation and Actual State of the Society of Jesus in Russian Dominions*. A forceful defender of the order, he was also at times a forthright critic, not least of the gentle General at the time of the suppression, Lorenzo Ricci.[26] Sweeping judgements were not uncommon in his assessment of people.

He was sixty years of age when he returned to religious life. The fact that he had lived in a wider world for nearly thirty years, was an excellent preacher, with a striking presence and a command of words, and combined with these experiences and qualities a bluff, sturdy spirituality, a wide knowledge of the history of the order and its constitutions, and a determination to revive the spirit of discipline he had experienced in his younger days – all rendered him an appropriate novice master for the time.[27] His outspokenness and hasty judgements made him many enemies, but those close to him like Archbishop Carroll and Bishop Milner, and many who survived his noviceship, retained a life-long regard for him and sense of gratitude to him. To certain young men, in whom he discerned a blend of strong virtue, intellectual ability, and qualities of leadership, he devoted particular time and attention. Peter Kenney, and two English Jesuits, Thomas Glover and Charles Brooke, were among these. He subsequently used his considerable gifts as a correspondent to keep in touch with them, and they, in turn, frequently sought his advice.

But, to return to the arrival of the young Irishmen who were to become his novices.

Novitiate and studies

The journey of the Irish students from Liverpool to Stonyhurst was circuitous. Eventually, amidst an undulating landscape of trees and fields falling away to the valley of the River Hodder, and then rising gradually to the foothills of the Pennines, they viewed the college on its slight eminence at the end of a half-mile long avenue. As they came closer, their attention was necessarily caught by an entrance dominated by high gatehouse towers surmounted by baroque cupolas, and approached by a causeway running between two great rectangular ponds or "canals".

When entrusted to the community in 1794 by Thomas Weld, the buildings had been untenanted for forty years. They were still in a quite ramshackle condition when the Irish arrived in 1804. Little, indeed, seemed to have been done to prepare for their arrival. Fr John Hughes, writing from the college on 29 September, remarked that nineteen youths from Ireland had been announced for several months yet scarcely a table or chair was ready. Five of them were for the noviciate at Hodder Place straightway, the others later.[28]

The five accepted for the noviceship straightway were Joseph Kavanagh, Michael Considine, Peter Kenney, John Ryan, and William Yore. They moved down the winding track from the college to Hodder Place: a compact, secluded house a mile distant, standing amid fields and trees above a leisurely river. In this sequestered spot, cut off from all communication with the outside world, even from the college, except with the permission of the novice master, the novices spent two years. Those who had presented themselves the previous September, were now in their second year. The five Irish, in company with a number of English youths, comprised the first year. At the same time, a small preparatory school was being constructed on the site to preserve its anonymity or, as Fr Stone put it, "to save appearances".[29]

The austere regime of the noviceship, added to the normal stresses occasioned by home-sickness, national and cultural differences, and confusion about the status of the vows to be taken, made their time at Hodder a particularly difficult period for the Irish. And those who had not a reasonably sound grasp of Latin faced additional difficulties. Plowden felt it necessary to undertake further tuition himself in order, as he remarked, to introduce into Ireland, at the second birth of the Society, "the abilities and learning, as well as the zeal and spirit, which distinguished the first".[30]

From the start, too, he left his novices in no doubt as to the high standards he expected of them in regard to "zeal and spirit". He sought to develop an attitude of service and dedication, and he set the tone himself. The noviceship commenced with the master of novices washing the feet of the new postulants, after which he read aloud the appropriate Gospel passage. This spirit, linked to a strong personal devotion to Jesus Christ, was imprinted and highlighted in the course of a thirty-day retreat, and it was further fostered by a routine which included daily mass and fairly long periods of meditation, spiritual reading – including the classic work by A. Rodriguez, *The Practice of Christian and Religious Perfection*, which was to remain part of the staple diet of novices of many religious congregations into the 1960s – and regular exhortations on the Jesuit rule and ethos. Such intensive preparation, with breaks for relaxation and periods of outdoor and indoor manual work, occupied the daily life of the novice. And great was said to have been the astonishment of neighbours when they sometimes perceived a gentleman's son engaged in truly menial tasks![31]

Plowden presented two exhortations every week on the Jesuit way of life, and each was followed by a repetition the next day. He brought to them a lifetime of reflection and experience, presented clearly and authoritatively. They were written out in his precise hand, and were so prized by successors as to be still in use more than 130 years later. He also wrote out numerous Sunday sermons which he lent to Jesuit friends.[32]

Renewing the ethos

It is pertinent to view some of the material covered in his exhortations, and to provide some indication of the spiritual formation given his charges. The Jesuit way of life as presented by him was based on two main documents: the Formula of the Institute of the Society of Jesus, as approved and amplified by Pope Julius III in 1550; and the constitutions of the order, approved by Gregory XIII in 1583. Kenney was moulded by these, and he was to become an authority on them.

The Formula of the Institute depicted the Jesuit as a soldier of Christ the King, answering the latter's call with generosity and dedication, and prepared to endure all hardships to carry out his instruction to go, make disciples of all nations. To follow him more effectively, and be more like him, the members vowed themselves to lives of evangelical poverty, chastity, and obedience.

The constitutions elaborated on the implication of these. The third vow, that of obedience, had a special place of honour. All superiors within the order were to be seen as in the place of God for their subjects, and hence obedience was to be not just in outward action but also, as far as possible, in mind and will. Part vi of the constitutions used a stark image to which Kenney was to refer on a number of occasions during his life – "Everyone who lives under obedience ought to allow himself to be ... directed by Divine Providence, through the agency of the superior, as if he were a lifeless body which allows itself to be carried to any place and to be treated in any manner desired, or as if he were an old man's stick which serves in any manner whatsoever in which the holder wishes to use it." And to bind themselves more fully to the service of their Lord, chosen members of the order took a fourth vow, one of special obedience to the pope, as Christ's vicar on earth, to carry out whatever he might order "pertaining to the progress of souls" and go, without excuse, wherever he might indicate.

The constitutions, therefore, envisaged the Society as a body of mobile, flexible men, free of the traditional demands of choir and cloister; its members ready to travel at a moment's notice, as indicated, wherever the pope, or their overall superior, commanded, provided the command did not involve anything sinful. And to enable the superior to judge accurately and allocate tasks wisely, and not burthen a man beyond his strength or place him in a position beyond his competence, all members were expected to make "a manifestation of conscience" to the relevant superior, that is to be completely open with him as to their strengths and failings.[33]

Not having the safeguards of the divine office in common and the fixed routine of the older orders, Jesuit documents, and generations of novice masters, placed particular emphasis on personal prayer and detachment, or inner freedom. The groundwork of prayer was laid from the first days in the noviceship, and especially by means of the aforementioned long retreat – based on a short book by the order's founder which he entitled "Spiritual Exercises", meaning by that term something which leads to spiritual health and strength, analogous to physical exercises which induce health and strength of body, and which involved various forms of prayer, reflection, and examination of conscience, which dispose the retreatant to rid himself (herself) of all inordinate attachments and discover God's will in his/her regard.

Long retreat and spiritual exercises

The long retreat of thirty days of silence, lectures, prayer and penances, opened with a consideration of the mysteries of creation and of sin as they related to the retreatant's own life and failings, and led on to a sense of gratitude to God and to an openness to his love and values as reflected in the gospel scenes of the life, death and resurrection of Jesus Christ. The intense, protracted, deeply personal involvement guided the novice towards inner freedom, or detachment, in decision making, and towards a frame of mind which sought God in all situations, circumstances and persons. Peter and his companions, like numerous men and women from the time of Ignatius to the present, were powerfully influenced and modified by the experience.

Plowden's gift of phrase and description, and his vigorous spirituality, enriched his guidance of the retreat, as did his first-hand experience from the days of the suppression of the pain and obloquy which could be the lot of a companion of Jesus. Kenney's own resolution and commitment to such companionship were to be tested in varied and searching ways during his time in Stonyhurst.

Each Jesuit made the long retreat once again at the end of his formal training, sometime after ordination; but each year he followed an abbreviated version in the form of an eight-day retreat. This, together with daily attendance at mass, periods of meditation, and a quarter of an hour of "examination of conscience", or prayerful review, twice a day, became henceforth part of Peter's life. And finally, he and his companions experienced not only in the noviceship but also during their later training on the continent, the custom of monastic silence, as an aid to prayerful recollection, in that part of the house reserved for the community, from a certain hour at night till after breakfast next day.

Plowden would also have been expected to impress on his novices, in accordance with the Formula of the Institute of the order, the importance of achieving a high standard in the traditional areas of the Society's apostolate: in study and scholarship, in lecturing, and in "the teaching of children and unlettered persons"; in the ministry of the sacrament of penance, by means of the confessional; in the careful saying of mass; in the preaching of the word of God; and in conducting retreats on the Spiritual Exercises. And there was the further reminder that, so far as it was practically possible, they were to endeavour "to carry out all these works altogether free of charge and without accepting any salary for the labour expended".

First report from Plowden

There were, of course, more mundane aspects to the days at Hodder. The intensity of the life, and the coldness of the first winter, led to a breakdown in the health of Peter's close friend William Yore, who was obliged to go home. Peter's own frail health suffered. His commitment was further tested by concern for his parents. A letter from Yore on 26 April 1806 told of a lawsuit in which his parents were engaged, and which had little prospect of a successful outcome. "Your father," Yore wrote, "is languid from age and weakly credulous. He bowed submissively to everything that came from his attorney, even

though the latter often contradicted himself and was 'confessedly not honest'."
Yore anticipated that the family would be reduced to a "state of misery ...
especially your dear mother, than whom a better woman does not exist". He
wrote to satisfy her as she was "not able to do it herself". She desired to know
how Peter would proceed in case of a failure in her business.[34]

On that last, assurance would have come quickly from Callaghan and
Plowden that he could stay on without any contribution from her. He had
greatly impressed his novice master. Already, Plowden, in the course of a
report to Callaghan on 29 January 1806, had declared: "Peter Kenney, a very
unexceptionable, steady and virtuous young man. He has the true spirit of the
Institute, has good talents, and is well grounded in his classical studies. His
constitution is delicate; during the first winter, his chest was much affected,
but since that time his health has been, and now is, sound. I wish Mr Yore
were here, to share the same character with him."[35]

Problems with the Irish – The Betagh connection

Plowden was not as happy, however, with many of the other Irish candidates.
The high standards he set for his novices is suggested by the large number
who left or were dismissed. Among those standards was academic ability, and,
as already indicated, competence in Latin. Many of Callaghan's élèves, Stone
remarked, were "good and pious but that alone" was "not sufficient".[36]

There were many Irish among those who left, or were dismissed from,
Hodder and Stonyhurst. The foregoing remarks might suggest that the reasons
were mainly academic. As against that, however, there are clear indications of
Plowden holding on to a number of men of very poor academic ability, in the
hope that "being virtuous" they might become useful missioners, if they could
obtain "the knowledge of moral divinity".[37]

Considerations other than academic, therefore, were involved in the case of
the Irish young men who returned home. Apart from ill health, the main consideration, in Plowden's view, was obedience; and a problem arose in that
regard because of Betagh's influence over the Irish candidates – who seemed
more committed to following his advice than to obeying their novice master.[38]
Betagh's position, indeed, was ambivalent. He revered the Society and cherished its spirituality above all, and wished his élèves to avail of it. At the same
time, he did not believe they could lawfully join the Society in England, since,
in his view, it was not validly established there, and hence he did not approve
of their taking Jesuit vows at Hodder. By communicating his ambivalence to
his candidates he caused inevitable confusion amongst them. The fact that the
noviceship was in England, that the novice master was English, and that they
would be taking vows in the English province, added a dimension of national
feeling to their confusion and resistance, and in this, too, they were reflecting
their revered mentor. The situation created considerable extra strain for all the

Irish students and novices, even those who, like Kenney, tried to avoid taking sides.

The problems among the Irish novices first appeared in 1805, and became really serious the following year. Concerned that the letters from Betagh seemed to be entering the noviceship through unofficial channels, Plowden attempted to find the source by obliging a first-year novice, John Smith, under obedience, to reveal publicly the name of the person involved. When the novice refused, he was expelled. Callaghan supported the novice-master.[39] Not long afterwards, three Irish novices left the noviciate.[40]

Betagh, incensed by Plowden's heavy-handed approach, upbraided Callaghan for supporting him, and went on to place the happenings in a wider context of criticism and grievance. Once again, he declared, as in the case of his transferring thousands of pounds "to foreign hands without even a security for their appropriation", Callaghan had acted as if he were "under the immediate dictate of the Holy Ghost". In supporting Plowden's "Inquisitorial tyranny" he had abandoned his young men and left them at the mercy of those who took every opportunity "to degrade them and revile their country". He would have been better employed looking to the wise conduct of "the holy Dr Carroll and his American brethren", who insisted on remaining independent when "the English attempted to extend their spiritual jurisdiction across the Atlantic". They ran their own college of Georgetown, and refused to emit new vows until the arrival of a more authentic sanction from the head of the Church. As to the unofficial letters, he assured Callaghan "on the word of a priest", that he had never sent any letter except through the regular channels.[41]

On Callaghan relaying these protestations and comments to Plowden,[42] the latter refused to accept Betagh's solemn declaration about the letters[43] and dismissed a further suggestion of his that the Irish élèves were experiencing from their English counterparts "the asperity of national prejudices"[44] – though subsequently he conceded that there may have been grounds for that complaint.[45]

At some stage in the cycle of cross-purposes, Stone sought to build a bridge by requesting the General to write to Betagh to express his appreciation of all the work he had done in the field of education, and in preparing young men for the Society. This the new Vicar-General, Thaddeus Brzozowski, did, writing from Petrograd on 14 June 1806.[46] Betagh was gratified, and wrote to Stone to express his appreciation and his devotion to the Society.[47]

The General's letter marked a turning point for Betagh. In Stonyhurst, however, he continued to be viewed for some time, particularly by Nicholas Sewall, a future rector,[48] and by Plowden,[49] as the source of all disturbance among the Irish students and as an enemy to the emerging Society.

Kenney, for his part, preserved a remarkable equanimity throughout the two years, even though his closest friend, William Yore, who had been happy in the noviceship, had been obliged to leave because of illness. He maintained his regard and esteem for Betagh, as will appear, while yet keeping his own counsel on the pope's verbal approval of the English Jesuit province. Writing to Callaghan on 13 July 1806, Plowden stated: "Br Kenney, if God gives him health, will succeed in everything. He has virtue, talents, and sufficient knowledge of Latin. His health has been good this year. He, Ryan, and Dynan, are the only three who have not wavered in their purpose, though they have been sorely affected at the departure of the four who left them."[51] Just a month later, he reported that "Kenney and Ryan, who make their vows next month, go on very steadily. Kenney is somewhat indisposed with some affection of cold, to which he is very subject."[52]

Kenney's testing in body and spirit

They made their vows on 21 September and were sent the following day to live at Stonyhurst. Kenney was assigned to study physics and mathematics for a year, after which he was to go on to divinity. Within a short time of arrival, however, he was "troubled with a painful swelling" which, when Plowden wrote to Callaghan on 4 October, had "much abated" but was "not yet entirely cured".[53] This heralded a long period of ill health in the still dilapidated buildings. Exposed as they were to the cold air of the Pennine foothills, they presented for the inhabitants a daunting ordeal during winter months. Peter sought to participate as best he could in classes (or schools, as they were called) and in the considerable demands of recreation. It seems unlikely, because of his poor health, that he took much part in the favourite autumn and winter game of football; and as he spent many of the winter months in the infirmary, it is likely that for long periods he was spared the junior divines and philosophers obligation to speak Latin during their ordinary recreation, and the general practice of talking French during dinner and supper. As regards the ordinary scholars, he had little opportunity of meeting with them. They appear to have been allowed to mingle with his group only "in a match of foot-ball". He could not but notice, however, their distinctive uniform, which later provided inspiration for that of Clongowes. In full dress, they appeared in "fur cap, blue coat with brass buttons, red kerseymere waistcoat, leather breeches, and blue or grey stockings".[54]

In December 1806, he apparently and inexplicably went completely blind. Shortly before Christmas, in Plowden's words, "he was sent to Preston to Dr Alexander's house, where he recovered his sight".[55] He was to experience various problems with his eyes during the remainder of his time at Stonyhurst. No sooner had he recovered his sight in 1806, than he experienced "a slight return of his usual winter complaint on his chest".[56]

Palermo proposal

On 17 March 1807, Plowden summed up "the case of the Revd P. Kenney" in a letter to Glover at Palermo. Having again praised his steady virtue and his attachment to his vocation the previous year "when others of his countrymen ran wild", he reported that his eyes were much affected by the recent cold weather and east wind. "Poor Kenney," he continued, "cannot apply to study and is, therefore, unhappy. He thinks that a mild climate would relieve him, and with proper submission seeks to be sent to Palermo".

Hence, Plowden continued, "Mr Stone wishes you to enquire if Fr Angiolini [the procurator-general of the Society, who had been sent from Russia to assist in the negotiations leading to the canonical restoration of the order in the Kingdom of the Two Sicilies] will be willing to admit him, on condition of a pension being paid for his maintenance; and you will be pleased to return as speedy an answer on this as you can." Glover might further assure his superior in Sicily "that Revd Kenney, though not educated among us from childhood, is a very unexceptionable and virtuous youth", with "a strong attachment to the Society".[57]

A precedent had already been set with regard to going to Palermo for reasons of health as well as study. Walter Clifford had previously been sent there on such grounds, and Glover had gone with him as a companion. There was also another consideration in favour of sending Kenney there. As matters stood in England, the vicars apostolic would not ordain Jesuit students as religious, that is under the title of religious poverty. They would ordain them only as secular priests, with an oath of obedience and promise of service to the respective vicar apostolic. In Ireland, too, as Plowden informed Glover on 10 March, the prelates would "never grant dimissorial (letters) otherwise than under an oath of returning, each to his own diocese, as a secular priest".[58] Because the Society had been formally re-established by the pope in Sicily, however, there was no problem about being ordained as a Jesuit religious there; indeed, anyone taking their vows there was unquestionably a Jesuit and religious, and could hope to be ordained as such anywhere.

Plowden: Kenney and Sicily

Plowden's laudatory assessment of Kenney's behaviour during his noviceship did not mean that he had been easy on him. On the contrary he seems to have applied traditional methods of "testing his humility" with particular brusqueness. A fellow-novice, Fr Postlewhite, recorded that when Kenney's time came to preach his first sermon from the refectory pulpit, his eloquence and conviction held the novices spell bound at the expense of their dinner – a very considerable feat, if true! "When he had finished a long exordium and first point", however, the novice master interjected, "We have got quite enough of your points", and told him to stand down. He did so, Postlewhite explained, "to snub and humble him, as Kenney was known to be an orator".[59]

On this, and on other occasions, Kenney's response appears to have been such as to assure his novice master of his "steady virtue". Plowden tended to be severe on all who sought concessions from the demands of common life, unless there was genuine cause on grounds of health. Then he could be very sympathetic as was evidenced in the cases of Clifford, Glover and Kenney. In such cases, especially when he felt those involved had leadership or/and scholarly potential, he showed himself ready to advocate sending them to the warmer climate of Sicily. It has been suggested, indeed, that he favoured the sending of better students there, irrespective of health, as he did not consider the atmosphere of Stonyhurst suitable for young men just out of their noviceship.[60]

More than a month later, while Stone was writing to Callaghan that as Kenney spoke Latin with "tolerable fluency", and was "very ready in learning", he would soon be able to speak Italian,[61] Plowden was once more pressing Kenney's case with Glover. He had virtue, ability, and a "happy temper", he declared, and he had "succeeded better than any of his countrymen ... and we look up to him as the most likely person to forward our business in Ireland, where a steady and intelligent man is essentially necessary". He emphasised again that it was Kenney's own wish to study divinity at Palermo and that he wished to depart before the autumn. He made his request, Plowden added, "with proper submission" and "not with the rambling spirits of his countrymen". The request was approved by Frs Stone and Callaghan. The latter would pay the pension. All depended, therefore, on Fr Angiolini. Plowden could not finish, however, without a wry remark on the cost of Kenney's ill-health: "I think the charge of drug bottles and gally pots of only last winter would almost freight him overseas"! And then he reiterated the central issue involved:

> A main point will be gained by sending Br Kenney to you; *it will facilitate his ordination*, and this is a matter of main importance, at least with respect to all the Irish, which Mr Stone and I most earnestly request you to keep in view, and to recommend to Fr Angiolini's zeal.[62]

While these letters regarding Kenney's future were being written, developments of perhaps even greater consequence for that future were taking place in Dublin. Fr Callaghan was in the final months of his life and was experiencing renewed pressure concerning the disposal of the ex-Jesuit property in Ireland.

DEATH OF FR CALLAGHAN – SECURING THE SPIRIT AND THE PROPERTY

On 21 March 1807, Dr Troy wrote to the prefect of Propaganda stating that a considerable sum had now been accumulated and was "in the hands of the octogenarian ex-Jesuit" who was "proving difficult to deal with". As the matter hinged on whether the Society could be said to be restored in the British dominions, he requested a definitive ruling by the Holy See on the matter.[63] On 30 May, the prefect, Cardinal di Pietro, replied that it had not been possible to obtain a papal rescript; but that he enclosed a letter which might be shown to Fr Callaghan to persuade him to change his attitude. The enclosure declared that unless they could produce a papal document to show that the Society was restored, the Irish ex-Jesuits, being reduced to less than three, were obliged, in accordance with their earlier agreement, to hand over the property to the Irish bishops – three or four of whom would be nominated and constituted trustees and administrators of the property, and would ensure it was applied to the good of religion.[64]

On 14 June, Luke Concannon OP, who acted as an agent in Rome for the Irish bishops, expressed his astonishment at Callaghan's obstinacy. He believed that the old man would now plead that there were more than three Irish ex-Jesuits still alive, that the Society survived not only in himself and Betagh, but also in Rome in the persons of the ex-Jesuits Abbé O'Connell and Abbé Plunkett.[65] The following day, Richard Callaghan escaped from it all. Writing to Strickland on 20 June, Fr Stone observed: "Good old Fr Callaghan died on the 15th of June. Please remember him in the prayers of ours." He added that he and Fr Sewall were travelling to Ireland on the 22nd or 23rd, as there was no time to lose with regard to the Irish property. He dreaded explanations with Fr Betagh, who did not know, as he thought, that Callaghan had made any will, much less that he had made Stone his heir and one of his executors.[66]

The "good Mr Stone" had a pleasant surprise in store. Everyone seemed to know about the property. Betagh, despite his adverse comment in the previous letter to Callaghan, was most obliging and helpful, and directed them to an eminent Catholic attorney, Mr Browne, who advised them to take possession of Callaghan's effects and papers.[67] And there in the old man's rooms, in a secret repository to which, fortunately, Callaghan had previously alerted Stone, they discovered some £4,000 in cash, bonds and promissory notes.[68] The days of the English Jesuits in Dublin were marked, moreover, by gargantuan hospitality. "We dined on Monday at Mrs Doyle's," Nicholas Sewall wrote on 7 July from their lodging at 76 Church Street, "with five bishops and twelve or fourteen clergymen. The bishops were Dr Reilly, the primate, Dr Troy (Dublin), Dr Moylan (Cork), Dr Bray (Cashel and Emly), and Dr Milner. We had Lisbon vin de grave, hoche, port, claret ... If you empty your plate you are sure to have another great portion on it directly. I often think of D's story about fighting rather than eat any more. With all this eating and drinking we are both very well, but I think my pulse beats higher than it did at Portico" (near Preston). The pressing invitations were so numerous that they did not know what to do.[69]

On 18 July, Sewall, like Stone, expressed surprise at how different Betagh was from what Fr Callaghan represented him. He informed them that he was leaving £200 by will to Stone, and his library for the Society on the Irish mission; and he also mentioned that all were much pleased with "the mild and humble conduct of Mr Stone" and were glad that the money was in such safe hands.[70]

Despite such favourable comment on Betagh, Peter Kenney at Stonyhurst felt obliged to write, on 22 July, a defence of the old man against an apparently tasteless and supercilious attack made at table by an English Jesuit recently returned from Ireland. It is not clear who the offender was. Only the draft of Kenney's letter remains, and that does not give a name. But it does mention that the man had welcomed him at Preston the previous winter and had recently come from Ireland, and this suggests, strangely in the light of the letter just quoted, that the offending person may have been Nicholas Sewall, who was stationed at Portico.[71] If it were Sewall, Kenney's uncompromising and eloquently forceful reprimand says much of his personality and independence, for Sewall was a notable figure, an anglicised American, soon to be rector of Stonyhurst and a future provincial. In its own right, the letter merits consideration for the light it sheds on its author at this stage in his career.

To Betagh's defence

He had lived in Dublin for twenty-one years, Kenney wrote, and had known Fr Betagh from his earliest days. He knew him "to be equally esteemed by our prelates, beloved by the clergy, and venerated by all orders of the people". He went on: "For you, Sir, it has been reserved to represent as destitute of civility, as a liar and not an upright man, him whom I never heard mentioned but with veneration." In "the account of your late visit to Ireland, with which you favoured us yesterday evening, your observations on the person and character of Mr Betagh seemed to be delivered with jocular wit and freedom of expression."

It was said that "old Betagh was a rough, surly piece", and that he had "unpolished manners". And "this expression", Kenney added, "was followed by a description of his person in which, I am sorry to say, I beheld a priest mimicking his senior in the sanctuary and attempting a ludicrous imitation of the usual effects of hither to ever honoured old age: his shoulders rising higher than his head, so that we must get at the other side of him to see it, his long stick and tremulous gait, were all aptly described to extort a laugh at the exotic figure. In his conversation with you ... you allege that he told a parcel of lies so that on the whole you concluded he was not an upright man."

He had been enraged by this attack, Kenney stated, but had remained silent: respecting the clerical character of the speaker even though the latter had not done the same in relation to Betagh. He personally could not see any grounds for the attack. Such grounds as were mentioned were very insubstantial and likely to be due to a misunderstanding. "As to his not being an upright man, whatever you meant by this equivocal term," he declared, "I really blush to repeat it. To refer it to his moral character would constitute a calumny, of which I cannot suspect you," while to refer it to "the lowly position which advanced age has given to his venerable head would be to outrage the feelings of every well bred man. And yet you complain that Mr B. has more of the Jesuit than the gentleman in him!" In the scholastic schools, Kenney remarked, he would not admit such an inaccurate distinction. Every Jesuit he had met left him with the impression that a Jesuit always acted as a gentleman!

Having thus highlighted his grievance, he embarked on a peroration:

> Had you any acquaintance with Mr Betagh you would soon own that few priests conduct themselves more like a gentleman or are better acquainted with the etiquette of polite life than he. Had you enquired of those archbishops, bishops etc whom you visited they would have given you different notions of him ... Such is his character that I dare to say you could not utter one half of what you said at our table in any company in Ireland without giving offence. I question if you would find abettors of your opinion even among the enemies of our faith. Indeed, the company who last heard you could not refrain from expressing their dislike of the manner in which you spoke of him.

Finally, he trusted, in the traditional way, "that these reflections might be received in the same spirit of charity with which" he had "delivered them".[72]

It was the controlled response of a young man, yet it conveyed a greater depth of feeling than might be expected in a spirited defence of a venerable fellow religious. It mirrored once more national differences, reflecting in miniature the propensity for tension and misunderstanding between even the best motivated Irish and English colleagues. The hyper-sensitivity of the Irish and their readiness to take offence, baffled many Englishmen and Anglo-Americans; while generations of Irish had marvelled at the unconscious insensitivity of their English masters and neighbours where Irish matters were concerned.[73] In this instance, it did not seem to occur to the unhappy recipient of Peter's letter that to ridicule Betagh was not only to mock a prominent Irish churchman but was, in effect, to assail the Irish students themselves, who had all been educated, and perhaps financially assisted, by Betagh, and been encouraged by him in their Jesuit vocation. Such inherent proneness for misunderstanding added, as has been indicated already, to the difficulties of Irish novices and élèves while at Hodder and Stonyhurst. They were to encourage Kenney in later years to establish a separate Irish noviciate.

Meantime, there was pleasant surprise at Stonyhurst at the warm welcome experienced in Dublin. Within a matter of weeks, however, the issue of ownership of the property flared up again, and Betagh found himself poised between loyalty to the archbishop and the hopes and commitments of would be Jesuit colleagues.

Jesuit property controversy – "The glare of gold"

Despite his graciousness to the English Jesuits, Dr Troy had not given up his designs on the now considerable ex-Jesuit funds.[74] He wished to ensure that the money was put to work in Ireland, not England. All depended, as has been indicated, on whether the Society could be said to formally exist in British territories. On 14 July 1807, Luke Concannon sent him the reply from Cardinal di Pietro which required the English Jesuits to hand over the Irish funds to the bishops if they could not produce a papal rescript re-establishing the Society in England and Ireland.[75] Dr Troy requested Betagh to forward di Pietro's reply to Fr Stone. He did so on 20 August. Callaghan, he declared, had informed the bishops of the extent of the funds, and this had whetted their appetites. Di Pietro's letter, he added, was but a letter "from an individual in office" who could not enforce final submission to his doctrine.[76]

Stone consulted Strickland, who also advised that di Pietro's letter carried no weight, and wondered that nothing was said to them when they visited Dublin. He marvelled "how much even pious people can be blinded by self-love where interest is concerned".[77] Dr Troy and his advisers, especially Concannon, had their own thoughts about Jesuit self-love and duplicity. In the new year, his Grace decided to intervene personally. He sent a very challenging letter to Stone: informing him that two queries had been sent to the Holy See by the prelates of Ireland, and that he felt under a necessity to communicate them to him, and the answers to each.

The queries were: 1. Whether the Society of Jesus was canonically re-established in Ireland and England "in consequence of any Apostolic Rescript, or any *vivae vocis oraculum* of his Holiness"? And 2. If it were "not canonically re-established in these kingdoms", should not the property of the deceased members of the suppressed Society "be committed to the administration of three Irish prelates, as trustees of the Irish mission", in accordance with "the determination of the Irish ex-Jesuits in an instrument signed by them in the year 1773"?

The answers which he had received, stated that the Holy See had not approved or acknowledged Jesuits anywhere "except in Russia and the Kingdom of Naples", and that the Sacred Congregation (once again) required of Mr Stone the title by which he retained the funds left by Mr Callaghan, and that he transmit an authentic copy of any Apostolic rescript and proof of any *vivae vocis oraculum* of his Holiness re-establishing the Society of Jesus in Great Britain and Ireland, and that meantime he refrain from disposing of any of the said funds.

The archbishop confirmed that Fr Callaghan had shown him the agreement between the ex-Jesuits, and that he had appointed himself, Dr Moylan of Cork, and Dr Delany of Kildare, as trustees of the Irish mission, but that afterwards, having been led to believe that the Society was canonically re-established in these kingdoms, Callaghan "renewed his vows and transferred the fund" to Stone. Finally, Dr Troy remarked that he had not mentioned the claims of the Irish prelates when Stone was in Dublin, because he wished to avoid any scandal arising from a dispute over a will, and because he had not then heard from Rome and knew the funds were safe in Stone's hands.[78]

The mild rector-cum-provincial felt aggrieved and betrayed by the archbishop's actions and letter. He later told Betagh that in the spring of 1803, in response to a friendly query from Dr Troy, he had informed him in a confidential letter that the British ex-Jesuits had petitioned to be united to the Society in Russia, and that the pope had granted the petition – "secretly, indeed, and by word of mouth only, for fear of drawing upon himself a persecution from the enemies of the Society both in Rome and elsewhere". He had asked the archbishop to signify his support for the union by writing to the pope in person. Instead, he had written to the strong opponent of the Society, Cardinal Borgia, who, as noted, had forthwith issued a condemnatory letter. Now, his Grace was appealing once more to the Congregation: this time "to wrest from the Society the means of re-establishing itself in Ireland".

With this background very much in mind, and their struggle in England to preserve their funds, Stone had set about replying to Archbishop Troy.[79] His response, written on 22 April 1808, was uncharacteristically strong. It had been stiffened by legal advice and, in all probability, by assistance from the forthright William Strickland.[80]

Stone's reply – Impact and effect

With reference to the Society being re-established in the British dominions by rescript or by *vivae vocis oraculum*, no ex-Jesuit, Stone stated, advanced any such pretensions. True, in a confidential letter to his Grace, under a recommendation of strict secrecy, and written in consequence of his Grace's assurance of friendship, he had used the term *oraculum* in a loose manner, trying to convey an explanation without measuring his words. When he had done so, he had no idea that his Grace harboured motives other than interest and friendship. But, he added, "Cardinal Borgia's severe letter" a few months later "discovered to me the use which your Grace had thought proper to make of my unsuspecting confidence". Stone continued with cutting irony:

> I cannot conceive why your Grace should search for rescripts and *oraculums*, when the high authority of Cardinal Borgia, which you certainly cannot mistrust, has assured you that none exist. It appears to me

equally extraordinary that the Sacred Congregation should search for such things in England and Ireland, while they can so easily know the truth from the Sacred Personage, from whom, if they existed, they must have come.

He then pointedly begged leave to express his surprise that his Grace "invoked the spiritual power, which we so highly revere, to invalidate the will of a British subject conveying property". He earnestly hoped, in sincere friendship, that no future circumstance would compel him to bring forth his Grace's deed to public knowledge. Finally, he assured Dr Troy that if his, Stone's, pretensions to the property of the late Revd Mr Callaghan rested on grounds that required his will to be set aside, he would not demur to surrender that property without troubling the Sacred Congregation about it. "But nothing of this sort appears."[81]

It was bare-knuckle fighting dressed in polite language. Plowden, a fortnight later, expressed the intent in his own direct and somewhat arrogant manner: "At present we think we shall keep the archbishop in awe, by the dread of discovering to public knowledge his very indiscreet act." For to invoke the spiritual power to invalidate the wills of a British subject, and to cite the appointed heir to answer before a foreign and spiritual court in a cause of litigated property, were "such gross violations of our oath of allegiance that nothing but the glare of gold could have blinded the prelate – but we know the words of our oath too well to pay any regard to his citations."[82]

The letter bewildered and upset the archbishop. Coming from the mild, inoffensive Fr Stone, it had a particularly disturbing effect. Dr Betagh objected strongly to Stone about the tone of his letter, and in particular about the "indecorous threat to make public his Grace's attempt to invalidate the will of a British subject conveying property". The aggravation was all the greater in that the letter reached Dr Troy during a serious fit of illness. Stone, with his usual deceleration, did not reply till 9 July, and then having expressed his regret that his letter arrived at a time when his Grace was so situated, he went on to give the background, indicated earlier. He then hastened to assure his Grace and Betagh that in maintaining the right of the Irish province of the Society of Jesus to the property in question, "no other motive than that of duty, justice, and conscience, and the good of the Irish mission ever have or shall influence any proceedings of mine in that affair."[83]

Without any sense of embarrassment or self-consciousness, he went on to inform Betagh of the progress of the élèves for the Irish mission; adding that he had received a letter from Mr Kenney off Malta, in which he said that he and his companion expected to be at Palermo in a few days. He concluded by requesting that Betagh would "please to present my best wishes and respects to Dr Troy, and assure him of my unalterable regard and esteem", and also to remember him kindly to Mr Browne whom he hoped to see at Stonyhurst shortly, and he wished Betagh would accompany him. It was very difficult to remain angry for long with "the good Mr Stone".

In fact, the archbishop appears to have been disposed for a while to go no further with the matter, accepting Stone's assurance that the money would be used for the Irish mission. And he apparently wrote to Rome to that effect. His adviser there, however, Luke Concannon, recently appointed bishop of New York, an agitated man, with an anxiety about Jesuits bordering on obsession,[84] insisted on seeking further letters from Cardinal di Pietro. He persisted for two years more, with at least the tacit approval of Dr Troy. In October, 1809, di Pietro sent another long missive.[85] When Stone eventually replied, on 25 April 1810, the matter had become largely academic. It was not possible to arrive at any satisfactory solution, he declared, until the Holy Father was released from French captivity. Meanwhile, he promised to preserve the funds carefully for the Irish mission, but emphasised that at the present time any claims on a British subject's property would be extremely unwise as government vigilance under that head was very acute, and particularly since his Eminence and other ministers of the Holy See had "become subjects of the public enemy, Buonaparte"![86]

By then, however, the Roman congregations were in disarray. Moreover, at the end of November 1809 – nearly two years after Kenney had gone to Sicily, where, nevertheless, he still followed the course of negotiations with interest and concern – Plowden requested Glover to let Kenney know that he had supplied "our good friend, Mr Grainger" with "a triumphant refutation of the pretensions and requisitions of Cardinal di Pietro, and a full justification of what Mr Callaghan and his heirs have done". Subsequently, Grainger informed Stone that Dr Troy had declared himself satisfied that Stone would fairly employ the property in question in its proper use, the service of the Irish mission, and that, as a result, the entire affair might be considered "closed and settled".[87] Time was to show, however, that the archbishop remained ill at ease until the funds were put to work in Ireland on the return of Peter Kenney.

Conclusions and departures

A satisfactory outcome to the dispute about property was essential to the future of the Irish mission and, in consequence, to Peter Kenney's work. One of the side benefits from the point of view of the bishops was that very clear assurances had been given that the funds would be used to the benefit of the Church in Ireland; and the funds were in fact to be conveyed to Kenney in 1813, following his return from Sicily. As he was leaving Stonyhurst, however, the issue was far from resolved. He felt personally concerned not only about the security of the property but about the validity of his vows and status as a Jesuit.[88] These issues were to come into sharper focus when he had settled in

Sicily and had opportunity to discuss the recent history of the Society with Fr Angiolini, who had been at the forefront in negotiations.

During his final year at Stonyhurst, Peter enjoyed better health. It was said of him that his bouts of blindness, which made reading impossible, had encouraged him to concentrate on the lectures and to reflect on the material. As a result, he acquired a grasp and assurance above the ordinary, particularly in philosophy. His knowledge was what Newman was to call "real knowledge", something "thought out and thought through" by himself. He was to bring the same approach to the study of theology. Before leaving Stonyhurst he had faced a public examination and a public defence of theses in philosophy. The account of his performance, sent by Stone to Betagh, was described by the latter as "most flattering and comfortable to the well wishers of the Irish mission".[89] He also informed Stone that he considered it a wise measure to send Kenney and Ryan to Sicily in that it would facilitate and secure their promotion to holy orders.[90] In this, at least, he was of one mind with Kenney's other principal mentor, Charles Plowden. Writing to his regular correspondent, Glover, in April 1807, Plowden had remarked that Fr Stone was sending Kenney and Ryan, the one very able, the other of but mediocre talent, that they might gather the genuine spirit of the Society in its source and also because it would secure their speedy and easy promotion to holy orders.[91] Nine months later, as they were about to set out, he entrusted a letter to Kenney which put the motive for their journey beyond all doubt. It was his belief, he declared, that the bishops, despite their opposition over the property, were most unlikely to refuse faculties to men returning to Ireland after being ordained in the Society, where it was undoubtedly established. So, "you now see," he concluded, "Mr Stone's motive for sending the bearer of this to Palermo; for his health, which has not been much affected this year, is a *secondary consideration*."[92]

Much later again, in September 1809, Betagh was to confirm Stone's thinking. A letter from Archbishop Carroll, he claimed, had brought home to him the insufficiency of aggregated Jesuit vows and the necessity of the voyage to Sicily. He urged, therefore, that all those sent there should renew their vows immediately on their arrival, and that "those of age receive subdeaconship, and then if obliged by the circumstances of the time to return home", they would come washed clean of any censure and qualified for further promotion.[93]

In this letter, Betagh acknowledged that he had earlier expressed to Stone his reservation about the journey to Sicily. At that time he had been concerned for the safety of Kenney and Ryan. Buonaparte seemed invincible. French privateers were recently at the mouth of the Irish Channel, and he had trembled at the dangers and uncertainties of their voyage and the insecurity and lack of permanency of their situation in Sicily.[94]

In January 1808, the two young men set out on the first stage of their long journey. Kenney appears to have nerved himself for the discomfort and danger of the voyage and the uncertain future in a besieged land. He, after all, was going at his own request. Poor Ryan, on the other hand, was travelling purely out of obedience, and he underwent a degree of anxiety which heralded future mental instability. A letter from Liverpool filled with incoherent phrases betrayed to Betagh the "violent conflict agitating his mind between nature and religious duty".[95]

At Palermo, meantime, their arrival was eagerly awaited by Thomas Glover. He had been ordained the previous year, and viewed his priesthood at this stage to be for the sake of Irish sailors and soldiers serving with the British forces on the island. And he had prepared the ground well for future foreigners – for he had not only established good relations with the Jesuit community, he had also made a good impression at the highest social level, even to the point, Plowden reported, of the queen sending for him to say his first mass in the royal chapel and showing "great regard and attention to him".[96]

III

Where two seas meet:
Stimulus and strain in Sicily

Sicily – I am drawn to it as by a lode stone. ... It was the theme of almost every poet and every historian and the remains in it of the past are of an earlier antiquity and more perfect than those of other countries ...

John Henry Newman

The political context

Betagh's fears about the voyage to Sicily, and that island's political future, were shared inevitably by the Jesuits at Stonyhurst. During Peter's years there, the struggle with Napoleon had been constantly in the news. Throughout 1805, indeed, fear of invasion hung over England until dispelled by Nelson's victory at Trafalgar. Thereafter, Napoleon sought to bring England to its knees by means of the continental blockade: attempting to cut it off from all trade with the continent of Europe. Britain, for its part, involved itself in coalitions against the French emperor. The Kingdom of the Two Sicilies, encompassing the state of Naples and the island of Sicily, joined such a coalition: admitting British troops as part of the arrangement. The Kingdom was ruled by the Bourbon king, Ferdinand IV and Queen Maria Caroline. They had been prominent in seeking the suppression of the Society of Jesus, at which time the queen, the beautiful but imperious daughter of Maria Theresa, empress of Austria, and sister of Marie-Antoinette, was much influenced by Jansenist views; but more recently they had led the way in western Europe in obtaining, on 30 July 1804, the restoration of the order in their dominions: an event with an impact on Roman curial officials that Peter Plunkett was happy to convey to Strickland – "the doings at Naples have humbled the purpled leaders of Propaganda to a degree you cannot conceive, They are reduced to silence and to a knashing of teeth."[1]

Ferdinand paid the price for defying Napoleon. The latter declared him deposed on 27 December 1805. He retreated to Sicily, where he indulged his fondness for the chase, and the provision of public spectacles. Napoleon appointed his brother, Joseph, as king. The Jesuits were driven out of their houses and banished from Naples. Some of them fled to Sicily to join their confrères there. The British navy set about protecting the island. Napoleon, meanwhile, took over southern Italy, so that a mere thread of sea, two miles broad, became the only barrier to the all-conquering French leader.

In these years, too, the relations between the pope and Napoleon became increasingly strained. Pius VII had opposed the extension to Italy of the *Code Napoleon* because it authorised divorce, and he had rejected Napoleon's request to have the apparently happy marriage between his brother, Jerome, and Miss Patterson of Baltimore, annulled. In 1806 the pope further asserted his independence. He refused to expel all enemies of France from the Papal States and to close the papal ports to British trade; protested at the appointment of Joseph Bonaparte as king of Naples, over which the papacy claimed suzerainty; and refused to appoint Napoleon's nominees to Venetian bishoprics.

The French emperor was too busy coping with a grand coalition of Russia, Prussia, Sweden, and Britain to respond immediately. With the defeat of Russia at Friedland in June 1807, however, he achieved the zenith of his power. He and Alexander of Russia at the treaty of Tilsit, 9 July 1807, virtually divided Europe between them. Napoleon extended his continental system.

The blockade rendered communication to and from Sicily uncertain and haphazard. Plowden wrote frequently, and repeated himself in his letters, to allow for correspondence going astray. He used various expedients to get letters through – sending some by bearer, some post-paid by Malta, others carried to Malaga and posted from there; yet in July 1807, he was complaining that he had sent nine letters without any of them being answered. That summer, before Kenney and Ryan set out, the correspondence to Glover was heavy with gloom and foreboding. Plowden wondered if Britain were to "be overthrown ... and suffer for its schism of 270 years", and he bemoaned, in that eventuality, the destruction of "all the meritorious labour of Fr Angiolini and his associates" in Sicily;[2] Stone, somewhat confusedly, instructed Glover to return home in the event of the Jesuits being forced to leave the island, and, if possible, to bring four or five students with him to finish their studies at Stonyhurst;[3] while Sewall, to whom Glover had expressed his fears of a revolution in Sicily, responded with the scarcely comforting news that it was "the constant opinion" that Sicily would fall to Napoleon by assault or revolution, or by arrangement with the Russians. The same letter expressed the view that the manufacturers and merchants of England would soon be calling out for peace, and that the government would not be supported if there was no trade.[4] And in May 1808, soon after the two young voyagers had arrived at Palermo, the overriding sense of confusion and isolation was conveyed vividly by Plowden. He denounced "the lying newspapers" for "deceiving the public with forged tales of naval victories in the Mediterranean", and for current alarming reports of the inability of British naval forces to defend Sicily. "The truth is," he exclaimed, "we are now *toto divisi orbe Brittani* [Britons cut off from the whole world], we have no intercourse with any part of the continent ...".[5]

In that overall situation, sending Kenney and the unfortunate Ryan to Sicily was entrusting hostages to fortune; and the sailing journey itself was sufficiently hazardous to evoke memories of the travels and travails of intrepid missionaries of the old Society.

Setting out and arriving

Even before Kenney and Ryan left England, their resolution was tried. They set out for Falmouth, staying at inns along the way. When they arrived "on the evening of 14 February" after "a painful journey", there was no sign of their ship and the convoy had sailed that morning. Two days later, they met the captain of the *Salerno* on which they were to sail. Kenney insisted on going aboard, as he and Ryan now had no lodging. At 10.30 that night, their captain, "soberly bedewed with grog", brought them to the ship; which they reached about midnight, after first running aground! Two frightening days and nights followed. "The cabin windows were smashed to pieces," Kenney reported to Fr Stone, "and the sea rushing furiously in set my bed afloat which lay underneath ... The cable anchor was lost and the vessel almost on her side. Our trunks, and as far as I can see our wine and porter, are safe." To add to the strain, the press-gang came aboard and took away one of the men. There had been only six and a cabin boy, which were barely enough. He continued: "The captain and mate are this instant abusing each other and I hear dreadful work. Altogether we have a blessed prospect before us. May God be our protection! Our hope is in the good prayers of our friends." His concluding lines were: "Midnight, or rather 1 o'clock Friday morning, February 19 1808, the fight is over. All is quiet. May the God of peace be with us. All the transports are sailing out. We are pulling up the anchor."[6]

The experience was unnerving for two young men whose only previous acquaintance with sea travel appears to have been one or more journeys between Dublin and Liverpool. It was an unforgettable start to a voyage that was to last for two months. Unfortunately, there is no account of the journey. Kenney kept a journal from his arrival at Palermo, but wrote nothing of the voyage. A letter from Stone to Betagh in July 1808, mentioned, as noted earlier, that he had had a letter from him off Malta, and that he and his companion expected to be at Palermo in a few days.[7] Stone, however, gave no date for Kenney's letter. It, presumably, was written early in April, for he reached his destination on the 16th of that month.

Malta was a focal point for British convoys in the Mediterranean. Kenney was to find himself there also, and for some time, on his homeward journey. From there, they took ship, or availed themselves of the same vessel, to Messina: traversing the deep, cool waters of the Ionian Sea, and sailing up the historic straits between southern Italy and Sicily to where, north of Messina, the Tyrrhenian and Ionian seas meet between the headlands of Scylla and Charybdis made famous in Homer's great epic. It was Kenney's first direct contact with the world of the ancient classics which Sicily so vividly evokes.

There was no stop, it seems, at Messina, nor, after rounding the top of the island, at the garrison town of Melazzo. They sailed past Capo d'Orlando and, closer in, along the variegated and picturesque coastline until they reached the town of Termini. Kenney was later to describe it as "worthy of notice for its antiquity and no way contemptible for its present situation". They made a short stay there. A pre-Roman settlement, celebrated for its hot springs, from which came its name, it stood on three levels. Visiting it again on 20 October 1809, he noted in his journal that he was better received on that occasion at the Jesuit college than he and Ryan had been when they paid a night visit there on their way to Palermo. On that occasion, the librarian, Fr Contantio, appears to have given them a cold welcome. Eventually, towards midday on 16 April 1808, they entered the majestic bay of Palermo.

The whole northern coast of Sicily presents from the sea dramatic views of unusual rock formation and sandy beaches against a backdrop of mountains. The entrance to Palermo – situated between two lofty promontories, Monte Pelligrono on the west and Monte Alfano on the east – comes as a fitting finale. As Peter's ship turned into the great bay, the city lay before him, spread out in a wide plain encircled by hills. He would come to know the expanse as the *Conca d'Oro*, the golden conch shell, because of its shape and the fertility of the soil. As the vessel drew closer, the steepness of the encircling hills became apparent; while in the foreground his gaze was held by a variety of tall buildings, of church spires, domes and minarets, all glittering in a bright sun against a sparkling sea, and conveying the image of an exotic, almost oriental city. From its foundation by the Phoenicians to its more recent experience of Spanish, and Bourbon rule, it had been a crossroads of civilization.

Sicily was, indeed, a fitting region to provide a width of European experience to students from a more remote island country. And the experiences were sharpened and deepened by the drama of the present, the imminence of a French invasion. Peter's years there were to give a special interiority to his appreciation of classical culture and of the classical languages, especially Latin; for it was no longer just a necessary medium of communication between countries, nor something to be mastered in order to understand the lectures and read the textbooks in theology and philosophy, it was part of a living tradition. Reminders of the radiance that was Greece and the majesty that was Rome were to be encountered on almost every shore of the island.

Early impressions

From his journal, which he kept intermittently from 16 April 1808 to 1 September 1811, it appears that they arrived unheralded. The first entry, at the date of 16 April, stated: "Arrived at Palermo about noon, and was conducted to the college by a clergyman and two secular gentlemen whom I met on the street." He and Ryan entered "as the fathers were coming out of the refectory" from dinner, and were "immediately recognised by Fr Glover and embraced by him and the other fathers". In the evening, they were "introduced to Fr vice-provincial in the professed house"[8] and, presumably as the first Irish Jesuits of the revitalised Society, "all the novices came to salute" them. The following day, Fr Glover said mass in thanksgiving for their safe arrival, and Kenney sent two letters in Latin to Syracuse. This, he noted, "much encouraged the inflammation in my eye which was soon communicated to the right one, and both every day grew worse". On 22 April, he and Ryan put on their "religious dress" for use within the college and community, and received confirmation that their ordinations were being brought forward because of the uncertain political situation.

By the middle of May he was fully involved in the life of the college and community. Able to study again, he took part in the public disputations on 20 May, during which students defended theses and answered objections in the presence of fellow-students, members of faculty, and some invited guests. In the community, he noted as a highlight of Ascension Thursday, 26 May, that there was ice-cream and talk in the refectory for the first time. He had a sweet tooth, and tended to comment in the journal when desserts were added to the menu; but he seldom expressed criticism despite the general sparsity of the diet.

Outside events soon imposed themselves on the confined horizons of lectures, discussions, study, and religious routine. He noted on 24 May that "an explosion of gunpowder destroyed several houses and people" close to the Franciscan convent; while further afield the occupation of Rome by the French general, Miollis, on 2 February led to the archbishop of Palermo on 10 May, "in compliance with the king's order", instructing that major litanies be said after the last mass everyday for the pope, that a further collect (prayer) be added to every mass, and that "for three successive days" there should be "exposition of the Blessed Sacrament" in every church for a few hours each day. At the end of the month variety was joined to stark reality with the arrival in the bay of "two English men of war, which gave two broadsides and hung out all colours". Their presence added further to the bustle, activity, and noise of the great marina, which provided one of the great spectacles of the city, especially at evening, when pulsing with the excitement and suppressed violence of chattering and gesticulating crowds of men, women, and children walking, sitting, or bartering by the wide harbour side.

The house of the professed fathers of the Society, or *casa professa*, and the Jesuit college, or *collegio massima*, were centrally located. They stood on one of the main thoroughfares, a street of high buildings, of palaces and churches, now known as Corsa Vittoria Emanuele, which runs down from the Porta Nueva, beside the royal palace, to the great harbour. On the way it traverses the Via Maqueda at one of the city's best known landmarks, the Quatro Canti, or Four Corners, where each corner is occupied by a statue of a Spanish king and a depiction of one of the four seasons. Close by this busy crossroads stood the Jesuit college and professed house.

As Kenney and customary companions[9] walked the surrounding streets and visited the local churches, they quickly became aware of contrasting architecture and of the city's varied history. The overall contrast to life at home could scarcely have been greater. During the summer months of 1808, long detailed entries in his journal reflected the novelty of his experiences. During June he wrote in detail of the solemn Corpus Christi procession,[10] in which the king and courtiers walked; of the celebration of the Forty Hours devotions[11] in the Jesuit church; and of the triduum of prayer and instruction for the Jesuit scholastics.[12] The very detail indicated, perhaps, a wish to record practices and procedures with a view to future application in Ireland. The two most significant entries during the month, nevertheless, were of he, Ryan, and others receiving the tonsure and minor orders; and, towards the end of June, of Ryan showing evidence of a persecution complex. His suspicions and accusations became so disordered that Kenney was prevailed on by Glover and the Fr Minister – who was in charge of the health of the community – to write to Fr Plowden about him.

The event which featured most *prominently* in the journal during 1808, however, was the great annual feast of St Rosalia, the principal patroness of the city. The festivities commenced on 11 July and continued for some days, drawing great crowds then as now, only that then there was a degree of pageantry, pomp and preparation, not sustainable under a democratic system. A temporary balcony was constructed along the front of the college, lit with flaming torches at night, to facilitate the viewing of the celebrations. One of the traditional highlights was the great opening procession, which had as its centre piece a great float or "triumphal car" bearing the statue of the patron saint to whose intercession the cessation of a plague in the seventeenth century was ascribed. The construction and decoration of the car varied from year to year, thereby adding to the excitement of the occasion. It was all so new and stimulating for him that he recorded almost every detail of the processions and celebrations during the civic feast. Not surprisingly the "triumphal car" caught his immediate attention. He described at length this ship-like structure rising in tiers to the great statue of the saint, and, on the tiers, rows of seated "musicians who played a pleasing symphony whenever the car stopped". This "grand machine", he observed, "whose height was equal to a house of four storeys, was highly ornamented on every part with tinsel, guilding and tapestry hung in festoons". It was drawn by 20 pair of oxen, and "was preceded by a large body of cavalry in a brilliant uniform with trumpets and kettle drums", who were followed on horseback by "one of the principal senators, who with a bell gave the signal when the car was to stop and when to proceed".

The large Jesuit college also encompassed a boarding school for sons of the nobility. After supper that evening, he was allowed go with these pupils "to see the fireworks at the sea shore". It was his first time with them. They walked in "a blaze of light" as "each of the nobles had at his side his own servant, lent by his parents, to attend him with a flambeau" (flaming torch). There was strict supervision, but the pupils, "conscious of their dignity, were as willing to keep good order as the prefects were to enforce its observance". En route, they drew up in a straight line to salute the on-coming royal carriage. The king returned their salutation by raising his hat, while the queen acknowledged it, in Kenney's perhaps naieve comment,[13] "by a most gracious smile which indicated the pleasure she felt at the sight of so many noble and virtuous youths". The college group then continued to the great crescent-shaped arena by the peaceful sea, and occupied, on an elevated platform, convenient seats near "the scene of the action". The discharge of two rockets from the royal platform signalled the start of the entertainment. There followed a battle of fireworks from one side of the marina to the other, succeeded by volleys of guns, and a vast fire of light which brilliantly lit up the whole scene. All then proceeded to the nearby public gardens to enjoy the illuminations there. Later as they walked home, Kenney marvelled how the great street was lit by streams of light extending in straight line for a mile and then rising with the road to form a pyramid of light over the gate to the city.

Next day, there was the excitement of horse races on the road in front of the college. The crowds pressed on either side, while the military were stationed at a very short distance from each other along the route to keep the course clear. It was a real *horse* race. There were five horses, but no riders! The animals had "bladders and other trappings hung from their manes", and at the starting shot, amidst the shouts of the crowd, the frightened horses ran the course, the crowd surging forward after they passed. There were three races. At the end of each, the name of the winner was brought to the king. After dark, the triumphal car was brought down the hill from near the royal palace. It stopped and played music in front of the illuminated balconies of the college, from which, as Kenney concluded in his account, "we saw all the public diversions".

By the following evening, 13 July, he seemed to have tired of it all. "I went to the villa of San Giuseppe," he wrote. "The diversion there was a ridiculous puppet show." Subsequently, there were "races, illuminations, and fire works" which he does not appear to have attended.

On the 26th of the month, he was delighted to have the opportunity, in the company of Frs Glover and Magnani, of visiting the king's villa. He wrote enthusiastically of the square four-storey cottage, "painted on the outside in various colours" and presenting "within and without something new, curious, delightfully pleasing and elegant, yet simple". On 1 August, the day after the feast of St Ignatius, the royal family, without the king who was unable to attend, visited the Jesuit church. As she alighted from her carriage, the queen remarked to Fr Angiolini: "I have come today to testify my esteem for all of you. I wished to come yesterday, but could not." Kenney's attitude to the visiting royalty, despite the queen's unpopularity in Sicily, was positive – "A number of Ours were drawn up within the two files of soldiers to receive them, where I with the rest had the honour of kissing the queen's hand." With Irish perversity he seemed less enthusiastic about the monarch of Great Britain and Ireland. His comment for 5 June 1809 merely stated: "The king's birthday was celebrated by the English here. The guns were fired, and the ambassador gave a most splendid dinner."

Meanwhile, poor Ryan's health continued to deteriorate. On 8 August he drew attention to his condition in a manner which the community found very embarrassing. Kenney wrote that, while they were having their siesta, he "stole out of the private gate ... and strolled about the streets in the domestic dress of the Society to the astonishment of everyone who beheld him. In this state he went to seek the queen's confessor", the bishop "who had promoted him to minor orders. The attendant refused him admittance, saying the bishop was asleep. He afterwards met with a secular priest, who, promising to find a confessor for him, took him to the madhouse." Seeing a naked man at the window, Ryan, as Kenney remarked, "had sense enough to discover what the place was ... and escaped from his uncharitable conductor." He returned to the Jesuit house, but, not being able to get in, he went to the villa of one of the royal family about three miles from the city, where he asked for "a Neapolitan gentleman of the prince's household" whose name he knew. That "good gentleman soon saw his disease and conducted him to the college two hours after nightfall". It was "an unlucky circumstance", Kenney wrote, that while this gentleman stood talking with Ryan, "the prince passed by and more by his looks than his words expressed his surprise to see a Jesuit at that hour, in that dress, and in that place". He continued: "Our trouble and confusion at home cannot well be conceived. We were as yet searching for him in every hole and corner of the great house when he arrived." A brother was appointed to sleep in his room to care for him that night, "but the next day the provincial, fearing to increase his insanity, ordered that he should not be confined to his room". The physician prescribed a cold bath for him each day. His health seemed to improve for a while, and then he fell back once more: believing that he had "been dismissed from the Society", and that the members of the community were "everyday reading, speaking, and publishing bills, decrees and proclamations against him". It was decided to send him home.

Writing on 15 September 1808, to Nicholas Sewall at Portico, near Preston, Thomas Glover told of Ryan's departure, and remarked that to judge by his condition of melancholy while at Palermo he would "never be capable of receiving holy orders".[14] Fortunately, it was not an accurate prognosis.[15]

In the same letter, he mentioned in some excitement a mysterious and dramatic adventure in which Kenney was involved. It was, in retrospect, to be one of the most memorable occurrences in the latter's career, bringing him for a short while close to an international incident.

Rescuing the pope

With the occupation of the Papal States in February, 1808, Pius VII became virtually a prisoner in Rome. It had been the wish of the Sicilian court for a considerable time, Glover wrote on 15 September, "to withdraw the pope from Rome and from French territory". On 24 August "Fr Angiolini received a private commission from the court", and embarked very secretly on an English frigate taking with him a Spanish priest, and Kenney as interpreter. "Last night," Glover continued, "they returned but they are all so tightly tongue-tied that it is impossible to draw a word from them: they only say in a short time we shall know everything, even the *very cats of Palermo.*"

Glover then went on to say that members of the community were amusing themselves giving their own interpretation of events or, as he put it, "building castles in the air". His own interpretation was that they were cruising off the papal states, that somebody was sent in disguise to Rome to contact the pope, but that he refused to leave.[16]

His construction of events came close to the reality as presented by Kenney in his journal, and as later conveyed in the history of the Sicilian Jesuit province.[17]

The annals of the province, in hagiographical style, pronounced that "the religious-minded King Ferdinand", concerned at the danger to the pope, determined to invite him to Sicily; and to this purpose he called on his friend, Fr Angiolini, who was known to Pius VII.

To him the king added as companion "Fr Fra Gian Maria Procida, OFM, a man of experience and good sense. Angiolini, as a result, was accompanied by him and by the Spaniard, our Giuseppe Gonzalez, and the Irish student, Pietro Kenney, who would serve as an interpreter for him on the English vessel in which they embarked on 25 August."

Peter's account of how he became involved was, naturally, far more personal and immediate. His entry of 25 August stated:

> About an hour before sunset, Fr Angiolini called me to his room and, having enjoined the strictest secrecy, told me I was to quit the college and go to sea with him that night about an hour after dark.

At the appointed hour he went to his room and found there Fr Procida, and two laymen, one a native of Rome, the other, Cavacciali, the marquis of Cacerelli's secretary. Around midnight, the Jesuit priests Angiolini and Gonzales, together with the others, boarded the English frigate *Alceste*, which lay at anchor in the harbour.

The next two days, sailing north east through the Tyrenian sea, "passed miserably", Peter commented, "as we had neither place of repose nor anything that we could eat or drink with comfort".

His entries for subsequent days, unfortunately, are illegible in parts. On 30 August they were off Ostia. Procida and one Capucetta, not previously mentioned, "wearing secular dress", were landed by a brig three hours after sunset. Peter's account provides no information about what happened at Rome. The province annals add, however, that Procida penetrated "in disguise through a thousand guards ... first at the gates of the city, then on entry to the castle", before he reached the pope. Angiolini, meanwhile, being "too well known in Rome", stayed aboard in the harbour.[18]

Cardinal Pacca, the recently appointed secretary of state, provided further details in his *Memoirs*. He recalled how one dark night he came across a frightening looking fellow lurking in the Quirinal, whom he took for a Sicilian bandit, but who assured him he was a Fransciscan friar in disguise and that he had come off an English frigate. It had sailed from Sicily, he declared, in accordance with an arrangement made with the English cardinal, Erskine, with Pacca's predecessor, Gabrielli (who had been expelled from Rome at short notice by the French), and with King Ferdinand, and it would lie off Fiumicino for three more nights. Pacca enquired of Erskine and the pope, both of whom confirmed the truth of the story, though the pope claimed that he had never consented to the plot.[19]

The annals rounded off the account in their customary style, stating that "the pope expressed his gratitude to Procida, to Angiolini, to the king, and to the kingdom of Sicily ... but refused the invitation, saying it was not appropriate for a pastor to abandon his flock, for a prince to abandon his subjects, or a father his children. Procida returned to Ostia, and they set sail for Sicily."

As might be suspected from the style, the annals' rounded presentation of the pope's calm, eloquent decisiveness does not correspond with the sense of confusion conveyed by Peter's account of subsequent events. Although Pius VII refused a number of offers of rescue, and although his secretary of state warned that to place himself under English protection would make it easier for Napoleon to declare him an enemy of the empire, and might bring about a schism in the church,[20] he does not appear to have given a categorical refusal on this occasion. This is clearly implied by Peter's entries. He has Capucetta and Procida returning to the ship "about three hours after midnight" on 2 September, that is three days after their departure. The frigate remained at its station, and a boat was sent to the shore "at the appointed time" on 3, 4, 5 September, "but in vain". On the 6th the day was spent sounding the shoalings off the fort of Fiumicino; and the next day again, Kenney observed that "Fr Procida refused to go ashore as had been previously agreed", having been upset by the fears expressed by Fr Gonzales.

At this stage, many of those present appear to have lost heart and purpose. On 8 September, Kenney noted: "strong remonstrances made to the captain by all except me to return. I declined signing the remonstrance." Two days later, Fr Angiolini and a count, who was also in the party, and whose whereabouts during these days is not clear, rejoined them; and two hours after sunset they set sail.

The annals mention that on their homeward journey "their English vessel was attacked by a French one. They managed to get away, and on 14 September arrived at Palermo, obtaining rather merit than fortune from their expedition. Angiolini gave the king a faithful account of what had happened." Kenney's final entry was more sober. He said nothing of danger from a French vessel; nothing at all, indeed, about the journey home. The next entry after 10 September is for the 14th. Then, in the most mundane of epilogues to a considerable adventure, he merely stated: "Wednesday. Arrived at the harbour of Palermo before dinner, but were not allowed to descend until after sunset – arrived at college at second table."

A colourful postscript was provided by a later story going the rounds in Dublin, that the captain of the frigate, Captain Cockburn (subsequently admiral), used to joke with his fellow officers that he had had the unique honour of receiving the orders of his sovereign to hold himself and his ship at the orders of two Jesuits, and for the purpose of carrying off a pope to England![21]

As if in reaction to the intensity of the previous three weeks, there was scarcely any entry in Kenney's journal for the second half of September. It had been a testing experience during which once again, despite asthma and proneness to eye infection, he showed a capacity to absorb great physical discomfort; and also manifested considerable independence and moral courage in standing alone against more senior members and refusing to support their remonstrance to the captain.

Towards ordination and first mass

Much of October was a holiday period for students. He spent some time visiting places of interest. The month closed with the eight-day annual retreat based on the spiritual exercises of St Ignatius Loyola. In November, the academic year commenced. He attended lectures on sacred scripture, and moral and dogmatic theology. Then, on 25 November, the rector informed him that his ordination was to take place within a few days. The cause of "this extraordinary haste", with which he was displeased, was the anxiety of many of the theological students. They had frequently "petitioned for orders", he wrote, because of their alarm at reports of a French invasion, even though "they had not yet arrived at the time usual in the Society, which is the third year of theology and the fifth of religion". They had prevailed on the greater number of consultors to the provincial to advise in their favour; and once the permission was granted the bishop of Gaeta, then in exile in Palermo, was immediately engaged to perform the ordinations as soon as possible.

On 27 and 30 November, respectively, Kenney and eleven other theologians received the orders of subdiaconate and diaconate. Ordination to the priesthood, however, was reserved to just four of them. This took place on 4 December, the second Sunday of Advent. It marked the fulfilment of a strong desire and single-minded persistence. Despite the solemnity of the occasion, Kenney's critical mind found expression in an unexpected comment. The bishop, he wrote, "performed the ceremony of this day with unusual devotion, his tears more than once interrupted those *pathetic exhortations* which the church gives the new priests".[22]

Instead of offering his first mass in the days after ordination, he decided to prepare for it at length. He deferred it until Christmas day. Meanwhile, his journal reverted to the regular daily entries. The octave of the feast of the Immaculate Conception of the Blessed Virgin, from 8 December, was celebrated with demonstrations of piety throughout Palermo. He was struck by the devotion of the people on this occasion, and was to express even more admiration two years later when, despite continuous, driving rain, the main procession was fully attended and the multitude, barefoot and bareheaded, at every step renewed "their devout shouts of praise to Mary and gave incontestable proofs of real devotion".

On 20 December he obtained permission to absent himself from the schools for four days to prepare by spiritual exercises, and the study of ceremonies and rubrics, for the celebration of his first mass. As priests are allowed to offer three masses on Christmas day, his first venture included three consecutive eucharists, in each of which he was assisted by the rector and Fr Angiolini. The intentions for which he offered these first masses reflected priorities that remained dominant throughout his life. The first, he "offered up to obtain the grace of ever faithfully and fruitfully exercising the ministry of the altar; the second for the ministry of the sacrament of penance; the third for the ministry of the divine word". On 26 December he offered the mass for his parents, and was attended by a consultor to the provincial, Fr Goja. Finally, two days later, he said mass for the first time unattended. It was said, not at the Jesuit church as the others had been, but in the nearby San Giuseppe, the baroque church of the Theatines. The arrangements were made by a member of that order, Don Agostino, who had a brother among the Jesuit theologians. The invitation included what Peter described as "a most famous breakfast together with all the theologians in the house of the Theatines".

With the new year, 1809, much of the novelty of the city and its celebrations had worn off. His entries in his journal became briefer, except where something new, or of special import, occurred. He had not previously experienced Holy Week and Easter in Sicily, and hence those days were written about in some detail. On Holy Thursday, following high mass in the Jesuit church, there was a procession to the altar of repose where the blessed sacrament was enthroned. All over Palermo, churches and convents had altars of repose bedecked with lights, flowers, and ornaments; and crowds, including the royal family and court, went from church to church to pray and "to adore our Lord". On Good Friday, after long ceremonies, he went to view the large public procession in which images were carried of "our Saviour" and of the "Madona Dolorata", in which nobles, city dignitaries, clergy and military participated, the military with arms reversed as was the custom during those days. Easter Sunday was marked by a sense of excitement and anticipation in crowded churches. At the mass at the Jesuit church the crowds surged forward at the "Gloria" to see the great purple veil before the altar suddenly fall and disclose the altar "in all its lustre and ornament, with a statue of Jesus risen from the tomb". Afterwards, he walked to the great cathedral and took careful note of all the ceremonies there. It had had a fascination for him from the time of his arrival. Situated close by the college, its golden stone, and its dramatic blend of Sicilian-Norman architecture and eighteenth century additions, rendered it distinctive in a city of majestic buildings, and it enshrined a wealth of historic associations.[23]

First invitation from Irish troops

A few days later he was visited by Captain Philips, a naval officer with whom he had become friendly, and who, as well as other naval and military personnel, had begun to come to him. Around this time, too, he came across a letter from the military fort at Milazzo, further east along the coast. It had been written by a Sergeant Richard Mulcahy, a native of Cork, 27 years of age, and, in Kenney's words, "a virtuous young man, though exposed to all the dangers of a soldier's life". It marked the beginning of the second great adventure of a semi-public nature during Kenney's time in Sicily. Mulcahy's letter lamented "the want of a priest who could speak English". He had heard of Kenney and expressed the hope that he would come to Milazzo. Kenney raised the matter with Fr Angiolini, who expressed interest but deferred decision. Kenney then wrote to Mulcahy, and in the journal for 8 April noted that he was a sergeant in a company of the 27th Grenadier battalions, and that there were also the 44th and 81st battalions, and also the remnant of the 31st which had escaped from Egypt, and that the greater part of all those were "Irish and Catholic". His interest and zeal, and that of his friend Glover, were aroused. The latter, indeed, had been involved in assisting members of the forces almost from his arrival at Palermo. Already on 10 March 1807, shortly after he had been ordained, the bluff Plowden had told him that he wished "the rough mission among the rabble of Irish sailors and soldiers" could be consigned to someone with more strength than he possessed, so that his course of studies would not be impeded.[24] Both men looked forward to active involvement at the fort at Milazzo, even though the expedition had to be deferred for the present.

Meanwhile, a matter of great consequence had arisen. Kenney, as has been indicated, had been kept informed by Fr Plowden of the claims to the property of the Irish mission being pressed by the Irish bishops and Cardinal di

Pietro of the Congregation of Propaganda. He had discussed the issues with Angiolini, and the latter had been moved to make a disclosure which promised to undermine the very foundations of the revived English Jesuit province. Kenney, after consulting Glover, felt obliged to send a long letter to Plowden conveying what Angiolini had said. "Kenney's ten pages," Plowden wrote to Glover at the end of June 1809, "have perplexed and disturbed us beyond measure".[25]

Probing the foundations

Kenney wrote his letter on 8 February 1809.[26] It presented with considerable assurance and precision the views of the procurator-general of the Society, Fr Caetanus Angiolini, who had originally been sent from Russia to treat with the pope and his secretary of state, Cardinal Consalvi, in 1803.

He and Glover regretted having to convey such afflicting news, he wrote, but after much deliberation they felt it necessary to do so: in brief summary, "it appears certain that the pope has never given *any leave whatever* for our aggregation to Russia, nor ever approved of it after it had been formed". This appeared impossible to Glover and him when they first heard it, but the detailed statement of the case presented by Fr Angiolini left no room for doubt.

By way of premise, Fr Angiolini suggested that two things be kept in mind: one, that the pontiff was a "sincere friend" to the Society, but a kind and timid man who wished "to send every petitioner away satisfied or at least in hopes", but whose timidity prevented him giving "a decisive answer, where any opposition was to be feared", and hence he "would do everything for Jesuits if no remonstrance were to be feared from kings, cardinals, bishops, and vicars apostolic"; secondly, the General, Fr Gruber, was so zealous for the propagation of the Society that "an appearance that the pope was not *against* a measure was as strong a motive to adopt it, as if the pontiff had openly declared *for* it".

The papal brief recognising the Society in Russia, Angiolini said, empowered the General "to receive postulants of whatever nation, who *should go to him* for that purpose". The General interpreted this as embracing not just those who went to him in Russia to be united to the Society but all who approached him by petition; and so he took it that he had the power of aggregating or creating new provinces. Cardinal Consalvi, however, had denied that any such power could be drawn from the pope's brief, and had stated that it was not part of His Holiness's intention. While Angiolini was on his way to Rome from Russia, the English province and other ex-Jesuits were aggregated to the Society. When he arrived in Rome, he found the pope knew nothing about it. When he approached Consalvi and, without mentioning what had been done, mentioned the desires of the English fathers to be united to their

Russian confrères, "the cardinal replied with a degree of warmth that such an attempt would be most imprudent and impolitical". Angiolini said nothing to other Jesuits about this response, because he felt they had acted in good faith and he still hoped matters might be set right.

Later, when the pope allowed an individual ex-Jesuit at Pekin to privately renew his profession in the Society as he could not travel to Russia, Angiolini raised the question of aggregation for other ex-Jesuits. "The pope coolly replied," Kenney wrote: "If they wished to observe the rules of St Ignatius in their own house, who can hinder them? The rules of St Ignatius are holy", and then added, 'provided they do not unite in a body'." When Angiolini left Rome, other Jesuits, including the well-known author Mazzaretti and Joseph Pignatelli (later canonized), took up the case, but without success. The nearest the pope came to a concession was when he said to Mazzaretti, who was complaining of the limitations of the Russian brief: "Well, well, *the substance of things is safe*; you must be content until the times will permit us to give a bull for the *universal Church*". The pope had been informed in more recent times, Angiolini said, of the aggregation in good faith of the English province, and had made no comment. As matters stood, therefore, the English province did not have papal approval, the validity of the vows of its members was in question, and there was no way its members in England or Ireland could be ordained under the title of poverty. And the pope's temperament was such that he would make no definite decision while any opposition existed.

"I am now quite sick of the subject," Kenney went on, "and I am sure you are equally tired and afflicted. I only add the motive which has principally induced Fr Angiolini to let me write this sad history, after having so long kept it secret. It is that you may know with what arms you are to fight the Irish bishops." The Jesuit property could not be safeguarded by any *vivae vocis oraculum* authority. The only solution was to send a number of Irish youths to make their vows in the Sicilian province of the Society, and after that have them return to Ireland by order of the General. In this way the claims of the Irish bishops would be frustrated, for these youths would be Jesuits for the Irish mission – the very fulfilment of Fr Callaghan's aims and "indisputably his heirs", even according to the 1793 declaration.

Smoothly and firmly, Kenney then moved on to discuss who should be sent from the Irish candidates. He excluded three, Messrs Dinan, Gahan, and Connolly: the first because he would be unable to manage the studies, the other two for health reasons, because of their particular complaints they would never survive "the garbage of our kitchen".

Before he concluded the letter, there was an insertion from Glover stating that what Kenney had written relating to Angiolini's disclosure was "a just and accurate statement of the facts". Kenney ended with a brief, and felt peroration which could not but move Plowden and dispose him to receive the hard news. "Need I, dear Sir," he declared, "end this melancholy letter by assuring you, that be the event what it may, my attachment to the Society and respect for superiors in England shall ever remain unshaken. I trust my conduct towards them shall never vary and that their commands shall ever be received by me as if they proceeded from that plenitude of authority from which alone religious obedience can arise." Finally, he remarked, that as what had been written was "not *official*", everything might go on as usual, except where there were reasons to the contrary as in the case of the Irish etc., "at least until the General speaks, who has been told all".

It was, indeed, a "melancholy letter". Many years later, in 1826, when being questioned by the Commissioners of the Irish Education Inquiry in relation to Maynooth College,[26a] Kenney, as noted earlier, was to state that he had retaken his vows in Sicily to ensure that he was truly a Jesuit; and even at the time of questioning he was still doubtful whether the English members of the Society were Jesuits, given that the papal bull of the restoration of the order, 1814, had not been accepted in England by the vicars apostolic.

Meanwhile, the letter left the good Mr Stone full of anxious questions. The "contents of your letter" and that of Mr Kenney, "received a few days ago ... are really distressing in the extreme," he wrote to Glover on 1 June.[27] "I must entreat you to desire Fr Angiolini to consult with the ablest Jesuit theologians in Sicily" as to "what is henceforward to be done by us? Must it be signified to those who have already taken their vows, that their vows are null? ... Can we admit any henceforward to the noviceship or to their vows?" And what of those who had been members of the old Society and had renewed their vows? He was to ask Fr Angiolini to send an answer to these questions as soon as possible, and to help with his advice.

Glover replied on 6 August reiterating Kenney's message. Fr Angiolini had sent on all the material to the General, he said, and Fr Pignatelli, the Neapolitan provincial, "had a conference with His Holiness" on the English province, the result of which was unknown, though the General had no doubt been informed. With regard to Fr Stone's queries, Angiolini's advice was "to go on as usual according to the (original) orders of the General". He was averse to consulting theologians because the matter was still secret. Glover, however, could not see, personally, how persons could be admitted in future to make their vows under the persuasion that they were becoming religious of the Society of Jesus.[28]

In the meantime, on 24 June, Angiolini had written himself to Stone. He, too, confirmed what Kenney had stated, and explained how the prolonged queries of the Irish bishops had caused him much anxiety and moved him to propose a solution to secure the future of the Irish Jesuit mission, even though this meant revealing the doubtful situation of the English province and thereby causing much hurt and concern. He urged that the twelve students for the Irish mission be sent to Sicily as soon as possible. Frs Kenney and Glover, he added, were in good health, and were working hard at philosophy at which they had given clear evidence of ability and impressed all their audience in public disputation, "in which Fr Kenney was particularly outstanding".[29]

The aftermath; and Irish performance at Palermo

As Glover was writing in August, a group of six Irish were already en route for Palermo, and, following an adventurous journey, involving a passage of arms with a French frigate, arrived about a week later. Writing to Plowden on 22 August, Angiolini expressed satisfaction with the six young Irishmen recently arrived at Palermo. Any others of their quality would be most welcome. And he concluded with a eulogy of Glover and Kenney, and particularly of the latter.

> Frs Glover and Kenney continue to give the greatest satisfaction. They have lately passed an excellent examen in theology; and it must be said that among our students in divinity, they are the two foremost. Fr Kenney, without any hesitation, is the first. What gives lustre and merit to all this is their remarkable religious fervour, and the genuine interior spirit with which they act. What fervent workers are being prepared here for your mission! May God preserve them and increase their number.

He added that they both enjoyed very good health, except for "some slight inconvenience which Fr Glover suffers from time to time from the great heat".[30] Three weeks later, in a further letter to Plowden, he once more assured him that Glover and Kenney were doing very well at theology, and that "Kenney undoubtedly surpasses all the others". He should do very useful work in Ireland, and like Glover would be "a true Jesuit". Both, he concluded, would take their final vows at the college at the end of two years.[31]

It is interesting at this point to diverge for a moment with respect to the references to the good health of the two men. It was all the more surprising in that Sicily was inevitably feeling the pinch of the French blockade, and the quantity and quality of the food available to the Palermo community seems to have been quite unsatisfactory. Kenney made very few references to this aspect in his journal, but Glover seems to have made a number of criticisms. So much so that on 25 February 1809, Plowden wrote to him that his and Kenney's "steady perseverance in spite of climate and domestic penury amounting it would seem almost to distress" were admired at Stonyhurst. "I really never go to table," he continued, "without wishing my plate before you." He was "equally edified at the exertions of the good Sicilian fathers amidst such poverty".[32]

The heat presented other possible grounds for complaint. Although it occasioned inconvenience to Glover, the warm dry climate seems to have suited

Kenney. The burning summer sun which reduces even the cicadas to silence received no mention in his journal. The hot gusting sirocco wind which filled the air with grit and sand, got into eyes, hair and clothes, infiltrated every nook and cranny, strained nerves, and rendered all action burdensome – even that seemed not to distress him unduly. Sirocco in "a most terrible degree" he wrote on 3 July 1809; walking outside "my eyes were almost turned in my head". The only other reference, four days later, merely stated – the sirocco, "which for two days had ceased, returned with new fury: the heat of the air alone was 100 degrees Fahrenheit." And he came virtually unscathed also through winter rain and snow, and even earthquake tremors. It was, perhaps, the healthiest period of his life.

Uncertainty continued, however, to disturb and stimulate for several months those English Jesuits who had learned of the doubtful status of their province. Fr Strickland was, perhaps, the first to recover. After some time in a trough of despondency, he bounded back to assert that while the aggregate was "canonically invalid" they had never pretended otherwise, and it was certainly not unlawful or sinful, and in support of this pointed out that "the head of the Church has explicitly declared that the constitutions and rules of St Ignatius are laudable and virtuous and that any individual who undertakes to observe them does well. We have done no more ..."[33] This, of course, was to turn a blind eye to the pope's alleged statement to Angiolini that it was laudable for them to follow the rule of St Ignatius "provided they do not unite in a body".

The General, Fr Brzozowski, on hearing of the disturbances caused by Angiolini, moved straightway to calm the waters. On 13 October he wrote to Strickland, emphasising again the clear signs of the real mind of Pius VII, explaining that the letter of Cardinal Consalvi in 1802 had been correctly interpreted and urging the English Jesuits to go on as they had been doing, to accept novices, allow them to take the religious vows of the Society, and regard those who were ordained as religious aggregated to the Society in Russia. The pope, he said, could, of course, have spoken clearly and publicly, but his difficulties had to be remembered.[34] Those difficulties, indeed, had become such as to render the future of many things very uncertain: for Pius had excommunicated Napoleon in June, following the French annexation of Rome, and on 6 July the emperor had had him arrested and carried off to prison in Savona. Fr Brzozowski, in the course of his letter, pressed firmly for the ordination of "our Irishmen" to the priesthood, since they were "truly religious in the eyes of the supreme pontiff" even if they did not appear to be "in the eyes of the archbishop of Dublin".[35] This led to the despatch to Sicily of *all* the Irish candidates, including those whom Kenney had advised against.

Well before the General's letter, however, the focus of Kenney's and Glover's attention had been diverted to ministering to the many Catholics, mostly Irish, serving in the British forces at Milazzo. This marked a distinct interlude in their careers.

MINISTRY AND MISTRUST AT MILAZZO AND MESSINA

Preparing the way

Their hopes and plans had met with various vicissitudes. Already in his long letter of February to Plowden, Kenney had mentioned that he and Glover still hoped to go to Messina or Milazzo at the autumn vacation "for the aid of those poor Catholics, who have none to minister to them the food of spiritual life". Then in April came Sergeant Mulcahy's letter, which was followed at the end of that month by another directly to Kenney. He presented the case made by Mulcahy to his rector and provincial, and on 10 May it was agreed that Glover and Kenney, accompanied by a Sicilian Jesuit, could go to Milazzo, but on certain conditions: that they had "some certain assurance" that English officers would not offend them, and that they take their examination in that year's theology course before they left. Complications then arose. An expedition was clearly being planned against the coast of Italy. Consequently, on 29 May Kenney noted in his journal that the rector had refused them permission to have the date of their theology examination brought forward "until it should be known whether the Irish were to go on the intended expedition". On 10 June signs of embarkation were evident. Kenney heard that all the Irish and English regiments were to go except the 44th, which remained at the castle to guard it. Thus, the entire project was deferred once more.

On 31 July, however, he observed that the troops had returned. A week later, Glover informed Fr Stone: "General Stuart is returned to Sicily with his army, abandoning the two small islands Ischia and Proscida, which he had taken in the bay of Naples. The expedition seems to have failed entirely. We know not what were the orders or the intentions of the general, but in the eyes of Sicily and Italy he has covered himself with ridicule. Since the English troops are returned it has been resolved to send us to Milazzo and Messina shortly." At the end of the letter, he added, "Fr Provincial has now decreed to send Fr Kenney and myself to Milazzo, to afford spiritual assistance to the poor soldiers there."[36] Next day, 7 August, Kenney noted that the provincial had applied to the archbishop of Messina for faculties for Glover and him to hear confessions at Milazzo. On 10 August, a Carmelite friend wrote to book three rooms for them in a monastery of his order in Milazzo.

During the next fortnight, as they awaited the archbishop's reply, there were letters from Mulcahy, and another Catholic soldier, Prestamburg; and the six Irish students arrived at Palermo and were placed in quarantine. Kenney visited them, brought them food, and said mass in thanksgiving for their safe arrival. On 29 August, the archbishop of Messina refused the request for faculties. At the start of September, Kenney wrote to Mulcahy and Prestamburg suggesting that they raise the matter with the archpriest of Milazzo. On 18

September, he noted that permission had come from the archbishop to confess the English-speaking troops. All was now ready for his and Glover's departure. And then, the day before they set out, he briefly entered in his journal: "Letter to me from Fr Plowden announcing my father's *happy* death – dated 29 July."

Departure and arrival

On the evening of 23 September they moved out from the shore and turned the east promontory. Next morning, the wind being contrary, they went ashore for a while between Termini and Cefalu, the sailors preparing a tent on the strand where they dined. That evening they journeyed on. Late the next day, they stopped at the foot of an abandoned castle near Capo D'Orlando, with its great mountainous rock "of sea-green colour mixed with streaks of white". On 26 September, before sunrise, they turned the cape of Milazzo and arrived early in the port.

Standing on the beach soon afterwards as they waited for the officers to come ashore, Kenney viewed the ancient town spread across an extensive level area until, on the north side, it ascended a steep incline to the summit of the promontory, where a vast fortress dwarfed the town and dominated the channel between Sicily and the Aeolian isles. First developed by the Arabs, and then by Normans, it was expanded and fortified by Emperor Frederick III, and continued to be strengthened by the Spaniards into the seventeenth century. Within a few days he was to discover that its massive walls covered several acres, and held in their embrace a castle, a sixteenth century church with a distinctive mosque-like dome, and a great courtyard which easily accommodated tented regiments and from which there was an unbroken vista of blue waters and distant encircling mountains.

They were "kindly received" by the governor, to whom they had two letters of introduction, and also by the archpriest "who removed two priests from the oratory of San Felippo" to provide them with "two miserable rooms". Kenney and Glover occupied these, and further accommodation was found for Fr Salemi, the third member of the party. Kenney said his first mass in the town at the Carmelite convent on the central plaza. After the mass, Sergeant Ward, one of the Irish soldiers, came to see him. On 29 September, the three men began to hear confessions. Ward was the only one who came to them that day. The regent of the Franciscans, meanwhile, spoke about them to an officer of the garrison, who stated that they should make a visit to the general in command. Later, Sgt Mulcahy called; "the first time I had seen him" Kenney noted. Next day they visited General McFarland. "He kindly received us," Kenney wrote, "said fine things of the Society, spoke of Catholic tenets but in such manner as to show that he was not very well acquainted with them." All seemed to be well. They began to hear the confessions of many of the soldiers. Everything proceeded smoothly, almost casually, for some days.

Orders to quit

On 1 October, they went to see the castle. Ward communicated at Kenney's mass, and another sergeant, named Mahony, came to see him. Three days later Kenney said mass at the Capuchin church, half-way down the steep slope from the fort to the town. He was warmly welcomed by a Fr Angeleh. On 6 October, Sgt Mahony decided he wished to commence a general confession of his whole life; and on the following day Kenney went to the Capuchin monastery to visit Fr Angeleh who was sick, and from there went on up the hill to the castle. He was accompanied by Fr Salemi, who wished to hear the confessions of the galley slaves. Kenney endeavoured to get into the garrison church to hear such of the soldiers as might come to him. He knew the 58th regiment quartered there were almost all Irish Catholic. He was unable to get in, but became involved in a long conversation with a young soldier. Fr Salemi, meanwhile, went off without him. And Kenney, revealingly, confided to his journal: "I had to return home alone – being the first time I had ever appeared without a companion. Happily," he added, "our custom was not known in the little town." On arrival home, his discomfort faded before a really serious setback. Fr Glover was closeted with Captain della Giustiza, the chief officer of the town, who announced an order from the English commander there "that we should quit Milazzo that night or the next morning".

Kenney, as has been indicated, had a strong sense of justice, was not lacking in moral courage, and could be very persistent when he felt an important issue was involved. "No reason for this strange order being assigned," he wrote, "we went after dinner (it was then a little before noonday) to Col Smith of 27th Inniskillings regiment, who said he knew no reason for it, that he did not even know there were such persons in the town, that the order came directly from General McFarland, then in Messina, but given in Sir John Stuart's name." They then "boldly but politely represented the high injustice done" them "by such an order, but as he could give no answer about it" they told him they "would go as soon as possible to Messina and expostulate with Sir John". They added, however, that they could not set out either that evening or the next morning. He did not insist. They planned to go next morning and hired horses to that end. The archpriest, who wished to keep Salemi for a sermon he was appointed to preach, argued that they could not set out without first informing the archbishop and their own superiors of such an order. They should wait till Monday. He, meanwhile, would send a courier to the archbishop who would be back in Milazzo on Sunday evening. Kenney consented on condition that the archpriest notify the motive of their delay to the captain and colonel concerned. This being promised, he noted, "we set about finishing the confessions of those poor soldiers and had not a moment's respite till the date of our departure".

On 8 October, he wrote in his journal: "said mass as usual and a good number of soldiers communicated at it. Mulcahy came to confession having the preceding evening learned the story." Fr Salemi preached in the church of St James, to which there was a public procession. Kenney and Glover were going to attend but decided otherwise when the archpriest advised against it. They learned that instead of intimating to Col. Smith the real cause of their delay, he told him the reason was that horses could not be procured. That evening, according to Glover's later account to Fr Stone, Capt. Giustiza sent word that if they had not left town by early next morning Col. Smith would send a picket of soldiers to accompany them out.[37] Hence, the journal continued: "seeing ourselves between enemies and weak friends, we determined to set off the next day". That evening the courier arrived with the answer from the archbishop that he did not wish to interfere.

Confronting the Scotch generals

They said mass before daylight, and were riding out of Milazzo at sunrise. As there was a wind against them, Kenney tied his cincture about his hat, to the amusement of passing soldiers. As they rode on towards the north tip of the island, and then around to Messina, "unpleasant reflections", Kenney remarked, "were sometimes interrupted by the charming prospect" for "we had in view almost all the way the seas, the Lipari isles and the smoking Stramboly,[38] and on the land the continued succession of hills, dales and precipices". And as they rounded towards Messina and faced across the straits, the view of Calabria was "most pleasing as it burst at once upon the sight". They stopped at the residence of a local nobleman who was friendly to the order. He insisted on they staying with him. Following a discussion with him and his friend, Don Luigi, they visited General Danero, governor of Messina, at his palace on the waterfront. He, too, was well disposed to the Society, and received them kindly; but when he heard their story, he excused himself from going in person to Sir John Stuart. He said, however, that he would arrange an audience with him by means of the Marquis de Palermo. They presented Danero with a summary memorandum of their case. They then went to see the bishop, who was "too busy" to see them but sent his vicar to them, Monsignor Belvivo. "He expressed a fear," Kenney wrote, "that we might have assembled the soldiers for private instructions and that some Protestants in disguise made an evil report of the meeting. On being assured that we never had such meetings or any instructions out of confession, he seemed satisfied and approved of our application to General Danero." They then went off to see the cathedral with its distinctive bell-tower. On their way home they were summoned to see Danero. He had presented their memorial to Sir John Stuart, even though it had been intended solely for Danero himself. He showed them Sir John's order for their departure. Writing indignantly to Fr Stone on 6 December, Glover observed that Sir John's order stated that "for particular reasons known to himself, he had ordered us from Milazzo, and that for the same reasons he begged the governor to order us away from Messina immediately; forbidding us to appear any place occupied by English troops". Not content with sending that in writing, Glover added, "he sent word that we must not dare to approach him, for he would not see us. Could anything be more despotic!"[39]

Danero, according to Kenney, said there was nothing he could do. He advised them to bring their case before the king, and counselled against going to see Stuart or appearing in public where they might receive an insult for which there would be no remedy. Kenney was "for going to or writing to Sir John personally", but Salemi and Glover did not approve. They spent the afternoon inside with the family of the baron, their friendly nobleman, as Fr Salemi did not wish them to go out. After nightfall, however, they went out for exercise, though even then the baroness had them cock their hats like secular priests that they might not be known. Thus, Kenney remarked in frustration, "on the one hand we had to suffer tyranny and injustice, on the other (were) obliged to yield to fear and weakness."

Next day, 11 October, the strange story took a stranger twist. Fr Salemi, not mentioned in Stuart's order, decided to call on him. The latter seeing him in his ante-chamber, retreated back into his room and sent word that he could not see him. Salemi replied that he was not one of the English fathers but a Sicilian who wished to speak a word to his Excellency. He received the answer that his Excellency would not see him but that he might speak with the general's secretary, Major de Sade. Salemi expostulated with the major, Glover noted, "on the injury done to us as individuals and particularly as belonging to a very respectable body". The major, belying his surname, received him graciously, and assured him that he had nothing against the Society or any of its individuals. Salemi pressed to have a declaration to that effect in writing from Sir John. De Sade promised to speak with his Excellency on the matter, and meantime declared they might stay until the weather allowed them to sail. That night the baron hired a boat to show them the harbour, and particularly the straits "with the famous Charybides", but the weather being unfavourable they had to content themselves with the circuit of "this noble port surrounded by land on every side except the entrance".

The following day they visited the archbishop who "kindly received" them and excused himself for not having taken a part in this affair on account of his infirmities. His apprehensions had been similar to those of Monsignor Belvivo, but he declared himself content with their assurances. He wished to know the result of the interview with Major de Sade. A second interview with the latter had taken place that morning. Once again, Glover wrote, when Salemi arrived "the same ridiculous scene of the general running back when he saw him took place". De Sade did not have the declaration drawn up, and asked to see the note sent by General Stuart to Governor Danero. Later that day, however, while they were at dinner, "the wished for declaration" arrived. It was a far from satisfactory document, but to have received anything at all was something of an achievement. It read:

Messina, 12 October 1809

Gentlemen,

In consequence of your application to the Commander of the Forces on the subject of the motives which may have induced him to have it intimated to you, through the means of General Danero, Governor of this place, that it was his intention that you should not reside in any of the garrisons or ports occupied by the British troops in this island — I am directed by His Excellency to acquaint you that this measure has not been prompted on his part on account of any grounds of complaint which may have appeared before him against either your private proceedings or personal character, but that in so doing he has merely acted upon certain principles of a general nature ...

Signed by Major de Sade, General Secretary. [40]

"These general principles", Glover commented, "must be of a very peculiar nature indeed to oblige Sir John Stuart to brand with public infamy two individuals, who he acknowledges to be innocent as well in their personal character, as in their private proceedings."[41]

They contracted with a boat owner to take them to Palermo, and sailed from Messina at 4.00 p.m. on Saturday 14 October, "with thoughts too serious and heavy to be much diverted by the classical and pleasing reflections which should otherwise arise from the near view of Charybides, Scylla, Calabria, and the beauteous port of Messina".[42] And as they reached the top of the straits between Faro and Scylla, Kenney's "thoughts became more affecting from the sight of so many British soldiers", whom he could see "along the coast of the promontory". The wind soon took the boat round the tower of Faro and they noticed a number of gunboats and transports, in which were "the fine regiment of Grenadiers" which they had left at Milazzo, and among them Sgts Mulcahy and Ward. This they learned when a change of wind obliged them to shelter at Milazzo on 15 October. They were warmly welcomed by the governor and the regent of the Friars Minor. Having learned that McFarland had returned to Milazzo a day or two after they had left, they determined to visit him, but were suddenly called on to embark. They left, however, Kenney noted vehemently, "a copy of the famous declaration for him; and about 8 o'clock bid an eternal adieu to the town of Milazzo ashamed of the vile timidity of the Sicilians, melted with pity for poor Irish soldiers, and disgusted at the unjust and tyrannical treatment received from Scotch generals."

Their feelings of frustration were increased by the captain of their boat who, in their view, was wasting much time stopping at "miserable places along the coast". Eventually on 20 October they landed at Termini, where they were well received at the Jesuit college and given rooms which had been prepared for four fathers who were soon "to begin a mission there for the first time since the return of the Jesuits".[43] The captain then decided he would go no further, but as he had contracted to take them to Palermo he supplied them with a chaise. They arrived at the college gate about 6.00 p.m. "to the joy of our Brethren and young friends". Two days later, "though fatigued in body and still more in mind", they entered on their annual eight-day retreat.

Seeking redress – The aftermath

The account of their experience had been sent to Angiolini by Kenney. He called on the Marquis di Circello about the matter, only to find that he had already been informed by letter from General Danero. The marquis, termed by Kenney "the timid secretary" [to the king], "resolved to have nothing to do in the affair and advised Fr Angiolini to pass all over in silence". A letter from the Marquis Cardill, of Palermo, to Angiolini added to what Kenney called "this general panic" by quoting a letter from the archbishop expressing his fear that perhaps Kenney and Glover by some incautious step had drawn the persecution on themselves, even though, as Kenney remarked, "this was directly contradicted by Stuart's own acknowledgement". This remark from the archbishop prevented "any interference" in their favour. Angiolini asked Kenney for a full account of the business. This he wrote during the retreat, and it was sent to the marquis. On 2 November, Kenney penned a letter to General McFarland; and three days later composed an extended one to Sir John Stuart. Glover, in Kenney's account, favoured sending it but, fearing the after effects, suggested showing it to Angiolini. The latter "liked the letter, but thought it better not to send it"!

The last word on their "unfortunate mission to Milazzo and Messina" was provided by Glover in his letter of 6 December to Fr Stone. On arrival at Palermo, he wrote, "we had some hopes of being supported; but we were deserted by all here, as well as in every other place. Mr Kenney then drew up an expostulary letter, very well written, which he wished to send in our joint name to Stuart. I objected to it for two reasons: first because, as Mr Kenney himself confessed, there was no prospect of him ever recalling his order; secondly, because he might very easily intimate to the court his wish of sending us out of Sicily, and ... I am sure we should be obliged to go, not only Mr Kenney and myself, but perhaps even all the other Irish. Stuart knows too well that all are afraid of him, and he avails himself of their timidity for his own ends. The conduct of the bishop of Messina from beginning to end of the business has been exceedingly shabby."[44]

How to explain what Kenney termed "the unjust and tyrannical treatment received from Scotch generals"? Apart from the obvious intimation that "Scotch generals" signified anti-papist, there was a further clue provided in a discussion which the three Jesuits had at Messina with the baron's friend, Don Luigi. Kenney, in his journal, under 10 October, noted that Don Luigi heard from a person connected with Sir John's secretary that they had been removed from Milazzo, and would be driven from Messina, not simply for having heard confessions there, which was of little interest to their military commanders, "but because being Jesuit our habit [*sic*] came from Russia, now the friend of France, and therefore some evil correspondence might carry on". It was vague and opaque, but a combination of Jesuit, Russia, and papist, were, perhaps, a likely concoction to stimulate a dictatorial, contemporary Scottish general to order expulsion from any of the garrisons or ports occupied by British troops on the island. Challenged to provide a rational explanation, he was reduced to "certain principles of a general nature". An overt statement of religious discrimination would have been unacceptable in a papist kingdom, especially when the monarch was known to have sought the restoration of the Jesuits, nor, indeed, was it likely to win much support at home where the pope's independent stand against Napoleon was esteemed. Sir John's bizarre and undignified attempts to avoid Salemi acknowledged the vulnerability of his position from a purely rational point of view.

The matter, however, did not stop there. Kenney and Glover wrote home in vigorous terms, and Plowden broadcast the story. The news spread in Ireland and occasioned anger. Ever since 1782, the Irish Catholic Committee had criticised "the want ... of religious toleration to Roman Catholics engaged in the service of their king and country".[45] The incident further confirmed the Irish bishops in their opposition to a government veto in episcopal appointments. They had little confidence in the government, Dr Moylan of Cork wrote on 3 April 1810: "the treatment of Catholic soldiers in the forces proves the bigotry of those in power".[46]

In June, just as parliament was prorogued, following the agitation of the Catholic Question in the House of Commons, there appeared in the newspapers a letter purporting to be written by either Kenney or Glover which, in Plowden's words, "was anonymous, cautiously written, and related the behaviour of Sir John Stuart to Messrs Glover and Kenney without any bitterness of expressions". Plowden was of the view that its publication "was so timed purposely to prevent it being brought forward in parliament".[47] It may have played a part, nevertheless, in the heated atmosphere of religious debate, and with the captive pope seen as a political ally, in the appearance on 5 July 1811, of a "General order of His Royal Highness the commander in chief" directing "the commanding officers of regiments" to be "particularly attentive that no soldier professing the Roman Catholic religion ... be subject to any punishment for not attending the divine worship of the Church of England"; and that any such soldier should be at full liberty to worship, "according to the forms prescribed by his religion; when military duty does not interfere".[48] An important principle had thus been conceded, though its application thereafter appears to have been left to the discretion of military/naval commanders and officers who were non-Catholic and, not infrequently, anti-Catholic.

MINISTRY AND STUDIES – PRAISE AND CRITICISM

Following the Milazzo expedition, Peter's life became focused on Palermo – his studies, and his role as a religious and priest. In the last, his attention was concentrated on the three ministries for which he prayed at his first masses: the ministry of the eucharist, of the sacrament of penance, and of the divine word.

The opportunity of exercising his gifts as a preacher were severely limited by language difficulties. His continued interest in developing his skills were suggested by his request of Plowden, in the course of the long letter of 8 February 1809, to send him a copy of Bossuet's expositions, and his frequent references and comments in the journal to sermons and panegyrics he had attended. The ministry of the eucharist did not present the same problems as the mass was everywhere said in Latin. He made frequent reference to offering mass in convents and churches throughout the city, including the cathedral, and the great Dominican church at the Piazzo Dominicana. His care in the celebration of the eucharist is clearly implied, and there are many indications of a deep reverence for the sacred host both at mass and exposition. Almost his first action on his return from Milazzo was to undertake a novena of masses for his father. On 31 December 1809, the entry ran: "Have just completed the number of thirty masses for my poor father." His main ministry at Palermo, however, was that of listening, instructing, and offering peace and reconciliation by means of the sacrament of penance. The archbishop granted him and Glover faculties to hear the confessions of all English speaking people in the archdiocese. His ministry grew as his name became known. Apart from passing visitors, he had a regular procession of soldiers, sailors, and ships officers, calling to him, most of them Irish, and a number stayed on to chat and drink coffee with the young Irish Jesuits at the college. Shortly before his return to Ireland, he was sent to hear the confessions of the Italian artillery at the castle, and was pleased to find that he could easily understand the Neapolitans and, with difficulty, the Sicilians. Arising perhaps from his early background, he possessed the common touch to an uncommon degree; and had also developed a facility to relate to all sections of society.

One of his most rewarding, and perhaps arduous, apostolates was that of visiting the hospitals, which then were far from being centres of hygiene or professional care. His concern for the sick sometimes led to conversions to Catholicism. One such in the weeks after Milazzo was "a poor black American of the United States" to whom he was called at St Bartholomew's hospital on 27 December. He died shortly after he was baptised *sub conditione*. Kenney received a number of Protestants into the Catholic Church, and each one, in accordance with the order given by the vicars apostolic in England, was rebaptised *sub conditione*, in case their original baptisms had not been valid. On each occasion he was careful to obtain the approval of the archbishop.

Another constant activity was letter writing. A number of letters were sent out each week. The recipients included Frs Plowden, Stone, and other Jesuits in England; Fr Betagh, and his mother, brother and sister in Ireland; people he had met as they passed through Palermo or on the journey to Messina, and in a special way Sgts. Ward, Mahony, and, above all, Mulcahy, who kept writing to him and who, in a sense, became his emissaries to the soldiers he could no longer directly contact. He endeavoured to procure books in English for them, and in September 1810, was able to send to Mulcahy – "a small packet containing 10 catechisms for the use of the Catholic soldiery, *Grounds of the Catholic Doctrine, Mayne's Conversion [sic]* copies of the "Acts" and prayers for those who wish to know the truth, for himself *The Poor Man's Catechism*, to Ward a nice prayer book, and to Mahony *The Spiritual Combat*."[49]

Sicilian comments on Irish students – "L'incomparabile P. Kenney"

A feature of life among the Jesuits at Palermo in those years was the frequency of death in the community. Many members were elderly, relics of the old Society. The blend of old and young, however, appears to have been mutually enriching; and the young, lively Irish group fitted in well most of the time. Kenney had been a good ambassador, and those who came after him experienced warmth and understanding from superiors. Fr Angiolini, though not superior when Peter arrived, carried considerable influence because of his early role and because he was procurator-general for the whole order. His empathy for the Irish, and his particular regard for Kenney helped to create a favourable climate. His comments in their regard might be considered excessive, as he seemed to have an un-Irish compulsion to be the bearer of good news and a reluctance to convey any bad tidings, but, as against that, the Annals of the Sicilian Province were almost fulsome in their praise.[50]

Angiolini's comments, therefore, in a letter to Plowden, 10 February 1810, probably reflected a fairly general perception in the community at that particular time. All the Irish were exemplary, he declared, in good will and religious virtues. He then added: "Fr Kenney excels all the others – he has gifts of nature; vigour, active and effective zeal for souls, and outstanding prudence. May God preserve him for His glory and the Irish mission." Glover, he continued, had considerable natural ability but was suited more to eloquence and poetry than to speculative pursuits.[51] And in April, he was assuring Plowden that "the likeable and edifying Irish ... were an honour to their master of novices", while Kenney was once again praised for his ability, ardent zeal, and true spirit of the Society, and he termed him "l'incomparabile P. Kenney".[52]

But the image of a happy band of brothers was to fade before long. Angiolini himself was to undergo much pain and hardship at the hands of fellow Jesuits, and Kenney, as a close friend, was to endure criticism from Sicilian brethren while also finding himself at odds with his own countrymen.

Criticism, death and division

Bitter criticism of Angiolini rose to the surface in the community during 1810. The cause is not clear. Kenney's journal suggests that it was related to some critical comments Angiolini made about the province, to his views on the Society in England and Ireland, and to his comments on the former General as reported in Kenney's letter of February 1809, and to some indiscreet criticism by Plowden which Kenney described as "misunderstood". Kenney was questioned by superiors regarding the letter of February and Plowden's criticism. The recent revival of the claims of the Irish bishops, by means of a strong letter to Fr Stone from Cardinal di Pietro, had raised anxiety levels in England, and this had eventually reached Sicily and played a part, it seems, in stimulating opposition to Angiolini. Some of the more virulent opponents also turned part of their anger against Kenney as his friend. The entire province became involved and distracted.

Writing to Glover, now back in England, on 20 October 1810, Kenney told of "continued and increased embroglios", and declared that "the General, continually beset with complaints sent from every quarter of this turbulent province, appears more than ever adverse to Fr Angiolini". He had removed him from the role of consultor, taken from him the character and employment of procurator general for the whole Society and reduced him to procurator and curator of the province, subject to the provincial and his assistants in everything, "and all", Kenney added, "without giving him the least notice, or room to justify himself from the accusations that have been written from all quarters".[53] Earlier, indeed, on 14 September, after Angiolini informing him of his demotion by the General "in consequence of fresh complaints made against him", and following on some problems with his own countrymen, Peter had written feelingly in the journal – "God preserve me from having any authority in the Society, and above all over the Irish!" The prayer reflected a sentiment that was to be frequently repeated during his life.

The following April, Plowden noted that Kenney thought "Fr Angiolini injured by a cabal, who by misinformation had prejudiced the General against him", and he, Plowden, feared that Kenney might have taken sides, or be suspected of having done so, against the provincial. A recent letter from the latter had presented Angiolini in a very bad light.[54] That there may have been some grounds for Plowden's fears that Kenney might at least be misrepresented is indicated in the latter's letter to Glover in October, 1810, when he remarked: "I am more than apprehensive that they have written to the General against me or at least to Fr Stone. Thank God", he added, "I have no post to be deprived of."[55]

That letter, however, contained other news which temporarily overshadowed all else. On 15 October, Edmund Cogan, from Cork, one of the ablest and best liked of the Irish students, was buried. He to whom Plowden had expressed the hope that God would at Palermo form him and his companions "into true *'filii resurectionis'*, genuine sons of the revered Society",[56] fell ill during the annual retreat, and died after "a horrible fever of eight days and a quiet peaceful agony of a few hours".[57] It left his companions in Kenney's vivid words, cast down under "thick clouds of distressing grief".[58]

The shared grief did not heal, however, the fissures that had developed during the year between him and the other Irish. He confided to Glover at the close of the same letter, that he feared they may have complained of him to the General for leading Fr Stone astray. The reference is obscure. It seems to relate to Stone's intention of appointing Kenney their superior. A position, which ironically and evidently, he did not welcome. "If Fr General send me back to the novitiate", he declared ruefully, "he will do me a great favour."[59] A consciousness of social distinction and background appear to have partly inhibited his attitude towards those of his companions from more privileged backgrounds, such as Esmonde and Aylmer; and though he struggled strongly against this, there remained an unease and tension. Consequently, the stress of feeling responsibility for the Irish constituted one of the main pressures on him in his final year in Sicily.

It originated with a letter sent from Plowden to Angiolini on 28 April 1810, which the latter read to Kenney on 26 June, and which contained orders from Fr Stone desiring, as Kenney reported it in his journal, "that we should all go home ordained and with patents signifying that we are Jesuits of this province, and I with a particular one should be constituted superior of all those who should come after me". From that point on, Kenney seemed to assume already some of the responsibilities of a superior. He considered it part of his role to keep Frs Stone and Plowden informed as to how his companions were getting on. His journal recorded some of their activities, instances of their illnesses, and also items of disagreement – from minor issues like Mr Connolly not coming to recreation, and spending money given for other purposes on wine and cakes for himself; and Mr Aylmer also displaying a proprietorial attitude towards money and complaining bitterly behind Kenney's back at his impudence in taking on himself "to act as superior and doing the contrary to what they wanted";[60] to an issue of bartering books which involved the provincial and left Kenney blamed by both sides.

This last arose in February, 1811, when the Irish bartered books with the other students of the college. The provincial, Fr Zuñiga, was informed that *one* of the Irish students, Connolly, had exchanged books which were not his, and he determined the books should be recalled. He referred the matter to Kenney. The latter, being asked by the provincial, put aside his reluctance to inform against one of his companions. He said that he had long heard that the books were not really Connolly's, but that he claimed that a dead student, named Jones, had left them to him. This was disputed, however, by Mr Dinan, a friend of the late Jones. Fr Zuñiga expressed his displeasure at Kenney's previous silence on the subject, and stated that he would himself "put his hand to the affair" which he considered "a great evil". Kenney, thinking "to save the parties a blush", suggested that he call together privately the few involved. He understood the provincial to agree to this. Instead, to his surprise and embarrassment, Fr Zuñiga issued an order to the immediate superior "that *all* books between the Irish and the other students should be immediately restored to their former owners".[61] The result, where Kenney was concerned, was hurtful and frustrating. He confided to the journal:

> My Irish friends, in conformity with the treatment I have received from them from the day that our first four were increased in Carlow College, displeased to lose their books, which they thought great bargains, vented their spleen in cutting hints against me, whom they thought to be a principal author of the affair.

The cause of the error, he believed, was that when they began to ask "who was the cause of the order?", the guilty ones took advantage of the fact that he "observed profound silence" and depicted him as "a principal author of the general order with regard to the Irish, and thus shifted a share of the blame from themselves."

Studies, examinations, and internal and external politics

Even in his studies the final year was stressful and disenchanting. On 7 May 1810, the day following the departure of his friend Thomas Glover, he unwisely sought permission from the provincial to be "freed from the school of Fr Goig" for the remainder of the year and to apply for the Canon Law class. Fr Zuñiga referred him to the rector whom he wished to discuss the matter with his consultors. The decision was in Kenney's favour. In jubilation he bade goodbye in his journal to the tedious professor and his distinctions – "Adieu, Dear *principium formale quo proximum.*" It was an unfortunate move on his part. There was already criticism of him in the house, as has been seen, because of his friendship with Angiolini. His outstanding ability and facility – in his very first year Angiolini had commented that he spoke *da maestro*[62] – and the latter's overt praise of him, left him open to envy; and the presence of so many Irish in the community provided scope for resentment, especially if they sought any exceptional privileges or exemptions. He attended his first Canon Law class on 12 May.

The following day, a letter arrived for the rector from the provincial, complaining "of certain disorders occasioned by the leave" granted to Fr Kenney. "This was the fruit," Kenney commented "of some misrepresentations sent to the provincial." On 18 May, the rector informed him that he and the provincial had conferred about him and decided that he should not go to either school of theology, but study canon law and prepare for his final examination covering the entire course of theology and philosophy. It was an arrangement which left him free of classes, with several months to revise the whole programme, before facing a stiff two-hour oral examination, followed by a public defence on a range of theological themes. For the public defence a long list of such themes was presented to him, from which he was to choose a certain number, and from which again his examiners would make their own choice. He completed his selection of "the conclusions", as they were called, on 26 October.

Meanwhile, the course of political events, as interpreted in England, was set to disrupt his final examination plans. Fears about the future of Sicily, joined to the opening provided by Archbishop Troy's agreement to ordain Ryan *sub titulo paupertatis*, on the grounds of legitimate vows taken in Sicily,[63] led Plowden and Stone, prompted by Betagh, to press for Kenney's speedy return.

Looking back from the vantage point of Waterloo and subsequent developments, it is difficult to visualise the fear and uncertainty felt in those years by opponents of France. Plowden managed to convey something of the deep unease and insecurity felt in Britain. In September 1809, he envisaged the possibility of his country having "to drink deep of the revolutionary cup". The government were "distracted by disappointment in all their enterprizes", its ministers were "quarrelling among themselves", and a plentiful harvest was "rotting in the ground with excess of rain".[64] And the following June, he was writing to Esmonde that the hay and corn harvest which looked scanty all over England, would be supplemented "by the plentiful arrival of corn from America" – but that other news was very bad. He expected the entire Spanish peninsula to fall to French troops, despite "a temporary respite" gained by Wellington; and generally there was "reason to fear everything". Though he claimed never to read newspapers, his letters to Sicily frequently referred to them. He continued: "Our public prints throw out alarms, even for Sicily. They suppose that a grand attempt to subdue it is in preparation all over Italy," and, he added, "the reflection that the defence of the island will be guided by the persecutor of your two excellent missioners [General Stuart] almost damps confidence in the protection of him, who dwells on high."[65]

Murat, Napoleon's king of Naples, was, indeed, preparing for an invasion of Sicily in the summer and autumn of 1810;[66] and, according to Kenney's somewhat fanciful entry in his journal and a subsequent letter to Glover, up to 4,000 French troops landed within six miles of Messina on 17 September.[67]

They were so fiercely resisted by the Sicilians, he said, that on the arrival of the British forces some 1,200 surrendered. The rest managed to get safely back to Naples "under their commander, who is said to be an Irishman named Kavanagh".[68] Kenney, who was away at the community's country villa during the invasion, returned on 28 September to Palermo to find that all the college were still "full of dismay, notwithstanding the capture of 1,200 Frenchmen". Fear ran close to the surface, and increased the Sicilian government's dependence on Britain and the avoidance of all occasions of offending its representatives. This fear, tension, and dependence, necessarily added an edge to relations in the Jesuit community, and it is not fanciful to suggest that Kenney's association with his English friend, Glover, may have been a shield against criticism while Glover remained at Palermo.

The concern in Britain was much heightened by news of the attack. And it moved Betagh to press strongly for Kenney's recall. Writing to Stone on 27 September 1810, he expressed his joy at the news of the flourishing state of the Society in Sicily, but added that "the joy ... was much abated by the dreadful uncertainty of a continuance; if once the French make good their landing in force, the dissatisfaction of the natives with their present government will make the whole island an easy conquest." He went on to "earnestly request Mr Kenney be sent as soon as possible" as "he is the only person I could think of making a trustee for the Society, in case of my death, which cannot be very remote. I even have in contemplation for him," he continued, "a situation in the chapel formerly half of which was appropriated to the Jesuits. The other new ordained priests will require a longer time of preparation for this mission; they may be spared for a time." As a further inducement to haste, he concluded: "The deluge of friars, pouring in on us from every corner of the continent, will seize upon every vacant situation, especially here where our Ecclesiastic Superior is partial to them."[69] His intervention seems to have been decisive in the determination to call Kenney home. The latter noted on 11 March, 1811, with reference to a letter received by Drinan from Fr Plowden, that Fr Plowden "supposes me to be already on my journey". Arrangements to find a vessel home were made next day. One was expected in about ten days.

On 15 March, the Sicilian provincial and his consultors decided that all four Irish priests – Kenney, Connolly, Dinan, and Gahan – should return home. The haste occasioned confusion about Kenney's final examination. There was a strong difference of opinion between Fr Goja, who had long been a supporter of Kenney, and the prefect of studies. The latter ruled, however, that "it was impossible to combine" Kenney's 'sudden departure with the public act". On 26 March 1811, Peter took his two-hour oral examination before four examiners on the entire programme of philosophy and theology. Knowing that it might be very important in Ireland to have evidence of degree qualifications, Fr Goja appealed to the provincial on 3 April to have Peter graduated. This necessitated a public defence. The provincial approved highly and urged him to go directly to the prefect of studies. As a result, Peter was told to prepare certain "conclusions" for the public act, and the required four examiners were appointed. The defence took place and was successful. And then graduation was refused!

Two days before his departure, that final frustration took place. His entry for 3 April, the last day in Sicily, was made without comment:

> An hour before supper the prefect sent for me and told me that the provincial, finding that the rector had some objection to graduate a Jesuit (a thing never before done in Italy or Sicily), held a *consulta*, thinking it would be in his favour. But he was disappointed. He and his companion were the only two who wished to give such an example. The others were all against it, and quite fiercely, not considering that any particular circumstance rendered this measure not a mere *spagnolata* (boasting) but a prudent step.

Wishing, however, to testify that they believed he merited the degree, they ordered that he should be presented with a declaration signed by the chancellor, the prefect of studies, and the secretary, and confirmed with the same seal which would have been on his degree.

Accordingly, under the date, 3 April 1811, there was issued to him the compromise document: a parchment from the Pontifical and Jesuit University of Palermo, signed and sealed as ordered, and stating that he had successfully completed a four-year course in theology and successfully defended the theological theses in public disputation.[70] He took home with it, a letter from the archbishop of Palermo, and one from Emmanuel de Zuñiga, provincial of the Society of Jesus in Sicily, testifying that he was a religious of the Society, and a priest without any impediments which might prevent him celebrating mass anywhere, hearing confessions, or preaching, and, furthermore, that he was suitable for all the other works of the Society, including that of colleges.[71]

Two days later, Angiolini wrote to Fr Stone expressing his sadness at the departure of "the outstanding and incomparable Kenney".[72] But on 26 March, the day Kenney sat examination, the provincial sent a more qualified comment. "Fr Kenney," he wrote, underlining the words, "is a man of fine intellectual qualities and devoted to study, so that he holds out the highest hopes in regard to his future. He is also a man of religious observance but, endowed, as he is, with a perhaps too vigorous character, he at times gives the impression of being unduly wedded to his own judgement."[73] The cautionary note was not lost on Stone and Plowden; and they were to have occasion to recall it.

Although the final year in Palermo was a very difficult one, the brief entries in the journal give no indication of depth of feeling. In a letter to Glover, however, there was a comment which conveyed a considerable degree of disillusionment. He urged him to caution Fr Stone "not to admit any petitions from the Sicilians to be admitted to Stonyhurst or to be sent to America". Those who talked of making such petitions were men "who would spread tales, and infallibly create scandal", and they seemed to assume that Stone would pay for all their journey.[74]

Assured but vulnerable

It was significant that it was to Glover that he gave vent to his feelings. He had few confidants. Glover appears to have been the nearest to being a close friend. As not infrequently happens when an Englishman and Irishman find themselves far from their respective countries, they got on well together. And given the rule of not going out of doors without a companion, they were thrown together a good deal, especially before the other Irish arrived. Besides, they shared similar apostolic work, mainly with soldiers, sailors, and English speaking residents and visitors. Indeed, they sought out work together. The Annals of the Sicilian Province for 1810 suggest that the result of their work, and that of the succeeding Irish Jesuits, was such that the Jesuit church "was always full of soldiers, to the edification of everyone, who went there for confession, to pray, to receive communion". The Irish, the annals continued, and this included Glover, "gave them the spiritual exercises [of St Ignatius], taught the catechism, and frequently visited their hospital and were sought and loved by them".[75] Allowing for the hyperbolic style, there was undoubtedly a memory of much zeal exercised to considerable effect. Their closeness led to two of the longest entries in Kenney's journal, both concerned with moments of rare disagreement in their friendship. They merit mention as providing a glimpse of the inner person behind the eloquent, controlled, seemingly self-assured exterior.

The first concerned an attractive woman called Mrs O'Higgins, wife of a British officer. She lived at Palermo. He was stationed at Messina and, despite his Irish name, was vehemently anti-Catholic. She decided to become a Catholic and sought instruction. Glover was recommended. He and Kenney visited her fairly regularly for purposes of instruction. After a while, Kenney felt uneasy about the whole process, and thought Glover was getting out of his depth. He expressed his misgivings to him, but without effect. He refused to accompany him in future. Again without effect. Glover's "too frequent and incautious visits" to the woman gave rise to unfavourable rumours in the city. She was baptised. Her husband returned and, angry at her conversion to Catholicism, threatened to kill her and the Jesuits. Glover was instructed not to visit her again. He obeyed with great difficulty. Meanwhile, he had kept much from Kenney, including his resentment at Kenney's attitude to Mrs O'Higgins. He began sending off his post for England, without telling his friend. The exclusion hurt Kenney who felt he had only tried to act as a friend, and wished

Glover would confide in him. He confided to his journal, in a lofty pretence at detachment: "True I felt his conduct; but am not too offended. The innate goodness of his heart and upright intentions must atone for a want of generous sincerity and experience. Poor fellow! little does he know that I have been made acquainted with everything that has occurred and with every step he has taken, and am only concerned that he has displeased so much his superior without wishing to do it, and thus deprived himself of his best friends."[76]

A further example of this kind of infatuation, with its accompanying sensitivity, not unusual among young celibates living close together, was provided by a long entry about something far less momentous. Glover, about to leave the house for a day or so, brought to Kenney's room a bottle of wine which they had bought together "for private use". He brought it along lest his friend should want it the following day in his absence. Kenney, however, took umbrage. "I took it to be a clear indication," he wrote, "of his unwillingness to trust me with the key of his room. I know no cause I have ever given for this want of confidence ...".[77]

Something of the sensitivity and vulnerability betrayed in these private entries remained throughout life, and, though shielded by a carapace of competence and confidence, were, perhaps, reflected in his reluctance to take on the government of others, and also in the empathy which added to his attraction as a confessor and preacher, and rendered him revered and warmly regarded by students at Maynooth and young boys at Clongowes.

JOURNEY HOME – VALETTA INTERLUDE –
CONFIDENT TO ENDURE AND ACHIEVE

On Saturday, 6 April 1811, Peter and his three companions set sail in convoy from Palermo. At first, the wind was favourable for Gibraltar. Then a heavy gale scattered them, and forced their ship back to Malta. There they had to await another convoy. Their stay at the city of Valletta was a pleasant experience for all four, but especially for Kenney. The bishop of the island, Ferdinand Mattei, was so taken by him that he determined to retain him "for the good of the British Catholics in the island". He wrote for that purpose to the provincial, Fr Zuñiga. The latter sent a polite refusal, together with orders for Kenney to hasten his departure. That reply came on 31 May. By then, the other three had sailed. As there was no convoy sailing in the month of June, he was obliged, probably to his relief, to wait until one "was appointed". Everybody, clergy and laity, made much of him. A generous monsignor provided him with "lodging and table". Two families combined as one to show him welcome: "They were never happy but when they had me in their house," he wrote, "and never was I there that they did not treat me with sincere friendship and with as much liberality as if I had been their greatest benefactor." A woman and a religious brother provided the furniture for his bedroom, washed his linen, and "were ever sending" him "little presents". And there was also the feeling that he was doing useful work, not only for the clergy and strong Christian families but for homes where marriages were under strain and for military personnel; and there were opportunities of assisting people wishing to become Catholics. All in all, the interlude provided a much needed period of affirmation, affection, and healing after a stressful and demoralising year.

On 1 July he set out in a convoy of seventy sail, after "bidding adieu to the last of those dear and firm friends" to whom he felt so indebted. He made daily entries on sailing conditions as they toiled towards Gibraltar, which they did not reach until 26 July – having being held back by "many bad sailing vessels in the convoy". After four days there, they embarked on the final stage of their journey on 1 August. Into the third week out, and still 800 miles from home, their provisions had nearly run out. "The little accidental adjuncts, which made sea-fare less unpalatable, have already disappeared," Kenney observed on 18 August. They struggled on, depending on fishing to keep them in food. It was with special pleasure, therefore, that he woke on 31 August and saw "the view of Dublin Bay from Dalkey round to Howth". They came to anchor in Poolbeg, and found themselves in quarantine without any food. He managed to send word to his sister, who came with some friends and provisions. He was home. The long period of preparation was over.

Effects of the long preparation

His training had sought to provide him with a spiritual depth and strength to face most eventualities, and with a wealth of knowledge and skills to do so with some grace. The Sicilian part of that training was particularly appropriate to the Irish context. Not only did it ensure that he would be accepted as a Jesuit by bishops and clergy, it also gave him a continental background not dissimilar to that of many Irish diocesan priests, and provided him with comparable experiences of foreign travel, climate and culture, and of the reality of French power and intention. In addition, it brought an uncommon exposure to archaeology and history from Palermo in the north-west right round to Syracuse,[78] the city of Archimedes, in the south-east, and enriched his appreciation of classical writings and locations; of sculpture, painting, and architecture; of philosophy and literature; of church ceremonies, liturgies and music; all of which, joined to his "amiable manner" and positive personality, made him welcome in both secular and clerical polite society.

To these general accomplishments were added the more clearly pastoral attributes of theological ability and sureness, rare oratorical gifts, already extensive experience as a priest, and a deeply based and zealous spirituality – a combination which, allied to that confidence in himself which had been so much affirmed by Angiolini, whose judgement he greatly valued and who remained something of a hero to him all his life, were destined to make him a figure of prominence and influence within a short time.

On a more academic level, his distinctive gifts ran to the then much prized facility of writing original Latin verse;[79] and to a width of reading relatively rare among clergy – he and Glover having been given the required episcopal permission which expanded their range of reading "to all prohibited books except any written *ex professo* against the sixth commandment".[80] In the social sphere, the intense, confined world of Sicily in those years had brought opportunity to meet with royalty and episcopacy, nobility and military commanders, as well as the rank and file; while at a personal level the crucible of criticism and intrigue had seared and tempered him, and added to an already strong sensitivity to injustice. And, not surprisingly, his time abroad had intensified his sense of being Irish; and also helped to align him with the new breed of priests who, despite their abhorrence of the excesses of the French Revolution, were touched by its independent spirit of justice and equality.

And lastly, and far from least, was the circumstance which he recalled with gratitude to the end of his days – "It was my stay in Sicily that removed the debility both of my chest and my eyes and enabled me to get through my studies and my labours ever since."[81]

The overall result was a man of thirty-two years, extended by many experiences, confident of his abilities, and eager to accomplish. In a relatively short space he had fulfilled much. He had travelled far from Stonyhurst, and the tutelage of his novice master. He still revered him and would consult him, but would go his own way. His faith in Charles Plowden's judgement had been shaken, and he was less tolerant of his unhappy practice of sowing tares among the wheat, introducing into his much valued correspondence exaggerated and at times irresponsible comment and criticism.

Despite the litany of qualities and acquirements, he himself was, of course, far from realising how prepared he was for future events. Indeed, as he chafed in extended quarantine, allegedly due to the absence from Dublin of the Lord Lieutenant, he came close to panic as he envisaged problems ahead. He was concerned, he wrote to Stone, on 6 September 1811, about the vagueness of his situation. What was he, and his companions, to answer if asked: "Who sent you hither? And for what purpose?" The provincial of Sicily had sent them off with ill-defined letters of introduction and without a word of instruction. They did not know whether their "immediate dependence" was on the provincial or on the General; nor in what part they were to settle, nor to whom they were first to offer their services.

And requesting Stone to excuse his freedom of expression, he announced that he could not be seen to be in a position of subordination to him, since his authority rested on the *oraculum vivae vocis* which, after long study, he, Kenney, could no longer accept as authorising "any act or public station" he might hold. As things stood, he could not envisage it being admitted "as a just ground of authority by any ecclesiastical court in the world", and, indeed, when he had cited it in Palermo it "raised the laugh of the ecclesiastical court" there. Furthermore, he could not even appear to have Stone as a counsellor because of "past ruptures, still existing prejudices, and ... suspicions mutually entertained on both sides of the water".

This did not stop him, nevertheless, complaining that he had hoped that a letter from Stone would have anticipated his arrival – "so that I should not be here a moment without having my mind formed, my system arranged, and my answers prepared for everyone from his Grace down to his curate."

Speaking as an individual, Kenney added, the many difficulties "terrify me". Much more, then, would they oppress him as a superior. "Believe me, Sir, I am not the person who can commence the mission in the present most intricate circumstances of the Society in general and of its mission in Ireland." And, he concluded: "In this new Society may I never be superior."[82]

It was a wish reflecting unhappy past experience, and enunciating a plea that was to become a *leit-motif* for the future but was to continually fall on deaf ears. In spite of many achievments, he was persistently to underestimate his own gifts of leadership and enterprise, though, fortunately, this did not prevent him exercising them.

IV

"All depended on the beginning", 1811–14:
Asserting identity – Maynooth – Castle Browne,
Sir Robert Peel, and political pressure

> The Jesuit at Castle Browne is likely to do more mischief than a rebel army on the Curragh.
>
> Report of informer to Sir Robert Peel, 24 June 1814

Despite his fears, Peter Kenney found a welcome on many sides when he came ashore. Apart from family and friends, lay and clerical, with whom he had maintained some correspondence, he was welcomed by those whom Betagh had kept informed of his progress at Stonyhurst and Palermo, including the archbishop and his coadjutor, Dr Murray. He had learned of the old man's death while he was at Malta, he now learned of the widespread mourning at his passing and of a funeral attended by an immense multitude of up to 20,000 people.[1] Betagh' praise of him, moreover, created a reputation which led to Dr Everard, president of St Patrick's College, Maynooth, in the spring of 1811, before Kenney arrived home, requesting Fr Stone to have him as his assistant and "second superior of the whole house";[2] while Kenney himself wrote from quarantine that "scarcely had the news reached Dublin" that he was in the bay than the superior of the Carmelite monastery went to the bishop to engage his services for his chapel.[3] He also found that he had further reasons to be grateful to Betagh. His old teacher had left him his lodgings, with the rent paid up in advance for twelve months to preserve in it his papers, books and furniture for the use of the Society to which he conceived them "inviolably to belong".[4] Before long, however, he found himself sharing something else of his mentor, namely, his suspicious mistrust of what was done at Stonyhurst.

This last was shared by a number of churchmen. It was believed that the superiors there would, as Plowden put it, "*per fas et nefas* retain in their own hands the management of the affairs of the new missionaries".[5] The belief reflected in part, of course, the traditional mistrust of England and things English, which was increasing amongst all sections of the Catholic population at this stage.

Mise-en-scène

That mistrust had been intensified by the refusal of the promised Catholic emancipation after the passing of the Act of Union; and at the time of

Kenney's return the politico-religious issue of Catholic emancipation was agitating the country once more on the question of the veto – whether the government would be granted the right of veto on the appointment of bishops and the right to pay the salaries of the diocesan clergy, in return for removing Catholic disabilities? Rome had granted such concessions elsewhere in Europe. The English vicars-apostolic, with the exception of Dr Milner, were prepared to concede. The Irish hierarchy, however, and the lay Committee of the Catholics of Ireland, were adamant in their opposition. Nothing reflected this more clearly than the words of the suave and gentle Dr Francis Moylan of Cork, who was known as a critic of republicanism, despite the fact that his brother, Stephen, had been secretary to George Washington in the American war of Independence and remained one of the latter's close friends.[6] Writing to Mr E. Jerninham, secretary of the English Catholic Board, on 8 April 1810, Moylan proclaimed uncompromisingly that Irish Catholics were prepared "to drag their degrading chains forever" rather than surrender influence in church affairs to men irreconcilably opposed to it.[7]

The clergy generally were becoming increasingly active politically on the issue, and the assumption that emancipation was primarily an Irish matter since England had so few Catholics was extending the traditional mistrust even to English Catholics. Kenney, despite his years abroad, soon found himself responding to the attitude of his coreligionists. Moreover, his uncertainty as to his status, and his insecurity with regard to the future, were further inducements to find grounds for "a suspicious mistrust" at what appeared to be in train at Stonyhurst with regard to "the new missionaries" of the Society in Ireland.

FIRST GREAT TASK:
ASSERTING THE INDEPENDENCE OF THE IRISH MISSION

Because he and his companions were members of the Sicilian province, which was recognised by the Irish bishops, he had hoped, in more sanguine moments, that they could operate openly, if discreetly, as Jesuits in Ireland and, indeed, establish a college to which the Irish at Palermo would come. To this end he had expected a definite commission from the General, with somebody formally appointed to act as superior. He had understood from Fr Plowden that this was how it would be. Instead, he found that nothing had been done to obtain a directive from the General or to have him appoint a superior for the Irish mission; and Plowden had even advised Fr Dinan to seek work under the bishop of his own native diocese. So, after all their travelling and labour, they were left with nothing distinctively Jesuit to accomplish, and Frs Stone and Plowden seemed happy to have them swallowed up in diocesan duties and demands. In the atmosphere of suspicion in Dublin it all began to look like an effort to keep the Irish mission in a very subordinate position to the English province and, in the process, preserve control of the Irish funds. The more he thought about it and discussed it, the more incensed Kenney became. He despatched a letter to Stonyhurst which, though no longer extant, appears to have been very forcibly expressed, to judge from Plowden's aggrieved reaction.

Frs Plowden and Stone found themselves in a difficult position. For so long they had been the controlling figures, the masters of formation, where aspiring Irish Jesuits were concerned, and now they found four of them returned as priests and members of the Sicilian province, conscious that they were Jesuits beyond question and, in Kenney's case, openly doubtful about the status of the men at Stonyhurst,[8] to whom, nevertheless, they looked for shelter and spiritual assistance. With Kenney, besides, there was a further factor. He had been given to understand earlier, through Plowden, that Stone intended him to be the first superior of the Irish, but Stone, probably because of Plowden's subsequent advice, did not fulfil the intention. Plowden, following a request for his opinion, had written on 21 April 1811, that Kenney was no doubt "a man of bright talents and sound virtue", but as he seemed to have sided with Angiolini it might offend the Sicilian provincial to give him any position of power, and hence he would advise against "giving any authority to Fr Kenney".[9] Now, ironically, here was Kenney, a member of the Sicilian province, and appointed by the same provincial as superior for the time being of the men on the Irish mission. And he was expressing strongly critical sentiments to his old master of novices.

Plowden was taken aback, and defensive to the point where he wrote rather dismissively of Kenney to one of the Irish students at Palermo destined to be one of Kenney's subjects! "I am not without some anxiety about the opening of this important mission," he wrote to Robert St Leger on 31 October 1811. "Mr K. had been but a few days in Dublin when he wrote hither a letter, full, as appeared to us, of unfounded alarms and imaginary difficulties, arising from his lively imagination and delicacy of sentiment. Before he could receive an answer, he appeared at Stonyhurst."[10]

It was after some three weeks, not a few days, that Kenney appeared at Stonyhurst. He met with Plowden, and then arranged a meeting with Stone, with whom he planned to speak "freely and candidly"; and to that end he also put his thoughts in letter form. Writing helped to clarify his thinking, especially when he was feeling strongly on a matter. The results of such discipline could be very powerful, as had appeared in his defence of Betagh, and in his outlining of Angiolini's views on the position of the English Jesuit province. Now, once again, clarity and intensity of feeling were combined to telling effect.

A controlled explosion

He understood from Mr Plowden, he observed, that as the General had not appointed any superior for the Irish mission, he and the other Irish Jesuits would be going thither "without any order or direct mission" from his Paternity. On their going back to Ireland from Stonyhurst, therefore, there would be two alternatives: either to present themselves, "each to his own bishop", telling him that having been sent from Sicily without specific direction or immediate superior, they were "at his Lordship's disposal"; or else that one of them should act as if he had the authority of a "constitutionally appointed" superior. He, Kenney, considered both alternatives to be unconstitutional and highly unbecoming. They were recognised by the Irish bishops precisely because they had lived and taken their vows in an area under the General's authority, hence it was necessary that their mission be seen to come from the General and that there be a superior "authentically appointed" by him. Such action would secure respect for their religious character and prevent them being individually attached to their native diocese. Mr Plowden had assured him verbally in the past, and by letter more recently, that this would be done, and it could be done easily. The question was – "Why had it not been done?" In Ireland, he added, "the question would be answered very soon ... Bishops, priests and people would one and all say" that they were thus scattered and neglected "to prevent the speedy beginning of any collegiate establishment, in order that Stonyhurst might further benefit from the delay" and that they might retard as long as they could "the return of the Irish property to its original source". However false this might be in itself, Kenney continued, they would spread it abroad with such an appearance of truth that, given the prejudice and mistrust in Ireland it would pass "for noon-day evidence". But others apart, what of themselves. "Might we not ask, with due deference, why were we sent to Sicily? To be Jesuits for a year or two and live the rest of our lives secular priests!" For the Irish episcopal system was so strong that what was started would not be easily changed. "All depended on the beginning."

Must we, he added with obvious feeling, "after having refused the offers of our bishops years ago, ... after having made long voyages ... through a love of the religious life, must we now be drafted and *curated* about by those very bishops, with our vows on our back ... Can the General thus secularise us? Has the Holy See deprived us of her immediate protection, which we enjoyed the other day ? What a consoling prospect ...! What fine encouragement to our juniors here and in Sicily, who are looking with fixed eyes on the beginning in Ireland!"

In conclusion, he poured scorn on a compromise suggestion of Plowden, that one of the Irish four who had returned to Ireland should "act as superior *in confidence*". Such dissimulation, he declared, could not long be hidden from the bishops; and besides it would be destructive of domestic discipline since the members would know that the superior was not really their superior and could not "give them an order of obedience". Would not such a superior, he declared indignantly, be in practice as Punch in the puppet show? He would be deemed a dissembler, pretending to a commission he did not have "whilst in fact he was your secret agent to deceive the bishops, and we should all have the honourable commendation of playing the comedy composed at Stonyhurst: nor should we any longer be called *second rate Jesuits*: our name would be *mongrel Jesuits*. I feel too much," he exclaimed, "and must finish."[11]

Even at a distance of nearly 200 years, both the intensity of feeling and the righteous indignation still stand out. A meeting after such an outpouring was a daunting prospect. And it was compounded rather than eased, by Kenney's appearance and personality. For, although in those years following his time in Sicily, he was described as "lank and lean as a bag of bones"[12] and though he was only 5 foot, 7 or 8 inches, in height, and would be spoken of on occasion by Plowden as "little Kenney",[13] the energy he exuded, and his presence and "dignified carriage", rendered size and girth irrelevant and focussed attention on his striking features and what he had to say. His face was not regular, but it was distinctive: a wide forehead in a large size head, a long nose, wide mobile mouth, and cleft chin, provided the setting for massive eyebrows over bright, piercing, often winning eyes, one of which was partly closed since his student days at Stonyhurst. And with all that went the alert intelligence, and fluent, at times caustic speech. And although there seems to have been some irregularity in his bone structure, certainly in later life, "few seemed to have noticed this, they were so carried away by the sweeping effect of his strong personality".[14] Usually an amiable companion, when the depths were stirred the controlled explosion was almost intimidating in its impact.

It has to be kept in mind, however, that in this temporary clash with his former superiors the combination of local suspicions and national feeling was only part of the motivation. There was also present – despite his aversion to assuming authority – the impatience of a young, energetic and zealous man to get things done, to ring changes straightway, and disposed, as a result, to view the caution of older people as obstructive, or timid, or out of touch with the real situation. And the situation in Ireland was much more favourable to religious orders than in England, as noted earlier, and Catholicism was more open, assertive, and less apprehensive. Hence, the possible grounds for disagreement were many as to what policy to pursue, and how secretly or openly.

Towards a modus vivendi

Though there is no record of the meeting with Stone, Kenney left a document which appears to chronicle the terms of an agreement between them. Rules for living in community and standards of behaviour were agreed, and Stone promised to write as speedily as convenient to the provincial of Sicily requesting him to declare by patent what authority he gave Mr Kenney pending the arrival of the General's order. He also promised to request the provincial that the Irish students be given a patent conferring theological degrees since such were important on the Irish mission, and also that patents be sent conferring the degree of doctor of divinity, previously approved, on Messrs Glover and Kenney.[15]

A further indication of the positive effect of the meeting was reflected in a letter from Plowden. On 26 October, five days before he ridiculed Kenney as alarmist in his letter to Robert St Leger, he wrote carefully to Kenney, blending bluffness with blandishment. To ensure the success of the mission, he warned, everything possible to gratify the bishops should be done, and any mention of the Society's privileges, or exemptions, should be avoided; but he wished that the Irish Jesuits should always be "religious men", and he requested that they consider as unsaid whatever may have fallen from his lips or pen that seemed in anyway contrary to that.[16] In his letter to Robert St Leger on 31 October, moreover, he mentioned, after referring to Kenney's "unfounded alarms and imaginary difficulties", that, in the light of suspicions and mistrust in Dublin, Mr Stone would not presume to assert, or to assume anything like jurisdiction in Ireland and had concluded "that the superiority vested in Mr Kenney" by the provincial of Sicily must continue until the General could make an appointment. He then expressed the view that today's Irish Jesuits were in a situation similar to the early Jesuits "who went forth to distant countries", singly, in pairs, or in companies, "and, by the eminence of their services soon obtained establishments for the Society".

In the same letter, he told St Leger that all four Irishmen were at Stonyhurst. Three had completed their thirty-day retreat. Kenney, after a month there, was now about to commence his at Hodder. Mr Stone wished him, after the retreat, to precede the others to Ireland and to send for them as soon as necessary arrangements were made; and he advised that, if it could be made convenient, and the archbishop did not oppose it, they all live in one house.[17]

About this time, Kenney decided to write personally to the Sicilian provincial – conscious, no doubt, of Stone's dilitariness – requesting him to send on papers showing him to be the superior of the Irish mission.[18] He and his companions felt embarrassed at the prospect of returning to Ireland without a commission from the General, or even a patent from the provincial of Sicily.

Appeal to history and to Petrograd

Following his retreat, he planned to cross over to Dublin to proceed with what had been agreed with Fr Stone. Even as he did so, however, there occurred a further flare up of mistrust and misunderstanding, which this time was to go over and back to the General before a resolution was found. The manner in which Kenney dealt with the issues involved casts light on his mind and personality as, free from years of formation and supervision, he strove to assert his own independence and that of the Irish mission.

Soon after he returned to Dublin, he gave vent to bitter feelings, mingling serious with bitter complaints. He had been frequently assured by Mr Stone, he informed Plowden, that he could draw from Mr Wright or Mr Sewall whatever money he required "to hire and put in order" a house for his companions. When he applied, however, both men refused to give out any money, saying they had no commission from Stone to do so. As a result, he was left with just £10 for his passage to, and expenses in Ireland. Again, Stone had given him a chalice of Fr Callaghan, which he left in Stone's press with the assurance that the key was always available. When he went to collect it, however, he found that Stone had gone off to London with the key. It all churned up national feeling and a sense of having been treated off-handedly, hence, having vented his grievances, he concluded: "I dare say it is of little consequence to some at Stonyhurst how we feel on this side of the water; but it will at least prevent my heart from bursting when I let out ... what I and others here feel, in being thus sent without a roof to put our heads under, without a prospect of that college so often promised by you and him, nay without any ostensible authority, or even the knowledge of our superior."[19]

There were also some heated exchanges with Nicholas Sewall, who told him that his "letters were filled with ill humour ever since" he "came from Sicily".[20] And he wrote trenchantly to Mr Wright, procurator of the finances of the English province, complaining of how he had been treated at Stonyhurst and alleging that the English province had done well out of the Irish money.

His writing to others than Stone indicated, it would seem, the virtual impossibility of getting a quick return from the English provincial. Wright responded by immediately arranging with La Touche bank in Dublin to hold £500 at Kenney's disposal, and then wrote in defence of Stone, and of the careful and fair administration of the Irish funds, and expressed surprise that he felt he had been poorly received at Stonyhurst. It seemed to him when he met him there, that he "concealed a dissatisfied mind under a cheerful appearance".[21] This last, Kenney refused to let pass. He was satisfied with Wright at that time, he replied, because he believed his promise that the draft of the money to purchase the house would be forwarded before long. But he had to write letter after letter and had eventually felt obliged to comment "that if we had treated others as we had been since our arrival from Sicily ... we would hear much of Irish blunders and mismanagement". He made no apology for this.[22]

In March 1812, in far distant Petrograd, Thaddeus Brzozowski, the Vicar-General of the order (there would be no one with the full title of General until the Society was fully restored) addressed a letter to Kenney and his companions which added to the confusion they already experienced. He had heard of their being sent from Sicily to their "Fatherland". The Society, he assured them, existed in "the British missions", and he reminded them of the spirit of their predecessors in the order and of the onus on them to live up to that same spirit of zeal and obedience. They had a superior in England, and a provincial, and they were to "obey them as though they were Christ the Lord"; and any doubt about their authority should be immediately dispelled. And they were to be very discreet in their speech. This was not "the time to be preaching from the roof tops ... about the Society in the British mission", and they were not to speak with the Irish bishops, or "with anyone outside the Society", about his letter or about their link with Stonyhurst.[23]

He was clearly not in touch with the Irish situation, and he would later chide Fr Stone for not informing him of the background. Kenney was upset at having Ireland treated as part of the British mission, at the General's lack of knowledge of the position with regard to the Irish bishops and Stonyhurst, and with regard to the attitude of the Irish hierarchy to Jesuits coming from Sicily as distinct from those in England. He suspected that the General had been misinformed from Stonyhurst that Ireland was part of "the British mission" and that this was a means of keeping control over the Irish funds. He was, in fact, partly correct in his suspicions. On the same date, Brzozowski wrote to Stone to say he had written to Kenney in the way he (Stone) had indicated. He hoped they [the Irish presumably] would in future be "docile, cautious and obedient".[24]

Kenney's response to the letter to him could scarcely be called "docile". He wrote at length to the General, and prevailed on a French ex-Jesuit, Fr Jautard, who knew the background, to do likewise. The latter had come to Ireland after the suppression and worked as chaplain at George's Hill convent. Their letters told the history of the Irish funds, how they had passed to Fr Stone, and of his commitment to protect them. But now, Jautard wrote, to judge from the ambiguous answers Fr Kenney had received, it was clear that the English province sought to deprive the Irish mission of its rightful property. He also wished to point out that the English Jesuits were seeking to bring the Irish into unity with them. They had tried this in the old Society, but their efforts were refused "because of the rivalry and jealousy which existed between the two nations". The Irish clergy were steadfastly opposed to such a union, and the Irish bishops would "not allow into their dioceses any religious who" were "under an English superior". Hence, he requested the General to ensure that the funds, which came to over £30,000, were restored to Fr Kenney as superior of the Irish mission, and that the older decrees were confirmed so as to shelter the Irish Jesuits from future encroachment by their English brethren.[25]

Kenney's letter went into more detail on the history of relations between the English province and the Irish mission, and on the case presented by a Fr Young in a previous century which had led to the General of the Society at the time issuing a decree against unification. He also expressed his doubts about the legitimacy of the English province.

On 30 September 1812, Fr Brzozowski replied to Kenney and also wrote to Stone, enclosing copies of Kenney's "prolix letter" and that of Jautard. He assured Kenney that the good of the Irish mission was dear to him, but reminded him that "the Society rejects and hates the spirit of nationality" among its members. He was examining the matter fully, for justice required that he hear both sides. He requested that Kenney send him the names of his companions, their dates of birth and other details about them; and meanwhile he confirmed him in the office of superior, and left them "joined to the Sicilian province for the time being". He added that when writing to him Kenney was to take care "to write plainly, clearly and distinctly" since it was "very troublesome to read and understand indistinctly written letters on matters of the gravest importance".[26] It was not to be the last reminder from a General about his handwriting.

In his letter to Stone, Fr Brzozowski sought his views on the Irish funds and on the historical independence of the Irish mission. He asked, in particular, about the manuscript written by Fr Young. (Writing from Russian territories, he had no way of knowing that John Young [1589-1664] had been superior of the Irish mission, had gone to Rome after the Cromwellian devastation, and had made out there a report for Fr General Oliva on the need to have the Irish mission separate from the English province.) Fr Brzozowski went on to say that he was making no decision for the present, except that he had confirmed Fr Kenney for the time being in the office of superior to which he had been appointed by the Sicilian provincial. "It seems to me," he added perceptively, "that Fr Kenney is devoted to the Society, has a good heart, and in this is not to be pushed but rather to be led along pleasantly, because he has ideas from the letters of Cardinals Borgia and di Pietro, from conversations with Fr Angiolini and the Irish bishops, from the rivalry that exists between the Irish and the English, and finally concerning the temporal funds which he considers to have been mishandled, and should not be retained by the English fathers." He wished to remove all prejudices from the matter, Brzozowski concluded, but for that he needed to be briefed by Stone on all aspects. He was distressed that the latter's letters to him "concerning this situation" had "ceased in the space of the past four years".[27]

The reception of this letter raised the whole issue above the level of individual differences and national feeling. The points of view of both sides had now to be taken into account. In particular, it brought Plowden to lay aside spontaneous dislikes and comments and to focus his attention on the seriousness of the disagreement and its possible causes. He assisted Stone by drafting a letter for him to Kenney which squarely addressed the latter's complaints; but at the same time he sent to Stone himself a very strong and critical comment on his leadership and his share in the confusion and bitterness that had arisen between Irish and English Jesuits. Stone's lack of energy, his procrastination, and his frequent saying that he did not know what to do, had bred "discouragement and uneasiness". "Mr Kenney," Plowden continued, "not knowing your real views, most freely attributes your conduct to the worst of motives, a design to defraud Mr Callaghan's heirs." And calling on his experience of the young Irish superior, he added:

> I am greatly inclined to think that the present Irish complaints would have been in great measure prevented if last Autumn, during a month which Mr Kenney spent here, you had explained to him your views, designs and intentions, if you had shown him some eagerness ... to provide in the meantime for himself and co., in a word if you had inspired some confidence. His main complaint is that you neither acted nor spoke to him, and he attributes this very wrongly to a design of wrongdoing the Irish mission.[28]

Despite the blunt advice, it was not till three weeks later that Stone finally wrote to Kenney. His letter was almost a verbatim copy of the draft made out by Plowden three weeks earlier.

From the reports which had reached him, he wrote, it appeared that Kenney thought that the English province sought to rule "the business of Ireland". In this regard he wished to point out that from the period when Fr Young, in the 1660s, warned against the union of the English province and the Irish mission because of "the inveterate aversion in those times of the Irish to the English nation",[29] down to the suppression in 1773, "the junction was never more mentioned"; and he believed that Young's argument applied even more forcibly at the present time because of "the odious union of the two kingdoms", odious because the Act of Union was seen pretty generally "as against the wish and will of the Irish nation". No English Jesuit, therefore, sought any "superiority", which, in any event, "in our present miserable and trying situation would be worse than folly".

Why, then, Stone asked, had he not surrendered Mr Callaghan's bequest to Kenney? He had defended the bequest against claims from all sides, he observed, and had been exposed to much recrimination; but he would remain true to the wishes of the donors, that was to say he would comply with the wishes of Fr General as soon as he was duly informed. But even then, as a trustee, he would not part with the funds until the General had appointed at least three people to receive them. He was now about to write to Fr Brzozowski to appoint, without delay, three people, "not Englishmen", to administer the bequest and "never to alienate it from its original destination". Meantime, if there was anything Kenney required, he would most readily concur "so far as the stock of property" would allow.[30]

Within a few months, Stone's communication was buttressed by a trenchant letter from the General, which summarised for Kenney all the queries he had put to Stone, including all Kenney's suspicions, and all the replies he had received. The responses, Brzozowski stated, showed how unsubstantial Kenney's case was, and hence he should put aside suspicions and trust the assertions of the English provincial. He reminded him once again that he was still waiting for particulars of his companions.[31]

Kenney and Stone corresponded during the summer regarding the purchase of land and premises for a college; and, on 29 July 1813, the English provincial sanctioned £20,000 for the purchase and refurbishment of Castle Browne,[32] destined to become Clongowes Wood College, and on 20 August signed a certificate to the effect that whatever monies he had remitted to the Revd Peter Kenney were "at his own sole and free disposal".[33] And although the previous autumn, Plowden had declared all the four Irishmen "equally unfit" to "conduct business in Ireland",[34] he now, in August 1813, exchanged friendly letters with Kenney on spiritual and academic matters, and assured him that he possessed the qualities of "great prudence, judgement and accuracy"[35].

Kenney, however, remained on his guard, and continued fearful lest the General be unduly influenced by members of the English province to the detriment of the Irish mission. In October 1813, he forwarded to Brzozowski the required particulars about his companions, reported that he had consulted with Fr Stone, and conveyed, with some temerity, his fears of the General being induced to favour the English province. The forceful reply from Brzozowski, on 10 July 1814, left him in no doubt as to where they both stood. Having first expressed his joy that Kenney had sought the advice of Fr Stone, he then took him seriously to task. "Dear Father, your letter is scribbled; neither revised, nor corrected, and I cannot read it. You should not write like that to me". And he then continued:

> You say that I seem to be more favourable to the English. A childish remark ! Is it that ... you want me to stop trying to foster intercommunion between you and the English, as though a superior should desist from promoting union of hearts among his subjects. When you write, dear Father, give more thought to what you write, to whom, and about whom.

He then pointed to the example shown in Russian territories where Jesuits of many nationalities worked together, united in what Francis Xavier called "The Society of love", and asked him to try to do likewise. Let him await the balance of the money, and "not prejudge, either through hastiness or impetuosity". Finally, he exhorted: "Do not condemn your brothers, whom you ought to revere on account of their virtue and experience."[36]

Despite it all, the sense of security on the Irish side remained very fragile. In September 1814, Kenney was again upset. He had received a vague report from Stonyhurst that Fr Stone planned to revive the claim to religious jurisdiction over Ireland, on the basis of the decision of the former Vicar-General, Fr Gruber, in 1803, to reconstitute just one province for the Jesuits of England and Ireland. Conveying his concern to Plowden, he revealed that he had earlier written to the present General, at the request of his companions and following close questions put to him by the Vicar-General of the diocese, to have the pre-suppression status of independent mission restored to the Irish Jesuits. Fr Brzozowski had replied, however, that they now belonged to the Sicilian province, that he appointed him, Kenney, superior of all his companions, and "enjoined him alone to write to him on business, and gave him all necessary faculties for the government of the mission". He advised him to consult with Fr Stone where appropriate, "but clearly indicated that this was not a duty, and that Mr Stone had no right of authoritative interference". Hence, Kenney had conceived the system of Fr Gruber to have been perfectly reversed, until the recent report which seemed to declare this to be a misconception, and, in the process, suggested that the present General was disingenuous.[37]

Summarising the letter for Stone, Plowden observed that he had "fancied that Mr Kenney's superiority was quite a settled point". He begged him not to write to Kenney without first speaking to him.[38] Three months earlier when Stone upset Kenney by precipitate action, he had had to remind him of the persistence in Dublin of the jealous suspicion of Fr Betagh that we were "attempting to jokey the Irish".[39]

On 30 September, Plowden wrote to assure Kenney that there was no question of any "claim to spiritual jurisdiction in Ireland", and that he and Stone were at a loss to know how the rumour arose. With more than a little cajolery, he then remarked that since Kenney among many other good qualities had "a candid and open heart", he was sure that "the circumstance in question" would not "be a source of lasting discord between the sons of the restored Society". And with less than candour, he averred that they "were perfectly glad" at his appointment, would consider it a misery to be loaded with such a responsibility, and that, in his judgement, it was much more probable that with Kenney's "virtues and talents" the Society would "rise to eminence in Ireland before the fallen English province" would "be able to recover a decent degree of constancy".[40]

Thereafter, "Kenney's superiority" remained "a settled point", and the Irish mission was free to proceed with its own affairs, without English Jesuit interference yet with assurance of English Jesuit support. The road to the satisfactory conclusion, however, may have left Stone reflecting wryly on intimations of the General regarding Kenney, and on an earlier comment of the Sicilian provincial. Writing to Stone on 22 July 1813, Brzozowski had remarked of Kenney that "although he was gifted and very suitable for our ministry, he wished and hoped that he was docile, for without that the other gifts did not avail, indeed could be dangerous".[41] It was, perhaps, what the Sicilian provincial had in mind when he observed that at times he gave "the impression of being unduly wedded to his own judgement".[42]

While all these difficulties in relationships were being raised, discussed, and ironed out, Kenney was also searching for suitable premises, serving a church and parish, winning a reputation as a preacher and spiritual director, planning to buy land and property for a college, acting as vice-president of St Patrick's College, Maynooth, and establishing Clongowes Wood College. And in the wider sphere of politico-religious affairs, the disharmony generated by the veto controversy was spilling over into attacks on both the Irish Catholic Church, and the Jesuits, especially at the hands of one, Sir John Cox Hippesley. And also, and most important for Kenney, the Society of Jesus was formally and universally restored by the pope.

These various developments in his story unfolded more or less chronologically, and at the time were usually centre stage in his daily life. They commenced soon after he took up residence in Betagh's old house at 92 Cooke Street. His old friend had also left him £200, as well as his papers and library.[43] Thus established, his next step was to arrange with Dr Troy about pastoral work in the diocese.

BEGINNING PASTORAL WORK: GEORGE'S HILL TO MAYNOOTH

By arrangement with the archbishop, he and Fr Gahan were deputed to work in St Michan's parish. The two other Jesuits would work in chapels nearby, "to favour the design of living together".[44] After some months, perhaps on the expiry of the lease, to have more space, and to be nearer the parish church, they left Betagh's house, crossed the Liffey, and lodged at 3 George's Hill; where Fr Mulcaile of the old Society had lived. There were just three of them, it seems: Kenney, Dinan, and Gahan. It was a busy area. Close by was the corn market and the notorious Newgate prison. St Michan's was just across the road from their house. It had cherished associations for them. Jesuits had worked there throughout the eighteenth century.

In this old church, soon to be replaced,[45] Kenney and his two companions assisted with masses, confessions and sermons. From time to time Kenney also preached and helped out in other churches. Indeed, he was under heavy pressure from the moment of arrival seeking to meet the bishops' demands for assistance in "teaching in the schools" and "the missions": the last referring presumably to a course of sermons and religious instruction promoting spiritual renewal in different parishes. His companions were not much help when it came to preaching. On 10 December 1813, he confided to Stone: "Gahan and Dinan are excellent religious men. In their duty in the confessional, masses, private catechisms, visiting the sick, they are indefatigable. But since their return, Dinan has not once attempted to speak in public; Gahan has done it once and trembles at the thought of doing it a second time". For assistance in teaching and preaching he would have to depend on the men still in Sicily.[46]

It was a time when sermons were critically evaluated in the public press and their preachers compared. His two companions appear to have mustered courage to preach, at least occasionally. Watty Cox's *Irish Magazine* bore out Kenney's estimation of their abilities, though without his redeeming qualifications. Under the heading "Veto Priests of Dublin", it spoke of Fr Dinan as "ignorant and superficial, unlike that celebrated Society", and of Fr Gahan as "incapable and dull". It also scrutinized Fr Ryan, at Arran Quay church, and dismissed him as "another stupid Jesuit – from Connemara"![47] Although the magazine did not mention Kenney, the tradition is strong that, even at this early stage, his preaching began to attract people to the church. This was to be a feature of his career. Social curiosity, as well as devotion, was reflected in his congregations. And even the acknowledged rhetorician, Henry Grattan, was said to have been drawn to attend. Kenney's eloquence differed from the prevailing tendency towards grandiloquence and declamation. It was said to have been calm, reasoned, and persuasive. His words were remembered for their substance rather than their flourish.[48]

The house at George's Hill was next door to the Presentation convent, which Fr Mulcaile had founded with Teresa Mullally in 1794. Kenney made himself available to the nuns for conferences and advice. He was impressed at the way in which devotion to the Sacred Heart of Jesus was practised at the convent. The devotion had been preached in Dublin from the 1740s, and must have been familiar to him as a boy.[49] It appealed to many Jesuits, whose own spirituality, as has been seen, was much concerned with personal devotion to the person of Jesus Christ. During the late eighteenth and early nineteenth centuries, as if in reaction to the harsh, juridical emphasis of Jansenism, confraternities and religious bodies bearing the title *Sacred Heart* sprang up in different parts of the world. Inevitably, with the passage of time, the devotion succumbed to some over-pious accretions. Hence, when Kenney during the summer of 1813 corresponded with Plowden about bringing out a new edition of a standard work entitled *Devotion to the Sacred Heart*, his English mentor sent him a number of books and emphasised the importance of the material being doctrinally "solid and well grounded". "Books of prayer and tracts of devotion," he added, required "great prudence, judgement and accuracy", qualities which he suggested Kenney possessed.[50]

The latter's work with the sisters and his growing reputation, led to him being consulted by other religious congregations. One recorded instance concerned the Carmelite convent in the Dublin suburb of Ranelagh, where the mother prioress sought to bring about a tightening of discipline and observance and ran into difficulties with some of the community. She consulted him, and also the coadjutor archbishop, Dr Murray, and, during 1813, decided to leave Ranelagh with seven or eight others. They moved to Mill Street in the parish of St Nicholas.[51]

Kenney and Dr Daniel Murray were to work harmoniously together. They were both past students and friends of Fr Betagh, but how well they knew each other prior to Kenney's return to Dublin is not clear. Certainly, within a short time of his return they became friends and mutual admirers. This was facilitated by their close co-operation as president and vice-president of St Patrick's College, Maynooth, 1812-13.

Vice-president of Maynooth

One of the immediately consoling things for Kenney on his return to Ireland, was the good will of the hierarchy and their desire to avail of the new Jesuits' services. A number of the bishops sought to have a Jesuit college in their diocese. Bishop Plunkett of Meath offered Dunboyne Castle, where he already had a school. Bishop Moylan of Cork, and Dr Power of Waterford, made repeated requests.[52]

Fr Stone, having reminded Kenney on 7 September 1812, that "it was the wish of the General of the Society that a college should be set up in Ireland as soon as possible," expressed his own preference for a college away from the Dublin area.[53] Kenney, however, was clear that he wanted an establishment fairly close to Dublin; and as he had a boarding school in mind he sought a large premises with sufficient land to make it mainly self-sufficient in the provision of food. His experience was of Stonyhurst and Palermo, both imposing edifices. His thoughts were of a foundation on a similar scale. And unlike Betagh, devoting his days to educating the deprived citizens of Dublin in penal times, he looked to the education of the new Catholic middle class, who were assertive, well-to-do, ambitious for their children, and interested in removing obstacles to their active participation in the social and political life of the country. But he was conscious of the need for haste. He wished to have a location for the able group of young Jesuits scheduled to return in 1814, who were to form the staff of the longed-for college.

In the midst of his search for locations, and his expanding work from George's Hill, he indicated little enthusiasm when the archbishop of Dublin approached him to accept the presidency of Maynooth. Dr Everard, the president, had become seriously unwell. In June 1812, however, Dr Daniel Murray agreed to accept the position for one year, pending Dr Everard's recovery.[54] Murray determined to have Kenney as vice-president. He argued, as had the archbishop, that the greater glory of God would be more effectively procured there[55] than in Kenney's present situation. What seemed to have succeeded, however, was the argument that what was involved was but "a conditional and temporary employment" which would not deflect him from "the setting up of a college of the Society whenever an opportunity offered".[56] His reluctance was because he was, at that point, awaiting a letter from Stone regarding the house at Dunboyne and regarding the availability of funds to purchase. Despite his request for haste, the reply from Stone was much delayed. As a result, he felt under pressure to make a temporary commitment to Murray's request. Had Stone's reply came on time, he later wrote, he would have refused the bishop's invitation, and the latter would not have pressed him if he knew he were employed on his "own line".[57]

He commenced work at Maynooth at the end of August. He and Murray stayed for only one year, but it proved a memorable interlude at a time when the college was beset with internal problems. On 31 October 1812, after several weeks experience of what was involved, he wrote a formal letter to the archbishop to place on record the grounds on which he had taken up the position and to preserve his freedom of action.

> Nothing could be more foreign to my intention, and to the wishes of my religious brethren, than a situation in Maynooth College. I, however, yield to Your Grace's desire and opinion that in my actual circumstances the greater glory of God may be more effectively procured there than in my present situation. ... I promise to go for the ensuing year, provided a duty more directly mine do not necessarily call me thence before the expiration of that time.

"I must, however, earnestly request," he continued, "that if Your Grace meet in the interim with a person who would accept the proposed situation, I may be allowed to spend in the humble domestic library of George's Hill, not as yet arranged, the hours I can spare from missionary labours."[58]

At this stage, the college had approximately 205 clerical students; of whom more than three-quarters were the sons of farmers, and the remainder from the ranks of tradesmen and shopkeepers, the lower professions and small-scale business.[59] Life within its walls, as with most seminaries then and long afterwards, was Spartan. The day commenced at 5.00 a.m., and was fully regulated. Students made their own beds, swept their own rooms, cleaned their own shoes, and so on. Silence reigned, except at certain times. There were no fires in the rooms, heating was provided only in certain areas; food was simple, even coarse; and students survived from 5.00 a.m. to 3.00 p.m. on what one ex-student termed a "sorry breakfast".[60] They were not easy to govern. They had not been through any preparatory seminaries. Most were "quite unbroken in the ways of discipline and obedience, and were not accustomed to regard any constituted authorities with sentiments of affection or esteem", and tended to resort to "disorderly scenes ... instead of legitimate means of redress".[61] Not surprisingly, a position of responsibility in Maynooth was not something eagerly sought in the early years of the century.

Student disorders tended to reflect times "when the public mind was excited"; for the students were said to be "Irish to the bone".[62] Hence, during 1798 sixteen were expelled; and from 1807 to 1810, in the first heat of the veto controversy, there was considerable turmoil. Special rules were drawn up making incitement to riot, disorderly noise in the prayer hall, and the circulation of defamatory letters against the president, professors, and fellow students, grounds for expulsion. It was noted that newspapers were being read in the prayer halls. A special enquiry was held into the state of the college, and in June 1810 the president and dean resigned.[63]

On 29 June 1810, Dr Patrick Everard was appointed president. He was away for long periods at a school which he had founded in England, yet in his two years as president he appears to have produced an abiding improvement.[64] Plowden, writing to Robert St Leger on 5 August 1811, remarked that when in London, in the spring of 1811, Everard had applied to Fr Stone to have Kenney as his assistant and "second superior of the whole house". Stone could not agree to this, Plowden added, and "Mr Everard returned to Maynooth and at one stroke dismissed 30 seminarists, said to have been turbulent, or marked for bad principles, even infidelity."[65] The trustees strongly supported Dr Everard and congratulated him in October 1810, on the improvement in subordination and piety since his appointment.[66]

The following year, however, there was much upset when the acting dean and professor of scripture, Mathias Crowley, defected from the Catholic Church. According to Plowden, he "read his recantation, or in the fashionable phrase, had 'renounced the errors of papacy', in one of the public churches of Dublin". The newspapers rang "with this scandalous triumph of error", and asserted "that many of the community of Maynooth" were expected to follow his example. From private accounts, Plowden continued, it appeared that Crowley's defection was a stroke of revenge against M. Everard, and he had heard that many were now leagued against the president, and that since "the horrid scandal of Crowley", he had, in fact, "resigned his superiority".[67]

When, therefore, Murray and Kenney took over after Everard, it looked as if they might be faced with a difficult time. For Kenney, as the first of the new Jesuits, the situation must have appeared particularly delicate, especially as the two most prominent professors, Dr Delahogue in dogmatic theology, and Dr Anglade in moral theology, were formerly of the University of the Sorbonne, and could be expected to be Gallican, perhaps Jansenist, in outlook, and, hence, anti-Jesuit. The issue of Gallicanism and Jansenism at Maynooth was, indeed, to surface prominently at intervals over the next hundred years.

Kenney and the French professors: Gallicanism and Jansenism

Dr Troy expressed concern early on about Gallican tendencies in Dr L.A. Delahogue's teaching on the Church[68] and later in his career sent texts in use at Maynooth to Propaganda for examination. Later still there were other complaints, and in 1853 the Congregation of Propaganda would recommend the withdrawal of his textbook.[69] In fact, Delahogue's expression of Gallicanism was moderate for the time, and the ever vigilant member of parliament for Sudbury, Sir John Cox Hippesley, queried at the time of the veto controversy if he were not, indeed, over favourable to absolute papal authority.[70]

Where Jansenism was concerned, there is no evidence of its existence in

Maynooth in the doctrinal and heretical sense of teaching doctrines such as the total corruption of human nature by original sin, and effectual predestination. It does seem, however, that the rigorism associated with Jansenism, was reflected in the moral theology taught in the college. This was marked by a negative view of human nature and a tendency to so emphasise the sinfulness and unworthiness of the human being before God as to discourage frequent reception of holy communion. The rigorist, as a result, viewed with grave suspicion the teaching of probabilists who sought to bring Christian mildness and understanding into the confessional. Bishop Healy, the first historian of Maynooth, accepting that there was evidence of rigorism in the early moral teaching at the college, and attributing it to the French professors, especially Dr Anglade, and French text-books, eloquently described rigorism as: "the moral system of those who" drew "too tightly the reins of law in restriction of a man's natural liberty of action; who" were "inclined to make precepts out of counsels, and mortal sins out of venial sins"; who "in cases of doubt whether as to the law or the fact", held the law to be binding and thereby imposed "an intolerable burden on men".[71]

To Dr Anglade, the idea that liberty was in possession 'till the opposite was proved, or, to put it another way, that "a doubtful law does not bind" in conscience,[72] was a form of laxism, a yielding to "the passions of men". He was, in practice, so strongly opposed to the probabilists that he told the Commissioners at the Irish Education Inquiry on Maynooth College, in 1826, that he "never read their works", and would never cast his eyes "on a theologian who maintains such a doctrine".[73] Ironically, though the Jesuits were known as champions of probabilism, the "overly severe" text in use while Kenney was at Maynooth was by a Jesuit, Paul Gabriel Antoine.[74] The French professors, however, substituted for it in 1813 an edition of the work of the secular priest, Ludivico Bailly, *Dogmatic and Moral Theology* (1789),[75] which was a standard manual in the seminaries of France, was Gallican and extremely rigorist, and was eventually condemned and placed on the Index of Forbidden Books in 1852.[76] The tone of the moral teaching in the college's first sixty years, therefore, necessarily contributed to that spirit of repression and scrupulosity in Irish spirituality which moved Patrick Kavanagh more than a century later to mourn how on "the green tree of humanity"

> The sharp knife of Jansen
> Cuts all the green branches
> ...
>
> Not sunlight comes in
> But the hot-iron sin
> Branding the shame
> Of a beast in the Name
> Of Christ ...

And yet, those who were "the true spirit of Ireland" managed to "joke through the death-mask".[77]

Despite having had, as his text-book at Palermo, the *Medulla Theologiae Moralis* of the classic probabilist, the Jesuit Bausenbaum, who had been much criticised by the anti-Jesuit party in France,[78] Kenney and the two French professors appear to have got on well together. He worked hard to establish good relations; and later, at Clongowes, he frequently invited them to college functions. Delahogue's defence of the order against Fr Fitzgerald of Carlow has been mentioned; while where Anglade was concerned, it is noticeable that at his appearance before the Commissioners of Education in 1826 he not only refused to be drawn into criticism of the Jesuits, but with reference to Kenney spoke of a retreat he gave at the college for five or six days which he attended and where "the subjects of mental reflection" were in his opinion "very good". The general tenor of the retreat, he declared, was "very edifying", and from it he hoped he "derived some benefit".[79] This, indeed, pointed to Kenney's most influential role during his year at Maynooth, that of spiritual guide, preacher, and retreat giver.

Spiritual guide and retreat giver

At Maynooth, as at most seminaries, the candidates for the priesthood had, in addition to vocal prayer, what was called mental prayer. The mental prayer, Dr Anglade told the commissioners, consisted of "reflecting and meditating on some particular truth, consisting chiefly of their state of life, or concerning the general principles of salvation". The material was given the evening before, and meditated on in the morning.

From his extant journals, it is evident that right through the year, Kenney provided points for these meditations, preached at mass, and gave two retreats of six or more days. The language used in the meditations and retreats sounds dated to present-day ears, but at the time it spoke vividly to its hearers; and the material was well organised, and presented in a convincing and personal way. Reading through notebooks of these meditations, based on what listeners took down, one finds a range of themes. Often the subject related to the liturgical season, as during Advent and Lent, when an appropriate scriptural quotation was taken for each day and a presentation or lecture given on it in the form of three points to be reflected on, prayed about. Among the themes of a specific nature, one notes: talks on sin, judgement, and the special solemnity and demands of the priesthood – the need for apostolic zeal, for obedience and purity, and the need to prepare for this exalted calling by prayer, mortification, and serious study. Again and again, the gospel scenes provided the setting for instruction or contemplation; and the appeal of the person of Christ in his life and passion was held before the students to encourage them to get to know him and his values better so that they might follow him more closely in their lives. In order to help each one advance spiritually, a period of examination of conscience was encouraged at mid-day and at night, with special reference to overcoming particular failings in behaviour or character.

Much depends in spiritual talks and homilies on the "presence" of the speaker, on the nuance of inflection and gesture, the capacity to create a mood and relate to the audience; nevertheless, something of the challenge Kenney presented to his young listeners may be indicated by some brief excerpts from, for example, an address on "Affection for Prayer" and a homily on St Patrick. He set the standards high, and conveyed expectation of a generous response.

"No man," he declared in the address, "can advance or persevere in God's service without prayer. It is then indispensable in a priest; and can a minister of God refuse an hour every day to this exercise? To be a man of prayer is the objective; to control one's thoughts and imagination is the great secret of a spiritual life. When you have practically learned it, your whole life, whatever be your occupation, will be a life of prayer ... It is of the greatest importance that every student labour to attain ... affection for prayer; he must ask it earnestly of God: prayer obtains the gift of prayer."

The homily on the feast of the national apostle and patron of the college rose to heights of fervent eloquence. They had been "chosen out of thousands", he reminded his audience, "to be depositories of the inestimable treasure of Christ's redemption, ministers of truth and mercy and the light of the world". Patrick was their "apostle and pastor" in a special way. And recalling the saint's determination and zeal in bringing the faith to the Irish people, he suggested that Patrick saw in them "the perpetuated fruit of his labours for Jesus Christ", the means to "the perpetuity of the faith in this his favoured land"; and he apostrophised their patron saying to them: "Be thou heirs of my spirit, as well as the successors of my ministry." If you wish to follow him, Kenney concluded, with practical application, "the first fruits of your zeal should be to promote virtue and learning in this house, this only hope of Catholic Ireland".

Kenney's six-day, or eight-day, retreat followed the general framework of the Ignatian Exercises: commencing with reflections on the end of man and purpose of life, and moving on to a consideration on sin and the mercy of God, and thence to contemplations on the call of Christ, scenes from his life, and his passion, death and resurrection. The presentations contained many references to books of the old testament and the psalms, as well as to the gospels and epistles, and always they looked towards action – towards amendment and improvement of life, and towards a deeper understanding and closer following of Jesus Christ. And frequently, too, there was a challenge to emulate the saints. Patrick, Francis Xavier, John Francis Regis, Vincent de Paul, he pronounced, were all men dead to everything but God's glory, the manifestation of His presence. "They were once precisely what you are now. Why may not you be what they became?" (Meditation on "Two Standards".)

To the members of religious orders there would have been little new in all this. To the seminarians and many of the faculty, however, it came across with great freshness. The meditations were eagerly written down, passed on to succeeding generations of students, and carried through life by many. One of the most highly regarded of Maynooth's theologians, Dr Patrick Murray, was among those. He wrote that the first trace of Dr Kenney's "luminous and powerful mind" he came across was "in some manuscript meditations which he composed during the short period of his holding the office of vice-president in this college, copies of which were handed down through some of the college officials". It was, he continued, "on the second or third year of my course (I entered college in the end of August, 1829) that I was fortunate enough to obtain the loan of a copy of some of these meditations. I remember well that I was quite enchanted by them – they were so different from anything of the kind I had, up to that time, ever seen. I transcribed as many of them as I could – they were given to me only for a short period – into a blank paper book, which I have still in my possession." He subsequently attended a number of retreats given at the college by Kenney, and was impressed at how the latter's style added to the content of what he said, for he "aimed not at the ear or the fancy, but through the understanding, at the heart. Not to steal it; he seized it at once; and in his firm grasp held it ... in ...willing captivity".[80]

Generally, the impression he made on the students seems to have been very positive. Even the Revd T.W. Dixon, who had been a student at Maynooth and had been ordained for some time before conforming to the Established Church, and who, from his evidence was patently anti-Jesuit, even he, when asked by the Commissioners of Irish Education for his recollections of Kenney, and whether he liked him "the better or worse for being a Jesuit", replied: "We thought a Jesuit was a very fine thing; a most holy character; and we considered him a very talented, clever man, and had much respect for him as such."[81]

Reflections on his vice-presidency

By his talks and sermons, his mingling with the students and listening to them, his assurance, energy, and firm but fair discipline, he helped to change the atmosphere in the college.

During this period of the Murray presidency, no student was allowed home on vacation without the special permission of his bishop, and also of the president of the college. Apart from this further tightening in discipline, it was reported that "the year was otherwise uneventful", which, as Dr Healy remarked, spoke well "for both the discipline and studies of the college".[82] A further indirect compliment was paid later that year, 1813, when the formal triennial visitation of the institution was conducted by a group of four judges and archbishops O'Reilly and Troy. One function of the visitors was to invite students to air grievances, and substantiate them, against any member of the administration. On this occasion, "no charge or grievance whatever" was made;

which was so unusual, it seems, that the "visitors broke up the sitting, and the chancellor expressed in flattering terms his satisfaction at the prosperous and orderly state which this silence so loudly proclaims."[83]

A more comprehensive, if florid, acknowledgement of Murray and Kenney's achievement in so short a time was conveyed by Bishop Murray's biographer, Fr William Meagher. "They found the discipline of the college ... sadly relaxed," he wrote, "and a spirit anything but ecclesiastical too widely diffused among the inmates – insubordination, and moroseness, and foppish estimates of independence, supplanting the modesty, and docility, and respect for order, and reverence for legitimate authority, which religion demands. *The vigour, and vigilance, and high ascetic tendencies of Dr Kenney, together with his reasonableness and moderation, and respectful and friendly bearing towards the students, soon wrought wonders amongst young people naturally so pious and tractable.*" The "suavity" of Dr Murray, and his "courteous treatment" of all, "completed the happy revolution ... Worldly-mindedness of every sort became unfashionable, discipline was re-established, and studies prosecuted with assiduity." Dr Murray rarely addressed the students, Fr Meagher continued, and when he did his words were treasured. Dr Kenney, on the other hand, "very often exhorted the community on their various duties, and in that strain of fervid elocution and lofty sentiment so fitted to kindle up the imagination of his young auditors." For them, Meagher went on, "he composed his series of meditations – one of which was produced each evening for almost the entire period of his stay in the college". To this day they "are as prized, by many in far advanced life, and as recently perused as they were listened to in their prayer hall at the college".[84]

One of the greatest tributes paid to Kenney in his life was that of Archbishop Murray before the Commissioners of Education in December 1826. Asked about the persons selected to give the spiritual retreats to students at Maynooth, he replied that they were chosen "on account of their talents, their zeal, and their knowledge of a spiritual life and of the spirit that ought to animate an ecclesiastic". And then asked whether Kenney was frequently called upon to preach because he was a Jesuit, "or as being a man of very considerable powers", Dr Murray replied:

> Solely in my opinion as being a man of very considerable powers, of very extensive information, of ardent and enlightened zeal, possessing an accurate knowledge of the springs which move and the virtues which elevate the human heart, together with a great facility of communicating his sentiments to the public in an impressive manner.[85]

It was an assessment which went far towards explaining Kenney's success at Maynooth and in later years.

While he was there, he continued to look for suitable premises for his college. During the final months of 1812, he explored the possibility of a property at Inch, near Balbriggan, Co. Dublin, belonging to Lord Gormanstown; and also considered the purchase of Rathfarnham Castle nearer the city. In January of 1813, the elderly bishop of Meath, Dr Patrick Plunkett, wrote him a warm, encouraging letter, in which he recalled his education by the late Jesuit, Fr Austin, and expressed his desire for the order's revival in Ireland. Then with regard to Kenney's quest for a suitable site, he counselled that active zeal needed to be accompanied by "patience, prudence, caution and foresight", since "few great undertakings advance fast to maturity", and he went on to add, with a wisdom which Kenney may not then have appreciated: "In the meantime, your actual highly respectable occupations do not estrange you from your vocation ... I am inclined to think that the esteem and respect entertained for you in the college, and the reputation you there and throughout the kingdom enjoy, have a closer connection than is apprehended with the designs of the divine founder of our holy religion."[86]

His time at Maynooth gave Kenney, indeed, a special standing with the hierarchy generally and with many priests from dioceses across the country, and was an effective means of presenting members of the partly restored Society in a favourable light. Such perceptions were to prove very important in the months and years ahead as he purchased and established a college. For he was embarking on this challenging enterprise at a time when the Catholic cause was weakened by internal divisions concerning the veto; when the government, with the defeat of Napoleon, was no longer dependent on thousands of Irish Catholic soldiers and sailors; and when the new chief secretary, Robert Peel, was conducting a powerful defence of the Protestant ascendancy and an assault on the cause of Catholic emancipation. In this unfavourable climate, the Jesuits in England and Ireland were loudly assailed by Sir John Cox Hippesley MP, Charles Abbot, speaker of the House of Commons, and their supporters.

Fortunately for Kenney, they also attacked the Irish bishops and Catholic Board, which encouraged the closing of ranks; while Hippesley's personal allegations against members of the Society, became eventually so vehement and strident that he lost credibility even among opponents of emancipation. But for some years the future of Kenney's enterprise looked very uncertain, and the present was tense.

RELIGIO-POLITICAL ALARMS: FACING SIR ROBERT PEEL
AND "HIPPESLIAN WARFARE"

The purchase of Castle Browne – Opposition to it

Throughout 1812, Sir John Cox Hippesley was vehemently active in promoting the veto. On 24 April he openly castigated Drs Troy and Milner for their stand,[87] and in May reached the point of declaring that Milner "ought to be hanged".[88] During 1813 and 1814, much of his energies were directed against the Jesuits.

In his final days at Maynooth, Kenney's search for a college was concluded. The chosen location was Castle Browne, near the town of Naas, Co. Kildare. It was the property of General Wogan Browne, then in the service of the king of Saxony, who had inherited it in 1812 on the death of his brother. He wished to pursue his career in Europe, and was eager to sell. On 19 July 1813, Kenney informed Fr Stone that the terms of the treaty for purchase were happily concluded. It remained to lay title and securities before counsel. He had chosen counsellor Dominick Rice, a Catholic who had studied at Liege, and "for greater security" had asked counsellor Denis Scully, who had "written the *Statement of the Penal Laws*", that "by his aid everything may be done to avoid the least expression that might implicate us in the penalties of that odious code".[89] Mr Wright, at Stone's request, wrote to La Touche bank to have £20,000 in readiness,[90] and in August, as noted earlier, all the monies remitted by Stone were at Kenney's "sole and free disposal".[91] This was a necessary arrangement since under the penal legislation no trust could be created, no endowment allowed, for a school for Catholics. Land and property could only be used for such purposes if bought by individuals, and continued to be their property. Kenney could buy Castle Browne safely only as an individual purchaser.[92]

After the purchase, Scully recommended him to safeguard "the legality of the purpose" for which the purchase had been made by expressing his willingness to admit any Protestant pupils who might seek admission.[93] That was on 19 December 1813. Well before then, however, Fr Stone was writing contentedly to St Leger and the other Irish at Palermo about the purchase of "Castle Browne in the county, I believe, of Meath [*sic*], with a considerable quantity of land". The price was also considerable, he said, "but Mr Kenney's friends and well wishers" thought "the bargain a very reasonable one". They would, therefore, have a dwelling ready for them when they returned from Sicily.[94]

The castle, and 219 acres of land immediately around it, were obtained for £16,000.[95] Once word of the purchase was confirmed, there was an extreme reaction on the part of some members of the Protestant population. The editor of the *Hibernian Magazine* proclaimed on 19 November 1813, that "the magnificent edifice", which cost £26,000 to build, had been bought "by a party of Jesuits for £16,000" and, as a result, Ireland was in "imminent danger". For, if popery continued to succeed, the country would "once more witness days worthy to rank with those of Bloody Mary".[96] Details on the purchase, provided by "a neighbouring gentleman", were sent on 9 January 1814, to the speaker of the House of Commons, Charles Abbot,[97] whose views on the Jesuits matched those of Sir John C. Hippesley.

Already, the previous summer, the latter had, as Stone wrote St Leger on 30 September 1813, inveighed against a college of Jesuits at Stonyhurst, and their sending students to Naples (then in French hands), and he was planning to raise a motion in parliament against them.[98] He had also held forth on the dangers of Jesuitism in Ireland, on a great sum of money gathered by sub-scription to endow a Jesuit college, and on the order possessing great property in Ireland at its suppression, property which should have been confiscated as was Jesuit property in Canada. Despite the verbal assault, Kenney, at this stage, felt no trepidation. He determined, however, to bring the matter for-ward by going directly to the Chief Secretary.

Meetings with Sir Robert Peel

He arranged an appointment for 23 February 1814. He did not inform Fr Stone of his intention, however, when he wrote him on 17 February 1814. It was not likely to fit into the latter's cautious, retiring approach to the charges of opponents. He did mention the encouraging remark of Lord Fingal that Hippesley would be silenced if he raised his voice against the Irish Jesuits because there were many who welcomed the dissemination of religious and moral instruction in Ireland. And where he himself was concerned, he added, he did "not fear anything", though his companions were "much alarmed"; but, then, they did not have "the advantage of combating with Sir John Stuart as Fr Glover and I have done; else they would think very little of Sir J.C. Hippesley, of whom no one cares a jot".[99] The self-confidence was to wilt in the face of Hippesley's persistence, but fortunately for Kenney it was still strong when he met with Sir Robert Peel. He prepared himself very carefully for the meeting: consulting Scully and two other "most eminent lawyers". Later, indeed, he was to say that Scully "almost dictated every word" he said to Mr Peel.[100]

The day following the meeting, the Chief Secretary wrote to Hippesley in reply to three letters of almost "indecipherable hieroglyfics" requesting infor-mation "in regard to the proposed establishment of a Jesuit college at Castle Browne in the county of Kildare". He had had an interview yesterday with Mr Kenney for a considerable time, he wrote. In answer to questions he had put to him, he stated "that he belonged to the order of Jesuits, that he had pur-chased the house and demesne of Castle Browne in the county of Kildare out of funds, £30,000, exclusively his own property, and that he intended to estab-lish a lay school for education of Protestants as well as Catholics, if it should be legal for him to receive a Protestant scholar; and that, although he did not educate his scholars in any other religious principles than that of the Catholic faith, he had no objection to their receiving such education from other quar-ters". He had asked Mr Kenney, Peel continued, "whether he had acted in this transaction on the part of others or merely as an individual on his own account". He understood him to say that he acted "merely in the latter capaci-ty". When asked if he had any objection to informing him (Peel) whence came the funds with which the purchase was made, and which he stated was exclusively his own property, Kenney had "declined answering that question".[101]

From such excerpts of Kenney's own account as have survived, in secondary sources, this last part of the meeting seems to have been the most detailed and searching. Peel, apparently, asked: "Are you not aware that we can confiscate that property?" And Kenney is said to have replied that "to a mercantile nation like England a character for honesty and good faith" were as necessary as they were to an individual trader. Hence, while he granted that the government had the power to confiscate, he did not believe they would "effect such a violation of the rights of property"; for to do so would be to violate the maxim of the greatly esteemed Lord Chatham. And he recalled how on it being suggested to Chatham, at a time of war with France, to lay hold of the monies of natives of France which were lying in English funds, he had replied: "No, No. If the devil had money in English funds, it should be safe for him."[102] To a further question, whether his vow of poverty precluded him being the proprietor of such funds, Kenney is said to have replied, "No, since his vow was a simple, not a solemn one."[103]

In his further information to Hippesley, Sir Robert Peel stated that Kenney studied in Sicily, not in Naples as Hippesley had asserted. Kenney had further told him that he (Kenney) understood there were "some severe strictures in an intended publication of Mr [Francis] Plowden, and that he feared these strictures would be attributed to him – but he disclaimed solemnly all participation". He also said "that it was reported that the object of his proposed establishment was the revival of the order of Jesuits in this country"; and Peel understood him to state that this was impossible, even if it were desired, for there had to be the express authority of the pope for such a revival. He complained that there had been misrepresentation, too, concerning the object of his institution, and he said he would publish a prospectus, as was usually done in other similar cases, which would explain the general plan.[104]

Peel in a subsequent meeting with Abbot, according to the latter's memoirs published more than 40 years later, stated that to all questions, Kenney "generally answered by putting some other questions instead of giving an affirmative or negative"; and that "he admitted that he was in early expectation of two from Sicily, Wolfe [*sic*] and Esmonde, whose father and brother respectively had been hanged in Ireland as traitors, and that he proposed to employ those two men as professors in his college." It would seem that Abbot's memory had suffered the ravages of time. Kenney had answered most of the questions very directly, to judge from Peel's account to Hippesley; and five, not two Jesuits, were expected from Sicily, and there was no Wolfe. Aylmer was probably meant. His father had not been hanged, but his brother took part in the 1798 rebellion; whereas Esmonde's father, Dr John Esmonde, had been executed in Dublin, the day after the commencement of insurrection at Clane and Prosperous, Co. Kildare.[105]

Kenney had sent an account of the interview to Plowden.[106] That bluff friend commented on 15 March: "I do not mean to arraign your avowal to Mr Peel that you are a member of the Society of Jesus. I must suppose that you had good reasons for this open acknowledgement; but I own I do not see them. In general, I would suppose everyman to be a foe, whom I did not certainly know to be a friend, and I would tell them nothing, unless I knew that they could other wise prove it. I cannot doubt of Mr Peel's being your enemy ... In every other part of your interview with him, I think your conduct was manly, dignified, and honourable." He then went on to put his finger on the point of future concern – "I conceive your enemies may yet wish and try to teaze you into some avowal of the source from which you derived your property ... No doubt you will be very stiff upon this head."[107]

The months of March and April 1814, were periods of intense activity and pressure for Kenney. Hippesley's attacks continued and received much publicity. On 10 March Kenney wrote to Sir Robert Peel enclosing a copy of the prospectus, which he had promised, and requesting a further interview. From a rough draft of the letter and other notes of his, it is possible to reconstruct the ground covered in the letter and in the subsequent interview during the third week of March.[108]

He was mainly concerned with defending the Society from Hippesley's attacks, especially what he termed the "famous speech" made in 1813 during which it was alleged that there was "constant emigrations to Naples" and a resultant "progress of Jesuitism" in Britain and Ireland emanating from there. He expressed "the humble hope that his Majesty's government would place more reliance" on his statement "than on the angry and incorrect representations by Sir J.C. Hippesley". He then went on to treat of the latter's claims of "constant emigrations to Naples" and the "progress of Jesuitism" in Britain and Ireland.

The Society had remained suppressed in every country since 1773, Kenney stated, except for Russia, and from 1804, Naples and its Sicilian dominions. In 1805 an English priest at Stonyhurst was ordered to a warmer climate because of advanced consumption. Joined by a young ecclesiastic as companion, he set out for Naples, then free of French control. They landed first at Palermo and there learned that Naples had fallen to the French. They stayed in Sicily. The priest died. His companion finished his studies, received ordination, and sent home favourable accounts. Since then, nine Irishmen were received amongst the Jesuits in Sicily. Three or four had returned home. Five remained there. Thus the "Progress of Jesuitism" emanating from Sicily, Kenney continued, amounted to this that there were to be found "five Jesuits between England, Ireland and Scotland", and when the five presently in Sicily returned there would be "eight or nine Irish Jesuits amongst five million of his Majesty's subjects in Ireland, and one English Jesuit", that is to say, he went on (not counting his other English colleagues as truly members of the order), there would be "six British Jesuits through all his Majesty's dominions in Europe, Asia, or America".

As to Sir John's further allegation of "a great sum gathered by subscription for endowing a Jesuit college", Kenney had never received a subscription, nor ever heard of it before Sir John announced it. He was equally ignorant of any endowment. There could not be such. When he had previously met with Sir Robert, he continued, Sir John Hippesley's assertion that the Irish Jesuits possessed great property at the suppression of the order had been raised, and he had said that he did not know that they possessed any such. He was now able to assure the Chief Secretary, however, that at the suppression "there were only 17 Jesuits in Ireland and that amongst them they had not as much property as would support them in their humble manner of life". In every other country where their property was seized, "the brief of suppression enforced the dictate of justice that each should be allowed a sufficient pension for life". The Irish Jesuits, as "they were unknown to the laws", were left "unmolested by the government", and without special provision. They lived doing good. They were all now dead; but their memory was cherished.

He then ventured to speak of his English colleagues. They had been violently persecuted for a century and a half, he said. "Their only safe home" had been away from home, in a foreign land. Yet their affections were never alienated from England. For the past twenty years they had lived there as missionary priests or directors of the college of Stonyhurst. They were about forty in number. They ceased to be Jesuits some forty years ago, but had imbibed the order's principles and maxims, and were "ever loyal, peaceable, useful men". Finally, he sought Mr Peel's advice as to whether Catholic schoolmasters could legally accept Protestant scholars, as he found "a great difference of opinion amongst learned lawyers on the question".

With regard to his interviews with Peel, he divulged to Plowden the uncertainty he experienced behind the bold front. Responding to his friend's letter of 15 March disagreeing with his "open acknowledgement" of being a Jesuit, he replied on 20 March that he had understood from an earlier letter of Plowden that he agreed with his approach. In any event, he said, he had many times received "legal and friendly advice on this point and was told" that he "might publish it to all the world", if he pleased. "I wished, moreover," he continued, "to be candid where nothing was risked by being so, and I well knew that the fact being notorious it would cause more suspicion to have refused to answer a question that must have been the first in the conversation."

Had Plowden's letter, however, arrived a day or two earlier, he added, it would have helped him in his second conversation with Mr Peel. For "others thought more favourably" of that meeting than he himself did. He was now of the view that Plowden was right in his estimation of the Chief Secretary. And he requested him, and the fathers at Stonyhurst, to put their heads and hearts together and tell him, as precisely as they could, what he was "to do, what to say, what to refuse". His state deserved commiseration: "I have not a creature to give me advice – my companions, timid, inexperienced, say not a word when asked but 'do what you think best'. A lawyer, now out of town, and Dr Murray, are the only consultors I have." And on many occasions, he did not feel he should have recourse to them. Finally, he assured Plowden of his firmness with regard to the latter's observations on the property and disclosure of its source: "I am prepared to suffer anything if the property, or any part of it, can be saved, at which I am sure a powerful grasp will be made this session."[109]

A time of tension and uncertainty

All this time, he was endeavouring to get the new college ready, assisted by five Jesuit brother postulants; and was travelling between there and Dublin, where he was still doing church and chaplaincy work from George's Hill. And he had prepared and was sending off the prospectus to various people, was conducting correspondence, and was becoming increasingly concerned about a motion Hippesley was bringing forward in parliament calling for confiscation of Jesuit property such as had been effected in Canada after the suppression.

It was a lonely, as well as exhausting and tense time for him. He was drawing on reserves of nervous energy; and felt very much on his own. Even with friends he had to be careful what he said, especially about the source of the property – lest it get out that it was left expressly for Catholic purposes and hence was subject to confiscation. He tried to get "some of the leading people" in Dublin to interest themselves in his case, but he found "everyone timerous". He applied to three bishops, whom he conceived to be well inclined; but they contented themselves with good wishes. He had strong suspicions of being under scrutiny; so much so, indeed, that he was afraid to write to the General lest his letter go astray. And for security reasons, too, he did not refer to problems when writing to the Irish in Sicily.[110]

The tense atmosphere had been increased by the attack on Hippesley by Francis Plowden, about which Kenney had given advance notice to Peel. It had taken the form of an open letter, and had received much publicity. Joseph Tristram informed Kenney from London: "Hippesley is quite sick with the perusal of Mr Plowden's letter", and not surprisingly as it was "a strong emetic".[111]

In this siege climate, Kenney was greatly consoled by a letter from Fr Plowden. The latter had approved of his recent letter to Peel and his account of the meeting. Kenney wrote back on 29 March to express his thanks, and in the process revealed how deeply the on-going pressures were affecting him. "Since this weighty business began to press heavily on my shoulders," he wrote, "and particularly since the Hippeslian warfare commenced, my days pass in anxious thoughts, and my nightly repose, often disturbed by gloomy apprehensions, suffers much from the impression made on my brain and nerves during the day. I have been uneasy," he continued, "at the possible disposition of Divine Providence to permit us to be once more plundered; ... but I now indulge the view that God has other views in our regard." Despite that optimistic note, he concluded with the words: "People here dread some prohibitory measure. We are certainly in a storm."[112]

A similar mood, and sense of urgency, was reflected the following day in a letter to Lord Donoughmore seeking his lordship's protection for his college "in the name of the sacred right of individual private property most honourably acquired and legally gained".[113] That same day, however, Plowden was sending him indications of an apparent change of attitude on the part of Hippesley towards the English Jesuits. He had mentioned to Lord Clifford that he intended to drop his motion against Stonyhurst. But Plowden went on to warn that Kenney might still have trouble "if the ministers were malicious and sought to prove that your property was formerly property of the Society of Jesus". He then provided a valuable presentation of the reasons, used later by Kenney and Stone, why the property could not be said to have legally belonged to a corporate entity, but was such that Kenney could genuinely swear that it was his.

"The Jesuits who were in Ireland," Plowden wrote, "did not form a body capable of having property. They were neither a province, nor a vice-province, they had no superior vested with constitutional powers according to the institute of the Society. They were merely individuals detached from different provinces, to which each one always belonged – Fr Betagh to the Champagne province, Fr Callaghan to that of Andalusia ..." Whatever possessions each had "was either the fruit of personal industry, or it was eleemosynary, intended for their individual support. It belonged then not to the Society at large, nor to any portion or division of the Society capable of having property." In Canada, to which Sir John alluded, "the case was very different. The colleges of Quebec ... with their respective property were a part of the province of France, as much as the colleges of Rouen and Amiens, all subject to the provincial at Paris", and so subject to confiscation at the dissolution of the order. In Ireland the small amount of the property could be left to the missioners without raising jealousy or alarming the government. After the suppression, they were individual secular priests, and any accessions received were from their private industry or from the benefactions of friends and family, and no one could lawfully hinder any or all of them disposing of these as they liked. Hence, Plowden declared, at the close of his tightly argued attempt to evade the application of unjust penal legislation, "no man can prove that your present property ever belonged to the Society of Jesus. Before you got it, it was as much private property as it is at present." The persecution might die away, he added, so the less said the better. But if ever necessitated to answer questions, as Mr Peel seemed to threaten, then Kenney should make his stand "on the point of it having always been private property".[114]

Elsewhere in that letter, and in others from Plowden and Stone around that time, Kenney had received private word of a rescript from the pope re-establishing the Society. All three felt obliged to conceal the news and their joy, however, lest it add to the storm stirred up by Abbot, Hippesley, and their supporters. On 21 April, however, Kenney was writing to Stone that the Irish bishops knew of the forthcoming rescript through Dr Milner, who was unable to keep a secret.[115] And four days later he proposed to Plowden that the General of the Society should write personally to Archbishop Troy, thanking him for his goodness to the Jesuits, and sending an authenticated copy of the rescript. And he added, revealingly, that it was important that the archbishop get the formal news from Russia rather than England, because despite his "fund of episcopal virtue and Christian charity" there was no one who could have "a more declared and obstinate hatred to everything to which the word English is added." His feelings, in this regard, were wounded by his "intimate knowledge of the sufferings of the poor in the immense tract of which he has spiritual charge".[116]

April had been a most significant month. On 5 April, Kenney, with the five brother postulants, took formal possession of the house and estate which he had termed Clongowes Wood, and dedicated the future college to the young Jesuit saint, Aloysius Gonzaga.[117] And on the international stage, Napoleon had abdicated on the 11th of the month; and there was news of the pope's release and of the papal rescript. But occasions of jubilation were soon overshadowed by a succession of discomforting events.

On 28 April, Lord Donoughmore, replying to Kenney, assured him of his assistance but warned that Hippesley was "very persevering in anything of a public nature to which he lends his hands";[118] and a week later came the publication in Dublin of a letter favourable to the veto from Monsignor Quarantotti, vice-prefect of Propaganda. It was dated 16 February 1814. On 13 May, Ignatius Rice, founder of the Irish Christian Brothers, commented from Waterford that there was great confusion about the Roman document and that if the pope had concurred in what had been done the Irish respect for the papacy would suffer. He prayed that this "wicked veto" would not provoke schism.[119]

In this disturbing setting, the moving of a motion in the House of Commons on 17 May by Hippesley occasioned little immediate interest outside the circle of those directly involved, such as the Jesuits and their supporters and opponents in the House.

The Hippesley motion and its effects

The motion, which was carried, requested that extracts from "Sir George Prevost's instructions as governor and commander-in-chief in Lower Canada, dated 22 October 1811", be printed.[120] In moving the motion, however, Hippesley ranged far and wide.

Although his proposal was directed at the Jesuits, and particularly those in Ireland, he devoted much of his time to an attack on the Irish Catholic Board; to drawing attention to "the novel spectacle of synods, composed of Catholic bishops and Catholic priests", established contrary to law in Ireland; and to criticism of Spanish Catholicism. On the Society of Jesus, he largely repeated what he had previously stated – a mixture of fact and fiction. "Nearly £30,000 had been remitted from Rome to Ireland" to purchase the lands of Castle Browne. Of that, £16,000 had been spent on the purchase; and on the site "a building had been erected as a seminary, which was under the superintendence of a professed Jesuit." He talked of the confiscation of the order's property in Canada, and of the Jesuits being "much more devoted to their own general than to the pope"; and he cautioned "the British government to be on its guard", for though he had the highest respect for "the moral character and general good disposition of the present pope", the Jesuits had always been "a powerful means of influence, a formidable band of intriguers" and "he therefore would wish to protect his country against the *fiat* of any pope for the resurrection and reorganization of such an order".[121]

Mr Peel's response to Hippesley covered ground already noted. He mentioned, however, that he had received a prospectus of the college from Kenney, and reiterated that the latter had not revealed the source from which he had derived his funds. He informed the House that he had told Kenney "that he was not to infer from the communication which had passed that the Irish administration acquiesced in the existence of the institution, but that they should continue to watch it with jealousy".[122]

Sir Henry Parnell, one of the ablest and most respected debaters in the parliament, took Hippesley to task. He had spoken to Kenney, he said, and seen the prospectus. What was envisaged was merely a lay school from which not even Protestants would be excluded. The talk of danger from the Jesuits, he added, was quite absurd considering "how very few of that sect were now in existence, and how much opinions upon religious topics had changed of late years". The proceedings followed "by that gentleman, whose motives had been distorted", were "justifiable and legal".[123] With reference to Peel's statement regarding Kenney "refusing to state whence he derived the fund", he wished to observe that Peel was not "entitled to catechise him on his private affairs. As a British subject, he had a right to set up the institution ... provided he did nothing which appeared dangerous to the state." "He had willingly answered all that concerned the public interest, but when the right hon. gentleman went so far as to inquire into the means by which he made the purchase, which was penetrating directly into his private affairs, he felt it was not proper for him to give an answer."[124]

Peel responded that he had not asked any question of Kenney "in a tone that evinced a desire to catechise him"; and then went on to state that "at the interview he had with Mr Kenney, he particularly told him that he must not be surprised if the same feeling which had induced the British government to confiscate the property of the Jesuits in Canada, should induce them at least to watch with the utmost vigilance and suspicion an institution established and superintended by one of the order, supported by funds, the origin and nature of which were totally unaccounted for."[125]

The warning note was clear. And Hippesley continued his attack in public pronouncements. It led Plowden to comment lugubriously on 26 May that many in England considered this to mark "the beginning of a serious persecution, and they expect new penal laws. In Hippesley, Titus Oates seems to be revived!" And he added that the current persecution against the Society was "at present *publicly*, and always had been *secretly*, forwarded and fomented in England, especially in London, by Catholics, laymen, priests, and prelates. The cry against us from these hallowed mouths is just now particularly loud." Bishop Milner, he said, had been "often upbraided by his mitred colleagues for protecting and showing friendship to Jesuits". He advised Kenney, once again, to stand firm on the issue of private property; to defy Peel to prove he had any vows; and to remember, besides, that his simple vows left him "capable of inheriting and possessing".[126]

The grounds for anxiety, and the sense of pressure and attack where Kenney was concerned, were further heightened from an unexpected quarter. Fr Stone, in a sudden panic, decided to break his long silence, and made a response to Hippesley's speech of 1813, which he then sent as a supplementary paper to Lord Clifford for enunciation in parliament. In a letter to Kenney he mentioned that in his response he had revealed the source of the Irish Jesuit money! How £7,000 had been left at the dissolution, which had later grown and been bequeathed from one to the other. And he also asked Kenney to say he had not received any money from England.

The latter, not surprisingly, was deeply angry at this intervention into Irish matters, without prior consultation, and at the fact that it went counter to all his legal advice and to that of Plowden, and also left him in an impossible position *vis-à-vis* Peel, and the Irish members of parliament, who might now feel, understandably, that they had been deceived. It also exposed him, he declared, to "a suit in chancery"; for the commission established by the Irish parliament "to hunt all legacies or donations made by Catholics for Catholic purposes" was quite active, and had recently instituted a suit for a lesser sum against Dr Power of Waterford. Besides, there was no way he could deny that he had received money from England. Clearly, there was divided opinion at Stonyhurst, he declared, and the interests of the Irish mission were being sacrificed. All this he wrote to Stone on 2 June,[127] and then wrote to Plowden[128] and to Scully.[129]

As a result of his strong response, Lord Clifford withdrew the paper.

Plowden pressed Stone to write to Kenney "to quiet his alarm" by assuring him that there was no essential difference of opinion between him and Stonyhurst. And he reminded him yet again of "the suspicions of Fr Betagh", and that there might well be "persons disposed to revive such false suggestions".[130]

In the meantime, the relevant articles on the confiscation of Jesuit property in Canada had been published. Kenney, who had been quite apprehensive about the publication because of the manner in which Hippesley and Peel had referred to the Canadian example, was at first relieved and then indignant when he read the relevant articles. In considerable annoyance, he informed Scully on 19 June that Peel had read to him at his interview only a part of the Canadian document, the part that seemed to threaten him. He had omitted "the latter part which inhibits not only Jesuit missionaries but every other Romish ecclesiastic to speak against the Protestant religion in their seminaries, and orders all missionaries amongst the Indians to be withdrawn and Protestant missioners established in their stead! Such an instance of ministerial bigotry," Kennedy added, "would appear incredible if we were not indebted to themselves for the information."[131]

The articles in question, as noted, concerned an order made in 1811, but this was itself the renewal of an order given by the governor of Quebec in 1763, following the expulsion of the Society in French possessions that year. Its printing now, in 1814, proved counter-productive for Sir John Hippesley and his supporters. Public opinion had moved a considerable distance since the 1760s. Thus, on 2 July, Plowden reported to Kenney that he was told "that the London papers try to apologise for the Canadian orders, which Hippesley and Peel have brought forth to light, because they are generally blamed by all who have read them as ungenerous, illiberal, and bigoted". It now seemed to be agreed that there would be "no parliamentary motion this year, either for or against Catholics or any portion of them". If such were brought before parliament, he added, "Lord Donoughmore will be our advocate in the Upper House, and in the Lower House, apart from the Irish members, there will be Mr Whitbread and Mr Canning." Having quoted a respected English legal opinion that Kenney's property was safe, Plowden concluded that the prospect looked good for Kenney. He was "covered for Peel and Hippesley" and could do what he willed "quietly within doors, under the favour of a good and friendly prelacy"; whereas the Jesuits in England, even if the Society were fully restored that year, lived under a hostile government, and had, moreover, "no worse foes" than three of their four bishops, and many of the clergy.[132]

The reaction to the Canadian articles marked, in many ways, the beginning of the end of that pivotal and anxious period, which Kenney termed the time of "Hippeslian warfare", and during which the advent of Irish Jesuits gave rise to all kinds of alarmist language and extravagant criticism. Peel, in the circumstances, found that he had sufficient on his hands trying to police "disturbed areas", and to cope with real problems without giving credence to informers reporting that " the Jesuit at Castle Browne is likely to do more mischief than a rebel army on the Curragh",[133] or to the outburst of a vehemently anti-Catholic member of the Aylmer family calling for the destruction of "the Jesuit college near me at Castle Browne ... a nest of villany ... a sect interfering in political as well as religious temporalities, and that by assassination and every horrid means".[134] Such fulminations seemed grotesque and hallucinatory in the context of his personal experience of the able, eloquent, urbane and gentlemanly Mr Kenney.[135] And strongly as he supported the Protestant ascendancy and opposed Catholic emancipation, it was scarcely politic to be associated any longer with one so partisan and hyperbolic as Hippesley, to whom, as Sir John Newport remarked, nothing was "too absurd to appear to him incredible when it relates to Jesuits, who like phantoms haunt him by day and night".[136]

English Catholic foreboding – Irish assurance

To Kenney, however, it was not yet clear that his position was fully secure. Plowden kept him primed with gloomy forebodings. There was agreement, he suggested, between the ministry and three of the English bishops and their supporters "to exterminate Jesuitism", and "Hippesley, and some of their agents" filled the daily papers "with extravagant rants against Jesuits" in order to prepare the public for a bill confiscating Jesuit property.[137] Concerned, Kenney forwarded the stark interpretation of events to Denys Scully as the remarks of "a very intelligent gentleman on the other side of the water".

Scully's response laid Kenney's immediate fears to rest. It was a striking manifestation of the assurance felt among politically conscious and professionally and materially successful Irish Catholics as compared to their counterparts in Britain. "With regard to the communication from your correspondent in England," he wrote:

> I believe it to be pretty correct, save what relates to the Jesuits. Any attempt of the kind would be so absurd, and so outrageous, that no political man of any weight would venture upon it. Indeed, those gentry have already sufficient on their hands, in the financial embarrassments, the humiliating peace with America, the broils of Congress [of Vienna], the contest about Belgium, the Corn Bill etc. without burning their fingers in your concerns.

"Some idle menaces," he went on, "have been thrown out by that wretched and ridiculous coxcomb, Hippesley, because he just knew that the English Catholics are as timid as hares, and have neither the energy to oppose, nor the spirit to punish an insolent man of his stamp. But, I have not the most distant apprehension of any hazard impending over your house." "And permit me to observe from experience," he added, "that I have never known an Englishman (however intelligent your corespondent may be) able to form a sound judgement upon any branch of Irish affairs, or to utter just opinions for one half hour consecutively upon the present or probable events of this country. This I say, not out of prejudice, but from a course of observation, frequent and various, during eighteen years."

Such sentiments served not just to quieten Kenney's unease, but also to fortify his self-confidence in relations with friend and foe from "the other side of the water". And Scully rounded off his instruction with some practical political advice. For the further security of the property, if there was any danger, "laymen would probably be less suspected in the capacity of trustees", he suggested, "than clergy or members of the order exclusively". And it might "be wise to court more publicity, and appear less fearful – occasional vindications, popular anecdotes, and other articles relating to the order historically and otherwise, might appear in the popular prints." For, he declared, there were "few better fences for such an establishment than public opinion – which even in these degenerate times" was "pretty just, with the aid of a little honest industry and a reasonable contribution of correct information".[138] Like most effective advice it enunciated what the recipient already sensed and wished to hear.

Although the Hippeslian concerns were in the forefront of his mind during 1814, that year also brought the two events for which Kenney had longed and prayed: the opening of an Irish Jesuit college; and the full papal restoration of the Society of Jesus.

OPENING OF THE COLLEGE, CLONGOWES WOOD, AND THE RESTORATION OF THE SOCIETY OF JESUS

One of the first pleasant tasks following agreement to purchase the Castle Browne estate was to decide on a name for the college. Both Kenney and the former owner wished to avoid the former name. Kenney reverted to an old title for the area, "Clongowes". At first there was a suggestion that the word "castle" be added. Denys Scully, when asked, would not hear of it. The term had become "vulgar in Ireland", he said, "by the indiscriminate assumption of it".[139] The name "Clongowes Wood" was chosen; and the early prospectus was headed: "College, Clongowes-Wood, The Rev Peter Kenney, Principal".[140]

This first "prospectus", which had been sent to Peel and various others, was not really a prospectus, as Kenney openly acknowledged, but a plain, single page printed statement "solely intended to satisfy the inquiries of those parents" who wished to know the terms of the college. It merely stated that pupils were admitted between the ages of seven and fourteen, that those under twelve were to pay fifty pounds a year, those over twelve, fifty guineas. And after some advice on necessary clothing and some extra charges, parents were reminded that the young student should not be removed from the school even during time of vacation. With regard to subjects and a programme of studies, the usual concerns of a prospectus, the printed sheet merely said: "It does not seem necessary to detail here the plan of education adopted by Mr Kenney. The system is sufficiently known, and highly esteemed." He evidently had so many calls on his time and energy, that there was no opportunity at this stage to draw up anything more elaborate. Apart from the worry and sleeplessness induced by the "Hippeslian warfare" and its heavy demands on time in correspondence, travel and meetings; there were on-going requests for retreats and missions from prelates, whom it was important to please; and there were regular requests for information about the college from all over the country, from bishops, clergy, and well-off laity.[141] The level of interest, indeed, indicated a high demand for places and this placed additional pressure on the work of adapting, restructuring, cleaning and furnishing the college.

By the middle of July there were some forty boys in the school, which appears to have been run by Kenney, assisted by Frs Dinan and Gahan, and six Irish Jesuit scholastics sent from Stonyhurst,[142] and the five religious brothers. The five Jesuits from Sicily were not to arrive 'till the following year. By September, 1814, it was clear that pupils were coming from different parts of the country: from Dublin, Cork, Limerick, Galway, Clare, Tipperary, and the midlands; and the parents tended to be drawn from the ranks of merchants, professional people, and farmers.[143] And however make-shift the accommodation in the early months, there was no faltering in demand for places. It was, indeed, to reach remarkable proportions within a short space of time.

Meantime, the five young priests from Sicily – Charles Aylmer, James Butler, Bart. Esmonde, Paul Ferley, and Robert St Leger, all doctors of theology – had arrived in Rome and were present at the historic restoration of the order by Pope Pius VII on 7 August 1814. Also in attendance at the ceremonies of restoration were the coadjutor archbishop of Dublin, Dr Murray, as well as Dr Milner, the Irish bishops' agent in Rome and England.

Decree of restoration of the society – Its application in Ireland

The five arrived in Rome for the feast of St Ignatius, "which was celebrated", Aylmer wrote to Fr Plowden, "with great pomp and solemnity". It was expected that the bull for the universal re-establishment of the Society would be published on that day, but the publication was deferred to the octave of the feast. On that day, Aylmer explained, "at about 8 o'clock in the morning his Holiness came in state to the church of the Gesu, where he celebrated mass at the altar of St Ignatius, attended by almost all his cardinals, prelates, and about 70 or 80 of the Society". Afterwards, they went to the nearby chapel of the Sodality of the Nobles, where the bull *Sollicitudo Omnium Ecclesiarum*, "which re-established the Society all over the world, was read": the old pope affirming that in his pastoral obligation to the church he would be guilty of a capital crime if he neglected to employ the skilled rowers for the storm-tossed bark of Peter which the Society could provide.[144] There was no reference to Jesuit privileges, but the houses and churches of the Gesu and the novitiate were given into their possession. "Drs Murray and Milner were present," Aylmer continued, "also the Queen of Etruria, the King of Torino, and many other persons of first rank. All the Society present then went up in order and kissed the pope's feet. He spoke to several of them ... and ... continually smiled at the number of old men who came hobbling up to the throne, almost all with tears of joy in their eyes."

For the young Jesuits, too, it was a highly emotive occasion. Aylmer was moved to hyperbole. "Yesterday," he exclaimed, "was truly a day of jubilee and triumph for the Society ... I could not refrain from tears. Little did I expect, or hope to be present at so consoling a ceremony in the capital of the world, and attended by such circumstances. Never was an order established in this manner; never such marked attention paid by any pope; never so great a triumph."[145] Plowden later informed Kenney that Bishop Milner had said mass in St Ignatius's bedroom, and Dr Murray in his private oratory, and that the Roman College, with the church of St Ignatius, was soon to be restored to the order.[146] Aylmer further commented on how well all five of them were received by Drs Milner and Murray, who showed great interest in them.[147]

In Ireland, meantime, Kenney rejoiced in this crown to his hopes and wrote to many of the bishops, who joined in his sense of joy and thanksgiving. Archbishop Troy, in a lighter vein, remarked to Dr Murray with reference to Dr Lanigan, the celebrated author of the *Ecclesiastical History of Ireland*, who had recently been released from the insane asylum at Finglas, that if recovered "the news of the restoration of the Society will probably cause a relapse into his former state! I wish his jansenistic principles were confined to himself."[148] Dr Power of Waterford, in his response to Kenney's letter, congratulated him on the restoration, and then struck a note of realism and caution. The Jesuits, he wrote, "have had, and still have, many enemies. The Society was too distinguished not to have some. It may be true that there were among them some carried away by a wrong spirit; I believe there were, but who of us will throw the first stone."[149] It was a reminder of a need of which Plowden and Kenney were very conscious. When he first heard of the likelihood of the revival of the order, in April 1814, following the pope's release from captivity, Plowden commented to Kenney that some of the old fathers were expecting that the restoration would be marked by much praise and flattery. He personally hoped this would not be so, and added that "if past humiliations do not at length produce humility among us, the Church will have no need of our services."[150]

The General's letters to the Irish Jesuits in the aftermath of the restoration were, in fact, far from triumphalist. "We must strive with all our might," he wrote, "not to be found unworthy ... of the splendid hope invested in us." He urged them to keep in mind the dedication, suffering and patience of their predecessors in their own country, and to strive to excel in all virtues, especially those which constituted them as religious and to which they were bound by vow, namely, chastity, poverty, and obedience. And though their religious dress in Ireland did not differ from secular dress, "their external behaviour, modesty, conversation and entire conduct" should identify who they were.

Turning to the role of the superior, he emphasised that "whoever he may be, whether talented or not," the superior "holds the place of Christ ... He has authority from God, he commands in his name." The superior, for his part, was to bear in mind whose place he occupied "so that he use his authority correctly and reasonably". It was "his duty to oversee religious observance". Transgressions, no matter by whom, were not to be passed over in silence. And he was to remember that he himself would have to give an account of his stewardship and would be found guilty if he allowed his authority to be spurned by his subjects. It was a reminder that made the position of superior so very difficult for Kenney.

The letter arrived in Clongowes on 11 January 1815, on the eve of three days prayer prior to the renewal of vows. Kenney read it "to all the Fathers assembled" the following night.[151] He was to endeavour earnestly to follow out the ideals and guidelines presented by the General, and to earn the serious displeasure of a number of his subjects for his efforts

"All depended on the beginning," he had written soon after his return from Sicily. He had particularly in mind at that stage establishing their distinctiveness as Irish Jesuit religious, while yet preserving and developing the tradition of close relations with the hierarchy set by the members of the old Society. Now, three frenetic years later, the separateness of the Irish mission was evident, a college had been founded, and a wide range of friendly and pastoral contacts with bishops and clergy had been established. It remained to consciously respond to pastoral opportunities, so that he might be able to present to the young men coming from Sicily not just a college apostolate, but a range of possibilities for more directly priestly work. To this end, during 1813, and the very busy and historic subsequent year, he took on additional work for the bishops, and also prepared the way for the establishment of a church in Dublin. And never far from his mind, as well, was a location for a noviceship, so that the Irish Jesuit mission might be more fully self-contained. For this, too, episcopal support was important.

Episcopal power and Jesuit ministry

The first steps towards establishing opportunities for the members of the restored Society to act publicly as priests were taken almost as soon as he arrived at Clongowes. He sought faculties to preach and hear confessions in the diocese of Kildare and Leighlin in which the college was situated. Bishop

Delany was supportive and generous with permissions.[152] In September 1814, Kenney approached successfully the prelate of the adjoining diocese, his good friend, Dr Plunkett of Meath, for the wider "faculties usually granted to missioners" to hear confessions in that diocese.[153]

Although he could ill afford to be absent from a school struggling to be born, he considered it important to respond towards the end of June 1814, to the request of the primate, Dr O'Reilly of Armagh, to give a mission at Drogheda. It proved so successful, that the archbishop proposed to him the establishment of a national Jesuit mission team, a concept not to find concrete expression for another thirty years. Kenney was sufficiently interested to relay the invitation to Plowden, who responded enthusiastically, reminding him that mission teams had been a regular feature of the continental provinces of the old Society.[154] Being at the service of the Irish hierarchy, however, was not without moments of intense frustration. Kenney sought to preserve a basic independence and a freedom from subservience, but at times he found himself faced with a peremptory summons which gave little or no option. Thus, after declining in November the invitation of his Grace of Dublin to preach a charity sermon in the bishop's parish on the grounds of having a bad cold, he was told to forego inconveniences, get rid of his cold, and preach the sermon.[155] Not without reason did Cardinal Litta write to Dr Troy the following January, conveying complaints to Propaganda from generals of other religious orders that some Irish bishops acted severely, even unjustly, towards the regular clergy.[156]

The spirit of Catholic assertiveness at that period, joined to his own exceptional energy, ability, and expansive vision, had prompted Kenney to embark on ambitious enterprises and to achieve a great deal in a short time. He was enabled to do so by the fund of money passed on by Fr Callaghan, by the good relations with the bishops, and the virtually free rein he enjoyed in the years immediately before and after the restoration of the order, when the General was far away in Russian territories and the turmoil of war made communication particularly difficult and unreliable. The superiors in Britain and Ireland, as a result, were largely autonomous. The deficiencies in communication also meant, however, that when the General did make a decision directly affecting such areas, there could be much confusion and upset. News of such a decision threw Kenney's plans for the mission into disarray. He only learned of it well after it was first issued, and then, almost in passing, from one of those on their way home from Italy.

Problems of communication and authority in the restored Society

A letter from Charles Aylmer, written in July or early August,[157] mentioned that the General had instructed Fr Zuñiga, the Sicilian provincial, to send Fr St Leger, one of the most able of the group, to the North American mission;

and he understood that St Leger was already on his way. The provincial, feeling it seems that he had not authority to dispose of the young Irishmen, had written for clarification. This presumably led the General to remember to write to Kenney on 3 September.[158] He also wrote to Fr Stone. He was looking for two men for America.

Greatly concerned, Kenney wrote first to the Sicilian provincial, and then, on 13 October, to the Vicar-General at Rome. Fr Brzozowski had not yet been able to come from Russia. Kenney, on behalf of the Irish mission, conveyed congratulations on the restoration of the Society, and then went on to relate how greatly the mission would be weakened by the removal of Fr St Leger. He had sent detailed explanations to Fr Aylmer, who would personally discuss the matter fully with him.

His eloquent explanatory letter to Aylmer provided an informative glimpse of the state of the Irish Jesuit mission at this point and of his plans for it, and also of the condition and some of the needs of the Irish church.

He requested Aylmer to use all his endeavours to prevent St Leger's departure for America. He was not expected there. Fr Grassi, superior of the North American mission, who had been writing to him, Kenney, for the past two years looking for men, had acknowledged within the past month that now that a college was being opened in Ireland, he had no prospect of obtaining anyone from there. Kenney then went on to points of more general relevance. He had, he stated, but eight priests to serve a large boarding school and a national mission; and funds were now so diminished by the purchase of the college, that he could not receive any more postulants until those who had been admitted had completed their education. At present, in fact, he did not know where to find money "to pay the pensions of 8 novices, 4 juniors, and three scholars presently at Stonyhurst", and yet he had to make such payments before he could fulfil his hopes of forming an Irish noviceship, and chairs for higher studies in Ireland. And the overall needs of the Irish mission had to be kept in mind. There were scarcely sufficient secular clergy to provide the basic sacraments of baptism, marriage, and extreme unction. The bishops, for their part, were calling out "for retreats, annual missions in one or other diocese, extraordinary confessors, the direction of diocesan seminaries", and there was not in Ireland any body of religious men for this purpose. Hence, it would seem very strange, at the very opening of the Irish Jesuit mission, if, after so much expectation and expenditure, "any one useful man should be withdrawn" and sent to another mission which "had long subsisted and was well founded, having already a noviceship, and two colleges".[159]

The General responded on 3 November 1814, permitting St Leger to "return to his native land". But he instructed Kenney, in the light of the great needs of the Society in North America, to confer with Fr Stone with a view to sending at least one Irishman and one Englishman, who could teach rhetoric and philosophy.[160] A decision regarding Fr Brzozowski's request was deferred, as sailing from British ports were cancelled because of war in the Chesapeake in North America.[161]

The General's change of mind with regard to St Leger ensured that Kenney would soon have his expected complement of men for the Irish mission. In the midst of all his plans and activities, and used to running a one-man operation, with the approval of his two rather limited companions, he neglected, unfortunately, keeping adequately informed the five able and potentially censorious young priests due from Sicily. The memory of his past experiences with them may have inhibited him, but, in any event, his deficiency in writing to them, in telling of his endeavours, his need of them, and the roles he envisaged them playing, sowed the seeds of serious future dissension.[162]

Meantime, however, Kenney had fulfilled his vision of a pastoral, ecclesial presence in Dublin by acquiring a *chapel* in Hardwicke Street, on the north side of the River Liffey. The small building had belonged to the Poor Clares religious congregation who had built it, and its attached accommodation, during the eighteenth century. In 1804 they moved across the city to Harold's Cross, and their chaplain, Fr Bernard MacMahon, took a lease on the chapel and its accommodation for his lifetime. At the end of 1813, Kenney, acting incognito through a solicitor, but with the permission of the archbishop, bought out MacMahon's interest in the chapel and living area.[163] He would take possession of the property following Fr MacMahon's death in 1816. There, his reputation as a preacher would become speedily and publicly established: for by then he was something of a celebrity; known fairly generally as the Jesuit who had founded the new college of Clongowes, who had been spoken about in the House of Commons, and whose name was in the papers.

V

"What an intelligent and active man can achieve." Public acclaim and domestic denigration, 1815–19: Clongowes – Hardwicke Street – Tullabeg – Focus of visitation

We hear our hearts grate on themselves: it kills
To bruise them dearer. Yet the rebellious wills
Of us we do bid God bend to him even so.
G.M. Hopkins, "Morning, Midday, and Evening Sacrifice"

The years from 1815 to 1819 were make-or-break years for the young Jesuit mission. A good beginning, followed by consolidation, was essential to the College of Clongowes Wood; but Kenney, as has just been seen, also sought two other key foundations – a public church in Dublin, and a noviceship. Their combined demands, however, were to stretch the mission's resources to the limit, and to exacerbate division within Jesuit ranks.

Peter Kenney's name has been indelibly associated with the story of Clongowes College. That story has been told at length elsewhere.[1] Here it is referred to only so far as it contributes to an understanding of his life, character, and achievements.

STUDIES, EDUCATION AND TRIALS AT CLONGOWES

As he embarked on establishing a prestigious educational foundation, he took it for granted that it was imperative to have clear objectives, appropriate structures, and a definite programme of studies. Such thinking had been transmitted to his followers by Ignatius Loyola, who had been helped, in his belated academic efforts, by the well-ordered system of studies and tight organization at the University of Paris, as compared to the more haphazard Spanish universities of his experience. As a result, he recommended that all Jesuit colleges should have a common, well-organized plan of studies in a suitably structured situation. After many years of elaboration and adaptation, a definite programme of studies, or *ratio studiorum*, was launched in 1599. For the next hundred and seventy years it provided the framework of the order's reputation in the field of education. Kenney looked to the principles of the *ratio* for guidance not just at Clongowes, but also later in the course of his two visitations to the Jesuit mission in the United States of America. It was central to his thinking as an educationalist.

In the *ratio studiorum* the overall objective was – the education of the whole person. The main means of achieving this, between the ages of, say, twelve to seventeen years, was by the teaching of the classical languages, Latin and Greek, over five years: the first three years being termed grades of "Grammar" (in accordance with the pupil's progress in knowledge of grammar, in readings, and even versification); and the final two being called "Humanity" or "Poetry" (concerned with advanced readings and fluency in the languages), and "Rhetoric"(the study of the principles and practice of rhetoric, involving oratorical and poetic composition).

In the fuller curriculum envisaged by the *ratio*, the student would then advance to a study of the philosophy of Aristotle, and thence to theology according to St Thomas Aquinas. Such a curriculum was seldom achieved in practice. Some schools never got beyond the study of language and literature, some combined literature and philosophy. Something of this last prevailed in the early years at Clongowes, where at least some of the senior students moved smoothly in their study of classical authors on to the works of Aristotle.

The teaching was not confined, of course, to the classical languages. There was a range of subjects, as will appear. What at least one parent expected Clongowes to provide was clearly stated in a letter to Kenney within six months of the opening. The author was Daniel O'Connell. On 4 January 1815, he wrote from Merrion Square, Dublin, to say that he wished to entrust two of his sons to Kenney's care. One was twelve, the other ten years. He wished their time to be devoted "to the acquisition of much classical learning; a solid formation in classics, especially Greek, being ... of great value to real education". He would also wish them, he said, "to acquire the French language, and as much knowledge in the simpler branches of mathematics, and as great a familiarity with experimental philosophy – including, or rather placing at the head, modern chemistry" – as might be consistent with Kenney's "plan of education". He was, of course, "most anxious that they should be strongly imbued with the principles of Catholic faith and national feeling". And "these advantages" he entertained "sanguine hopes of", if they were placed under Kenney's care.[2]

The "sanguine hope" of Kenney imbuing his charges with the significant conjunction of "Catholic faith and national feeling" reflected, it would seem, a personal acquaintance with, or well grounded trust in Kenney, rather than any expectation of a special emphasis on Irish history. The teaching of history at this stage was very much in an ancillary place. And some years later, alas, if one is to believe one celebrated past student, there was little evidence among the staff of the college of any interest in Irish history and little sign of "national feeling". Thomas Francis Meagher, who had fond memories of Clongowes in the 1830s, and who became the militant Young Ireland orator, and subsequently raised and led the celebrated Irish Brigade in the American Civil War, wrote of the Irish Jesuits of his school days that it was "an odd fiction" which represented them "as conspirators against the stability of the English empire in Ireland. With two or three exceptions," he observed, "they were not O'Connellites even. In that beautiful, grand castle of theirs, circled by their fruitful gardens and grain fields, walled in by their stately dense woods, ... they lived and taught ... rather as hostages and aliens, than freemen and citizens ... Ireland was the last nation we were taught to think of, to respect, to love and remember."[3]

But to return to the actual programme of studies in Kenney's day. Fortunately, he left his own description of what was taught. He did so under unexpected and distasteful circumstances: in response to rather peremptory queries from the Lord Lieutenant.

It all began with a letter from Youghal on 10 October 1815, sent by an Irish Jesuit brother, Philip O'Reilly. He had arrived there after a voyage of 75 days from Palermo, aboard a ship under a captain who was "a drunken rascal". He had not laid in sufficient provisions, and had endangered the vessel during his drunken bouts. They were bound for Belfast, but had struck on the bar at Youghal. O'Reilly wrote not only to tell Kenney of his whereabouts but also to report on his cargo – over three tons of books and some polished stone and agate crosses! All of which had been collected by Frs Aylmer and Esmonde,[4] and were left to the luckless brother to bring home. From Youghal, the boat sailed for Belfast. Again it was caught in a storm, and was eventually driven on shore in Dundrum bay, near Killough, on 23 October. Not surprisingly, the size of the personal cargo in the charge of a Jesuit gave rise to queries at customs. The goods were held up. The matter was brought to the attention of the Lord Lieutenant. This, at a time when the English newspapers were printing nefarious allegations against Jesuits.

Kenney spent five expensive and anxious weeks in Dublin, at the Enniskillen Hotel much of the time, negotiating about the goods, and composing three memorials to the Treasury Board of Customs and the Lord Lieutenant.

To the latter, he explained that the books, bound and unbound, were for the college library and for the Jesuit community. The Lord Lieutenant asked for a copy of the prospectus. Kenney found he had no copy left of the original which he had sent to the parents and Mr Peel. So, in its place, he sent a description of what was being done and planned to be done at Clongowes. It represented an application of the *ratio studiorum*, adapted to circumstances, and so presented as to placate the formidable recipient. It also necessarily reflected, in its practice, his experiences of the Jesuit colleges at Palermo and Stonyhurst.

"The education," he declared, "comprises all the branches of classical knowledge without neglecting the requirements necessary for the merchants' office." In "the plan of conducting this general education," he continued, the classical department comprised seven schools (or classes), each of which required a proper master, who made the pupils assigned to him, and the exercises allotted to his school, the subject of his undivided care. Each pupil was supposed to remain one year in each school. The schools were arranged in ascending order, according to the degree of information supposed to be acquired in them: there were two elementary schools, three grammar schools, two schools of rhetoric.[5] In these the pupil was gradually conducted "from the first rudiments of grammar to a very sufficient knowledge and practice of poetry and eloquence in the English, French, Latin and Greek languages". He added, that he was sure it was unnecessary for him to say that he "would not direct any plan of education that had not religious and moral principles for its basis and great object".

He went on to remark that he charged "a very moderate pension" so as "to put a suitable education within the reach of the decent classes of society", and hence he was "at present very unable to meet the expense of the duty which", he was told, would "amount to £280".[6]

In the end, the memorials and negotiations led to a reduction in custom duty from the feared £280 to £161 4s. 8d. But when all expenses were paid, including Kenney's stay in Dublin and the expensive transport from Killough to the Grand Canal harbour, James Street, Dublin, the overall cost was £234 0s. 5d., and with that many of the books were badly damaged.[7] It was a cost which pressed particularly heavily in a year when the need for additional building to accommodate pupils had already led Kenney to borrow £300 from an old friend, James Bacon.[8]

The books contributed, however, to those wider aspects of education long associated with Jesuit schools. They went towards building up a library, which already had a nucleus from the works donated by Fr Betagh. They included texts on philosophy and theology, for Clongowes had classes in these disciplines for its Jesuit scholastics, or students for the priesthood. By the middle of the following year, indeed, there would be a community of ten priests, six brothers, and eighteen scholastics; the last-named taking the lectures in philosophy and theology, in addition to their work of teaching and their task of supervision when the pupils were not in class. The college was to continue as a centre of higher studies into the mid-twenties, and was to provide for a while for members of the English Jesuit province, who sought to complete their studies in Ireland so as to be ordained as religious (*sub titulo paupertatis*), courtesy of the Irish episcopacy since their own vicars apostolic still refused to recognise their existence as Jesuits and religious.

Encouraging pupils to read widely, think clearly, and express themselves fluently in speech and writing, were important features of the wider education just mentioned. The expansion of the library necessarily facilitated reading; and the school's emphasis on this aspect during these first years is suggested by the evidence of a student from that time before the Royal Commissioners of Irish Education Inquiry. William Rogers, interviewed on 13 November

1826, regarding Maynooth where he was a student, was also subjected to detailed questioning about his time at Clongowes. His answering appears to have been lucid and fluent. A native of Cork, he was four and a half years at Clongowes, from 1814 to 1818. They were encouraged to read widely outside the course, he said, by means of a boys' library. The books were mainly in English, and generally concerned with English literature: Sir Walter Scott's poems, Burke's works, the usual collection of British essayists, all Miss Edgeworth's works, Sheridan's speeches, and many other works, including some on history of which he recalled only Robertson's *History of Charles V* which was read publicly in the students' refectory. As regards his own reading, it was extensive. "I read most of the English classics," he said, "and several portions of the Greek and Latin classics, which were not included in the class business, but in which I stood a second examination, called the Academics, which were public."[9] His interview also indicated that his "class business" included some algebra, and Italian, as well as the study of a large catechism full of "texts or references ... to scripture".

The mention of "the Academics", or Academy, however, focuses attention on another distinctive feature of the *ratio studiorum* which Kenney introduced to Clongowes and which excited much interest. It involved a public presentation by some of the abler students and a readiness to answer questions on a whole range of texts of classical authors, and sometimes also French and Italian texts.[10] The occasion was attended, at various times, by professors of Trinity College, Dublin, and of Maynooth College, by Archbishops Troy and Murray of Dublin, by the bishop of Kildare and Leighlin, by local magistrates, the families of the boys, and friendly neighbours like the local clergy, and Lord Cloncurry and the Duke of Leinster. All were entitled to examine the candidate of the day on any portion of the elaborate programme presented. The public ordeal of declamation, exposition, interrogation, often lasted over four hours and seems to have greatly impressed visitors. The third Duke of Leinster, a regular attender, when questioned about Clongowes some years later, before a committee of the House of Lords on the Catholic question in Ireland, remarked: "It is the most curious establishment I ever saw, as the boys are well brought up. A public examination is held there every year and Fellows of Trinity College are invited to go down: the Fellows are given a list of what classics they are to examine in, and the answer is wonderful."[11]

The *ratio studiorum* provided for lines of organization and authority, as well as for the actual plan of studies. As noted, there was a particular master in charge of each class, and instructions were provided for him. The overall charge of the classes, the curricula and the students was entrusted to a prefect of studies or headmaster. He was a key figure. The school took its character from him and from the rector of the entire establishment. The centrality of Kenney to the early developments may be gauged from the fact that he was both prefect of studies and rector, and superior of the mission.

In accordance with the application of the *ratio* at Palermo, the prefect of studies at Clongowes, at the end of each term, read out a report on the progress of each class. A flavour of Kenney's approach, and of the ethos of the school at the beginning, is provided by the survival of the "Public Terminal Reports of the Prefect of Studies", especially those for the years 1816 to 1821.[12] The earliest of these are in Kenney's handwriting. A perusal of the first eleven pages shows him, not surprisingly, displaying characteristics almost endemic to headmasters – a serious demeanour and exalted language to dramatise the importance of study, the iniquity of neglecting it, and to inculcate the virtues of hard work and discipline. The models presented as examples of style, taste, and diligence were, inevitably, the classical writers and orators.

In the Christmas report for 1st Grammar, he found much to praise in the standard of their classical studies, and in their work in English, French, Geography, and Declamation. Where the 2nd Grammar class was concerned, however, he observed that their compositions generally "reached only a wretched mediocrity", and this led him on to expound on a favourite theme, namely. the importance of composition in the whole area of education, and particularly in a classical education. It was an emphasis he was to reiterate in his American visitations, and he bequeathed it in a special way to Georgetown University.[13] Composition, he declared, was meant to reflect a reading of the classics with careful attention, with a view to imitating them, so that in the actual composition there would be unity and perspicuity, ... and such features as irrelevancies, plagiarism, and purple passages, which but disfigured the overall unity, would be avoided. Adherence to the requirements of good composition, made also for good English writing. Composition, in fact, was "a main feature of a literary course", and on no other system had there been formed at any time "luminaries in the Senate or the State". To neglect composition, therefore, would be, from a literary point of view, "a high disorder ... a neglect of duty to yourselves, to your friends, to your country, and to connive at such neglect would in wise be criminal"!

Exalted language was also brought to bear on the "senior schools", as he counselled them to emulate the great models of Grecian eloquence, especially Demosthenes; and reminded them that by entering into the feeling and "into the full spirit of the great models" laid before them they would form their judgement, and their taste, and rear their souls to greatness. Finally, it was important to keep in mind that "the lights of Greece and Rome" were "men of unparalleled industry, men ... of the most highly cultivated talents, men who spent the time, which others gave to sleep and amusements, in profitable studies"!

In the first year of Clongowes there were 110 pupils. The following year the numbers rose to a remarkable 200,[14] although many were lodged in improvised accommodation. Kenney's triple role, and his widespread reputation, led to his frequent absence from the school; but a gift for detailed organization, and the fact that the structures were similar to those experienced in Sicily and Stonyhurst by a number of the community, ensured that the college functioned without notable damage under a delegated authority. Most Sundays, in effect, he was present to address the assembled school and to enthuse his hearers with his vision: with the values and high standards of life, work and discipline which he expected from a Clongowes Wood boy.[15] His reputation, energy, commitment to pupils, assured manner, and organizational ability, created an ambience which attracted parents, and promoted a spirit of study and firm, yet relaxed discipline. Mothers, like Daniel O'Connell's wife, Mary, were impressed by the happiness and contentment of their sons and by the fact that Mr Kenney "seemed to be more like a kind parent than anything else to them".[16] The fathers were kept informed by letter of their sons' progress in diplomatic, yet forthright words. Extant letters, which survived mainly in great collections such as that of O'Connell, mirror this careful expression as well as further evidence of personal interest. Even as busy a man as the Liberator read the rector's letters with care, passed on the comments to his wife, and encouraged his sons to observe carefully school rules and discipline.[17] "What a comfort to us, Darling," Mary O'Connell wrote after one report, "that they should deserve the praise of such a man."[18]

All the signs, then, from early on were of good order and good spirits, and a certain impressiveness suggested and reinforced by a rather resplendent school uniform – "a cap made of rabbit skin, a blue cloth coat with brass buttons, yellow cassimere waist coat and corduroy trousers".[19] Already, indeed, by the end of the first year, 1815, such favourable accounts had reached Stonyhurst that Nicholas Sewall wrote to Kenney, on 2 December, to express his joy at "the high commendations", he had heard, "of your college, of the good order and regularity, of the spirit of devotion and learning practised in it"; and in January 1816 Fr Stone referred to reports of persons coming from Ireland on "the prosperous and flourishing state of your college".[20] But most pleasing of all to Kenney was the tribute paid by the bluff Plowden, following a visit to Clongowes by Fr Anthony Simpson, a Frenchman by birth and destined to become provincial in France, but then a prominent figure at Stonyhurst. Plowden wrote on 12 October 1816:

> I must next tell you, that the most heart-felt comfort which I have enjoyed these many years, comes from Mr Simpson's report (which fills Stonyhurst!), of the excellent arrangement, order, progress, and success of your new establishment. I bless God for it, as being highly useful to religion and creditable to the Society. *It shows what one intelligent and active man can achieve. Crescat in mille millia.*[21]

Kenney, then, had good grounds for a sense of satisfaction, a glow of achievement; and yet he was far from peace of mind. Despite the outward marks of success and well-being, he was conscious of criticism and disharmony within the Jesuit community. The revelation of his concern was made to an English Jesuit friend. For Kenney, who seemed defensive and uneasy with the two Irish Jesuits of distinguished family background, was quite unambiguous in his relations with representatives of two far more prominent English families: the Plowdens, whose roots ran deep not only in England but also in North America – Charles alluding almost in passing to Long Island being known formerly as Plowden Island;[22] and the Welds, who managed to preserve more than 12,000 acres of land and their Catholicism during the penal laws, and enjoyed royal visitations to their great estate in 1789 and 1791. His letter was to John Weld, the young rector of Stonyhurst, with whom he was friendly since their days as novices together.

Stress and problems as superior

On 12 February 1816, in a long overdue letter to his friend, he gradually unveiled something of his unease as prefect of studies and superior. He first addressed an enquiry from Weld as to whether Fr Esmonde could go to Rome to represent Irish and English interests. He was clearly exercised that neither Esmonde nor St Leger were currently available for work at Clongowes: Esmonde, because of his health, staying at home at Ringville, near Waterford, with his brother, Sir Thomas Esmonde; and St Leger working in Waterford at the request of the bishop, Dr Power, and visiting an ailing member of his family.[23] If Esmonde were able for active service, he stated, he would be much needed at Clongowes. But one could not rely on his health. Kenney's own sentiment was that he "would rather have him at Rome sickly, dying or dead, if you will, than have him as he is", for though he gave and received edification from his family it was "no way for a Jesuit to spend his time" and afforded "a very bad precedent to us". As long as the Irish bishops stayed so well disposed, he continued, the Irish Jesuits had no need of a representative at Rome, but he was conscious that some such person was necessary for the English province. Hence, he was well inclined to give Esmonde to him, if he deemed "such agency *really necessary*" for the good of his province and had not another to send. He presumed the entire expense involved would rest with Stonyhurst.

His exasperation with Esmonde may have been reflected in his attitude towards him. Esmonde was among those who later spoke of his severe discipline.[24] But his uneasiness about the two Waterford members did not explain his further candid remarks to Weld:

> I frankly confess, as I write in confidence, that I should be quite ready to embrace the opportunity of being liberated from the cares of this mission. In truth, I ever disliked, I now abominate the office of superior.

Were he relieved from it, he went on, he believed it would add twenty years to his life, He had matters so arranged that his "presence and service would be less missed than others might think". He had not intended to say all this, he concluded. He feared it indicated that he was not completely resigned to God's will, and he asked Weld to pray for him.[25]

He did not know when writing that his English friend was experiencing much severer trials with his larger and very divided communities at Stonyhurst. Worn down by work and pressure, he was to succumb to a fatal illness within a number of weeks. It says something of Kenney's closeness to him, and perhaps of his own tiredness as well as sensitivity, that on the morning of 8 April he is reported to have informed the community at Clongowes that he expected bad news from Stonyhurst; that he had seen Fr Weld in his room during the night. The night and the time of the alleged apparition, coincided with Weld's death at Stonyhurst.[26]

Where Kenney himself was concerned, his problems as superior appear to have been a mixture of his former strained relations with "the five from Sicily", and his long and frequent absences from the community and college in relation to the acquisition of the Hardwicke Street chapel, and the acquisition of a suitable place for a noviceship, in relation to the books already mentioned, and in order to meet the many demands on him from bishops and religious – demands to which he either felt constrained to yield, or wished to yield, while yet feeling that his presence was required at Clongowes. He who complained of the precedent set by Esmonde's long absence with his family could scarcely have been unaware that his own absences were giving rise to comment and criticism within the community, not least from his second-in-command, Fr Aylmer. The latter, who was the minister of the house, responsible for the day to day running of non-academic matters, complained in his diary, which covered the weeks from 1 November to 13 December 1816, that Kenney was frequently away from the college, and he chronicled his absence from 10 to 12 November, and from 29 November to 13 December.

This last long absence appears to have been partly related to the illness and death of Kenney's twelve-year-old nephew. Also there was reference to demands on him to give charity sermons for the bishops of Cork and Limerick. Charity sermons, it is important to recall, were often a crucial means of financing charitable bodies at the close of the eighteenth century and the first half of the nineteenth century, and, hence, preachers of high reputation were sought after in order to attract a large and well-to-do attendance. It was difficult for someone in Kenney's position to turn down such requests. The previous year he had declined a request from Cork.[27] This time he appears to have accepted both invitations.[28] From Aylmer's diary it is also evident that part of Kenney's long absence from the end of November was devoted to securing the Hardwicke Street chapel for the Society following the death of its tenant, Fr McMahon. and also the adjoining residence where he had lived

with his sister. On 8 December, Aylmer remarked that there was much opposition "by the priests of the parish" to the establishment of a Jesuit chapel at
that location, and five days later he noted that they had heard "that Mr
Kenney had got possession of Hardwicke Street chapel" but that "as yet"
there was "no account from himself".[29]

It was a recognition of their difficulty in working together, perhaps, that
led Kenney soon afterwards to move Aylmer from Clongowes to the new
appointment of resident priest at Hardwicke Street. Frs St Leger and
Esmonde, meantime, had returned to Clongowes, and Kenney appointed the
latter a consultor of the mission.

Pressure of external demands

The new year brought no lessening in the demands on him. Arrangements for
novices was a pressing concern. In March 1815, he had obtained permission to
open a novitiate in Ireland.[30] This had followed negotiations with Mrs Maria
O'Brien who owned Rahan Lodge, near Tullamore, in the midlands. She had
the approval of Bishop Plunkett of Meath for her plans.[31] Kenney seems to
have first met her and her husband through Archbishop Murray, near whom
they lived in Dublin. Through him he also met Miss Matilda Denis, who was
to be a strong supporter and a generous patron of Jesuit ventures, and Mary
Aikenhead and her followers who were committed to working with the poor
and lived in community at Summerhill, not far from either the archbishop's
house or the Hardwicke Street residence and chapel. The O'Briens were noted
benefactors of Catholic charities, and Mrs O'Brien had the reputation of being
one of the most attractive and best dressed women in Dublin. She was prepared to make available to the Jesuits, near her lodge at Rahan, a house and
104 acres of land at a moderate rent, in return for their providing religious
services for her own farm workers and the large Catholic population in the
area. The offer was attractive to Kenney as a means of establishing a noviceship in a location unlikely to attract government or public attention. Mrs
O'Brien, however, was not above extorting forms of interest. Thus, on 12
September 1815, she informed Kenney that Dr Plunkett had given full
approval to members of the Society giving spiritual instruction and hearing
confessions in the parish, and in his public instruction "alluded to your
coming here" next Sunday. She regretted the short notice![32]

Negotiations regarding Tullabeg dragged on into 1818; and, in the meanwhile, there was a regular flow of letters from Fr Plowden commenting on the
Irish novices at Hodder. To the normal problems of motivation and suitability
of temperament, there continued to arise those relating to national differences
and attitudes to authority. Arising from this last, Kenney was distressed in
October 1816 to find that two young men had been sent home without being
told that they were dismissed. The unpleasant task fell to him. He was

informed of their arrival by Fr Gahan, now serving in Hardwicke Street, on whom they had called. Gahan remarked, in a jovial but revealing aside, that one of them was a very nervous type who reminded him of a friend at Clongowes, "where no kind of noise must be heard, much less loud laughter, as Mr Ferley knows".³³ It was another indication of Kenney's efforts, when he was at home, to create in the Jesuit community's part of the building an atmosphere of recollection "proper to a religious house", even if it meant correcting one of his consultors, Fr Ferley. As he told Alymer, in a slightly different context, "what is observed this year may be considered as a standing rule or custom of the house".³⁴

A further example of outside events encroaching on his time and drawing him away from Clongowes, was the importunity of Dr Murray, who involved him in assisting and drawing up constitutions for Mary Aikenhead's community of women soon to be known as the Irish Sisters of Charity. Kenney's work for and with religious organizations is treated in a separate chapter; but something of the pressure it placed on him at this stage is indicated by a letter from Archbishop Murray, written from London on 15 April 1817, complaining, half in jest yet fully in earnest, that Kenney had been avoiding him when in Dublin, that he could "travel about the world at the beckon of everyone" who invited him – and Bishops Corcoran, of Kildare and Leighlin, and Murphy, of Cork, were discretely indicated – while his "own little family at Summerhill" was "left in a state of confusion and disorder" uncertain of what was "to be the result of all this unexpected delay". So, Murray continued, "I now beg of you to take up your pen in earnest and enable me to present the new constitutions to the sisters at Whitsuntide." He also sought his opinion as to whether the two most recent applicants might "be admitted to the novitiate at Whitsunmonday. And in that case," he added, "I would expect you to say a few words on the occasion"; indeed, "at whatever time the reception shall take place I will expect it of you."³⁵

Within a fortnight he was being called away again, this time by Mrs O'Brien wanting to discuss the map of the Tullabeg (Rahan) estate, the location of the projected noviceship, and wishing him to stay over to preach at the local church on Sunday and also to discuss with her some points raised by her friend, Mary Aikenhead.³⁶

It was all proving too much for both Kenney and leading members of the community at Clongowes. Apart from the wear and tear on himself, he felt oppressed, as his letter to Weld had indicated, by the tension and criticism of the community; though it is not evident that any of its members, not even Esmonde or Aylmer with all the assurance and poise of their inherited social status, had as yet faced his strong personality with direct criticism and challenge. On 9 April 1817 he wrote to the General asking to be relieved of his position as superior of the mission and rector of the college.

His letter reached Fr. Brzozowski on 28 June. The General replied in terms of considerable exasperation on 9 July. It was remarkable, he said, that Kenney, having neglected to answer his letters again and again, now expressed the desire to be freed from the burthen of superior. "How can I accede to your wishes?" he asked. "How can I appoint a successor when I know nobody? Shouldn't you have sent me a catalogue with: 1. names, surnames, age, grade, office, entry; 2. some sort of short briefing on health, strength of body and soul, proficiency in letters and virtues; suitability, in the case of young men, for study; in the case of priests, for governing and various offices? Thus informed, I could determine something, instead of being totally blind. Now the prudent thing to say is that all should remain as they are, until I receive due information." It also displeased him, he added, to have individuals writing to him for permission to go overseas without first going through Kenney. The latter, accordingly, was "to inform the writers of the correct way of doing things, then examine their wishes and all the circumstances and, after mature consideration, determine with Fr Grivel, now on visitation at Stonyhurst, to see if what they seek can be granted; and then," he concluded, "there is no need to write to me on the matter again."[37]

The announcement of the visitation of the English province by Fr Grivel had been made on 14 May. Born in France, and destined to die in the United States of America, his presence close by provided opportunities to members of the Irish mission to more readily convey their grievances to a higher authority. The announcement also appears to have stimulated Kenney to repeat his request to be relieved of government.

On 23 July 1817, the General, Tadeusz Brzozowski, wrote to Grivel to inform him that as Fr Kenney had again asked to be relieved of his office as superior of the mission and rector at the college of Clongowes Wood, he judged it wise to act on his wishes. Therefore, after hearing the consultors' views on informations about possible successors, he should appoint a vice-superior.[38] On receiving the letter, Grivel asked Kenney to come to England to see him. When Fr Esmonde heard this, he wrote to Grivel asking that some consultors also have an opportunity to visit him.

The impending release from office, which Kenney had sought, was not to bring him, however, the relief and peace he expected. Instead, the months ahead were to be marked by turmoil, hurt and misunderstanding.

LEAVING OFFICE – COMPLAINTS – ACCUSATIONS – AND NEW PROSPECTS

On 4 August 1817, he replied to the Visitor's letter. Before he could set out for England, he said, he had to fulfil a promise made to the archbishop of Dublin, namely, "to preach at the clothing on 21st of this month of the Daughters of Charity, a recently founded congregation". As Grivel was not due to return to Paris until the end of September, he hoped this delay would not inconvenience his "very important work". If the cause of the delay were approved by his Reverence, he, Kenney, would set out for England on the evening of the 21st itself.[39]

Eleven days later, 15 August, Esmonde wrote to the Visitor, quite unaware that Kenney had asked to be relieved of office. On one matter, he said, he wished to speak "urgently and vehemently", namely, that all the goods of the mission were in the name of one man, and if anything happened unexpectedly to him all would pass by law to his brother. That "one owner of all our goods," he continued, "is the Revd Fr. Kenney ..." A man certainly (if I may add a word about him) of outstanding ability, virtue, and piety, and with an eloquence of considerable power for which he is famous among outsiders. But we are men, and it is better to be over-timid than imprudent." And he went on to complain that in the ten months since Kenney nominated him as one of the consultors, he had been given no information on "temporal affairs". The same applied, so far as he knew, to the other consultors. It would help if some one of them, together with Kenney, were called by the Visitor to England, "to speak more clearly of all matters" in his presence. He was not available to travel himself, but he recommended a fellow consultor, Fr Ferley, and also Fr Aylmer, who, as noted earlier, was a close friend. Even though the latter was not a consultor, he was "for a long time minister of the house" and was well versed in the college's affairs. Esmonde concluded by saying that he had just heard that the Visitor was coming to Ireland, hence, if he wished to have any of the consultors go to England, it were better that "the request be seen to come from his own initiative" by public letter, "without informing Fr Kenney".[40]

About this time, the consultors and Fr Aylmer appear to have despatched a joint communication to the General. Fr Brzozowski was later to speak of their writing about Kenney in such a way as to make him believe that he would bring about the ruin of the Society.[41] A copy of the letter seems to have been sent to Grivel, and was a factor in inducing him to go quickly to Ireland without prior approval of the General.[42]

When the Visitor met with Kenney in Ireland, the latter was mystified and deeply upset to find himself facing "accusations of having visited a certain female, and slept outside the [Jesuit?] house in the locality". The "certain female" was presumably his good friend, and benefactress of the Society and other religious bodies, Miss Matilda Denis. Kenney was able to convince Grivel that there were no grounds for concern or suspicion, but it had been a harrowing experience. It was only much later that he discovered that when the Visitor read the Latin letter, from Aylmer and the consultors, with its complaints, he read *propter impuritatem* for *propter impunitatem*. He also learned at that later stage, and with some annoyance and disenchantment, that his colleagues had described him as "more Jansenist than Jesuit".[43]

Apart from such indications picked up from an examination of later letters, there is no extant account of what happened when the Visitor arrived in September 1817. Kenney was to say subsequently to Grivel that he had been too indulgent to the dissidents in Clongowes;[44] but the grounds of his complaints have not survived. Following consultations and interviews, Grivel appointed Charles Aylmer in Kenney's place, and formally announced his decision to the assembled Clongowes community. The appointment awaited a patent of approval from the General.

One young scholastic who was present, Robert Haly, destined himself to become rector of Clongowes and a well known preacher, left the only account of the Visitor's announcement. He did so, however, some fifty years after the event. What he particularly remembered at that stage was that, following the announcement, "Fr Kenney threw himself on his knees, asked pardon of all for any offence he might have given in the course of his administration, and then kissed the feet of all his religious brethren." It was a type of action associated with structured situations such as penitential exercises or expressions of humility and service during Holy Week. Its seemingly spontaneous performance in this instance might conceivably have evoked a critical response, but what Haly remembered was "how much the members of the community were edified".[45] And that, in its own way, said something, perhaps, about the genuineness of Kenney's response, and his style.

On 28 September 1817, at the conclusion of the visitation, Fr Grivel formally "gave thanks in the name of the Society and of the Jesuits of Clongowes to Fr Kenney for the wisdom, vigour, and the shrewd and patient administration which, within three years, had raised the college to such remarkable heights".[46]

That the formal tribute was not just a formality was evidenced in subsequent private letters to Aylmer. Thus, writing from Stonyhurst on 12 October, he praised the developments at Clongowes and added: "I feel more and more the great service rendered to your college by the governing with strength of the good Fr Kenney. My dear father, I pray you for the love of God to keep his (achievement?) well, using the same means with all suavity." And he thanked God for enabling him to fulfil the General's wishes by appointing a new superior, and for "Fr Kenney who has put in excellent order the instruments which assure to the members of the Society their temporal goods".[47]

Exclusion under the Aylmer administration – The noviceship squabble

For Aylmer it was an impossible performance to follow, and, unfortunately, he did not have the ability and temperament to make a strong contribution of his own. He sought like most successors to assert his independence of his predecessor's ways; but to a considerable extent he appears to have succumbed to the temptation of the weak executive, to assert himself by denigrating his predecessor. And there is some evidence that his consultors, at least at first, abet-

ted him in this. Part of the temptation was to reverse some of Kenney's decisions, even though they had been approved by the Visitor. Aylmer was, moreover, both indecisive and stubborn. He kept in touch with Grivel, seeking the
assurance of his advice, yet frequently went his own way.

Kenney, meantime, had gone to work at the church in Hardwicke Street,
with a view to going eventually to Tullabeg as master of novices. This was the
arrangement which Grivel made with him, and which he understood Aylmer
to have confirmed. At Hardwicke Street, not content to wait for people to
come to him, or to draw them by the power of his preaching, he went out to
meet people of all classes, talked with them, and drew them towards the sacraments, especially the sacrament of penance. In this way, his reputation and the
demand for his services grew. The months passed, and there was not a word
about his appointment to Tullabeg. He noticed that the provincial behaved
with "great reserve" towards him, and on the two occasions he visited Clongowes he found the priests unwelcoming, and even his old friend, Fr Jautard,
had "become a sworn enemy". It was indicative of the change in spirit in
Clongowes, Kenney felt, that the old man, as spiritual father, now displayed
"an anger against the lay brothers ... and treated them as a joke".[48] Unknown
to him, Aylmer had been writing to Fr Grivel, who retained his authority as
Visitor at the command of the General, complaining about having to have a
foundation at Tullabeg, "an ugly region ... with many marshes and bogs", and
giving reasons why "Fr Kenney's plan" for there "was useless and impracticable".[49]

On the last day of April, or start of May, Kenney heard from the provincial, to his dismay, that Fr St Leger was to take charge at Tullabeg and that
he, Kenney, was to stay at Hardwicke Street, and that the provincial was surprised that he expected to go to the midlands.[50] Kenney wrote to Grivel. The
latter ordered Aylmer to send him to Tullabeg. He was not long there, however, when he was informed by the provincial and his consultors that they had
decided to go against the Visitor's instructions and that he was to return to
Dublin.[51] The consultors next decided that he should be moved to Clongowes
to teach theology to the Irish scholastics, who were shortly to be joined by
their counterparts from England. Esmonde, as a consultor, wrote to Grivel to
argue that such a change would do Kenney good. He was living on his own in
Dublin, almost like a secular person, dining outside the house every day
except Saturday, and not returning until nine or ten o'clock most nights. Lay
people had commented that he had "almost forgotten his own in the college".
If he came to Clongowes, Esmonde concluded, "not as before, but in a subordinate position, he would acquire a little more of the confidence and love of
ours."[52] It was perhaps indicative of the new leadership that they emphasised
the need for Kenney to teach theology as a support to the resident theologian,
Fr Butler, without ever consulting the latter. When he heard of the plan, he
wrote to the Visitor to state that he did not approve of Kenney's "broad

views" on books permitted to students, and did not want him teaching theology at Clongowes.[53]

In October 1818, angry at the way he had been excluded, at the chopping and changing, and the flouting of the Visitor's authority, Kenney wrote to Grivel protesting that he was being too indulgent, and providing him with the entire history of the projected noviceship since he had left Ireland. He pointed out that "the whole affair" was "a succession of equivocations, of orders, of counter-orders, insincerities and contradictions"; and the suggestion that he teach theology, he continued, was "like another scene in the same comedy". He had not read a book of theology, or spoken Latin, for seven years, and yet he was being asked to come and teach without preparation, and a month after the term had commenced. In any event, his responsibilities in Hardwicke Street, he added with some exaggeration, would keep him there until Christmas. He then revealed that he knew of the former complaints of the consultors about him and of Grivel's misreading of their letter, and this further indicated to him "that Clongowes for some years should not be the vineyard" of his labours. Nevertheless, if his Reverence sent him, he would go to Clongowes but "without enthusiasm, without preparation", and against his own judgement.[54]

Grivel responded by warning Aylmer against "possible jealousy and rancour" towards Kenney on the part of some of his consultors, and informing him, with perhaps a sly smile, that Fr General had confirmed Kenney's appointment as novice master for the coming year,[55] and that meantime Kenney was to go to Clongowes after Christmas, not to teach theology but as superior of the theology students, spiritual father to the community, and admonitor to the superior![56] Hoist with his own petard, Aylmer twisted about to find reasons for Kenney not coming to Clongowes: if he were to replace Fr Jautard as spiritual father, it would greatly upset the old man, and, besides, members of the community would not have "that confidence in Kenney that one should have" in a spiritual father; and as admonitor, he would not be able to carry out that role properly as he would be away frequently giving retreats, and especially during Lent when Archbishops Troy and Murray would want him in Dublin.[57] In the event, Kenney was still at Hardwicke Street as the new year, 1819, commenced.

Turning of the tide – A prospective bishop

Esmonde, meanwhile, had become quite concerned at the quality of leadership exhibited by his friend, Aylmer. The latter spent too much time on details and neglected basic problems, he informed Grivel on 19 February 1819. His main difficulty was "indecision". He continued – in a lofty tone of regret concerning Kenney which displayed no awareness of the latter's experience of hostility and rejection from "the five" – "How sorry I am," he protested, "that Fr

Kenney did not spend this year with us ... He would be a treasure for us if he were more united with his own, and they with him". The numbers had fallen from 250 to 200, but neither he, nor Fr Ferley, had been able to fulfil all their functions. "If Fr Kenney had been with us," he continued, "he would have helped us, and his 'activity' might perhaps have remedied the indecision of Fr Aylmer"; moreover, "being acknowledged everywhere as a man of great talent, his name would" have helped "the college much". He dearly wished to have him in Clongowes as professor of theology and companion to Fr Aylmer. The previous appointment as admonitor, but not professor of theology, was impossible; though the superior clearly needed an admonitor![58]

In a subsequent informative, but undated letter, written from Hardwicke Street, and hence probably during Lent, Esmonde spoke in gloomy terms about Clongowes. It had "lost public esteem". It was necessary for us, he observed, to "be guided by the needs of the country", though he did not specify what these were. He hoped he was a false prophet, but it seemed to him that they would "soon have 100 instead of the former 240-250" pupils. "Fr Aylmer", he continued, "is a man of great piety, but easily entangled, indecisive; *who feels he has gained much if something is postponed*".[59] Turning to Hardwicke Street, he remarked, almost in surprise, that Fr Kenney did "honour to the Society" there. If he went to Clongowes after Easter, as Grivel had recently suggested, it was important that whoever came to Hardwicke Street in his place should be prepared to the maximum so as to preach "to the most cultivated people in Dublin" who came there to hear him.[60]

He went on to talk of a wider issue, that of possible Jesuit candidates for vacant episcopal sees. Fr Aylmer's name had been put forward as a successor to Dr Corcoran, bishop of Kildare and Leighlin. There was no danger of his being chosen, in Esmonde's view. There was some danger, however, of Kenney's name being put forward, not only for a bishopric but for the vacant primatial see of Armagh. Dr Curtis, professor at Salamanca, was said to be too old; and another candidate, Fr Carr, too young. He continued: "Archbishop Murray, who has much influence in these things, makes a big case for Kenney"; and Esmonde felt that Dr Curtis "would willingly cede the mitre" to Kenney because of his "great esteem and affection" for him. It would be a bad thing for the mission if this happened, he warned, for "things will not get better without the return of Fr Kenney to the college. If the others are not of this opinion I hope that time will show that they are right, and I am wrong!"[61]

Kenney was not destined, at this stage, to return to Clongowes, or go to any other Irish destination. Something quite unexpected was in store.

Mission to the new world – Bishop of Kerry?

On 23 April 1819, the General, Fr Brzozowski, wrote from Polotsk to Fr Aylmer to say that the condition of the Society in North America required a

Visitor, and that he had selected Fr Kenney for that office. He appreciated that Aylmer was short of numbers, but he would have to bow to necessity. The absence would be "only for a few months", and then Kenney would return to Ireland. Meanwhile, he was to pronounce his four vows of final profession as soon as possible, after the customary triduum of prayer, so that there should be no delay in his departure.[62]

The same day he wrote, at greater length, to Kenney. He was very concerned, he announced, at the information he was receiving on the state of the Society in the United States. He had decided to send a Visitor to deal firmly with the problem, and Kenney had been his eventual choice.

"Reverend and dear Father," he declared, "as I am entrusting to you a very serious office, I ask you above all to consider before God the great importance of the task and with what diligence it must be carried out." And he went on to paint a stark picture: "The mission of the United States in America, which formerly counted saints and martyrs" had "been brought to such a pass that it could be called a wretched parish". He elaborated:

> Nationality has taken possession of the spirit of Ours, and so has discord. The native-born Jesuits cannot put up with either an Italian, or a German, or a Belgian superior. They insist on having either an American or an Englishman. Are these the voices of religious men? Are they Jesuits? Absolutely not ... To stamp out and eradicate this spirit I am selecting you as Visitor to the College of Georgetown and to the Mission of North America.

He added that the present superior, Fr Kohlmann, was a good religious, but that he knew little about temporal administration. And this, the General believed, was "the principal cause of the discord", which was "a scandal to seculars and about which the bishop of Baltimore" had written to his Assistant at Rome. Kenney was to investigate everything; and a list of specific instructions was provided.[63]

This major, convoluted commission gave him a new lease on life. He had the vision, energy, and application to thrive on large challenges; and the fact that he had been shunted to one side in the home mission made him all the freer and readier to respond to the honour and trust shown by the head of the order.

He set about right way making arrangements to clear his commitments, so that he might sail as soon as possible. By 9 June he had written to Plowden for advice on the best port of departure and on the situation in North America. On the 12th, Plowden recommended Liverpool as the port; and continued: "Certainly I will give you all the information in my power on the sad state of affairs in that country". Kenney's mission thither seemed to indicate, he remarked, that the General had yielded to the request of the Vicar-General,

Fortis, and the Roman provincial, to have detained at Rome, Fr Grassi, the able president of Georgetown who had come for what was meant to be a short business visit. "The General in his last letter to me," Plowden concluded, "seems almost to despair of saving the diseased limb of the Society in America. It will be a blessing if you succeed, but Oh how I regret that Ireland must lose you."[64]

On 16 June, Kenney was professed of the four solemn vows, in accordance with the instructions of Fr Brzozowski;[65] and the following month he went to England, where he spent some weeks with Plowden and other Jesuits[66] before sailing on the appropriate date, 31 July.[67] Writing to Grivel a week later, Aylmer stated: "Our dear Fr Kenney has left for North America, where Fr General has sent him. He left for New York from Liverpool on St Ignatius' feast. We are in great difficulties and sorrow after his going, especially the people of Dublin and elsewhere. After his departure, he was chosen by the clergy of Kerry as bishop 'in partibus', and the nomination was sent to Rome for the approval of the pope." He urged Grivel to take up the matter at Rome "so as to block the nomination, which would certainly cause jealousy among the secular priests and would be injurious to the Society". There was no need to remind his correspondent that in the constitutions of the order there was a prohibition against seeking directly or indirectly any position of authority within the Society, and "an equally severe order not only not to seek, but even to refuse, any prelacy or dignity outside the Society, unless the same had been commended by the highest ecclesiastical authority".[68] Kenney's aura and reputation was to expand amongst his brethren as his absence was increasingly experienced at Clongowes.

Decline at Clongowes – End of a beginning – Reflections

By the late autumn of 1819, indeed, Esmonde's gloomy predictions about the college seemed about to be fulfilled. The numbers had declined greatly, partly due to an inaccurate diagnosis of scarlet fever at the school,[69] and also to "the deprived state of trade and low prices of grain".[70] But for at least one member of the community, writing at the end of October 1819, the "desertion" of the college was due to the "weakened and lax government" which had prevailed since Fr Kenney's departure. The latter, he observed, "was known to the people, and he knew how to gain and keep their confidence. He was able to manage people, and whatever were the prejudices against his formidable austerity there was a general feeling that he was the man to govern the house, to overcome the difficulties, and to become respected. The resolute alertness and the energy of soul which were characteristic of him" were in marked contrast to "the lack of energy" of his successor, who "took up his burden without being known to the people" and never knew "how to win their confidence. Indifference and indecision have been a mark of his progress." He ignored the representations and warnings of the staff, and like "a reckless pilot" slept quietly "in the midst of rocks and waves".[71]

The writer, William O'Brien, was a third-year theology student, and there are grounds for suspecting exaggeration on his part,[72] but his was but one of many letters of criticism sent to the Visitor or to Rome;[73] and certainly by the end of 1819, it is clear that Kenney's standing had been fully restored at Clongowes, and the memories of his "formidable austerity" had mellowed. On 3 January 1820, Fr Rosaven, assistant to the General, commented wryly to Plowden on "the inconsistency" that while Kenney "governed Clongowes complaints used to arrive" of his conduct, but now "all Clongowes redemanded" him "loudly as indispensably necessary for the support of the Irish mission".[74] At that stage, of course, Kenney was deeply engaged in the affairs of the North American mission and there was talk of his not returning, and the serious decline in numbers had greatly focussed the minds of the Clongowes community.

In the summer of 1819, however, when Kenney was leaving Ireland, signs of insecurity at the college were not so evident, and he could happily feel that he had placed the new Jesuit mission to Ireland on a sound footing. The flagship, the College of Clongowes Wood, had dwindled but was surviving. The property was "secured by every existing law";[75] and where the school itself was concerned, he had fulfilled the requirement which Archbishop John Carroll had emphasised with respect to his college at Georgetown: "The fate of the school will depend much on the first impression made upon the public, and a president of known abilities and reputation would contribute greatly to render that impression a very favourable one."[76] The initial favourable impression he had made secured the foundation. In addition, premises and land for a noviceship and small college had been acquired at Tullabeg in the midlands, and a small but popular church had been established in Dublin. And he had fostered a careful system of administration by means of a simple form of book-keeping, which anyone could apply: with entries only under two headings "charge" and "discharge" (*illata* and *ablata*) a method he subsequently introduced on the American mission.[77] Moreover, thanks largely to his personal links with Betagh and the survivors of the old Society, to his success at Maynooth, to his special efforts, varied gifts, and wide reputation, the revived order was accepted in the country; and its members were well-regarded and welcomed by the bishops, secular clergy, and other religious. So much was this so, indeed, that Dr Troy, in 1818, was to say of the opposition of the English vicars apostolic to the Jesuits that he found their "conduct ... unaccountable", since here in Ireland, without any formal publication of the bull of restoration, the Jesuits "are acknowledged and employed in the ministry with great benefit to religion. They have a public chapel in this city, they are ordained *titulo paupertatis* etc. etc. There is not a whisper of opposition against them, either from the clergy, nor laity, from Protestants or the government."[78] It was, in effect, Kenney's very standing with Drs Troy and Murray that encouraged the English province to approach the archbishop of Dublin through him, when they sought to have their theology students ordained in Ireland *titulo paupertatis*.[79]

The happy change in fortune which attended him in 1819, seemed prepared to accompany him to the New World. Just before his departure, "fresh letters", which Plowden had received from the American superior, Fr Kohlmann, "gave him spirit". For the letters indicated, as Plowden informed Aylmer on 5 August, that Kohlmann's vigorous measures had quieted the alarming disorder in the American mission, and that Fr Kenney would "find his work almost done to his hand". Kohlmann stated "that order, regularity, and studies" were "re-established at Georgetown, that the peccant members" acknowledged "their past misconduct", and that they were "already of one mind and heart with their superior".[80] The advent of a Visitor from the General, especially one with Kenney's redoubtable reputation, had helped to concentrate minds on self-reform.

Hence, when he arrived he was relieved to find that matters were not as serious as the General had feared, though closer acquaintance would indicate that there was much room for reform and that the mission was in fact in a parlous condition. Throughout his at times painful sojourn, however, both the indigenous and foreign Jesuits were to be disarmed by his unassuming manner, impressed by his oratory and powers of organization, and won over by his obvious desire to understand and be of assistance. He had evidently benefited from his setbacks in Ireland; and availing of the Society's emphasis on discernment, and examination of the well-springs of behaviour, he appears to have realised that some, at least, of the negative reaction of his colleagues towards him resulted from insensitivity in his manner of applying his "formidable austerity", and from a self-sufficiency and energy which rendered him neglectful about consulting others and keeping them adequately informed. He was always, however, to be more at ease and more appreciated in positions of authority by those who were not fellow Irish Jesuits. The latter viewed his personality, ability, and reputation with more awe than he realised; and their collective memory remained focussed on his early reputation for severity.

His journey to the United States passed without event, apart from bouts of sea-sickness. An extant letter, written from the ship, recalled how happy he had been at Hardwicke Street, and then directed his thoughts ahead with the characteristic reflection: "But am I not still more happy to do the will of God with less consolations than those with which Hardwicke Street superabounded. I should have had some attachment had I remained longer."[81]

VI

A man sent. "Visitor to Georgetown and the mission to North America", 1819–21: Emissary to the United States, and to Rome

> There is no other land like thee,
> Thou art the shelter of the free;
> The home, the port of liberty
> Thou hast been, and shalt ever be.
>
> James Gates Percival, "New England"

THE PREPARATION AND INSTRUCTIONS

In the weeks of his uneventful voyage across the Atlantic, Kenney had ample time to consider the General's detailed instructions and to relate them to the background information which he had obtained from Plowden, who, as part of his "joy in writing", had kept up a regular correspondence with Jesuits in the United States and especially with his old friend and contemporary John Carroll.

Bishop John Carroll – The early years of Georgetown College

As he related his instructions to the information supplied by Plowden, Kenney could not but be conscious of the extent to which the scene had been set by John Carroll, from the suppression of the order in 1773 to his death in 1815.

The British territories had been served almost exclusively by Jesuits of the English province during the eighteenth century.[1] At the time of the suppression, about twenty of them, in Maryland, Pennsylvania, New Jersey, and New York, ministered to some 30,000 Catholics. They stayed on at their posts as secular clergy, and soon experienced, with the success of the American revolution, the end of penal legislation and freedom to teach, preach, and administer the sacraments. Carroll was quick to see the opportunities presented to the church under the new regime. He rallied his fellow ex-Jesuits, and got them to undertake three tasks: 1. To organise together in a Corporation of Roman Catholic Clergymen to preserve the lands and funds of the Jesuit mission against the day when the Society would be restored – an initiative not unlike what occurred in Ireland; 2. To erect a college which would raise up Catholic laity and foster priestly vocations; 3. To establish some form of definite connection with Rome.[2]

In 1784 the Holy See acknowledged his leadership qualities by appointing him prefect apostolic in the United States; and five years later he was designated the first bishop of Baltimore.³ For some years he had been planning a college. Agreement was reached with the trustees of the corporation to draw on the Jesuit funds to get it underway. In 1789, the year of his episcopal nomination, and the year of the ratification of the American constitution and of the inauguration of the first president of the United States, he received the deed to the property at Georgetown on the Potomac River. He placed it in the hands of the ex-Jesuits; and drew on his experience of his Jesuit studies to formulate a syllabus based on the humanities and philosophy. Although the new academy, which held its first classes in 1792, was "open to the students of every religious profession", he looked on it as the "hope of permanency and success to our H. Religion in the United States". It would, in effect, prove to be the mother of a long line of Catholic colleges and universities, supplying thereby one of the essential needs of the young American church.⁴

Bishop Carroll's close ties with a number of the leaders of the revolution was a major factor in the college's favour. In 1797 the United States, first president visited the Georgetown campus. It was a token of General George Washington's personal regard for John Carroll. Such close links benefited, in effect, the entire church, including the Society. The last was in particular need of such good will. Powerful figures like John Adams and Thomas Jefferson viewed the order's restoration as "a retrograde step from light towards darkness".⁵

Before Kenney left Liverpool, he had also learned that though Georgetown was the centre of Jesuit activity in the United States, it had been in difficulties for most of its twenty-eight years. Despite Carroll's great desire to get off to a good start and, as part of that, to have a college president "of known abilities and reputation",⁶ the academy, from its opening in 1791 to the current year, 1819, had had eleven presidents, was almost always short of funds, and experienced wide fluctuations in student numbers.

Part of the problem was caused by Carroll himself, and subsequently by other prelates. There was a duality in his thinking about the purpose of the college which led to confusion in action and policy. His appreciation of the religious freedom and pluralism of the United States, induced him to present the institution as one catering for all religious denominations; while at the same time he saw it as the main means of providing priests for the expanding Catholic Church. Successive presidents struggled with the inevitable tensions: the emphasis placed now on humanist, academic studies and liberal discipline; now on the more rigorous discipline and narrower curriculum appropriate to a seminary. In his own lifetime, the archbishop's ambition for the college continued to vie with his need to meet the demands of his vast diocese. There was a great dearth of suitable priests and, unfortunately from Georgetown's point of view, the men most sought after by the bishops for pastoral work were those who were active and gifted in the academic sphere and American born. Carroll's partiality for native clergy was stiffened by the church's necessary dependence on what he called "missionary adventurers": men who had been failures and troublesome in Europe and had been despatched by their bishops or religious superiors to the United States.

Kenney, indeed, was to remark on the prevalence of Irish clergy among these problem priests. Responding to Dr de Barth, the Vicar-General for Philadelphia, who asked his advice about a priest claiming to have a recommendation from the bishop of Raphoe, he commented: "You have had quite enough of Irish and Germans to be more cautious in admitting them than you would be with any others ... Priests from the northern and western dioceses of Ireland should excite even more caution." And he further cautioned regarding his countrymen of "a great facility with some of our good prelates to say all the good they can of a bad man to remove the scandal of his conduct from their own flock".[7]

Carroll's suspicion of non-Americans, however, extended even to men of exceptional calibre. Thus, of Fr John Anthony Grassi, the one eminent president Georgetown had had, who could not easily be faulted, he judged that he let himself be mainly influenced "by foreigners, that is, his brethren from Russia, Germany, Flanders etc., all of them good religious men but not one of them possessing an expansed [*sic*] mind, discerning enough to estimate the difference between the American character and that of the countries which they left".[8] Carroll's nativist tendencies, however, in no way lessened his attachment to the papacy; though he tended to keep his distance from the Congregation of Propaganda Fide, whose understanding of things American was very limited, and whose hostility to the Jesuits he had personally experienced during his visit to Rome in 1773, the year of the suppression.[9]

American nativism and Kenney

Given the impact of American culture, history and ambience on a personage as sophisticated and cosmopolitan as Archbishop Carroll, it was not surprising, in the early years of the restored Society, that American-born Jesuits displayed strong nativist tendencies. Kenney, in reporting to the general congregation of the order at the close of his visitation, was to say, that "the American fathers were madly patriotic and freedom loving, firmly believing that their race was wiser and more blessed than other nations",[10] and that, "as religion had not captivated their hearts and minds, they resented being governed, or corrected, or instructed by foreigners". But he was careful to add that the foreign Jesuits were mostly aged, and unable to speak English, and some of them were only a short while in the order and had little knowledge of the institute, and some were quite odd. "With such material pupils were to be taught, novices formed, scholastics educated, and twelve missions serviced". Not surprisingly, then, "seeing the quality of the immigrant priests", the American Jesuits and students, "despised them, and were reluctant to confer with them on any important matter, nor entrust any secular business to them. 'We begged for learned Jesuits,' they said, 'and we got ignorant monks. There was need for strong and energetic workers, and aged and infirm men are sent'." And while the foreign priests, with some justice, complained to the General of a secular rather than a religious way of life, of native nationalistic attitudes, incompetence in government and the management of temporal matters, these would not have been so prominent, Kenney thought, if they themselves "had been what the native priests were looking for, and if they had not meddled in temporal affairs".[11]

As indicated earlier, he proved very much the right person for the situation and time. He had imbibed the spirit of the old Society in its European setting, and was at home in the traditional world of monarchy and hierarchical authority; but at the same time he was consciously Irish, had experienced the reality of national differences when at Stonyhurst and again in asserting independence from the English province, was friendly with leaders of the Catholic popular movement seeking emancipation, and far from having problems with the concept of democracy and a republic, as many Europeans had, he welcomed the opportunities it offered to the Catholic religion, the Society, and his countrymen. In fact, considered comments of his on this theme, nearly two years after he left the United States, were unusual for a clergyman of the time and might almost have been penned by the young Lamennais or a liberal democrat like Daniel O'Connell.

Writing to his friend John McElroy at Georgetown, and referring to a letter from the new superior of the mission, the recent arrival from White Russia, Fr Dzierozynski, in which he spoke of the American students at Rome as the hope of the future if they "did not retain their republican spirit", Kenney observed that such an expression could not fail to vex the young men. "Was it not extremely imprudent," he asked, "to tell this to Americans? Surely it is of more consequence to gain their affections, increase their piety and docility, than to lessen their attachment to their republican government! If they are to have any opinion on politics, why should it not be in favour of their native government?" And he went on: "Those who have fled from an absolute tyranny in Europe, should be the last to complain of the spirit of a government that gives fair and equal advantage to the Catholic religion. It is the glory of the Catholic Church that it is adapted to every form of government and not dependant on any. It conciliates the spirit of every constituted authority with the spirit of Christ's spiritual kingdom, and in this sense repeats to them all the words of the psalmist – 'Every spirit praises the Lord'."[12]

Not surprisingly, then, he was able to adapt to both factions. And, moreover, as Robert Emmett Curran commented in his magisterial *Bicentennial History of Georgetown University*, he quickly won their trust "through his fairness, openness and prudence. He saw quickly that both were to blame: the

Anglo-American Jesuits for their undisciplined life style and illegal desire to control their own finances through the corporation, and the continental Jesuits for their rigidity and imprudence."[13]

Fr Grassi's presidency – From Carroll to Marechal

The General's instructions to Kenney mentioned a foundation at New York, and raised a question about a debt being owed by Fr Kohlmann. The development in question was a church, residence and college, which was served by Frs Kohlmann, Benedict Fenwick, and James Wallace and which flourished in 1809–14. It cost the Society nothing. There was a debt, but this was being paid off steadily. While it was expanding, however, Georgetown took on a new lease of life under the dynamic leadership of Fr John Grassi. He became president of the college and superior of the mission in 1812. Curriculum and discipline were revised, student numbers increased, and, as a result, there was a shortage of teaching staff. He decided to close New York in order to develop Georgetown. Bishop Carroll supported him, though he suggested that both academies might have been kept open were it not for "a narrow jealousy against admitting others than old or new Jesuits" to man the colleges.[14] The decision was a painful one. Grassi assumed the New York debt of 10,000 escudos as a debt of the Society. Kenney, together with Kohlmann and many others, lamented the departure from New York. It brought down "the greatest odium" on the Society, he told the General, and caused factionism and scandals. Indeed, he declared, "religion lost more in sacrificing New York than Georgetown will gain in ten years";[15] and he was careful to emphasise that it was Grassi, not Kohlmann, who was responsible for transferring the debt to the Society.[16]

Immediately, however, as Kenney understood, Georgetown benefited. Benedict Fenwick and James Wallace who had done trojan work at New York, joined the staff, and Anthony Kohlmann, who had been administrator in New York and had had rather strained relations with the other two, was made master of novices. Although not many years in the Society, he had considerable pastoral and educational experience in Europe as a Paccanarist, spoke a number of European languages, as well as English, and was a devout religious. Georgetown's standing under Grassi's presidency was formally recognised in 1815 when Congress granted it its first college charter, empowering it to grant degrees in "the faculties arts, sciences and liberal professions".[17] Then, in this year of high acclaim, Archbishop Carroll died. Fortunately for the college, his successor, Leonard Neale, was also a former Jesuit and, in fact, a former president. He was faced, however, with a problem which dogged bishops of the period. In places lay Catholics owned the land on which a church and presbytery were built, and in a number of instances exercised their legal right of determining who occupied their property. In such instances they pressed prelates to remove priests whom they disliked, or were otherwise perhaps unsatisfactory, or else demanded that a man stay on whom the bishop wished to remove. Irish priests and laity figured prominently in such confrontations, and at times they took their case to Rome. This had occurred in part of Neale's large archdiocese, at Charleston, South Carolina, in the case of two refractory priests, Gallagher and Browne, whom he had removed, and whose case Propaganda appeared to be supporting.[18] Faced with a veritable schism at home, and misunderstanding at Rome, he asked Grassi to go to Rome on his behalf. The latter was reluctant, but felt an obligation to go. Good relations between the college and the archbishop was essential, and, besides, the visit would also serve to further three other aims: to persuade the assistant-general of the need for English-speaking priests in the United States; to arrange for the reception and training of a number of young American Jesuits at the Jesuit college, Rome; and to seek European benefactors for the American mission.[19]

He set out in 1817 and, as has been seen, was detained in Rome. Bishop Neale, meanwhile, died, and was succeeded in 1818 by the Sulpician priest, Ambrose Marechal, who, as a Frenchman, was not viewed sympathetically by many of the American population. A former lecturer at the college at a time of tension between the nativist Jesuit trustees and the French Sulpicians, he was interested in the college but had little of Carroll's or Neale's practical empathy for it or for the Society of Jesus. Before long he laid claim, as Kenney was to experience at first hand, to jurisdiction over the Jesuits and their disposal, even though there could be little doubt as to their exemption as religious ever since the restoration of the order; and he also claimed the Society's property for the archdiocese. This last claim was to go to Rome and result in almost a decade of controversy before the combined efforts of the General, Fr Grassi, and the corporation's trustees won through. The latter, for obvious reasons, were key figures in the early history of the restored Society in the United States.[20] It was they, and Kohlmann's involvement with them, that the General had in mind when he instructed the Visitor to investigate the temporal administration of the mission. Of this rather complex background, too, Kenney had been informed by Plowden.

The mission's dependence on property and the corporation

From the beginnings of the Maryland colony, considerable amounts of farm land had accrued to the Jesuits, by means of grant or purchase.[21] From these properties, and revenues from them, they supported themselves and their apostolic activities. This was then necessary because Catholics were relatively few, widely dispersed, and not accustomed to providing for the upkeep of their pastors; and also because the Jesuits from their inception were not supposed to charge fees for the tuition of their students nor accept stipends for pastoral services. They managed to run their colleges across Europe and in other parts of the world during the seventeenth and eighteenth centuries by means of subsidies from the nobility or governments. This type of aid was no longer readily available in the nineteenth century, and it had always been a problem in the largely non-Catholic English speaking world. Hence, after the suppression, John Carroll's special care to bring the order's lands in Maryland and southern Pennsylvania under the ownership and control of a corporation composed of ex-Jesuits, from whom trustees were appointed, who were required by law to be native Americans.

At the time of Kenney's departure for the United States, some 12,000 acres remained in the hands of the corporation; and the trustees, notably Francis and Charles Neale and Leonard Edelen, took their responsibility for its administration very seriously. Carroll had envisaged the corporation as having complete power over temporalities, even as against the authority of the local bishop or the Roman Congregation for the Propagation of the Faith (Propaganda Fide) which had responsibility for mission countries. He had expected, however, that the superior of the mission would be a member of the corporation with power to administer the funds. In practice, the superior had no authority over the funds. The corporation functioned independently of him. The circumstance that he was usually a "foreigner" weakened his position.

Precipitating a visitation

In 1818 the General intervened and ordered the corporation to make the superior, Fr Kohlmann, not only a member of the board of that body "but also to give him unrestricted power to act as its agent in transacting business". This the corporation did, but the arrangement soon gave rise to such blatant difficulties between the trustees and the superior that it proved a major consideration in sending the Visitor.[22]

Anthony Kohlmann was appointed superior of the Maryland mission by Fr Brzozowski after Giovanni Grassi had been detained in Rome. The latter, on leaving Georgetown in 1817, had named Charles Neale acting superior of the mission, and had appointed Benedict Fenwick president of the college. The decisions were, in large part, to exclude Kohlmann, whose volatility and difficulties with the Anglo and Irish Americans were well known to him.[23]

Following his appointment by the General in 1818, Kohlmann also took over charge of the college. He had long held that there was no prospect for a successful general academic establishment at Georgetown with its small population of 15,000, as compared to New York with some 96,000 inhabitants. He disapproved, moreover, of the liberal ethos associated with the scholarly "core" of the faculty assembled by Grassi: namely, Benedict Fenwick, outstanding in Latin and Greek, fluent in French, and competent in theology; Roger Baxter, an Englishman, teacher of English literature and rhetoric, and a noted public lecturer; and James Wallace, an Irish immigrant, highly regarded as a mathematician, and writer of a widely used textbook on astronomy. Kohlmann's emphasis was on the college as a place for the formation of seminary candidates, and this influenced his approach to discipline and the curriculum, and created a climate disagreeable to Protestant students. The curriculum he sought was one dominated by Latin and Greek grammar. To the "core" members he appeared to be confining education to clerical preparation, and they continued to follow their own preference in the use of texts despite his orders. As a result of this, and other provocations, he transferred them out of Georgetown. Archbishop Marechal co-operated by assigning Baxter to a parish at Richmond, and Fenwick and Wallace to a parish at Charleston.

To the Anglo-American trustees, Kohlmann was associated, besides, with financial extravagance and poor judgement. They recalled that he had left the mission with a debt of $10,000 in New York; that he, and his treasurer, John McElroy, had for some time favoured selling the plantations; and they now considered that they were using funds erratically and excessively for such purposes as the support of future novices. When McElroy later, during 1820, refused to open the financial books of the college to the corporation directors their worst suspicions seemed confirmed.[24]

Already, indeed, in the early summer of 1818, Charles Neale, whom Grassi had appointed as superior, complained to the General that Kohlmann's behaviour was threatening the very existence of the mission. "He has thrown out on his own authority," he said, "Father [Benedict] Fenwick and the mathematics professor Wallace, most learned men. He has built a novitiate in Washington city ... [and] he is so changeable by nature that what he builds today, tomorrow he will tear down. He alienates by his German customs Americans, so that there is a great danger ... that the whole Society will perish here."[25]

Occasions of anxiety were not confined to such instances. The new superior's discipline, as president of the college, which was heavily enforced by the conscientious and sensitive Stephen Dubuisson, a French emigré, who had many pastoral gifts but little capacity for administration, gave rise to a student revolt in 1818. It was believed that there was a plot to kill Dubuisson; and six instigators were expelled. The new regime, moreover, unhappily coincided with a recession and financial panic in 1819, and the combination brought about a marked decline in student numbers.[26]

The bitter divisions between the native (Anglo and Irish) American Jesuits and their superior and his "continental" supporters occasioned widespread scandal. Letters were sent to the General from both camps. In Kohlmann's letters, the disobedience of Baxter and Wallace featured prominently. The disruption and threatened collapse of the college, eventually moved even the archbishop, late in 1818, to convey to the General in Russia, through Plowden, his belief that the Society "must absolutely sink and fall in the United States" unless there was immediate relief.[27]

Not surprisingly, the General became "increasingly disturbed" at the reports from America about the factional ethnic discord,[28] and decided, as a result, to send a Visitor who would provide him with an objective account and serve to alleviate and, hopefully, even solve the prevailing problems.

The restricted commission

Fr Brzozowski's detailed instructions to Kenney required him to begin his visitation in each place by having "an account of conscience from each one" – a personal interview where each was expected to give an account of his spiritual and moral state, his work, relations with others, achievements, hopes , and problems. This, in the Jesuit tradition, was meant to provide the superior with an in-depth appreciation of his men and their work, and enable him to make the best possible use of their abilities. He was also to look to the spiritual observance of the members, to establish and guard the authority of the superior and correct what needed to be corrected. And he was "not to excuse himself on grounds of age". He was "the Visitor", and must undertake seriously what was to be done for the glory of God, and God's blessing would follow. In financial affairs, he was to scrutinise the situation carefully, appoint a suitable procurator from among the native Americans, and limit the power of the superior in temporal matters as he judged fit. As there was a report that Fr Kohlmann had contracted a debt in New York, which he stated did not involve the Society, Kenney was to investigate and establish the truth of the matter.

He was also to nominate consultors to the superior (i.e. four men with special advisory, not deliberative powers), and remind them to write to the General at stated times; and he was to determine if there was any native American who could succeed Fr Kohlmann. Such a man, however, would need to be able to promote the spiritual progress of his subjects; since among former superiors, in the General's view, there had been a neglect of the ways of spiritual formation This had improved somewhat in recent times, but it was essential that when young men came from the noviceship into the college they came to a place where discipline and regularity flourished. The Visitor, therefore, was to ensure that only those were appointed to the college who by their example would spur the young men towards regularity of life, and promote the growth of love in their hearts. In this context, he was to "look into the behaviour of Frs Wallace and Baxter" about whom complaints had been made. He was also to talk with the local superior to see if some novices, "who had been well trained" by Fr Kohlmann himself, when he was novice-master, "could be sent to Italy to do their studies there, and thence return to America fortified in piety and knowledge".

Finally, he was to call on the archbishop, immediately after his arrival, and salute him in Fr Brzozowski's name stating "that he had been sent to improve everything" and would "neglect nothing that would promote union of hearts", a goal which was much emphasised in the Institute of the Society. It was not possible to determine the length of his sojourn, the General added. He might remain a number of months, if necessary; but right through he was to keep his Paternity informed.

As time passed, Kenney became increasingly aware of the problems and frustrations inherent to these instructions. He had been given a formidable task, which the General seemed to wish him accomplish within a matter of months, but he was given little freedom of action. He might appoint and confirm personnel, he could recommend whether the superior, Kohlmann, should be changed or not, and might suggest the replacement, but he had no power to remove him. He was expected, during what was meant to be a brief visitation, to keep the General informed of everything, and to await his responses before making the final report; but as letters to and from Russia had to go through England, an interchange of letters could take up to six months.[30] Hence, it was difficult to see how the commission could be fulfilled within a short space. Moreover, as Plowden would ruefully remind him, "the change of circumstances" before the General's answer arrived would often render "the execution of his orders almost impossible".[31]

These inherent restrictions were not immediately apparent, however, when Kenney arrived in North America. His basic mandate, as he understood it, was threefold:

1. To settle temporal affairs; and also to restrict the authority of the superior if necessary;
2. To secure and strengthen discipline in the Society;
3. To bring delinquent priests to a more productive and fruitful life.[32]

He faced the daunting, unfamiliar task with considerable trepidation, nerving himself to proceed carefully, but firmly. The General's injunction about age, must have brought to mind St Paul's instruction to Timothy: "Let no one disregard you because of your youth, but be an example to all in the way you speak and behave ... Do not neglect the spiritual gift given you ... Be conscientious about what you do and teach ... Never speak sharply to an older man, but appeal to him as you would to your own father, and treat younger men as brothers."[33] Time would demonstrate how assiduously he followed that advice.

ARRIVAL – FIRST IMPRESSIONS AND APPROACHES

When his ship docked at New York on 9 September 1819, he learned that the principal towns had been visited by yellow fever and that Baltimore was severely afflicted. This upset his original plan of an immediate call on Archbishop Marechal. It was necessary to take a circuitous route to avoid the city; and he had his first experience of the inconvenience and bone-shaking discomfort of the horse-drawn travel and spartan inns which were to become a feature of his time in this new country. Hence, it was not until 25 September[34] that he reached the small bustling port of Georgetown, in the District of Columbia, some five miles from the new capital city of Washington, and saw above it on a high, wooded hill, the two buildings and octagon towers which constituted the college. The prospectus for the following year described the campus as: "situated on an eminence on the Maryland side of the Potomac", commanding "a full view of Georgetown, Washington, the Potomac, and a great part of the District of Columbia". The situation, the readers were assured, was "peculiarly healthy".[35]

One of his first actions on arrival was to present Fr Kohlmann with a copy of the first volume of John Lingard's scholarly *History of England*, which had just been published.[36] Awaiting himself was a file, with "details and information on every point, left by Fr Grassi";[37] and also, then or shortly afterwards, news from England and Ireland that the priests of the diocese of Kerry had chosen him to be coadjutor to their ailing bishop, Dr Sughrue. Plowden, in his account, assured him that he was writing to Rome to have the election set aside.[38] A subsequent letter from Fr Aylmer, moreover, made it clear that Dr Sughrue was not too pleased with the selection. He had one of his own clergy in mind; and proposed to Aylmer a range of obstacles, practical and fanciful, with all the guile and calculated flattery for which the natives of his county were justly famous. He believed that the government would resist the appointment of a Jesuit; that knowledge of the Irish language would be essential; and that a man of such talents and piety as Fr Kenney would have "a field more commensurate to his talents than Kerry" in the great American mission, and surely who would not readily make every sacrifice to see "a new Paraguay ... formed in the wilds of North America".[39] In effect, Sughrue was accurate in his estimation of the government's reaction. A letter from Plowden a month later informed Kenney that the Lord Lieutenant had publicly stated that his election to a bishopric was disapproved by the government. "What a dreadful man you are!", Plowden exclaimed impishly. "It seems your conference with Mr Peel terrified ministers."[40]

Plowden's communication made good time. It arrived on 5 October just as Kenney was writing his first letter home from Georgetown. By then, he had worked hard to get a grasp of essentials, and was already sensing the great needs and possibilities of the mission. Despite the tension between the Jesuits and Dr Marechal, and the latter's problems with some Irish priests and people, Kenney sought to bring a fresh, unprejudiced vision to the archbishop's vast concerns: greatly sympathising with his struggle to minister with only 52 priests, of whom but 27 were natural English speakers, to a diocese which embraced Maryland, Virginia, North and South Carolina, Georgia, and the "vast territory contained in the limits of Georgia, the Floridas, Tennessee, and the Mississippi River".[41] And he was also beginning to suspect what in

fact Archbishop Marechal had already reported to Rome, namely, that there
was probably "no part of the Catholic world in which the Society of Jesus
could exist more securely, spread more widely, and produce more abundant
fruits".[42]

First impressions

On 5 October he wrote to Aylmer giving his first impressions as Visitor. An
almost tangible note of relief was discernible. "Matters are not so bad as they
were made to appear. The poor General has been more plagued than he ought
to have been." He then admitted, however, that there were "great disorders
amongst some young priests, who wished to live in the college in a way that
suited themselves", and that there were some old priests who, "being trustees
of the corporation for the management of the property", made regulations
which tended to undermine the authority of the superior. The latter, fortunately, "by one courageous act", had obtained more from the trustees than Fr
Grassi had been able to do. He hoped that what remained to be done would
"be peaceably accommodated" since all the parties seemed glad that a visitation had been instituted by the General.

At this stage he was much influenced by the views of Fr Kohlmann, who
was personally gratified by his courtesy and co-operation. These qualities and
his unobtrusive adaptation to the customs of the country and to the age and
background of each one, were already beginning to quell apprehension and,
among the Americans, to disarm the potential for anger against examination by
a "foreign"authority.

With particular reference to Georgetown – with its mixture of lay pupils
studying humanities and philosophy, and Jesuit novices and scholastics – he
observed that "bad times", the current economic recession, had contributed to
the decline in the number of pensioners, or boarders. They were now only 60,
but they had never been as high as a hundred. As to the Jesuit personnel:
there were 21 scholastics and 13 novices, but the number of Jesuit priests in
the college and entire mission was only 22. To increase the teaching power in
the college, he had recalled Fr Baxter from parish work at Richmond.

As to the temporalities, or farms, of the mission, he went on, these were
large but generally in a bad way. This was because there had not been any
general system of management and economy.

Despite these negative aspects, he assured Aylmer that he believed that
great things would yet be done by this mission once "perfect union" was
restored, "stability secured" to the discipline of the college, and one system
"adopted by the various managers of the plantations". He feared, however,
that there would be difficulties arising from certain pretensions of the archbishop. Since he had commenced the letter, his Grace had written to Fr
Kohlmann opposing Baxter's recall from Richmond. As the bishop had already

enough to trouble him, he felt that they might have to yield to him. Then, with further empathy, he went on: "His Grace makes a grand battle for his people ... I admire him. And really the desolate situation of his flock, still more desolated by the enormous scandals of so many bad priests, plead this excuse for any trespass on the rights of others."

In that same letter to Kohlmann, Dr Marechal had expressed his upset that the Visitor was not remaining in the United States, and he asked the Jesuit superior in presenting his, the archbishop's, respects to Kenney to let him know that he would be doing all in his power to ensure that he stayed in America. Retailing this to Aylmer, Kenney said he had no idea what his Grace had in mind to do, but he did not wish Aylmer to "take any measures to prevent the success of his efforts". Elaborating on this, he revealed how much he had already been moved by the need and challenge of the American apostolate.

He had tried in strict impartiality, he said, to contrast "the wants of this country" with his "obligations to the Irish mission", and had resolved, in accordance with their founder's teaching on obedience, "to guard carefully that religious indifference that leaves the subject" at the superior's disposal "like a stick in an old man's hand". Were he at his own disposal, he "should think it almost a crime to return from any motive of affection or attachment to those comforts and sympathies" which he should "never enjoy out of Ireland". Indeed, "were a man fit to do no more than catechise the children and slaves", he ought to consider his being on the spot by the will of God a proof that it was most pleasing to God to remain amongst them, and "to sacrifice every gratification under heaven to the existing wants of catholicity". He did not plan to touch on this subject again while he was in America. "I shall not even lift my hand to influence the General one way or the other," he added, "because I am unwilling and unable to decide between the claims of the Irish mission and the wants of this, when I am myself the object of discussion".[43]

Aylmer, a poor correspondent,[44] was stirred by the letter to remind Kenney that the General in writing to him about his (Kenney's) commission had spoken of it as occupying only some months, and hence he urged him to return to Ireland immediately he had completed the object of his visitation. He admired his indifference, he said, but he must not forget "the wants of this weak and young mission or the many claims it had on his services". Ireland was "really deserted" since he left it. He sent the kindest regards not only of the Jesuit communities, and his numerous friends, but also of Drs Murray and Troy, and of the new archbishop, Dr Everard, all of whom, he insisted, were anxious for his return.[45]

Kenney continued throughout October to interview Jesuits at Georgetown and to make contact with men at mission stations not too far distant. To all he sought to impart a sense of involvement in a common purpose. One of the trustees, Fr Edelen, called on him. As he was about to return to St Thomas Manor, an old estate south of Georgetown, near Port Tobacco creek, Charles

County,[46] Kenney asked him to carry a letter to another trustee, the elderly and partly paralysed, Francis Neale, a former master of novices and president of Georgetown.

The letter offered a good example of the respect and diplomatic sensitivity with which he approached older men used to a largely independent existence, and sought to win their support. Fr Edelen's return to St Thomas Manor afforded him, he said, "the opportunity of saluting you in the name of Fr General"; and he personally viewed "with no small gratification", in "the present large congregation at Georgetown, the lasting fruit of your zeal and the proof of the important service which your ministry has rendered to the American mission". He was greatly grieved to hear of his infirmities, but hoped to find them alleviated when he would have the consolation of visiting St Thomas Manor.

"In the meantime," he continued, "I should be happy to receive from you any opinion or suggestion which you might think proper to give me on the affairs of this college, whether literary, spiritual or temporal." He would have much to say to him and his brother, Fr Charles, on the general interests of the Society, and he hoped "to receive such assistance in the final arrangements of the temporalities of our missions" as would contribute to their "being prosperously managed for the great object for which our venerable fathers had transmitted them". Having thus quietly emphasised the purpose of the mission funds, while graciously acknowledging the Neales' important role in preserving them, and assuring them of his interest in they being prosperously managed, he moved on to enlist their assistance in a matter of some delicacy.

Fr Baxter was on his way from Richmond to St Thomas Manor to make his retreat. Francis Neale had formerly been his confessor. Baxter was greatly needed at the college. There was no one else to teach philosophy. Hence, it was hoped, he said, that he would return from retreat "fervent in his desires to serve the *common cause* more effectively than Richmond Manor can do". It was a great pity to have to abandon any area in this most important mission, Kenney concluded, but "the most essential interest of religion, not less than common justice to the Society", called for his return to Georgetown.[47]

The retreat, in effect, appears to have disposed Baxter to accept change with more equanimity. Plowden, to whom he wrote, found his letter full of good sentiments, and he urged Kenney to take a more positive view of him than Kohlmann did.[48]

At the end of October, Kenney sent a letter to the General telling of how well he was received, of the gentle approach he was pursuing, and saying that he might need to stay on till Easter. He promised a full report before long. The General, who was ailing, replied on 3 January 1820. He was pleased to hear of the "good religious spirit" and of Kenney's friendly reception. He approved of his gentle approach, but warned that it would need to be mixed with due firmness and severity when required. He urged him to place temporal affairs on a firm footing since from that tranquillity would follow in the Society, and also to seek to win the favour of the archbishop. Kenney might stay till Easter – longer if necessary. He wished to be remembered to "the excellent Fr Kohlmann".[49] The letter, unfortunately, never reached Kenney. By following, however, the original instructions, he kept in practice to the letter's suggestions. On 5 November he completed his visitation of Georgetown. He decided to defer his report to Fr Brzozowski until he had visited some of the farms, and had personally presented his Paternity's respects to the archbishop.

Dr Marechal, meantime, had commenced his campaign. In a letter to Fr Grassi at Rome on 31 October, he reminded him that not only had he not brought back reinforcements to the United States, he had not even returned himself. Now he understood that Fr Kenney, who "came here about two months ago and seems to be a man of talent", was also not staying. The mission could not stand this kind of neglect. He requested Grassi to impress on the General "the absolute need we have of Mr Kenney", and also to ask him to send two or three young men as soon as possible.[50]

Some three weeks later, following a visit from Kenney, the archbishop wrote personally to the General. As soon as the scourge of pestilence had passed, he said, "this excellent father has come at once to pay me a visit". He was grieved that Kenney had probably received from his Reverence an order to return to England as soon as he had examined with care the spiritual and temporal affairs of the mission. This was detrimental to the entire mission. First Grassi, now Kenney. Hence, he pressed that the latter remain forever in America, or until further help came; and that the General send two English Jesuits to Georgetown, and, not to drain that province, two other Jesuits from any other nation. It was important, he added, that these be young, of good health, and, between them, be capable of teaching theology, logic and mathematics. He realised this was a big sacrifice to ask of the General, but it was necessary.[51]

Kohlmann was meanwhile adding his voice to that of Marechal. He wrote through Plowden, who informed Aylmer, that he had forwarded to the General both their "reasons for possessing Kenney. He must decide." In the same letter to Aylmer, Plowden passed on the most recent news he had received from Kenney as he came to the end of his Georgetown visitation. The college had, for its various students and the novices, only four masters of humanities. Fr Kohlmann was at once rector, minister, and professor of philosophy. There was one teacher of divinity; a procurator; and a young master of novices, who yet knew no English". There was a complete absence of pastors on some of the Jesuit missions, temporal affairs were in bad order, and the Catholic religion was being "sadly degraded from New York to Charleston in South Carolina by scandalous priests and friars, French and Irish. One named Egan" had "lately apostasised and married the widow of a Jew!" These

men, he said, were in Kenney's view "sent hither from Europe by the destroy-
ing angel".[52]

Aylmer was probably as much amused as impressed. He tended to sit light-
ly to Plowden's grave and doleful accounts and interpretations, and was not
averse to calling him "a croaker".[53] Kenney's actual report to the General,
however, made painful reading.

First report to the General

He submitted his report on 2 December 1819. It was an account of the mission as he saw it at that point, with particular emphasis on Georgetown. His
judgement on certain people and situations would change with increased
knowledge and understanding. He was still much influenced by Fr Kohlmann.
He followed in his presentation the order indicated by the General.

He had interviewed each one at Georgetown and some from the farms and
found that all were content in their religious vocation. Some of the native-born
in the younger age group, however, were tepid; but this, he believed, was
largely due to the discords and the bad example of some of the priests. He had
hopes of their improvement.

As an example of the kind of difficulties which could arise among the
young native-born Jesuits, he cited the case of George Gough, a first-year philosophy student, who had entered the noviceship four years earlier. He suddenly fled the college at the end of September without a word to anyone.
When brought back, he refused to stay or give any reason. "To this day,"
Kenney wrote, "I have been unable to find any cause ... but this: a character
that abhors any manifestation of himself because he would trust himself to no
one." From his companions, he also learned that young Gough had been "so
carried away by personal dislikes that when he found that he would have the
good Belgians as companions, as soon as they finished their noviceship, he
detested them so much that he preferred to leave rather than put up with their
conversation". Thus, Kenney commented, "the Society has this obstacle to
overcome in these parts – namely, that Americans have such an ardent passion
for liberty and for their country that it approaches madness, and they have of
their nature an intense hatred of manifesting themselves or others to superiors".

With regard to procedure, he was careful, he said, to ensure that the superior carried on as usual, and he so worked with him that it appeared they were
in complete agreement. Before he had promulgated the ordinations of the visitation on 5 November, he arranged with the superior that the opinions of the
other fathers were heard.

The discipline of the community improved, he continued, from the time Fr
Kohlmann was made superior, at least to the extent that morning prayer and
the two daily periods of examination of conscience took place. But in many

ways the customs of the Society were not observed, and there was a constant changing of the order of time. To counter this he composed a custom book. In it everything happening through the whole year was arranged, with particular days and times determined. He consulted widely in the process, and submitted the outcome to the votes of all. That being done, he admonished the superior that the book "was to be observed as a rule of discipline" so that people could no longer change everything "at their whim".[54]

In keeping with the General's emphasis, and the reality of the situation, he devoted much space to temporal concerns. He prefaced his treatment of this section with the comment that there was hardly any hope of his arranging such affairs if he were to return to Europe in the near future, because it would be necessary for him to visit all the houses and farms and endeavour to induce the fathers who were in charge of residences "to take up one single system by which farming operations could be better served, and the produce kept more carefully for the common use".

To bring about this change would be exceedingly difficult, he continued, because superiors in charge of residences were infected with a crazy fever with respect to what concerned farming operations. Every residence had a very extensive farm, but the superior, "who first of all should be a missionary" wished above all to be a farmer and to conduct affairs in his own way. It was not enough for them that they be a priest and superior; the custom of the country demanded, they said, "that they also be 'managers', that is a farm steward". And they would not tolerate a religious brother, or a layman, running temporal affairs. The latter's function was to work the fields under the direction of the superior. The result was a great amount of inefficiency and waste: "one man goes to enormous expense in providing unnecessary farm buildings; another in new experiments which turn out useless; a third in introducing a new agricultural system which does not work. Hence, amidst much wealth there arises the greatest poverty, and all the farms, with one exception, are burdened with debt."

As if to match this pen picture, the Vicar-General of Philadelphia was to remark nearly a year later, that as St Ignatius's famous institute was supposed to be a masterpiece to cover every eventuality, surely he must have guided his sons "against the devil's temptations in this country, namely, that the devil, in order to hinder the children of St Ignatius to become good missionaries, would try to make them bad farmers, and thus", with one stone hitting two targets, "the spiritual is neglected and the temporals ruined, and thus farewell the Society. It is come near to the point at present."[55]

Kenney, continuing his report, remarked, indeed, that the Institute of the Society clearly indicated what should be done; but that did not remove the practical obstacles. A competent procurator, or treasurer, priest or brother, should be appointed to each area by the superior, and there should be an overall procurator for the entire mission on whom the mission superior could depend. This general procurator would visit the individual farms at fixed times, examine how they were being run, and keep the superior of the mission informed. In practice, however, there were no priests or brothers skilled enough to be individual procurator-managers, and no one competent enough to be overall procurator. Previously, his Paternity (the General), when appointing Fr Kohlmann superior of the mission, had appointed an Irishman, Fr John McElroy, general procurator. The latter was an excellent religious, and a good college procurator, endowed with many talents, but he knew nothing about agriculture and was a "foreigner" and hence not acceptable to the trustees. Among these, the Frs Neale and Edelen were particularly important, Kenney continued. They had to be won over, for they were key members in that "civil body ... called a corporation in which" was "invested all our title to property and without whom nothing can be possessed by us, according to the civil law".

"When your Paternity reviews all this," he went on, "you will see that the matters entrusted to me will take considerable time." He had not, so far, nominated a general procurator nor consultors to the superior, because of the complexity of the situation and because he was not sure what changes his Paternity would make before he had completed the visitation of the entire mission.

In the context of temporal affairs, he reported also on the New York foundation; and, as mentioned earlier, exonerated Fr Kohlmann with respect to the debt incurred there.

He next turned to the General's request for the names of indigenous priests whom he could recommend to become superior of the mission. He reviewed each possible candidate (with the exception of the two he had not met, Benedict Fenwick and Wallace), made observations on each, and found none suitable. He gave particular attention at this stage to two men: Adam Marshall, and Enoch Fenwick. Marshall was a teacher of humanities and physics, who worked hard, and alone among the indigenous priests lived spontaneously at the college ... He was, however, weak in theology, not long acquainted with the Jesuit way of life, and had some peculiar views "derived from liberal and promiscuous reading". In the future, he might be a candidate for promotion. Fr Enoch Fenwick was a vicar-general of the archdiocese. He lacked neither talent nor learning though he had not completed his studies. Kenney judged, however, that he did not have that prudence, that holiness, that charity needed in a superior, and there was a suggestion of intemperance. Of a third man, later to come into the reckoning, Charles Neale, whose name had been suggested to the General and who was the pivotal member of the trustees, he observed that he had been superior previously and that during his term things were in a dreadful state, and, besides, he was not prepared to be detached from his chaplaincy to "his nuns".

Moving to the hope for the future presented by the novices and their training, he reported that he had transferred them from the unsuitable surroundings of the college to the old White Marsh estate in Anne Arundel County, 25 miles east of Georgetown, which he understood was a more fitting situation, though he had not yet visited it. In seeking out a novice master he had found the choice so limited that he felt obliged to opt for a 32-year-old Belgian, who was only four years in the Society and could not "as yet speak English without many mistakes". In his favour, however, it could be said that Van Quickenborne was very devout and "knows the institute and our spirit well, for he was splendidly trained in Belgium".

In a later letter, he was to add that the young Belgian scarcely rendered authority agreeable, was "by nature too vehement", and had little skill in governing others, but in time might make an outstanding spiritual father.[56] The assessment was probably more accurate than the prediction: for though Van Quickenborne became legendary for his commitment, and was to be spiritual guide to a canonized saint, Sr Rose Philippine Duchesne, he was to tax and challenge excessively not only her, but also himself and a generation of novices by his unbending asceticism.

The scholastics, Kenney reported, were given excellent example at the college by the priests there, with the exception of Fr Baxter, now teaching logic and metaphysics, who in many ways behaved "in a purile and worldly fashion".[57] In accordance with his Paternity's instructions, and the requirements of the college, he had recalled Baxter from Richmond and Wallace from Charleston, some 600 miles distant. Baxter took the transfer badly, but complied. When, however, Kenney wrote to Wallace, and gently pointed out that the General wished him assigned to the college, Wallace challenged his authority and poured out complaints against Frs Kohlmann, McElroy, and German members of the community. The fact that Wallace challenged his authority, and particularly the fact that he, Kenney, could not change the superior whom he, Wallace, considered the main source of the college's problems,[58] brought home very clearly to him the limitations of his powers as Visitor.

Reference to Baxter and Wallace led on to an account of the disedifying breakdown in discipline at the college after the departure of Fr Grassi. The latter had appointed Ben Fenwick as rector, though complaints about his prudence had been previously made by "trustworthy fathers". On Fenwick's return from summer vacation in New York, he found that the General had made Fr Kohlmann superior of the mission, and that Kohlmann had already made changes in the timetable of the Georgetown community and required all to attend the community meal together. Irate at what he saw as interference in his area of authority, Fenwick assigned his own hours of dinner and supper and was joined by Baxter and Wallace. Thus, they went their own defiant way "before the eyes of novices and scholastics from 1817 till August 1818".

Faced with this situation, Fr Kohlmann, after eleven months, arranged with the archbishop that Fenwick go to Charleston and Baxter to Richmond. He did not wish Wallace to leave, as he was a gifted mathematician, but gave way when he insisted on going with Fenwick. "You Paternity can judge," Kenney remarked, "what is to be thought of this pair." As to Baxter, he had so complied with religious discipline that it might be said of him that at the same time he both "reluctantly accepts and does not accept it".

Against this background, and that of the mission generally, he was of the opinion that it was altogether necessary to send scholastics to Italy for proper training. The superior ought to send five or more. In fact, there was no alternative. There was only one professor of theology, Fr Rantzau, who was frequently absent because of illness, and the only one who could supply for him was the superior, Fr Kohlmann, who was already overburdened. "My heart is saddened," Kenney continued, "when I see the Society in such dire straits for men who can offer useful service." That somewhat despondent note ran through the concluding section of his report. He gave expression to a strident request for help for the mission, and especially for Georgetown.

"It is necessary to inform your Paternity," he declared, "that the visitation will produce little improvement because there is no one to instruct the youth, no one to govern wisely, discipline and give orders. I have looked and searched here and there, and found no one suitable to be minister of a college, or for a chair of theology." Up to that point there had been no minister. The procurator of the house sought to fill the office, but he had never seen a college of the Society, and had been ordained priest only two or three years, and hence could achieve little in the position. Among the "missionaries", those working from the farm estates, there were only Frs Maleve or Carey who might make a minister, if they were first trained. But the mission stations were short of workers, and to withdraw priests from them would lead to an outcry from both bishop and populace. Hence, he concluded, "I beg your Paternity on bended knees, and pray you to think again about this vineyard of the Lord, and raise it up from the wretched state its in. Do you send workers of a kind whom St Francis Xavier would not reject. Men who speak English. The fruit of effort in many areas is lost because missionaries are not understood, they speak so badly that they are not heard, and not being understood they are despised."[59]

It was a limited report, as previously noted, confined strictly to the headings indicated by the General, and dependent for interpretation at times on second-hand information – especially that supplied by Frs Kohlmann and McElroy. Kohlmann, indeed, viewed Kenney as still just commencing his work. As late as 7 December 1819, he was writing to Fr Grassi that "Revd Fr Kenney, our amiable Visitor, a man truly of great merit, has begun his visitation".[60] From a wider perspective, therefore, the historian and discerning reader might well experience disappointment at the absence of reference to such items as popular religious devotion and practice, and to an aspect of the Jesuit farms so relevant to their viability, namely, that they were part of a plantation economy which depended on slave labour. On this last, however, as will be seen, he would write in subsequent correspondence and in his document "ordination on temporalities".

To Charles Plowden, Kenney's report to the General was disappointing from a different point of view. Shortly after he received it for transmission to St Petersburgh, Plowden conveyed his views clearly, if circumspectly. It was evident, he told him, that he had ahead some troublesome work, but he warned that it looked as if some people were seeking to mislead his judgement. He was also of the opinion that the General would not consider his report as adequate. His Paternity sought a great deal of information, and to judge by the directives he sent to Stonyhurst, he would expect decisive measures. His principle seemed to be "that young men, who will not assume the true spirit of our business, ought to be discharged". Plowden rounded off the letter, however, with the news that Fr Grivel had recently told him that he had advised the General to reappoint him, Kenney, as superior of Clongowes and of the Irish mission, as soon as he returned, or at least as soon as Fr Aylmer's three years tenure had ended.[61]

As the year drew to a close, Kenney found a welcome outlet in two favoured areas: preaching and curriculum organization.

Preaching and studies

Archbishop Marechal, in a detailed report on the state of religion in his diocese made to Cardinal Litta, prefect of Propaganda, in October 1818, remarked of the population – "the eagerness with which they listen to the divine word is almost unbelievable. Any priest of even mediocre influence is certain to attract to himself a multitude of eager listeners in our churches."[62]

Kenney's reputation as an orator preceded him to the United States, and, though there is no reference to him preaching on a regular basis, he was certainly called on for special occasions. No unusual preparation was required. Recent research into the Catholic preaching and piety of the period shows strong similarities to what he would have been accustomed in Ireland: "a purgative spirituality in which human weakness and a self- and world-denying asceticism was emphasised";[63] in which there was devotion to the person of Christ, often under the symbol of the Sacred Heart, to Mary and the saints; where preaching placed emphasis on scripture and on the Roman primacy; and where, as elsewhere in the post-tridentine Church, doctrines and devotions attacked by the Reformers, such as the eucharist, the Virgin Mary, the nature of the Church, received special attention. As in Ireland, the devotion of American Catholics found popular expression in the rosary, and in veneration of the blessed sacrament, especially during the octave of Corpus Christi.[64]

Kenney's standing as a preacher found formal recognition coming up to Christmas 1819. He was invited by the archbishop to preach at a special ceremony in the cathedral at Baltimore. The continuously mild weather facilitated the journey from Georgetown.[65]

Writing to Fr Grassi in the quiet of Christmas eve, Anthony Kohlmann told of the liturgical event just five days earlier. The occasion had been the presentation to Dr Marechal of the pallium: the circular band worn over the chasuble about the neck and shoulders, which signified the special jurisdiction of a metropolitan or archbishop.[66] Marechal invited Kohlmann to present the pallium. The latter wrote succinctly: "On 19th I gave the pallium to our venerable archbishop; and R. Fr Visitor on that occasion carried off, by the unanimous voice of all the clergy and laity, the singular praise that never such a sermon was heard in Baltimore. He joins solidity to a most flowing and unaffected language. Is it possible that we should lose such a man?"[67]

Kenney's American reputation for pulpit eloquence was to lead the following year to an invitation to give the oration in St Patrick's church, Washington, at the funeral service for the Duke de Barry. Fr Nerinckx, the much revered Belgian diocesan priest, who did so much for the North American mission, was present. He reported that the service in this large church, accommodating three thousand people, was attended by "all the foreign ambassadors and the most prominent members of the United States Congress, which was just then holding its sessions"; and that "Revd Father Kenney, Visitor of the Jesuits, and an Irishman of uncommon eloquence, preached the funeral oration to the admiration and delight of all present".[68]

The question which Kohlmann posed about losing such a man reflected the increased desire to keep Kenney in the United States. Kohlmann, wishing to enlist Grassi's support at Rome, referred in his letter to a report that the Visitor was named for a bishopric in Ireland, and then gave Kenney's reaction, namely, "that such a precedent, at the beginning of our infant Society particularly, would have most dreadful effects on the whole Society". The order would never be re-established in the United States, Kohlmann concluded, if the men able to establish it were taken away "to fill an office which will never remain without subjects and applicants". Fr Kenney was "essentially necessary here".[69]

Following the Baltimore celebration, Kenney returned to Georgetown to a wet and moderately warm Christmas. A few days later, as the weather changed suddenly to frost and snow,[70] he was working at what Fr McElroy in his diary spoke of as "the rearranging of the various classes".[71] It was part of his contribution to a new prospectus which drew on his knowledge of the *ratio studiorum*, his experience of the Jesuit colleges at Palermo and Stonyhurst, and his practical application of that experience at Clongowes which, it has to be remembered, was larger than Georgetown at this stage.

Details of studies in the early years have been well chronicled in histories of the college. Here, it is sufficient just to touch on some general features relating strictly to Kenney. In the system he proposed there were six years of general education, termed respectively – Rudiments, Grammar 1, Grammar 2, Grammar 3, Humanities, and Rhetoric: traditional names which were to last for another seventy years. Pupils moved on each year, provided they gave evidence of sufficient proficiency. This was established by means of examination; the results being closely related to the aggregate merit of one's compositions.[72] The compositions were written in each of the languages taught. Insistence on composition was central. If the student at the end of six years was sufficiently proficient, he might proceed to the Bachelor of Arts degree, and then, after longer and successful study in the higher branches of mathematics and philosophy, might take the degree of Master of Arts. This reference to post-graduate studies in the 1820 prospectus was the first such reference in any prospectus of the college.[73]

A distinctive feature of Kenney's approach, and in keeping with the spirit of the *ratio* and what he sought to achieve at Clongowes, was the assigning of the same teacher for the subjects Greek, Latin, French and English, in each year. He was meant to go up with his class year by year. This placed considerable demands on the teacher himself, on teacher resources, and on timetabling, and it is not clear to what extent it was applied; but it had the distinct advantage that the teacher really knew his charges and could adapt to their individual needs; and this was particularly relevant at a time when elementary schooling was not organised and pupils entered at various stages of knowledge and age. The importance of individual attention may be estimated from two entries in the college register a few years later. An entry for 16 October, 1827, lists a new student aged eight who "could read words of three syllables"; while on 19 January 1829, there is mention of another new student aged 19 who "was received and placed in the second class of Rudiments".[74] The reference to a "second class" for beginners clearly indicated a necessary system of grading, at least in the first year.

Kenney entered on the New Year determined to try to win over Baxter, Wallace, and the two Fenwicks. As an earnest of his good will, he appointed Baxter prefect of schools; hence, with a key role to play in applying the new programme throughout the college.[75] An even higher priority with him, however, was the creation of a solid framework for harmony between the superior and the corporation with a view to solving the temporalities problem.

Towards solving the temporalities

Already in mid-November, there were signs of positive developments with the arrival of Fr Charles Neale in New York "to settle his temporal affairs". From there, he wrote to the Visitor declaring his intention to come on to Georgetown.[76] Their meeting began the process of co-operation.

In February 1820, with improved, if still inconstant weather,[77] Kenney visited a range of farms. Among those expressly mentioned in surviving letters and documents were: St Thomas Manor, Port Tobacco, Charles County;[78] Newtown, one of the better run estates, in St Mary's County;[79] St Inigoes, at the extremity of that county where a peninsula juts into the mouth of the Potomac as it meets Chesapeake Bay;[80] and in southern Pennsylvania, what he described as the most pleasing of all the properties, the "*tout ensemble* of the church, house, and farm of Conewago".[81]

By 19 February, his visitations and discussions had reached a point where he wrote to Enoch Fenwick, at St Peter's church, Baltimore, to say that he now wished to speak to him, as executor of Archbishop Carroll's will, regarding an arrangement between the corporation and the superior of the mission. The matter was too detailed for an exchange of letters. It required discussion. "A forced measure" would not bring satisfaction. The Frs Neale and Edelen knew of his proposals, he said, and recommended their adoption. He then commented on Fenwick's delay in coming to the college, and remarked "in candour" that he, his brother, and Fr Wallace, did "not seem to manifest that interest for the concerns of this house and of our missions which every Jesuit ought to feel ... Occurrences should not lessen our attachment, whether they prove us to have been faulty or blameless."[82]

A few days later, he was writing in a partly optimistic vein to Fr Maleve at Fredericktown, north west of Georgetown, to the effect that though the difficulties at the college were many they were not insuperable and "with a little patience and concord" might be made better, though not as good as one might wish. He then added that the articles which Fr Kohlmann made the trustees sign did not stand up as a general rule of action, and that, in consequence, it would be necessary to draw up another arrangement which would have for its object "to secure that respect ... of the rights of law given to the trustees, and at the same time secure that respect and obedience which is due to the superior". He then stated firmly: "*the outlines of this arrangement will be as follows*".

The "*outlines*" contained seven headings, and covered three and a half quarto pages. In summary: they made the trustees consultors to the superior of the mission, on the lines of special advisers to a provincial, and various provisions were made for the filling of vacancies, and to meet occasions of disagreement between the superior and his consultors; a procurator-general of the missions, or farms, would be appointed by the superior of the mission, but the latter's choice had to be approved by at least three of the five trustees; this procurator-general (who, as noted, was a key figure in Kenney's plans) was to be the agent of the corporation and to present regular accounts to them, and if not a trustee himself was to have right of attendance at all consultations on the temporalities of the mission; he was not, however, to incur any extraordinary expenses without the consent of the superior, who, in turn, was to consult the trustees before granting or refusing permission. The superior was also to consult before appointing any one to be manager or superior at any residence. Moreover, property, in future, might not be alienated without the approval of the Holy See. And superiors of residences were not to be procurators or managers of the farms, if others were available; but in all other domestic concerns they were the director; and the manager, if a priest or religious brother, was to be subject to them in all matters of domestic discipline.[83]

Under these heads, he drew up his carefully balanced "Ordination for the Regulation of Temporal Affairs", and, as he later informed the general congregation of the Society: the material "was discussed over and over again"; he "heard the views of all so far as this was feasible"; and "it was accepted by everyone". After much deliberation, the man he opted to present for approval as procurator-general was Fr Adam Marshall, who had previously done mission work from the farm residences and now, as noted, taught humanities and physics at Georgetown; and, as he lived at the college, Kenney had had a chance to get to know him.

SECOND IMPRESSIONS, AND RECOMMENDATIONS TO THE GENERAL

Between visits to the farms, he engaged in considerable correspondence during February and March. On 4 March he wrote to the General, recalling that he had written the previous October, and December, and on 5 January. He now wished to convey his most recent impressions and recommendations.

First, he reiterated that out of the twenty priests he found no one suitable to be rector of the college *and* superior of the mission. Everything went to pieces, he observed, when Fr Grassi left. There had been complaints about him, especially from the foreign priests, but "those who opposed him were light weight in comparison to him". He asked that Grassi be obliged to return.

Speaking of the Jesuits individually, he pointed out that he had seen each one, but had not yet met with B. Fenwick and Wallace, who lived six hundred miles away. He then mentioned that he planned to have a special meeting during April with the priests of the corporation and the superior of the mission, and to "promulgate an ordinance relating to the authority of the superior in temporal matters, and the freedom of administration which the civil law of Maryland grants to a clerical corporation". He would send a copy to his Paternity.

Next, he spoke at some length about the superior, Fr Kohlmann, but in a manner very different from his previous report. All the fathers agree, he stated, that he should not hold executive authority. "Indeed," Kenney continued, "I myself am concerned about his extraordinary instability. When I see that he can so easily persuade himself that your Paternity's commands need not be carried out in certain cases,[84] how can I believe that my prescriptions will be observed. He is an exceptionally changeable man. He serves God wholeheartedly, believes firmly what the church teaches, he loves the Society and promotes it vigorously, but in other respects he will not be tomorrow what he is today. This is so, not through disobedience, but from a mental disease from which, as I hear, he always suffered and always will."[85] Pin-pointing the deficiency, in a subsequent letter to Fr Grassi in Rome, he observed: "the man who has last spoken to him gains him, and the last plan is always the best ... He is the victim of anyone who will only study to dupe him, nor need the intriguers study much."[86]

Kenney concluded the letter to the General with a fairly explicit reminder: "Fr Aylmer wants me back but I won't be able to leave before the end of April. And if I don't receive a command from your Paternity before that, I will wait till the beginning of June".[87]

Letters from Plowden had cautioned him against ending his visitation before hearing from Fr Brzozowski. Mentioning this in a letter to his contemporary in the Society in Ireland, Mathew Gahan, on 6 March, he added that "the necessity of the case, Fr Plowden's advice", and "the cry of all, say I ought not to stir before I hear from him". The simple, rather timid, but much loved Gahan, destined to become "the apostle of the Isle of Man", evoked from Kenney the few extant letters which conveyed some of his more general impressions of aspects of life in the United States during his first visitation.

Impressions on some more public issues

In the letter of 6 March he mentioned an item of Irish interest, namely, that he had received an affectionate letter from a mutual acquaintance, one Patrick Corrigan, who was, alas, "deeply engaged in a most scandalous schism", which had been developed by "Mr Carbery, the Dominican, formerly curate of St Michael and John", Dublin. Corrigan had wreaked dreadful havoc among the Irish in Norfolk, Virginia, as Carbery was doing among the Irish in New York, "by persuading them that every Catholic except themselves belonged to a French Sulpician or Jesuitical party combined against them". And this roused into fury national spirit and Irish pride.

On an issue of wider significance, which also had a particular relevance to his own role in the United States, he wrote:

> I have been several times to Congress! Great speaking! Oh! dear, 200 American republicans disputing *pro aris et focis* whether the state of Missouri should have slaves or not.

The issue excited an intense ferment, he continued, and threats to dissolve the union were quite common in Congress and elsewhere. It was eventually decided that Missouri would not be required to abolish slavery, but slavery would not be permitted in any new territory to be settled between Missouri and the Pacific Ocean. This compromise was considered essential by the politicians to prevent the separation of the southern from the eastern states and the emergence of two federal republics. "In fine," he concluded, "slavery is so interwoven with the actual existence of the freeborn American in the middle and southern states, that it cannot be touched ..."[88]

Slavery and the Jesuit farms

The entrenched nature of slavery, its intricate. involvement in the economic and social life of much of rural America, and the intensity of feeling as to its rights and wrongs, were brought home to Kenney not just by debates inside and outside Congress, but by the actual dependence of the Society in the United States on slave labour for the survival of its farms and its financial existence. He was conscious, too, as observed earlier, of the sensitivity of American Jesuits to criticism from foreign members of the order, "ignorant monarchists", who appreciated neither the country's republican traditions nor the Society's peculiar position in Maryland as a large landholder.[89]

Hence, he proceeded very cautiously on the question of slavery: knowing that he could undermine his whole position and influence as Visitor by moral strictures on the system. He contented himself with seeking to bring about improvement in the farms and in the condition of the slaves on them, while pointing ahead to a future without slave labour. And there was much room for attitudinal as well as material improvement, for as Cyprian Davis noted in his *History of Black Catholics in the United States*, "the assumption of black inferiority was an accepted part of the social and cultural landscape, a conclusion not to be questioned. On this point the majority of Catholics differed little from their contemporaries, whether in the south or the north."[90] And Kenney, almost inevitably, came to share something of that attitude.

The issue, indeed, begot ambivalence and confusion amongst the best intentioned. Christians, on both sides, quoted scripture in support of their viewpoint; and vehement supporters of human freedom in other contexts were divided on this. Thus, Irish nationalist, John Mitchell, who condemned Daniel O'Connell as half-hearted in his quest for liberty, proved a strong defender of the system of slavery in the United States; while O'Connell was one of the most principled and outspoken champions of abolition. And Bishop John England of Charleston, a noted supporter of Catholic emancipation in Ireland, and an extoller of freedom in the United States, stoutly supported the system against his old friend O'Connell. "Many bishops", indeed, "were slave owners; and inevitably some of them did engage in buying and selling slaves, just as many priests and religious did."[91]

John Carroll, himself, had been a slave owner, but uneasy about it; and he and the corporation made a number of resolutions about changing from slave to free labour, even to freeing the slaves, but never got around to enacting them.[92] Part of the reason, apart from the very considerable economic problems involved, was a sense of responsibility for the slaves, who were spoken of as "the family" in each farm. The Maryland Jesuits, indeed, appear to have conscientiously tried over the years to treat their slaves benignly, and to influence fellow-Catholic slave holders in that direction by word and example. As far back as 1749, George Hunter, the Maryland superior, wrote: "charity to

negroes is due from all, particularly their masters. As they are members of
Jesus Christ ... they are to be dealt with in a charitable, Christian, paternal
manner; which is, at the same time, a great means to bring them to their duty
to God and therefore to gain their souls."[93] Accordingly, slaves, in their eyes,
had certain basic rights: to adequate food, clothing, shelter; proper care when
they were old or sick; and Christian marriage in which the spouses were not
separated by being sold off individually, or split up for economic purposes.[94]

Dependants of the slaves were also looked after, and, indeed, the high per-
centage of underage or superannuated slaves was one of the factors making for
the uneconomical state of Jesuit farms.[95] Jesuit slaves, as, indeed, the slaves of
many churchmen, were generally considered to be underworked, and to have
"a soft life".

This treatment was blamed by some for the licence and indiscipline in evidence on a number of the farms. Neither moral offence nor laziness were punished, William Beschter wrote from Georgetown some years later, and so "our
slaves corrupt ... with impunity", and the proverb was warranted "he is as bad
as a priest's slave".[96] Promiscuity was prevalent; and in places a high percent-
age did not attend religious service.[97] One plantation manager, Br Mobberly, a
native of Maryland, who had thought and written about slavery, had ambivalent feelings about it existing on a Jesuit mission, and had experienced the
growing discontent and corruption among the slaves at St Inigoes farm
between 1806 and 1820. The real problem, in Mobberly's view, lay in lack of
discipline.[98] He set himself to rectify the matter, but found that his Negroes
had the last word.

The slaves of the Jesuits had the, perhaps, unique opportunity of voicing
their complaints and problems to a superior higher than their local master.[99]
They grasped the opportunity eagerly at Kenney's visitations; and he, as will
appear, brought their complaints about the brother's severity before the corporation, and Mobberly was removed within a month.[100]

Despite the evidence of benign treatment, the living conditions in 1820
were generally very poor. The economic recession added to the squalor and
debts of farms already crippled by bad management.[101] The well-being of the
slaves, therefore, was inextricably linked to the condition of the farms. In
trying to solve the problems of the latter, Kenney was also improving the lot
of "the family".

The 12,000 acres of Jesuit land was mainly disposed in estates in the southern counties of Maryland, and in two smaller plantations on the eastern shore.
They also included, however, two farms, totalling more than 1,700 acres, at
Conewago and Goshenhoppen in eastern Pennsylvania. Kenney's initial overall
impression of the plantations, as indicated in his first letter to his Paternity,
was of "so much apparent wealth and real poverty ... complaints of land mismanagement, unprofitable contracts, useless and expensive experiments and
speculations".[102] The impression was subsequently confirmed by Adam

Marshall, in a measured report to the new General, in 1821, following a visitation of all the plantations and houses.[103]

When, therefore, Kenney met with the corporation in April 1820, preparatory to finalising his "Rules and Ordinances on the Administration of Temporal Matters",[104] he was concerned to emphasise that proper management was a basic requirement. Good order and regularity were essential. And with regard to complaints about the disorder and low work rate of the black people, he expressed the belief that when regularity was established in a house, the servants too would become regular.[105] After much discussion, there was agreement on the ordinances on temporal administration, which followed, though in greater detail, the outlines given earlier in his letter to Fr Maleve. That achieved, he made out, perhaps towards the end of April, an important overall statement for "The Consultors of the Mission on its Actual State and all its Concerns".

Statement and recommendations to the consultors

This document embraced in its compass "Religious Discipline" and "Studies" among the members of the Society, but the main focus was on "Temporalities".

Under that heading he touched on the points mentioned previously, the general inefficiency and bad management at the farms, and the absence of a uniform system of book-keeping. Moving to the central issues covered by his ordinances, he emphasised that the wishes of all had been consulted, so far as possible, and that the intention was not "to make farmers or teach agriculture", nor to instantly remove every evil, but to "establish a system of cooperation, a uniformity of action, regularity in the accounts, and a constant inspection over all the farms". In fine, "the principles of regulation" were being established. The details would be worked out by good sense, good will, and experience. The ordinances aimed to ensure that "authority and subordinate co-operation" were "so poised as to prevent excess in any party"; so that no one need mistrust and all might "strongly confide in each other".

His statement then dwelt on the choice of a procurator of the mission, who would also be the agent of the corporation. He went through various names, requesting their advice. Strangely, he did not mention Adam Marshall at this stage.

Having dealt with the overall principles and framework for the farms and their management, he moved on to the sensitive issue of the slaves. From his meetings with them, from general observation, and from discussions and advice, he was clear about what could be done. He determined to be quite pragmatic, never censorious, not to appear to take side with the blacks, and to get the consultors themselves to take on responsibility for policy. That way, decisions had a chance of being both effective and lasting. The matters to which he felt it necessary to draw attention were themselves a commentary on the situation of the slaves in the prevailing culture – even in reputedly "softer" plantations.

"The consultors are requested," he stated, "to make an arrangement on the treatment which the slaves are to receive on all our farms"; an arrangement "from which the local procurator", or immediate manager, "cannot depart". As things stood, there was "a sort of arbitrary regulation", which differed from farm to farm, and could be changed by any new manager. And this, he said, "gives these querulous creatures cause to complain, even when they are not ill-used. They are in general disaffected towards their immediate manager."

At St Inigoes, he continued, they were "furious against Br Mobberly", and there was scant hope that he could "do good by remaining". Indeed, he added, "there have been instances of undue treatment, even allowing for exaggerations". All this should be prevented; and it could only be done effectively by the corporation.

He then instanced areas where he thought the consultors should intervene with respect to the treatment of the slaves.

1. "Let their rations be fixed – (in some places they have only had one pound and a quarter of meat: often this has not been sound)."

2. Say "whether they are to be allowed to rear poultry or not, and hogs".

3. "Whether they are to have half of Saturday to themselves."

4. Insist "that pregnant women should not be whipped.

5. "That this chastisement should not be inflicted" on any female in the house where the priest lives – sometimes they have been tied up in the priest's own parlour, which is very indecorous."

6. "That they should all be sent to church on Ash-Wednesday and Good Friday, and on the patron saints of the church or places, if kept with solemnity; though, of course, they may be made to work the rest of the day."

7. The consultors need "to devise more effective means to promote morality and the frequentation of the sacraments"; because "the crimes that are reported of our slaves, and their neglect of duties the most sacred to a Christian, are a reproof to a Society that taught sanctity to savages; but when these crimes are committed in the very threshold of the sanctuary, the scandal is enormous."

After this, he moved to the general problem of slave ownership: directing the attention of the consultors, or trustees of the corporation, to the possibility, and desirability, of having other means of working the plantations.

"Great zeal, piety, prudence and charity, with a regular system, are requisite," he said, "to check the evils attendant on the possession of slaves. As long as our farms are cultivated by them, such constant exertions alone can keep them from becoming scenes of iniquity and disorder." And, in peroration, he added: "Should the day ever come that the corporation will deem it feasible to get rid of the slaves, either by employing whites, or letting out their lands to reputable tenants; or any other way in which it can be effected without injury to the property, it is unnecessary to say *that such an event will relieve this mission of an immense burthen, and a painful responsibility, and the whole Society of the odium which is thrown on it by people who speak without consideration or the knowledge of the actual state of things in this country.*"[106]

He rounded off his statement on "the actual state" of the mission and all its concerns, by saying that he considered it expedient to make such to the consultors, not just to convey details with which they might already be acquainted, "but rather to put them in possession of the view which" he had "taken, and the opinions" he had "formed, from all that" he had "as yet been able to see or hear".[107]

A further comment on the temporalities and the slaves, also during the month of April, was made in a letter to Fr Louis De Barth, vicar general, Philadelphia, and an agent of the corporation. Having remarked that he would feel "quite happy" if he had a procurator-general of the missions and a rector for the college, Kenney added:

> All the trustees are quite content with the arrangements I have made on the temporalities and are desirous to have them carried into effect. They seem inclined even to part with the slaves and to let the lands out, or to manage them without Negroes. This, of course, is no order of mine. I leave this quite to themselves, but such a change cannot suddenly take place or ever without a sure prospect of its being for the better.[108]

It was an approach reflecting a salutary circumspection, which was to be sadly lacking many years later, 1838, when the slaves were sold *en masse*, much to their disadvantage, the shame of the Society, and public scandal. In the immediate term, Br Mobberly was removed, and three other managers had been removed or demoted within a period of two years as a result of his report and ordinances and the subsequent recommendations of the man he chose for procurator-general, Adam Marshall.[109]

Writing to the new General, Fr Fortis, on 22 June 1823, one of the trustees of the corporation, Fr Leonard Edelen, remarked of Kenney's contribution to the farms and the well-being of the mission:

> Upon the whole, I think our spirituals and temporalities have been much amended, since the ordinances of the Fr Kenney, late Visitor to this country, have been adopted. They place things in a more regular order and permanent state. By strictly adhering to them we may hope still for better times.

He added, however, that one thing to be still "mostly lamented is that unity and charity are not yet entirely restored among us ...".[110]

The reference to deficiencies in "unity and charity" at that time reflected the continuance of the tension between "foreigners" and native born Americans; though it was nothing like as intense as during Kohlmann's term as superior. Kenney's changes had eased matters; and it also appears that changes he instituted in attitudes to management and in personnel led, by the 1830s, to a significant improvement in the revenue and general condition of the plantations.[111]

COLLEGE SURVIVAL OR CLOSURE? STRAINING AT THE BRINK

In the meantime, where Georgetown College was concerned, he was finding it difficult to see his way. The General's restriction on his changing the superior, and the archbishop's opposition to any withdrawal of men from pastoral work in the archdiocese, presented immense obstacles. He went through moments of intense gloom, as his first letter to Fr Brzozowski indicated, and as Plowden perceived in the letters he received from him. The objections of Wallace, Ben Fenwick and Baxter to Kohlmann's rectorship, and the archbishop's opposition to their return to the college, led Plowden, indeed, to advise him "to abandon the idea of a college as a forlorn hope".

His English friend, now carrying the burden of provincial, proposed instead that the existing institution be reduced to "a day school, or a pension-ate for little boys", which could be run by the German Jesuits who were readi-ly available. From these, he could select a band of youth of ability and good will whom he could bring over "to undergo a complete Jesuitical education, noviciate and studies, partly at Clongowes, partly at Rome". After a number of years, these would be "formed men" able to renew Georgetown College. Plowden concluded: "all this may seem impracticable; you will know best, but for our part I see no other chance".[112]

Although Kenney would be reduced, even as late as the end of May, to wishing that when Kohlmann put Fenwick and Baxter out, he had also "closed the college at the same time, for then our credit would have been saved, and we should not now be so puzzled how to keep it open";[113] there is no evidence that he actually contemplated closing it. Indeed, by the time Plowden's letter arrived on 7 April he was already beginning to see the way forward. Towards the close of that month he wrote to Francis Neale and Louis De Barth, and the consultors, in such a way as to indicate that he envisaged Fr Kohlmann giving up the office of president, or rector, of the college and moving to the Society's house in Washington as superior of the mission – to which, also, the masters and Jesuit theological students might move, thereby giving much needed room to the residence at Georgetown where "the masters and scholas-tics and lay-brothers" slept "all together like boys in a dormitory".[114]

Kohlmann's departure to Washington would make way for a new president at Georgetown, and the possibility of an amicable return of B. Fenwick and

Wallace, and the tiding over of the college till the young men returned from Rome.[115] If the Fenwicks and Wallace were available, Kenney confided to his friend De Barth, "matters would soon be in great part adjusted". But unfortunately the archbishop was so much against any one missioner being recalled, that he, Kenney, was driven to "the alternatives of displeasing him, or of letting all here go to ruin". "Had we," he concluded, "a procurator of the missions for the college, I should feel quite happy."[116]

Braving the bishop

His reluctance to assert his right to recall the Fenwicks and Wallace was based on the experience of two previous stressful encounters with Dr Marechal. For much as he disliked exercising authority and the occasions of confrontation to which it gave rise, he had nerved himself to go against the archbishop with respect to two men whom he considered essential to the college and community.

The first encounter concerned Baxter's recall from Richmond to Georgetown, alluded to earlier; the second arose from the community at the college. He had composed the new custom book with the assistance of the community; but to secure its observance there was needed, in accordance with the order's tradition, a Fr Minister responsible for the "regularity of religious observance". Such a man, in Kenney's view, should be allowed to "grow old in the job" so as to ensure stability in religious discipline. For this key role there was, he believed, only one proper person, Fr Carey, who, though he had no experience of college life, was a man whose piety, popularity, prudence and mild manners would supply for other deficiencies.[117]

Although Fr Carey was active in pastoral work from a Jesuit mission station, and his withdrawal was likely to excite strong opposition from Dr Marechal, Kenney went ahead. On 20 March 1820, in a letter home to Fr Esmonde, he reported: "Our good archbishop has commenced a war because I took a father from the mission to be minister of the college. I keep in the shade and let Mr Kohlmann fight the battle *fortiter* and *suaviter*" (strongly and agreeably). The bishops of America, he added, had issued what they called an "article of discipline" whereby no missioner from a religious congregation could be recalled unless he appeared to the bishop to be entirely necessary to the existence or progress of the said congregation. Hence, if the two men most necessary for the college were withdrawn from Charleston, there would be a major commotion. So, he observed ruefully, "we find ourselves in perfect slavery in this land of liberty".[118]

The situation revived all his longing to be free of the government of others. He yearned to be quiet again on a mission, though it were in Connacht or on the banks of the Missouri. There was indeed "an enormous overflow of Irish" in every state of the Union, and he understood that great numbers flock to the new settlements in the west, where they and their children might live and die without sight of a priest.[119] His spontaneous reaction did not prevent him, nevertheless, from providing, from "the shade", for Fr Kohlmann, a lengthy memorandum in response to Dr Marechal's co-ordinated complaints and claims.

Among its forthright declarations was the reminder that what was essentially involved in the case of Fr Carey was the removal of a Jesuit from one Jesuit house to another. If the consent of the bishop were required for this, he observed, the spiritual privilege, or exemption, of all religious orders was at issue. But their privilege of exemption was granted by the Holy See and could only be revoked by it. Again, there was the matter of the religious vow of obedience. In refusing a man permission to leave the diocese, or a part of the diocese, was his Grace stating that he exempted him from his vow, that he was not to obey his religious superior? But that, surely, was a matter beyond episcopal jurisdiction.

Dr Marechal's claims, Kenney continued, would seem to make him a kind of general superior of the various houses of the order in the United States, so that religious superiors would not be free to recall men even to save their own houses from ruin. That would be an intolerable situation, and would destroy all discipline in religious life. Faced with such subversion of the government of the order, Kenney declared, Fr Kohlmann should not hesitate to make clear that the Society would sooner withdraw its subjects from America to be employed where ecclesiastical authority would put no obstacle to the practice of their religious way of life ... And he provided two historical instances where the Jesuit General had taken such action, once in 1600, and once in quite recent years.

He remained unbending with regard to Carey; but the trouble and stress involved made him painfully conscious of a more extensive and intensive "war" in the event of Benedict Fenwick and Wallace being recalled. Yet he could not see how he could fulfil his commission without them. They were essential to the college, and had even come to feature in his plans for a new rector.

Search for a rector

All were agreed, he wrote Fr Grassi on 31 May, that the college would never succeed while Fr Kohlmann was rector. "The manner in which the masters have been appointed, the changes made on the complaints of the scholars, would be enough to ruin any regulated house, and yet he does not see this." People outside now took little interest in the university. "It were to be wished that a native should be rector, and *then it would not be of much consequence who were superior of the mission.*"[120] There were four possible candidates: Benedict Fenwick, Adam Marshall, James Wallace, and Enoch Fenwick.

Benedict Fenwick would be the man most desirable for the reputation of the house, Kenney continued, but all the foreign fathers disliked the prospect and a greater impediment was the disposition of that father himself, who, he feared, was alienated from the Society and seemed disposed to accept a bishopric. Earlier, in writing to the consultors of the mission, he had made it clear that with regard to Fenwick he could speak "only … from the reports of others" as he had avoided coming to see him and was evasive in his correspondence.[121] Marshall lived in the college, and if he were more known to the world, better acquainted with its manners and the Society's rules, he would have little difficulty in choosing him for rector.

Wallace and E. Fenwick were the only two left, he remarked as he concluded this section of his letter to Grassi. "May God direct, which I should choose. If Wallace were *less American*, the choice were easy."[122] The fact that Wallace was now in the running was an indication of the extent to which Kenney had freed himself from Kohlmann's influence, how much, in effect, he had put aside his own feelings after receiving a hostile letter from Wallace, and how limited the choice was. Wallace, too, had avoided coming to meet him.

He decided to recall Benedict Fenwick and Wallace to Georgetown, and to decide between them there. Having taken the decision, he wrote firmly to Archbishop Marechal on 11 June pointing out that he wished to appoint either of the Fenwicks or Wallace as rector, and that if matters went on as they had been at Georgetown there would "not be twenty scholars in the house this year". The remedy would have been had sooner, he said, had not a fear of distressing and displeasing the archbishop deterred the superior from recalling Frs Benedict Fenwick and Wallace. He recognised his Grace's great needs, but it had to be stated that "if the college be not better supported it will sink, and your Grace will consider who it is that withholds the only devisable remedy".[123]

After such straight talking, he suffered the chagrin of the two Jesuits not coming to Georgetown. Fenwick never refused. He just kept deferring his arrival, making one excuse after another as to why he could not get away. Wallace, on the other hand, bluntly refused to come until Kohlmann and McElroy were removed from the college, and he quoted from the institute of the Society disputing Kenney's authority over him. Further correspondence ensued, and a refusal to obey a formal injunction. Kenney was placed in the position not only of dismissing any thought of him as rector, but of dismissing him from the Society.

He sought the advice of the consultors, delayed and pondered, and then reached the point of writing a letter announcing his dismissal on 30 July 1820. He had used a gentle approach, he declared, tried to be a friend, but found his express injunction met by a formal refusal and that repeated. Disobedience that was "deliberate, formal and avowed" such as this was deemed "incorrigible" and called for the extreme remedy of dismissal. He added that a Jesuit who searched the institute only to read lectures to his superior was like the man who studied the scriptures to find an apology for his own conduct.[124]

He mentioned in the letter that he was imposing on the superior the task of dismissing him. This may have been partly due to the fact that he felt he had only a little time left in the United States. In the event, he abandoned his written communication: influenced, perhaps, by consultors like Leonard Edelen who felt Wallace should get another chance – a period on probation until a new superior was appointed.[125]

In fact, James Wallace took the decision himself in September: applying to Kohlmann for dimission.[126] After his departure, he, ironically, returned to teaching mathematics and philosophy: receiving an appointment at Columbia College, South Carolina. He remained a priest in Bishop John England's diocese of Charleston until his death in 1851.[127]

Long before this, of course, it was clear that Enoch Fenwick, vicar general of the archdiocese, was the only candidate left. In his letter to the General of 2 December 1819, Kenney, relying on what he had been told, had spoken of him as having talent and learning, though he had not completed his studies, and was lacking in the prudence, holiness and charity needed in a superior.[128] When he met him, however, in April 1820, he liked him and wished he were available for the college. At that stage he felt that if Fenwick made it clear that he wished to return to Georgetown there would be some chance of the archbishop agreeing.[129] He subsequently appears to have coaxed the reluctant Fenwick to that end; and then on 7 July raised the matter himself with the archbishop. The latter was dining at the college in the company of three Indian chiefs, one of whom made a speech honouring him as his "Great Father". In this benign climate, Kenney pressed that Enoch Fenwick be freed from the cathedral at Baltimore to be president of the college. When Marechal objected and pointed to the great difficulties this would cause in the Baltimore congregation, Kenney remained adamant. His Grace could not refuse, he declared, without exposing the most important of their establishments to a certain ruin.[130] On 26 July, the publication of the new prospectus of the college served as the means of announcing Enoch Fenwick's appointment as president.[131]

The quiet manner in which the whole business was conducted was typical of the visitation. "As yet," Baxter wrote to Grassi as late as 4 June 1820, "Fr Visitor has not done much ostensibly."[132] And this from one who had been uprooted from Richmond. He hoped, nevertheless, that Kenney would be the new rector of the college. And just three days later, as a further comment on the favourable, if unobtrusive, impression made by the Visitor, John McElroy, the procurator at Georgetown and an evident admirer, wrote to Grassi urging Kenney's appointment as both rector and overall superior: "Never was there a clergymen in this country," he said, "more universally esteemed, particularly by the native Americans, and indeed by foreigners. His perfect knowledge of the English language, his particular talent for government, his amiable and unassuming manners, has endeared him to all persons to whom he has been introduced." He warned Grassi to be on his guard against the representations of the Irish Jesuits to have Kenney return home, even though there was no comparison between what he could do there, in a country with so many priests, and what he could achieve in America; and he concluded with the hope that the Revd Fr would order him to remain.[133]

The reference to the "Fr Vicar-General" introduced an element that changed the situation very considerably for Kenney and, indeed, for the whole Society: for it reflected the recent announcement to the Jesuits in the United States of the death of the General, Tadeusz Brzozowski.

The interregnum – "To stay or return?" – Pressure to conclude

Towards the end of April 1820, Kenney had received a letter from Plowden dated 25 March, which confided to him in strictest secrecy 'till official confirmation came, that "Fr Brzozowski, the General, after nine days illness, died as he had lived, most piously, at Polotsk, on 24 January, that is on February 5th" by western measurement. The powers of a Visitor expired with the death of a General, Plowden continued, but this did not apply in Kenney's case, as the provision was made in the institute of the Society that "the faculties and powers of Visitors *out of Europe* do not expire at the death of the General" but continue as if he were still living.[134]

The news added to Kenney's concern about the duration of the visitation; and where before he wondered when he would receive a reply from the General, his concern now was whether his letters had ever reached him, and if they had whether they had then been forwarded to Rome, or had they gone astray. And with the further news that the order had been expelled from all Russia's dominions, came the added anxiety that the letters might have fallen into unfriendly hands and be misused. Unable to speak with any one about the matter, he eventually, on 31 May, wrote to Grassi, with the intention of sending the letter with the six young men destined for Rome.

He hoped, he said, that his letters of January and March had been sent on to Rome "since the decease of our chief, known only to me here". He then summarised what he had put in the two letters to the General, and added the solution he had come to about separating the office of rector and general superior. He pointed out also that Fr Kohlmann was due out of office in September, and that the General had asked him to recommend a successor. He had reported to Fr Brzozowski that the only suitable person among the native Americans was Fr Charles Neale; and that of the foreign priests, Fr Kohlmann, with all his defects, was the least objectionable.[135]

The occasion of the scholastics' departure was used to send several letters to Rome. Some amounted to pointed documents in praise of Kenney and requesting his retention in America. Fr Maleve wrote from Frederickstown, north west of Georgetown, where Kenney had written his letter of 31 May, to inform Grassi that the Visitor had given "an excellently great sermon on the Real Presence yesterday [Corpus Christi day] ... His eloquence attracted all our Catholics, and many of the best informed Protestants, who were present at the procession. May he remain in this country for the sake of our Society and the mission in general. There is nobody here who can bring things together again."[136] A further encomium on Kenney's pulpit eloquence was penned the same day, 2 June, by Kohlmann writing from Georgetown. Having given the names of the six scholastics, made comments on each,[137] and expressed the hope that their sojourn at the very centre of the Christian world would enable them "to become the very pillars of the Society in the new world", he added, almost in passing, the remarkable tribute: "Fr Kenney is still here, and has acquired in the short time of his residence in this country a higher reputation as a preacher than ever anyone before him is known to have enjoyed."[138] Also destined to travel with the young Jesuits was Baxter's letter, already noted, with its request for Kenney's retention.

To the latter's relief, official confirmation of the General's death arrived from Plowden at the beginning of June.[139] He immediately set about informing the various houses of the mission, and his letter also mentioned that the order had been expelled from Russia on 31 March. Writing to the Neale brothers on 6 June, he expressed relief that "the tedious and precarious ... Russian correspondence" was at an end, informed them that Fr Aloysius Petrucci had been appointed Vicar-General by the late General, and brought them fully up to date with the news that "our six good youths left us an hour since ... on ship from Georgetown to Gibraltar".[140]

He was undoubtedly aware that the young men were bearing letters calling for his retention in the United States. What he probably had not foreseen was that the news of the General's death, the anticipation of change, and the sense of relative proximity to Rome, as distinct from Russia, would generate new expectations for the American mission, and an increased demand for his retention there. John McElroy's eulogy and request was written the next day;[141] and the following day again Kohlmann wrote to Vicar-General, Petrucci, asking that Kenney be allowed to stay, and stating that in this request he had the unanimous support of the consultors both of the mission and of the college. There was a great shortage of manpower on the mission, he declared, but especially of those with skill in management and authority, and hence there was great need of Kenney, "with his firmness in action and gentleness in manner, to stabilise our Society for action". The need was much greater than at Dublin. There was a daily increasing number of Christians looking for leadership and catechising, and the Indians ardently begged for Society missionaries. Fr Grassi could confirm all this, Kohlmann told the Vicar-General, and also that America was unique in the world in this, "that it can never happen that the Society here will ever suffer persecution, not unless the fundamentals and constitution of this state are completely overthrown". Hence, their united prayers beseeched for the progress of the Society, that Fr Kenney be ascribed to this mission in place of Fr Grassi.[142]

Kenney was in considerable doubt as to whether to stay or return.[143] After reflection however, he determined to press on with completing his commission; and so, a few days later, on 11 June, he wrote his forthright letter to Dr Marechal on the need to recall Frs Ben Fenwick and Wallace to the college.[144] He sought to adhere to the timescale to which he had adjusted himself before he heard of Fr Brzozowski's death, and which envisaged a return home in August. The impetus towards return appears to have been increased, moreover, by the awareness that the archbishop, despite their differences, was pressing hard to have him appointed to the new see of Philadelphia.[145] And although he was probably not aware of it, his position and reputation had also led to his name being put forward for the see of New York. On 26 August 1820, Bishop Du Bourg, then resident at St Louis, wrote to Bishop Plessis of Quebec to support his petition. "I find all the qualities which so difficult a commission requires united in Father Kenney," he said, "provincial or visitor of the Jesuits in Maryland. He is an Irishman, a thing essential to turn aside national jealousies; and, if I am to believe all the reports about him, he is a man of rare talent, vigour and prudence ... I have had the assurance to write about him to Rome."[146]

Later, Kenney was to justify his departure from America to the General on the grounds that he wished to avoid the see of Philadelphia; and also because he had accomplished as much as could be done, considering that he had no authority to replace the superior; because his commission left it unclear how long he should stay, and his return was sought in Ireland; and because, and this seems like a reason after the event, he wished to place before his Paternity, or the Vicar-General, the needs of the mission.[147]

During June and July, meanwhile, he continued to work quietly and persistently: persuading, consulting, asserting in the case of the archbishop, in an attempt to finalise the choice and appointment of a rector of the college and a procurator-general of the mission. As throughout his visitation, his colleagues continued to be impressed by his patience, prudence, energy, and what McElroy termed his "amiable and unassuming manner";[148] and yet, as noted many times already, Kenney expressed his own abhorrence of government, especially the government of ecclesiastics.

A tenuous clue to the apparent contradiction was, perhaps, presented the previous March by a passing remark to his old friend, Gahan: "You know my impetuosity, and also the facility with which I can content myself with even unexpected results."[149] If for "impetuosity" one understood the mixture of driving energy, and that impatience with the circumspection and hesitancy of others which was reflected in his railing at "the vile timidity of Sicilians" in the face of "tyrannical treatment ... from Scotch generals", and in his assertion of the independence of mission from the English province, then the patience, prudence and amiability expected of a religious superior were exhibited by him only at the cost of persistent self-vigilance. The outward ease indicated by the reference to his "amiable and unassuming manner" was probably assisted, however, by his stated facility to easily content himself. This more passive, undemanding side was further suggested in another letter to Gahan, in which he remarked that he was almost penniless but was loath to ask for any money from the mission. They were so miserably poor in the midst of wealth, that he was sure it would be difficult to get what would send him home. "It is true, I want nothing; equally true that I have not a *cent* at my disposal."[150]

By the beginning of July, as seen earlier, he had persuaded a reluctant Enoch Fenwick to accept the position of rector; and by the end of the month had encouraged an equally reluctant Adam Marshall to be procurator-general.[151] He obtained the support of the various consultors, and of Fr Kohlmann, for his choices.

Meanwhile, on 20 July, Plowden wrote to say that he had been called to Rome to attend a general congregation to elect a new General, and that the Vicar-General had issued an order for Kenney to remain in America until the future General gave him further instructions. He presumed that the order had been forwarded to him.[152] It is not clear when such orders were sent. For there was a letter sent to Kenney from Vicar-General Petrucci, as late as 7 September, instructing him to stay on in the United States until matters were fully in order, and promising to send him some professors of higher studies.[153] It is also not clear, that Kenney received any such instructions while he was in the United States.[154] Certainly, he was well on his way to Europe by the time Petrucci's letter of 7 September was written. Already on 30 August 1820, Fr Kohlmann had written his valediction in a letter to the Vicar-General:

> Fr Kenney has departed, having completed his visitation. He has won the hearts of all.[155]

He was not fortunate in his choice of men, or rather, perhaps, was unfortunate in having so few suitable candidates available. Enoch Fenwick as rector was not a success. He seemed to view his task apathetically as building up "a college which has one foot in the grave".[156] He lasted only two years. In 1822 he was succeeded by his brother, Benedict, who returned to the college after Charles Neale replaced Kohlmann as superior and transferred McElroy to a parish in southern Maryland. He first took McElroy's place as procurator, and then became rector or president. He, too, made little impact, and happily left to become bishop of Boston. Baxter, whom Kenney chose as prefect of studies, left the Society in 1824; and Adam Marshall, his choice for procurator-general, did likewise the same year.[157]

The visitation, nevertheless, had a number of beneficial and lasting effects.

It brought order into the temporal administration, improved discipline and introduced structures and customs promoting order and team-effort, separated the office of college rector and superior of the mission, and managed, at least, to keep the college open, and then ensured the future by approving the sending to Rome of the six scholastics – William McSherry, Thomas Mulledy, John Smith, Charles C. Pise, George Fenwick, and James Ryder – three of whom, Mulledy, McSherry, and Ryder, all first or second generation Irish Americans, were destined, on their return in 1828, to revitalise the college and, between them, to occupy the president's office for almost twenty-two years between 1829 and 1851.[158]

And what of the impact on Kenney himself? He was left with warm and abiding memories. On the feast of his patron saint, 29 June 1821, he recalled "the goodness and affection" with which he was treated "last St Peter's day by Mr Kohlmann and the community at Georgetown". "Salute everyone for me," he requested John McElroy, "write about everyone to me."[159] And two months later, he wrote James Ryder at Rome that not even the public entry of George IV into Dublin, and the shouts of 300,000 voices rending the air, could distract his thoughts from America. "Had there been no danger of being made rector or superior, I should have asked to go back before I left Rome."[160] The following year, he longed once more for "a quiet mission in the US" but dreaded the prospect of "colleges and the government of ecclesiastics".[161]

So there remained a strong emotional attachment and attraction, but restricted by that recurring plaintive note: that turning of a blind eye to the demands of historical living; a persisting enigma in an otherwise pragmatic and hard-headed man. It was as if he carried within himself, apart from other considerations about authority, a romantic image of mission work as direct ministry to people, unconfined by the demands of organization and discipline, and the burdens of finance and careful diplomacy. With all his practicality in many fields, that side to him, where the United States was concerned, found exulted stimulus in the Jesuit tradition of 150 years of apostolic endeavour and martyrdom among Indian tribes. During his Visitation he shared with his friend, Gahan, an account of two recent occurrences which evoked that tradition and added to the lure of the new world mission. The bishop of Bardstown had told him that at the extremity of his diocese, near Detroit, Indian tribes still revered Fr L'Allemont and the other Jesuit martyrs and had recently erected a cross at the spot where he was killed; and Kenney related further instances of Indian tribes cherishing the memory of the Black Robes and preserving an identity with Catholicism despite their abandonment following the suppression of the Society.[162]

The instances were the stuff of romance, joined to the Gospel call to leave all and follow. The appeal of America, as a result, had become part of him. It was to move him to preserve a live interest in developments there, and it disposed him to make a further valuable contribution in a later Visitation.

But the months and years ahead were very much unknown territory as he departed the United States after his first period as Visitor. It was a distinct possibility that he might be ordered by the new General to return straightway.

BRINGING THE MISSION TO ROME

He arrived at Liverpool early in September, unexpected, almost penniless, and without any clear idea as to what to do next. He did not know, it would appear, about the general congregation, since his first action was to write to Plowden at Stonyhurst. As the latter was on his way to Rome, the superior, Fr Tristram, answered the letter and invited him to Stonyhurst.[163] There, as Kenney put it, he found that it was "the decided opinion of everyone" that his "late commission" required him to go to Rome. It was also, he admitted, his own mind. A written report on the American mission was unlikely to have much effect. This was evident, he believed, "from the notion, or rather no notion, which the late General seemed to have of the true state of things there, not withstanding all that Grassi wrote". Besides, he feared that his previous reports to the General had perished in the commotion that shook Polotsk soon after their arrival there.[164]

Given his shortage of money, Fr Sewall, and other members of the community, formed a subscription towards paying his expenses; and in consideration of the position in which he stood in consequence of the Vicar-General's letter, which they understood had been sent to him, the superior thought it better that he set out immediately for Italy "both to relate the success of his visitation, and recruit members for that very important station". It was also hoped that he would render assistance to Fr Plowden in his business at Rome.[165]

He left straightway: enduring with his customary energy and determination the hardship of horse-drawn travel and indifferent lodging, not just across Britain but along the winding roads and mountain passes to Rome. On 16 September, after staying overnight at the Union Inn at the foot of the white Dover, he set sail at 11.00 a.m. in fine weather. Before leaving, he wrote to Esmonde, in the absence of Aylmer at the general congregation, informing him and the Irish Jesuits of his plans. He mentioned that his health had been very good up to quite recently. "I passed the winter much better than I should have done in Ireland," he wrote. "I never once coughed, but had not been two days in Liverpool when I began again."[166] The respiratory infection accompanied him to Italy.

He found he was in good time for the congregation. It had been postponed by papal mandate during September, and then unexpectedly recalled by the pope on 4 October. Aylmer, writing home three days later, was not sure when the congregation would be able to get under way. Kenney had not yet arrived, he said, and then, in an ambiguous sentence, observed that the Vicar-General's letter to Kenney was written on the supposition of the congregation being deferred until spring.[167]

At the congregation, subsequently, Aylmer was admitted to represent Ireland, and Kenney "on American business".[168] Late in October, he grasped the unique opportunity of presenting to representatives of the entire Society an "Account of the State of the Jesuit Mission in America".

Report on the mission

After an historical introduction to enable the assembly to understand why he was sent to the mission as Visitor, he outlined the threefold mandate given him by Fr Brzozowski:

1. To settle temporal affairs, and also to restrict the authority of the superior if necessary.
2. To secure and strengthen discipline in the Society.
3. To bring delinquent priests to a more productive and fruitful life.

He then indicated the main steps he had taken under each heading: providing a summary, in effect, of what he had accomplished.

On the administration of *temporal affairs*, he made out a procedure, he said, which, if executed exactly and firmly, would eliminate all quarrels about temporal affairs. With respect to discipline, he had removed the novices from the college and set up a separate noviciate twenty-five miles away; had transferred the scholastics, theologians and philosophers, from the college to a spacious house (in Washington) which had been derelict for three years and was in danger of being lost to the order; and for the overall good of the mission had separated the offices of rector of the college and superior of the mission. The latter took up residence in the new house of studies in Washington. To standardise discipline in the college and noviceship, he had composed appropriate custom books; and had also found it necessary to lay down rules on obedience, silence, and fraternal charity, and also with regard to the studies of the scholastics. On the issue of *"delinquent priests"*, he reported his experiences with Baxter, Wallace and Benedict Fenwick, (without mentioning names) and the steps he had taken.

He then went on to speak more widely of the mission: dwelling on its problem aspects, presumably to emphasise its need of assistance. Of the 24 Jesuit priests in North America, he remarked, not one was suitable to govern or to teach theology or philosophy, and the mission residences were not producing good results because many of the Jesuits had an inadequate knowledge of the language and customs of the country, and the secular priests with whom they worked spread hostile rumours about the Jesuits among the people. A third reason for the ineffectiveness, he declared, was because there were in the Society's houses a type of servant called "slaves", many of whom constantly complained about the Jesuits, and lived in such an abandoned manner that they were a scandal to Catholics and heretics alike. Finally, there was shortage of manpower, and Jesuit missions, houses and churches were being given over to the use of secular priests, and were in danger of being lost to the Society.

Such, he concluded, was "the miserable state of a mission" which had been in existence for 200 years and presently possessed 12,000 acres of rather good land, a college, a noviceship, a house of studies, 12 residences or missions, and 14 public churches. It contained, he added: "24 priests, 20 approved scholastics – including 8 who are in Rome,[169] 20 brothers, 10 novice scholastics, and 7 brother novices. In all 81." He finished, however, with a message of hope and a recommendation. Despite "the evils" from which the mission suffered, "future progress should not be despaired of," he declared, "provided help and opportune remedies" were "quickly adopted". To this end, he recommended:

> Either the congregation should set up a deputation concerning American affairs, or refer the entire matter to the General so that he can, as soon as possible, approve of the ordinations, adopt remedies, and send assistance to America.[170]

The new General, Fr Luigi Fortis, was to be in a better position to understand the United States mission because of the reports of the Visitor, and because he was stationed at Rome and had Grassi available for advice; and he was also in a better position to provide practical assistance because the expulsions from Russian territories had provided a supply of Polish Jesuits, some of whom would do invaluable work in North America.

The work of the congregation dragged into the new year, and during much of the time Kenney's future destination was in abeyance.

Whither Kenney?

Early in November, he was giving two talks a day during a retreat;[171] and then was confined to bed for four days with a heavy cold. At this point, Aylmer was concerned that he would be returning to Georgetown and was labouring to prevent it. The General, he observed, had promised that he would return to Ireland if possible.[172] At the end of the month, almost all entered on a retreat made and directed by the General. Kenney by then was quite well, and old Fr Plowden was stated to be in wonderful good health. Aylmer expected, however, that they would not be leaving Rome earlier than the middle of January.[173]

On 10 January 1821, he was still unsure about Kenney's destination, though the latter, he noted, was now anxious to return with him. He observed, in passing, that the discipline at the Roman College was so strict that the

American students were refused permission to speak to Kenney.[174] Twelve days later he made a special plea to Fr Fortis to secure Kenney. At this juncture, he declared, the Irish mission could not afford to be without him any longer. Apart from shortage of manpower, a further key factor in Ireland, as in England, was friendly relations with the episcopacy, and Fr Kenney was essential to that. The bishops had been much opposed to his going to America. The archbishop of Cashel and two other prelates seriously attempted to block his departure. The archbishop of Armagh, who was a regular visitor to Clongowes when Kenney was there, had not crossed the threshold since his absence. Archbishop Murray, in conversation with Fr Esmonde, remarked that with the recent death of the talented Fr Butler the only hope for the Society was the return of Fr Kenney. Quite apart from this, and from the mission's shortage of manpower, and the protection of its property and assets of which he was a master, Kenney dealt with the influential people in government in England and Ireland, overcame the efforts of the Society's adversaries, and founded the first college. In his absence, questions concerning the temporalities might easily be raised again in the English parliament.[175]

Whatever the effect of such special pleading, and his own refusal to express a personal preference, Kenney was not sent back to America. He and Aylmer left Rome for Ireland towards the end of February 1821.[176]

BACK HOME – END OF THE BEGINNING

The journey home was arduous, especially for Kenney. He was quite unwell, and also managed to leave some of his luggage behind at a wayside inn.[177] "He was ill for seven days," Aylmer remarked, and in the voyage from France to England suffered a great deal. Their ship was battered by a raging sea, and was in great difficulties when a fishing vessel went to their aid and brought them to a beach.[178] By 11 April, however, Kenney was writing from London to the ebullient Fr Dunn at Preston, expressing his regrets that he had been unable to effect much on his behalf, but offering a remark about the General's curia likely to stimulate Dunn's interest. It unwittingly measured a future General against an old friend: "Roothaan knows English very well though he does not speak it. He is the most clever and the most active of the four consultors. [But] There is not one equal to Fr Angiolini among them all'.'[179] On 15 April, he and Aylmer arrived back at Clongowes.

Within a week, he was active in the little church in Hardwicke Street, Dublin, and already engaged to "give the Spiritual Exercises to the bishop and clergy of the diocese in August".[180] Indeed, he was so busy before long that he remarked that he had scarcely time to read his breviary.[181] And by October, not only had he given retreats to the clergy of Dublin and of Meath, but it was commonly said "that some of the bishops and all the clergy of Cashel"

had sent a request to Rome to have him as archbishop. Aylmer, feeling beleaguered once again, appealed to the General to use all his authority, if the
report were true, to ensure "that Fr Kenney is not taken from us".[182]

The latter, meantime, kept in touch with America: exchanging letters, as
has been seen, with McElroy and Ryder, and also with others who were less
dependable in their replies. Not being sent back to the United States was a
rubicon in his life, and as if to affirm that a significant era had come to an end
there came the report of the sudden death of Fr Charles Plowden. The day
after learning the "very melancholy news" he wrote of it to McElroy.[183]

End of an era: death and burial of Charles Plowden

The death had taken place on Plowden's return journey from Rome at 5.00
a.m. in the mountain village of Jougne, close to the French border with
Switzerland, on one of the ancient routes of access between Italy and Gaul.
There, at the hostelry of the Three Pigeons, still inhabited, he suffered what
appears to have been a major heart attack. He was 79 years of age. The suddenness of the death occasioned an investigation by a judge and the Procureur
de Roi, in the course of which some reference in Plowden's letters, or a
remark of his servant, regarding the election of the General of the Jesuits,
resulted in his being recorded in the mayoral archives as "Monsieur Charles
Plowden, general des Jesuites", and, accordingly, he was buried by the munici-
pality with particular care and honour![184] He was laid to rest in the quiet valley
below the town: a place of sloping meadows around the ancient Roman church
of St Maurice, close by the old Roman road and a tree-lined stream where
birds sing and water sparkles on June days.

More than a year later, Kenney still grieved: "I every day regret him"; but,
like many others, he could not but comment on the irony surrounding the
death of one who, though he asserted that a Jesuit had no nationality, was yet
very patriotically English and known for his strong anti-French sentiments.
"Without being superstitious," he remarked to Fr Dunn, "I think there is
something very singular in the will of providence, which has decreed his
respected ashes to mingle with those of Frenchmen."[185] Had Kenney been able
to look ahead one hundred and seventy years, he would have been further
bemused and pleased by the final bizarre twist provided by providence and
circumstances, which resulted in the old man's "respected ashes" being
brought home to English soil and his family's seat, at Plowden Hall,
Shropshire.[186]

With Charles Plowden's death a significant link with the years of formation, and the planning and restoration of the Irish mission, had been removed.
He had at times irritated and provoked Kenney and the first generation of
Irish Jesuits of the restored Society, but without forfeiting their regard and
respect. After his passing, they would not again feel so close to Stonyhurst.

They were on their own, as it were, but he had channelled to them the ethos of the old Society, and had bequeathed them something of his own robust spirituality and call to high endeavour.

For Kenney, it marked the end of significant beginnings. Possible new fields of mission had closed with his return to Ireland. He sought to remain "detached" with regard to future areas of work; to be a man sent: not one who chose his own career, for such a one never knew whether he was following God's will or his own. Meantime, his days in Dublin were filled with a ministry prescribed by his religious superiors.

PART 2

Years of consolidation and development, 1821–33:
Ireland, Rome, Maryland, and Missouri

VII

A time of agitation, renewal and emancipation, 1822–9: Superior again – Domestic strains – At odds with Dr Doyle – Preaching and retreats – Seeking change

When Calvin's Christ made antichrist had caught
Even the elect and all men's hearts were hardened,
You were called profligates because you pardoned
And tools of ignorance because you taught.

G.K. Chesterton, "To the Jesuits"

Home to a turbulent land

The Ireland to which Kenney returned in 1821 was marked by agrarian distur-bances sufficiently violent and widespread to lead to the reintroduction of the insurrection act and a temporary suspension of *habeas corpus*. The news of the violence was broadcast by the press, and excited interest in North America. John McElroy enquired about it, and evoked some of Kenney's infrequent comments on contemporary Irish social and political events.

"The disorders are bad enough but not near so much as the English papers make them," he responded in March 1822. And he continued:

The crimes and murder and burning houses have been frequent and cannot admit of any excuse or palliation. It is however true that the people are goaded to desperation by the sad effects of the tithe system, the high rents, and absentee landlords. *Your slaves, even in the south, are better provided for in many respects than a great portion of our peasantry.*

In the same extenuating vein, he went on to refer to the result of the popula-tion census issued the previous May. It concluded that the real number of the population had to be about 7,500,000 people. But this great crowd, he contin-ued, occupied an area that scarcely had more arable land than Pennsylvania. "If we were not Catholics, nothing could restrain us; and yet with unblushing impudence we are told that Catholicity is the cause of our disorder."[1]

Some weeks later he wrote again from Hardwicke Street, in response to another communication from McElroy: this time with a mixture of information about himself and about social and political matters. An earnest of his eager-ness to keep in touch with his friend, he remarked, was that after a day's labour yesterday, he was sitting down to write to him "instead of going out to break the air" on the only fine day they had had that spring. The full weight of the work in the church had fallen on him. He was again quite alone at Hardwicke Street, "without any sure prospect of having even one religious companion". Following this introduction, he went on to contrast aspects of life in the United States with the existing situation in Ireland.

McElroy's reference to Bishop Conwell's triumph against the lay trustees gave, he observed, "a great proof of the justice of your laws, and the fair, equal and equitable manner in which they are administered without any distinction of religion or prejudice of party". If the unfortunate Irish peasantry were persuaded that the laws affecting them, and their administration, had equal claims on their respect and submission, the recent flagitious and atrocious deeds in Limerick, Cork, and Tipperary would not have taken place. Unhappily, however, the penal laws had long since made the Irish poor look on the laws as their oppressor.

Finally, he could not conclude without his familiar regret for what might have been, and his reiteration of dislike of positions of authority. He would wish to be in a remote congregation in the United States; but such "humble prospects" had been more than once marred by those "who would fain force" him into episcopal dignities or the office of superior. He trusted he had escaped the former for life, and that he might happily stay clear of the other was his greatest wish.[2]

His "greatest wish" was, of course, not fulfilled. Some four months later, he was informing his American friend: "On the 26th inst. I received the General's order to take up the heaviest cross that I can find on earth, the government of which I was disburthened five years ago. Pity me and pray for me. What I would give to be an humble missioner in Frederickstown, Conewago, or even Goshenhoppen." In future, he added, his address would be Clongowes Wood College, Clane, Ireland.[3]

Superior again – Temporalities and spiritual problems

At Hardwicke Street, as has been noted, he had been kept very busy. There as in other Catholic churches the daily services included mass – for which the priest, and anyone receiving communion, fasted from food and liquid from the previous midnight – the sacrament of penance, or confession, and the preaching of the word of God. Such free time as he had appears to have been devoted to retreats – though only some of those, for example to the clergy and Christian Brothers,[4] are recorded; to correspondence; and occasional visits to Clongowes for special events such as the annual academy. Not surprisingly, he was always happy to pass on good news about the college. His own health, however, was again being undermined by asthma – something which added to his nostalgia for the New World: "I seldom pass a winter without having colds and pectoral complaints here," he informed McElroy in March 1822. "The winter I passed (with) you was the most healthy since I left Sicily."[5]

The consolations of pastoral work which helped cushion the bouts of asthma, were now removed, however, as he took up once more the overall responsibility for the Irish mission. And within a matter of weeks he felt weighed down by the extent of the practical problems he had inherited.

On 30 October he wrote to an English Jesuit, Edward Scott, who had been ordained at Clongowes and was familiar with the Irish province. He asked to be allowed to write to him freely and in confidence about matters he could not divulge to others. It would be "a great comfort to me," he wrote, "to have a father or two unconnected with the house whom I could consult on matters of importance." Presuming the permission, he went on to say that when he arrived at Clongowes on 29 September, he found that there was a debt of £6,000, and "not one shilling in the house". On "the other side of the book" there was "at most £2,500 of good debts"; but these were now most difficult to collect. Meanwhile, there was a want of everything, including coal and farm stock. "In spirituals," he continued, "we are scarcely better off: – a constant habit of indulgence in amounts of every kind – punch almost every day for all – recreation days often with long dinners out of the refectory, at which 1 dozen or more of wine is taken by a community of 20 or 25 young men. All this engendered a love of shooting, coursing, and almost everyone after the villa [the community holiday] goes to his [own] vacation or drives off somewhere or other."

He was convinced, he said, in what at first sight seemed a peculiar conclusion, "that the main cause of this decline in both points" [temporal and spiritual] was "the change of the dinner hour from 12.00 to 3.30 p.m."! For, he explained, after-dinner time was "night for nearly four months of the year"; candles were lighted before dinner was finished, the whole evening became "a lounge", and the community felt less disposed for study. And he understood that the increased consumption of meat since the change had added greatly to costs, and there was also an increase of indigestion and illness. "May God forgive Fr Grivel," he exclaimed, who had introduced the change. He concluded his letter to Scott with the actual number of scholars at Clongowes. It now stood at 125. "They once were 245." At the "little school" at Tullabeg, there were just twenty-five.[6]

From the journal, which he wrote up fairly regularly from his return to Clongowes, it is evident that little more than a month later he managed to return to the old practice of dinner at 12.00 noon. The only protest seems to have been from some of the senior boys, and he had little difficulty in coping with that.

The journal's entries, though brief, provide some insight into his views and preoccupations and into aspects of life at Clongowes. Thus, on 3 November it is recorded that the opening of a new chapel was marked by special celebrations. A number of guests came to dinner, Afterwards, cards were played till the bell for examen of conscience, night prayers, at 10.00 p.m. This common means of filling the long winter evenings in country areas, was not encouraged by Kenney except on special occasions. At Christmas, his entry mentioned a midnight mass, followed by an hour's meditation at 1.00 a.m. and then by a public mass at 2.00 a.m., which was attended by a "vast crowd". On 29 December he was off to Dublin to fulfil a preaching engagement, though "bad with cold".

While in the city, he devoted a considerable amount of time to assisting the new teaching Institute of the Blessed Virgin, which the previous November had taken a house, later known as Loreto Abbey, in Rathfarnham, outside Dublin. The foundress, Frances Mary Teresa Ball, was a sister of Mrs Maria O'Brien, mentioned earlier in connection with Tullabeg. She was encouraged by Archbishop Murray, as had been Mary Aikenhead of the Irish Sisters of Charity, to consult Kenney for spiritual guidance and for his assistance in drawing up constitutions and a programme for formation. He was to provide a similar service to Ignatius Rice, founder of the Irish Christian Brothers. This important aspect of Kenney's career will be dealt with separately; but at this point it is chronologically appropriate to pause to take note of the archbishop's distinctive contribution to the spiritual revolution which was taking place in the second and third decades of the century, and also to note Kenney's links with the new Institute at Rathfarnham during 1823, at the archbishop's request.

Working with and for the Loreto Sisters

During his long episcopate, Daniel Murray was the virtual founder of the Sisters of Charity and the Institute of the Blessed Virgin, commonly known as "Loreto". He also played an important part in the formation of the Congregation of the Irish Sisters of Mercy, founded by Catherine McAuley; reorganised Maynooth College, in conjunction with Kenney; founded All Hallows College for the education of priests for the English-speaking foreign missions; introduced into Ireland the Society of St Vincent de Paul for the assistance of the poor; and convened the first diocesan synod to be held in Ireland for 150 years. In the formation of the religious congregations, the preparation of constitutions, and ways of proceeding, he sought Kenney's assistance, as has been noted, and frequently pressed heavily upon him.

Thus, in January 1823, following on his arrival in Dublin from Clongowes, Kenney was writing to him about the situation in the new house of the Loreto community. When he reflected, he said, "that the entire charge of this very complicated and extensive establishment" depended "on the exertions of three very delicate ladies", he had to view "the preservation of their health as a duty of religion". Given their delicacy of constitution and their labour and solicitude, he did not think that any of them should be obliged by the precepts of fasting and abstinence, though such a suggestion might not be welcome to them. As for the Reverend Mother, Teresa Ball, he recommended that she be placed under obedience in everything that regarded her own person, such as the quality of food, the nourishment she required, how far she ought to attend the sick, and the hours of rest she should take; for he was convinced that "between her great solicitude to discharge the numerous duties of her station in the best manner, and the many wants inseparable from a new establishment", her health could not be "in worse hands than her own".

Kenney and Teresa Ball became staunch friends. He readily gave what advice and support he could. In June 1823, in response to a request for his guidance on a programme for the novices, he wrote a long and detailed letter, drawing on his experience of Jesuit noviceships as a model. Thus, having offered suggestions about preparing the night before for the next morning's meditation, he proposed such other duties as: a half-hour's meditation in the afternoon, a half-hour's reading of Rodriguez each morning, which he deemed "indispensably necessary for novices", and a half-hour's lecture or reading on the "Lives of the Saints" in the afternoon.

As to the mistress of novices' exhortations or instructions on the rules and constitution, these, he recommended, should not be given four times a week as proposed but only twice, and they should not exceed a half-hour in duration. Two other days could be given to exercises: where the novices would be asked to recount the substance of what they had heard the previous day. He envisaged the novices making their meditations in common, and the subject matter of the afternoon being a repetition of that of the morning.

On these and other suggestions, however, he took care to add in conclusion: "You must consider all that I have said as a mere private opinion, not to be adopted till the archbishop approves the suggestion to whom you ought to convey your own remarks on the matter, notwithstanding delicacy or fears in differing from me."[7]

It is clear that Mother Teresa took too much on herself, especially in the early years. In the process, she gave too many instructions to her novices, and was in danger of wearing herself out. Hence, as one of her biographers observed, she was fortunate in having the moderating influence of such experienced advisers as Dr Murray and Fr Kenney. The latter "was one of the 'unequalled friends' of whom Mother Teresa spoke on her death-bed".[8]

Pressures political and financial

But returning to 1823. Kenney's stay in Dublin during January did nothing to improve his cold. On 1 February he wrote in the journal that the cold which he had had since mid-December had finally obliged him to take to his bed.

The remainder of his entries during the year reflected a variety of cares and interests, though the journal usually recorded only bare facts, giving little indication of the strain or stress which might be involved. It is clear that he understood his overall concern for the mission as involving considerable attention to the day to day administration of the college. This appears in references to pupil arrivals, their illness and visits to physicians, the visits of members of community and pupils to Dublin; in the mention of visitors to the college, occasions of special dinners and the amount of wine consumed; in records of meetings with teachers and prefects of discipline regarding the progress of pupils. And there is even a reference to his making a 5.00 a.m. visitation to the rooms of the Jesuit scholastics to check that all were up and at their prayers.

Among items of special note in the journal were the visits of bishops to the college, especially Archbishop Murray in February, and Dr Doyle and some of his clergy, who came for dinner on a number of days during June while he was engaged in diocesan visitation in the area. In July, as he reviewed the academic year, he made a note for particular consideration in the coming year: one familiar to generations of headmasters, namely, that the method of teaching French should be altered, and that no Latin, Greek, or French, was to be taught before the young student knew how to read and spell English, and had a grasp of English grammar!

Two items, however, which caused him particular concern were only mentioned in passing.

The first referred to a petition from the township of Ross and the town of Armagh presented to the House of Commons during February, "against a body of Jesuits in the south to whose machinations the disturbances and the ignorance of Ireland were to be ascribed". Challenged in the House, the presenter revealed he knew nothing about these Jesuits or where they were to be found. Kenney, however, was worried at the fact of the attack. He consulted the local bishop, the redoubtable Dr Doyle,[9] and wrote about the petition to his good friend, the primate, Dr Curtis. The latter counselled him to treat such attacks as those of "vulgarian adversaries, that can only kick and bray like asses", and pointed out that if the Society was not a corporate body, in the eye of the civil or statute law, he should also understand that neither were the parish priests, bishops, or the Catholic Church "recognised here or privileged as such". Hence, he should not worry, but carry on as heretofore; and if all came to all, he, Curtis, would be happy to have a Jesuit college in the province of Ulster, but particularly in Drogheda or some other leading town of the archdiocese, where such was "extremely wanted".[10]

The second item was of more immediate import, though, again, the reference in the journal, for 12 August 1823, was simple and sober: at a consult "on the means of remedying the state of temporal affairs of this house, Messrs Aylmer, Gahan, Ferley, Dinan were present and advised me to go to England to borrow £5,000 at legal interest, even at 6 per cent if necessary, on a mortgage of the house and demesne".

His earlier letter of October 1822, to Edward Scott, indicated his concern about the temporal state of the mission as he took up the position of superior. How much more the current situation weighed on him was displayed to another overseas Jesuit, his regular correspondent, John McElroy. On 4 September 1823, he wrote from England saying that he had come thither on a business of a very painful nature, to meet with Messrs Sewall and Wright of the English province "to borrow a large sum of money on a mortgage" in order to pay off "the debts contracted by our establishments".

Something of his earlier confidence and independent spirit seems, indeed, to have deserted him for a while. "I have my fears," he said, "that we shall never do well by ourselves." There was no source of income from farms, as in America, and so everyone not active in a college was a financial burthen. Moreover, there were too few men to provide the change of people which the many offices and laborious duties required. Hence, he no longer had the strong objections which he had "formerly entertained" against a union in one body with the English Jesuits, and he was only deterred from proposing it to the General, whom he knew favoured such a measure, by the reluctance his own brethren would have to it, and by the unauthorised status of the Society in England, where though the vicars apostolic did not attack property in the manner of the archbishop of Baltimore, they did worse —"they attack our existence".[11]

The almost complete silence of the journal on another matter of major proportions in 1823, and especially 1824, is quite remarkable It is almost as if it were too serious for comment. Indeed, the only reference to the grievous difference of opinion with the bishop of the diocese, Dr Doyle, is a passing and indirect mention under 20 July 1824, to "the vile observations made by Revd McMahon on us to James Colgan and to some of his family".[12]

DR DOYLE AND THE SOCIETY: CONSTRAINT AND CONFRONTATION

Kenney's friendly relations with the episcopacy have been mentioned again and again. It was strikingly acknowledged in he being asked to preach at the funeral of Dr Troy; while his friendship with the primate, Dr Curtis, was evident in the letter of 6 March, quoted above, which furthermore carried the personal request – "stop with me alone while you remain here, like a true friend, though you could be more splendidly provided for elsewhere".[13] The succession of Daniel Murray to the archbishopric of Dublin, 11 May 1823, strengthened further the links with the bishops, and increased the number of episcopal visits to Clongowes. Murray frequently brought others with him. In June 1825, indeed, he was to rendezvous there for dinner with Dr McHale, recently appointed to the see of Killala, with Archbishop Kelly of Tuam, Bishops Coen of Clonfert and Logan of Meath. Kenney's journal also chronicled regular visits from Dr Murphy of Cork. As might be expected, therefore, he worked particularly hard at cultivating good relations with his own local ordinary. The former bishop had been very friendly; but Dr Doyle exhibited from the start a certain guardedness and unease towards the college and the Jesuits who ran it.

James Doyle: background and training

James Warren Doyle OSA, had been consecrated bishop of Kildare and Leighlin on 14 November 1819, while Kenney was in America. He later combined his Christian name and that of his diocese in the initials J.K.L. with which he signed his influential writings. He was only 33 years at his consecration: a man of energy, high ideals, intellectual power, fluent speech, and vigorous, assured opinions. He had joined the Augustinian order at Grantstown, near Carnsore Point, Co. Wexford, in 1806, and the same year was sent to Coimbra in Portugal where he attended university lectures.

His education was interrupted after a year by the French invasion, and he was left with a scrimpy and fragmented grounding in theology. He largely educated himself by voracious reading. "The genius of the place, the spirit of the time", as he put it, exposed him to the writings of d'Alembert, Rousseau, and Voltaire,[14] but also to writings and attitudes having a strong Gallican-Jansenist emphasis, especially in relation to moral theology. Like many of his generation he took as accurate the caricature of Jesuits and ridicule of "Jesuit theology", particularly probabilism, to be found in Blaise Pascal's brilliant satire, the *Provincial Letters*. And although the *Provincial Letters* had been condemned by Pope Alexander VII in 1657, their accusations of Jesuit moral laxity and duplicity were still believed by many.

Dr Doyle on his return to Ireland, associated members of the order, as a result, with laxity and undue lenience in their moral teaching, and in their practice as confessors. His own leanings, as indicated, were towards moral rigorism – which made less allowance for human frailty, and betrayed something of a Jansenist unease with, and suspicion of, all forms of sense pleasure. Nevertheless, despite his theological doubts about and imbibed hostility towards the Society, he exhibited from the start of his episcopate a deep attachment to Fr Bartholomew Esmonde both as adviser and friend.[15] Part of the attraction may have been the social standing of Esmonde's family, but there was also Esmonde's refusal to be overawed by his learning, height, and dominating presence, and his ability to bring out the human and humorous side of Dr Doyle's personality.[16]

The personal contacts and kindness received at Clongowes, indeed, almost disarmed him. Writing to a close friend, a nun at Clane, Mrs Teresa Brenan, on 6 May 1823, he exclaimed: "How they do overcome evil by good! They are always heaping favours and attentions upon me, and you know how badly I repay them. However, for the sake of Xavier, if for no other cause, I shall be converted." Yet, continuing the letter the following day, he was again divided between hostility and appreciation. As he moved from the poverty of the bog of Allen area to the "respectful mansion of the Jesuits", he was disturbed by the setting of "trees, lawns, flowers, superb halls and apartments, a simple but neat church with a superb organ and delightful music", all that might gratify "the desires of a sensual man". He subsequently "officiated at vespers and gave benediction" and wished that he "could deserve to be in heaven", but the Lord, he wrote, "left me where I generally am, low and miserable". Afterwards, all proceeded to dinner which, compared to his own regular meal of "a scrag of mutton",[17] scandalised him by its profusion. Taking for everyday fare what was put on in his honour, he ventured to whisper his criticism on one such occasion to Esmonde, and received the reply: "My Lord, if you could only glide in some day, and conceal yourself beneath this table, you would find that the Jesuits' fare is widely different from that served up on a day that J.K.L. is expected."[18]

In his letter to Mrs Brenan he added: "Mr Kenney is all goodness and piety, and the whole family as happy as virtue and temporal blessings combined can render them"; and then continued revealingly that they oppressed him by their kindness. Their "constant occupation" enabled them to serve God well, but he had to confess that "their place, the recourse of visitors, and the luxuries which surround them" were "great incentives to passion", and he "should not like to be one of them chiefly on that account".[19]

His lordship was not beyond airing his criticisms of the order in company, careless of the weight and protection given his words by the dignity of his office. At this point in his biography of Dr Doyle, W.J. Fitzpatrick relates one such mildly dramatic incident, which he attributes to a memoir by the Revd John Lynch SJ.[20] On an occasion when both Archbishop Murray and Dr Doyle were present at Clongowes, the latter, in the course of discussion after dinner, put an intricate question on canon law to Dr Murray. The archbishop, "who was a most cautious man, and never gave a direct answer when he could possibly avoid it, said 'Well, my Lord, I don't think you need pass your neighbour, Fr Kenney, to receive a satisfactory reply'. The Jesuit and the bishop then began a discussion which continued, with varying success, for a considerable time." Dr Doyle, "accustomed not to mince his words in discussion with fellow priests", as Ftzpatrick puts it, and speaking with a customary authority bordering on arrogance, appears to have expressed a point of view which was very critical of the Society of Jesus and its moral teaching. It was too much for Kenney. Loath to accept dictation from anyone, least of all regarding his own religious order, "he stood up, exclaiming, 'I am unused to such language at my table', and walked out of the room".[21]

The bishop's inherent unease, and his suspicion of Jesuit moral teaching, received a decisive push in the early months of 1824 from the clergy of Clane and Kill parishes, whose congregations, in large numbers, were availing of the services of the Clongowes priests as confessors.

The parish clergy appear to have had mixed feelings about the Jesuits. Fr McMahon of Clane had written to Kenney on 21 February 1823, to say that the "gentlemen of the college" had his permission to do all the good in their power in his parish. They could "preach at mass or in the evening at all times, also attend to the sick, hear confessions, same as myself or the curate, for which I shall feel thankful".[22] Yet, as Dr Doyle later stated, he had received many representations, some of them often repeated, that the observance of discipline was breaking down because of the people's recourse to the Jesuits for confession.[23] The gist of the clergy's complaints was that their rights and functions were being undermined, and that the Jesuits were being taken advantage of in the confessional by all sorts of reprobates. Moreover, they impressed on Dr Doyle that a desire to withhold dues from the parochial clergy was not infrequently a cause why some withdrew from their jurisdiction, and influenced others to do likewise.[24]

Restriction of faculties, and response

Disposed as he was to expect undue leniency in Jesuit confessors, Bishop Doyle felt obliged to act. In March 1824, he wrote to Kenney withdrawing permission to hear confessions except of those who came with a letter of permission from the pastor of their own parish.[25] A prohibition on attendance at Clongowes for religious services was proclaimed to the public from the altars of Clane and Kill.[26] Yet on 15 March, the parish priest of Kill, Fr Thomas Nolan, wrote to express his indebtedness to the priests of the college for their kindness to the people under his care, and stating that some who had been away from the sacraments for years had come back due to their efforts. He mentioned the names of certain people who informed him they wished to go to the college for confession and asked that his letter be considered as "a note of permission for them and every other of the people of this parish who trouble you".[27]

The parish priests, it would seem, were coming under pressure from their parishioners following the bishop's decision; and the latter had himself received a number of letters of protest in support of the Jesuits. Among the community at Clongowes, meanwhile, the episcopal stricture had occasioned consternation, and no little anger. Esmonde later told Dr Doyle that his "extraordinary stricture" was "the most painful wound which has affected us since the opening of our college".[28]

Kenney was dismayed by the bishop's attitude. He considered himself, and the other confessors at Clongowes, to be wholly orthodox and circumspect in their teaching and their administration of the sacraments, and certainly where he himself was concerned such was the view of the general body of bishops.

True, he advocated "frequent communion" as a great help to "tepid souls" – a practice far from universal in the church at the time; but he bound this about with the proviso that there had to be careful preparation for the reception of the sacrament, and even then his advocacy was confined to saying that even those who prepared carefully for the sacrament should not communicate for more than three days without going to confession![29]

In his approach to the penitent, however, he perhaps exhibited more compassion than Dr Doyle would approve. He was quite convinced that in doing so he was being true to the mind and practice of Jesus Christ; and in retreat after retreat, and conference after conference, placed emphasis on gospel scenes which reflected mercy and compassion. Not surprisingly, the parable of the prodigal son was a favourite source of insight in his perception of God. On different occasions he pointed out that "the Father of mercies" was "more ready to forgive than the prodigal to ask for pardon", that he went forth to meet him, raised him from the earth, and pressed him to his heart. "No reproaches, no reprimands." In short, Kenney presented a God who delighted "to exalt mercy above judgement".[30]

Dr Doyle's stricture, in consequence, appeared intolerably high-handed; and in conflict, indeed, with the church's law and its tradition of allowing the public the freedom of choosing a confessor. "I should like to know," Kenney remarked, "to what canon Dr Doyle can refer in justification of this mandate." And to the prelate's imposition that penitents required a letter of permission, he is alleged to have stated baldly: "My Lord, I will accept no such conditions. I have not hitherto heard many penitents, I shall hear fewer for the time to come."[31] Shortly afterwards, presumably following a meeting of consultors at the college, Esmonde wrote to Dr Doyle to say that he begged leave, "in compliance with the instructions of our superior, Dr Kenney, to resign into your Lordship's hands the faculties by which the Jesuits at Clongowes have officiated as priests since 1819".[32] As a result, the "gentlemen of Clongowes" withdrew from all confessions.

Knowing, however, that his Lordship, though believed to be headstrong, was yet ready, in the face of "proper evidence", to modify his opinion, Esmonde, encouraged by Kenney, kept up correspondence with his friend.[33] He strongly argued the case: defending the liberty of the individual, and expressing the hurt felt by him and his colleagues, and the damage inflicted on the order's reputation. Dr Doyle replied on 5 April. He thanked him for his "unreserved freedom" in communicating his sentiments. "Candour is always commendable," he said, "but in our intercourse with each other it is a duty." He had written the regulations "with great pain", but he deemed it necessary to do so, and he then gave the reasons previously noted. No charge, he insisted, had been made "against the confessors of the college, who were supposed to be deceived or misled", and, he added that he had not "been actuated by any feeling of distrust or enmity" towards the Clongowes community whom he loved and cherished; and he found that similar sentiments prevailed amongst the clergy generally. If there were a few who spoke improperly. they must be allowed for since one could not expect all the clergy to agree in their feelings and opinions. "And should any of them dissent," he continued, "from many maxims of your institute or your theology, and I am one who do, this should be tolerated in us; but we should not put down as evil or erroneous what the church leaves untouched."[34]

It was a response that left matters much as they were. An exchange of letters followed during the month, which went into various aspects of moral theology, and where some of Dr Doyle's prejudices of a Gallican-Jansenist nature were expressed. "The decay of morality and consequent defection from religion in latter times may be traced to the relaxed morality of the Society"; and this expansive charge was propped up by reference to Jesuit teaching on probabilism and mental reservation.[35] Esmonde pointed out that Jesuit theologians enjoyed freedom of opinion on questions which had not been definitely pronounced upon by the church. They could be found, indeed, on opposite sides of a question; though generally in moral theology, and especially with regard to probabilism, they stayed close to the teaching of the revered founder of the Redemptorists, who had recently been beatified, Alphonsus Liguori (1696-1787). And going on the offensive, he suggested that Dr Doyle was aligning himself with the accusations of Pascal and the Jansenists, who were not just enemies of the Society but of the Catholic Church.

The two friends got together in May, and came close to resolving the differences. Writing to Esmonde on 23 May, the bishop stated that almost every day since he had the pleasure of seeing him at Clongowes, he thought of writing and apprising him of his "almost entire conversion" to his opinion. He then went on, however, to refer to a religious sister, who wished to avail of the services of her confessor at the college but now was unable to do so, and he requested that that gentleman "and the other gentlemen might have the goodness to continue their exertion for the good of souls, and might be induced to assist not to thwart me in my endeavours to unite the pastors with their flocks", and be, he added, again with scant understanding of the Jesuit and religious vocation, what the church intended religious to be, "assistants to the bishops and the parochial clergy". He never intended his regulation, he declared, to exclude persons from confession at the college who had a "special reason" for not fulfilling their Easter duty in their parish church. Why then, he asked, "have your good gentlemen, whom I have always met not only as friends but as brothers, why need they have created and published amongst the poor obstacles which I certainly never contemplated?" He did not presume to blame them for this, he concluded, but he hoped that Esmonde would "dispose them to resume their wonted charity to the poor and rich".

Esmonde's comment, written on the back of the letter, was that "Dr Doyle, without rescinding the restriction, seems anxious to explain it away, but in an unsatisfactory way for all parties as I tell him in my answer of June 2nd."[36] That "answer" traced the experience of the Clongowes Jesuits in their work in the confessional. They had been almost overwhelmed by penitents, Esmonde stated; and people came long distances to them, many of whom had been absent for years. Because of their devotion to the sacrament, his Lordship's strictures were particularly painful. As to his Lordship's present request that the community "resume their wonted charity to the poor and rich", it was not clear that he was withdrawing his restriction, and even if he were it was not going to be easy now to work in harmony with the parochial clergy. As an appropriately friendly conclusion, he offered a gentle inducement: "In case my arguments may have induced your Lordship to modify your views, no one need fear that you will feel that pain which is sure to pierce little minds when avowing an altered opinion."[37]

Dr Doyle did, indeed, reverse his decision. And, as sometimes happens after a disagreement, relations between him and the college became closer than they had been. The final healing of the breach, however, was not without one further embarrassing incident: the one referred to in Kenney's diary.

Final hiccups before resolution

Sometime in the second fortnight in July, Esmonde wrote to the bishop to extend Fr Kenney's invitation to him to attend the annual academic exhibition to be held on 2 August; and he added apologetically, an item which might be as disagreeable to his lordship as it was painful to him, Esmonde.

On the occasion of a charity sermon at Clane, he stated, the parish priest, Fr McMahon, in the presence of a number of ladies and gentlemen, including a pupil from Clongowes, passed derogatory remarks about one of the pupil's Jesuit teachers, and then extended his criticism to the college and to the Society of Jesus generally. He supposed, Fr McMahon remarked, that he would be invited to the approaching academies at the college. "I have been there but five times in my life and can't bear the sight of the place." And when the pupil tried to defend his teachers, "the reply was to this effect. Poor child! You don't know them. For my part I don't like them. I quite agree with Doctor Doyle in his dislike of them …"[38]

On 30 July, Dr Doyle replied in what had become an almost characteristic style: giving graciously with one hand, and then seeming to take all away with the other. He had more than once impressed on Fr McMahon, he declared, the necessity "of his cultivating the favourable opinion and good will of the gentlemen of the college". He was aware that "by talking overmuch", Fr McMahon "commits faults"; and "this is doubly painful to me," Dr Doyle continued, "when my own name is introduced to prejudice the mind of anyone against men whom I highly esteem". But what was he to do? It was not in his power to govern the tongues of those who were not always guided by their own good sense. He, personally, always spoke well of Clongowes whenever he could.

And then, following those healing words, he indulged in another of those seemingly unconscious chameleonic utterances which helped explain his clergy's confusion as to his real attitude to the Jesuits. He remarked that if he had thought less favourably of the Society than many others, as Esmonde knew he had, and had sometimes reasoned or spoken on those matters in their history which he could not justify in his own mind, as others had done, yet, he continued:

> I have been at the same time ever careful to commend what I thought commendable in the body at large, but above all in the members of your college, so that if priests in this diocese show an unkind disposition to so useful an establishment they are not warranted by my example!

In conclusion, he remarked that he had heard of a direct and public attack made on a certain publication of his by a Jesuit in Dublin, and the clergy in the Clongowes area "heard of it, they believed it, and they felt it", but he, when he heard of it, "desired it to be papered over" since he regarded it as common sense "to return good for evil and to overlook what friends do to us as well as what is done by opponents".[39] He also mentioned that because of conferences and the visitation of the parishes, he regretted that he would be unable to attend the approaching academy day.

After this rather ambiguous communication, and his Lordship's absence from the academies on 2 August, Kenney was in some anxiety about the future. Consequently, it was with a mixture of relief and trepidation that he saw a few days later a letter from Dr Doyle addressed to Esmonde, who was temporarily absent from the college. "As I knew that you had no secrets with the bishop," he informed Esmonde, "I opened the letter, and was agreeably surprised to find him still desirous of your views. You must go to him."[40]

Dr Doyle's letter, written on 7 August, was an invitation to Esmonde to spend a few days with him and advise him concerning a suitable altar for his chapel.[41] His friendship with Esmonde led, indeed, to many visits to Clongowes by Dr Doyle; while Esmonde, for his part, assisted the bishop in dealing with proselytism by the bible societies,[42] and in his powerful advocacy of the cause of Catholic emancipation.

Esmonde's key role in the order's links with the bishop, almost necessarily increased Kenney's reliance on him and his appreciation of his many qualities. Kenney's virtual dependence on him underlined the almost chemical unease in his own relations with the bishop. Around this time, however, interchanges between them appear to have become more relaxed; though it is difficult to assess the real situation, since the stories that have survived are centred on occasions of real or imaginary confrontation; and these, in different ways, reflected contemporary, or near contemporary estimations of Kenney.

Fitzpatrick's account of him leaving the table has been mentioned. Other sources talk of an occasion when Archbishop Murray invited Dr Doyle and Kenney to his house in North Cumberland Street, Dublin, with the object of correcting some erroneous views held by Dr Doyle. And it is alleged that after the issues in question had been discussed "with the greatest fullness and candour" by Kenney and Doyle, the archbishop was well pleased with the result.[43]

Fr Henry Lynch sj (1812–74), who was a pupil at Clongowes under Kenney, 1825–9, and later prefect of studies there, told, in his later years, of a further passage between the two men: which may, indeed, have been another version of the interchange which Fitzpatrick attributed to "Revd John Lynch". When dining at Clongowes among a large party of distinguished guests, Dr Doyle, so the story went, "let fall some very loose sentiments about the Society". The prelate, Lynch continued, "despite his great talents and piety", not infrequently adopted erroneous positions about matters even of grave moment, due, perhaps, to an over confidence in his intellectual powers "partly arising from being largely self-educated". From a person who was present, Lynch was told that "Fr Kenney, finding that no one else in the community would dare contradict Dr Doyle … could no longer restrain himself. And though he was doing the duty of host at table, and the remarks disrespectful of the Society were made by the bishop of the diocese, already so famous and, I shall add, so feared not only by his opponents but even by his own clergy, having, as he had, the name of being uncompromisingly rigorous, Fr Kenney burst forth in a torrent of transcendent eloquence in defence of the Society." And having referred to the criticisms made by Rousseau and Voltaire, he concluded with the query: "Surely, my Lord, it cannot be that your Lordship means to adopt the frightful principles of Rousseau and Voltaire?" The company, it is alleged, "were utterly dismayed, and Dr Doyle shifted his position with a boyish laugh, trying to pass it off … He ever after showed a reverential awe of Fr Kenney and later became much devoted to the Society".[44]

Despite the elderly Fr Lynch's rather simplistic and partial reminiscence, Dr Doyle and Kenney do appear to have established a relatively smooth working relationship, at least from 1825 on when they appeared before government commissions.

Doyle and Kenney and government commissions

In March 1823, at the time of the accusations attributing to the Society responsibility for the outrages in the south, the bishop asked Kenney about the order's status in Ireland in terms of civil and ecclesiastical law. Kenney provided a long and closely reasoned reply on 6 March 1823. There was a very small number of Jesuits in Ireland, he observed, and they did not constitute a province or vice-province of the order, and as these were the only parts of the Society recognised by its institute as corporate entities, the Jesuits in Ireland could not, in ecclesiastical law, be considered a corporate body, no more than any three or four Jesuits would be in the missions of China or California. Similarly, of the establishment at Clongowes it might be said that it was "not an establishment of the Society of Jesus", no more "than would a small house in Dublin which any three or four of ours might take for the purpose of keeping there a day school".[45]

Dr Doyle accepted the argument; and two years later, in his magisterial performance before the Lords' Select Committee on the State of Ireland – which ended, as the Duke of Wellington wryly remarked, in "Doyle examining us"[46] – he responded to certain questions on Clongowes and the Jesuits with the answer: "the Jesuits in these countries are not recognisd to exist as a corporation like the other religious orders; and if they be Jesuits, as I believe they are, they do not seem, as far as I can understand, to act in any other capacity than that of individual clergymen collected together ... I do not know in an official way that they are Jesuits at all; I even on one occasion ... applied to Mr Kenney in an official way to ascertain whether he was or was not a Jesuit; I have communicated ... the substance of the reply he made to me in what I have just said."[47] Kenney's explanation had also been presented to the other key Irish witness, Daniel O'Connell, who expressed the view that the Jesuits in Ireland existed there not as an ecclesiastical order but as a body of individuals who had established a "seminary" there.[48]

In addition to the briefing of witnesses before the Lords' Committee on the State of Ireland, Kenney found himself facing the prospect of being a witness himself before a Royal Commission on Irish Education, set up by George IV in 1825. It was remarked by a contemporary, Fr James McDonnell, that he tended to be unusually nervous and absorbed a few days before preaching a major sermon.[49] He was something of a perfectionist in his preparations. The tension occasioned by the commission, as a result, must have been intense. In the event, he and Dr Doyle were subjected to a detailed, unfriendly examination by Foster, the leading commissioner, for some eight hours.[50] According to Richard Lalor Sheil, writing in 1829, Kenney remained outwardly unperturbed by Foster's sarcasms, who, in turn, was baffled by his ready responses.[51]

On the appearance of the lengthy first Report of the Commissioners, Dr Doyle was so incensed that he wrote a devastating letter to the one Catholic member, Mr A.R. Blake, chief remembrancer and confidential friend and adviser to Lord Wellesley,[52] in which he regretted that Blake had affixed his name to a report which clearly bore the marks of "the old no-popery system" where "no gentleman of honour or integrity had had a place".[53] It was an unjust and ungrateful remark to a man who had encouraged him and given him confidence when facing the Lords' Committee.[54] Fortuitously, it fell to Kenney to smooth the resultant strained relations.

In his journal for 1825, he noted that Mr and Mrs Blake and some friends had arranged to pay a visit to Clongowes on a particular day. Sometime later,

Dr Doyle, on his visitation to that part of his diocese, appointed the same day to call on the college. Hearing he was coming, Blake expressed the wish to meet him. The bishop agreed. When they met, before his Lordship could speak, Blake "with great earnestness stretched out his hand". Thereafter, "they conversed a long time together and alone". Subsequently, the ladies and Mr Blake lunched, and returned to town about 4 o'clock; while the remainder – 13 Jesuits and 12 guests, including Dr Doyle – dined at 5 o'clock, and accounted for 20 bottles of wine, between port, claret and sherry. The journal notes that there was "no punch", which was part, presumably, of the economy campaign![55]

In concluding this account of the bishop and his relations with the Irish Jesuits during Kenney's time as superior, one notes such immediately perceptible factors as the influence of Dr Doyle's background, and the strength of mind and character of both men. Less perceptible, but perhaps more disturbing, was Esmonde's remark that a number of the local clergy were making critical comments about the Jesuits and the college; and the implication was wider than any mere concern about loss of dues and attendances in their parishes, or any comments from the bishop.

Why they indulged in sniping remarks is not clear, but one suspects that there was an element of social distinction involved. The Jesuits with their wide acres and castle had taken over "the big house", the Wogan Browne estate, were visited by the great landed proprietors of the region, and had become identified, to some extent, with the landed establishment; an identification which could readily have been made under the superiorship of Aylmer, himself of landlord class, who spent much of his time at Clongowes visiting his own family's nearby demesne. Something of the social unease reflected in Fr McMahon's remarks, might also be read into Dr Doyle's private comments on "the respectful mansion of the Jesuits" and the "luxuries that surround them"; and it is not unlikely that some at least of the community compounded matters by insensitivity to the image being presented to the local priests and people.

Meantime, while the foregoing were taking place, Kenney continued to be subject to outside demands of a more directly apostolic kind as well as pressures of a domestic nature.

PUBLIC SPIRITUAL RENEWAL, DOMESTIC STRESS, AND EMANCIPATION

Almost every week-end was devoted to assisting at the church in Hardwicke Street, counselling individuals, or working with the new religious congregations situated in Dublin. And for a number of special episcopal occasions his services were sought as a preacher. He had been called on at the obsequies of Archbishop Troy in 1823, as has been mentioned, and now, two years later, was requested to preach at the consecration of Dr Crolly, the new bishop of

Down and Connor, in Belfast on 1 May. He had first met Crolly during his time at Maynooth. The primate, Dr Curtis, wrote to Kenney on 25 April requesting him to call on him on his way to Belfast, and to accompany him on the remainder of his journey from Armagh. He wished to meet with him not just out of friendship but "to have some private conversation ... on the very interesting and delicate affairs of these momentous times".[56]

The "affairs" in question probably related to the Unlawful Societies (Ireland) Act, which had been brought in on 9 March and which had led within a matter of days to the formal dissolution of the Catholic Association and had also placed Orange Lodge meetings in breach of law. And there was also the excitement generated by Sir Francis Burdett's Emancipation Bill, introduced on 25 March with O'Connell's support, which contained "two major securities" – to defranchise the 40-shilling freeholders in Ireland, and to remunerate the Irish Catholic clergy – which had given rise to heated debate.

At the episcopal ordination, Kenney took for his text Psalm 89.35, and before the large congregation of Protestants and Catholics preached on the unchangeable nature of the Church, its divine authority, and the continuity of Petrine jurisdiction within it. The following day he attended the special dinner given by the new bishop for some 250 guests, most of them Protestants. The occasion was punctuated by a seemingly endless procession of toasts, which extended the celebrations over six hours and enveloped the participants in a haze of benevolence and good will.[57]

That year, also, there were considerable additional inroads on his time and energy resulting from the declaration of 1825 as a jubilee year at Rome. For centuries the popes had declared a jubilee every twenty-five years, which meant that pilgrims going to the holy city within a specific time, visiting the four basilicas, and receiving the sacrament of penance and communion, were declared absolved of all their sins and the temporal punishment due for them. And the custom had grown up of extending the indulgences of the jubilee year throughout the world the following year, on condition that the congregation received the sacrament of penance and communion, and fulfilled certain conditions such as a number of visits to specified local churches, and some fasting or works of charity. As the jubilee was to be extended to Ireland in 1826, there were additional requests during 1825 for preparatory retreats for clergy and religious.

Retreats and spiritual principles

Those which Kenney undertook were exacting on him and on the participants. The timetable which has survived from a retreat he gave to the clergy of Cork during that year, shows the spiritual exercises commencing on Monday evening and continuing till Saturday morning. During that time, silence was to be observed. Each day commenced with morning prayer at 7.00 a.m. and an hour of meditation, followed by mass at 8.30. Breakfast at 9.00 was followed by a short talk at 10.00. At 10.30 there was a consideration on aspects of a priest's life and duties. At noon there was another meditation, followed by "examination of interior" and a visit to the Blessed Sacrament. A further meditation commenced at 3.00 p.m. Dinner was at 4.00. At 6.00 there was a short talk on the statutes of the diocese, and at 6.15 a second "examination of the interior" for half an hour. At 7.15 points were given for the morning meditation. At 8 o'clock there was night prayer, and fifteen minutes later – all retired in silence to their respective lodgings. At all free periods during those intensive days, Kenney was available for confession, advice, and consultation. And, of course, every address had been prepared with meticulous care.

From examples of talks which he gave to clergy at different times, it is clear that among matters likely to be emphasised were the devout celebration of mass, compassion and patience in the confessional, fidelity to the breviary, frequent confession, self-discipline, and commitment to prayer. His instructions on prayer invariably included, apart from methods of meditation and contemplation, an emphasis on "the second-method of prayer" – whereby, for example, the person praying took the Our Father word by word and continued to meditate upon one particular word as long as he/she found "various meanings, comparisons, relish, and consolation in considering it", then on to the next word and so on. The period entitled "examination of interior" was a time of prayerful consideration of one's predominant failings, what Kenney termed the "homebred foes", the enemies within, with a view to remedying them.

And whether with religious congregations or secular clergy, he tended to bring to their attention what he called "the four cardinal points of the spiritual life":

1. *Recollection*: which "avoids dissipation of heart and mind from God".
2. *Generosity towards God*: seeking to be responsive to divine grace at all times.
3. *The Exercise of the Presence of God*: which he termed "the foundation of the spiritual life".[58]
4. *Purity of Intention*: so that one's motives and intentions are directed to God. (This point, he observed followed readily once the habitual state in no 3 had been acquired.)

The additional retreats to religious congregations occasioned by the jubilee preparations were usually of eight days duration. They followed the usual structure of the Spiritual Exercises, though in the lay-out of the retreat he differed on occasion from what was general practice. The theology of the resurrection of Christ was relatively undeveloped in the nineteenth century and, in consequence, meditations on the risen Lord were usually confined to the last day of the retreat, a practice which persisted into the second half of the present century. The one complete retreat of Kenney that has survived from these years, however, has him devoting two days to meditations and contemplations on the risen Saviour and on the coming of the Holy Spirit and the commencement of the church.

The challenge to live up to the highest ideals of their state in life, which he presented to students, priests, and bishops, were applied unremittingly to those in religious life. They were reminded that their vocation was "to practise the virtues peculiar to the saints": "a total detachment from worldly pursuits, self-contempt, due subordination to those whom God, or your superior, have appointed to direct your steps in the paths of virtue and inspect your exterior conduct; indifference to what merely concerns your own person, love of religious knowledge, recollection of heart, and ardent zeal to promote God's glory[59] by your own perfection and the salvation of others".

Kenney's popularity as a spiritual director and preacher certainly could not be said to rest on any dilution of the ideals and doctrine of the period. He was, however, never wooden; and those with problems and failings could usually expect to be met with understanding, compassion, and encouragement.

But as well as these involvements, there were to be met, day in, day out, the ineluctable requirements of school and community.

The rector and the scholars

The new year, 1825, indeed, had opened in school with an incident which called forth the prompt and decisive qualities his colleagues valued in him. His journal for 27 January noted, without any further explanation, that on that night, after supper, the pupils of the two final years, poetry and rhetoric, instead of going to night prayers, "closed and barricaded the door of the playroom with tables, benches etc. and caused musical instruments to be played with shouting, riots etc." When the news was conveyed to the rector, he immediately recognised the serious implications. He came straightway to the spot, posted a person at the door to distinguish voices, and then ordered the door to be forced with a sledge. "Soon the panels were in and the culprits handed out through the breach." They were placed on their knees along the wall in the long gallery. Kenney addressed a few words of reproof to them, and then, to save them from "the warmth and just anger of the masters and prefects", ordered them to be allowed go to bed quietly. "The whole riot, and its suppression, did not last half an hour."

Next day, the six known ringleaders were singled out and "severely chastised" at the place where they had rioted, and then confined in a room under a special prefect. The rector, meanwhile, met with the house consultors. The latter recommended the dismissal of the three of the six against whom the evidence was strongest. Kenney let it be known that they were to be expelled, and waited. Soon there were urgent pleas for leniency from the classes involved, and from the majority of the students. He allowed himself yield to the signs of contrition. He drew up a formula of apology to be read out by the chief culprits in the study place, and prefaced the occasion by a few words. Afterwards, "in punishment of the general guilt of the two schools", he suppressed the sodality, which was composed of Poetry and Rhetoric classes, suppressed their private library, and forbade these schools be taken out on coursing, or to be allowed feasts at Carnival – "until the rector should be advised by the prefects to allow these indulgences in consequence of their good behaviour". Thus, rough justice and discipline were applied with flexibility, and the main offenders saved the ultimate stigma of expulsion. All effected expeditiously, yet without undue heat or haste.

Another, less authoritative side was depicted by Henry Lynch, who commenced as a young boy at the college that year. "I have seen him," he said, "after he retreated early from a party of prelates and other personages who were being entertained in our college, order the servant to conduct to his private room several of the smaller scholars. What was their delight to see his table covered with parcels of fruit and cakes he had early in the day ordered to be prepared for them … I remember how he stooped to chat most charmingly with us … asking us to explain to him the best method of making a bow and arrow, and getting us to show him how to make a ball, and enchanted all the while at seeing us enjoy our little feast …"[60]

Rector and the community

His main concern, however, continued to be the community. Life in a boarding school in the early nineteenth century, as has been noticed, offered few opportunities of getting away from the pressures of teaching or/and supervision. Such activity took up most of the day, and much of the rest of the time was occupied by spiritual duties, class preparation, correction of exercises, organizing school activities, and so on. And the academic year, it must be remembered, ran for eleven months. It was a tiring life, unrelieved except by occasional visits to Dublin, special dinners and libations on feastdays and when distinguished guests came to dine, and sometimes games of cards on such evenings. But such interruptions introduced a secularising element and the danger of weakening the spirit of recollection and prayer in the house. The balance was difficult to attain.

To achieve it, Kenney, with in mind, perhaps, the decision to send the young Americans to Rome, became convinced of the advisability of educating a number of the young men in France, where they would receive a strong formation which would enable them to cope with such a life. This would cost money, as the foreign provinces were no longer prepared to educate Irish Jesuits free of charge as many of them had done in the old Society. Nevertheless, he felt it necessary to make the financial sacrifice. Ever since the

Visitor's arrival, the quality of religious observance had, in his view, seriously declined.

Writing to his English Jesuit confidant, Edward Scott, then in Paris, on 12 August 1825, he asked him to convey to the French superiors the special need of care and patience in correcting the faults of the Irish élèves, which were "contracted in the anomalous way of life which it has been our lot to live here" and which, he could not resist adding, were brought on the house by a Frenchman, Fr Grivel, who, Kenney claimed, "temporised with every difficulty, flattered everyone's weakness, promised to realise everyone's wishes, disappointed everyone, and his name at last becomes as little respected, as his measures were greatly injurious".

The French superiors, he continued, need to be aware of the "curious mixture of secular and religious life which we have here to live". And in speaking to them, Scott should keep in mind how widely Clongowes differed from Stonyhurst, especially in two particulars; and he outlined what these were.

First, "we are more exposed to the world than you are. The Catholic gentry about us. The vicinity of the capital. The influx of strangers. The necessity of keeping an intimacy, at least an acquaintance with the families of our people. All this brings us under the eye of secular persons much more, and much oftener, than we should be were we situated as Ours in Stonyhurst". Hence, it was necessary, on the one hand, to prepare the young men "for the secularising eye of the secular" that they "may not undervalue our ministry"; and, on the other hand, there was required "a deep love of retirement, an aversion for secular amusement", so that they might not be drawn to imitate a secular way of life.

The second point of difference from Stonyhurst was one mentioned earlier, namely, that in Ireland there was no means of changing situations and few of changing offices, for there were no alternative missions to which men could be changed as in England. Thus, the result was that the same teachers, for the most part, had been "employed the past eleven years in the lower schools" (in Clongowes), "others the same way as prefects". This sameness produced "languour and disrelish of labour, then desire of change and love of outdoor diversions, amusements etc.". And there was no place to send someone who was troublesome, even "highly injurious", in the college.

All this, Kenney emphasised, rendered "a love of solitude and of labour, unassisted by variety, change of scene or occupation, indispensable". He concluded his letter to Scott by suggesting that Fr Glover at Rome be requested to obtain from the General "a form of domestic discipline" for Clongowes and Stonyhurst, whereby "systems of eating and drinking and living more *da signori* than *da Gesuiti*, should all be restrained"; otherwise, education abroad would not bear fruit.[61]

The sending of young Jesuits to Europe for education emphasised the international character of the Society and helped counter a colonial or island mentality; but the kind of views and plans he had outlined to Scott, or maybe his way of expressing them, certainly reflected his reputation for austerity and were unlikely to win much support from those prominent members of the community who had opposed him so often in the past. In the event, the accumulation of work and various pressures induced a state of exhaustion which moved him a few months later to seek a complete change.

Seeking a change

On 22 December 1825, he wrote to the General asking to be relieved of his superiorship. His mind was tired out, he declared, by many concerns, including the demands on him for sermons, and his body had become "too heavy for lack of time to take exercise". His desire was to go to the United States as an ordinary missionary, but first he would welcome a year at Avignon to recuperate and to do his tertianship – a year of spiritual renewal usually undertaken following the years of study and ordination – which he had had no opportunity to undertake up to this. Eleven of the past 14 years had been spent in positions of authority. He went on to suggest that instead of the superior of the mission being also rector of Clongowes, there should be two offices. It was an application of the solution he had introduced in America. He recommended Robert St Leger for superior of the mission, and Bartholemew Esmonde as rector of Clongowes.[62] At a later date, in support of Esmonde's appointment, he mentioned not just his piety and general suitability, but also his popularity with outsiders, and especially with Bishop Doyle, "who ought to be numbered among the enemies rather than the friends of the Society, but who, nevertheless, thanks to Esmonde, often requested the spiritual exercises for his clergy".[63]

Meantime, as he awaited the General's reply, he faced into another very busy year. He commenced on 1 January with a sermon at St Michan's Church in Anne Street, to fulfil an earlier promise. It brought back memories to him and the parishioners. Crowds flocked to hear him. Then on 23 January, he made the long, cold, and weary journey to Kerry in response to a request from a man who was dying. When he reached Ballingar, near Listowel, the man was dead. He stayed on for a few days, renewing acquaintance with members of the local clergy; reflecting, no doubt, how he had been the choice of many of them for bishop.[64]

On 23 February 1826, Fr Fortis replied to his letter. He approved, on Kenney's recommendations, that St Leger be made superior and Esmonde rector. Each was capable of filling the other's office, if change were necessary. He also approved of the superior not living at the college; but where should he live? He requested Kenney to let him know as soon as possible, so that the new man could be soon appointed. "As to your request to be allowed go to Avignon," Fortis continued, "and live a quiet life in holiness, justice and study, spared the preaching of sermons or other apostolic ministries, I am not at all adverse to granting it." The rector of the house at Avignon was a holy and excellent man. Nevertheless, care must be taken, the General reminded him, lest the Irish bishops, or the Jesuits, or their friends, oppose his departure for France. "I leave that to your prudence and skill," he continued, "recommending that you apprise the French provincial of your plan ..." While there, he should pray to the Holy Spirit for guidance regarding the American mission. Fortis would also pray about it. He would not entirely deny the permission, or fully consent to it before the end of the year. As to Kenney's criticism in his letter of Fenwick's appointment as bishop of Boston, he had strongly opposed it, but it was clear that Fenwick was not "altogether unwilling to accept the honour.[65] Before the General's letter had a chance of reaching him, however, Kenney found himself embarked on one of his most demanding, yet rewarding, experiences as a preacher.

The jubilee celebrations

The extension of the Roman jubilee, already mentioned, gave rise in Ireland to unprecedented popular expressions of faith and fervour. In Dublin, it commenced on 8 March 1826, at St Mary's Church, the pro-cathedral, Marlborough Street. The papal bull announcing the jubilee was read out, and Archbishop Murray preached on the graces and indulgences available during the week of devotions. The Church, he declared, in virtue of its tradition and the commission given to Peter (Mt 16:18f), granted removal of temporal punishment for sins already forgiven, that is if certain conditions were first fulfilled. Here, he referred to those noted above, prayer, together with the reception of the sacrament of penance [reconciliation] and of the eucharist.

Two days before the jubilee, according to the *Freeman's Journal* of 7 March 1826, "the mass of the Holy Spirit was celebrated in the metropolitan Catholic church, Marlborough Street. ... after which the Revd Mr Kenney preached. The crowd was immense." The public devotions during the week, consisting of prayers and instructions, commenced each morning at 7.00 a.m., and were repeated at midday and in the evening.[66] Kenney's personal impact seems to have been exceptional. His sermons, as was noted early on, were usually "very well constructed ... [and] powerfully presented";[67] and though he was not a tall man, he somehow, as one observer recalled, looked taller than he was by virtue of his strong physique, presence, and erect bearing; and his enunciation was clear, he had a controlled and varied delivery, and a commanding voice "of rather metallic bass".[68]

Something of his contribution is suggested in the rather unctuous language of William Meagher, the biographer of Archbishop Murray. Each day, he wrote, "Fr Kenney harangued the people ... on their duties in those effusions of commanding eloquence which never failed to achieve the most signal victories over sin; while on Sundays, his Grace addressed them with the same gratifying results ." The confessionals were crowded almost without interruption, Meagher continued. On the first morning of general communion, as a result, the pro-cathedral presented a spectacle such as Dublin had probably never previously witnessed. The building was packed to overflowing, and every member of the congregation seemed to receive communion. At the conclusion of the ceremonies that morning, Kenney led the people in the renewal of the baptismal promises. At a distance of a quarter of a century, Meagher still recalled the scene with emotion and grandiloquence. "Beholding the sight that met him as he ascended the pulpit, Fr Kenney burst forth into such strains of jubilation and thanksgiving, as made his overflowing audience almost beside themselves, while with uplifted hands and streaming eyes they literally shouted aloud their eternal renunciation of Satan and his works. It was, indeed, a jubilee that morning in Dublin ... a bright epoch in the lives of many a wanderer, who never before had knelt at the holy table, and thenceforward never strayed away from their father's house."[69]

Because of the public response and demand, the period of the jubilee was extended again and again, and similar ceremonies were celebrated in "almost every parochial and every conventual church within the city".[70] The archbishop introduced the same imposing ceremonies in each church, and it is to be presumed that he managed to involve Kenney in at least some of them.

The jubilee was also held in various parts of the country. Kenney, telling of some of the demands of life in Clongowes to his friend, John McElroy, on 2 July 1826, remarked: "We are obliged to go out to jubilize the country – Mr Aylmer gave the public exercises in Athy, Mr Esmonde in Clane, and is this moment giving them in Bray, the Orange bed of Ireland."[71]

Establishment criticism and suspicion

The enthusiasm generated by the public gave rise, not surprisingly, to concern, misunderstanding, and hostile criticism in the unionist press. The *Dublin Evening Mail*, of 8 March, denounced "the foolishness hourly executed" at the pro-cathedral; and portrayed the "blasphemous ... sin-forgiving jubilee" as a cynical exercise thought up by the clergy to keep the people in a state of ignorance. And as the jubilee ran on, the paper extended the implication of indulgences to the possibility of papal absolution of subjects' oath of obedience to their lawful monarch;[72] and greeted the joint pastoral of the bishops, written by Dr Doyle, with a scare-mongering scenario for the future. Doyle was assuming the power of the sovereign pontiff, it was alleged, and, though he was a loyal subject, was it not possible that a future pope, hostile to Britain, "might send to this country a wily and insidious Jesuit, a bigoted and intolerant persecutor, a deep and designing hypocrite", who would issue "a pastoral", signed by all the bishops, in favour of a bull calling for "the extermination of all heretics"![73]

Such inordinate suspicions and fears were inevitably influenced by the new vigour of the Catholic emancipation movement which was receiving perceptible support from the sense of cohesion and fervour fostered among the Catholic population by the country-wide jubilee. In the general election during June-July of that year, 1826, the political significance of a disciplined, united, Catholic vote was to become apparent for the first time. O'Connell joined the campaign of Henry Villiers Stuart in Co. Waterford, a Protestant favourable to emancipation, and, by mobilising the Catholic electors, contributed to the defeat of a seemingly invincible Lord George Beresford.

To be an ordinary missioner in North America?

In a letter to the interested McElroy, on 2 July 1826, Kenney chronicled with some relish the obvious discomfiture of Orange supporters in parts of the country during the election. He then went on, however, to remark that he hoped to be soon relieved of his "present burthen" which had nearly exhausted all his energies and left him "good for very little".[74]

The possibility of going as a missioner to the United States seems to have stimulated him to renew old contacts. On 2 July, as well as writing to McElroy, he also wrote to Fr Dubuisson, now rector at Georgetown, giving him some information from Ireland and Europe, but mainly asking for news from different parts of the American mission. Among other enquiries, he wished to know particularly about "good Fr Van Quickenborne", now in Missouri; and asked to be remembered to "good Fr Dzierozynski", if he were at Georgetown, for he remembered his kindness to himself and Fr Aylmer at Bologna. Much of his Irish news, moreover, had an American flavour. The late Mrs Paterson, neé Caton, the granddaughter of Charles Carroll, was now the Marchioness Wellesley, Lady Lieutenant of Ireland. She was much liked, for Protestants not less than Catholics admired her prudence, condescension and amiable manners. The archbishop, whom she met at Clongowes, had become "her confessor and great friend".[75]

Despite his talk of change, however, nothing further seems to have happened. An extant portion of a letter of his to the General, Aloysius Fortis, on 29 April of the following year, appears to be a reiteration of what was proposed and accepted, at least in principle, two years previously. He requested once more to be released from his position of authority, and that the office of superior be separated from that of rector of Clongowes. He concluded with a sentence which indicated, perhaps, a reason for Fr Fortis's delay in deciding about sending him as missioner to the United States: "My own affairs proceed not badly even though slowly, and things seem better this year."[76] Was it, indeed, that he had been discussing with the bishops and fellow Jesuits about his departure, and that the live possibility of leaving had both eased the burthen psychologically for him, and, at the same time, rendered his colleagues more conscious of the pressures on him? Besides, in that momentous year, 1828, there were many dramatic public happenings to distract his attention and that of his colleagues from in-house issues.

Countdown to Catholic emancipation

The Catholic Association commenced 1828 with simultaneous meetings in some 1600 parishes as a challenge to the government; and in July the gauntlet was thrown down with O'Connell's sweeping success in the Clare election to become the first Catholic elected to parliament.

Unfortunately, very little of Kenney's correspondence during this year has survived. What remains refers but briefly to the political scene. Yet, one of the most frequent topics of conversation at Clongowes had to be the religio-political developments – given the many friends of the community, as well as past students, involved in the emancipation movement, and the fact that Kenney had made the college a centre of hospitality not just for visiting clergy, but also for prominent laity, and the most prominent of these was O'Connell himself. The kind of relationship which had been established between them was reflected in a letter of Kenney on 16 December 1823, which, having expressed his pleasure at having O'Connell's third son, John, at the college, went on: "I am much gratified by your promise of spending a day here before the expiration of the Christmas holidays. As the days are short, I hope that you will make up your mind to sleep here that night that we may have more leisure to enjoy your company and conversation."[77] The college, in fact, became a regular port of call on the Liberator's journeys. Some nine years later, he would tell of arriving at Clongowes with two of his children after nine o'clock at night, and the three of them settling down to an improvised dinner, where he ate "a quarter of beef" while his daughter, Cathy, "helped to demolish a turkey and a ham". He slept at Clongowes, while Cathy, and his son, Morgan, were billeted with Fr Aylmer's family nearby.[78]

A key factor in the community's lively interest in O'Connell's campaign was his enrolment of bishops and clergy as active supporters and allies. It was a conjunction which enabled the emancipation movement avail of the close ties between clergy and people, which had been forged during the years of persecution, and which, by the 1820s, were opposed to any concessions to the government·in terms of veto or salaried clergy. The mutual regard and affection of people and priests for each other was, in the judgement of the experienced French traveller, Alexis de Tocqueville, the real key to basic social order in Ireland.[79] O'Connell had sensed this. Among the Irish clergy, moreover, Tocqueville encountered a spirit of democracy found nowhere else in Europe, a commitment to the separation of church and state which he had previously observed only among American priests. It was a concurrence which Kenney instinctively reflected in his time in the New World.

Sadly, Kenney's only extant reference to political happenings in 1828 was, as mentioned, virtually in passing; and then was confined to the autumn period of uncertainty and relative inactivity. It occurred in a letter to Fr Robert Haly, at Fribourg, on 30 September. The country had become, he wrote, "the land of spouters". Orators were doing wonders collecting the Catholic rent. "All the feuds existing among the different tribes of the south are quelled by the Catholic Association; and the frequent exhibitions of strength and numbers are said to terrify the government." On the other side, an association of Protestants, termed Brunswickers, were collecting rent for Protestant purposes. The leading Catholic lawyer in England, he continued, "Charles Butler of London", had "published his opinion that Mr O'Connell's admittance to parliament cannot be refused according to law".[80] The year closed, in fact, with hopeful prospects for emancipation. Following a letter from Archbishop Curtis to the Duke of Wellington, with whom he had been acquainted during the campaign in Spain, the duke let it be known that he was concerned "to witness the settlement of the Roman Catholic question".[81]

The year also closed for Kenney on a happier note. Letters of Fr General Fortis, posted on 9 November, made his Christmas joyful with the information that St Leger and Esmonde were to take up the respective offices of superior and rector. Replying, belatedly, on 3 February 1829, he expressed his "many and repeated thanks" for the freedom which he now anticipated with joy.[82] By then, however, Fr Fortis was already six days buried;[83] and the promised arrangements were in abeyance. The Society's temporary disarray was deepened a week later by the death of its staunch supporter, Pope Leo XII, on 10 February.

Expulsion of Jesuits and other (male) religious orders?

Where Kenney was concerned, at this point, public issues nearer home were almost monopolising his attention. The new year had opened in Ireland with renewed expectations and tensions. Before long, more as a concession to fear rather than principle, it became clear that a Roman Catholic Relief Act was about to be introduced. It was also evident that it included restrictive provisions in relation to members of (male) "religious orders, communities, or societies of the Church of Rome, bound by monastic or religious vows" and "resident within the United Kingdom". In accordance with the provisions, all the foregoing gentlemen were to provide particulars of themselves to a relevant official within six months of the Act, and any member coming into the country after the commencement of the legislation was to be "deemed and taken to be guilty of a misdemeanour" and, if convicted, might be banished for life. A licence to enter might be obtained through "one of His Majesty's principal Secretaries of State, being a Protestant". In addition, it was enacted that none of these bodies might receive novices, or administer "any oath, vow, or any engagement".[84]

As these clauses threatened the very future of Clongowes, seventy prominent past students met at Hayes Rooms, Dawson Street, Dublin, and signed a petition against the offending section of the proposed bill. The Duke of Leinster spoke up in support of the Irish Jesuits in the House of Lords, and headed a petition of twenty-four signatories from "the nobility, magistrates, and gentry of the Co. Kildare, Ireland", which praised their eminently useful employment of instructing youth, and claimed, with more rhetoric than logic, "that since their establishment in this county there has been less party spirit, less political agitation, and less religious animosity in this than in any other county in Ireland".[85]

Kenney travelled to London to meet with Fr Charles Brooke, the English provincial, to ensure a united approach before the common danger. They decided against procuring formal petitions to parliament lest such opposition "impede the great measure of emancipation". But as the character of the Jesuits, as distinct from other religious orders, had been attacked, Brooke and Kenney decided to present a defence against the imputations which had been made.[86] The resultant document was signed by Brooke alone. He sought to place particular emphasis on the Jesuits' loyalty and allegiance, and to this end quoted Kenney to effect: "The Revd P. Kenney, superior of the Jesuits in Ireland, in his examination before the Commissioners of Irish Education Inquiry, says 'allegiance is a duty which a subject owes to his sovereign before any other obligation is contracted, whether to bishop, or superior, and he is therefore already bound by that prior duty'."[87]

Despite all such efforts, and also a generous testimony in favour of all the male religious orders from the archbishop and clergy of Dublin,[88] the provisions remained. Kenney took the matter calmly. He had stayed on in London from early March until April to watch the progress of the bill and discuss its implications with its supporters. He returned there in May, and called on O'Connell,[89] who appears to have previously assured him that the provisions were inoperable. He had already, on 6 March, informed his wife, and his friend, Edward Dwyer, secretary of the Catholic Association, that he would "drive a coach and six" through such restrictions.

"The great measure"

O'Connell himself was enthusiastic about the Act. "I tread on air," he wrote his wife. "Whoever thought we could get such a bill from Peel and Wellington ... Catholics can be judges, mayors, sheriffs, aldermen, common counselmen, peers of parliament, everything in short, everything."[90]

Yet even in these moments of heady excitement he had to acknowledge "the only blot" on the bill, the fact that the vote was being taken away from the 40-shilling freeholders who had sacrificed their future for him and made his movement irresistible. Henceforth, the vote was denied them.[91] The Act became, in effect, a measure mainly benefiting the middle classes.

Such negative implications were not widely evident, however, at the passing of the bill. The measure was hailed as a great achievement throughout Europe and in North America. O'Connell's stature abroad became such that Honoré de Balzac would later comment: "I would like to have met three men only in this century – Napoleon, Cuvier, and O'Connell";[92] while the Earl of Clarendon was to remark that had O'Connell "ceased agitating when Emancipation was carried he would have been as great a man as Washington".[93] To the large majority population of Ireland, the Act marked the first major victory after centuries of defeat and subjection. It lessened the sense of political inferiority, demonstrated what organization and discipline could achieve, lifted morale, and remained across the century a pillar of light in dark times. For Catholicism in Ireland and England it marked the beginning of an era of expansion. The "second spring", hailed by John Henry Newman, was to come in England; while among the Irish there grew an abiding sense of mission, a sense of having survived centuries of persecution in order to be, in God's providence, bearers of belief to other lands.

The exultation and sense of achievement that characterised the mid-April days of 1829 stayed in the memory; and even a young Protestant boy of ascendancy stock, Aubrey de Vere, retained romantic recollections to the end of his life of the rejoicing that charged the countryside around his father's estate in west Limerick following the passing of the Act:

> The hills were covered with bonfires celebrating the passing of the Bill. I was then fifteen, and I well remember climbing to the top of a high pillar on the summit of a hill opposite our house ... and standing upon it for many minutes, waving a lighted torch around my head in the gathering darkness.[94]

His success confirmed O'Connell in his quest for liberty and in his belief that it could only be obtained by "moral agitatory force". His regard for liberty led him, as has been noted, to speak out in support of the emancipation of the slaves in North America. It also led him to serve as parliamentary spokesman for Jewish emancipation.[95]

Kenney was heir to convictions similar to O'Connell's. He was a constitutional liberal in political affairs, so far as one can judge from rare passing comments. One such straw in the wind, apart from his favourable reactions to the American system, was a remark in September 1830, after Charles X had failed to overthrow the constitutional and parliamentary system in France "The whole world," he informed John McElroy, "celebrates the triumph of the principles that achieved the downfall of Charles."[96]

On political matters at home, however, as frequently noted, there is a dearth of extant comment. And as the only reference to events in 1828 occurred in a letter to Robert Haly at Fribourg, so was it also in 1829, apart from the brief reference to his visit to O'Connell in London. On 31 July 1829, he wrote to Haly instructing him to return home, and reminding him that he would have to register his name within six months of his arrival. He continued: "Were the other clauses rigorously enforced, they would in time cause the extinction of all the religious orders in Ireland, ... but it is the general opinion that so much of the act will remain a dead letter."[97] The "general opinion" proved accurate. Kenney had written from Lyons. He was on his way to Rome for the general congregation to elect a new General of the order; and, unwittingly, for a new major undertaking.

VIII

Impact at 21st General Congregation.
Opposition to departure for North America,
1829–30

> Were it not contrary to the usages of the Society, it would raise a monument to him as a sign of perpetual gratitude.
>
> John Roothaan, General

Before leaving home, Kenney carried out the instructions of the Vicar-General of the order to hold special meetings with his consultors to discuss the state of the Society's mission in Ireland, and to bring to Rome the views expressed.[1]

"General state of the mission"

He and the consultors met on 6 and 7 May. The result of their deliberations was a sanguine report, and two requests of major importance for the future of the order in Ireland.

The general state of the mission, they declared, gave hope of much improvement. It had commenced in 1811 with three men. Now it had 65 members, of whom 22 were priests. Its temporal affairs were in a healthy state. Such debts as there were did not involve Clongowes or Tullabeg, but arose from the purchase of land to build a church and larger house in Dublin. The church would provide work for six to eight men and "easily sustain them". The venture was presented as having the approval of the archbishop, though the latter, in fact, appears to have been less than enthusiastic about it.[2] Clongowes and Tullabeg, the report continued, were also capable of sustaining more men. Hence, there were well grounded hopes for the future. To secure these, however, two conditions would have to be met. These constituted, in effect, their petition to the General Congregation and the General.

The first request was that the mission be raised to the status of a province. As matters stood there was a hiatus. Technically they could be subject to a superior from another kingdom, one at war perhaps with England, as was pointed out to Kenney when he appeared before the Royal Commission in 1826. Admittedly, their present numbers were fewer than existed in other provinces, but as concessions were often made in new foundations they requested such a favour. It would be a recognition of those earlier fathers by "whose blood and sweat the Irish mission was initiated and propagated", and would give solace and spirit to present members and bring about an increase in numbers.

The second request also bore the marks of special pleading. Jesuit colleges were in great demand in Ireland. There was much need of them, especially in the cities, where the sacraments were widely neglected by young and old, and in the north of the country where "an unbelievable number of Arians, Socianists, and Deists were to be found".[3] In short, that religion which had endured persecution for three centuries was now in danger. Jesuit schools could provide an effective remedy; but the problem was that wealth in Ireland lay mainly in the hands of non-Catholics, and Catholic colleges could not be supported as the colleges had been in Catholic countries. Hence, the only practical solution was to charge fees, and they requested the special concession required to do so.

To bolster their report, Kenney approached the archbishop for a formal comment on the work of the Society in Ireland. He received a glowing testimonial from Dr Murray on 14 May, and set out on his journey that afternoon.

Just over two weeks later, he entered Lyons "two hours after sunset". He eventually arrived in Rome at 3.00 a.m. on 15 June, having deeply experienced once more the discomforts of contemporary public transport. Between Bologna and Rome, he informed Esmonde, they travelled for three nights without rest and two days without dinner. The duration of his journey from Dublin to Rome was precisely one month.[4]

AT THE GENERAL CONGREGATION

In the days following his arrival, as members assembled, there was time to visit various places of interest. From extant fragments of a diary he attempted to keep, he visited a number of churches, was given a detailed tour of the Vatican Library, and joined a queue of prelates and other distinguished clergy waiting to say mass on the feast of St Aloysius Gonzaga in the saint's room at the Roman College.[5]

When the Congregation had fully assembled and conducted preliminary business, it set about choosing a new General. The choice was announced on 9 July. It was Fr John Roothaan, a native of Amsterdam, whom Kenney had singled out at the previous Congregation as the most able of the General's assistants. He was in his 44th year, and his election, in Kenney's view, was clearly a mark of divine providence.[6]

To the new General and Congregation, the recently elected, and very short lived, Pope Pius VIII, expressed his esteem and good wishes, and advised the order not to extend itself for ten years until its young men were properly formed. He also intimated his wish that in Jesuit schools history, geography, as well as mathematics, be added to the classical languages as a necessary part of contemporary education.[7] The advice was taken very seriously. The members were conscious that in the previous ten years so many colleges had been accepted that many priests had been overburdened, and young men had been put forward too soon. It was the unanimous voice of all, Kenney reported, "to let our young generation be perfectly formed" before their sphere of exertion was enlarged. Hence, he thought it likely that the next ten years would be "comparatively years of repose".[8]

The Congregation, as was customary, elected new assistants, following the election of the General. These were primarily associated with regions where the Society was most numerous. Those chosen were: Fr Pavani for Italy, Rozaven for the French assistancy, Landes for Germany, and as the extensive Spanish assistancy could not provide a nomination at the time, the congregation chose as a substitute an Englishman, Kenney's old friend, Thomas Glover.[9]

Defender of scholasticism

Having a friend near the seat of decisions, gave Kenney additional confidence in putting forward the recommendations of the Irish mission. Another factor, moreover, worked strongly in his favour. He and the new General shared an enthusiasm for the scholastic theology of St Thomas Aquinas. Kenney, indeed, was remembered from Maynooth days as frequently absorbed in Aquinas's *Summa Theologica*.[10]

At the Congregation, when philosophical and theological studies were under review, and there was discussion about abandoning scholasticism for more "progressive" approaches in those disciplines, Kenney made an intervention which proved decisive.

Writing of it, in *Giovanni Roothaan* (Rome, 1930), Pietro Pirri related in his rather florid manner that "Fr Peter Kenney, superior of the Irish mission, an impressive speaker, made his intervention with a forceful and spirited defence of scholasticism. He recalled how much the Church and the Society owed to that system, how the order's most illustrious men were formed according to the scholastic method, and how it was the very decline of the strength and perfection of that method that provided openings for the enemies of religion. He concluded by stating that in rejecting this method, the Society would be involved in a process of destruction not reconstruction. All," Pirri continued, "were carried away by the eloquent address of Fr Kenney; so much so that the congregation decided by a unanimous vote that, as in the past, the scholastic method should remain as a sacred patrimony of the Society." Fr Roothaan, the author added, "applauded the words of the eloquent speaker" with animation. "He conceived such an affection and sense of gratitude to Fr Kenney that he considered him an outstanding benefactor of the Society in having recalled it to its true method and doctrine. He declared that were it not contrary to the usages of the Society, it should raise a monument to him as a sign of perpetual gratitude."[11]

Kenney could be sure, as a result, of at least a sympathetic hearing to his requests for province status, and freedom to charge student fees. And his spirits were further raised by his current physical well being, even though many others were being laid low by the heat and food of Rome. He felt sufficiently expansive to exult to Robert Haly on 25 July "I am, thank God, made for all weather, climate and food: though not insensible to many inconveniences, I am in good health."[12]

Seeking province status and school fees

To give weight to the argument for recognition as a province, he drew up what he described as "A brief history of the mission in a few folio pages from the days of St Ignatius to the present." In doing it, he was helped, he wrote, "by many ancient papers which I found in our archivium and [by] others got elsewhere".[13]

This "Brevis Notitia de Missione Societatis Jesu in Hibernia" brought the story up to the death of Betagh and the beginning of the restoration. It concluded with a quotation from St Ignatius to counter the objection that the fewness of numbers and houses in the Irish mission did not justify it being raised to a province.[14]

With respect to the other issue, "the pension for schools", he had asked Aylmer to consult with Archbishop Murray and others who might have information about schools run by Irish Jesuits before the suppression, 1773, to find out if fees were required then.

Writing to him, on 24 July 1829, Aylmer reported that he could get no information on the matter. His Grace, however, desired him to tell Kenney "to use his name and influence in urging the great necessity and utility of our having day schools in this city, and the impossibility of having them otherwise than is generally practised, viz. the scholars paying a pension": – which might be accepted not as fees for tuition, but as expenses for house rent, the building of school rooms, the support of servants and assistants, and, indeed, towards providing pupils with books, paper and so on. This last was particularly relevant as a form of payment in day schools. His Grace added that in Ireland, where the greater glory of God was so much in question, he believed that every allowance should be made, and would , indeed, have been made by Ignatius himself. He seemed astonished, Aylmer continued, that there should be any difficulty about charging fees, given that a stipend for masses was permitted to enable them meet financial needs. In the last analysis, he suggested that an application might be made to the pope who, he had no doubt, would grant permission at once.[15]

Armed with this, and other letters from Aylmer, Kenney translated the relevant parts into Latin, "particularly Dr Murray's opinion", and laid them before the General's assistants. He saw each of these in private, and though Fr Brooke, the English provincial, would not join with him, or make fees a matter of interest for his province, he yet proved helpful in sounding out provincials and leading men of other provinces. He was taken aback in the process by the French avowal that "they not only supported their masters in the convittos [boarding schools], but even their novices, by the proceeds of the pensions of the convittori".

Following this preliminary work, and the perusal of the above mentioned documents, the General, the assistants, and others, including Kenney, were decidedly of the opinion that neither of the questions should be put before the Congregation. The question of province status properly belonged to the General; while to raise the question of pensions at the Congregation was likely to "give rise to a strong contest, which would embarrass the General, and end most probably by a negative decree".

The assistants advised Kenney to wait on in Rome until the provincials had gone home. By 1 September, he thought that vice-province status at least would be granted, and that on the fees issue the General would permit him to apply to his Holiness, or might do so himself.[16]

His wait in Rome was longer than he expected. Provincials were slow in leaving, and then the General had to go to Naples for a while. It was 6 October before he was able to send a final report to Ireland. He had been present at the consultations between the assistants and the General, and the result, he observed, was "most satisfactory". The General's secretary, Fr Joannes Janssen, presented him with a formal response in writing on 11 October, the day before he was due to leave Rome.

It stated that with respect to the schools, a pension could be tolerated "for the present" provided there was no obligation on parents to pay, and that no child was "excluded because his parents, otherwise honest", could not "afford the fee". On the issue of status, Ireland was declared a vice-province, with the possibility of shortly being a province. Janssen availed of the occasion to remind the provincial and superiors to observe carefully the regulations about writing to the General so that he might have "reliable knowledge on the state of the vice-province".[17] The letter also conveyed the appointment of Batholemew Esmonde as rector of Clongowes.

MISGIVINGS, OBEDIENCE, OBJECTIONS, AND THE AMERICAN MISSION

Before leaving Rome, Kenney was informed that he was to be sent to North America, and that the General would confirm it by letter in February. He was to keep the matter to himself. He interpreted this as applying to Ireland. In an undated fragment to an overseas correspondent, possibly Fr Moran at Buenos

Aires, he confided: "I am to wait for further letters, but it is arranged that I go to remain in the United States for some years at least. No one here knows as yet anything of this; but on receipt you may address me: College, Georgetown, District of Columbia, US. You may direct another to this house for fear that plans may be altered before April, when I (am) to sail."[18]

He said nothing of how he felt about the decision. A few months earlier, however, he had been less than enthusiastic. Writing from Rome on 1 September 1829, to John McElroy, regarding the new General's great interest in the American mission, he remarked that he was aware that Fr Roothaan had serious thoughts of sending him to America again. He, however, had not asked for that mission. Some years ago he had asked for one year's repose to prepare himself for it or any other mission, "but now I am grown so heavy and old," he remarked, "I fear that I shall not be able for any work worth the trouble of crossing the Atlantic." Nevertheless, there would not be any opposition on his part to the designs of the General.[19]

In this last, he was giving expression again to the principle of detachment, "indifference" or internal freedom – the on-going endeavour to divest himself of "self-love, self-will, and self-interest". And he was to live it a year later as, with a worsened chest condition, he set out from Liverpool.

Homeward journey and serious illness

The "worsened chest condition" was occasioned by, or at least became more evident, during the homeward journey from Rome. As noted earlier, he had rejoiced at his good health during his time at the Congregation. At this period in his life, however, "good health" was a relative matter. His chest was chronically impaired. In a letter to Thomas Glover, while he was enjoying this "good health", he let drop that he had deferred collecting some items – "having a dislike ... to annoy my chest by going up to my room".[20] But even the relative good health deserted him on the morning he was leaving.[21]

He contracted a severe chill; which seemed to leave him, however, after some days. He determined to cross into France by the Italian west coast in order to avoid being delayed by snow. The route was a perilous one, and the road being less travelled, the schedule of coaches was infrequent.[22] He took a month to reach Paris. There he stayed for eleven days: not viewing things of interest, as he later assured the General who had queried the length of time he took to reach Ireland, but seeking alms from Irish Catholics in the French capital for the fabric of the new church of St Francis Xavier, Gardiner Street. The only places he visited were the Royal Library and the cemetery of Père La Chaise, and for the rest his time was spent in laborious questing, which took so much out of him that he attributed to it the severe illness which overwhelmed him on setting foot in England.[23]

In a further letter to Glover, on 1 January 1830, he related how on his arrival at Dover on 30 November 1829, he had felt so ill that he had to go straight to bed when he called on his friend, Fr Scott. The latter looked after him for a fortnight. He arrived back in Dublin on 16 December, and was laid up for another week. Eventually, he reached Clongowes on Christmas Eve, still with a severe cough and chest infection.[24] The illness was completely unknown to him, he told the General. His heart and liver, as well as lungs, were affected and he had to take his rest sitting up.[25] Nevertheless, he hastened to assure Glover on 1 January that in all other respects he was well. He had "no fever, pain or ache". And if the weather only became like that of Italy, clear, dry and mild, he would soon be himself again.[26]

Uncertainty, delays, and complications

On his recovery, he was straightway caught up in administration; and this included the painful trauma of expelling from the Society a priest, Charles Frazer, who had been twenty years in the order and was a prominent member of the staff at Clongowes. In addition, now that he had moved from Clongowes on the appointment of a rector there and was living adjacent to the Hardwicke Street church, he had become involved in a heavy programme of pastoral work as if he had no physical impairment. He was continuously engaged in sermons and the hearing of confessions from the beginning of Lent until the feast of St John the Baptist (24 June). "All this time, and every single day, I sat in the confessional for three, four, and sometimes five hours", he reported, and the circumstances seemed to be such that he could not reduce this activity.[27]

Meanwhile, the months passed without the expected letter from Roothaan regarding America. From the United States, however, came word that the divided and dwindling college at Georgetown had taken on new life with the appointment as president in September 1829, of Thomas Mulledy, one of those he had sent to Italy: a man of imposing presence, exuding energy and confidence, who combined high aims with a shrewd business sense and the flair of a natural salesman.[28] Kenney took his superior-general's silence "as a change of heart". He hoped, he wrote John McElroy, that the good news which had reached him about increased numbers and improved prospects at Georgetown might have caused Fr Roothaan to believe that he was not necessary for the good of the rising mission.[29]

At the end of May, his Paternity wrote. Kenney was not only to go to the United States, but was to go once again as Visitor. The patents of office were enclosed. Further instructions would await him at Georgetown. Fr St Leger was to succeed him as vice-provincial. And Fr Grivel, the Frenchman who was at Stonyhurst and had been a Visitor to Ireland, and for whose judgement he had little regard, was to go to America with him. Kenney was to leave as soon as possible.

He received the letter on 10 June. Before that, however, news of his destination was circulating at Rome and in the United States. Fr St Leger had heard about it in a letter from Italy, and embarrassed him with questions. And a visiting American Jesuit, Fr McEnry, was able to tell Fr Esmonde on 9 June, the day before Kenney received his letter.[30] Replying to the General on 29 June, Kenney emphasised that he was in no way responsible for any leakage of information: "I place a higher value on ready obedience in difficult and burdensome matters than my country, my friends, my brethren." If it were God's will, however, he would wish to be setting out without any authority; but, he added, "not my will be done, but the will of God and of your Paternity". The rest of his letter was devoted to defending himself against Fr Roothaan's complaint about not hearing from him and his consultors, to explaining how he took so long returning from Rome, and to giving a general report on the state of the vice-province.

In his report he told of how he had been obliged to expel from the Society on 24 May, Fr Frazer, who had been prefect of studies, and a teacher of some of the senior classes, at Clongowes.[31] He would write more at length on that matter, he stated, in a letter addressed solely to his Paternity. Apart from this sad and serious news, he painted an optimistic picture. At Clongowes all seemed to be going well. The number of boarders had increased from the previous year, and religion and piety among them, as well as union and charity among the Jesuits, had shown growth. The seminary at Tullabeg was flourishing under Fr St Leger and a new chapel had been built. The church of St Francis Xavier, Dublin, "rises higher as the days pass" and would, hopefully, "have a roof before the winter". On the Isle of Man, Fr Mathew Gahan had built small schools for the sons of the most wretched and poorest Catholics and was now engaged on plans for a second chapel on the opposite side of the island. He had received a letter, he said, from Fr Moran in Buenos Aires. Everything was going well with him, and the vicar capitular (there being no bishop there) had drawn up plans for a church for the use of English and Irish Catholics, for whose sake he had undertaken that distant mission.[32]

This positive depiction reflected how he saw the situation. He believed that he was leaving the new vice-province in a much healthier state than when he had received it as superior. But, he was not yet ready to depart, he informed the General. The burden laid upon him he accepted with a willing heart, and he was getting ready to sail as soon as possible, but he had not yet handed on the reins of office to Fr St Leger because he would be unable to leave Ireland before August. This, he explained, was because the archbishop of Dublin had him tied down to give the annual retreat to his clergy in July, and he felt obliged to keep his promises lest there be danger of giving offence to that "excellent prelate whom both on his own merits and for our own good we ought to respect very highly". By the end of July, however, he would have everything settled to the best of his ability and placed in the hands of Fr St

Leger. He hoped to arrive on the shores of America towards the end of September, a suitable time for travellers as the summer heats were wont to lessen about then.[33]

This time-table meant that July became a month of hectic activity. He sought to conclude outstanding matters relating to Clongowes, Tullabeg, the Dublin residence and church. This included drawing up the status for the coming year: changing men, allocating new personnel, and such other adjustments as seemed necessary – and all the while making no reference to his departure. On 12 July he went to Maynooth to commence the annual retreat to the Dublin clergy.[34] A month later he was still in Ireland. Final arrangements, he informed Glover on 16 August, were deferred because of the academies at Clongowes on 2 August; "and since then many things happened to cause delay. Amongst others, the terrible affairs that threatened to disturb France created new puzzles for us." He outlined the kind of problems created by the July revolution in France: some men had to be brought home, arrangements had to be made to send others to safe destinations, and there was continued concern at the absence of news from the young men who were at the novitiate in Avignon. In the light of all the demands on him, he did not think he would be free to leave for another ten days. He added: "By Mr St Leger's own wish I have not yet announced him at Clongowes Wood as my successor; but, unfortunately, from America and Stonyhurst the news of my destination has been prematurely published. But the General may depend on my alacrity and obedience. I am making every exertion; but the order came suddenly after all; for when no letter came in February as the General promised, I concluded that he had changed his mind."[35]

He had in Glover a more sympathetic ear than in Fr Roothaan, or, indeed, in his colleague, the new rector of Clongowes, the forthright Fr Esmonde, who privately, and occasionally to his face, expressed his criticism of him and of his record as superior.

Running the gauntlet of Esmonde's criticism

The establishment of a separate rector for Clongowes was intended to reduce Kenney's work load. In practice, it gave over the running of the major house, and its finances, to a very independent, outspoken and hyper-critical personality who took his responsibilities very seriously, not only with regard to the academic and pastoral life of the college but also with reference to the productivity of the farm and the history of expenditure in all aspects of the enterprise. He pressed Kenney for an account and explanation of his expenditures while rector of the college as well as overall superior, and challenged his freedom to avail of college funds for the general needs of the mission .

Within months of Esmonde's appointment, differences between them were in evidence in relation to these finances. Letters were exchanged. And on 6

February, Esmonde committed to his journal vigorous comments about Kenney's character and stewardship. With reference to the latter's response to his queries about expenditures, he accused him of "affected ignorance, that is a species of lying", and expressed his resentment at Kenney speaking to him, and of him to others, about his "want of candour". This type of personality attack, Esmonde continued, was the kind of language he had frequently heard from him in his own room, and it pained him "more to see a man of such superior qualities in most points lower himself to such unworthy language". And he went on: "the fact is no one ever speaks to him the plain, honest truth, and thus he strangely deceives himself in his estimation of things and persons". The exception, of course, was Esmonde: "I respect and esteem him, but never could make up my mind to flatter him. On the contrary, I often tell him plain truths, though sometimes in an impertinent way; but really he often forces it from me by contemptuous abuse as in the present instance".

It is difficult, in that presentation, not to envisage Kenney as somehow in retreat before Esmond's assertive personality, an assertiveness stamped with the assurance of hereditary landed gentry. It is an impression that is deepened by his engaging in a drawn out exchange of letters when a more direct face to face discussion seemed called for; and by his delay in telling him, even in strict confidence, about his departure for America – fearful, perhaps, of his opposition. His secrecy about America did indeed incense Esmonde, especially as all Dublin seemed to know of Kenney's departure though his own colleagues had received no information about it. He first heard the news on 9 June 1830, from an American Jesuit visitor. He immediately wrote to St Leger, as Kenney's expected successor, to protest that Kenney could not be spared from Ireland.

Among the reasons he gave were that the Society was not yet consolidated in Ireland, and was much in debt; that Kenney's influence with the archbishop was particularly important at present because Fr Aylmer "seemed to have commenced" the church in Gardiner Street "without leave of the archbishop", who was "by no means friendly to it", and it also had "many clerical and lay opponents". Moreover, the shortage of manpower underlined that "the first requirement was to strengthen ourselves at home, and then lend help to the Isle of Man, Preston, Buenos Aires, and America". In short, he exclaimed, let Fr Kenney "forget America, and give himself to us, become one of us, live with us".

It was an indication of the state of his knowledge of Kenney's mind, as well as an indication of Kenney's close-mouthedness about his commission, that Esmonde, at least on 10 June 1830, seemed to think that the decision to send him to America was at Kenney's own instigation! St Leger, not surprisingly, does not appear to have made any representation to the General on the matter.

In the light of this overall background, it is not surprising that Kenney's eventual disclosure met with a very cool response from Esmonde. On the evening of 26 August, Kenney called the consultors to his room and there formally announced his departure and the General's appointment of Fr St Leger as vice-provincial. He was visibly moved, but declared that he was happy that the prospects of the Society were now better than when he received the government of it in 1822. St Leger then spoke, praising all that Kenney had done as superior and saying that he thought him "a man specially raised up by God in these difficult times for the good of the Society in Ireland", and he agreed that the Society was in much better state now than when Mr Kenney received the government of it.

"All this astonished me," Esmonde wrote. And the following day, in the presence of St Leger, he accused Kenney of leaving the college far worse off than when he took it over in 1822-3. Infuriated, Kenney requested St Leger to make a thorough investigation of the temporalities of the college and to do him justice against this "unfounded calumny", and went on to declare, it seems, *"that from this out he had done forever with Mr Esmonde"*.

Despite the apparent animus in his journal, little more than a week later Esmonde noted: "I went to Dublin to bid Mr Kenney good bye previous to his departure for America."[37] Seemingly unmoved by confrontation himself, he appears to have expected others to emerge unscathed from his enunciation of "plain truths" expressed in an "impertinent way". A man of different temperament like Kenney felt undermined and maimed by such behaviour, and sought relief from the burden of governing such colleagues. Yet, like Dr Doyle, he sensed the absence of malice in Esmonde and was conscious of his physical frailty, and accordingly, despite his assertion that he "had done for ever" with him, it was to Esmonde and "all our good brothers and friends around you" that he wrote from New York on 3 November 1830, to give an account of his voyage and announce his safe arrival.[38]

In the event, he did not leave Dublin till 12 September; and then went directly to Liverpool and changed the booking to a later packet, as Fr Grivel was not ready.[39] This gave him breathing space to write some letters, visit friends at Preston and Stonyhurst, and generally slow down. He was more exhausted than he wished to admit.

Parting letters – Preparing for the way ahead

His first letters, naturally enough, were to American Jesuits. To his fairly frequent correspondent, James Ryder, who had done so well at his studies in Italy, he wrote on 14 September of his imminent departure and asked him to let "Dr Power and his friends at New York know that we are coming by the packet that sails on the 24th from Liverpool". It would be "too formal" for him, personally, "to write or let them know".[40] The following day he wrote to his friend McElroy, and to him, not for the first time, he spoke frankly of his inner feelings and motivations.

"You cannot imagine," he wrote, "how much I dread the onus imposed on me. Had I, as I told the General, been sent to help you in any way that would not carry with it the responsibility of directing others, or of arranging your very difficult temporalities etc., I should go with great pleasure. God is, however, all sufficient."[41] Two points, however, consoled him. First, that the decisions to send him, and appoint him Visitor, were contrary to his own feelings and wishes; and secondly, that he had never put himself in the way of these decisions. Again, the emphasis on not seeking his own will, not wishing to bend the superior's will to his, so that he could truly feel that in obeying, especially in matters not to his liking, he was journeying with him who said – "not my will but thine be done".

Within a few days, however, his overtaxed body made its needs felt. Writing to Robert Haly in Dublin, he remarked that Fr St Leger had urged him to take a rest. He had thought the advice "supererogatory", until for three days, from Saturday to Monday, he was laid low by a sharp pain in his side.[42]

On 24 September, as the ship was delayed, he availed of the time to write to Fr Roothaan. The pain and trauma surrounding the dismissal of Fr Frazer had clearly contributed to his exhaustion. Although he had already sent a full account, he could not help referring to it again as he felt "much embittered" about it. "Since the apostasy of the too famous Andrew Saul in the seventeenth century," he wrote, "we have not had a blow like this." The esteem and reputation which the outstanding fathers of the Irish mission had left, and which had spread throughout the whole country, had led to "benevolence and good relations with the-bishops ever since the restoration of the Society"; and this thankfully remained despite the damage caused by this "unhappy person". Dr Doyle alone, had "spoken badly of our institute". The "excellent archbishop" had not said a word though he (Kenney) feared "the impression such awfulness may have made on his mind". What the "awfulness" was is not clear. Frazer was later said to be "in Aberdeen preaching controversy, and much followed".[43] Kenney's detailed letter on the matter to the General cannot be traced, though a letter from the latter to Kenney, dated 24 July 1830, indicated that he was not surprised that Frazer had to be dismissed.[44]

Having spoken of his distress concerning the dismissal, Kenney turned to his American mission. He was under the impression that Fr Grivel was to be his assistant in the United States. This arrangement was quite unsuitable, he declared. Grivel's English was poor, he did not know America, and he was 61 years of age. A great deal was required where the Americans were concerned to assure their fidelity, and their prompt and effective agreement with the things that would have to be done. And if in himself there were certain obstacles, because he was "so inadequately instructed in their affairs", was "not from the country", and for other reasons "not now necessary to mention", how much more was this the case with Fr Grivel. What was needed was one of the Americans, someone who knew the country, the language and customs, and could make smooth the paths. He then proceeded to make suggestions, which unwittingly confirmed how "inadequately instructed" he was "in their affairs".

He suggested Fr Dubuisson as a possible assistant, apparently unaware of his limitations in the English language, his criticism of republican ways, and his association with the continental rather than the native American "camp". Later in the letter, he remarked that if there were no suitable native born American he would recommend Fr McElroy who, though not born in the United States, was an American citizen; and although he had not done sufficient studies to be made a professed father, he had "a good head", was "well accepted and active, well thought of by the academic people and" had "done a world of good on the mission". This seemed to be a plea to have someone he knew well rather than an informed assessment: for McElroy again was strongly associated with those critical of native Americans, while his academic standing was undermined by his limited education and "particularly (by) his social status as a former lay brother in the order".[45]

Finally, with an eye, no doubt, to the General's instruction to examine carefully the temporalities of the mission, he made a point of remarking that "the temporalities are the great evil of ours in America". There was no one who was experienced and able in temporal matters – such as the guardianship and development of investments, nor anyone who knew much of other matters of a similar nature. After this careful reminder of how difficult was his task, he concluded on a note of detached obedience: that whatever his Paternity decreed with regard to Grivel, Dubuisson, or McElroy, was acceptable to him.[46]

The strength of empathy and heritage

Despite the "certain obstacles" in himself, and his awareness of the difficulties in gaining the prompt and effective agreement of Americans, and also the fears he had expressed to McElroy, he had at another level an instinctive confidence in his ability to handle the situation, partly based on previous experience of the people and country. Intuitively, he had absorbed the relevance of the kind of advice which his friend Ryder communicated to his fellow-American, McSherry, as the latter returned home from Europe.

> You know better than I ... that far more good is to be done in America by reason and good example than by authority and force. Accordingly, all the true spirit of the Society you have imbibed in Italy infuse into Ours without letting it appear that it is imported from Italy, and be "to their virtues ever kind, and to their faults a little blind".[47]

Ryder, indeed, from the time of his own return to the United States, in 1829, importuned the General to send Kenney to America as superior;[48] and McSherry was to be appointed Kenney's assistant.

And there were other intangible considerations which helped surmount psychological diffidence, and the physical fear induced, in his state of health, by the thought of six weeks of confinement, tossing and turning in a wooden sailing ship on a great ocean. These included his sense of political and social affinity with the United States: which, in O'Connell's phrase, had been raised from being a "pitiful province of England" to the position of "an independent and mighty nation",[49] and in which Irishmen could contribute as equal citizens – aspects which held a great, and almost romantic significance for men of Kenney's generation.

In his case, moreover, there was a further dimension, a transmitted ardour, where America was concerned: that sense of a common religious-family tradition, noticeable in his previous visit to the New World, which linked him with men of the Society who had travelled vast distances and endured intense hardships: from Francis Xavier in Japan and the Maluccas in the sixteenth century, to the North American martyrs, and Jacques Marquette tracing the course of the Mississippi, in the seventeenth, to Eusebio Kino living in the saddle and dominating the religious history of Sonora-California-Arizona into the eighteenth century. And that link merged, more readily in 1830 than in 1819, with a national heritage which now had taken on a Catholic identity. The combined cocktail was one to buttress resolution, straighten shoulders rounded by respiratory restriction, and master a cough that could whine and rasp like a saw through the living trunk.

IX

Maryland revisited: September 1830–October 1831

If ye would that in your graves
Your free sons would bless their sires,
Make the Far Green West your home
Cross with us the Atlantic's waves!
James Clarence Mangan, "America's Invitation"

The smooth and rough at sea

On 26 September 1830, Kenney and Grivel eventually set sail from Liverpool. Their ship, the *Sylas Richard*, was a vessel of 400 tons, 125 feet long, but "not wide in proportion". For the next thirty-five days they gazed at sky and water. Kenney, who kept a journal through much of his second American visitation, chronicled the events of each day. They were well looked after, he remarked. The beds were reasonably comfortable, sheets were changed thrice during the voyage, and the meals were gargantuan. He marvelled at the abundance of things to eat; and how so great a quantity and variety of food, dressed and served in a most excellent state, could be prepared in so small a kitchen. He detailed, in letter and journal,[1] the extensive menu for each meal with an enthusiasm which offered a clue to his overweight. For breakfast alone, there was: French rolls; teas, green, black, mixed; coffee; meal with milk; cold ham, beef, and rashers and eggs; with one other hot dish of meat – liver, chops, pork or mutton". Claret, milk, and water were available to drink instead of tea or coffee.

In addition to these attractions, the voyage had many days of calm sailing. Nevertheless, he had a difficult passage. "Nothing can reconcile me to eating or sleeping on a ship," he observed. His difficulty with his chest coloured his experience. "Two persons sleeping, one above another in a little room, with … a door and window through which air has never passed", was such a trial for him that he would not undergo it for a month for any other motive than that of duty. Although he slept and ate well, nothing seemed to refresh him; and for the first time he experienced "a swimming in the head", partly occasioned by a greater number of high seas than he had ever previously experienced.[2] In one of these, as he stood on the sheltered side of the deck, the vessel gave a sudden heave which threw him violently to the opposite side. The result was only a sprain,[3] but there was much pain for a few days, and some anxiety because no one could diagnose what exactly was wrong.[4]

Reflecting on the problems posed by the voyage, he faced the reality that he was ten years older than when he had last crossed the Atlantic, was not as strong physically or as vigorous mentally as he had been, and that he had set out already "greatly fatigued in mind and body". In that condition, the motion and smell of the ship affected him more than usual, and he found that to write or read for an hour upset him. He noted gratefully, however, that Fr Grivel – whom he had so often criticised – had been "a great comfort".[5]

En route to Georgetown

When they eventually arrived in New York on 31 October, they were relieved to be met by Dr Power, vicar general of the diocese, whom Ryder, as requested, had alerted to their arrival. A greatly esteemed figure in New York, whom many thought should have been bishop,[6] he greeted them most hospitably and would not hear of their staying in a hotel, but had them conveyed to the bishop's house, where he acted as their host in the absence of his Lordship in Europe.[7]

They spent a week in New York, then two days at Philadelphia, and from there moved to Baltimore. From Baltimore, on 12 November, Kenney wrote to McElroy in a confidential vein, seeking his advice as a friend. His patent, he said, was that of "*Visitor cum potestate superioris* (Visitor with the power of superior) for the present". He expected further instructions from the General to await him in Georgetown. What ulterior views his Paternity had in mind, he did not know, but he felt he would "very soon make these missions a province or, at least, a vice-province". Meanwhile, he (Kenney) sought a socius or assistant, and would welcome McElroy's advice.[8]

He and Grivel arrived at Georgetown on 13 November to a warm welcome. Straight away, Kenney became involved in his role. The General's instructions, sent from Rome on 3 July, awaited him. They set his agenda for the time ahead. He read them with some trepidation.

THE GENERAL'S INSTRUCTIONS

Tuition fees

Fr Roothaan commenced with a disappointing comment from Georgetown's point of view. The college had charged tuition fees for boarders and day pupils alike until 1827, when formal dispensation to do so was sought. It was refused by the then superior general, Fr Fortis. This led to appeals on the grounds of financial need and of the American people's mistrust of those who charged nothing for education.[9] Now Roothaan stated that it was clear from letters sent to him that the number of scholars had greatly increased that year, and that among them were members of prominent families. Consequently, it would appear "that the prejudice against free schools attributed to that people either does not exist, or, if it did, has ceased". Accordingly, he reiterated what Fr Fortis decreed with respect to the non-acceptance of emoluments for instruction, as laid down in the constitutions.

The bishops

From there, the letter of instructions moved to a recommendation to Kenney which, the General said, he had more than once commended to the American fathers, namely, that he should "take very special care in every undertaking to consult the bishops"; and he was not to make use of the special faculties and exemptions granted the Society by the Holy See, if doing so would in the slightest way cause displeasure.

Temporal matters: farms and slaves

These items, however, were preliminary to the main issue to which Roothaan wished to direct his attention as Visitor, namely, "the state of temporal affairs".

At first sight, it may have seemed to Kenney that he was back where he started as Visitor ten years previously. The present General, too, was concerned about the large farms, the amount of time and trouble taken by their administration, and the "sense of proprietorship" which they generated and which constituted a danger to the spirit of poverty. As he read on, however, it became evident that Roothaan's main focus was on the productivity of the farms and the problem posed by the slaves. "The corruption and immorality" of the later was almost proverbial, the General declared. They lived together like animals, and this necessarily so, it seemed, "because of the their numbers and the insufficient productivity of the farms". Some of them, moreover, were "difficult to govern" and sooner or later would "lay claim to their liberty". In the circumstances, he asked, "would it not be to the temporal and spiritual good of the Society to sell the farms with the slaves, and allocate the money in a different way to other useful purposes?"

This was the question, he continued, to which Kenney was to especially apply his mind, so that being "precisely informed" he, Roothaan, might make a decision. So long as the situation remained uncertain, the discipline of the mission must necessarily suffer. He was to examine the temporal affairs most carefully, and avail of the assistance of Fr McElroy or any other Jesuit said to be skilled in such matters.

Finally, the General commended to his "zeal and charity" a special love for the American section of the Society, and requested that he seek "with full judgement, yet gently and prudently", to restore gradually the flowering of religious discipline, and the genuine spirit of order, so that abundant fruit might be brought forth to God's glory. In a postscript he informed him that his con-

JESUIT RESIDENCES, 1830–1833

MAINE

miles

0   50   100

V T.

Indian Mission •

N . H .

NEW YORK

MASS.

CONN. R.I.

PENNSLYVANIA

Goshenhoppen •

Conewago •

Frederick • Bohemia

Georgetown • White Marsh

W . V A

Alexandria
St Joseph's

St Thomas Manor

Newtown

St Inigoes

N CAROLINA

sultors were to be: Frs Grivel, Dzierozynski, Dubuisson, and Mulledy.[10]

Kenney immediately contacted the new consultors, and called a meeting for the following day. As soon as the names were known, there was immediate comment among some of the Anglo-Irish-Americans that only *one* of their number had been appointed; and it was assumed that he was appointed merely because of his office of president, or rector, of Georgetown. The assumption was well grounded. Fr Roothaan, at this stage, was highly suspicious of the Americans' spirit of independence, and especially where Mulledy was concerned. "Keep an eye on this new rector," he counselled the superior, Dzierozynski, in May 1830, "let him not do everything as he pleases."[11]

First consultors' meeting

Kenney presented his patent to the consultors on 14 November 1830. It was dated 29 May 1830. Straight away, certain words in the document gave rise to discussion. The General had written: "*Te in Visitatorem Americanae missionis cum potestate superioris eligimus*" (We have chosen you as Visitor of the American mission with the power of superior). Dzierozynski asked the Visitor if the words "cum potestate superioris" (with power of superior) did not "constitute him superior of the mission with the ordinary authority annexed to that office?" Kenney replied that there was no further information on the matter in the patent, or in the further instructions which had awaited him at Georgetown. The words were new to him, he stated. They were not in any other patent he had seen. Fr Dzierozynski was of the view that the words clearly indicated that Kenney was both Visitor and overall superior, and the fact that new consultors had been appointed supported this interpretation. All the other consultors came round to the same view.

So, Kenney, who was always so concerned to shed the burden of authority, found himself reluctantly saddled with a dual responsibility. In his report to Roothaan the following day he sought clarification. The reply, eventually sent from Rome on 10 January 1831, stated that the General saw no reason to add anything to his original words, since their meaning was "patently clear"![12]

From Kenney's standpoint, this was the first of a number of disconcerting experiences arising from the at times precipitous style of Fr Roothaan's government. Instructions which were not clear were to be followed by instances of decisions taken, even radical changes in policy, without consultation, sometimes without forewarning or explanation, so that he would justifiably feel on occasion that he was being bypassed and his authority undermined.

Taking stock and settling in

Meanwhile, on the evening of 14 November, Fr Dzierozynski had it announced in the refectory that Fr Kenney was superior as well as Visitor, and the Visitor's faculties were declared. Next day, Kenney visited the community chapel and the "scholars chapel" and spoke briefly on the General's interest in the welfare of the mission and on his own role as Visitor. It was then made known that it would be some time before he could start seeing people in private interview. A pause of some days was deemed necessary for repose, to experience "the general state of things", to receive and return visits, and to write to the General.

In his communication to the latter, he told first, as has been seen, of how his letter patent had been interpreted, and then went on to speak of the central part of his commission. He clearly felt daunted by the extent and density of the issues. "The question of selling, or not selling, our property," he wrote, "is very serious and, at first sight, frightening." Much time and application would be required to marshal opinions and arguments so as to enable his Paternity to have the required clarity to make his decision. There were also other issues to be addressed, "regarding studies, the novices, and individual missions", which were affected by the particular circumstances of the country. Indeed, many of the difficulties experienced by members of the Society arose from their not understanding the customs and spirit of the people. Because of this, he requested that Fr McElroy be his socius or assistant.[13]

Some unpleasant experiences

His first days in Georgetown were also marked by some unpleasant experiences arising from his dual role as Visitor and superior.

Almost immediately after his arrival, he was requested by the Revd Joseph Fairclough, a secular priest who was pastor of the Jesuit church and residence at Alexandria, south of Georgetown, to come and visit him. The latter had been made pastor as there was no Jesuit available. The previous archbishop, Dr Marechal, had recalled his faculties, and ordered him to give up the church. He obeyed the suspension, but stayed on in the church and residence and rallied the congregation to his support. This was clearly unacceptable to the Jesuit owners. He railed against them as a result, and wrote very critical letters about them to the next archbishop, Dr Whitfield, and suggested to him "that if he sent a non-Jesuit there, the premises, by means of the congregation, would pass into the hands of the archbishop". Fr Neale, who held the deeds of the property for the Society, sought legal assistance. Arising from this, Fr Fairclough asked to meet the Visitor.

The latter made it clear by letter[14] that he did not approve of what he, Fairclough, was doing, but that he was prepared to meet with him. So on 20 November, a week after his arrival, Kenney departed Georgetown by steamer: travelling down the Potomac, and then taking coach to Alexandria. It was a vain journey. "The gentleman had the effrontery to require that Mr Kenney would cause Mr F. Neale to cede his deeds to the archbishop in order that he might send a secular priest to Alexandria." Kenney returned next day.[15] He would later remark that Fairclough had "done more than is known to poison the mind of the archbishop against us";[16] and it was, indeed, to dispose Dr Whitfield favourably that he subsequently agreed to spend Christmas at Baltimore, away from his own house and community.

Also of a pressing and unpleasant nature in the early weeks was a meeting of consultors on 5 December, which led to his having to dismiss from the order Brother James Fenwick, who had been a steward to a number of farms, but appeared to have been enticed by the lure of commerce and to have lost his desire to continue in religious life.[17]

First major decisions: relocating the noviceship

There were so many matters arising, so many calls on him in his dual role as Visitor and superior, that he was soon concerned at their impact on his visitation of Georgetown College. Hence, when he received a letter from John McElroy inviting him to Frederick to assess its suitability for a noviceship, he replied, on 23 November, that he was engaged in the visitation of the college and was determined not to stir from Georgetown before Christmas.

He had promised the archbishop, he continued, that he would spend Christmas day with him, but as soon as he could leave Baltimore he would go on to Frederick. He cautioned, meanwhile, that McElroy's plan for the noviciate did not seem feasible, as there was no certain income indicated for the support of the novices. He went on, however, with the courtesy that marked all his relationships in the United States, to assure him that there would not be "either decision or impression" contrary to his view, before he, Kenney, had "the pleasure of seeing Frederick with all its improvements". He then added that he thought it might be necessary to take him temporarily from Frederick, as the General had emphasised the need for competent advice on temporal affairs and had mentioned him by name. On the issue of selling the farms, his Paternity had also instructed him to scrutinise carefully the reasons for and against. It was a large undertaking, Kenney continued, and not to be rushed: "We must take our time, make our plan, and, in order, see everyplace and everything." As a start, however, McElroy must accompany him on his visits to the mission stations. He would do his best, in his absence, to supply for the needs of Frederick. He requested that, if possible, McElroy come to see him in the first week of December.[18]

The last request was easily met, for McElroy was due to arrive at Georgetown on 6 December to give the annual retreat to the students. Kenney participated in the religious exercises: giving on different days, an instruction on the sacrament of penance, on prayer, and on holy communion. On one of those days he also found time to receive the religious profession of a sister of the Visitation convent, in a ceremony lasting two hours.[19] The retreat finished on 10 December; and next day there was a meeting of the consultors which McElroy attended. The subject was the location of the noviceship. It was generally agreed that Georgetown was too distracting and busy, and that an alternative place was urgently needed. McElroy was present to put forward his proposal of Frederick as the location.

During the discussion, there were different views as to whether the location should be in a city or in the country; and then all agreed that there were only two possibilities, Frederick, or the White Marsh farm and residence. Most of the consultors were impressed by McElroy's presentation, but Mulledy held out for White Marsh. Kenney deferred decision, saying he would carefully weigh the reasons on each side.[20]

As McElroy's new house at Frederick could not be ready for some months; and curious to see how matters stood at White Marsh, which he had instituted as a place for novices during his first visitation but which had proved unable to provide for them, he decided to visit it with Mulledy. They set out on Mr Neale's chaise, and managed to mix business with some pleasure. The next day, Sunday, Kenney was asked to preach at the mission. Subsequently, he dined with some of the prominent local Catholics, and that night Mulledy made a "punch with butter, which he called a Virginian stew". Next morning he made a different variety of punch which fortified them for the journey home.

Next day, 14 December, Kenney wrote to McElroy to convey his views on White Marsh and the location of the noviceship. He had had a good meeting with a former Jesuit scholastic Dr Jerome Mudd, who was in charge of the farm. The latter had assured him that it was "the most healthy of all the farms in Maryland"; and had shown, in considerable detail, how it could accommodate 15 novices, and feed them well from the produce of the farm. Moreover, he had pointed out that the presence of a novice master, and of any priest who might be a novice, would be of great assistance to the mission station, as it would release the missioners to serve distant congregations. The obligation under the constitutions for the novices to teach catechism and visit the poor, could be met there by their "catechising" on Sundays the blacks, and children sent by members of the congregation; while in the 100 blacks at White Marsh they "could not fail to find substitutes for the poor". Kenney, as a result, proposed to send the novices there for some months as a trial, at least until McElroy's house was ready.[21]

Three days later, 17 December, the matter was considered at a consultation. A further meeting was required, on 21 December, before the proposal was accepted. The novices were to go to White Marsh in the spring or before it.[22]

Planning on temporalities

This final consultation of the year also demonstrated that the Visitor had a definite plan on the issue recommended so strongly to his attention by the General, namely, whether it was expedient to sell, or otherwise dispose of the landed property. In each house he determined, he said, to present a range of questions on the subject, and provide an amount of information. The responses would be placed before the consultors, together with the arguments pro and con, and with the names of the fathers who favoured each side. In this way, the consultors would have both reason and authority for each side of the question. They would then give their own opinions on the case, and write privately to the General. Kenney's minute of the consultation on the issue concluded with the comment: "This plan was approved and agreed to by all."

At this stage, he had also a scheme of visitation laid out. From Baltimore he proposed to go directly to Frederick, and, following visitation there, go on a circuit to the outlying missions – farms and residences – in Pennsylvania; and thence to White Marsh on the way back to Georgetown.

The final question discussed at the meeting of consultors on 21 December, which was likely to be the last meeting for some time because of his programme of visitations, was a question of major import, which was to surface in different forms during his time in the United States.

Day scholars, boarders, and tuition fees

At this stage it concerned "prohibiting the further increase of day scholars at Georgetown college"; but in the background was the fact that there was an increased demand for boarding places, which offered a greater prospect of making the college financially viable – given the continuance of Fr Fortis's decree against tuition fees. Boarders paid 150 American dollars annually for board and lodging; whereas the day scholars, who used to pay 50 dollars annually, now, since Fr Fortis's instruction, were charged only 5 dollars, and that under the heading of "fire and servants".

Although such financial considerations were not put forward in the consultors' deliberations, and could not be because of Fr Roothaan's confirmation of his predecessor's decree, they remained part of the hard background. And, significantly, when Kenney wrote about the issue to his friend Thomas Glover, at Rome, he was careful to introduce it by saying that while he did not seek the revocation of Fr Fortis's order, he did feel that it was due to the General to let him see that the information on which he grounded his resolution to confirm that order was completely erroneous – the information, namely, that the scholars who received a gratuitous education at Georgetown were much increased in numbers and that many of them were of the more respectable ranks of society. In fact, the increase in numbers had been among the boarders, who were also the ones who came from many of the more respectable families. There had not been an increase of late among "the 5 dollar boys", and an examination of their parents' occupations[23] showed that very few could be called the sons of respectable families. He drew attention to all this, he said, "as a proof of the facility with which even good men exaggerate or misrepresent facts which they would wish to establish".[24]

His minutes on the consultation relating to "prohibiting the further increase of the day-scholars" show that, prior to meeting his own consultors, he met with the consultors of the college, with whom he discussed the state of the different school classes and the influence of the day scholars on the college. With regard to the last, he noted that they all agreed that day scholars were an injury to the boarders – and should be discontinued.[25] At his own consultors' meeting, the proposal to prohibit the further increase of day scholars was put forward with many supporting reasons by the rector, Fr Mulledy.

Kenney subsequently indicated what these were in the course of a letter to Glover – who, as noted previously, he availed of as a channel to the General on sensitive issues, and also as a means of defending himself against complaints and misinformation. "All the American fathers", wished to get rid of these day scholars, he reported, "firstly because, with their limited number of masters, they cannot attend to them and do justice to the 102 convittori [boarders]; secondly, because the place is so little adapted to keep up a strict separation, they find it most difficult since the increase of the convittori, to prevent the externs [day scholars] from bringing (in) prohibited articles, and otherwise keeping up private intercourse with the convittori; thirdly, because parents of the convittori, and other friends of the college, have represented to them that these day scholars will ultimately injure the reputation of the college, and are even now a motive with many not to send their children to it, notwithstanding that it has risen to notice so much since Fr Mulledy's appointment and the return (from Italy) of the other fathers. Lastly, they observe that as these boys are all, or nearly all, Protestants, who never come to prayer, mass, or catechism, they have no opportunity of infusing any moral principles into their heads; and that the end of our education in their regard cannot be realised, while, on the other hand, the college is reproached with their misconduct when they behave amiss."

In the light of these remarks, Kenney continued, he had proposed to the consultors that it be left to the rector to decline to receive any new day scholars, but Fr Dzierozynski, who had encouraged the influx of day pupils, wished them to continue; while Grivel "got frightened, or, as is usual with him, pretended to think the matter of such importance that it should be postponed". And so it was, Kenney concluded, lest anyone might conclude that he had "acted precipitately" in the matter.[26]

He was not, it would seem, fair to Dzierozynski, who suspected that financial and class considerations were influencing the decision. He had earlier made his position clear to Fr Roothaan: "the Society must preserve its tradition of educating both rich and poor alike according to their promise, and not according to their ability to pay".[27]

The decision, which Kenney so evidently sought, was eventually taken in 1832; and also in that year there was to be a new approach to the tuition fees – as will appear in the next chapter.

Meanwhile, there was a sense of unfinished business. Despite this, and the fact that he had not completed his visitation of the college, he was sufficiently happy with the situation there to feel that he could, at this point, interrupt his scrutiny, not just to go to Baltimore to honour the archbishop's invitation to preach on Christmas day in his cathedral,[28] but also, as already noted, to go on from there to commence his programme of other visits. How he actually viewed Georgetown at this point was conveyed in a report he sent to the General early in the new year.

First report on the college

He wrote from Frederick on 10 January 1831.

> In the college I have summoned all individually according to the rule; and, by the grace of God, everything is going so well that I have found little to change. Fr Mulledy is an active rector – he gives satisfaction to the members of the house, and strongly upholds discipline both among the boarders and the religious, and is highly regarded by outsiders, especially the native Americans. He has now more than 100 boarders, who are well organised and obedient; and almost all the college's debts have by now been wiped out. So, I have affirmed him in his office as far as I could; and I ask your Paternity to declare him rector *de jure*.

He was aware of Mulledy's defects, he continued, but his "extremely impetuous enthusiasm and excessive patriotism" were daily becoming more moderate, and he loved and upheld the true principles of the Society's discipline and sincerely sought to serve God in accordance with his vocation. He, Kenney, had admonished him to amend certain things, and had appointed as his consultors Frs Ryder, McSherry, Young, and Fenwick – all of whom remained in the college.

He went on to say that he had made Ryder minister of the college, and admonitor to the rector. McSherry had been minister, but as there was great need of another master, and there was no one else to hand, he was appointed to a teaching position. In any event, he was "not endowed with that shrewdness and energy of which a minister has need". The distribution of the hours of meals, he continued, and the discipline of penances, had been brought into line with the Italian model. And the custom, which had grown up, of having talk three days a week during dinner and supper, had been terminated. The rector, of course, still retained the power to grant such a favour on some occasions during the year. "Only this and similar matters needed to be put into better order", he added, as the essentials of the Society's discipline had been restored, or preserved, through the piety and care of Fr Dzierozynski.

Rounding off the first weeks

In the same letter, he spoke of the choice of a novice master. He had to speak

1   Peter Kenney sj, from a portrait in his later years

2   Stonyhurst in 1794

3   Jougne church, and the graveyard where Charles Plowden SJ is buried

4   The fort at Milazzo, Sicvily, as it stands today

5   A view of the St. Rosalia procession, Palermo, much as described by Kenney

6 Clongowes Wood College, c. 1819

7 Maynooth College, c. 1810 from a painting by G.P. Coddan in the library

8 Daniel Murray, archbishop of Dublin, from a portrait in Gardiner Street church

9 Blessed Edmund Ignatius Rice,
founder of the Irish Christian
Brothers, from a contemporary
engraving by W. McDowall after
a painting bt R. Kennedy

10 Thomas Betagh sJ, 1738-1811

11 Mary Aikenhead, foundress of the Irish Sisters of Charity, at the age of twenty

12 Mother Frances Mary Teresa Ball, 1794-1861, from Joseph Haverty's portrait in 1834 in Loreto Abbey, Rathfarnham, Dublin

13 St Regis Seminary, Florissant, Missouri, 1830, from a
sketch by John B. Louis SJ

14 St Rose Philippine Duchesne, 1769-1852, of the
Society of the Sacred Heart, friend and benefactress of
pioneer Florissant Jesuits

15 Thomas Mulledy sJ, twice president
    of Georgetown, 1829-37 and
    1845-8, from a daguerrotype

16 John McElroy sJ, Missionary,
    chaplain and founder of Frederick
    and Boston colleges

17 Georgetown College in the 1830s, as Kenney would have known it;
    an engraving by W. Harrison after a design by S. Pinistri

18 St Louis College, *c.* 1829; a sketch by C. Bosseron Chambers

19 St Louis waterfront, *c.* 1840; a sketch by Norbury L. Wayman

20 "The Missioners Welcome" an illustration of an event in the life of Peter J. De Smet, the "Black Robe," friend and missioner to American Indians

21 Peter J. De Smet sj, an engraving by J. Franck after a painting by N. de Keysey

22 Joseph Rosati, bishop of St Louis, 1827-43, from a contemporary portrait

23 St Joseph's, the oldest Catholic church in Philadelphia, which Kenney received back for the Society and where he ministered

24 Scene from a bicentennary celebration at St Joseph's

25 John Roothan, General of the Jesuits during the
latter part of Kenney's life

26 St Francis Xavier's church, Gardiner Street, Dublin,
from the front

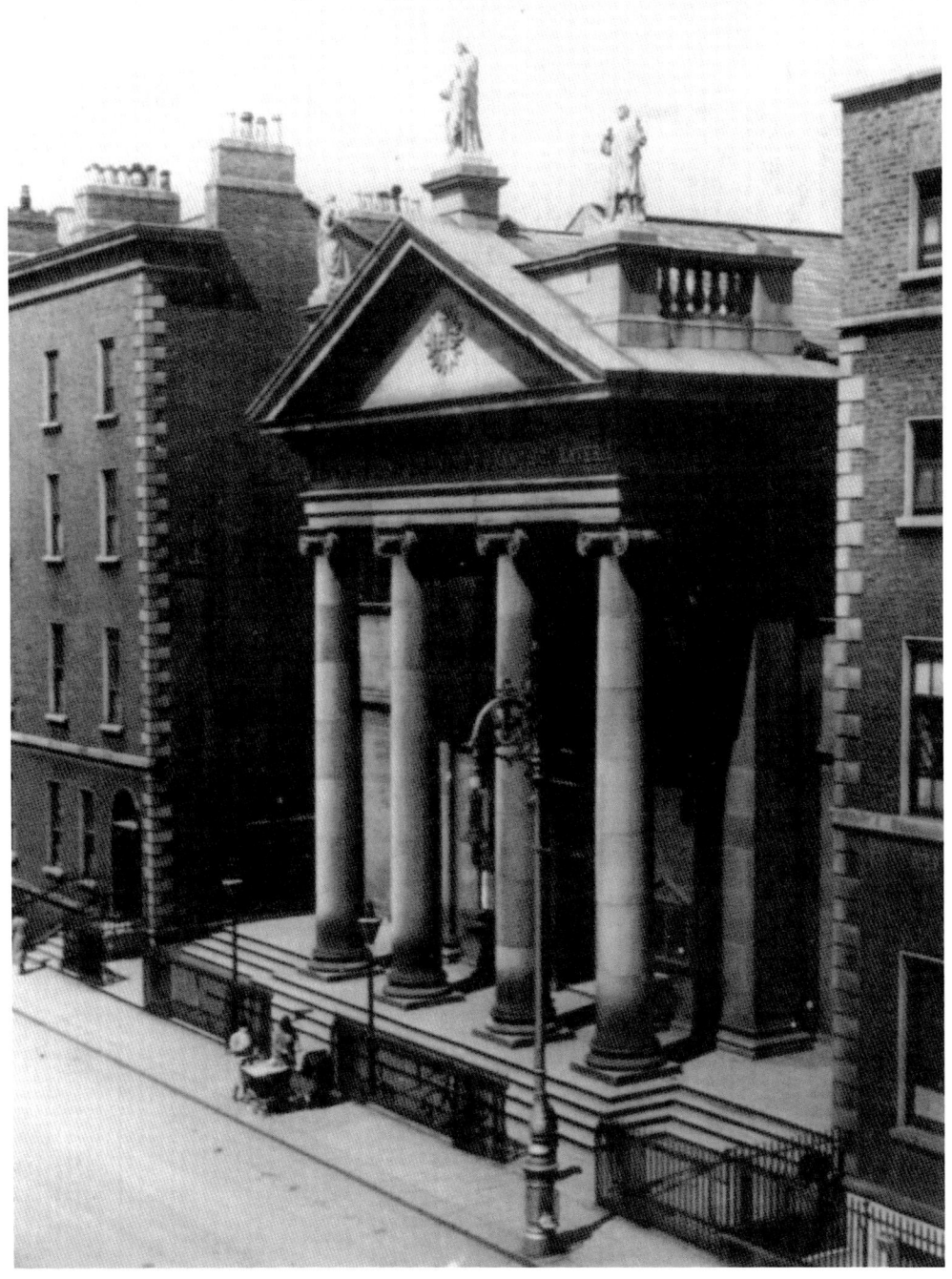

27 Crowds at a Novena of grace in the Gardiner Street church

individually to consultors on the subject, since some of them were likely candidates for the position. Most considered that Fr Dzierozynski had been too indulgent in that office towards the young men and did not understand their character, and hence they preferred that the position be committed to Fr Grivel. This Kenney had done; though he could not resist adding: "he is not the man I would select out of thousands for such an office!" Dzierozynski was made professor of theology at the college, and chaplain or "spiritual prefect".

Three young Belgians had arrived to join the Society, Kenney continued. They were sent by that most zealous Belgian layman, Peter de Nef, together with a large number of books, mass vestments, a large bell, and gold and silver coins to the value of 16,000 French francs. De Nef's zeal, manifested in contributions of men and material gifts, was a mainstay of the Jesuit mission in the United States, and was to receive regular mention in Kenney's letters.

As to his writing from Frederick at this stage, he took care to explain that the archbishop's invitation to Baltimore had obliged him to set out from Georgetown when his visitation of it was not yet finished; and that once in Baltimore it seemed expedient to visit the residences, which were in that region north of Georgetown, before returning to the college. It was also appropriate to visit these at this early point in the visitation, since their temporal affairs were less complicated than those of other missions, and hence the information required by his official instructions could be more easily garnered there. He planned to bring Fr McElroy with him, moreover, so that the condition of the northern missions might be better discussed and understood.[29]

Public relations role

There was one important matter he did not mention: namely the public relations side to his role as Visitor and superior. His journey to Baltimore, indeed, was part of a public relations exercise with the world outside the college. As the Jesuit General's official representative in the United States of America, his fellow religious were inclined to push him forward socially, and people in Washington and other cities were usually eager to meet him. For his part, he was disposed to be as available and as agreeable as possible for the sake of the benefit to the college and to the order. He found himself invited to dinner in various houses; and among the list of people he recorded meeting were ambassadors and dignitaries from other lands reflecting the college's proximity to Washington. In the six weeks from his arrival to the end of December, he included among those he met: at Philadelphia, Dr Conwell, bishop of Philadelphia, and Dr Kenrick his coadjutor; at New York, Dr McNevin; at Georgetown, the Chevalier Forrledi, "Portuguese minister to the United States", and a "Madame Sturlede, ex-empress of Mexico"; at Washington, the French ambassador; and at Baltimore, the Mexican minister, and, of course, Archbishop Whitfield and his priests and friends. The visit to Baltimore, as indicated earlier, was of particular importance. Tensions remained from the long controversy with the previous bishop, Dr Marechal; and the behaviour of Fr Fairclough had added to them. As Kenney had prepared to set out for Baltimore, the court case against Fairclough was in session.

The visit to Baltimore

He commenced his journey by moving into Washington on 23 December, spending the night at the Indian Queen hotel, so as to get the early morning stagecoach. It proved an unpleasant experience. Next day, however, he forgot his discomfort when warmly welcomed to Baltimore by the archbishop. As the next day again was Christmas day, he said his three masses in the cathedral. The first at 7.45 a.m. was said in almost complete darkness. At midday he preached. That evening, Dr Whitfield provided a splendid dinner for him and "the gentlemen of the seminary".[30]

On 26 December he preached at St Peter's Church, and then had dinner with Mrs Caton, Mr Carroll, Mrs McTavish, Mr Caton, Mr Wharton, and the Revd Mr Chance. "We were quite in the family way," Kenney wrote in his diary, referring to the Carroll ambience. "The archbishop was not invited to this party," he added. During the next four days he dined at a different place each day: meeting again with members of established families like the Catons and Carrolls; renewing old contacts and making new ones; being hosted by Dr De Barth, vicar-general of Philadelphia; and by friends of the archbishop, at a dinner which the latter also attended together with the superior of the college, Fr Samuel Eccleston, a future archbishop of Baltimore. Apart from the entertaining, he was largely housebound because of the very bad weather.

He left for Fredericktown, or Frederick, by stagecoach on 31 December. The town was not far distant, yet the journey westward proved taxing. "Such jolting I never before experienced," he wrote in his journal. Even though the thoroughfare was called "a turnpike, and said to be a good road", the wet weather had made it quite uneven.

With this journey he embarked on several months of detailed examination of all aspects of Jesuit life – in residences, school, mission stations and farms. The attention to detail in covering this period makes for heavy reading, and for any hapless general reader an almost necessarily boring experience, but it seems necessary to convey the diligence and thoroughness which Kenney brought to implementing the General's commission, and to appreciate the success, pain and frustration, he subsequently experienced.

HOUSEBOUND AT FREDERICK: GUIDING AND PLANNING

His friend, McElroy, sought to make him feel at home at the Frederick residence; and showed his esteem by actively involving him from the moment of his arrival in the liturgy, and in meeting members of the parish. He preached at high mass on 1 and 2 January 1831; supped with the choir – "ladies of singular worth", on the 4th, and preached again at high mass on 6 January.

He had earlier complained about the weather, but now he began to experience in a new way the severity of an American winter. From the beginning of the month there was continual frost. By 15 January he was commenting that a very great quantity of snow, about eight inches deep, had lain frozen for some days. Two days later he noted that snow lay two feet deep on the level, and in some places it was "higher than a man's head on horseback". There had been no mails east or west for three days.[32] Not surprisingly, his day book recorded the purchase of warm gloves, and socks.[33]

The sad plight of Irish labourers

"This, I think, is the severest winter that I have witnessed in my life", he wrote in his journal on 15 January; and he went on in sombre tones to speak of the effect of the cold on the many Irish labourers in the area.

> I have been here at Frederick since the afternoon of Dec. 31st, and in that time many poor Irish died in the neighbourhood. A great crowd of them are employed in the canal from Pittsburgh to Georgetown, which passes close to this place. The severity of the weather, bad lodging, and ardent spirits, kill a great number.

The influx of these Irish labourers had multiplied the sick calls, he added, and placed the priests concerned under much pressure. Fr Peeters from the Frederick community was "laid up through exhaustion".

This sad situation, with its effects on fellow Jesuits as well as fellow countrymen, weighed heavily on him. He conveyed his concern to Thomas Glover in a letter on 10 February. "A transient but powerful increase" in the already extensive labours of this residence, he confided, had been lately occasioned by the making of the canal from Pittsburgh to Georgetown, which attracted "a vast crowd of the poor Irish, who are the great white labourers of this country". They endured the exceptional heats in the summer, and the equally terrific frosts and snows of winter. About twenty had been buried in the graveyard of Frederick residence within the past six weeks, and many more in other places. To them the missioner was frequently called by day and night, 6, 12, and 16 miles along the canal. "In short," he concluded, "from here to Georgetown, more than 40 miles, the missioner here, and our two in Georgetown, Frs Von Lomel and Lucas, are the only priests within the reach of these poor men, who, however they may live, will not die without a priest, if they can get one."[34] Some days later, in a letter home to Fr Haly, to whose prayers he recommended the ailing Fr Peeters, he added the information that the Irish labourers, because they had no villages near them, were forced to lodge "in miserable huts tightly constructed of thin boards" which were "called chantees" [*sic*]. Snow and wind penetrated the crevices, and this, conjoined with ardent spirits, had led to the death of a great number of them.[35] Fr Dubuisson some weeks later put the number of Irish working on the canal and roads at around one thousand.[36]

The Peeters tragedy

To the severity of the winter, and the harrowing plight of the labourers, there was added for Kenney a sense of personal loss with the death of Fr Peeters. He had grown close to the zealous young Belgian, and was deeply upset at the waste of such a gifted life: a death brought on almost entirely by overwork. In several letters, during the young man's illness, he asked for prayers for his recovery. He had been but two years in the country, he informed Glover on 1 February, and had not known any English when he arrived, yet he now spoke very well, and at one of his mission areas, called the Tract, he had made thirty converts. Consequently, he added: "if the General send us missioners, they ought to be natives of the British Isles or young Belgians – no foreigners learn English with equal facility, and in goodness and activity they more than compensate for every deficiency."[37]

When Peeters died twelve days later, Kenney's sense of loss was such that he felt the need to write at length about him to Glover, and in the process conveyed something of the demands of missionary life, especially in Frederick, and of the need for understanding and compassion on the part of superiors. He also revealed more of his own humanity than he perhaps realised. The memory of the young Fleming was to remain with him, and to influence his thinking.

In his references to the young priest's work load it has to be kept in mind that church law required then, and for more than a century to come, that the celebrant of mass had to be completely fasting from the previous night, no matter how late in the morning the mass was celebrated or what other work he was required to undertake before it.

"On the 10th of this month, a few minutes before three a.m.," he wrote, "I received the last breath of good father John Francis Peeters, a native of Flanders." He entered the Society in 1828, at the age of 29, and after only ten months noviceship at Georgetown, he was sent to Frederick. The labour of the missions attached to Frederick and, perhaps, his "overzealous efforts to discharge his duties" hastened his death. Although not much accustomed to ride previously, he rode several miles three Sundays of the month, sometimes staying three or four days ministering to the Catholics scattered over the region, and instructing and hearing confessions of up to 200 blacks. Kenney stood in for him on one Sunday during Peeter's illness, and though he travelled by sleigh and only heard confessions, he found those three or four days among "the hardest missionary days" he ever had. In addition, Peeters taught French and Latin in McElroy's secondary school, St John's seminary, at Frederick, and this meant that his journey to the mission stations on Friday or Saturday had often to be made "under a burning midday sun". "Last Christmas day (Saturday)," Kenney continued, "after the fatigue of hearing confessions on the vigil and in the morning, and after fasting to dinner in order to sing high mass here, he had only a hurried dinner before he rode to his six mile mission ... to sit down to fresh labour on that and the succeeding day." On New Year's day he was off again and stayed away till the Epiphany. The Saturday after that, although not well, he went to a small congregation where there was no church. "He returned sick, and the following Saturday took to the bed on which he died."

"I think it necessary to be thus circumstantial," Kenney continued, "because he often said that this mission was very good to kill priests, and yet nothing was done to alleviate his labours, though in my mind all this fatigue was far from being absolutely necessary; and I am justified in declaring to you that the good man died with the belief that his life was unnecessarily sacrificed. I am certain Fr Dzierozynski never understood the extent of his labours. Fr McElroy did not feel for them sufficiently to make a proper statement of them, and Fr Peeters was too religious to complain. I must add, that others who were witnesses of the details believe that Fr Peeters persuasion was too well founded."

He made this statement, he informed Glover, that the General might perceive the need of exhorting local superiors in America to have the *viscera misericordiae* [the bowels of mercy] with regard to the strength and health of those under their care. Fr McElroy was a man of strong constitution, fond of everything involving great exertion, who did not weigh sufficiently the effect of such exertion on strength, health, time and studies. "He and Frs Quickenborne and Dubuisson" and he feared many others, stood "much in need of all the checks that authority can give on this point, and of all the tenderness that charity can infuse into the heart."[38]

The demands of the excellent McElroy

McElroy's zeal and indefatigable energy, which made him heedless at times of the strain on others, was to become proverbial. He was endowed with a powerful constitution which enabled him to spend nights in the woods and to ride sometimes a hundred miles to attend someone who was dying. Indeed, it has been remarked that "practically all of western Maryland and much of western Virginia became his parish". At the age of sixty-four he took on the position of the first commissioned army chaplain during the American-Mexican war; and some years later founded Boston College and the church of the Immac-

ulate Conception.[39] He lived on to the age of ninety-five, joking in his final
years: "The angel of death has passed me by. I'm afraid Our Lord has forgotten to call me home."[40]

That same energy and zeal built in the town of Frederick, in the Frederick
valley, a "Catholic Free School" for boys, introduced religious sisters to open
a girls school, ran a church with regular services, served a number of mission
stations, and, while Kenney was on visitation, was planning a new church
which was to be an exact copy, but in larger dimensions, of the new Jesuit
church of St Francis Xavier in Gardiner Street, Dublin.

Kenney found himself in wonderment at what his remarkable friend had
accomplished in Frederick; but he could not but be concerned at the price to
others, and at the future prospects. Soon after his arrival, while Fr Peeters was
still alive, he wrote to Dzierozynski: "It's a great consolation to me to see all
the things which the excellent Fr McElroy has achieved"; but where was the
help to come from to continue this good work? Two scholastics had been kept
teaching at Frederick well beyond their allotted time: even though one of
them, Mr Curly, was now 37 years old and had not yet begun his studies in
logic; and the other, Kelly, aged 30, had not yet had an opportunity to begin
his noviceship. And McElroy himself and Peeters were almost worn out with
labour. In short, he concluded, "neither priests nor scholastics are equal to the
work".[41]

Yet, a month later, and despite Peeters death, he was reporting to Glover
that he found "the greatest difficulty in getting Fr McElroy to lessen duties
that he has really created for himself and others to the great consumption of
their time, strength and health". It was important, therefore, to examine carefully the overall demands at Frederick, and to limit activity to what was essential.[42]

A problematical school

This led him to inform Glover of the problems posed by the school, or *collegium inchoatum*, which Fr McElroy, with so much zeal and credit to himself,
had established. Although concerned about academic standards, and in particular the too little emphasis on Latin, Kenney was mainly troubled by the work-
load of the three Jesuit scholastics, Van Sweevelt, Curly and Kelly.

Their united labours on behalf of the school population of 70 Protestants
and 26 Catholics, were, he observed, "enough to shake any constitution".
From 8 o'clock in the morning to 4.30 in winter, 5.00 in summer, they were
almost continuously with these 96 scholars every day of the week. Although
some of the children were too young to study, the scholastics were expected to
teach them, or bring them to play, even in the evening. "You have some idea
of the fatigue of the schools in the Roman College in the months of June and

July", he reminded Glover, but the latitude at Frederick was 39.24 degrees, and its situation, "far from any sea breeze or great river", was "a cause of terrific heat". If the school were to continue to be conducted in its present manner, he could not see how the scholastics would have any strength left for their later study and work.

The public were being so well served, he continued, that he did not wonder that in America, where interest was well known to prevail over religious feeling, that even German Lutherans sent their children to Jesuit schools. But whether the good achieved, and the possibility of future good, were sufficient to justify the cost, was for him "as yet problematical".[43] The problematical aspect was added to by the fact that the town was "a very bigoted place" and the parsons "jealous and watchful". As a result, McElroy had not yet "hazarded to teach the Catholics the catechism in the presence of the Protestants", and no pupils had become Catholics in the boys' school.[44]

Consultors' comments on his progress

He spent two months at Frederick. This led one consultor, Fr Grivel, to write in his annual letter to the General: "Our Father Visitor seems to want to be based in Fredericktown. It is his practice, and that of Fr Brooks [the English provincial], to do things all alone. But I have always seen that things went well in that way because they are not hasty in action, and sometimes the consultors only serve to hinder business."[45] The discursive and elegantly circuitous Grivel was the only one to refer to the long absence at Frederick; and he was also the one least consulted by Kenney! The other consultors made just brief reference to the Visitor, all of it complimentary.

Dzierozynski, who differed from him on a few matters, described him "as an outstanding man, the kind of person which America long wished for";[46] Mulledy, who readily accepted his advice and correction, wrote that "the arrival of P. Kenney has brought the greatest consolation to all";[47] while Ryder, who replaced Grivel as consultor, spoke mainly of the impact of the Visitor on Georgetown: "the presence of P. Kenney as superior and Visitor has proved a true blessing to all. People are well disposed towards him. The college is now better regulated, there is devotion to silence and religious duties, there is peace and contentment".[48] Finally, Dubuisson remarked that he showed great understanding and patience with the impetuosity of McElroy, and then paid a revealing tribute: "Fr Kenney seems to proceed with plenty of prudence and without the slightest national bias. He has showed me a lot of confidence".[49]

What, indeed, kept Kenney so long at Frederick was a combination of factors: the variety of ministries there; his determination to give time and detailed study to every place he visited; its accessibility to Georgetown – being but 42 miles distant; and a factor which he did not allow for, the severity of the winter. "To day," he wrote to Robert Haly on 16 February, "the snow, by which I have been surrounded since the 14th January, began to melt." The first snow had fallen on 5 December, and from then to 16 February, with the exception of three or four days, there had been "a continual and intense frost ... accompanied with a terrific n.w. wind". In and about Frederick, he added, the height of the drifts was frightful. One hundred horses were employed to take the stage with the mail out of the town, and in a whole day they scarcely made ten miles. The mail from Baltimore to Philadelphia, with the long delayed western bags, was frequently dug out of drifts of snow. Many lives had been lost. It had been the most frightful winter that he had ever passed.[50] The enforced stay gave him time, however, to work out the most effective means of fulfilling his role and mission.

Organising for change

By the end of February, he was prepared to move on. Before doing so, he was expected as Visitor to present a *memoriale*, or memorandum, commenting on the situation as he found it and leaving instructions for the future. He was conscious, however, as he informed the General shortly after departing from Frederick, that he might be seen as an issuer of regulations, and he felt that "regulations" would be not only unwelcome but that, after being put into execution for a few months, local superiors would try by every means to exempt themselves from them just as much as their subjects, or else allow them to fall into disuse. Hence, after he had weighed the state of affairs and considered alternatives, he had decided on a two-pronged approach. He was insisting:

1. That in each house, as the Jesuit rule prescribed, there should be drawn up a custom book containing rules and requirements to determine domestic discipline, the running of the missions, and the functions of any attached church.

2. That he, acting "not just as Visitor but as superior provincial", following his visitation of each house, as the Society's constitutions required, would leave behind in each house a *memoriale*, a written comment and instruction as to what should be done or corrected in each, with an injunction that the memorial and custom book be in future inspected by the superior of the mission, or province, on his annual visitation. Up to this, he added, these two requirements had been almost overlooked. In restoring them, he was acting not as a Visitor, but rather as superior provincial, and thereby setting a pattern for provincials in the future.[51] In effect, it ensured a regular review, and proved a shrewd and far-reaching decision.

One of the main functions of the visitation, and, as a result, of each *memoriale*, was, in his view, to establish order, cohesion, and "uniformity of practice in the various houses of the Society in these missions". To this end, he took what he termed "5 rules" for his guide in writing his different *memoriale*.

1. To see what the institute of the Society said, or seemed to suppose, on the point in question; 2. Which side the general usage of the Society most favoured – as far as such usage could now be ascertained; 3. To inquire what usages were introduced by the Jesuits of the English province, who had founded these missions. 4. To determine whether the customs of the Roman province provided a model; 5. Lastly, to consider, other things being equal, what was most practicable and useful in the actual situation and circumstances.[52]

All this received its first outing at frederick at the end of February 1831. It was prepared for by a detailed examination of the various aspects of the church, residence, missions, and schools;[53] and was presented in a style which gave acknowledgement and praise where possible, and presented change, or reproof, in a veiled and gentle manner.

The model memoriale[54]

The document which he left "at the Residence of the Society of Jesus in Fredericktown, Maryland, on 28 February 1831", opened with an expression of satisfaction at the great improvements which had taken place since he visited Frederick in 1820. He then went on to observe that as the residence, the missions dependent on it, the church, and the school, were all, as it were, united in one establishment, it was most important that "the duties and usages of all these departments" be carefully set down to ensure "regularity and stability". Accordingly, he wished that the custom book, which had been commenced, be begun anew and that it indicate the manner of proceeding, the distribution of time, and duties to be carried out in each of these four areas. Having dealt with this ordered framework in some detail, he issued a number of instructions to be followed.

The first of these, as might be expected, was aimed at protecting members of the community from the driving zeal and energy of the superior. Thus, no new duty, office, function or practice, was to be added to those presently in operation "without the express leave of the provincial superior". Where the records of accounts were concerned, he insisted, as he would do in each place, that, in addition to the account books for different areas, there was to be one overall double-ruled book which gave the general picture of income and expenditure, or "charge and discharge", as he termed it, and which could readily be consulted by the superior, the procurator, and provincial superior wishing to learn quickly and clearly the state of the finances. He expressed his approbation of the remarkable economy exhibited in the expenses of the community and servants, which, including maintenance and wages, "in 8¼ years did not average $100 per annum"! He formally restricted the number of hours of work that might be demanded of scholastics, and instructed that the Jesuit brothers should not be employed digging graves for the public in the

Jesuits' churchyard, nor in any occupation "in which their labour would have the appearance of being used as a source of income". Finally, Fr McElroy was required to transfer the entire charge of the girls' school, and the convent, to the sisters to be exercised by them according to the rules of their institute.

And to ensure that the *memoriale* received maximum, and continued attention, he decreed that when the next visitation was made "this memorial is to be shown to the provincial superior, or Visitor, that he may see that its provisions have been carried into execution".

On 1 March he left for the old mission of St Francis Regis at Conewago, some forty miles away: a property of some 650 acres in Adams County, Pennsylvania, not far from the towns of Gettysburg and Emmitsburg.[55]

THE PLANTATION AND MISSION OF CONEWAGO

He went by Emmitsburg, probably to visit the Sulpician seminary of Mount St Mary, and did not reach Conewago until 3 March.[56] One of the better kept plantations, it had been one of his favourite places during his 1820 visitation.

On his arrival, he found that the improved weather had brought a backlog of post forwarded from Georgetown. Accordingly, correspondence vied for his immediate attention with the practical details of visitation. Most pressing was a confidential letter from Bishop Conwell of Philadelphia, written some weeks earlier, offering to secure for the Society its former house and church at Philadelphia, and suggesting that he be empowered to act for the order in the matter. The erstwhile opponents, his coadjutor, Bishop Francis Kenrick, and the parish priest, had moved to different locations in the diocese. Kenney, on the very day of his arrival, wrote to McElroy, asking him and Dubuisson to discuss the letter privately and advise him as soon as possible.[57] Subsequently he wrote to Mulledy for his views on this and a range of other matters, including the offer by the bishop of Bardstown of his college, capable of taking 150 boarders, together with teachers, if only the General would send him "three or four men of talent and piety".[58]

Also calling for attention was the issue of alleged miracles at the Visitation Sisters convent. Quite sceptical, and not wishing to be involved, he indicated little enthusiasm for Dubuisson's part in examining witnesses,[59] or his subsequent printed statement.[60]

Conewago was Kenney's first opportunity to carry out Roothaan's instruction to investigate the farms and the situation of the slaves. In the midst of this detailed examination, additional correspondence was a strain, especially as he had not yet got a socius or secretary. A letter from McElroy seeking exemption from his instructions, within a few weeks of Kenney leaving Frederick, was particularly unwelcome. McElroy sought the retention of Mr

Curly, saying that Kenney's decision had taken him unawares. The latter responded frostily that he would not "incur the responsibility of allowing the delay of a single day. I do not, my dear Father, take you unawares. I did not come to any determinations until I had well thought on your circumstances, as well as his and ours. Two months have nearly elapsed since I decidedly told you that he should go to Georgetown." Now, "when I hoped Mr C. had reached Georgetown, I receive a letter calling for a further, and an indefinite prolongation of his stay! I must request that he go directly to the college!"[61]

His investigation of Conewago was very thorough, to judge from the scattered notes which have survived. There was a long interview with Fr Lekeu, the superior, and with a Mr Lely, who gave him the history of the church and residence. There had been missionary contact with the area since 1745, and the current church of the Sacred Heart of Jesus was erected in 1789.[62] He noted the number of livestock, the number of those employed and their wages, the additional people employed at harvest time: all with a view to arriving at as accurate a picture as possible of expenditures and receipts.[63]

The question raised by the General about selling or not selling property was constantly kept in mind. To avoid such a drastic step, he and McElroy had toyed with the idea of "letting out the farms". Considering this alternative in the context of Conewago, he found there were a number of difficulties. It would not be easy to get "solvent and honest tenants", or to overcome the opposition of some Jesuits, and there was the further practical difficulty about gathering information – since enquiries about the prospect for lettings in the neighbourhood were likely to lead to uneasy suspicions on the part of the manager.[64]

Despite the amount of ground to be covered, he hoped to have finished his visitation by 22 March; and already by 10 March felt sufficiently sure of general standards in his visitations to date to report to Fr Roothaan that in Fredericktown and Conewago residences he found "no scandal or evil of much import ... In fact many things were praiseworthy." In the same letter, he told the General that he now did not think Fr McElroy suitable for the office of socius,[65] and thought that Fr McSherry was the only one who appeared to possess the qualities mentioned by his Paternity. "He's a prudent man and acceptable to all, but is lacking in quickness of mind and, I hear, that when he is faced with many matters he is easily distracted and made weak." But as a better man could not be found, he proposed to take him from the school in July to be his socius, unless in the meantime his Paternity arranged otherwise.[66]

Thus an important decision was put in train. He also assured the General that he was gathering information as he went along on the major matter entrusted to him, but that the more people he listened to, and the more he heard, the more he saw the difficulty of the problem, but all would be reported to his Paternity in due time.[67] But his letter was destined not to be completed and posted for many weeks. His plans received an unexpected setback.

Plans awry: a prisoner of illness

From letters to Mulledy and Dzierozynski it is evident that he meant to leave
Conewago, as mentioned, about 22 March; and since he saw no urgency for an
earlier return to Georgetown, he intended to go on to the plantations and missions of Goshenhoppen, and of Bohemia, where he expected to pass the Easter
holiday, and thence to White Marsh on the way back to Georgetown.[68] But on
what was to be his final day, he was, as he later informed Mulledy, confined
to bed with a chest attack, which was rendered more severe by his habitual
asthma.[69] This was an understatement. He was more explicit in a letter to an
Irish widow, Mrs Dillon. She had recently lost her husband, and to console
her in the face of the seemingly haphazard cruelty of death, he recounted the
tragedy of Fr Peeters, commenting that it "was an awful instance of the law of
death to see so promising a labourer cut off from a vineyard where the harvest
was so abundant and the labourers so few"; and in that context, he spoke of
his own recent experience of the transience of life through an illness, which,
he said, kept him prisoner for a month, and for a time made him think himself
nearer the verge of eternity than he had ever before been. "I had a fierce
attack of fever, which truly irritated my habitual asthma and reduced me to
such a state of weakness that, after fever and cough and oppression on the
chest was finished, I remained a long time so feeble that to say mass in the
church at which I lived was a great exertion."[70]

When he got round to completing the letter to the General, on 26 April, he
explained that he had been laid low by an illness similar to what he experienced on his return to England from Italy. This time, he added: "a very
severe and lengthy winter provoked and increased the asthmatic condition with
which I've been troubled from infancy". He was 52 years of age, he continued
wryly, and feeling that he was not now the same as he was yesterday or the
day before yesterday![71]

The debilitating impact of this bout of sickness was illustrated by the
entries in his journal. It was not till 1 April that he felt able to make an entry,
and then it was merely to chronicle: "I was this day able to sit up so long that
I resumed the recitation of my office, which I had not said since the 22nd."
Seven days later, however, he rediscovered what a chest patient today would
take for granted. "Last night, and only then, I recollected the manner in which
for several months I contrived to sleep in my last illness in December 1829,
and January 1831, by keeping pillows at my back and sitting up. I adopted it,
and slept well, and this day for the first time I feel a return of strength." It
was the turning point. The weather too improved; and on 15 April he reported how the mildness of the preceding days had covered all the peach trees
with blossom, and the fields were quite green. On Sunday, 24 April, he was
able to record that he "preached for something less than half an hour ... on
the resurrection of the dead, was hoarse at the beginning, but a change of key
overcame it".

By the beginning of May he felt able to visit some adjoining areas in company with the superior, Fr Lekeu. "In an open four-wheel chaise" they visited Gettysburg and Hanover on different days. He was pleased with the appearance of the courthouse and the church in the former; and in Hanover, "a small, clean German town" with a population of 993, he made a few purchases.[72] He planned to leave two days later for his next stop, Goshenhoppen. As he did so, he formally left his *memoriale* at the residence in Conewago.

His *memoriale* for Conewago reflected his long stay there. He was pleased with the overall state of the house, church and farm of "this ancient residence and mission of the Society of Jesus". As at Frederick, he placed special emphasis on the overall account book, and on the importance of having and following a custom book. With respect to the latter, he wrote at some length on the three sections with which it ought to be concerned: domestic discipline – including the care of health and proper preparation of food; regulations for the church and missions; and the operation of the farm. This last section had a very practical function in his view. It would give the numbers employed, their wages, the markets, the times of sending to market, what happened at harvest time and so on. In fine, everything that the knowledge and experience of the manager had found to be most appropriate for carrying on the business of the farm. This section of the custom book would be, after some years, Kenney observed, "a sort of useful manuductor to the new manager" and prevent the situation, which hitherto had prevailed, of each new farm procurator being "a mere novice", having to spend years learning "what the experience of his predecessors should have at once conveyed to him". In effect, Kenney's practical approach was recreating one of the strengths of the old Society. It was able to move men around from place to place and from post to post, without unduly weakening its ministries, because it had a system of customs, or rules, for each post. New occupants had just to follow established procedures: thereby benefiting from the experience of the past until, in time, they were able to contribute their own amendments and insights; and meanwhile they had their areas of responsibility clearly defined and were protected from being seriously misled by designing customers or deceiving servants.

At Conewago, as at the other houses, he recommended that a diary be kept of the history of the house. The diary of the ancient mission was destined to chronicle a very special event many, many years later: the elevation of its church in 1962 to a minor basilica and its recognition as a mother church of Pennsylvania.

Finally, as at Frederick, the local superior was charged in conscience with the implementation of the Visitor's instructions, and again their perpetuity was cared for by the further instruction that the memorial and custom book be shown to the mission superior, or provincial, at his annual visitation, who would check that what was laid down therein was being carried out.[73]

Moving on

His hopes of leaving Conewago on 8 May were deferred by torrents of rain which prevented travel.[74] Within a few days, however, he was installed in Goshenhoppen plantation, in Berks County, Pennsylvania, where there was a church as a residence and some 780 or so largely wooded acres.[75]

There, his visit and *memoriale* followed the now established lines. He was appreciative of the considerable changes made since 1820, especially the "notable increase in the numbers of the faithful" attending the church.[76] He advocated the overall system of accounting, and the keeping of a custom book; and then, regretting that the accomplishments of the founders of the mission had been almost entirely forgotten,[77] he urged the introduction of a diary, or journal, of the day to day history of the house. In that diary two years later he was to comment once again on the improvements which had been made, and to add some further remarks which offered an insight into the way of life of the rural missioners. Their mode of operation had evidently changed little over many years.

The missioner on circuit

He observed that he had arrived at Goshenhoppen in 1831 in the company of Fr McCarthy, who had been absent for almost a year because of his work in Reading and Pottsville. He and the superior, Fr Corvin, served Catholics there, and also in areas such as Easton, Haycock, Massillon, and Lebanon. What this meant in terms of travel and endurance was indicated in Kenney's "scattered notes", which mentioned that Pottsville was 50 miles from Goshenhoppen and 30 from Reading; Easton was 36 from Goshenhoppen, and from Reading 54, and so on.

Thus, although by the 1830s the Jesuits had urban parishes in Washington, Georgetown, Frederick and Philadelphia, the Jesuit circuit-rider remained still prominent in Pennsylvania, as well as in southern and western Maryland, and on the Eastern Shore; and the typical weekend for such continued substantially as described by John Grassi in 1818, in the course of his report on the state of the Catholic religion in the United States.

> On Saturday, the missionary leaves his residence, and goes to take up his lodging with some Catholic living near the church. Having arrived at the house, he puts the Blessed Sacrament in some decent place, and also the holy oils, without which he never sets out on a journey. On the following morning he rides to the church, and ties his horse to a bush. The whole morning is spent in hearing confessions: meantime, the people from distances of four, six, ten miles, and even more, are coming in on horseback so that often the church is entirely surrounded by horses. Mass begins towards noon; during the celebration, those who

can read make use of prayer books; and pious hymns, for the most part in English, are sung by a choir of men and women.

Grassi went on to report that the sermon usually came after the gospel, and that the people listened eagerly to the word of God. When the mass was over, the children recited the catechism, infants were baptised, or the ceremonies were supplied in the case of those already baptised in danger, prayers for the dead were recited or the funeral services were performed over those who had been buried in the churchyard during the absence of the priest. Finally, the priest attended to those who asked for instruction in order to join the church, or who wished to be united in the bonds of holy matrimony.[78]

At the end of May, or the first days of June, 1831, Kenney left Goshenhoppen and made his way to Philadelphia. There he met with Monsignor Power and Frs Kiely and Levins who came from New York to meet him.[79] From there, on 6 June, he travelled south to the large plantation of Bohemia, in Cecil County, on Maryland's Eastern Shore,[80] where he arrived on the morning of 7 June 1831.[81]

On the Eastern Shore

As usual, correspondence awaited him. One letter required an immediate response. Fr De Theux, new superior in Missouri, required $732 for the month of July. Kenney wrote to Mulledy that afternoon to send the money "by draft or order of Georgetown Bank on the Bank of the United States, St Louis", and used the occasion to respond to another urgent letter, sent by Mulledy, regarding a scholastic named Gartland, whose continued unsatisfactory conduct left no alternative but dismissal. He enclosed a letter for Gartland. If it met with Mulledy's and Dzierozynski's approval, it should be given to the young man.[82]

Next day at 5.00 p.m. he commenced his own eight-day retreat, following an order of time from 4.00 a.m. to 8.45 p.m. His day included, apart from mass, rosary, the two examinations of conscience, and a fifteen-minute visit to the Blessed Sacrament, three meditations of one hour's duration, a further hour of consideration or reflection, two half-hour periods of spiritual reading, and also, presumably, though not mentioned, the recital of the divine office.

Shortly after the retreat, he was visited unexpectedly by Mr Gartland. He came "to make a last effort", saying that he had not previously been admonished about the consequence of his faults. Kenney was not impressed, and felt Gartland was resigned to leaving. He reminded Mulledy, however, that it must not be left in the power of others to attempt such an excuse; and he made it clear that he was concerned about the two other scholastics who had been in trouble. If there was any repetition of their behaviour, Mulledy would be advised to call them to his room and there quietly remind them that any open violation, not only of God's commandments, but of the Society's rules, must, if the fault prove incorrigible, lead to the worst extremities. And he went on to offer advice which had Mulledy's precipitous personality in mind, but which also reflected his own sensitive style. "I never should correct them, or any of the religious," he declared, "until I had prepared myself for it, so that they should not have to plead that their feelings were hurt by the manner, the time, or place, in which they were reprimanded. Above all, I should not allow a word to escape in time of recreation that might cause an unpleasant sensation either to them or to others."

He followed this sage advice with a request, and a further reminder on appropriate behaviour. When Monsignor Power and Frs Kiely and Levins came to see him at Philadelphia, they talked of visiting the exhibition at Georgetown and stopping at St Ignatius. It would be greatly appreciated, he told Mulledy, if he personally invited them to the exhibition. These men had been very kind to members of the Society, and so "gratitude to them" was a duty, "independent of the advantage of cultivating the goodwill of the clergy of such a city ... as New York."[83]

Bohemia was different from the previous mission stations in that secular priests operated the Jesuit churches. The considerable farm of 1,500 acres, however, was in the charge of Br Heard.[84] Much of it seems to have been let out, but what was in Jesuit hands was not functioning profitably. The main problem, however, seemed to be with the indiscipline of the small slave population. Kenney noted that there were seven of these bound servants : five males, two of whom were under eighteen; two females, one of whom was under sixteen. The three men were married, but their wives belonged to other owners. They behaved promiscuously, taking advantage of the benign rule under which they lived. They fought at home and abroad often; and one of them had turned his house into "a sort of tavern for selling whiskey etc. to ours and our neighbours servants". In Kenney's view the situation was a scandal as well as a very inefficient way to run a farm. "Not one" had been "to the sacraments for 12 years ... except the old woman". Seldom was one seen at mass on Sundays. All swore and cursed. Two were drunk 10 or 12 times in the year. Within months, he gave Br Heard sanction to sell off the slaves.

It had long been the practice among the Jesuits in Maryland, as noted earlier, to sell individual slaves. It was usually done only in order to keep families together or to punish troublesome individuals. Deferred emancipation had been considered the acceptable way of ending slaveholding in the Society's plantations: that involved the contractual renting out of slaves for a specified number of years which ended with their legal freedom.[85] This was the method followed by Br Heard. In October of the following year, Kenney would write: "Br Heard has disposed of all his slaves except a boy." The servants were sold to neighbours and tenants, and in their place Heard employed some negroes who had got their freedom earlier.[86] The farm became productive.[87]

To St Joseph's, Annapolis and 4th of July celebrations

On 26 June he moved to St Joseph's, in Talbot Co., on the Eastern Shore.[88] Here there were 340 acres.[89] At the residence, Fr Hardy was in charge. Kenney's impressions are not recorded. Hardy informed him, however, with regard to his eight or so servants that he had "little to say favourably". Very few frequented the sacraments, and he feared that most of them were immoral. He continued – tending to avoid like most Jesuits the word "slaves": "Admonition is of little avail with most of our servants, and surrounded as they are by Methodists, free blacks, and careless coloured Catholics, their reformation will be difficult." The (Jesuit) Brother was unpopular and would never rule the servants, who were "determined to oppose him in their sly way, right or wrong".[90]

Kenney spent only five days there. As usual he examined the accounts, gave instructions about receipts and expenditures, and examined the farm production and stock, the houses, barns and quarters, and all other temporalities, and endeavoured to put an evaluation on them if they were to be sold. It was all part of the process of accumulating information for the General.

On 1 July he left by gig for Easton, the main town of Talbot County. He stayed overnight, and next day took the steam boat which plied twice a week between Easton and Annapolis. They arrived at Annapolis about 4 o'clock on Saturday and went to Williamson's hotel. Subsequently he was prevailed on by Captain Neath, the steamboat captain, to stay at his house. On the Sunday he said mass and preached in the small Catholic church, and later at dinner at Neath's met with "Mr Taney, the present attorney general, Mr Johnson, first clerk of the court of appeals, a Dr Sparks, and Mr Du Bois". Next day was the 4th of July, the anniversary of American Independence. He attended the celebrations and appears to have entered into the spirit of the occasion.

Although so consciously Irish, Kenney, like most of his countrymen of the period, had an unquestioned loyalty to the British monarch. But he seems to have had none of that empty, patronising attitude of superiority towards the American independence celebrations exhibited by some visiting English gentlemen, including clergymen.[91] Kenney, as observed already more than once, greatly valued the freedom of religious expression and the, relatively, equal opportunity offered the New World, and hence had no adverse comments to make on the celebrations at Annapolis. He recorded objectively, almost impersonally, what stood out in his memory.

"Went to the courthouse," he noted, "to hear the oration pronounced by a German, long resident in the country." An orator's critical comment followed – "inanimate in his delivery; composition tame, though of some merit: examples abound of the benefits to commerce, literature etc. of the Union; the influence of the example of the independence and happiness of America on the European states. The apostrophe to Poland was very feeling." There was "firing from the College Park at sunrise and sunset; from the fort about noon.

A steamer from Baltimore brought 12 visitors, mostly young men, who created some disorder ... Many were cut, and a child said to be killed." He made no comment. The very next words were: "Left Annapolis before 5.00. Arrived about 9.00 at Queen Ann."

Impressions and omissions at White Marsh

He had written, care of the post office there, to Dr Mudd of White Marsh, hoping he would collect him. The letter was present. Dr Mudd was not. He clearly had not collected post for twelve days. Kenney set out to walk the seven miles to White Marsh. His "wanderings", as he remarked, increased it to nine miles, and he was "greatly tired" when he reached his destination. On the Sunday he preached, and met a number of men and women of the White Marsh congregation, including some from Ireland. That afternoon, Fr Mulledy came from Georgetown College with letters.

The White Marsh estate lay fifteen miles to the east of Georgetown. Its holdings spread into two counties: some 2,000 acres in Prince George's County, and 1,160 in Ann Arundell County, Maryland.[92] Although Kenney had visited it before Christmas and talked with Dr Mudd about the estate, it was to be expected that he would spend a long time there, not just interviewing clergy, novices, and staff, but inspecting the large plantation, with its "104 slaves, males, females, and children",[93] its stock, crops, buildings, accounts, and so on, in accordance with his practice in fulfilling the General's special commission. In fact, his stay was brief, and he appears to have focused his attention almost exclusively on the noviceship.

Views on noviceship training

In his *memoriale* he praised the arrangements made within such a short time for the comfort of the novices, and the amount of wholesome food with which they were supplied. That being said, he went on to make suggestions which were, by and large, a reflection on the training Fr Grivel was providing as novice master, especially with regard to methods of prayer. He also made detailed, almost pernickity observations on aspects of discipline: on how the novices served the meals at table, and other aspects of deportment and behaviour which were viewed by society as marks of "good breeding". After some further remarks regarding the practice of silence and training in obedience, he addressed Fr Grivel personally on one particular practice, which reflected the latter's French and Russian, and more recent Italian background.

"The statue of the Virgin dressed in female attire", he wrote, was such a novelty in America that it has made a very different impression from what it would produce in Italy. It produced ideas very remote from piety. Hence, he thought it would be well to exchange it for a picture. "In these Protestant countries," he continued, "even the Catholics have not that simplicity in the expression and practice of piety as would tolerate dressed statues of baptised saints." And he warned that such practices as "baptising" church bells or statues of saints would occasion ridicule; and concluded that if by any mischance the Protestant papers got hold of his "Virgin in petticoats", they would "make a piece of buffonery of it". Finally, since some of his recommendations would occasion changes in the time-table, he concluded his *memoriale* with a fully revised time schedule.[94]

The short stay at White Marsh, and the restricted nature of his inspection, was the result of a change of policy by the General. A letter had arrived from Fr Roothaan stating that he had decided against selling the properties.

THE FARMS AND THE SLAVES: CHANGE OF PLAN AND CONSEQUENCES

The sudden change in his commission

The decision, without warning, and without waiting for his report, upset and angered Kenney. It was very difficult to bring obedience of the understanding to bear; all the more so in that he suspected the decision was due to intervention from some of his own consultors. His detailed investigation of the estates had given rise to some apprehension, not least, it seems, among the slave population;[95] but the representation which changed the General's mind would have had to be sent before that examination got under way. He suspected the European members who were his consultors in the early months of his visitation. The suspicion was well founded. Dubuisson, Dzierozynski, and Grivel had all, at different times, written to express their opposition to the sale of the farms.[96]

They feared that Kenney would be unduly influenced by the younger Americans, Mulledy, McSherry, and Ryder, who were known to hold the view that the future of the Society lay in the expanding cities: running colleges like Georgetown, and the other colleges for which the bishops were crying out. They had little time for the farms, which in their inefficiency was a source of embarrassment to them. They were, Ryder declared, "an incubus upon our prosperity" which "only attract the sneers of the disaffected, or the compassion of those who wish us well but are forced to say that we know not our own interest".[97] That "interest" called for the sale of most of the farms to finance the colleges, or, at least, the leasing of the lands to tenant farmers. In either case, the sale of the slaves was also necessarily envisaged; and not just on an individual basis, as previously, but on a large scale. And that, it was argued, would remove another part of the "incubus upon our prosperity", since, as has been seen, the great majority of the slaves were dependants – children, legitimate and illegitimate, old folk, and the sick, while those who were active were not noted for discipline and diligence. Moreover, in this argument, such a sale would bring relief from the moral opprobrium increasingly associated with keeping slaves. Maryland was at this point experiencing particular pressure on the issue of emancipation. For some time a bilateral division of the Union had seemed likely, with the Potomac as the dividing line between the new federation of states; and in such an arrangement, Maryland, as the only slave state within the northern federation, would be obliged to emancipate its slaves or, perhaps, even face a slave revolt.[98]

So, the younger American Jesuits felt that the moral and political climate at home could no longer be ignored; and with their European experience, they were also conscious of the growing movement for emancipation in Europe, and especially in Britain. This, of course, was something very real to Kenney; and he naturally empathised with much of what Mulledy and his colleagues were feeling. He had been exposed in Ireland, as has been seen, to the views of two of the strongest proponents of emancipation, namely, Dr Doyle and Daniel O'Connell. The latter, in fact, would soon be actively engaged in the preparation of a bill in the British House of Commons for the abolition of slavery.[99]

And despite such practical considerations as Georgetown's natural affinity with the South, and that a preponderance of its students came from the southern slave states, and that many of the abolitionists were anti-Catholic, it was becoming increasingly clear that the moral case was unanswerable. Within the decade, Pope Gregory XVI would condemn all unjust molestations of "Indians, Negroes, or other men of this sort" and all attempts to reduce them to slavery, and would forbid any Catholic to defend or teach anything that supported the slave trade.[100]

The continental Jesuits, for their part, and the older American Jesuits, found their "holy cause" not in generalities encompassing "good feelings of humanity" and "the highest ... principals of Christianity", but in a more prosaic and immediate obligation to the bound servants on the farms. They were scandalised by the grand plans of the three younger men. The plantations, Dzierozynski argued, constituted "a perpetual good". The black folk residing on them were not an economic investment, but "children whose care and well being has been given to us by God". Like many of the European Jesuits, he tended to regard the slaves as simply American serfs whose living conditions were superior to those of most of the peasants in Poland, Russia, France, and to those of Irish labourers in the United States. And the Jesuits' Christian and pastoral obligation to them could not be gainsaid: they were a trust for whose salvation they would have to answer.[101]

This message was clearly conveyed in a long and enthusiastic letter from Grivel to the General, 20 January 1831, from the plantation of St Thomas Manor, near Port Tobacco; in the course of which he spoke very favourably of the 60 negro slaves there, and indicated that their good behaviour was representative of the situation in the other Jesuit farms. They were happy in their plantations, and dreaded nothing more than being sold.[102]

With the General's letter to Kenney, the "grand plans" of the younger men were suspended. "We had some time ago very brilliant prospects", Ryder wrote to his former master of novices, Kohlmann, now in Rome, on 30 September 1831, "for we were persuaded that Revd Fr Visitor would sell, as reason dictates, some of the immense waste of landed property belonging to the Society, but owing to *increased representation* made by some here to our Very Revd Fr General, poor Fr Visitor has been ordered not to think of so doing".[103]

The continental Jesuits, then, had reason to fear that Kenney was inclined towards the plans of Mulledy, McSherry, and Ryder; but they overestimated the latters' influence. For Kenney was determined not to be rushed. He wished to see the whole picture, and was conscious both of moral responsibility to the black servants and of the practical difficulty in selling properties which also involved selling large numbers of bound servants. Maryland's relatively small plantations (most slaveholders owned fewer than fifteen slaves) offered little prospect for a mass sale of nearly 300 slaves without an undesirable breaking up of families; so, if the slaves were to be sold they would have to go to planters in the Deep South, which was a very uncommon practice in Maryland, and also particularly hateful to the slaves.[104] Hence, he needed time for a full examination before reporting back to the consultors with proposals. And he was conscious, too, that circumstances might urge him to retain the farms.

What hurt and angered him, therefore, was that although the consultors had agreed to his plans for examining the farms and then reporting back to them, some of them had written privately to the General long before the examination was completed. This upset him far more than the General's decision. He did not know which of the three continental consultors, or how many of them, were involved. He suspected the ingenuous, zealous, but rather neurotic Dubuissson, but had no evidence. Accordingly, he wrote him a carefully crafted letter which conveyed his sense of hurt and betrayal, without making any charge or open accusation. He wrote from Georgetown on 20 July 1831. The message was clear.

Having first thanked him for an earlier letter of his, he announced that the General had decided that the estates were not to be sold. He, Kenney, thought that this was "the easiest and safest" decision his Paternity could make, but he regretted that he had announced it before he received the report which he had so often declared to "be necessary for the full discussion and ultimate decision of the question". Dubuisson would recollect, he went on, that he had submitted his plan of procedure to the consultors last December, and that it had met their approbation. This surely implied that they would wait to see all the relevant documents and reports before they again wrote on the subject to the General; and yet they, or some one of them, must have so written that Fr Roothaan decided without the enquiry which, up to that date, he declared to be necessary. "The consequence now will be," he concluded, "*that those who hold opinions opposite to that which the General has adopted will say that the question has not been sufficiently examined, and that the decision has been made before the investigation was well begun. All this will be used as an argument on a future day for the reopening of this discussion.*"[105]

The denouement to "the Jesuit slaves"

Unfortunately, as Kenney predicted, the closing of the examination did not lead to an end to the discussion. Those who favoured sale of the estates argued that the General had been inadequately briefed, indeed misinformed. Fr Roothaan, in fact, was to observe to Kenney in some indignation a few months later that the impetuous Mulledy had had the temerity to take him to task for letting himself be unduly influenced by some of the "continental" brethren.[106]

The debate continued long after Kenney had returned to Ireland. And in 1835, at the first official congregation of the Maryland Jesuit province, a majority of the ten delegates were to request the General's permission to sell the slaves as well as some of the plantations. "With the revenue to be thus gained, they asserted that the province could, among other things, strengthen its existing colleges in Georgetown and Frederick and establish new ones in other cities like Baltimore, Philadelphia, and Richmond."[107]

Most of the continental Jesuits in Maryland, nevertheless, vehemently continued to oppose the sale, as did many of the native American Jesuits. Eventually, in December 1836, Fr Roothaan, persuaded that "the subsistence of the province" depended on it, gave his approval to a general sale of the slaves, provided that their religious needs were looked after, their families not separated, and that the money from the sale was invested to support the education of younger Jesuits. Because the provincial, McSherry, was a dying man, it was not till 1838, when Mulledy was provincial, that action was taken.

In June of that year, and with scant regard for the General's provisions, some 272 protesting slaves were rounded up and shipped to a pair of Louisiana planters in the Deep South. It occasioned much protest. Individual Jesuits aided individual slaves escape the agents. Some complained forcefully to the General about "this tragic and disgraceful affair". Among complaints from outsiders was that of the archbishop of Baltimore, Samuel Eccleston, who protested vigorously to Roothaan at the scandal caused by Mulledy. The latter resigned his position and embarked for Rome to present his case personally to the General who, meantime, formally removed him from the office of provincial, and thereafter detained him in Europe for some years.[108]

"The tragic story of the Jesuit slaves," wrote the black American historian, Cyprian Davis, in *The History of Black Catholics in the United States* (1990), "presents to us not only the harshness of slavery as it really existed but also the moral quicksand of expediency and inhumanity that sooner or later trapped everyone who participated in the ownership and buying and selling of human beings." "The Catholic Church in the United States" in the nineteenth century, despite the prohibition of Pope Gregory XVI, and with some honourable exceptions, "found itself incapable of taking any decisive action or of enunciating clearly thought out principles regarding slavery."[109]

But to return to Kenney, and the years before the "tragic and disgraceful affair". Despite his disappointment at the General's unexpected decision, which removed the main focus of his visitation, and his conviction that the decision, in leaving the issue unexplored, would occasion on-going division and disagreement, he had some positive and consoling experiences during the summer and autumn of 1831.

Grounds for assurance

Two days after he wrote to Dubuisson, he received a long letter from Thomas Glover, who said he had faithfully translated his February letters for the General. The latter, he reported, was "sorely afflicted at the news of the death of Fr Peeters"; and he added that on the issue of the day scholars at Georgetown, his Paternity left the decision to Kenney and his consultors.[110]

Before the August meeting at which the matter was considered, Kenney had made important changes in the membership of the consulting body. On the grounds of their absence from Georgetown, Grivel at White Marsh, though not far away, was replaced by the Visitor's socius, McSherry; and Dubuisson, now at Frederick, by Ryder. Thus, where before there was only one American-born Jesuit among the consultors, there were now three. In consequence, Fr Dzierozynski was alone in opposing the decision against "the further continuance" of the day scholars.

The decision, in Ryder's view, gave a new sense of freedom and added to the college's aura of confidence. Something of his exultation was expressed in his letter to Kohlmann, at Rome, on 30 September. "Our college, thank God ... goes on swimmingly as to reputation and increase of students ... This year we shall have at least 120 (boarders) ... Of the day scholars we are at last rid." He went on to observe that "it required great consultation and great exertion to obtain from Revd Fr Kenney that regulation, owing to the thoughtless, or rather unfounded, opposition made by Fr Dzierozynski", but that now all, seeing the visible advantages, applauded the measure. The reputation of the institution was "certainly great", he enthused, the public papers made frequent and honourable mention of it, and seemed proud "that its professors etc." had "received their education in Italy".

After such rejoicing, he supplied some bad news. The first item, as seen earlier, was that the sale of the landed property had been put off by the General. He then added that the college had been weakened by the loss of "five valuable subjects" to Missouri, and the expulsion of three scholastics. Despite these and other problems, however, the overall situation remained hopeful and satisfactory: "*We are all very happy under the Revd Fr Kenney, and are confident that if America is ever to thrive she must date her commencement from the present.* We are only apprehensive that he may be removed before the machine has been made to work well, and a supply of engineers found to keep it – in operation."[111]

Male religious are not seldom deficient in affirming each other. It is not clear that so glowing a commendation was ever passed on to Kenney. It had to be evident to him, however, that the college generally was going well, and that the decision regarding the lay scholars was being viewed positively. About the same time, moreover, he received a revealing and endearing letter from Bishop John England of Charleston, which must have done a great deal for his personal esteem.

Writing on 6 August, England declared that he had laboured zealously for ten years, yet had made little progress. This he blamed on his own lack of "that interior spirit of piety and familiarity with God" which was "necessary for one holding the apostolic commission". This lack had been passed on to his priests, almost all of whom had been educated and formed by him. He had arranged that his priests meet at Charleston each November for a five- or six-day retreat. But it had "begun to degenerate into form." "I wish you to come to us on the next occasion," he declared. "God alone knows what blessings you may bring. You could rouse us, you could instruct us, you could animate us ... I can instruct, I can explain, but your style and manner I believe differ from mine and our joint efforts might do much in this city were it but for a week. Do not refuse me. Say that you will come and we shall easily regulate the details ... May God inspire you to confer this favour."[112]

It is not clear that Kenney was able to confer the favour. For he was scheduled to travel to Missouri early in October, and the physical possibility of getting to Charleston in November seems remote; but given his zeal, and his desire to accommodate bishops, it is most likely that he made some arrangement to visit Charleston on his return journey, if not on the outward one.

ORDERING AFFAIRS BEFORE GOING WEST

On 30 September, Ryder had mentioned: "Revd Fr Kenney is quite well, and in a few days will set out for his Missouri visit with Mr McSherry".[113] From at least the end of August his plans for travelling west had been fixed. And hence during September there was an atmosphere of temporarily rounding up affairs evident in some of his correspondence.

Writing to Fr Roothaan on 14 September 1831, he reported that the two Belgians, Frs Van Lomel and Van Sweeveltd, whom his Paternity had assigned to Missouri the previous year, were at last about to set out. Fr Van de Velde was to have travelled with the two, but had been detained by illness. The archbishop, Kenney continued rather caustically, was displeased at the removal of priests from his diocese. "He complains that we are rushing off to develop missions in the west, while Virginia remains uncultivated; and it is nearest to us, and under his jurisdiction. In fact, we have neither a position, nor a house, in Virginia, and if, by the sweat of our brows we were to gather from all directions and found a church there, he'd claim it for himself and demand that it be transferred to his control by drawing up a legal document!"

In the remainder of the letter he pointed out that Maryland had lost eight personnel "from death, dismissal, and going to Missouri". The "dismissal" referred to the three scholastics mentioned by Ryder. They had become quite undisciplined; over indulging in alcohol, and failing in obedience, among other defects, and were now quite unsuited to life in the order. And if it were asked, he said, "why so many" had "defected and why they were tolerated for so long in the Society", the reasons, in his view, were three fold. His analysis looked back to past experiences in Maryland, and to present and prospective developments in Missouri.

The first reason was that the noviceship training was not adequate. In 1819 he couldn't find a better master of novices than Fr Quickenborne, but he lacked *nous* (common sense) and experience in leading others. Even then his efforts might have produced a better result, if he had not immersed himself in his passion for agriculture. He neglected the formation of his novices, and this contributed to several defecting both before and after their vows. In writing this, he observed, he was also thinking of the problem of setting up a novitiate in Missouri, where, he understood, not one of the fathers attached to the mission had "completed his full two years in a house of probation".

The second reason for the defections, in his view, was that "all the time" that these three young men "were teaching school, or engaged in their studies, they were witnesses of the dissensions that flourished among the fathers", and became imitators of some of the less well behaved. And the third reason, was the attitude of the superior, the "holy and gentle" Fr Dzierozynski, to those in formation. He was, in Kenney's view, too indulgent. He "used to condone easily and scarcely ever punished".

Finally, in this last letter to Rome before concluding the first stage of his Maryland visitation, he made mention of the French Jesuits, who had come to Kentucky at the invitation of the bishop of Bardstown and claimed to be exempt from his, Kenney's, jurisdiction and subject only to their French provincial. He knew well, he wrote pointedly, that they were under his, Kenney's, jurisdiction so long as his Paternity had not indicated that they were exempt. He was saying nothing, however, "lest disputes arise – which certainly would have arisen, if love and peace were not regarded more than authority!"[114] Subsequently, while in Missouri, the issue of the French fathers came to a head, and, once again, he was to find the General less than supportive.

Although his own imminent departure was not expressly mentioned in this somewhat melancholy communication of 14 September, he had spoken of it a fortnight earlier in a consoling and informative letter to his sister. Writing from Philadelphia to express his sympathy on the death of a member of her community at Harold's Cross convent, Dublin, he concluded with one of his relatively few general comments on religion and the Catholic Church in the United States. Once again, his very positive appreciation of the opportunities presented in the new republic was evident.

It would edify the community, he wrote, to learn "that in this vast Republic, where the people are sovereign", the Catholic religion, unaided by wealth, education or influence, which were all in favour of the sectarians, and unprotected by laws, which recognised no religion but were equally favourable to all, manifested "every day the innate power of divine truth in the progress which it makes in every section of a country nearly 2000 miles in length". The "influx of the poor Irish, with all their faults", he continued, contributed "to this great triumph of our religion. In the course of the last year, nine Irish churches were erected in the state of Pennsylvania alone almost solely by the contributions of the Irish labourers working on the canals and public roads. These were pure acquisitions, for there never had been a church where they now stand."

He ended with a postscript regarding his immediate plans and his disposability in the future for whatever sphere was allotted by providence:

> Before this reaches you, I expect to be on the banks of the Mississippi, that is nearly 1000 miles further from you. When I am asked when do you return home, I can only answer – "It is not given to know the times which the Father hath placed in his own power"! On that subject, I neither receive instruction nor ask for any.[115]

He set out on the long journey westward on 4 October 1831,[116] accompanied by Fr McSherry, and the now recovered Van de Veld, feeling that he had at least won the good will of all on the Maryland mission. Even Fr Dubuisson, whom he had addressed in scarcely veiled criticism, was to confide to the General as the year drew to a close : "The administration of Fr Superior seems to be suited to the situation – prudent, tending more to take note so as to make improvements, rather than making changes abruptly."[117] It was an appropriate attitude to carry westward to a vast and unfamiliar region.

X

Westward to St Louis: Portal to far-spread prairies and flashing river, October 1831–June 1832

> The varied and ample land ...
> ... Ohio's shores and flashing Missouri
> And ever the far-spreading prairies covered with grass
> > Walt Whitman, "When Lilacs Last in the Dooryard Bloomed"

The prospect of a journey of over 1000 miles, by horsedrawn conveyance over broken roads and by steamer down hazardous rivers, was daunting ; and yet there was a lure and excitement about seeing the frontier country, and witnessing the surge of the covered wagons from the Missouri River to the Rocky Mountains. And a focal point for all that activity was their destination, the area around the expanding town of St Louis, where the Jesuits of the Missouri mission were primarily located. Fortunately, as they journeyed westward both Kenney and Van de Velde kept journals which reflected their wide-eyed observation and sense of new experience.

THE JOURNEY WESTWARD

At 2.00 p.m. on Tuesday, 4 October 1831, Kenney, William McSherry, and James Van de Velde set out from Georgetown. Next day, at Baltimore, their first stopover, he brought his companions to visit Charles Carroll, now in his 95th year and more honoured than ever as the only living signatory of the Declaration of Independence. He was delighted to meet Kenney once again. They were also made welcome by his daughter, Mrs Caton, and granddaughter, Mrs McTavis, the sister of the Marchioness of Wellesley.[1]

On the morning of 6 October, at 1.00 a.m., they "left Baltimore for the Missouri by way of Wheeling". It was a journey of three days, over poor roads, in what Mark Twain termed, in *Roughing It*, "a great swinging, swaying stage", which changed horses every ten miles or so and gave the passengers time to stretch their legs and counter fatigue. The breaks were all the more welcome on this journey in that the coach was so crowded that there were nine sitting inside most of the time, and also because of the presence among them of seven passengers, mostly "government controllers", whose conduct in de Velde's view was "revolting", and whom Kenney described as "the most indecent set of men in whose company I have ever chanced to be". He had "never met with anything so obscene as their conversation", and he also found their cursing, swearing, and defamatory stories about certain public figures, quite offensive.[2] Not daring to confront them openly, he and his companions tried to show their disapproval by their silence. Other memorable, but not unusual experiences on such a journey, was that the stage broke down at one point, and on another occasion one of the horses took fright coming down a steep hill and nearly upset the coach.[3]

With some relief they arrived at Wheeling at 3.00 a.m. on Sunday, 9 October. They had fasted since dinner the previous day with a view to saying mass later on the Sunday. They were disappointed. The fifty Catholic families in the area were without a priest, but as there was no altar they did not feel free to celebrate the eucharist.

The following afternoon, they boarded the *Emigrant,* a steamer scheduled to take them down the Ohio river from Wheeling to Cincinnati. Kenney hearing much in praise of such steamers was disappointed to find his boat greatly inferior in every respect to those that plied between New York and Philadelphia and Baltimore. Moreover, it was uncomfortably crowded. He spent some time observing his fellow travellers. The large numbers meant that there were three sittings for meals. The tables were crowded with dishes, and he noticed that all "eat with incredible speed, speak little or none, and the ladies (all honest white females above the peasantry are ladies) are as silent as the rest. The gentlemen, though some are their husbands, say nothing to them." On his third day aboard, the arrival of extra cabin and steerage passengers from the little towns on the banks of the Ohio led to four tables at breakfast; and "here for the first time," he remarked, "I saw blacks sit in the same room with whites." He commented critically on the absence of milk and sugar at breakfast and at the way his neighbours piled fish, flesh meat and fowl all together on one plate. He made up for the absence of milk by beating the yokes of two eggs which he put into his coffee; which led, not surprisingly, to "a gentleman American" remarking that "such a mixture was as bad as an emetic, and that he would not have any objection to take boiled, roast, fish, flesh all upon the same plate!"

On arrival at Cincinnati on Thursday, 13 October, they put up at the Cincinnati hotel. After dinner they went to see Bishop Fenwick who offered them the hospitality of his house, but in such a manner as to leave Kenney in doubt about their welcome. Next day the bishop invited them to dinner, but said no more of their staying with him. Van de Velde thought they had been received "very kindly". McSherry suggested to Kenney that his lordship's apparent lack of warmth was just "his way". It was an accurate analysis. Fenwick, in fact, had been so impressed by his meeting with Kenney that he was subsequently to lobby strongly to have him as his coadjutor bishop. Despite what he deemed a cool welcome from the bishop, Kenney was much taken by Cincinnati itself with its streets "wide and long, and footpaths well paved with brick", and with its buildings exceeding "in size, cleanliness and appearance anything that could be expected" and the newer ones "imitating the best style of Baltimore or the other cities". It epitomised the growth and change that characterised this new world. The town was, he thought, a prodigy of rapid progress and prosperity. Its population in 1805 had been some 750 people. Now, in 1831, it was reckoned to amount to 20 thousand or more.

After this encomium from his usually cool pen, he made no further entry till they arrived at Louisville, on Sunday, 16 October. There, all accommodation was occupied because of the crowds for the horse races next day, and because of a conference attended by large numbers of Methodist ministers and their families.[4] He found he had to share a room with four others. Going to a local hall to say mass, he was warmly welcomed by the one priest in the area, Fr Abel, who invited him to preach. Kenney agreed. Afterwards he was introduced to some of the parishioners. Among them were a Mr and Mrs Breen, and the latter's sister, a Mrs Kennedy, both from Ireland. They made him feel at home, and he gratefully accepted the offer of a room from the Breens. Their coffee was the best he had tasted for a long time, he wrote, but, alas, that night "between the coffee and the muschitoes [*sic*]" he could not sleep. The next two days were devoted to visiting and dining with many local people, a number of them with Irish names. Invited to visit a Captain Hall, he found no one at home. All were at the races. Invited on the Wednesday to dine with another captain, he found that he too was at the races. "It seems here," he remarked ruefully, "you can dine with a man when he is not at home!" His wife, however, received them with kindness. On 19 October, at 4.00 p.m., they bade adieu to their many new friends, and went on board the steamboat, *Charleston*, on the final leg of their journey. It was to take five days, and prove eventful.

The boat was greatly overcrowded. Van de Velde observed that there were thirty male passengers for sixteen berths, and fifteen or sixteen ladies and half a dozen children for only eight berths. As a result, people slept on mattresses on the cabin floors. In addition, there were eighty other passengers. It was all very unpleasant. "The principal object of the captain" was "to make as much money as possible regardless of the comfort of his passengers".[5] It indicated the movement of people taking place along the Ohio and Mississippi. There were some two hundred steamboats, according to Van de Velde, afloat on these waters.

Kenney noted once again that there was "no milk for coffee", but more important for someone with his chest complaint he had no pillow for his head, and a pane of glass in his window was broken. The second pane broke "when the boat got aground on a bank of sand in the Ohio"! Following that laconic entry, his next comment read: "In the Mississippi too she struck bottom." He added that on Sunday, 23 October, about midnight, the craft was driven close to shore in a storm which had the effect of upsetting the work of the wheels and "the waves dashed over the vessel". Some people remained up to be ready in case of danger, but he went to bed. The rain was pouring down. About two hours later the alarm went. He did not get up, though he began to dress. He commented: "The danger was greater than most people imagined ... A short time before the storm got up, the captain said to me that if the anything occurred half the persons aboard should perish." Van de Velde noted that later in the day they were once more on a sandbar, but only for an instant.[6]

The latter's account of the journey was much fuller than Kenney's. He made reference to places along the way and to the various rivers entering the Ohio, and, naturally, took a special interest in the confluence of the Ohio with the Mississippi, and in boat's entry on that "renowned river". They were, he observed, disappointed with their first view of it. It was as if it entered the Ohio, rather than the other way round, since above the large mouth of the latter the Mississippi was much narrower, and neither very wide nor very swift. "We expected to see a majestic river," he remarked, "much superior to the Potomac or the Susquehanna." It surpassed them in length, "but that was all".[7]

Kenney himself, however, gave no indication of his feelings on first seeing "the father of waters". He made no reference to width or flow, to whole trees floating by, to islands, or the towering bluffs on the port side as they drew nearer to St Louis; no reference even to the fellow Jesuit whose name was ever associated with the exploration of the Mississippi. His only comment on this final part of the journey was a heartfelt: "Thanks to heaven we arrived safe at St Louis at noon on Monday, October 24th".

ARRIVAL – FIRST IMPRESSIONS AND "MISE-EN-SCÈNE"

Describing the town that year, as she saw it from the dock, the American author and publisher, Anne Royall, wrote: "It rises gradually from the river, and terminates upon a most delightful even green, which commands a magnificent prospect of Illinois and the river".[8] On this grassy edge of the town stood Saint Louis College, a brick building, "three storeys high, with a trio of dormer windows in the garret, and a high rock foundation and basement".[9]

After the three Jesuits came thankfully ashore and began to find their land legs, McSherry sent for a carriage. There was much traffic and bustle, and the vehicle was a long time in coming. Growing impatient, and no doubt welcoming the opportunity of walking after five days of virtual inactivity, Kenney set out on foot and got to the college by the back door. Fr Verhaegan, the president of the establishment, seeing him endeavouring to get in, ran up and asked what he wanted. "And thinking me a stranger," Kenney remarked, "conducted me to the parlour. Mr McSherry," he added in the same wry style, "had to pay 1 dollar & half for his carriage!"[10]

In their relief at arriving, none of them gave any immediate indication of their impressions of the town and its atmosphere. Within a very short time, however, it was borne in on them that they were in the midst of a maelstrom of activity, that they were seeing history in the making, that St Louis was in effect "the gateway to the west".

Fortunately, Van de Velde conveyed something of their sense of wonderment in these weeks. Writing to George Fenwick, on 16 November 1831, he observed:

> (An) object of curiosity, to us three wise men from the east at least, is the almost continued influx of strangers from other states; the public road, which leads to the interior of this state, passes before our college, and along it you may see everyday, men, women and children, on foot, or in wagons and other vehicles, cows, horses, wagons, carts, emigrating westward and forming a complete procession.

Whole bands, he continued, had to wait at the ferryboat, which was a fairly large steam vessel, and was almost always crowded. As well as those arriving by road, others arrived from Pittsburgh, Wheeling, and other places on the Ohio, especially Louisville, in steamboats and flat boats. "Even this morning, 17 November," he added, "a part of an Indian tribe has arrived here from the limits of Canada, via Pittsburgh, and the remainder of the tribe is soon expected – they are all civilised, dress like white men, and are going to form a settlement in the Arkansas Territory."[11]

In the midst of all this movement and excitement, Kenney settled in. Before long, he considered it imperative to send some account of the strange world to Rome. Accordingly, he provided for Thomas Glover a brief summary of the region's recent history, together with comments on the inhabitants, mainly with reference to their religion and life style.

Development of Missouri and St Louis

"The population of this country, when ceded to the United States," Kenney reported, "were, the Indians, bordering on the settlements of the whites, and the whites descended from the French of Europe and Canada", known as Creoles. Previous to that date, "the whole country from the west bank of the Mississippi to New Orleans was called Louisiana, and this part was called Upper Louisiana. About 1764, a settlement was made for the first time on the rocks where the city now stands, on the west bank of the Mississippi, by a company of French men in the fur trade."[12]

In 1803 the United States purchased the whole of Louisiana from the French for 11,000,000 scudi ($15,000,000). Subsequently, in 1821, Upper Louisiana, in which St Louis stood, became "an independent state of the Federal Union under the title of Missouri"; and ever since, he continued, "there has been a great influx of that English population, which is here called

American – a denomination neither assumed by, or given to, the French settlers, no matter how long they may have been in the country".[13]

That "great influx" of population also reflected, it might be added, St Louis's development as a terminal and shipping point for the produce of the Missouri and Upper Mississippi river settlements, and also as a centre for outfitting and supplying farmers on their way west, and provisioning the western army posts, and also the large Jefferson barracks in the town itself. Its main source of income in the 1820s, however, continued to be the Indian fur trade.[14] An indication of the speed of its development is that already by 1821, St Louis boasted of three newspapers,[15] 57 groceries-cum-saloons, 13 physicians, and, significantly, 27 attorneys. Ten years later, when Kenney arrived, the town had been designated a port of entry for foreign goods and there were said to be 432 steamboat arrivals. On a Sunday morning in July 1833, the *Missouri Republic* counted 21 steamboats lying in port. "St Louis had become part of a transportation network that included Philadelphia, New York, and other eastern ports; New Orleans; and Pittsburgh, Louisville, and Cincinnati on the Ohio river."[16] Not surprisingly, travellers, like the Protestant clergyman and writer, Timothy Flint, found "the harbour ... extremely busy"; and he observed an incidental feature subsequently captured in a celebrated painting by local artist, George Bingham "almost every boat, while it lies in the harbour, has one or more fidles scraping continually aboard, to which you often see the boatmen dancing".[17]

Not surprisingly, the town's location, its quick expansion, and increased trade, brought problems. The 1830 census showed 5,853 residents, of whom 20 per cent were slaves;[18] but in addition, as has been indicated, there was a large passing population. By that date, as a result, there was no longer sufficient timber for fuel and building; the drainage was not adequate; the sewerage was deficient; stagnant water had collected; mosquitoes multiplied; and malaria flourished. Different diseases made their appearance. Cholera became a regular danger, and a cause of many deaths.[19] Nobody was safe from it, though the danger was greatest where people lived together in large numbers. This last, was to lead Kenney to press urgently for the provision of an infirmary at the Jesuit college in St Louis.

In his descriptive letter to Glover, however, his attention, as might be expected, focused less on the physical location and its problems than on the state of religion in the region.

The state of religion

"Of the population of St Louis, and its immediate vicinity," he commented, "the bishop counts 3,500 Catholics. The 500 are Irish, and some Americans from the middle states, and a few from Lancashire."[20]

The Irish, incidentally, included a number of well-to-do business men. In

1819, Bishop Du Bourg obtained pledges towards the construction of the first cathedral at St Louis from among others, 23 Irish immigrants, Protestant and Catholic. At Florissant, some seventeen miles distant, six Irishmen, led by the wealthy land-owner, John Mullamphy, were involved in building the local church, dedicated to St Ferdinand. Mullamphy, indeed, was a prominent figure in St Louis: a friend and patron to the bishop, to the Sisters of the Sacred Heart, and to the Jesuit college. Some years later, there was reference to 47 Irishmen appealing to Du Bourg's successor, Bishop Joseph Rosati, "for an English sermon at high mass every other week".[21]

The request indicated the predominance of the French language in Catholic worship. Some 3,000 of the 3,500 Catholics were Creole and French speaking. They also clung to the traditions of the Creole Sunday and feast-days, which were marked by a ball after mass, horse racing, card playing for money, billiards, and a general pattern of "gaiety and excitement" which, according to a recent historian of the city, "served the community well".[22]

Kenney, however, was far less positive in his remarks about them. Although the French settlers were the bulk of the Catholics in the state, they were not, in his view, "a vital portion of Catholicity". They had lost the activity and industry of their European progenitors and had adopted the disregard of religion "ascribed to the modern race of Frenchmen". Much of this was accounted for by their links "with New Orleans and … with the worst description of French emigrants". But even among the poorer classes, they were frequently absent from church, it was difficult to get them to support their church or pastor, and they were careless, "even for worldly goods", provided they could live in a poor hut, "and dance and frolic occasionally. They have in this regard," he continued, "approximated much to the savages with whom they have too much intercourse, and like them they have no anxiety about the education of their children."

As a result of these failings, the education and enterprise of the Americans had put these people in the background: "the Americans have got into almost all the offices, corporative, commercial situations, and thus a powerful influence has been created in this Catholic country in favour of all the mad errors which the Yankees and the British (brought) into the state".[23]

It is not clear what he meant by "all the mad errors" brought in by the Yankees and the British. Presumably, he had in mind the various forms of Protestantism which were at odds with "Catholicity"; while his concern at the disregard of religion "ascribed to the modern race of Frenchmen" might be presumed to include not only absence from church and decline in morals, but also the proclaiming of agnostic views among a section of the population. There was certainly a range of these influences in evidence during his time in the region. The Baptist preachers had arrived in 1818 preaching against "this citadel of Romanism". The Presbyterians and Episcopalians came a few years later.[24] Numerically, however, the Protestant population was small. The agnostic views, according to the Baptist evangelist, John Mason Peel, were expounded mainly by the officer corps in the area; while the other active agents of irreligion, in Peel's estimation, were that lower part of the Anglo-American population – the river men, petty artisans, and labourers – who poured out "scoffings and contempt on the few Christians".[25]

The background information provided by Kenney was designed to assist the General's understanding of the work and problems of the Jesuits in the region. That work, and its history and problems, was, of course, Kenney's main interest and responsibility in Missouri.

The Jesuit return to Missouri: concordat, and problems

He had acquainted himself as thoroughly as he could with the story of the Jesuits in the region, since they had returned thither a few years previously at the invitation of the zealous bishop of Louisiana, Dr Louis Du Bourg. The latter had already introduced the Sisters of the Sacred Heart to Missouri under Mother Philippine Duchesne, and the Vincentians, under Joseph Rosati, to promote education in the region. A former president of Georgetown College, he naturally sought Jesuit helpers but nobody could be spared from Maryland. Then in 1823 he made an offer which was very timely. The noviceship at White Marsh had reached such a degree of destitution that it could scarcely feed its novices. The superior of the mission, Fr Charles Neale, planned to send them away from the Society. The fact that they were "all foreigners", Belgians, made the decision easier.

Du Bourg, deeply concerned for the spiritual and material welfare of the Indian tribes in his vast diocese, offered "to the Society of Jesus for ever … exclusive care of all the missions already established, and which would be established, on the Missouri and its tributary streams". The grant also included, the bishop added, "the spiritual direction … of all the white population", and once the Jesuits arrived he promised to give such financial assistance as he could manage, and for their immediate residence and upkeep ceded a farm of 350 acres [212 acres in reality] at Florissant within twenty miles of St Louis. "

Fr Neale saw the offer as providential. The novices and their energetic and zealous novice-master, Van Quickenborne, all longed to work among the Indians, and all spoke French. He signed the agreement with the bishop, without waiting on approval from Rome. As his part of the concordat, he agreed to send immediately two Jesuit priests, seven candidates for the priesthood, two or three Jesuit brother-coadjutors, and four or five negroes to be employed in providing the additional buildings that might be necessary, and in cultivating the land;[26] and he also promised that two years after their arrival four or five missionaries at least would be sent to remoter missions, that is to Indian settlements in the vicinity of Council Bluffs, a considerable distance up the Missouri towards the north west.

The first years

The first party was composed of three coadjutor brothers, and seven novices, under the leadership of Charles Felix Van Quickenborne, and his assistant Fr Peter J. Timmermans. They were accompanied by six negro slaves, three men and their wives, who had been employed on the White Marsh plantation and were now assigned to service in Missouri. The seven novices were Belgians, and all, except for one who left, were destined to make a considerable contribution to the mid-western mission. They were Felix Verreydt, Judocus Van Assche, John Smedts, each of whom became effective missionary pastors; John Elet and Peter Verhaegan, who became noted educators and administrators; Francis de Maillet, who was sent away from the Society; and Peter De Smet, who gained world wide fame as a missionary among the Indians, as a peacemaker between the government and the Sioux, as a writer of fascinating accounts of the western country, and as a popular lecturer – crossing the Atlantic nineteen times to tell Europeans of the Indian mission.[27]

To a number of Jesuits the movement to Missouri seemed quite quixotic. Van Quickenborne's innate optimism, however, enabled him to remain unshaken; while Peter Kenney, back in Dublin after his first visitation, though he disagreed with the decision of the Maryland superior yet remarked, "I have strong hopes that God will do much with the little band gone to Florissant."[28]

The bishop provided no funds for the journey. The story of the thousand mile trek of the little band, walking, and navigating two flat boats down the hazardous Ohio river, has often been told. They left White Marsh on 11 April 1823, and arrived at St Louis on Saturday, 31 May.[29] Five days later, they moved to their farm some seventeen miles north of St Louis, near the village of Florissant.

They found that the buildings were quite inadequate for their numbers, let alone for the seminary and Indian school which the bishop had also envisaged. There was a square shaped cabin of hewn logs, and two smaller cabins also of logs. These, moreover, had not been vacated by the tenant, who bore the proud Irish name of Hugh O'Neill. While they waited his departure, they stayed at Florissant with the Sisters of the Sacred Heart, under their superior, Mother Philippine Duchesne. The sisters were to be a source of continuous support during the early years. Philippine Duchesne saw in Van Quickenborne a man of deep spirituality, whose spiritual guidance she valued. In the event, it seems likely that only a saint would have benefitted from the guidance she received. His dealings with her manifested characteristics which also created difficulties for fellow Jesuits and for Kenney.

Kenney, during his first visitation, had remarked of Van Quickenborne that he had "little skill in governing others", was "by nature too vehement" to render authority agreeable, but might "make an outstanding spiritual father".[30]

He was accurate in his assessment of his capacity to wield authority, but scarcely so in his hopes of him as a "spiritual father".

He was a man of highest ideals, ascetic, and hard on himself, but he lacked the flexibility emphasised by his order's founder, was demanding of others and incapable of delegation. His spiritual direction where Mother Duchesne was concerned was wooden, and, not unlike some other directors of the period, he seemed to see it as part of his role to humiliate her for her spiritual good, to help her grow in humility! Despite such treatment, she reported to the foundress of the congregation, Mother Sophie Barat, that they were "all very happy under his direction".[31] In a rather special way, Philippine Duchesne embodied the motto of her congregation – "be ready for anything and satisfied anywhere"![32]

Inflexible authority and excessive zeal

Van Quickenborne's poor judgement and other defects led to the decline of most of the ventures undertaken by him. The seminary training of the young Jesuits was neglected in the interests of teaching young Indians and of working the farm; the school for the young Indians foundered partly because of the severe and rigid regime he imposed; and his colleague, whom he considered lazy, died within a year from overwork![33] Van Quickenborne drove himself harder than anyone else. His health collapsed under the strain. In October 1825, the superior of the American mission sent Fr Theodore De Theux, son of a Belgian count, and Br John O'Connor, a native of Tullamore, in Ireland, to his assistance.

The following year, two of the Jesuit students were ordained; and the next year again the burden was further eased with the ordination of the remaining four men, subsequent to a visit from the overall superior, Fr Dzierozynski. In 1828, Bishop Joseph Rosati, who had succeeded Du Bourg as prelate of the Missouri region, offered the College of St Louis to Van Quickenborne. He accepted. The institution opened in new buildings at 9th Street and Washington Avenue in 1829. Fr Peter Verhaegen became its president and community superior, but, to his chagrin and frustration, Van Quickenborne reserved to himself the final decision in virtually all matters, and made a weekly supervisory trip from Florissant to St Louis.[34] Fr John Elet, one of Verhaegen's companions, wrote to Dzierozynski at this time that "the government of Revd Fr Van Quickenborne" was "deemed by all his subjects intolerable".[35] In 1831, the General appointed De Theux superior of the Missouri mission, which he made independent of Maryland.

Kenney had been apprised of, and not been surprised by the problems caused by Van Quickenborne's leadership. He was very relieved, therefore, when he received an assurance from De Theux, before he set out for the Missouri, that all were now content.[36] His disappointment was to be considerable, soon after his arrival, when he found that all was far from well, and that once again the hard pressed members of the mission laboured under a superior unsuited to authority.

As he began to adjust to St Louis, his impressions of the Jesuit college were not very favourable. He was impressed, however, by the good relations existing between the community and Bishop Rosati, which had been highlighted by the prelate coming to meet and welcome him on the very day he arrived.[37] Straight away, the two of them found a point of mutual regard, in that Rosati had met Dr Murray of Dublin in Rome and, like Kenney, greatly admired him. Kenney determined to do all in his power to assist the bishop and cultivate his friendship. The latter's diary shows Kenney preaching on purgatory on 2 November "with great eloquence and very great unction"; and the following Saturday he and McSherry journeyed with the bishop to St Charles across the Missouri, where next morning they assisted him at high mass. That evening Kenney preached. On their return to St Louis on Monday, Rosati dined at the college with the Jesuit community.

The following weekend the three men took the boat down the Mississippi to reach the diocesan seminary at the Barrens, near Perryville, where Kenney gave a number of addresses. He was to visit there more than once, and was later to write that he "spent a most delightful fortnight" with his lordship in his seminary at the Barrens. "In that desert," he went on, "he is erecting a noble church, the stonework of which is done by a lay brother, a Neapolitan." The bishop was also building a beautiful cathedral on the same lines at St Louis, only the stonework would not be as elegant as the Barrens.[38]

From Kenney's first visit to the seminary of this first month of his visitation, Rosati had eight other references to him preaching or otherwise assisting him; and, in the process, travelling for six days with him seventy miles south by the great river to conduct confirmation at the old French town of St Genevieve, and then on to the hamlet of Kaskaskia, a former Jesuit mission, some twenty miles from St Louis. Not surprisingly, given Kenney's health, the bishop noted on 5 December that he visited him, and other sick clergy, in the hospital run by the Sisters of Charity!

If Kenney's experience of the ecclesiastical superior of the diocese was relaxed and friendly, it was to be very much otherwise with the unfeeling, autocratic superiors of the Jesuits on the Missouri mission.

Autocratic superiors and a matter of dress

He had considerable powers of concentration, and very much adhered to the Ignatian dictum – "*Age quod agis*", do what you are to do, don't be distracted from your purpose. As Visitor, however, he moved, as Dubuisson had indicated, cautiously but thoroughly. He not only made himself readily available to the bishop, and met with such prominent people as the college fathers wished him to meet, he, above all, gave time and attention to each Jesuit on the mission. Overwork, and the severity of religious superiors, had occasioned tension, anger, and in some cases deep unhappiness.

One external ground of difference and complaint concerned clothing. Despite the strenuous work, irrespective of weather, the long black cassock, or soutane, was worn outside the house as well as inside. "We have four parishes to attend now and several congregations of Catholics scattered in the country", Van Quickenborne wrote to Fr Dzierozynski on 25 July 1823. "We all go in full Jesuitical dress at all times and in all places. It gives great satisfaction and edification to the people."[39] His successor, De Theux, had similar views. Most of the other Jesuits felt differently. Their experience was that the garb occasioned ridicule rather than edification, except among the Indians who cherished the memory of the former "Black Robes". Even before Kenney left for Missouri, he had received a letter from Verhaegen requesting that the wearing of the cassock outside the cloister be abandoned.[40]

Shortly after his arrival, the whole matter was placed before him. He discussed the arguments for and against with many people, and then, on 29 November 1831, brought the question to the consultors of the mission for decision. The consultors, in addition to Fr John Theodore De Theux, were Frs Felix Van Quickenborne, Peter Verhaegen, Peter Walsh, and John Baptist Smedts. Also brought into the discussion were the consultors of the college, Frs Peter de Smet and John Elet.[41]

In the course of the consideration, many reasons were put forward against wearing the soutane in public. It was contrary to the institute of the Society, since that required that Jesuit dress be that of the local clergy of the country. The long habit gave rise to insults and indecent expressions as members of the community walked the streets: this was the experience of Frs Elet, Walsh, Verhaegen, and de Smet; the latter, indeed, complained of people offering to raise the tail of his long robe to see if he had pantaloons on. The habit, moreover, was an embarrassment to respectable Catholic gentlemen, and even to students, when an occasion arose of walking with Jesuits in the town. It also made the religious brothers look the same as priests, while it singled out Jesuits from other priests, which was particularly inappropriate in these days and especially in Protestant countries. And whereas in many Catholic countries, many were said to have been drawn to the Society by the habit, in America the extravagance of the dress was likely to operate against a religious vocation to the order. Finally, if in winter the soutane was covered with a long whitish great coat "why should summer dress be such as to startle everyone"![42]

No reasons were put forward in favour of continuing the prevailing dress, though Van Quickenborne and De Theux were clearly opposed to any change. Kenney ruled that the dress was not to be worn henceforth in the street or public places. De Theux's only response was: "If the Visitor orders, I will obey."[43] Van Quickenborne informed Kenney that he had written to the General about the long habit and the latter had implicitly approved it. Kenney replied that nobody could be obliged to wear the habit in public.[44] Subsequently, in his report to Fr Roothaan, he emphasised the oddity of the figure cut by a Jesuit missionary in Missouri as, on horseback, he wore a Roman soutane tucked around his body and an American hat, a style neither strictly clerical nor lay.[45]

The intractable, inflexible De Theux

The silent, almost obdurate attitude of De Theux had concerned Kenney from the start. He was, he told the General, a man of excellent intentions but unbending judgement, almost unaware of his bias towards rigorism, and with a mentality which required a religious superior to rule by a steady and obtrusive show of authority.[46] Others expressed similar views. To Fr John Smedts he appeared "too severe, too biting in his words, and in correcting people publicly was too impatient, sharp and violent".[47] Fr Verhaegen also deplored his severity, while McSherry, remarking on his lack of gentleness, and his ignoring of his consultors, observed: "As long as I know him, and he was a novice with me, he always was this way."[48]

In later years, when not in authority, De Theux was to be reverenced for his humility, kindness, long hours of prayer, and good humour; but when dressed in authority, he was a very different person.

Kenney, unfortunately, had to treat with him in that guise. And he was a formidable figure: a man of imposing build, with an aquiline nose and an austere appearance, who exuded the unconscious hauteur of one born to position and power. His distant manner seemed removed from feeling, and his religious training added to this impression. For, according to the description penned by his former novice, Fr Isidore Boudreux, he had been brought up in a seminary which was influenced by the theology of Pierre Dens and other rigorists, before the advent of St Alphonsus Liguori's moral teachings, and, as a result, "had a great apprehension of the judgements of God". Later, though he tried to conform to the milder doctrines followed by the Society, it proved difficult "to rid himself of first impressions".[49] An apprehensive and timorous conscience, wedded to temperament, resulted in severity and a painstaking adherence to the law when in authority. One member of his community in St Louis, Fr Van Asche, frequently said of him that he was "a man who could understand only the letter of the law, and by that letter only did he govern".[50]

Kenney soon found that for all his religious observance and piety, De Theux was "open to no thought which did not arise in his own mind". All feared him, he reported. "There is scarcely anyone who loves him, nor anyone who wishes to manifest himself to him save as obliged by law ... He wants everyone to do things his way, and demands more than others can give."

Continuing his report to the General, Kenney indicated his dilemma. His efforts to suggest a milder approach to government fell on deaf ears. He reminded De Theux, then, that his function as Visitor was to hear everybody, and on matters of serious moment to obtain the views of the consultors. And if there were matters to be changed, he would discuss everything with him, and nothing would be done without his knowledge.[51] He sought thus to assure him and win him over, and though he could see that matters were very serious, and that there was unease and, in some cases, almost despair, he was loath to undermine the superior's authority by interfering personally.

Those who suffered most from De Theux's autocratic and unfeeling government were some Jesuit brothers. Two of them were so unhappy that they sought permission to return to Maryland. One of them was Henry Rieselman, at St Charles mission; the other, Br John O'Connor, at the college, St Louis. Kenney felt obliged to intervene in their regard.

The harrowing tale of two Jesuit brothers

Rieselman, who was seriously ill, and was teaching at an elementary school at St Charles, was told by four doctors that he would not recover his health unless he left Missouri. Fr Smedt with whom he lived and worked, did not wish him to leave. Rieselman spoke to Kenney who, he said, received him well.[52] This appears to have been in November.[53] As the brother was clearly very ill, Kenney brought the matter up at a meeting of the mission consultors. Three supported him with regard to sending Rieselman back to Maryland. De Theux and Van Quickenborne opposed it. Nothing was done. The brother wrote to the General on 1 January 1832, probably on Kenney's advice. The following month, in his own letter to Roothaan, Kenney outlined the story and remarked of De Theux and Van Quickenborne that they were "the two harshest and most unfeeling Jesuits of all I have ever known".[54]

The story had, however, a happy outcome where Rieselman was concerned. When Kenney visited St Charles in April, and saw that he looked "horribly ill", he decided to take matters into his own hands. He consulted three physicians in the area, and from one of them, a Dr Power, "received a certificate. ... in favour of removing Brother Henry to Maryland, which the other physicians *motu proprio* recommended".[55] The catalogue for the Missouri mission, 1832, with reference to the residence at St Charles, noted that Henry Rieselmann was transferred to Maryland on 2 May 1832.

The story of the other brother was very different. His health was not affected to the same degree as Rieselman, but his account of his experiences with Van Quickenborne and De Theux were so serious, indeed shocking, that Kenney helped him to write about them to Rome. He had him address his letter to Fr Glover, with a view to his bringing it to the General's attention.

John O'Connor introduced himself as a "temporal coadjutor" or religious brother, 50 years old, and 19 years in the Society. He had come to Missouri with Fr De Theux in 1825, and understood that as it was part of Maryland he could always have recourse to the superior there should any difficulties occur. He now understood from the Fr Visitor, he continued, that this opportunity no longer existed, as the mission of the Missouri was now a separate jurisdiction; and Fr De Theux would not consent to let him go, and the Visitor considered that he should not interfere.

He had been unhappy for a very long time, Brother O'Connor went on, and his prayer was that his Paternity would order his return to Maryland, because if it were left to the superior of the mission permission would never be granted. "Reverend Father," he continued, "I have lost all confidence in the superiors that have governed us since I came hither." The "mode of governing" made it impossible for him to reveal his motives or feelings to a superior.

He then proceeded to give examples of abuses of priestly authority rare in the annals of the order, but eloquent of the culture of time and place and of the corrosive influence of the institution of slavery.

> When Fr Van Quickenborne was superior he called me to assist at a scene that put my duty and my feelings in such opposition to each other that obedience became a most painful virtue. To see a priest of the Society, with his cassock off, standing in his trousers and flannel shirt, ordering the lay brothers to tie the hands of the Indian scholars like so many felons and take them out to be cruelly scourged on the naked back in the open air under his own eyes! ... One of these grown youths was stripped so naked, that he only had an handkerchief tied about his loins whilst his hands were stretched in the form of a cross fastened to a tree and a post.
>
> On another occasion I was called to attend the stripping and tying of a black woman, who would not strip herself to be flogged, and Fr V.Q., again in trousers and flannel shirt, ordered a layman to force her to strip; and in this contest she was so uncovered that her sister, who stood by, cried out 'My sister is naked'; on which I ran away, and hid myself in the woods, and gave way to my grief and vexation, not knowing what I should do. I was afterwards told by one of the priests, that Fr Van Quickenborne proposed my dismission [from the Society] to the consultors for this and other faults that he found in me.

Turning to De Theux's behaviour, Br O'Connor observed that he was minister a long time at St Louis and at Florissant, and was also his confessor until, with the leave of the superior, he felt obliged to leave him. At confession, O'Connor alleged, he would remind him of looks and words that occurred out of confession for which O'Connor had not accused himself, or about things he thought were "used in disrespect of him"; and when O'Connor told him that his life was being made miserable by such sermons, De Theux would often advise him not to go to Holy Communion, though he would not refuse him absolution. He also gave him excessive penances, such as not to leave the house for a whole day, and to say "mea culpa" publicly at breakfast, dinner, and supper. "My feelings are warm, my temper hasty", O'Connor admitted; and he acknowledged that "too often" he "couldn't restrain either one or the other", when he felt he had received an unjust penance, and in protest he would sometimes omit the customary address of "Reverend Father" when responding to De Theux. The latter would then remind him that he "was a professed Father of the Society" and should be addressed with due respect. De Theux, moreover, had told him that a consultation was held about his (O'Connor's) dismissal. This, it appeared, was the brother's main worry. He feared dismissal, and hence requested that he be sent where his vocation would "be secure".

Kenney's comment

As the letter was in Kenney's handwriting, he felt it necessary to explain to Glover how this came to be; and also to make it clear that Brother O'Connor's communication was to be taken seriously. This last was important because in many respects the latter's letter read like a litany of grievances, and it was clear that the good brother had his own share of failings, including a tendency to tantalise De Theux by a form of insolent subservience developed by his ancestors as a response to generations of imperious Irish landlords.

"The testimony of all the fathers of this house," Kenney wrote, "agree in denouncing Fr De Theux's mode of governing as most harassing. absolute, and unreasonable. ... The scenes of the Indian boys and black woman are too true. The penances at breakfast, dinner and supper, given in a tone of despotic command, and with the expression of much passion, in the presence of the community in the refectory, and of many other similar ones, are supported by the informations of all the fathers and brothers that I have yet seen.

"Fr Van Quickenborne himself was scarcely more obnoxious to all in Missouri during the time that he was vice superior, than Fr De Theux was whilst minister at Florissant. The rector [Verhaegen] told this father, the very night that his appointment as superior was announced, that the General could not have made a choice more disliked by the community. The fits of passionate emotion he strives to conquer because he knows them to be sins against meekness, but all the rest is as bad as ever, because his principle is – *that these Flemings are to be kept down; if you listen to them, you spoil them; if you grant them what they want, they will begin to quarrel among themselves; refuse them everything, and they will submit.*[56] These, his own words to me the first day I met him: and because I cannot in conscience follow this advice, he thinks that I shall ruin discipline. I have seen all but three or four of the vowed religious, and the three novices, and I can only say now that either his government must be reformed or an explosion must take place.

"I did not interfere for B. O'Connor. His health is now good. But I did for B. Henry Reiselman, whose removal the attending physicians advised, and who to me and Fr McSherry appeared to be pining to death. De Theux refused his consent. He, and Van Quickenborne, are holy men; but two such heads have rarely been set on human shoulders."

Kenney added an interesting postscript. Georgetown, he said, had "no wish to get O'Connor back; but he would not be objected to if the General allowed his return". And he added that "a kind letter" written in the General's name "would quiet" him, particularly if De Theux changed his approach; for "O'Connor, like all the Irish, is hot, and kindness would do anything with him". As things stood, he declared, all who came from Maryland wished to return except the Belgians. And the latter, despite having themselves suffered so much from national feelings, were said to harbour some national prejudices.[57]

Whether or not national feeling entered into De Theux's relations with Kenney, or whether he genuinely believed that Kenney was ruining discipline, or felt his position threatened by him, or for any mixture or combination of such factors, the Belgian superior certainly made little effort to smooth the Visitor's path, court his favour, or extend the expected degree of co-operation to a General's representative.

The failure of diplomacy

Kenney was to win almost universal acclaim among Jesuits in the United States for his sensitivity and tact in human relations. But it had little or no effect on De Theux or Van Quickenborne, who, as superiors, marched to their own private drums. This was particularly frustrating for the Visitor in issues of moment.

One such, and even more evident than at Frederick, was the overburdening of Jesuit scholastics with various duties at a time when they were meant to be studying theology. It was a practice quite contrary to the instructions of the Society's founder. Yet De Theux openly ignored his views on the matter.

Almost philosophically, Kenney related to John McElroy on 9 February 1832, how James Van de Velde, who had been fifteen years in the Society, most of the time teaching, "without being allowed to finish his theology", was "again condemned to teach for another year", though he (Kenney) had "specially warned Mr De Theux" against it. Again, Mr Van Swevelt, had been made clothes-keeper and sacristan, in addition to his teaching hours. When Kenney heard of these appointments, he had "very quietly remonstrated", but De Theux told him that both men could combine their theology and their work! "Everyone but himself saw the impossibility of such a combination," Kenney remarked. "I let the experimentation be made"; and now De Theux "finds that theology was lost in rhetoric, and in all the clothes, bed and table linen of the house, to say nothing of the duties of the sacristan and infirmarian: all of which Van Sweevelt had to do, whilst, without any professor, he was to prepare for his *examen ad gradum* in order that on the oath of four men he might become a professed father of 4 vows!!!"[58]

"*Bone Deus*, that men who are bearing the heat and burden of the day should be treated so! Excellent man though he be, he is by no means a good superior." Thus, Roothaan replied to Kenney on 12 May 1832.[59] He subsequently admonished De Theux on a number of occasions on the need of mildness in government, but did not remove him from office. Br O'Connor lived out his life in Missouri.

The "absolute and unreasonable nature" of De Theux's mode of governing strengthened Kenney's commitment to his practice of drawing up detailed regulations and instructions which would establish a pattern of order and procedure which could not be changed at the whim of a superior.

WINTER INTO SPRING: DEJECTION, INVIGORATION, REFLECTION

Enduring a long winter

Kenney's time in the mid-west was also rendered difficult by another form of severity, that of the climate once more. It was one of the region's worst winters for many years. "Since the 6th December," he wrote in his diary on 16 January 1832, "all sorts of vehicles" passed over the Mississippi at St Louis. In a letter to the General more than a month later, he spoke of "a horrible north-west wind, blowing almost continually, which almost congeals one's blood", and commenting again on the Mississippi remarked that it had been frozen over for almost two months, and that the supplies for the city, which came from the Illinois side, were being transported across the river. And this, he marvelled, at the same latitude as Palermo![60] This February experience followed false harbingers of spring. It was all rather depressing, and all the more in that he was marooned at the Florissant residence, from 24 January into March, where Fr De Theux was superior!

His sombre view of the time and region was conveyed frankly on 24 February 1832, to his old friend and benefactor, Miss Denis, and on 9 February to John McElroy.

To Matilda Denis, to whom a letter was long overdue, he gave some general information about the region and population, and said that he was writing his letter some three miles from the village of Florissant – so called "on account of the beauty of the country, which I hope I may be able to see when the snow is gone and the fierce north wester ceases to freeze the wine in the chalice whilst a pan of burning coals stands on the altar". His health was good. "Were you to experience," he continued, "the dreadful winter which I have had again to encounter and the miserable house in which I live, you would say, that an asthmatic old man is well off if he can struggle through a severe season."

He had arrived here on 24 January from St Louis, he observed. That day "a north west blast came on". It was so severe that their 17-mile journey took seven hours because of stoppages. On the final part they had to walk right into the wind. He had repeatedly to turn his back to get his breath, and was "shaking like leaves in a storm" when he arrived at the house. After this, he was "laid up for some time". It was the second occasion, and he hoped "the last for the winter". "Since then to this day," he went on, "I have not been 50 yards from this desk; not so much on account of my health as on account of the difficulty of going out. The ground has been constantly either covered with snow, or one mass of mud with rain and matted snow. In the whole of this state there is no such thing as a road in the proper meaning of the word ... Expert riders find it difficult to make their way." He had, he added, "the best private room in the house", which was a log house made of unsplit trees heaped one over the other. It was a little longer and wider, but much lower than Miss Denis's front parlour. "What exercise can be taken," he asked, "in such a place and in such weather? You see that I tell you everything quite candidly. You will then fully believe me, when I say that I am well. The change, particularly since I came to the Missouri, from my former habits and comforts is really so great that I thank God that my advanced age is capable of supporting the trial."[61]

Two weeks earlier, while still, perhaps, laid up from his journey, or still recovering, he gave vent, in a letter to McElroy, to a negative mood and style reminiscent of his old mentor, Charles Plowden. He told of the "most miserable, dirty, crowded, dangerous boats" they had to use from Wheeling to Missouri. There was less danger in going to Ireland than in coming to St Louis. And he exclaimed: "Pray for us, and make everyone pray, that we may get safe again to Georgetown; and do not believe the 10th of what you hear of the glories of the Western Waters; or of the richness of the soil, or the beauty of the scenery ..."[62]

Once the weather improved, however, and travel became possible, he set off, careless of age and asthma, to visit outlying mission stations.

To the mission stations

Earlier, in his journeys with Bishop Joseph Rosati, he had visited formerly thriving missions of the old Society in the Illinois country, such as Kaskaskias, Kaokias, and Prairie du Rocher, as well as St Genevieve.[63] Now, having ventured forth to the town of Florissant and preached there at the end of March, he took the steamer across the Missouri to the town of St Charles on 5 April; and the following day, Sunday, "preached on the veneration of the cross (for) about an hour".[64] From there he visited two mission stations which had been looked after by Jesuits from the time of the arrival of Van Quickenborne and his followers in 1823.

One was at the village of Dardenne, situated on a small tributary of the Mississippi, nine miles west of St Charles. At this time, its wooden church was in bad repair. It was served from St Charles twice a month by Fr Felix Verreydt. Kenney had not much to say about this station, but he wrote at more length in his diary about the other mission and its environs.

This was situated near the village of Portage des Sioux, on the right bank of the Mississippi, about twelve miles north east of St Charles. It stood in a fertile plain between the Mississippi and the Missouri, shortly before the two rivers met twelve miles or so further down. The village took its name from the legend that the Sioux Indians, being pursued by their enemies the Osage, and knowing that only two miles divided the great rivers at this point, escaped by carrying their canoes across this tongue of land. This portage, not known to their pursuers, was subsequently used frequently by Indians as a means of saving themselves 25 miles of back-breaking paddling.

As well as the legend associated with the name of the location, Kenney would also have learned of the strong religious spirit of the inhabitants of the village. Van Quickenborne and others extolled their religious fervour,[65] and later, in 1837, the *Annual Letters* would record: "Here, if anywhere in Missouri, the life of the first Christians is reproduced. None can be called rich and there are few who do not have to toil for a living."[66] When Kenney visited, and experienced the religious spirit of the people, the church was a frail timber barn, with "some benches" and "a hole in the wall between the sacristy and the choir to serve as a confessional".[67] In this settlement, among a people who "surpassed in piety all places in the neighbourhood", Van Quickenborne was to die on 17 August 1837, worn out by exertions, and much revered, at the age of 49 years.[68]

Subsequently, it may be noted, Portage des Sioux lost many of its Creole characteristics as American, German and Irish settlers took the place of the pioneer stock, but it retained its deep religious piety, which today is symbolised by a man-made causeway leading to a giant statue of Our Lady of the Rivers, rising on a pedestal fifty feet above the waters to dominate Alton Lake, a 40-mile stretch of the Mississippi River.

Acquaintance with the farming people of this region, and of the areas nearer Florissant and St Charles, made Kenney more conscious of the land they worked and of their way of living, and this evoked, almost inevitably, some comparison with Ireland. People married young, he wrote in his diary on Palm Sunday, 15 April 1832, and "the abundance of provisions and (the) thin population give great encouragement to these young people to settle, but the scarcity of money obliges them to live in such miserable sheds as they can make with their own hands." Many of these were as bad as "a poor Irish cabin". Yet, "in the midst of this poverty", the women tried to dress well on Sundays, and "it would surprise a stranger, he continued, "how many grand bonnets and cotton gowns go forth on Sundays from these uncomfortable abodes".[69]

These journeys and contacts in the springtime of the year lifted the mood of despondency which had gripped him during parts of February and March. It was not, however, just the weather, inactivity, and Fr De Theux that had upset him; there was also a sense of grievance against his superior general with reference to the presence of French Jesuits in Kentucky.

The French in Kentucky – Grievance with the General

He had previously been upset, as has been observed, by Fr Roothaan's changes of direction without reference to him; now a letter from his Paternity, which arrived on 10 March, made reference to the French fathers in a way which seemed to further undermine his position as Visitor to the United States.

The next day he sent off a long and vigorous letter of complaint to Glover, "as an adviser of the General", because, as he said, "I have no longer the courage to open my mind clearly and freely to him." He was sure that his Paternity meant to treat with kindness and sincerity those to whom he had "committed a share of his authority"; yet, he continued, "I have felt so much the want of these dispositions in my intercourse with him that I have more than once been on the point of entreating him to transfer my burthens to others, who might be more likely to merit his favour and his confidence." He had not done so, because it "might be taken as an act of feeling in me and of disrespect to him". He was not objecting to the measures which since his arrival the General had been pleased to adopt in America without his knowledge, but he did wish "to convey strong objection to the manner in which every one has been carried into execution". He then went on to "state facts"; going back to his first learning about the French fathers and the history of his subsequent relations with them.

In February 1831, or soon after, Fr Chazelle and two other French Jesuits arrived in New Orleans. As communication between the bishops was frequent and rapid, it was "soon rumoured through the United States" that they "had come to take possession of Bishop Flaget's college at Bardstown". No previous information had been addressed, or intimation given, on their arrival, "to the superior within the limits of whose jurisdiction they had appeared". Indeed, it was at the dinner table of Bishop Kenrick in Philadelphia that he learned of the developments at Bardstown. "I do not know how so cool a man as you, my dear Father," Kenney continued, "would have felt; but I confess my warm temperament made me regret that ... such an utter, though unintended disregard to the superior's office, was reserved for my administration." His obvious lack of information, gave the impression to outsiders of "mal-administration in the general government of the Society".

He went on to relate that letters to Frs Dubuisson and Grivel from the French fathers had seemed to suggest that they were aware only of the province of Maryland, which they said had no authority over them as they were under the French province. After Dubuisson and Grivel had pointed out that there was a Visitor who was "superior of the United States", and that they should have first contacted him, Fr Chazelle eventually wrote, in October 1831, what to Kenney seemed "an empty letter of pure formality"; and Bishop Flaget also wrote to say how providential it was that these French fathers had been able to come, and he asked, in all seeming innocence, that since their English was very poor, some Jesuits might be loaned from Georgetown until their command of English was adequate![70]

Kenney replying to Chazelle had pointed out that he was superior of the United States, and that if Chazelle and his companions were to be exempt from that authority he was sure the General would have informed him of it. He hoped, he said, to "visit him in charity" on his way to St Louis, "without making any inquiries into his affairs, which he had so studiously kept from" his "knowledge". At Louisville, on his way west, Kenney met with a Fr Evremond on his way to Georgetown to become a Jesuit, sent by Chazelle and Bishop Flaget, but with a view to entering the French province. Kenney told him that he had no authority to receive him into the French province, that if he wished to join that province he had to see the French provincial. He then explained the matter by letter to Chazelle, and put off his visit to Bardstown till on his return journey. Chazelle and his companions subsequently "advanced so far" as to request him, as Visitor, to "accept their obedience".

Meanwhile, Kenney continued, he had written to the General stating Fr Chazelle's claims to operate in Kentucky as a member of the French province, and declaring that he felt he could not recognise these claims until he had "an official intimation" that Chazelle and companions "were exempted from the jurisdiction within the limits of which they were living and acting". He felt sure that the General would say he was correct "in requiring an authentic intimation, which had been involuntarily omitted". This would save his position in the eyes of the American fathers. "A single line a year ago would have saved all the unpleasant work above described, and another line would have repaired the evil."

But what happened? Instead, Kenney stated with warmth, "I learn '*res minime nova est in Societate ut provincia Europeae missiones habent in America!*' ('It is nothing new for European provinces to have missions in America.')"[71] "Who said it was," he commented. "The only question was whether I was right or wrong in refusing to admit an exemption from the jurisdiction of this mission before I received due notice of its having been granted." The "*res minima*" answer suggested that the French fathers were right in disregarding his views; that the "French provincial ... had authority to set up a new mission in the very centre of the old mission over which I was appointed to preside!" The General's answer, indeed, was "evasive", and such an exercise of authority neither imparted kindness nor won confidence. Was it "nothing new", he went on, for a European province to have a mission in America, when there did not exist between the people of this country and that province either a common origin, a common government, or a common language? Was it nothing new that that province erected its new mission within the limits of the ancient and national mission of the country without giving any notice to the superior of that mission?! That, indeed, was the "newest" of situations, and it was "the only point in question".

What he wished to obtain, therefore, by his long letter, he informed Glover, was that the latter would "cause the General to understand that the neglect of due intimation justifies my refusing to consider the French fathers exempted from the authority of the superior in the United States, and that his decision be sent both to me and them. This is now the only remedy."[72]

It is not clear that Fr Roothaan did as he requested, though subsequently he did send a placatory letter. Having given forceful expression to his annoyance at being ignored and taken for granted, however, Kenney seems to have ceased to let the matter trouble him. On the way home, he was to call at Bardstown, whose bishop he admired, and give a retreat to the clergy there. He also availed of the occasion to remove any awkwardness between the French Jesuits and himself, and later, as mentioned, they expressed their obedience to him as Visitor.

The long winter at Florissant provided occasions for brooding, but it also gave him time to think about the needs of the mission and its missioners. One area of concern was health and factors related to it. His own bouts of illness left him particularly sensitive to Ignatius Loyola's instructions on the care of the sick.

Concern for health and the sick

His sensitivity extended to aspects linked to sickness and apostolic effectiveness, namely, overwork, inadequate or unsuitable diet, cleanliness, and opportunities for relaxation and exercise. All these were to feature in his *Memoriale*, or official recommendations to be observed for the future in Missouri.

In a region where fevers and diseases took a heavy toll of life, people weakened by overwork, undernourishment, unsanitary conditions, were ready victims. The death of the outstanding young missionary, Fr Peeters, while he was at Frederick, was never far from his mind; and at Florissant the memory was still green of Van Quickenborne's young assistant, the short-lived Fr Timmermans. To improve the situation, he was to insist at St Louis, despite the college's poverty, that an infirmary be provided; and that, in the face of a school year running for eleven months, from 1 September to 31 July, no Jesuit was to teach more than five hours a day, and all were to take some recreation each day and have time for self-improvement.

At Florissant he sought to get De Theux to soften his Spartan attitudes, and was prepared to intervene with vigour on occasion when all intercession failed. The case of Br Rieselman has been noticed. There was also the instance of Fr L.J. Rondet, a diocesan priest, greatly esteemed by the bishop, who went missing from Florissant where he was on retreat. When De Theux, despite requests, refused to make any effort to trace him, Kenney required him to do so.

In the matter of health, an aspect which exercised his attention, as has been noticed, was the quality and preparation of meals. In Missouri he found additional grounds for concern.

Meals, health, and celebration

Used to the "comfort" of a good table at Stonyhurst and in middle-class Dublin, he found the careless cuisine of frontier life difficult to accept. The waste of food in the midst of poverty, and the cooking of meat and poultry just killed, were, he declared, "most reprehensible". And he was critical of the lack of attention to the preparation and presentation of meals, even on special occasions. On Sunday, 1 January 1832, he noted in his diary: "Dinner at the usual hour. A boiled cheek of pork and cabbage, beef ill-roasted and quite hard. Cider ill-tasted and excessively acid. Such a dinner on New Year's Day I have never seen in the Society. The minister said the beef was tender, but though the rector carved the dish, and went even to search for a tender bit in other dishes for the Visitor, he did not succeed." And like many travellers to sea-coasts or the vicinity of great rivers, he marvelled at the dearth of fish! "I have been nearly five months in the country, and I have only once seen fresh fish, which was at the bishop's: it had been brought from St Charles, 20 miles distant from St Louis."[73]

The months at Florissant, and the subsequent experience of the mission stations, with their needs and possibilities, also encouraged him to question the relevance of the Society's emphasis on institutions of education in that time and place.

THE COLLEGE OF ST LOUIS: TO CLOSE OR CONSOLIDATE?

Introduction to the college

The Jesuit college was only two years in existence, when he was introduced to it. The same year, the controversial author, Mrs Anne Royall, described it as "the most flourishing college at this time in the United States, all the professors being not only of the first learning, but of the most polished manners". And she was particularly taken by Fr Verhaegen "a stout, noble, fine man ... with a smile which came from his heart."[74] Kenney had a high regard for the Jesuit faculty, but otherwise took a very different view of the college.

It was, in effect, at that time, but a restricted grammar school adapted to frontier conditions. There was no demand for Latin and Greek, and little appreciation of the value of knowledge apart from its use to commerce and trade. Yet the college's prospectus purported to offer an ambitious melange comprising an English course – involving "spelling, reading, writing, grammar, history, geography"; and also the teaching of "the use of globes, arithmetic, book keeping, mythology, poetry, rhetoric, basic mathematics, and French"; and a classical course said to include – "Latin, Greek, logic, metaphysics, moral philosophy, physics and advanced mathematics."[75]

Kenney was impressed by the care taken with the teaching of religion in the college; but highly critical of the gap between the reality and the pretentious and misleading descriptions presented by the prospectus. He wrote in some detail about it to John McElroy on 9 February 1832, knowing the latter's wish to learn how the school at St Louis compared to his at Frederick.

The school population, he remarked, was composed of "29 boarders, 6 half-boarders, 117 day scholars", and "of the whole number of 152, which through the whole of this severe winter attended school (with few exceptions) every day, only 51 are not Catholics". The superiority in numbers allowed the "masters to be bolder" than McElroy's teachers might be. They did not "oblige the non-Catholics to learn any catechism, but they made the Catholics recite their lesson in it in the class in front of the others". The lesson too was "explained to all alike", and they had "no difficulty in questioning the one, as well as the other, with regard to the meaning of what had been explained". Besides, the Protestant boarders joined in all the prayers, heard all the instructions, and had books and beads as well as the Catholics. "Thus," Kenney declared, "the most important object of our school is fully realised with regard to the greater number."

But where "the object next in importance", a classical education, was concerned, that object was far from being realized, and there was no immediate prospect of the department being more flourishing. Poor as McElroy's classical school had been a year ago, it had double the number of those studying Latin in St Louis College. There was, he continued, "great flourishing in the prospectus" about rhetoric, philosophy, classics etc., but the details of the reality told "more truth than the fine descriptions, glowing hopes, and brilliant course of studies found in the pages of a prospectus, or in the reports of any (academic) exhibition ... It is said that high sounds and a little boasting does much in this country. If it do, it will not last long. Such mists disappear as the sun rises."

He then proceeded to give some of the "details". There were five classes. The two lowest taught "the alphabet, spelling and reading". These were the most numerous classes. The next two had, in addition to reading, "geography, some notion of elocution, a little history, some elementary composition". Then "comes rhetoric (God bless us)". The pupils there, "when all together", might be twelve. They learned by heart elements of rhetoric. They studied and made abridgements. They wrote English letters or, alternatively, did a composition on some subject.[76]

Why not move to New Orleans?

There was, in fact, an unsettled air about the college in those early years. Its very continuance was in doubt. Hence, as he informed the General in April 1832, one of the reasons why the Jesuits were not promoting the study of Latin and Greek was that they feared the parents might withdraw their sons entirely if they did so.[77] Moreover, quite apart from the classical languages, the rector or president of the college, Fr Verhaegen, had earlier written to Fr Roothaan that – "all things in the state seem to take on a character of ... change and instability. On this account, we cannot hope for that solid zeal for letters which is elsewhere in evidence." There was little prospect at any time of a large number of boarders. The only hope of increase lay in Lower Louisiana.[78] Verhaegen, in consequence, favoured the acceptance of an offer from Bishop De Neckere of New Orleans to open a college there. He pressed strongly, indeed, with the Visitor that this opportunity should not be let slip by of "settling in one of the most important positions of the Union".[79]

Kenney, and also Fr Walsh, prefect of studies at St Louis, disagreed: pointing out that there were not enough men to supply the needs of the one college they had. Verhaegen, however, kept negotiating with the bishop, and subsequently went to visit him, without informing Kenney;[80] and on 25 August 1832, he proposed to the General that three men be sent to open a college in Louisiana which, he said, would be a livelier prospect for pupils and vocations than St Louis, since most of the boarders there came from Louisiana. And he warned that if some other group than the Society took on the Louisiana college, there would be a serious loss of students to St Louis.[81] Faced with such strong advocacy, Roothaan was in two minds. Writing to Kenney on 23 October, he declared that he had no men available to send to Bishop De Neckere, so the only hope seemed to be to send two or three men from St Louis College. What did he think?[82]

Kenney, by this time long back in Maryland, wrote to Missouri for the most recent information and for a full statement of the offer of Bishop De Neckere; and he made it clear that he thought the General would impose two conditions, namely: "no debts – a classical education". And he further confided to McSherry that he could not see how the Indian mission was ever to be serviced if another college was undertaken by the Missouri fathers – unless considerable help was sent to them.[83] Verhaegen, in reply, said he was waiting on the return of Van de Velde, who had spent the winter in Louisiana, and who would be able to give the most up to date information. When Van de Velde returned to St Louis, however, Verhaegen did not write to Kenney. Subsequently, one of the consultors of the mission told the latter that he had been put under pressure to support the New Orleans college, but that he (the consultor) had opposed it because of the shortage of men.

By 12 June 1833, Kenney was convinced that the shortage of men was beyond question, given the recent death of Van Lommel and Fr De Smet's impending return to Belgium.[84] And even though Verhaegen, in August, was still advocating the sending of men to Lower Louisiana with a view to opening a college which would eventually become, as it were, "the mother house";[85] the General had come by then to echo Kenney's views. In a letter to Van de Velde, the other main supporter of the New Orleans project, he warned of the need to "hasten slowly, lest by undertaking too many things you be unable to carry on and, in fine, succeed in building nothing but ruins". "And let us never forget," he added, "that it is better for us to do a few things well than most things badly."[86]

Thus, Kenney, by concentrating on the task in hand, might be said to have been, somewhat ironically, the rescuer of the University of St Louis. "Ironically" because he had doubts about concentrating men in a college when there was such a shortage of priests in the Missouri region as a whole, and so much missionary work to be done there; and in April 1832, following his visit to the mission outposts, he had given strong expression to these reservations in a letter to the General.

The wider need and larger question

Writing from St Louis, in Easter week 1832, he praised the manner in which the Belgian fathers had, with great industry, learned to understand, speak and write the English language, and had endeared themselves to the English-speaking Catholics of the city. But their very success raised the question: whether they were best employed in the college? The education of 150 boys, of whom 51 were non-Catholics, was engaging, almost to the point of exhaustion, a staff of seven fathers, one scholastic, and three religious brothers. Could the results be up to the energy expended?

"This question is an urgent one in these United States," he continued, "where, turn where one will, one finds Catholic families scattered here and there in very great numbers, who have neither mass nor sacraments, sometimes not even baptism. How many non-Catholics, too, would not seven priests of the calibre we have here bring to our holy faith, were they to occupy themselves in serving missions?" And, he went on: "The excellent Fr Peeters, whom I cannot name without tears, learned English and, in the space of two years, in one of two missions which he attended, converted 31 non-Catholics, even though he only visited there twice a month. How long would it be before 31 out of the 50 non-Catholic pupils in St Louis would be brought to the faith, even though seven priests were daily employed teaching them?"

Were the pupils taught the classical languages, he added, they would at least have the grounds of a serious education, and be prepared for a priestly vocation, and in that way serve the mission; but Latin was almost non-existent. Again, the future of the future of the college, in the full sense, that is, as a boarding school, was problematical. Few people in St Louis could afford such, so the existence of the college was dependent on the support of better off parents in Lower Louisiana. And a further factor against the college, was that its staffing made more difficult the fulfilling of the mission to the Indians promised in the concordat with Dr Du Bourg. The St Louis Jesuits now seemed preoccupied about many things, he observed, but few, if any, apart from Van Quickenborne, indicated any interest in the Indian mission. Yet, there was an obligation in this matter.[87]

Such doubts and questions, in one form or another, were among the grounds for concern experienced by churchmen throughout the United States; and the presence, in non-Catholic graveyards across the mid-west, of hosts of gravestones bearing distinctively Irish names indicates how real those grounds were.

Living with the college

Despite his misgivings, Kenney felt tied to the situation; and an important factor in the sense of restriction was the knowledge that the good and zealous, and well disposed bishop would not welcome closure of the school. So, he found himself with sentiments later expressed by Verhaegen: "The college of St Louis ... cannot now be abolished and so must be tolerated."[88] And having accepted that, he set about with characteristic determination to raise its level of education so as to distinguish it from other schools, and enable it to be a vehicle for the apostolate in Missouri. To this end, he appealed to the General, in the same letter, to impress upon the St Louis Jesuits the need to bring the education they offered into closer alignment with the standards of the Society, especially in the cultivation of the Latin and Greek languages.[89] This the General did the following October in a letter to Verhaegen;[90] while in a letter to Kenney, two days earlier, he agreed that the college could not "be terminated now and so must be borne with", but instructed that it "be drawn little by little to approximate to our system of studies". And in this respect, he added, let them "first of all ... study Latin more" and "perchance that sterile field will yet bear fruit".[91]

Because, then, of "the wants of St Louis College", and to avoid further delays in undertaking the Indian mission, Kenney turned down the invitation to open a college at New Orleans, and also abandoned the plans of Van Quickenborne and De Theux for a permanent mission residence on the Salt River, in north eastern Missouri, some 120 miles from Florissant.[92] And as a further earnest of his commitment to the development of St Louis College he was prepared to sanction the building of two extensions.

He returned to St Louis from Florissant for Holy Week: assisting the bishop and clergy with the ceremonies in the cathedral on the Thursday, Friday and Saturday, and preaching in English on Easter Sunday, 22 April. The following Sunday he preached again.[93] His friendship with the bishop led him to encourage the Jesuits at the college to offer to preach at the cathedral on alternate Sundays. It was an arrangement that did not survive. On another issue, however, discussions between Rosati and himself produced results which were to influence not only the future of St Louis College but also Jesuit colleges in other parts of the United States. This was the familiar but thorny issue of tuition fees.

PAYMENT FOR TEACHING?

What was involved, as will be recalled, was, on the one hand, securing steady financial support for the school and easing the teachers' and staffs' burdens; and, on the other hand, the principle of Ignatius Loyola, strongly reasserted since the restoration of the order by the superior generals Fortis and Roothaan, namely, that Jesuits were "to give freely as they have freely received, neither demanding nor admitting any reward or alms whereby any of the Society's ministries may seem to be recompensed".[94]

Naturally, Kenney adhered to the spirit of the rule. It was a matter associated with his vow of poverty; and professed members of the Society, moreover, by virtue of their special fourth vow, were not to permit any mitigation of the rule in regard to poverty. Yet, desks had to be provided, timber for fires paid for, maintenance costs covered, boarders fed, servants and lay teachers paid. A fee to cover essentials other than tuition was permitted for boarders, but the College of St Louis in the early years had a large majority of day students. How could they be covered? Faced with this problem even the austere, poverty-loving Van Quickenborne found himself reduced to the expedient employed in Georgetown: he made a minute charge of five dollars a year for the use of desks and candles. Kenney, however, initially deemed this pittance to be really tuition-money, and not acceptable. He was quite uneasy, nevertheless, about the economics and realism of the situation, as, indeed, he had been at Georgetown, and, conscious of the complexities, asked the General to make no decision on the matter until further information reached him.[95]

Among the complexities was the fact that the employment of lay teachers would have to be envisaged if Jesuits were to be released for work with the Indians or the outlying mission stations, or merely to ease the pressure on the Jesuits in the college. The General, in fact, was to suggest this to Verhaegen in October 1832;[96] only to receive the answer that the annual salary of one lay professor, 500 dollars a year, would absorb the current fees of a hundred day students.[97] This underlined the need to increase the number of boarders. To promote this, Kenney approved the sending of a Jesuit annually from St Louis "to lower Louisiana to settle accounts with the parents of the students, to buy provisions of sugar, coffee, wine etc. and to increase the number of boarders".[98]

The discussion of the issues, and negotiations, continued long after he left Missouri, and he was to be active within the order in seeking a dispensation from the Ignatian principle; but while he was still in St Louis he was unavoidably drawn into considering ways of seeking approval of tuition fees by his good friend, Bishop Rosati.

Unease among the Jesuits about the future of their college, and remarks by certain parents critical of free education, occasioned concern to the bishop, who did not wish to see anything undermine a key institution in his diocese. He naturally turned to Kenney as to how he, as bishop, might be of assistance. The two of them, as noted, had established a remarkably close regard and trust in a short time. Kenney spoke repeatedly in his praise; while Rosati testified to his regard in a number of practical ways, including the present of a set of breviaries,[99] and the appointment of Kenney, in his own absence, "to hold his place, until he returned".[100]

Kenney, at this stage, had come round to accepting the need for a tuition fee because of exceptional circumstances, as in Ireland and England. He explained to the bishop, however, the difficult position in which the General, and all professed fathers of the Society, found themselves with regard to seeking any mitigation with regard to the vow of poverty; but then recounted how their mutual friend, Dr Murray of Dublin, had raised the question of petitioning the pope for a dispensation from the regulation about tuition-fees in the Irish situation. This was the line Rosati decided to follow. He wrote to Cardinal Pedicini of the Congregation of Propaganda, Rome, seeking a dispensation; after first writing at length to the General outlining his reasons for doing so. It was a mark of his close contact with Kenney, that he urged, in his letter to Pedicini, that Fr Kenney be consulted on the matter.[101]

In subsequent months, while the request was being weighed in Rome, Kenney, with his consultors in Maryland, decided to press the case with the General for Jesuit schools generally in the United States. Early in September

1832, they entrusted Fr McSherry with certain "postulata", or petitions, to be brought to the congregation of Jesuit procurators at Rome and presented to Fr Roothaan; and these included a request, in Kenney's writing, for a dispensation from St Ignatius's ruling together with reasons why it should be granted. It pointed out that neither from the farms, nor from funds received from the missions, was there any money available to support schools. Hence, the Jesuits in schools in the United States did not have that basic provision for food and clothing which Ignatius required for his followers in the foundation of colleges, and were obliged "to have recourse to miserable expedients which degrade our colleges". It was invidious, Kenney argued, to be said to be violating poverty, when all that was sought was maintenance: a maintenance, indeed, which provided but a precarious subsistence from year to year, and was very different from that solid maintenance, secured by law, which was deemed in keeping with poverty in Europe but which "would be here esteemed a luxury". Again, if the labourer was worthy of his hire in the ministry of preaching, surely he also was in that of education. And in this context, McSherry was referred to some appropriate remarks made by Bishop Rosati. Also, it was evident that in the United States there was a need to use every lawful means to increase the facilities of spreading the Catholic religion, and these included financial assistance, since the main thing to be feared from the Church's adversaries in America was the facility which money gave them "to overpower us with hoards of fanatical or hypocritical preachers and thousands of books and pamphlets".[102]

The Congregation of Propaganda, after considering Bishop Rosati's petition, asked Fr Roothaan for his views. He, by way of reply, sent them a copy of the bishop's letter to him; and then petitioned Pope Gregory XVI as to what road the Jesuits were to take: careful not to express an opinion about, or to ask for, a dispensation. Rosati, who had come to Rome to plead the case, was granted audience by the pope on 13 January 1833, and was informed that his request was conceded as necessary on two grounds: inability of the Jesuit schools to support themselves without tuition fees; and prevailing prejudices, amongst some people, against free schools. It was left to the Jesuit General to decide how the dispensation might be applied.[103]

Writing from Rome to Kenney on 21 January, McSherry reported that the only one of their "postulata" to the Jesuit congregation of procurators which was approved was "the petition to take money for day-scholars ...". "Bishop Rosati, through the Propaganda," he added, had "made the same request for the Missouri, and the General will pray the grant to be extended to all America, Ireland and England, so that all doubt on this subject will be removed in future".[104]

The following day, in a letter to De Theux, as the superior in Missouri, Roothaan observed that Dr Rosati "wrote to his Holiness asking that the Society be allowed to receive school money [tuition fees] in view of the peculiar circumstances obtaining among you, as also in Ireland and England, to which petition his Holiness has graciously assented. As a consequence, there is no longer any difficulty on this score, and it is well, indeed, that the petition did not come from the Society."[105] To Rosati, he wrote a long letter which concluded with the wish that: "St Ignatius may not take it amiss that in a matter which he had so much at heart and recommended to us so warmly, we turn aside for the time being."[106]

Kenney also wrote to Rosati: thanking him for his recommendations to the cardinal prefect and the Father General. The bishop's gracious response was typical of him: "I wish I could render you and all the Society more important services; I am very glad to see that what little I may have done produces the most desirable effect, that of uniting us all with the sacred bonds of a still greater charity."[107]

Writing to John McElroy, on 14 April 1833, Kenney judged that this decision (on tuition fees) would in time "produce great results in our situation in these states".[108] It was certainly critical to the continuance of St Louis College. And it came at a most propitious time. For on 28 December 1832, the general assembly of the state of Missouri had recognised the college as "a body corporate" with "the name and style of St Louis University", and had constituted and appointed as its trustees P.J. Verhaegen, Theodore De Theux, P.W. Walsh, C.F. Quickenborne, and James Van de Velde.[109] It thus became the first university west of the Mississippi River. To Kenney, the thought of St Louis College as a university, able to confer all sorts of degrees, occasioned some amusement. "Certainly at present such an appellation has something of the ludicrous in it; but let us hope that one day it may verify the name", he remarked to John McElroy.[110] And, he added in a letter to McSherry, that what was truly valuable now and always was that the trustees were "without limit empowered to receive, and manage all the property, real or personal, belonging to the college; so that they can now receive donations, if they can get them, to any amount in money or land".[111]

Its third level status and trusteeship, and the new freedom in the Jesuit manner of conducting schools, together with much hard work and confident leadership, gradually enabled St Louis University to "verify the name", and to replace the prospect of day to day survival with one more appropriate to a city which was terminus to great rivers and portal to the far-spreading prairies.

THE MISSOURI MEMORIALE:
TOWARDS "PEACE AND RELIGIOUS HARMONY"

Well before the above decisions were made, Kenney, as has been remarked, had returned to Maryland and was deeply immersed in his visitation there.

Before departing Missouri, however, he had determined to impart as much order, harmony and stability as he possibly could to the mission. The means he planned to employ was a wider application of that already employed in Maryland, namely, a far ranging, clearly expressed set of instructions, which might not be changed without the superior general's consent. That there was a felt need for order and stability was clear to him, and had, in fact, been put forcefully to him by Verhaegen, rector of St Louis College.

"The grand object which, in my opinion, Your Reverence is to effect, by all possible means, is to prevent for the future the grounds of complaint and disunion which have existed in this mission for several years ... As these chiefly arose from the superiors of the mission interfering in the affairs and duties of local superiors", it would be "highly conducive to the peace and happiness" of everyone, if regulations were made and enforced which would confine everyone "to his proper department". So, "Reverend and dear Father", Verhaegan concluded with an almost prophetic ring: "Take ... the most effectual measures" to bring about the "treasure of peace and religous harmony, and, poor as we are, I dare say that we will deem ourselves rich enough."[112]

Kenney's answer was his *Memoriale*, which reflected his experiences and covered every aspect of mission life, and which, in its main text, ran to thirty-four, closely written pages.

"Most effectual measures"

By way of introduction, he emphasised that his instructions were in keeping with "the universally established customs of the Society", and that its institute prohibited provincials, let alone superiors, from changing whatever the Visitor had ordered, or revoking faculties which he had granted to individuals. He then went on to treat of a number of areas in considerable detail.

These included: a daily time-table which, in addition to the normal round of duties, indicated the required periods of prayer and recreation, and the numbers of hours of sleep; a section on diet, cooking, and health, along the lines noted earlier, together with a strong reminder to superiors;[113] a section on hospitality; and on care of the sick – including his approval of an infirmary at the college. He also dealt with a building addition to the college; with the wearing of the cassock; and the teaching hours of scholastics, and their opportunities for relaxation. Also, of course, there were, the two abiding requirements: the provision of custom books, conformable to the instructions of the *memoriale*, for each house, which would be examined each year by the provincial; and the careful keeping of accounts, which required having, in addition to the individual ledgers, "a general charge and discharge book".

As well as these by now familiar items, there were others more distinctly related to the region. Thus, he expressed special concern for the Indian mission. Although he was not in a postion at this point to give directions concerning it, he could not, he declared, "approve of any new mission, or measure being adopted, or obligation contracted", that would preclude the hope of achieving that great object "which the fathers had chiefly in view on their first arrival in the country". And in line with Verhaegen's early suggestion, he reminded superiors "not to restrict the authority of subordinate superiors within narrower limits that those prescribed by the rules of their respective offices", while provincials were instructed not to restrain "the faculties of rectors", and rectors those of ministers, "without great necessity", and never without due consultation. With Brother O'Connor in mind, perhaps, he decreed that henceforth "no one in ordinary conversation" was to be "styled 'Reverend Father' " and "no one below the minister" was ever to be "styled by the name of his office". Also in terms of office, and social distinction, he emphasised that Brother de Mayer, whom he had recently appointed procurator of the house and farm at Florissant, had "the same care and superintendance of all temporal things that are exercised by the procurators of other houses", and that "the circumstance of his being a lay brother" was not in any way "to limit the faculties ordinarily granted to the priest who generally discharged the same office". Finally, he turned to the most striking instance of social distinction on the mission, the presence of "the coloured servants", as he called them.

Care of the "coloured servants"

Six slaves, as has been mentioned, had come to Missouri with the Belgian Jesuits in 1823. By the time of the civil war most of the Jesuit houses in Missouri and Kentucky seem to have had slaves. But the numbers were much smaller than in Maryland or Louisiana; and to judge from Kenney's *Memoriale*, there was much that was praiseworthy in the interaction between the Jesuits in Missouri and their negro slaves. He commented on "the good conduct, industry, and Christian piety of all the coloured servants of both sexes", and remarked that "our houses of the mission are the only ones where no complaints have been made of the slaves". He urged the fathers to preserve "the same paternal, ... yet vigilant conduct towards those creatures, whose happiness here and hereafter so much depends on the treatment they receive from their masters".

And he proceeded – with an awareness of Br O'Connor's story, of his own experiences on his first visitation, and of the inhumanity all too evident in contemporary culture – to issue, as it were, "protective notice" for "the coloured servants".

"All our priests and non-priests," he declared, "will understand that it is most *strictly* and *solemnly* forbidden them to inflict any species of corporal chastisement on a female slave, or ever to threaten by word or act that they will themselves personally chastise them. Should such corrections ever become necessary, lay persons may be employed to do it. Neither are the priests to inflict corporal chastisement on the male servants, but this, when necessary, may be allowed to the lay brothers, who have authority over them. By this prohibition, priests are prevented from administering to any one corporal chastisement, however well deserved, which could be considered severe punishment"..

Finally, he expressed the hope that the College of St Louis would soon follow the example of the farm at the noviceship "by providing separate houses or chambers for each family of servants", and what was "still more necessary, separate places for the unmarried males and females".

To write, and represent

The remaining instructions in the *Memoriale* related to the bishop and to the Jesuit consultors.

The bishop had asked him to promote Jesuit support for his apostolate of the public press. In the *Memoriale*, as a result, Kenney encouraged the fathers of the college "to have published in the Catholic press", or in any other paper patronised by the bishop, such pieces as might be thought "useful to the public or an assistance to the editor of the papers". It was a form of ministry that was to prove an adornment to the mission, and subsequently to the Missouri Jesuit province.

In conclusion, Kenney reminded all that his commission as Visitor continued until terminated by the General, and that, consequently, all might write to him whenever they had sufficient reason, while the superior, the rector, and all their consultors were to send official letters to reach him at Georgetown before 1 August. And conscious that De Theux's subjects were fearful of him, he entreated the consultors to keep in mind "their strict obligation" to represent their views to the superior – "stating their opinions most fully and candidly" even when they feared that they might not "coincide with his private views".[114]

Effect of the Memoriale – Comments on the Visitor

With this final attempt to secure and rivet the directives of his visitation, Peter Kenney left St Louis. That same day, 8 May 1832, Verhaegen wrote to Dzierozynski: "We are all doing finely, but alas! in losing today our excellent Fr Visitor we lose a treasure."[115] And some months later, he informed the General: "The visitation of Revd Fr Kenney was of the greatest utility to our mission. He taught us a number of things which concern the spirit of our institute and left us with a memorial of regulations. As long as we loyally keep to it, as we are doing now, everything here will go on well."[116]

How "loyally" they kept to it overall has been indicated by a recent historian of St Louis University, who remarked that Kenney's "temporary schedule" came to assume equality with the ten commandments ... and was to continue from the agricultural, kerosene-lamp age into the age of electronics, with almost no recognition of dramatic changes in the American manner of living". He added, fairly, that: "it was not Father Kenney's fault this means to an end should eventually become a sanctified end in itself".[117]

The Visitor's weighty emphasis on the obligation of his instructions was with a view to their being taken seriously, not to they being set in granite; and even amidst the very directives there were reminders of the need for flexibility, for adaptation to circumstances and location. A factor promoting the persistence of his influence was, undoubtedly, the clarity of the instructions and the fact that they appeared to be a very practical application of the institute of the Society. Indeed, reading them today, more than 160 years, two general councils of the church, and several general congregations of the Society, later, one is struck not by the fact that some of the views seem quaint, some of the practices and directives obsolete, but that in so many instances his solid spirituality and enlightened common sense still ring true.

PRESERVING MISSOURI'S INDEPENDENCE – RETURNING EASTWARD

He had still one direct contribution to make to Missouri before he finally left America. He had told Bishop Rosati, in May 1832, that "the consolation and edification" which he had received at witnessing the progress of religion in his diocese had interested him in every aspect of that development.[118] That special interest in Missouri received practical expression some weeks after his return to Georgetown.

On 28 August, at a meeting there of the consultors, as well of the college as of the mission, the impetus to expand Maryland from a Jesuit vice-province to a province came to a head. It was agreed to petition the General to erect Maryland into a province, and under that heading to have it embrace the Missouri mission and, indeed, the entire Union so that it would be termed the province of North America or of the United States of North America.

Kenney, in forwarding this petition of the Maryland Jesuits to Rome, made it clear to Fr Roothaan that in his office as Visitor of the Missouri mission, of which he had not yet been relieved, he could not endorse such an important step as the reunion of Missouri with Maryland before the superiors and consultors of the western region had been consulted about it. Where he himself was concerned, however, his personal opinion was that the proposed reunion was not the appropriate step in the circumstances, and not likely to promote the overall Jesuit objective of God's greater glory.[119] His protest was contributory, at least, to the subsequent decision. When Maryland was erected as a province, just before he returned to Ireland, the status of Missouri remained that of an unattached and independent mission, and as such was left free to develop its own characteristic expression of the Jesuit ethos. Ironically, the very separation of Missouri from Maryland occasioned the only adverse comments on him as Visitor.

Praise – Not without criticism

On 23 October 1832, the General, responding to Kenney's earlier expression of being hard done by, commenced his letter to him with the words: "First of all, to console you I will tell you that from the various letters from Missouri they were delighted with the visitation, and it has had a great effect. It especially has led to expansion of hearts and union of souls. Someone has asked me if the jurisdiction of the Visitor over Missouri continued as long as he was in the United States. I answered affirmatively, as it could be necessary to consolidate the visitation."[120]

Despite this, and despite, as he saw it, his unremitting efforts to do what was best for Missouri and be even-handed between it and Maryland, Kenney was very conscious of criticism of him by certain Missouri Jesuits, particularly after he returned to Maryland. This weighed on him to the point that in his very last letter on American affairs he appealed to McSherry, as provincial of Maryland, to defend him from "the odious suspicion" of Fr De Theux, of Fr Verhaegen, and of Fr Smedts of St Charles – "who always says and thinks what Fr Verhaegen bids him". They complained of him and said he was "prejudiced against the college and mission". He asked McSherry, in "strict justice" to him, "to open their eyes and those of the General on this subject".[121]

The criticism was concerned with the allocation to the Missouri mission of candidates recruited for the Society of Jesus in North America by the munificent Belgian benefactor, Pierre-Jean De Nef, who regularly sent thither books, vestments, money, and prospective novices. Rivalry and dissension had arisen in the past between Maryland and Missouri about the destination of the gifts and the young men. Very conscious of this, and particularly concerned, as he informed Dzierozynski, "about the destination of subjects", Kenney while in Missouri arranged with the "fathers there" that: all Belgians who came to America with the intention of going to Missouri, should go to that mission; and that any who came "without any determination" for either mission, should make their choice before they entered the noviceship at White Marsh,[122] lest, presumably, the Maryland location of the noviciate might influence their choice. The noviceship in Missouri, under Van Quickenborne, it will be recalled had not been a success. The only other candidate for the position in terms of experience in the Society was De Theux, whom Kenney and all the consultors were adamant was not suitable, and whom the General thought should not be superior and novice master. So, it was agreed that the novices would go to White Marsh, and De Theux made no objection.

The immediate occasion of criticism against Kenney was the arrival of five Belgians in November 1832, who had been told by De Nef that they were to go to Florissant for their noviceship. He was unaware that it was no longer functioning. Kenney, as he reminded McSherry, had the five make their choice of mission. They chose Maryland. He gave it as his view, nevertheless, that two should go to Missouri at the end of their noviceship. After this was settled, De Theux wrote that he should get the young men immediately, that it should be "decided by lot" whom he should get, and that he should have three rather than two. Kenney refused to entertain the proposal. It would constitute, he declared, "an unconstitutional mode of election", it was disrespectful of the Visitor, implying that he was "incapable of making a disinterested appointment", and it was contrary to the arrangement regarding novices for Missouri made while he was there "with Mr De Theux's knowledge and with the approbation of the consultors".

That Verhaegen and Smedts "on this occasion" had joined with De Theux in criticising him, he found particularly unfair. He had laboured "to obtain for them a just and fair distribution of persons and effects" and found himself as a result "placed between two fires", since at Georgetown he was made to understand that he "was too much inclined to favour Missouri".[123] Ironically, the one consultor known to have spoken up in defence of the Visitor against the complaints in Missouri was Van Quickenborne, who, writing from St Louis to the General on 17 August 1833, gave it as his judgement that Fr Kenney "acted justly and fairly in all matters".[124] But, then, this holy and zealous man was said to find it difficult to "live in peace in the one house" with De Theux![125]

On leaving St Louis on 8 May, or shortly after, it is not clear what route Kenney took. His diary, or the extant part of it, does not recommence until 3 June. From a letter of Fr Grivel to Nicholas Sewall in England, however, it would appear that he arrived at Bardstown, Kentucky, south of Louisville, on 15 May.

The Bardstown retreat and visit

"There," according to Grivel, "he was to give a retreat to the clergy of the diocese according to the invitation of Bishop Flaget and his coadjutor, Bishop David." Moreover, "he was to inspect there, as Visitor, the first beginnings of the college of the French Jesuits, called by the bishop and sent by the General".[126] Grivel thought Kenney would give another retreat at Cincinnati, and that, though he would not remain indefinitely in the country, he would probably remain for two or three years as provincial of the new Maryland province, which would soon be announced.

As is evident, Grivel lumped together fact and surmise, and his information, even as to dates, was not always accurate. He had Kenney, for example,
leaving St Louis on 15 April. But that Kenney went to Bardstown is undeni-
able. Indeed, it would have been almost impossible to refuse the invitation sent
by the bishop on 26 March 1832. "All the people who have heard of you," he
wrote, "and, above all, my clergymen, are very anxious to see you, and hear
you preaching the word of God. Many of my missioners have begged of me to
solicit you and entreat you ... to give them a spiritual retreat of five or six
days! I conjure you, by all that is sacred and religious, to grant us such a
blessing; it will remove the prejudices still existing against your Society, (and)
it will serve considerably to alleviate the cares ... of an old missioner, who has
served all of 40 years in the United States".[127]

Despite the accumulated tiredness which he brought with him to
Kentucky, the retreat appears to have gone well. M.J. Spalding, the biographer
of Bishop Flaget, and himself a future bishop, recalled of the exercise that –
"the impression made by this truly eloquent man of God was deep and lasting".[128]

Kenney's suavity of manner, moreover, and his gift for personal relations,
smoothed immediate difficulties with the French fathers, and established a
lasting friendship with at least one of them; while he continued to have a way
with him which almost all bishops found both relaxed and respectful. As
already noted, he treated all with the deference due their office, but yet related
at a personal and spiritual level with equality and independence – and especially in the United States. It was a combination which American prelates met
seldom enough, even though formality was much less in evidence among them
than in Europe. At least one visiting Irish clergyman expressed pleasant surprise at the modesty of the American bishops, measuring them, presumably,
against his experience of their episcopal brethren in Ireland.[129]

Bishop Flaget, himself, continued to seek Kenney's spiritual advice in the
weeks after the retreat. And on 25 July, in fact, wrote to thank him for his
"truly kind and consoling letter"; adding:

> I avail myself of the first moment of leisure ... to return you my
> warmest thanks for the comfort you have given me and the people that
> are about me. Thus you continue, though at a great distance, to perfect
> the good work you so happily begun when you were in Bardstown.[130]

Rolling smoothly east

His first extant reference to the return journey has him at Lancaster, Ohio, on
3 June. They arrived there on a Sunday morning at 3.00 a.m. McSherry said
mass at 9.30, and Kenney at 10.00, after which he preached. The church was

small, but the congregation more than two hundred. McSherry found several relations in the town. They stayed, however, at the local tavern where although they "had a pint of good wine … and beer at dinner", their bill "for two nights, 2 chambers, and a day, was only $2.25 for both".

At 2.30 a.m. next day they left Lancaster, arrived about 6.00 at Somerset, and got to Zanesville, between Columbus and Wheeling, at 10.00 a.m. Delayed there for many hours, they made the acquaintance of the "resident minister", Mr Myles of the Dominican order, later to be mentioned as a candidate for the bishopric of Cincinnati. Kenney, having time to walk about, commented on the "very good, clean town", which was "like other towns in Ohio of any note, regularly built. "They departed on the mail coach at 9.30 that evening. As the road from Zanesville to Wheeling was the best made of any that he had experienced in the United States, the coach rolled smoothly and he slept well during the night. They crossed the Ohio in a ferry "moved by horses pulling in equal numbers at either side of the boat", and breakfasted at Wheeling, whence, after a change of horses, the stage set out again. This time the road was rough. They arrived at Pittsburgh at seven o'clock that evening.

His account finished there. A laconic narrative which made little effort to convey the exhaustion and hardship involved. A subsequent letter to Robert Haly, in Ireland, rounded off the journey, and his visitation of Missouri, with the remark: "I arrived at Georgetown on 13 June, after an absence of 8 months and 9 days, in excellent health."[131]

REVIEWING THE EFFECTS OF THE MISSOURI VISITATION

A consideration of the effects of his visitation on the Missouri mission, during not just those eight months but during his entire time in the United States, brings to mind many items of varied significance.

Of most general import, perhaps, was the fact that the separation of the Missouri mission from Maryland was announced to coincide with his visitation, and that he subsequently played an important role in preserving that separation when the new Maryland province sought to incorporate Missouri. Fr Roothaan agreed with his privately expressed estimation that an independent Missouri was more likely to fulfil the Ignatian ideal of promoting God's greater glory; and some years later the General held fast to that judgement when Frs De Smet, Verhaegen, and other Flemish Jesuits sought to make the mission part of the Belgian Jesuit province.

In the realm of more precise effects, one moves with different degrees of assurance.

The undoubted influence of his *Memoriale*, or guidelines to be followed, suggests that his emphasis on health and hygiene was reflected in greater care in the preparation and presentation of food, in greater care and empathy for the sick, in the limitation of teaching hours and greater provision of opportunities for relaxation. Again, his encouragement of writing might be seen as providing an early stimulus to what was to become a great tradition among the Jesuits of Missouri; while more immediately tangible manifestations of his visitation were such features as the college infirmary, revised clerical dress, and the provision of custom books and a fixed system of accountancy.

One of his most valuable contributions, however, was his invocation of an overall vision of what the mission might achieve, and how it might best use the resources available to it – so far as it was free to do so.

In terms of the best use of resources, his instinct at that moment in time, as has been indicated, was to deploy as many men as possible in what was called the rural missions, in missionary excursions to pockets of Catholics scattered over wide areas. But all he felt free to do was to encourage the few already involved in that ministry, and formally release Van Quickenborne to devote his immense zeal to that work. He was restricted by unalterable circumstances with reference to the College of St Louis and the mission to the Indians.

The staffing of the College of St Louis, as he saw it in 1832–3, was not an optimum use of resources, but he was saddled with it; and so he determined to make the college as effective as possible, and to that end he made it the focus of educational effort, and sought to prevent the dissipation of manpower on other educational ventures. As part of that concentration, he approved immediate building plans despite shortage of funds, approved the sending of Van de Velde to promote the college in lower Louisiana despite shortage of teachers, and participated himself in the attempt to secure the dispensation with regard to tuition-fees. The overall effort had immense repercussions for the future of the College and University of St Louis.

The other limiting circumstance was the commitment to the Indian mission, which had been built into the Du Bourg agreement of 1823 but which was being largely neglected in Missouri, and had been forgotten at Rome. It was part of his contribution to insist that there was a strict moral obligation involved, and that undertakings which would prevent the fulfilment of that obligation must be put aside. The General proved of like mind, and this paved the way for the later developments which resulted in a great expansion of manpower and funds for the Missouri Jesuits, thanks to the appeal of the Indian mission as presented to young Europeans by Peter De Smet, "the Black-Robe" par excellence, for whom the Redmen felt "a deep personal affection and absolute trust" extended to no other white man.[132] A future provincial of the Missouri vice-province was to comment on how much the order owed De Smet in terms of the "excellent number of young men" he attracted, the money collected for their support, his influence with bishops and prominent people, and the fame of his writings and journeys, which redounded to the good name of the Society.[133]

But Kenney had not only recreated the ambience for the Indian mission, he had also, unwittingly, prepared the impressionable and sensitive De Smet for it. When he came to St Louis he found the young priest in a distressed state, with a form of skin affliction which, while it had not affected his mental health or physical strength, left him with a leprous like infection on arms, chest, forehead and hair. His distress was added to by the lack of sympathy and care exhibited by his superior, De Theux, even though the scabrous disease had been in evidence for many months. He sought, on his physician's advice, a return to Europe, but the superior would not hear of it. Kenney did not wish to interfere, unless there was considerable danger in delay, which there did not seem to be. He also felt there was need of further medical opinion. He referred the question of the young man's return to the General. It was clear, however, that he felt that a return to Europe was the humane course.[134] The General's reply, which only came after Kenney was back in Maryland, gave him complete discretionary powers. Accordingly, on 14 March 1833, in response to two letters from De Theux regarding De Smet's petition, he gave his consent provided "physicians say that there is little hope of his recovery here, and that there is great hope of it if he go to Belgium".[135]

Meanwhile, unknown to Kenney, De Smet had obtained a second medical opinion which assured him that the Missouri climate had nothing to do with his ailment; and so, now that he was scheduled to return to Europe, he did not wish to go. De Theux, apparently following instructions to the letter, as was his wont, insisted, however, that he must go. He left in September 1833. On arrival in Paris, in December, he wrote to the General to be allowed return to Missouri. He disclosed the second medical opinion, and said that he had eventually been commanded to leave against his will. Roothaan permitted his return.

The restless and impressionable young priest, whose ailment may have been largely psychosomatic, and who now no longer seemed seriously afflicted, decided to devote time, prior to sailing, to travelling about Belgium lecturing with zeal on the Indian apostolate. As a result, he brought back to Missouri his first batch of "excellent young men", as well as a collection of money, books, paintings, altar vestments and furniture, and scientific instruments; and so equipped was made welcome by De Theux, whose mother in Belgium he had also taken care to visit![136]

As not seldom happens, however, it is possible that the most important effect of Kenney's visitation of Missouri was one not easily measured. He came to a situation where the superior of the mission was seen as severe, unfeeling, and interfering; where his subjects experienced frustration, anger, and unhappiness; and where there seemed to be no pattern, rules, or traditions to preserve subjects from the whims of a superior. Verhaegen had appealed to him as Visitor "to take the most effectual measures to ensure among us the heavenly treasure of peace and religious harmony, and, poor as we are, I dare say that we will deem ourselves rich enough".[137] He replied, as has been seen, with a set of detailed instructions, independent of the will of the superior, to provide a pattern of order, harmony, uniformity and stability, in the lives of the members; and to inculcate the ideals of respect for others, their opinions and work, and the virtues of hospitality and charity. And he painstakingly provided an example, in his own behaviour, of a caring, listening leadership, which availed of consultation, and respected the views of others. As a consequence, the General, as noted, was able to inform him that his visitation had had great effect, and "had led to expansion of hearts and union of souls";[138] and ten years later, the vice-provincial, Van de Velde, would speak of a harmony very different from the scene that met Kenney on his arrival at St Louis: "We have," he wrote, "French, Belgians, Americans, Spaniards, Irish, Germans, Hollanders; but all live together as if they were of the same country."[139] Even allowing for exaggeration, a great deal, clearly, had been achieved in a short time.

XI

Maryland, from mission to province: Concluding the visitation – Evading episcopal honours – The journey and the homecoming, June 1832–December 1833

> May you yet live many years to witness in the continued prosperity of this portion of the Society, now become a constitutional body, the happy fruits of a mission commenced two hundred years ago.
>
> Peter Kenney to the aged Francis Neale, 1833

Return to Georgetown

For a week after his return to Georgetown, he made no entry in his journal. Presumably there was physical tiredness, as well as a back log of correspondence and of meetings with individual Jesuits. The fact that there were now more than thirty members of the Society in residence, nearly half of the entire Maryland mission, increased the likelihood of problems seeking his attention.

On 21 June, however, the feast of Corpus Christi, he gave notice of his renewed involvement in public celebrations at the college. "Said mass for the scholars," he wrote, "at which eight made their first communion." A few days later he met with the 14 young Jesuits about to renew their vows, and heard their manifestation of conscience. The following day he gave an exhortation to the Jesuit brothers. On 29 June, the feasts of Sts Peter and Paul, he said mass at 5.45 a.m. for those renewing their vows, and then forestalled an attempt to use the date to honour himself. "The rector hinted this day as my feast," he wrote, "but I wished it would not be done, as I conceive such usage not prevalent in the Society." That evening, however, he and Mulledy had a visit from Chevalier Forladi, the Portuguese ambassador, who invited both of them to dinner on Thursday, 5 July.

A few important developments came together on 1 July. He had applied to Bishop Kenrick to be allowed reoccupy the Society's "ancient residence and little church of St Joseph, in Philadelphia", which had been served by secular priests ever since the suppression, though the legal right had always been invested in the Jesuits.[1] On 1 July Kenrick replied graciously: "I shall see with great pleasure the successors of those venerable men, who founded the Pennsylvanian mission, reoccupy the first church in this city." He requested, however, that the current pastors be allowed remain on until the spring as they were endeavouring to build another church in the south side of the city. All the Jesuits were quite pleased with this concession, Kenney subsequently informed Robert Haly. "It will be the first establishment of the Society in any of the great cities." But he added the practical note: "the house is very good, but the rest of the premises very little better than Hardwicke Street."[2]

On the same date, Fr Neale, a trustee of the mission, provided a boost to Mulledy's building plans with the information that he was prepared to "lend $12,000 on a mortgage to the college for any length of time that the college may wish to keep it, redeemable by instalments of not less than $1,000."[3]

On 4 July, Kenney, as usual, had a long entry to mark the anniversary of the Declaration of Independence. In keeping with the impetus given to patriotic celebrations by Mulledy, the flag was flown from the college tower, and the cannon was fired by the students from before sunrise to almost nine o'clock that night. The Declaration was read, and one of the rhetoricians pronounced what Kenney termed "a very good oration". There was a special dinner attended by Mr Daniel Carroll and other strangers, with "many patriotic toasts". Fr Fenwick "sang a few songs"; and great feeling was produced by a former pupil of the college, who spoke affectingly of his thoughts of Georgetown during life's vicissitudes in various countries. "Good Mr D. Carroll shed tears and other old persons were not less affected." It was, Kenney concluded, "a very gratifying day".[4] The dinner with the Portuguese ambassador next evening was attended by a number of well known guests, including the mayor of Georgetown.

His only extant letter from those days in Georgetown, was in reply to one from McElroy seeking his views on giving an eight-day retreat to some religious sisters. He had no problem in principle, Kenney replied, but warned against his over-committing himself. He added an admonition in the firm but disarming manner he used with the headlong McElroy: "I am sure that you would not like to make the superior cut what the Italians call, a bruta figura!" But why would you "deem it proper to speak to the archbishop and to your congregation, and to almost all in your neighbourhood about building a new church, before you could give a hint to the provincial superior? You see how plainly I act with you – I really have no other way – and, though without rashness, I think you have. Yet I cannot think that you will be displeased with my frankness."[5]

A few days later, 10 July, his journal recorded that he had set out for the residence of St Francis Xavier, at Bohemia, on the eastern shore of Maryland. He had arranged to meet with his socius, Fr McSherry, there. The latter had left him during their return journey to Georgetown in order to make his thirty-day retreat at Bohemia, prior to taking his final vows in the Society. He was due to take these in Kenney's presence, as representative of the order, on 16 July.

As he set out, Kenney was happy with the situation at the college, and relieved, perhaps, to get away just then as the work on the new building commenced. In a long letter to Robert Haly, from Bohemia, he remarked that the college was "flourishing" under its "indefatigable rector". And he went on to report that there were 130 resident boarders, not counting the half-boarders who spent the whole day at the college. Mulledy had built in the past year an infirmary of four storeys, which contained a fine kitchen among its features, and the workmen had just begun to dig the foundations of a four-storey addition to the "old college" which would provide cellars, a refectory, a study hall, and a chapel. The full length of the building would be more than 90 feet long. The dimensions would be a few feet longer, he thought, than those of the refectory and study at Clongowes. His detailed communication to Haly, however, had started out on a far less positive note.

Anxiety for news from home

With some time on his hands, and in a residence dedicated, like his Hardwicke Street church in Dublin, to St Francis Xavier, he had experienced a rush of homesickness, and a sense of hurt and anxiety at the absence of letters from home. The anxiety had been fuelled by reports in the public press of cholera in Ireland, particularly at Naas, just a few miles from Clongowes. "Why should I be forever doomed to complain of neglected correspondence?" he asked. He had written several letters. Yet the last direct news he had received from an Irish Jesuit "was penned in June 1831! And in the meantime the public papers frighten and excite our anxiety every day by reports of the ravages of cholera. Think what I must feel when I read that at Naas 16 died of the disease. All the consequences of the fatal illness of 1819 rushed to my mind; and *no one* will write what *everyone* must know." He blamed Haly particularly, because 15 months ago he had promised he would write soon again.[6]

Ironically, even before he wrote his anxious letter, Bartholemew Esmonde had written from Clongowes to assure him that matters were not as bad as they might appear in newspaper reports likely to have reached him. The first place cholera appeared was at Naas where "almost thirty were carried off". The parents of Clongowes boys, naturally, were very concerned, but the school established a strict quarantine and followed the instructions of "the first physicians of Dublin". It remained open and unaffected by contagion. Other colleges, such as Trinity College, Carlow, Maynooth, Navan, Tuam, had all broken up in the face of the cholera panic. Most of the main towns, in fact, had been visited, and at Tullamore "everybody who could ran off to the country spreading alarm on every side". In town and country, however, Esmonde added, "the conduct of our clergy, and of the Sisters of Charity in the hospital, has made a great impression on all parties. Many have become Catholics".

After further information on public and personal matters Esmonde dropped a remark which must have come as something of a shock to Kenney when the letter reached him: "I suppose you have heard ... that we may soon expect you; at least the General's letter to me [of April 14th] says – '*Redebit P. Kenney quam primum negotia in regione quam visitat composuerit*' (Fr Kenney will return immediately his business is completed in the region he is visiting). I hope these 'negotia' are by this time nearly settled."[7]

Haly, incidentally, replied immediately he received Kenney's aggrieved letter. He repeated much of what Esmonde said about the cholera, but added that Kenney's old friend, "the good Archbishop Curtis", had fallen a victim. He had good news, however, about the new Gardiner Street church. Miss Denis had been frightening them for some time that Archbishop Murray would not consent to open the church. Instead, "he consented in the most gracious manner". Although still with scaffolding, the building was impressive. "The ceiling and stucco work" were "greatly admired", and the structure was also "peculiarly favourable to the voice". Kenney would also be pleased to hear "that the collection in Marlborough Street church" (the pro-cathedral) had "increased" since Gardiner Street opened, so that "all feeling against us seems gradually subsiding".[8]

Bohemia and St Inigoes

Meanwhile, Kenney was pleased with affairs at Bohemia. He had been there previously for almost three weeks during June 1831; but now, as he informed Mulledy, he found that Br Heard, who was in charge of the farm, looked much better than he did last year. And he attributed "much of his renewed health to the peace, which the absence of his wicked slaves allows him to enjoy. All things go on well." McSherry, he continued, had made his final vows at 5.00 a.m. mass that morning, 16 July, and was of the opinion that it was "absolutely necessary to look into the state of St Inigoes before we make up our reports for Rome"; and as that might be done in a few days, he, Kenney, saw no difficulty in delaying the election of their representative to the congregation of procurators at Rome. He asked Mulledy to notify the consultors. He expected to be back before the feast of St Ignatius, 31 July.[9]

On 17 July, accordingly, he and McSherry left Bohemia for Frenchtown some 14 miles distant, whence they took the steamer for Baltimore, where they put up at Barnum's hotel. Next day they dined with the Jenkins family, and that evening went aboard the *Franklin* under Captain Jenkins, who was very kind to them during what proved to be a "rather long and rough" passage.

They entered the Potomac at nine next morning, and stopped near the mouth of the river.[10] The residence of St Inigoes stood at the southern tip of Maryland, and served the mission of St Nicholas.[11]

Kenney was impressed at the improvements since his last visit. "I am much delighted to see the total change in the house for the better," he wrote in his journal. "What a difference from its situation in 1820! It does not owe a single cent! It was then very heavy in debt."[12] For some reason – perhaps relating to Br Carbery's plans for involving the blacks in effective methods of working the farms – they stayed longer at St Inigoes than originally intended. On 25 July he wrote to Mulledy that he could not be in the college for St Ignatius's day; but would set out as soon as possible after that feast.[13]

Daily minutiae at Georgetown

He returned to Georgetown at the beginning of August, and soon was caught up in a host of details. A meeting with consultors on 5 August found it necessary to remove Fr Neale, for reasons of health, from managership of the farm at Newtown. Fr Young was appointed manager and rector on 7 August. On the same day, Kenney received three scholastics and two brother novices into the Society. A few days later, Fr Barber at Frederick applied for a newspaper for himself because he could not get a chance to read the ones that came to the house; and Br McGir asked again to be removed from Frederick because the housekeeper's daughter was allowed run a milliners shop in the basement! And to add to the plethora of minutiae, McSherry, on his return from St Inigoes on 9 August, stated that Nelly, one of the slaves, said that another servant, Peter, ought to be sold because "he steals a sheep very often, to take (one) to his wife, and the next to his sweetheart"![14]

On 15 August, Kenney received the final vows of the rector, Mulledy. A special dinner was held to mark the occasion, with some outside guests, including the Portuguese ambassador. That day, being the feast of the Assumption of the Blessed Virgin, Kenney preached at the high mass, as Fr Dubuisson was ill.[15]

In the midst of these and numerous other calls on his attention, there was the serious business of preparing for the procurators' congregation at Rome.

Preparing for the congregation: proposals

On 19 August, in a letter to McElroy, he mentioned that he planned to take Br McGir from Frederick to assist the ailing Br Heard at Bohemia; and he added: "We are sending Mr McSherry to Rome, with two of the young scholastics; but of news is not yet public."[16]

He was thus informing him that McSherry had been elected as the Maryland representative to the procurators' congregation at Rome. The congregation was to discuss the main trends, needs and developments in the Society across the world, advise the General whether a general congregation of the order was desirable at this time, and provide a forum for the discussion of important specific topics. It also gave the individual representatives of distant countries an opportunity to report personally to the General on their overall situation, and to clarify certain needs and press for certain permissions and exemptions. It was, therefore, an important event for the whole order; and particularly for the remoter regions in the young, restored Society.

During August, Kenney and his consultors of the mission, as well as the consultors of Georgetown, continued to meet in preparation for this conference. They wished to use the occasion, and McSherry's going to Rome, to bring to the General, for his consideration and approval, certain measures approved by them.

Putting these forward, Kenney first of all mentioned those proposals which were "recommended with ... the utmost unanimity". The most notable of these were: that his Paternity make the mission into a province of the Society; that he reunite Missouri to the Maryland mission and so have the new province, like the old mission of the Society, embrace the whole of the United States – though Kenney, in a private letter, recommended against the reunion, as noted earlier.

Other proposals of significance, though not supported unanimously, sought the General's sanction "for the adoption of some arrangements" that would "gradually liberate" the mission from slave servants "and substitute free labourers in their place" ; and his permission to allow the Society in the United States "to receive pensions from day scholars in places where the schools" could not "obtain foundations or other means of adequate support".[17]

On 5 September, McSherry and his companions set out for Rome.[18] The previous day, Kenney gave him detailed written instructions under sixteen headings. These concerned how he was to proceed in Rome, and gave particular attention to the proposal for tuition fees. He put forward eight reasons why pensions should be allowed for day scholars. These have been summarised in the previous chapter on Missouri. In addition, McSherry was requested to buy books and astronomical instruments at Paris, to present the "obedience, affection and respect" of all on the mission to the Fr General, and to remember Kenney to Frs Kohlmann, Glover, and all the Jesuit Assistants, the Irish Jesuits, and all others who might enquire for him. Finally, the by now probably overwhelmed McSherry was instructed to write at certain points on his journey, and to send "all sorts of news, once every six weeks".[19]

Assurance of support – Need of approval

Kenney's own relations with Rome received a boost within a few days of penning the instructions for McSherry. He received a letter from Fr Roothaan, in his own hand, assuring him of his regard and confidence.[20] It was a response to the letter of complaint and upset Kenney had sent through Glover. Writing to the latter on 18 September, Kenney thanked him for the good use he had made of his letter of 11 March. "It has procured for me," he said, "the consolation of a very condescending letter from Father General, 12 May, written by his own hand. I highly appreciate this act of kindness, which has its effect in giving me courage and exciting my gratitude."

He went on to confess his need of such support:

> Any office of government in any place has been, and always will be, painful to me: naturally speaking, I hate it; but it becomes quite intolerable if I were to bear it without the full confidence of him, to whom alone I am responsible, and to whom alone I must look for countenance and support. I am now quite free from all anxiety on that subject; and what I did feel was the greater pain because my feelings were not known to any, not even to my socius,[21]

At the same time, two of the consultors in their regular letters to Rome were praising his style of government. Dzierozynski briefly, as was his wont, spoke of his strong and motivating leadership in spiritual and temporal affairs.[22] Dubuisson, as usual, was more prolix and complicated. "The Lord seems to be blessing our mission," he observed. "I appreciate more and more Fr Superior [Kenney], his consummate prudence, his talents, his virtue, zeal, excellent mind, and his courtesy. This is a real treasure which you have given to America, and I hope that you will not take him back." He then went on to say that a short time ago he "had a slight difference of opinion with him" on the expenses of the church for which he, Dubuisson, had responsibility. He went into detail on the matter, not in order to complain, he said, but to enable his Paternity understand his "reasons for remaining in opposition to Fr Kenney's opinion". He did not wish his Paternity, however, to let Kenney know that he had "communicated all this". In the same convoluted way he proceeded indirectly to praise Kenney and criticise Mulledy, who, it would seem, was rather short and impatient with him. "As far as I can judge," he wrote, "things are going well in the college. Fr Rector [Mulledy] is truly a man of talent, a strong minded person – not that I am finding fault (I have communicated my observations to Fr Kenney), but I hope that although he is still a bit green he will mature with time, and with the example of the very amiable manner of the Fr Superior."[23]

Meeting others' needs; and obstacles

The issue of the slaves kept presenting itself in various forms. The aged Fr Francis Neale, who had long been a benign manager at St Thomas Manor, Charles County, and had been taken advantage of by some incorrigible servants, had sought permission, as has been indicated, to retire to St Inigoes. He wished to sell the troublesome slaves, and Kenney seems to have agreed to assist him in negotiating the sale. Not hearing from the old man for some time, he wrote him on 10 September. He first inquired how he was in "these sickly times"; going on to speak of several deaths from cholera at Georgetown, the "more general victims" being "poor Irish labourers and others of that class". Then he reminded him that he awaited his answer about the sale to two planters in Louisiana, who preferred Catholic slaves and lived in an area where there was a Catholic priest and church.[24] At the end of the month, Neale, presumably under pressure from his black "family", replied that he had none to sell. This seems to have been final, though Kenney wrote to him again, on 10 October, assuring him "that he might sell incorrigible slaves that were giving bad example to others and to the neighbourhood, though other managers were not to do so without leave from the superior".[25]

Efforts to meet with requests and needs, also met with obstacles from other quarters. His decision to send Br McGir from Frederick to assist Br Heard at Bohemia evoked criticism from McElroy. He left the latter in no doubt, however, as to his determination. "The members of the Society," he wrote, "do not pertain to any house ... They are never to be considered as *astricti glebe* [bound to the land] like the peasants in Russia ... The property is irrevocably applied to houses, but persons are to be as free as air in the hands of the superior, or General, to be wafted not merely from Frederick to Bohemia, but across the ocean to any part of the world where the greater service of God was to be hoped for." He would be going to Bohemia in a few days, and if he found that Br McGir was immediately required there then he was to be sent thither straightway – "for the importance of that place is far greater than the mere attendance to the cows and small, domestic drudgery of Frederick". He would, of course, try to supply someone in his stead.[26]

On 15 September the ceremony for "the opening of the schools", or commencement of the school year, took place. By the end of the month, the sense of summer was truly past. "Put on a new winter cassock made of very good cloth", he entered in his journal on 30 September. And on the day he wrote to Fr Neale, 10 October, he held what he called "the last consultation" concerning a holiday house "on the heights above Georgetown"; and next morning, at 8.00 a.m., set out for Bohemia, in Cecil County.

Presiding from Bohemia

Bohemia, like St Inigoes, was one of his favoured places. He presided over the mission from there for many weeks. On 10 December he was to explain, in the course of a letter to the archbishop of Baltimore: "I have been here for the last two months to afford the very small flock in the neighbourhood an opportunity of performing their religious duties until I should be enabled to place someone here permanently."[27]

One receives the impression in these weeks that he was marking time: waiting on McSherry's return from Rome with the answers to their petitions, and also with news of his own future destination – for he had recently learned of vigorous attempts by some American prelates to have him appointed bishop of

Cincinnati. It was in an effort to block this movement that he had written to the archbishop of Baltimore on 10 December.

FINAL EFFORT TO APPOINT HIM BISHOP: A CLOSE RUN

It had all started on 23 August 1832, when Dr Edward Fenwick, the Dominican Bishop of Cincinnati, whom Kenney had found somewhat cool in his welcome, wrote from a sick bed in Detroit to his friend, Bishop Rosati, to say that he was now 64 years, had much travel in his extended diocese with its growing Catholic population, and needed a coadjutor. He had "solicited the Holy Father to grant Father Kenney, superior of the Society of Jesus in the United States of America, for coadjutor of Cincinnati – his talents, piety, experience and other eminent qualities are well known and sufficiently recommend him. If stationed at Cincinnati as bishop," Fenwick continued, "he would no doubt much promote the cause of our religion in the western countries, (and) the honour and propagation of the Society of Jesus, which I respect and admire much as one of the most meritorious and useful religious societies to the church and the world at large." He had sent his request to the pope and the prefect of Propaganda through the Revd Mr Jeanjean. He asked Rosati to second his petition to the Holy Father and Cardinal Pedicini, and as he did not have Fr Kenney's baptismal name he asked him to include it in his letter to Rome.[28]

The bishop of St Louis complied within a short time: recommending Kenney's appointment to the cardinal prefect of Propaganda with the words: "He needs no commendation for it is clear enough ... to judge from the office assigned him by the superiors of his Society, that he is a man of no ordinary mark. For the rest, I had ample enough opportunity to become acquainted with his learning, piety, prudence, singular eloquence and suavity of manner when, during the past year, while visiting the houses of the Society, he spent several months with us to the very great edification of all. Eligible, therefore, as he is in every respect, I deem him most worthy of being raised to the episcopal dignity."[29]

Just three weeks later, on 26 September, Bishop Fenwick died: a victim of cholera while conducting a visitation of his diocese. The issue now became one of directly filling the see. Rosati pressed Kenney's name on Propaganda, and sought the support of Dr Whitfield, archbishop of Baltimore, and other prelates.

The first Kenney heard of these developments was on 4 December 1832, when a letter from Mulledy, written on 20 November, reached him at Bohemia. The archbishop, visiting Georgetown, had told Mulledy that the late bishop of Cincinnati had twice written to Rome seeking Kenney's appointment as his successor, and had sent a representative to Rome last August to plead the case.[30] Kenney was loath to take the matter seriously. "What a curious bit of news was that which the archbishop communicated to you!" – he replied to Mulledy. "Had it not come from him, I should have treated it as an idle rumour; but I still hope and believe that the threatened evil will not occur." He could not conceive that "a compulsive order" would be imposed on a person of his age, whose services, whatever they were supposed to be, could not be of long duration in any office, or any place. Nevertheless, he continued, it was right "to take all precautions", and hence he "determined to send to Rome" what Mulledy had written to him, although he expected that the proposition would be abandoned before it reached the pope.[31]

Although he did not mention it in his letter to Georgetown, he had also written to Archbishop Whitfield, mindful of his warm welcome from his Grace the previous Christmas. He asked him to use his "utmost influence with the Sacred Congregation to prevent such an appointment". The "good Bishop Fenwick", he declared, had not known him and his circumstances, he had only seen him "four or five times in his life", and then only in a passing way. "I had long since indulged the hope that I was no longer in danger of exercising the awful responsibility attached to an acceptance of the episcopal office", he continued, and nothing short of the certainty of offending God by sacrilegious disobedience would ever induce him to give his consent. He could not bear the thought, he declared, of being withdrawn from the jurisdiction of the Society, to which he was warmly and unalterably attached. He uttered these sentiments because they were most sincerely felt and constituted a just ground of objection to his appointment.

His second objection, he went on, was that he was in his 54th year, and subject to an asthmatic complaint which was "much irritated by the cold winters of this climate", and which, with his advanced age, already deprived him of the facility of making those exertions which some years ago he was able to make in the discharge of missionary duties. Indeed, he continued, "in the course of nature I cannot expect to be useful in any office, or in any place, ten years longer ... Why then force me into a situation, the dread responsibility of which must only tend to shorten my days in the midst of increased trials and solicitudes."

All this, was in addition to his own personal lack of progress in that state of perfection to which the holder of the episcopal dignity was expected to have already arrived.

Finally, he protested that "the diocese of Cincinnati with all its rising institutions" required a man of more vigour and influence than could be expected from him at his age, and, besides, the Indian mission, in the Michigan area, required a facility in speaking French which he did not have.[32]

On 17 December, the archbishop sent a rather cool response. "I have received your very edifying letter," he remarked. "I have written nothing yet to Rome concerning our late lamented bishop, and do not intend writing unless the S. Congreg. of Propaganda consult me." Other bishops may have written, however, since Bishop Fenwick had addressed some others on the matter. He added that from information received, it appeared that Dr Fenwick had envisaged that his vicar-general, the Revd Mr Reese, would suit better the Indian mission about Detroit, and that Kenney would be the fittest person for the Cincinnati diocese. He concluded with the dry comment: "Your humble sentiments of yourself, and the fears and repugnance you express, being common to the most worthy of a mitre, would not, I suppose, dissuade the pope from proceeding in such a nomination. But I know nothing from Rome concerning the matter."[33]

Not content with this response, Kenney wrote again, and then called on his Grace when passing though Baltimore – "without receiving the least consolation from him".[34] His persistence had been prompted by news that Bishops Rosati, Flaget, and, he suspected, Kenrick of Philadelphia, had joined forces in support of the late Bishop Fenwick's petition.

Dr Whitfield's "cold answer" led him to question his Grace's motives and intentions. These suspicions were to crystallise and harden within a few months. Already, however, an indication of his Grace's hopes and plans had been revealed to Bishop Rosati. Dr Whitfield, despite being a former Jesuit novice, or perhaps because of it, indicated little sympathy towards the Jesuits, and shared the attitude of his predecessor and close friend towards Irish clergy.[35]

Replying to the bishop of St Louis's request for support for Kenney, he said that he had raised the matter with Mulledy who said "that as Fr Kenney was a professed father he could not be a bishop unless the pope strictly commanded him, and, besides, Fr Kenney had already declined the coadjutorship of Dublin". He continued circuitously: that he had written nothing to Rome about Cincinnati, but that some hints received from Ohio suggested that it might not be to the good of the diocese if Fr Kenney were elected, since Bishop Fenwick had left two-thirds of the churches and landed property to the Dominicans; and "they" had proposed to him to recommend certain priests from his own diocese. However, he had done nothing as yet. But, he continued:

> Let us all be cautious. If possibly a good choice can be made let an American-born be recommended and (between us in strict confidence) I do really think we should guard against having more Irish bishops. I am really afraid of the consequences, and I hope my fear proceeds from no national antipathy but from motives God may approve. This you know is a dangerous secret, but I trust it to one in whom I have full confidence.[36]

A letter from McSherry, nevertheless, sent from Rome more than a fortnight later, indicated that Kenney had real grounds for concern. The Revd Jeanjean had arrived three days previously with many verbal recommendations to add to the late bishop's petitions to Propaganda and the pope. He told McSherry that Cardinal Pedicini was strongly disposed towards the appointment. "The cardinal," he said, "thought it must have been an inspiration in the bishop to make such a nomination, a *Jesuit to succeed a Dominican.*" As soon as the General heard about it, he went to see Pedicini; but, in Jeanjean's view, it was going to be very difficult to change the cardinal's mind. McSherry then went on to agree, with perhaps more honesty than tact, as to Kenney's unsuitability for the appointment. "Fifty reasons can be urged," he wrote, "against your appointment, independently of the chief one on your part. It would be a pretty thing to see a person of your age and delicate health learning to ride, and then travelling out to visit the Indians, subject to some of those fine north westers which you experienced last winter. I expect you would not return as far homeward as the bishop did."[37]

On 14 January, Bishop John England of Charleston, wrote from Rome to Rosati about the tangled situation regarding Cincinnati. "The Jesuits are working hard to prevent Kenney being named to its charge. The Dominicans are working equally hard to have it made an appanage of their order and are proposing Mr Miles ..." "Purcell of Emmitsburgh was mentioned also ... and ... I was thinking of Power of New York. But as yet it is impossible for anyone to see his way through the case."[38]

Eventually, the matter was decided at a meeting of the Congregation on 25 February 1833. It was a tight run, as Roothaan explained to Kenney in a congratulatory letter written three days later.

> The danger was undoubtedly very great and imminent. And although when I first heard what was afoot, in the month of November, I did not omit to carry out my duty in the matter, yet in these latter days there was increased need of negotiation. The Holy Father left me little hope. But in the end, in the Congregation meeting on 25th of this month, the reasons which I had earlier given carried the day: Your Reverence's health, and Ireland's need of you, for it never ceases to call you back. Thanks be to Him who snatched us from this situation and in whom we hope to safeguard us again.

He added later that "very probably health reasons alone would not have sufficed to avoid the episcopate, without the pressure from Ireland".[39] The appointment to Cincinnati went to Fr John B. Purcell, and Detroit to Fr Reese.

Joseph Rosati, knowing that the General and Kenney would have opposed his hopes, had bypassed them both and, early in December, 1832, had written directly to the pope in support of Bishop Fenwick's petition. Now, on the failure of his efforts, he made mention of his hopes in the course of a reply to Kenney; who had earlier written to thank him for his efforts with respect to the tuition fees.

"I congratulate you," he wrote, "for having escaped what I know you have always much dreaded." He hoped that providence would continue to protect the diocese of Cincinnati under "the young, zealous, pious and enlightened prelate" to whom it has been entrusted. He had received news of the erection of the new province of Maryland with great pleasure and he desired and confidently expected that many others would "flourish in these our western wilds". And he continued:

> The thought that a bishop belonging to the Society, of the merit and worth of a *certain dear friend* of mine, would have contributed to introduce it in Ohio, and put it in possession of a college, which was languishing, notwithstanding its spacious and beautiful buildings, and which could not fail to prosper in the hands of the Society, was one of the motives that had induced me to enter into the wishes of the venerable bishop of Cincinnati. But providence can do everything otherwise than we think.[40]

Resisting the demand for other Jesuit bishops

While Kenney's own personal anxiety had been removed, he still had, as Visitor, grounds for concern. Fr Dubuisson had received hints that he would be made bishop of San Domingo, Fr Verhaegen was rumoured to become coadjutor to Bishop Rosati, and Fr Van de Velde to Bishop de Neckere of New Orleans. There seemed to be almost a plan, he informed McSherry, "of converting Jesuits into bishops" which, though it might "appear to the bishops concerned to be required for a particular good" was likely to "be productive of much general evil", for it would stir up jealousy amongst the secular clergy against the Society. "The strong feelings which we saw among the few Kentuckians whom we met" with regard to the French fathers, would be immensely magnified if they felt that Jesuits could easily be made bishops.[41]

In the event, none of the three rumoured appointments materialised; but there was another development with regard to Dubuisson which gave rise to much upset. It turned out that Archbishop Whitfield had been playing a deep game of his own with regard to Cincinnati. Despite his talk of appointing an American-born prelate, he really had the French-born Dubuisson in mind for the bishopric, and seemed to think that the Jesuit opposition to episcopal appointments could be easily overcome.

He told Rosati, on 19 March 1833, that he had complied with Kenney's desire that he be excused for reasons of health,[42] but he did not mention that he had recommended Dubuisson as his first choice, and John McElroy, even though he was Irish, as his second choice.[43] The General termed this *novi genereris persecutio* (a new form of persecution); and Kenney, in the light of his personal experience of Dr Whitfield, was moved to an uncharacteristically acerbic attack. "Archbishop Whitfield", he confided to McSherry, seemed to set little value on the "principles of government" of the Society. He had told him some time ago, "with a sarcastic smile", that "he thought it was very easy for Jesuits to get quit of the vows that forbids the professed to accept ... ecclesiastical dignities". "I am happy that his efforts have failed," Kenney went on, as "it may convince him that Jesuits cannot be so easily withdrawn from the jurisdiction of their chief ... ". And it would also serve "to check, or prevent, that rising ambition amongst us, of which there has been already more than one instance".

He was also happy for Dubuisson's sake that the General was successful in opposing his election, because "all his merit would never counterbalance the want of cordial concurrence and support on the part of the clergy, which, inevitably, would be the torment of his life and the scandal of the flock".[44]

Subsequently, in an effort to alert the rather ingenuous Dubuisson, he informed him of the planning of the archbishop and his council with regard to the Cincinnati bestowal of honours which, he observed, could only be accepted at the risk of "being forced out of the path of humility and obedience".[45]

Much as Kenney valued "the path of humility and obedience", however, he had small capacity for humiliations and, as has been seen on a number of occasions, was very sensitive to any suggestion of slight or manipulation by a significant other person. Accordingly the sense of being used and misled by the archbishop and the Revd Deloul, the chief of his council, bit deep; and in one of his final letters to the new provincial, McSherry, written as he journeyed homeward in August 1833, he told of being deliberately misled by Deluol with reference to the character of a candidate for the Society; and encouraged McSherry to "make the General acquainted ... with the whole character and manner of proceeding generally adopted by the archbishop and his council."[46]

But the narrative has run ahead of itself. Kenney had been several weeks at Bohemia when, early in December 1832, he heard of his name being put forward for Cincinnati. He continued to govern the mission from there for some time, while also fulfilling the role of pastor for the small congregation.

CONTINUING TO PRESIDE FROM BOHEMIA

His journal records religious services during his weeks there, and visits to neighbouring places, and, naturally, almost every meeting with people from Ireland. These last included "wealthy peddlers called Sheridan and Brady, a store keeper called Doran, and, at the city of Wilmington, the Revd Mr Cavanagh, who had just returned from Ireland accompanied by "a convoy of men, women and children, amounting to 30". He stayed for a while at Wilmington, which had a population of 6,626, and noted that Cavanagh's church had a congregation of about 300 adults, mostly Irish. Among the other places visited from Bohemia were Philadelphia, and neighbouring towns such as Warwick, and Newcastle, and the Society's farm of St Joseph, south of Bohemia, on the eastern shore.[47]

Turbulent scholars and unsupported masters

During this period, he conducted the affairs of the mission mainly by correspondence. On 2 November he responded to a report from Mulledy regarding the conduct of some novices who were due to take their vows, and also to his wish to have one of his teachers, Fr Varin, removed from the college because of his failure to control his French class. Kenney took a very serious view of this last. Indiscipline was a problem in many schools in the United States, especially when many of the scholars, as at Georgetown, were from the southern slave states, accustomed to be served and to dominate, and ill at ease with discipline and obedience. Varin's class made life intolerable for him.

Holding firm convictions on the obligations of a headmaster or college president, Kenney considered that the conduct of the scholars had not been addressed in a sufficiently serious manner. "It does not appear to me creditable to the administration of the house," he observed, "that the pupils should be suffered to play the fool with any professor whom the authority of the house had placed in the master's chair, merely on account of simplicity of manner that did not affect either his knowledge or mode of teaching. It did appear to me," he counselled Mulledy, "that if you had appeared amongst them and insisted on their keeping silence and order, you would have been obeyed; and the effect of his simple ways would have been daily diminished ... Every master put in the schools should be supported by the whole authority of the house." He did not even venture to say that Mr Varin's removal would not have been necessary in the sequel, but support for him would have subdued the ill behaviour of the scholars, "and not have left it in their power to say that they caused a change of masters by playing the fool with the one that you had given them".[48]

Architectural considerations

John McElroy, his most frequent correspondent, kept him busy with ideas and proposals for his projected church at Frederick. Responding on 12 November, Kenney reminded him to make sure that the man he had in mind for the design was a good architect, a man of integrity and standing, and warned that while he might plan, discuss, and arrange for fund raising, he should make no contract, or final commitments, for the present. He then went on to give his own architectural preferences. He thought a Grecian church preferable to a

Gothic one. In the United States, in any event, there did not appear to be "a sufficiency of either artists or money to build a large church that would be a good specimen of Gothic architecture". On the other hand, "it would be quite easy to build a perfect church of the Ionic order".[49] Fr Dzierozynski had mentioned to him that the plan of St Francis Xavier's church in Dublin would be a good one for Frederick. He was not sure that in all points it was the answer, but it certainly was the first church in Dublin built "with due attention to style and proportion in any of the Grecian orders".[50]

Reminders for Mulledy and Ryder

On 15 November he wrote to Mulledy again. And, as so often, his letter contained a mild rebuke for the impetuous rector; this time with reference to the manner in which he had accepted five Belgians for the noviceship and sent them on to White Marsh without consulting the novice master, Fr Grivel. The latter, considering Mulledy his superior, restrained his anger, but complained to Kenney. Ironically, Mulledy had earlier asked the latter to return to Georgetown to interview the five young men to assess their suitability for the Society. "You were kind enough to suggest," Kenney wrote, "that I should return quickly to examine, admit etc. Now what a fool you would have made of me, if I had gone! The very time that I was reading your letter, they were on their way to White Marsh, or had already thrown Fr Grivel into the utmost consternation and disorder!"

He concluded with quiet words of practical wisdom which, alas, did not have a long-term effect. "It is good to profit by experience," he wrote. "We must not leave it in the power of any one to say that superiors unduly interfere in subordinate offices, or local superiors with the provincial authority. If we wish to enjoy peace and prosperity, we must remember that '*pax est tranquillitas ordinis*' [peace is the tranquillity of order]. If impetuosity in either language, or action, be indulged, we shall soon exceed the limits that our holy rules have set for both speech and conduct. These remarks," he added, "are made with great regard for you."[51]

He was far from finished, however, with the case of the five young Belgians. He had been appalled to learn from Grivel of a neglect of hospitality towards them during their stay at Georgetown. The person responsible for hospitality was the minister, Fr Ryder. Writing to him on 16 November, Kenney stated that he had learned from Grivel that they were five days at the college and had had no change of clothes. They came to White Marsh, Grivel stated, "with shirts on their backs, since a fortnight; no stockings, and no office books; and nobody in the college offered them a change or other accommodation". Was all this true? Kenney asked. Ryder knew that the young men's trunks were left behind "and, consequently, that coming from the sea they needed changes etc.". He was not to write to Grivel, but was to write speedily to him.[52]

After hearing from Ryder on 26 November, he replied that while the entire blame for the neglect in charity could not be laid at his door, yet "the minister's duty was not fully fulfilled on that occasion. He should have inquired into their wants immediately on their arrival and have seen that they were soon supplied", for nobody could "travel in boat or coach from New York to Georgetown without requiring an immediate change". He went on to sketch what charity and hospitality required of a minister with regard to someone coming to stay at the house. When he learnt from the rector that anyone was to remain in the house, even as a guest, "the minister in half an hour should see him brought to his room, or to some other room *ad interim*, there have him supplied with everything necessary, told when the next meal would be, and sent to bed if he wanted sleep; and then a person should be ordered to call or to guide him to the refectory and other necessary places, without giving the stranger the trouble of asking for anything." Such were "the prompt and delicate attentions" that should be paid in our houses to our own guests.[53] In a lighter vein, he enclosed a letter to Dzierozynski which asked, on behalf of Br Heard, for a good alarm clock which "strikes faithfully, loudly and constantly", so as to call him in the morning.[54]

Pastoral anxiety

During November 1832, Charles Carroll died. He was "in his tomb" before Kenney heard. He determined to spend a couple of days at Baltimore to visit "Mrs Caton and family on their ... affliction".[55] Having done so, he returned to Bohemia on 6 December to commence his annual retreat.

After the retreat, he stayed on for a week; during which he instructed a 29-year-old Catholic man, who had never been to confession and communion, and also "Billy, the black boy". On the day appointed to receive the sacraments, the man did not turn up. Kenney blamed himself for not commencing the instruction earlier out of fear of pushing himself forward too soon. Now he was due to leave, and was concerned that the man would not go to an American priest since so many of them had "a cool and reserved character which did not attract". Then, as he was about to set out, the man turned up, explained the doubts and scruples which had held him back, and received absolution and communion. A relieved Kenney concluded his account with much feeling: "He promised to write to me occasionally. The next morning I said mass for him and left Bohemia, very probably never again to see him or it ... He is in God's hands, and my only duty in his regard, as well as my wish and desire, is to pray for him all my life, which I mean to do, and hope that God will accept this intention, once for always." As for his own defects in not approaching him and "Billy, the black boy", earlier, he prayed for forgiveness so far as God might see him defective.[56]

GEORGETOWN AGAIN: NEWS FROM MC SHERRY

He was back at Georgetown for his third consecutive Christmas in America. Within a day or two he was immersed once more in consultation and correspondence. On 28 December there was a meeting of the consultors of the mission, at which an offer from Bishop Kenrick to purchase St Joseph's church, Philadelphia, was refused; as also "De Theux's proposal to choose by ballot those who were to go to Missouri".[57]

Very conscious of the importance of letters to people away from home, he wrote regularly to McSherry, giving him news of the mission. And during December he had been at pains to urge him to send information about "the Cincinnati business", and to insist on his unsuitability for episcopal office.

As he worried about what the new year might bring in this regard, McSherry was sitting down in Rome, on 29 December, to inform him of Mr Jeanjean's arrival and of Cardinal Pedicini's support for the wish of the late Bishop Fenwick. The news was not encouraging also regarding their proposals for the procurators' congregation and the General. "I am afraid," he wrote, "I will not be able to give you any news concerning the slaves etc. before Easter ... The last time I saw the General, he said he was so busy that he could not speak of American matters before next month. I had just then in my hands the motives why we should endeavour to change our system, and do away with the slaves. He appeared very willing to listen to them, but at some other time." For the rest, after some information regarding individuals, McSherry remarked that there was no news worth communicating. There were many reports, but these generally proved false. He assured him, however, that he had fulfilled his request to visit the Irish College and pay his compliments to the recently appointed rector. He completed his letter with the remark: "Dr Cullen also wished to be remembered to you." Thus, though he was not to know it, Kenney, in his desire to be friendly and establish contacts, had made amicable acquaintance with yet another archbishop of Dublin!

During this period, public attention in the United States was focused on a presidential election. Kenney, to judge from a letter to Fr Haly on 18 January 1833, was himself very interested in the contest, the techniques used to get votes, and the emerging political situation.

American politics: presidential election

"Here we have had a mighty contest for the office of President of the US," he remarked. Haly would be amused to witness "the arts employed to work on the feelings and prejudices of the electors". The Irish were mostly all favourable to General Jackson, who was seeking re-election, because he had the name of being the chief of the democratic party and because he really did beat the English at New Orleans! "To gain them they were made to believe that all the friends to the National Bank, to which Jackson is opposed, were

Orangemen, and that General Jackson was a great favourite with Bishop Conwell and Pius the 8th!"

Then he went on with news of "a more alarming contest" which had arisen. "The eastern states, with their white and dense population", were the manufacturers of the country. "The southern states, with large territories and a thin and black population", were "cultivators of the soil". The former, with a majority in Congress, "obtained a tariff of duties to keep British goods out of the market". This was warmly opposed by the others, and especially by South Carolina, which had now refused to pay the duties or to suffer them to be paid, and, in a full convention, had declared that if the US used "force to compel her, she, that very moment, ceases to be a member of the Union". The president had issued a proclamation declaring this doctrine to be unconstitutional, and had required Congress "to enable him to shut up the ports in any state".[59]

A further comment on the excitement caused by South Carolina was provided by an Irish-born Jesuit at Georgetown, William Grace, who lived in the room next door to Kenney. Writing to Edmund Ignatius Rice, who came from the same part of Ireland and was a friend of his, as well as of Kenney, he observed on 24 February 1833, that in response to "the wild belief" of the people of South Carolina "that they could nullify the laws of the central government, troops were dispatched by the president to see that order should be observed there, and now it is hoped that differences will be amicably adjusted ..."[60]

This observation constituted the final reference to American public affairs in papers relating to Kenney. Grace's letter, however, had a further, more immediate interest by reason of its comments on Kenney himself; placing him, indeed, albeit in rhapsodic language, on the heights of Georgetown when they still opened on a majestic, unrestricted panorama.

A room with a view

Kenney wished him to say, Grace continued, that he would write a long letter (to Rice) very soon. He then added regarding him that his health was "very good", the climate agreed with him, and above all he had a splendid view from his room. "From the windows he can every moment behold ... the clear Potomac rolling its limpid waters just beneath ... the college buildings. Here it is beautiful and wide, running in a south-easterly direction from the distance of four or five miles, and then it turns its course due south by the city of Alexandria, whose once commercial warves it washes ..." There was also to be seen from the college, Grace added, "the highly improved lands and mansion of Arlington, the property and residence of George W.P. Custis, one of the most ardent friends to the emigrants from the Emerald Isle that America ever gave birth to".

Then, after a glowing account of the college's "high repute", he proceeded in the same fluent, grandiloquent vein to speak of Kenney himself. With all the claims upon him, Rice should not expect to see him soon back in Ireland. "Besides," he observed:

> We want him here, his presence is sufficient to give tone to any community; his eloquence, his piety, his easy softness of manners have instantly won the hearts of those who heard him or had the opportunity of conversing with him.

It was "the source of something like national pride and complacency" to them, he added, "that those clergymen of the Catholic church" who were designated "as really eminent" were "true-born sons of Erin"; so that it was not only Father Kenney, but many others who were looked upon as great men.[61]

Despite the writer's evident bias in his favour, Kenney undoubtedly experienced, as indicated earlier, much recognition and affirmation, and blossomed and relaxed in the friendly ambience. At home, by contrast, he was more on his guard, especially, as has been seen, among his fellow religious. Soon, in Philadelphia, he was to experience a degree of warmth of acceptance, joined to pastoral opportunity, such as to make him wish to live out his days in that city.

WELCOME IN PHILADELPHIA

As the new year commenced, most of his extant letters show him largely taken up with immediate, often mundane, mission affairs – the obtaining of a government subvention for McElroy's school and the implications of being subject to government inspection; news of St Louis College being raised to university status;[62] discontent among the scholars at Georgetown, some of whom had run away; Mulledy's poor health and the fact that he was taking no exercise and "was daily growing larger";[63] and his own plans of moving to Philadelphia.

Sending news to McSherry on 20 February 1833, he remarked that he had written to Bishop Kenrick to say that he hoped to occupy the house at St Joseph's, Philadelphia, in Easter week. Messrs Mulledy and Dzierozynski had stated that he must go there as there was no one else who could be moved. "I must have another," Kenney added, "but who he will be I know not yet."[64]

Just before setting out, however, he received a letter from the General, dated 20 January, stating that McSherry was to "pronounce solemnly the four vows of profession" on 2 February, and would be the provincial of the new American province. Kenney, in his office of Visitor, was to give him the letter of appointment. It was left to his prudence how to make use of this communication.[65] A few days later, he moved to the church and residence, situated between Walnut Street and Willings Alley, in Philadelphia.

From there, he wrote happily to McElroy on 14 April 1833: "the bishops have been very kind indeed, and the clergy not less so. It is creditable both to the pastors and flock of St Joseph that they part with mutual regret." And he added that the pastors, Frs Donahue and Whelan, had given up their rooms to him, the former, indeed, leaving him his furniture till Kenney had time to provide for himself.

The sense of positive welcome at St Joseph's was confirmed two days later, when Bishop Kenrick invited him "to accept the office of vicar-general, if consistent with the rules of the Society. Otherwise, the bishop" wished him "at least to exercise the powers usually granted to vicars general in regard to the members of the Society".[66]

Consolation and disappointment

Very conscious of being the first representative of the restored Society in Philadelphia, and of the importance of being located in the Union's most historic city, he set himself to provide as good a service as possible for the people attending the church. He called Dubuisson to assist him. The latter came readily, though not without assuring the General – "My Georgetown flock are in a kind of uproar at my departure."[67]

Basking before long in the warm reception of the mainly Irish congregation, as well as of the bishop and clergy, Kenney began to hope that he might be allowed to spend his life there. Earlier he had spoken of the physical demands of the mission being too much for someone of his years and poor health, but here, at St Joseph's, in a city parish, he felt he could do rewarding work without undue physical strain. Such hopes were soon shattered, however, by an otherwise consoling communication from the General. Written on 28 February, it reached him on 26 April. It stated that Fr McSherry was already on his way home, and that he brought with him a decree elevating Maryland to the status of a province, and letters patent appointing him provincial. With this official backing, Fr McSherry would be firmly established and in a position to secure the effects of the Visitation. Consequently, in the autumn Kenney could at last return to Ireland where, Roothaan assured him, he "had been so very ardently longed for". The General continued:

> You have brought about much good in your American Visitation. You fulfilled your duty and mission thoroughly, and will be able to say of your labours, because of your merits, the words of Nehemene: "Remember me, dear God, for this ... Remember me favourably, my God." And so, I pray with all my heart, that the Lord reward you. I am able to give thanks and do so.[68]

Almost as if in response to the unwelcome news of his departure, Kenney sought to place his newly favoured location on a secure footing for the future. In an effort to elicit as much information as he could about the history of the premises and land between Walnut Street and Willings Alley, he requested Dzierozynski to search for all the deeds and documents relating to the area with a view to building on the site, expanding the church, and possibly opening a school nearby.[69] Then, leaving Dubuisson to hold the fort, he set out to fulfil some commitments in neighbouring areas.

He journeyed first to Pottsville, where he had a commitment to preach. A coal-mining town, north west of Philadelphia, and some 35 miles from Reading, it had grown in eight years from one house to 3,000 inhabitants, many of them with Irish names. It now had four houses of worship. He preached in a church which held a congregation of 400 people, and was served by a Cork priest, Fr McCarthy, from the mission at Goshenhoppen.

After a few days, he travelled with him to make his final visit to Goshenhoppen.[70] He rejoiced to see it cleared of debt, with a well run farm, and able to contribute more than one hundred dollars a year to the general treasury. The church was due to be enlarged the next year to cater for the "notable increase in the number of the faithful".[71]

Return of McSherry – Pastoral possibilities in Philadelphia

On 29 May, shortly after his return to St Joseph's, he learned that McSherry had arrived at New York; and immediately wrote to him "with joy and gratitude to God for his safe arrival".[72] Receiving a letter from him the following day, he replied to inform him of the position regarding the news of his elevation and the new status of the mission. "I think it well to apprize you," he wrote, "that though the General in his letter of January let me know his intentions in your regard, I have not communicated to anyone, as yet, the fact of your profession on 2 February." Similarly, he had been silent about his own return to Ireland. "This precaution", he continued, "I thought necessary *here*, where so sudden a change might cause talk; but good Bishop England wrote to Mr Purcell that the General in treating with the pope insisted on the necessity of sending me back to Ireland; and Mr Purcell, without any attention to my wishes, published it to the clergy of this city in a late visit made when I was at Goshenhoppen."

He added that they were not yet comfortably situated at St Joseph's. "The house was in such a state, that I have been obliged to get it refitted from top to bottom." He asked him to send particulars of his arrival, so that he might have him met. "We are near Chestnut Street warf," he concluded, "and I believe that it is there the NY boats stop."[73] On 1 June, about 4. o'clock, McSherry, and three companions, arrived at St Joseph's.[74] Two days later, Bishops Kenrick and Conwell, a Fr Kelly, "and the old bishop's nephew", dined with them. In succeeding days they dined at the residences of the local clergy, and on 7 June, McSherry and companions sailed for Baltimore en route to Georgetown.[75]

Kenney stayed on at St Joseph's. He appears, indeed, to have been kept quite busy with pastoral work throughout June; and one long entry in his journal for 14 June was illustrative of some of the problems facing clergy in the expanding urban centres of the United States.

"This day ... Fitzpatrick and Ellen Fitzpatrick were married by Fr Dubuisson in my room. They came several nights ago and wished to get married immediately, which is the general way that the Irish do here. They sometimes come after 9.00 at night and want to get married without any delay. With this pair I succeeded in deferring it for a few days. They both, in the meantime, came to their confessions and received [communion] this morning, and afterwards were made happy. They seemed to be good people and very simple, though with such curious notions about entering into the married state without any preparation. The clergy are very easy in admitting them to this venerable sacrament, even in this disorderly way, lest the parties, not having due respect and just notions, should go to the secular magistrates or to a Protestant parson. With all this danger, which most certainly does exist, it seems to me that additional efforts would put a stop to this horrid abuse, or at least greatly lessen its frequency."

It had been agreed with McSherry not to announce immediately the province status or the name of the new provincial, but to prepare for it over a number of weeks. Kenney, meantime, writing back to Ireland, and to the General, continued to express his fondness for the church and work at Philadelphia, and was at pains also to emphasise its strategic importance for the future apostolate of the Society.

In a letter to Esmonde at Clongowes, he first thanked him for sending the ground plan of St Francis Xavier church, and views of its interior, which he had forwarded to Fr McElroy, who was much taken by them. Then he spoke of "our ancient church of St Joseph". The residence of the Society in Philadelphia dated as far back, at least, as 1773; and "the recovery of this mission was most earnestly desired on account of the greater facility of doing good in a great city, but also on account of the advantage to be derived to the whole province from a residence midway between N. York and Baltimore". And having recounted the steps which led to the repossession of the property he related the many instances of the bishop's kindness.[76]

A similar enthusiasm was reflected a few days later in his letter to Fr Roothaan. Again, he commenced with words of thanks. This time for being relieved from his onerous position, and for the General's kind remarks written in his own hand. And he went on to state that he knew he could give no greater thanks to God and his Paternity "than to leave himself completely at his disposal to do with him what he wished like a stick in an old man's hands". He hoped to leave from the port of New York at the beginning of

August. Then, after some information about other parts of the mission, he wrote at length about negotiations and developments regarding St Joseph's, Philadelphia, which led him on to point out that although hitherto there had been no Jesuits in the great cities of the country, "now a door is opened to us in this very beautiful city with a population of more than 100,000 inhabitants", and noted for its wealth of literature and culture "so that among Americans it is frequently spoken of as the Athens of America". There were 25,000 Catholics. These were French, German, but mostly Irish in origin. "It was clear," he added, "that this new acquisition would be of considerable moment in giving greater glory to God."[77]

A sense of ease and relaxation is perceptible in his letters during this month. Regarding a young Irish youth he had admitted into the noviceship, he informed the Virginian Mulledy, that his name was James Kelly, and he was "from the Yankee part of Ireland", but had "no roguery in him like McElroy or Hughes"![78] And reflecting his benign spirituality, as well as his relaxed, almost playful, manner, was a letter to George Fenwick, the following day, which told him that the General had decreed that his profession of four vows would take place on 25 August 1834, and that he wished him to spend the intervening time "in earnest efforts to attain the perfection of our holy institute, and in the daily correction of those defects, which, as the lot of our mortality, are almost inseparable from our conversations, opinions, and dispositions". As he had so much time allowed him, he, Kenney, would leave it to Fr McSherry to draw to his attention those faults "more particularly observable" in him. "Let us give God thanks," he added, "that we are not worse; and beg his pardon for being so bad as we are."[79]

By the end of June it was generally known that McSherry was to be provincial, and that the Visitor was returning home. The occasion of the feast of Sts Peter and Paul, on 29 June, was used as an opportunity of honouring Peter Kenney, and treating it as his feast day. The only extant reminder of the celebrations, is a less than memorable poetic effusion by a Belgian scholastic.

At length, on the evening of 8 July, the decree elevating the mission to a province was publicly proclaimed at Georgetown College, and Fr William McSherry named the first provincial.

PROCLAIMING THE PROVINCE: 8 JULY 1833

Kenney's own account of this historic occasion was brief. A fuller reconstruction of events may be had by conflating contemporary reports given in two separate diaries of the College.

> The community were ordered to assemble at 6.00 p.m. ... Accordingly, at 6.00 p.m., Fr Kenney delivered an exhortation replete with eloquence and holy fervour, which he said would be his last. He then announced

to all that this mission is constituted a province by decree of the Revd
Fr General Roothaan, with all the rights of other provinces of the
Society. He urged us to enter with confidence upon our new life and
amid all our difficulties to press onward with good heart. Two hundred
years, he said, had already passed since our fathers first founded the
mission, and now at last was witnessed the crowning of their labours ...
In conclusion, he got one of the fathers to read the decree of Very Revd
Fr General Roothaan creating the American Mission a Province, with
the title of Province of Maryland, its provincial Revd Fr William
McSherry; next were read the patents of the new province (which was
done all standing); finally, Fr Kenney delivered them into the hands of
the new Provincial with a profound and respectful bow. Then the usual
prayer was recited at the end of the instruction, and Fr Kenney having
risen bowed to Fr Provincial to go first.[80]

The total membership of the new province in that year was 90: 38 priests,
20 scholastics, 32 brothers.[81] Fr Grivel, writing the following day to Fr
Nicholas Sewall in England, was careful to note that it was "the mission of the
Eastern US" that was erected into the Province of Maryland; and he added
the information that the spread of Catholic population among the main cities
of the east was: 19,000 Baltimore, 25,000 Philadelphia, 35,000 New York, and
11,000 Boston.[82]

Kenney, himself, sent a thoughtful letter to the elderly Fr Francis Neale
prior to the ceremony on 8 July. "To you surely, before any of the other
members of the new Province of Maryland, is due the intimation that at 6
o'clock this evening Fr McSherry becomes its first provincial." He went on to
express the hope that he would "yet live many years to witness in the continued prosperity of this portion of the Society, now become a constitutional
body, the happy fruits of a mission commenced two hundred years ago, and of
that zealous solicitude with which" he "contributed to its revival and to the
preservation of its property". And he concluded with the request: "May I beg
a share in your prayers and sacrifices, whilst I again plough the ocean on my
way to Ireland, which I shall do with God's help in the month of August."[83]

Departure and tributes

Not prone to linger once his task was done, he left Georgetown for good on
11 July. The diary of the college paid him a remarkable tribute. It stated:
"This morning, 11 July, 1833, we all embraced for the last time our beloved
and honoured Fr Kenney. He himself was very much moved at his leavetak-
ing. Never has a man lived among us whom all without exception so loved and
reverenced."[84]

The memory and respect lived on. Seventy-five years later a Jesuit historian of the Maryland province was moved to write eulogistically of his first and second visitations:

> Rarely indeed are such talents as were his united in one person … vision, courage, confidence in God, utter abandonment to the lead of obedience, these made Peter Kenney a man almost without compare in this country. Apparently he could not be frightened … It was a gigantic undertaking, and only a giant of God with the spirit of a child could bring it to the crown of success.[85]

A LEISURELY FAREWELL AND AN UNEXPECTED GUARDIANSHIP

He planned an unhurried progress towards New York. Next day he wrote from Baltimore to McSherry, saying that he could not pass through there without taking leave of Mrs Caton and family, and many other friends. He had called on the archbishop and informed him "that we were now a province of the Society with all the privileges annexed to that station". On hearing this, Kenney observed, "he seemed as much under the influence of apprehension as if I had said that you had been made *legatus a latere* in his diocese!" The archbishop, however, he had to acknowledge, "was more than usually kind" to him: taking him to the Catons in his carriage, and having him return to dine with him. Kenney concluded with the promise – "You shall have many a line from me before I sail."[86]

He went directly from Baltimore to his favourite Bohemia, bringing with him the archbishop's letter announcing the jubilee which he himself had preached in Dublin in 1826.[87] On 16 July, he took the steamer from Newcastle to Philadelphia, a distance of 32 miles, where he arrived at 3.00p.m.[88] Shortly afterwards, he sent a letter to McSherry, which informed him that he had "left good brothers Heard and McGir at 6.00 this morning in good health". He had sufficient travel money, he continued, but as McSherry was "kind enough to speak of a map of America", he would "purchase the best" and present it to the Irish vice-provincial as a present from McSherry. "Such acts of courtesy always promote charity, and indicate that we take great interest in each other." Finally, in his gentle, indirect way, he conveyed a warning: "You will not be displeased with me, when I add that the General's letters are never to be opened by any other than the persons to whom they are directed, so long as that person is within reach."[89]

On 19 July he wrote to his friend, John McElroy, of developments since he was last in touch with him. It was an informative letter. After speaking of the promulgation of the decree erecting the new province of Maryland, he reminded him that "the body is now formed. Long may it prosper. You are now a member, not of a mission but of a constitutional portion of the Society having all the privileges and rights usually granted to the transmarine provinces." He then continued on a more personal note: "It is no small consolation to me to leave it so formed, and with so great a prospect of doing much good … The General orders me to be in Ireland this autumn: and I am now on my way. I wait here Mr Dubuisson's return, and set off for N. York on the 25th, perhaps the 24th inst. I should wish to sail on the 1st August, but the great probability is that I shall not go until the 2nd from N. York to Liverpool."

The remainder of the letter dealt with an unusual request. McElroy had written to him of a Mrs Lowe wishing to send her son to school at Clongowes, and asking if the boy could travel with him. Kenney pointed out that it would cost her much to part with the boy, and if he did not like Clongowes what was to be done? If she still persevered in her intention, however, he would "with great pleasure take charge of him". If all was in order legally, he would write to McElroy from New York to say at what day the boy "ought to be there to join me, when I go aboard".[90] Unwittingly, his decision involved him for a time in the early development of a prominent American public figure. The thirteen-year-old boy in question, who was described as bright, energetic, and straight-forward,[91] was Enoch Louis Lowe. Following education at Clongowes and Stonyhurst, he was to study law under a former scholar of Georgetown, Edward Lynch,[92] and subsequently to be elected to the Maryland legislature and to become governor of Maryland before the age of thirty.[93]

On 9 August 1833, Mrs Lowe granted to the Revd Peter Kenney "the care, control, custody and guardianship" of Enoch for a period of three years, or until she revoked the said guardianship.[94] He seems to have fulfilled his role with sensitivity and care, but not without difficulty. The boy proved popular during his years at Clongowes, 1833–6, but he was fitful in his approach to study, and latterly to discipline so that it was only by the intervention of his guardian that he was saved from expulsion![95]

But to return to the departure from America.

Final adieu and advice

Kenney left St Joseph's, Philadelphia, on 26 July. Writing to the General the previous day, Dubuisson exclaimed: "Tomorrow good Fr Kenney leaves us to go to New York. What a loss for us. I am heart-broken. I have to struggle not to give way to melancholy."[96]

On arrival at New York, Kenney sent a letter to McSherry to congratulate him and Mulledy "on the receipt (from Rome) of the diploma for conferring degrees in theology"; and continued, in the hortatory, but concerned tones of one just out of office, to urge that the college never be reproached "with a facility of granting theological degrees to persons who are not worthy of the distinction". There had already been grounds for reproof at "the ease with which literary degrees" were bestowed. And though something might at present be "conceded to the usages of the country", the honour of the Society was not promoted by such practices. "The Jesuits would be justly censured if they lent their aid to a superficial system of education that will impart little of merit, and too much of the pride of knowledge. Georgetown," he added, "cannot too carefully guard its honour against any approach to such unworthy condescension." In conclusion, he expressed his appreciation of the picture of the college, which McSherry had sent him through the Kennedys, although, he added, – "it and you all are too deeply impressed in my heart ever to render such a reminder necessary."[97]

How deep was the impression made by America appeared in the most revealing of all his letters, written on 27 July to his old friend and benefactor, Matilda Denis, who, it would appear, had been urging him to return soon to Ireland.

In mourning at leaving America

"A few days since," he began, "I wrote to Mr St Leger, to whom the news was first due, that I have received my marching orders, which desire that I should be in Ireland in the autumn of this year."

On the 11th of this month, he continued, "I began this painful journey and went through a scene which I should not like to encounter again." It was not that he was "preferring new friends to old ones". She knew how much he loved "all those brethren and good friends" with whom he had been "connected by so many ties"; and neither was he insensible to the connection which he had with those institutions from which he hoped he would "draw some advantage in the great accounting day", nor could he ever forget "the exquisite consolation" which he felt among "those good people of Dublin" to whom the exercise of his ministry "was useful and acceptable". Yet, "with all this before me, I leave these States with great regret; and if the decision depended on me, I should never decide to leave them."

Then, he added didactically, even affectedly: "You will cry now, what a shame! But you, my dear Miss Denis, only see one side of the picture. You see Dublin, and know something of Ireland. I know Dublin, Ireland and America almost from east to west! How think you could any missionary priest determine to leave a country where there are hundreds of Catholics who are without mass, three, four, six months in the year? Where there are thousands who do not hear it more than once or twice in a month? Who could go from a place, where the weakest and oldest can render services, the more valuable because in many instances there is no one to do them better?"

She, and many others, he continued, put America in opposition to Ireland on this question. That was not fair. "The overwhelming Catholic population" in the United States was Irish; "and, in general, the emigrants are the most uninstructed of all the Irish whom I have known". He went on:

In the whole of St Joseph's congregation in Philadelphia, where I lived since the 12th April, there are not four families which are not Irish; and, of all other places in the US, I leave this congregation, and Philadelphia, with the greatest regret. The aid of the ministry is deeply, greatly wanted, received with the greatest ardour, blessed with the most consoling fruit, requited with the warmest gratitude.

He did not say "that in these last points" Philadelphia was superior to Dublin, "but the other points" were "decidedly in its favour".

And apart from all this, there were "our missions in the Missouri, in Maryland and Pensylvania" where, as he expressed it in the benign glow of departure, there were "so many dear Fathers and Brothers who, for three years, have never given me the least cause of trouble, and have afforded in innumerable kindnesses the sincere evidence of their respect and charity for me. When I think of the state in which I saw these missions fourteen years ago, and that in which they now are, is not the consolation, thence derived, a new cause of regret that I am no more to witness the progress of their prosperity? Those who were then sent to study at Rome, are now the able and indefatigable superiors and *operarii* [workers]; and the last consoling duty of my ministry was to induct Fr McSherry, one of their number, into the office of provincial and formulate the General's decree by which the new province of Maryland is erected, after all the vicissitudes of a mission that next year would have completed its 200th year!"

"What will you say to this letter? I know that I shall be happy in Ireland and delighted to see you all. 'Everything has its time' – I am not now rejoicing in the hope of seeing Ireland, I am mourning, as far as I dare, for leaving America!"

He concluded with more immediate news: "Hitherto, my health has been very good. Yesterday morning at five o'clock, and only then, I packed with my own hands three trunks and the old green bag, said mass at 9.00, was off at 10.00, and travelled 90 miles before 9.00 at night ... The night before, I stole an hour to pass it in the house of a humble Irishman, formerly a journeyman in employment, now likely to become in this happy city a richer man than his employer ...I sail on 16th August in the *Caledonia* ...for Liverpool. Send a letter before me to the post office there."[98]

Did he, one wonders, in the light of his sentiments of sadness, regret his practice of not seeking to influence the General's disposal of him; of leaving himself "like a stick in an old man's hands to be used as he wished"? Ignatius Loyola, after all, had allowed for, and facilitated the making of representation to superiors. Certainly, regret at the loss of a greatly desired opportunity was still agitating him more than six weeks after his arrival at Liverpool.

"Present my best and most affectionate regards to good Bishop Kenrick," he wrote Dubuisson on 28 October. "Assure him that I have never received a less gracious command of obedience than that which banished me from his beloved flock and his beautiful city of Philadelphia! Most willingly would I have spent the few years that remain of my life in cultivating, as far as my poor efforts could reach, that precious portion of our Lord's vineyard."[99]

The Catskills, the Hudson, and Westpoint

Meantime, his days in New York were filled visiting friends, many of them Irish, being entertained in different locations, and being shown places of interest in the vicinity. McSherry had advised him to visit the Niagara Falls, but he had to put this aside because of his distance from them and shortage of time. He contented himself with a visit to the Catskill Mountains, about 12 miles from New York, and to "the beautiful banks of the Hudson".[100] On 2nd August, indeed, he had a memorable journey up river.

In his journal, for that date, he gave a long account of his visit to Westpoint Military Academy, in the company of Monsignor Power, and Frs Kiely and Levins. He was "more than enamoured with the beauty of the Hudson scenery", particularly that which was "commanded by the hotel and barracks of Westpoint". They dined "most sumptuously on a fish dinner", and again he experienced an Irish dimension – "the waiters were all Irish". With his sense of now being a connoisseur of boats, he noted that those to Westpoint were 150 feet long, and the cabin of one of them, the *Albany*, "was nearly the full length of the boat and the most sumptuously ornamented that I have as yet seen – good and large paintings representing the battles of this young and admirable republic".

EMBARKATION, ARRIVAL, AND UNPLEASANT TASK

The time to leave the "young and admirable republic", however, came all too quickly. On 16 August, surrounded by friends, laden with presents, he met up with young Louis Lowe on the steamer which brought them out to their ship, an hour's sail from the wharf. Then, as he noted in his detailed "Memoranda of the Voyage, 1833":

> At 2.00 p.m. the pilot, all the visitors, took leave of us, got aboard the steamer, and soon were out of sight, leaving us to the providence that rules the ocean and traces to man his path in the sea.

In the early part of the voyage, both he and young Lowe felt sickish, then recovered, and had a fairly smooth passage. Kenney read through the second volume of the *Life of Christopher Columbus* by Washington Irvine, and was impressed by the "simple, elegant style" and the "solid and dispassionate manner" in which the material was treated. "Some years ago," he observed, "it would have been fatal to the success of the work to treat so favourably of so decided a Catholic as Columbus was, and to treat so impartially of persons and matters connected with the Catholic Church".[101]

The voyage, apart from some passenger complaints about the high spirits and sharp voice of thirteen-year-old Lowe,[102] was rather tedious. "The wind was generally very light and variable."[103] It was only when they arrived at Liverpool, on the afternoon of 10 September, that they realised how fortunate they had been. Storms of great intensity had raged nearer Britain and Western Europe on 29 and 30 August, while they were moving slowly some 1500 miles from their destination. The gales had "strewed the English, Irish, French and Flemish coasts with wrecked ships and lifeless bodies".[104] News of the scale of the disaster, and anxiety lest word of it might occasion fear and worry on the part of American friends, and especially Mrs Lowe, induced Kenney to write to McElroy at the first opportunity to assure him and Mrs Lowe of their safe arrival. As his young charge showed no interest in Liverpool, and was evidently bored and in low spirits, he put him on the boat for Dublin, having arranged for him to be met and brought to Clongowes. Before sailing, he reminded him to write immediately to his mother.[105]

He, himself, went on to Stonyhurst, where he was much pleased with all the improvements, and particularly with the house of studies for the scholastics, which they called "The Seminary". The old chapel was levelled to the ground while he was there. Indeed, it was reserved for him "to perform the last office of religion" in it. "On Monday, Sept. 23, I had scarcely finished mass," he wrote, "when I saw the altar at which I had celebrated borne away on the shoulders of the labourers, and the work of destruction soon levelled the whole fabric to the ground." The workmen laid "the timbers of the roof of the new church that very day". In all, "he spent 20 days in England". He subsequently informed the General that he delayed at Stonyhurst at the request of the provincial. On 29 September, he preached at vespers in the new church in Liverpool, opened that day by the bishop.[107] He arrived back in Dublin on 1 October to a warm welcome from fellow Jesuits.[108]

Eight days later he received a letter from Fr Roothaan, which was appreciative yet not entirely welcome. Hoping that he had arrived safe and sound in Ireland, the General went on: "I write this letter to congratulate you on your successful return, and to thank you again and again for your labours and all you endured in your American visitation to the glory of God and the great benefit of Ours." He had received his letter of 9 June, and was "very grateful" for his "detailed account" of the return of the Society to the Philadelphia station, and how he conducted that business.

He then continued: "No one doubts but that your return to Ireland has been very greatly desired by all, and will be most beneficial to their affairs. Your authority and acceptability is great because of your achievements. After a rest from your fatiguing journey, there will be a task for you that will be useful and much desired. If perchance you settle in Dublin, which I certainly would be glad of, I'd like to receive from you an exhaustive account of the condition of the Jesuits there, and of the college." He was concerned, he said, "at the perpetual silence of Fr Aylmer", and because he heard from other members that the life style there was "more elegant and luxurious than is customary among Jesuits even in Ireland". If this were the case, and there was a noticeable difference, especially in food, between that house and what was customary in other houses in the province, that, he observed, would be a matter of serious concern. Consequently, he requested him to help the vice-provincial by means of his advice and authority, both with regard to the Dublin house (if there is anything amiss there), and in all other matters pertaining to the best religious administration of this very dear vice-province." Would that its "spirit and members grew", he concluded, so that he could designate it a province. There had been progress, but there was still "something lacking".[109]

Rounding off the visitation – Problems at home

On 20 October he replied to Roothaan. His letter combined comment on Irish affairs as well as on those of Maryland and Missouri. It served to bring his American experience to a close, and to indicate his uneasiness at the role the General seemed to wish him to play in his native city.

He commenced with some local news. "It was a great consolation to me," he wrote, "to see our new St Francis Xavier church. It is indeed beautiful, and as regards style and ecclesiastical architecture ... there is none like it among Catholic churches in these islands." In terms of the large numbers of the faithful, it might "seem too small, yet in terms of our poverty it can seem too large". There was a "commodious", but unfinished, residence beside it. Both buildings were "a monument to the genius in these things of Fr Esmonde, and to Fr Aylmer's skill and perseverance in this very arduous ... work".

Moving on to American affairs, he reported that as regards "the new province, and the American provincial, the fathers and brothers were very joyful". He was given many indications of thanks, and signs of fraternal charity, up to the very day of his departure. And he added, in what was now a familiar expression of feeling:

> Certainly, nothing pertaining to that province and region can be unwelcome to me, nor was ever given me by holy obedience a mandate less welcome than that which ordered me to leave America and our Americans.

He cherished this affection, though he was aware that there were some who were not sorry to see him go; but he considered that he could ignore them because he knew that their feelings were opposed to his office rather than to him personally. They intensely disliked foreign interference in the conduct of their affairs, though this did not extend to the work of foreign missionaries. The latter could work happily, "invested by no prejudices, and not impeded by the cultivation of the party spirit of factiousness". The work was heavy , but the fruit abundant.

The reference to the absence of prejudice and party spirit was an implicit comment on some of his past experiences at home and on what he currently sensed among some of his brethren. He disliked the present role suggested by the General, and greatly feared the possibility of being put in charge once more. He endeavoured to steer his Paternity away from such a decision.

He had been ordered to stay on in Dublin by Fr St Leger, he continued. The latter, however, had not told him anything about the standard of living enjoyed by the Dublin Jesuits. It did not suit him to do so, since it was very well known what his (Kenney's) views were, and that they differed greatly "from the domestic discipline which Frs Aylmer, Ferley and O'Connor hold should be maintained in our houses". He did not know whether or not Frs St Leger and Esmonde had become of similar mind in recent years, if not, they appeared very indulgent on the matter. They had recently changed, he went on, a number of things in domestic discipline which had been fixed by him, in conjunction with his consultors. His opinion seemed to them "too out of date and too little conformed to the customs of the region". Consequently, they did not readily make known to him what was done in his absence. He had heard reports from lay people of individual Jesuits "living in too secular a manner", and of "splendid dinners" and "autumn vacations", but if these were true, it were best that emendation await the community's movement into the new house beside the church, and that then it be carried out by the present superiors who had "permitted certain practices". "What was needed was a change of practice, not of persons." Finally, he drew attention to the fact that there was a coolness towards him on the part of the vice-provincial, Fr Robert St Leger, based on an earlier misunderstanding.

He mentioned these factors, he concluded, lest his Paternity be under any illusion about his position and influence. He prayed, however, that he be not worried about the situation, nor hasten to amend matters. "May all proceed in peace. I do not refuse the cross, and your Reverence's mind is my mind."[110]

These final words, assuring the General of his always ready obedience and oneness of mind with him, were almost an invitation to a further period of authority over restless fellow-countrymen; who mainly valued him when he seemed to be about to be taken from them.

His time in America heightened, perhaps, his already strong awareness of the importance of historical roots and their relevance to a sense of identity. Less than two months after his return, he wrote to the English provincial,

Richard Norris, requesting the restoration of any letters that Fr Stone might have brought to England after the death of Fr Betagh. He offered to readily pay for a copy of any material in the English archives referring to Irish Jesuits and the Irish mission. "There exists such a want of information regarding the province that any little item becomes of importance. Tho' the number here was always small, still it is scarcely credible that after so many years there should not be found even one paper to throw light on past transactions." In the history of the Irish Jesuits, nothing could be found posterior to 1652; "and all my searches in the archives of the Gesu only obtained one document, the latest date of which was 1670".[111]

Volunteering for India

Before he had fully settled back in Ireland, there arose one final prospect of foreign missionary work. During November, he learned that the Holy See had requested the General to supply some Irishmen for Calcutta, where there was a great and immediate need to be met.[112] He thought no more about it until a letter arrived from Fr Roothaan on 30 December, which concentrated his attention. Two Jesuits priests were to go to India from England, and two from Ireland. He had chosen, the General stated, the St Leger brothers to go from Ireland. In the circumstances, he considered that he could not appoint anyone else but Kenney as a replacement for Robert St Leger. He was sure he would accept with "the same alacrity" with which he had undertaken the very much greater responsibility of Visitor, and would carry out the task to the end "very efficiently". He knew for a fact, he added, that the arrangement would be welcome to his fellow Jesuits in Ireland. The final arrangements would not be made till Fr Robert returned from England, so there was need for secrecy about the appointment for the present.[113]

Grasping at the straw that "final arrangements" had not yet been made, Kenney contacted the individual consultors and pointed out that the appointment of the St Legers was quite extraordinary, given Robert's very poor health and the fact that he was not particularly keen on going. He also wrote about the selection to Fr Norris, the English provincial. Finally, as he informed Esmonde, he wrote to the General, declaring that the St Legers had not the health for such an enterprise. Instead, he offered himself "to go most willingly", confident that the climate in India would be much more favourable to his asthma than that of Ireland. He asked the consultors to write in support of his offer, which he seemed to expect would be granted.[114]

Thus a year that marked the end of a mission to the New World offered briefly at its close the prospect of a mission to one of the most ancient civilizations in the old world.

It was not to be. The General thanked him for his letters, adhered to his decision to send the St Legers, and expressed his trust that this sacrifice would benefit the vice-province in service and spirit, that they would be empowered to look, as through a window in the ark, beyond their slender resources and gain in that expansiveness of heart so appropriate to men of the Society. "And my most excellent Fr Peter," he added, "has not been lacking, and is not lacking in such great-heartedness, and I have looked to him, and still do, to be the preserver of Ireland."[115] It was a daunting expectation, and, in many ways, too much for him.

The return from the United States, and his new appointment, marked the end of personal involvements in overseas missions and of demands for his episcopal preferment. A watershed had been reached, which provides a stopping point from which to look backwards and forwards to another major involvement, namely, his work for religious congregations, which, hitherto, apart from the Sisters of Loreto, has been mentioned only in passing. His final years, indeed, were to be devoted largely to such work, combined with intensive pastoral activity and spiritual guidance in his native city.

PART 3

Spiritual guide, preacher and pastor, and the final obedience

Honour is flashed off exploit, so we say;
...

Yet God (that hews mountain and continent,
Earth, all, out; who, with trickling increment,
Veins violets and tall trees makes more and more)
Could crowd career with conquest while there went
Those years and years by of world without event

G.M. Hopkins, "St Alphonsus Rodriguez"

XII

Confidant and adviser to new religious congregations: Irish Christian Brothers, Irish Sisters of Charity, and Sisters of Loreto

Invitation to Baltimore

During his time in America, Kenney wrote to, and received letters from Edmund Ignatius Rice, who was, as previously noted, an old personal and family friend.

In a letter commenced on 18 July, but not finished till 8 September 1832, he linked the need for the Christian Brothers, or the Brothers of the Christian Schools, as they were often called, to developments in the United States. Bishop John England had done much for the education of females, but there was a dearth of education for poor boys. "Would to God that Bishop England could bring a few of you here," he declared. The only problem was the obligation of teaching gratuitously, which, he feared, would leave them without means of support. But if trustees could take money by pension or contribution, and allow sufficient for "the maintenance of the masters", as was sometimes done by the Brothers in Ireland and was certainly done by the Sisters of Charity in America, then there could be no doubt of his institute's success.[1]

Kenney was presumably aware that already in 1828 Dr Whitfield of Baltimore had requested a foundation of the Brothers in his diocese.[2] It was refused on the grounds of scarcity of personnel.[3] Now, four years later, the American bishops in conclave requested Brothers for Baltimore. Kenney wrote from there in support of the project. Br Rice informed the hierarchy that it might be possible to grant their request, but at a later date.[4] Kenney's desire for an American foundation testified to his admiration for Rice and for the congregation he had founded. He, indeed, at the close of his first Visitation, had brought back the apostolic brief from Rome, 1821, which established the Brothers of the Christian Schools as "the first congregation of lay-religious men in Ireland".[5]

It was his privilege to be of considerable assistance to the Brothers in their early years, as well as to two other dynamic contributors to the revived Irish church, the Irish Sisters of Charity, and the Irish branch of the Sisters of Loreto.

IRISH CHRISTIAN BROTHERS, OR
BROTHERS OF THE CHRISTIAN SCHOOLS

Edmund Ignatius Rice was born in the small town of Callan, Co. Kilkenny, in 1762. By the time he commenced his work for poor boys in 1802, he was a tall, well-proportioned man of forty years, with house property in Waterford, an inn at Callan, and some 2000 acres of land in Counties Laois and Kilkenny.[6] He was friendly with Peter Kenney's brother in Waterford, and Peter described himself in 1841 as having been "in close habits of sacred friendship with Mr Rice for nine and thirty years".[7] He was closely acquainted with him, therefore, from the start of Rice's work of Christian education.

After his return from Palermo, he spent some time with Rice and his community at their headquarters in Waterford. Writing to Mother Mary Knowd, superior of the Presentation Sisters at George's Hill, Dublin, where Kenney resided, Edmund Rice remarked, on 2 November 1813: "Our good friend, Mr Kenney, proposes to take his leave of us on Tuesday. We shall feel lonesome enough after him. I think he is destined by Heaven to do a great deal of good."[8] The following year, on 11 May 1814, he wrote to Kenney asking how he was getting on since he went to Clongowes, expressing his fears that the veto controversy might lead to schism, and mentioning some prospective pupils for Clongowes.[9] Gradually, Kenney was drawn into a supportive role to the new congregation, which by 1812 had foundations already in Waterford, Dublin and Cork.

In 1816 a school was opened at Limerick. The city was described by the *Irish Parliamentary Gazetteer* of the time "as furnishing the very acme of those evils of starvation, disease and putridity, which render the poorer sections of the Irish population so many segregations of charnel houses of the living".[9a] Out of a population of 45,000, there were 17,000, over five years of age, who could neither read nor write. The bishop, Dr Tuohy, was concerned at the extensive proselytism being carried out by means of the Lancastrian schools. He invited the Brothers, welcomed them with open arms, but had made no provision for their accommodation nor for school premises. Eventually, classes were started in September 1817. Attendance was poor, because the children lacked clothes. The Brothers solved the problem by begging from door to door in order to build up a clothing fund. To help them in their severe poverty, Kenney came to Limerick in 1817 to preach the first charity sermon on their behalf. It realized only £67.[10] But the times were bad. Already, he had been to Cork to preach on behalf of the school there.[11]

In 1818, the constitutions and rules of the institute, with a memorial from the Brothers petitioning for their confirmation, were sent to the pope. They were accompanied by letters of support from Drs Troy and Murray, and other prelates; and within an unusually short period of two years, the request was granted. The approval of the congregation and its constitutions was recorded on 16 July 1820. The brief was drawn up, and was "signed by Pope Pius VII, 5 September 1820, and given to Fr Peter Kenney SJ, for transmission to Ireland".[12]

Edmund Rice received the brief from Kenney early in January 1821. It was an impressive document, but opposition was expected. Communities of religious, or "regulars" as they were termed, had had difficulty in being accepted in some dioceses "as being independent of diocesan control and imposing additional financial charges on the parishes" so that "the already miserable stipends for the clergy could be seriously diminished". As the first congregation of lay-religious men, known popularly as "the monks", they had already experienced such opposition. The brief, however, strongly discouraged any hostility from ecclesiastical authorities; warning, with considerable vigour, "We add the authority of Our Apostolic support ... depriving any judges whatsoever, ordinary or delegate, even the auditors of the Sacred Palace, and nuncios of the See Apostolic, of judging or interpreting otherwise..."[13]

During 1821 much time was given to discussion of the papal brief, and to preparation for a special meeting to give it formal acceptance in January, 1822. On Friday, 11 January 1822, the nineteen professed brothers assembled at the foundation-house, Mount Sion, Waterford. "That same evening," in the words of the congregation's historian, "they began a retreat conducted by Fr Peter Kenney SJ, which terminated on the evening of Saturday, 19th. The next day, 20 January, then the feast of the Holy Name of Jesus, Fr Kenney said mass in the Mount Sion oratory, at which all the brothers received holy communion and prayed for the light and guidance of the Holy Spirit."[14]

In the course of the chapter, Kenney's influence appeared in indirect ways. The office of the Blessed Virgin, which had been said daily, was now confined to Sundays, holydays, and the four principal feasts of the Blessed Virgin. This change – according to the History of the Institute, by Br J.D. Burke, an early historian of the congregation, 1891–1904, who lived with many who knew the founder[15] – was attributed to advice from Kenney: "that great man remarking to them that they would require twenty times more knowledge than they would ever have to communicate in the most advanced schools, in order that they may teach with power, ease and effect". The change, presumably, allowed additional time for study. Br Burke singled out a further contribution, in attributing the congregation's seal and motto to him. Asked to devise such, Kenney furnished the Brothers with: *Facere et Docere.*[16]

Up to 1822, each house was an independent unit, admitting and training its own postulants. The superior was appointed by the local bishop. Now, following the chapter, superiors henceforth were to be appointed by the superior general; and there was to be a central novitiate, with a training school, at Mount Sion, under the supervision of the superior general. Brother Patrick Ellis was appointed the first novice master, combining the position with that of assistant to the general. As a result of arrangements made by Kenney, Br Ellis resided at Clongowes for some time "in order to observe how novitiate life was carried on".[17] Thus began the close links between the Society of Jesus and the Christian Brothers which were to be maintained into the twentieth century.

After the chapter's decisions, Kenney spoke to the members on the theme – "In silence and in hope there is my strength." He pointed out in a vigorous manner, the line of conduct each brother ought to pursue personally, and in relation to his fellow brothers, his superiors, the children entrusted to him, and with regard to the other duties he had to discharge. He emphasised "that silence ought to be a favourite observance of a religious order, and that hope in God's providence should be one's anchor in all one's difficulties". At the conclusion, the brothers knelt to receive his blessing;[18] and on Sunday, 27 January, the day after the dissolution of the chapter, all the brothers waited on him to thank him for his assistance and guidance.[19]

During the 1820s it is likely that Kenney was frequently consulted by Edmund Rice in preparing the rule book of the congregation, which was issued in 1832. Comparison with the Jesuit rule is evident in places, even to similarity of wording. Thus, there is a similar emphasis on detachment, or inner freedom, so that one is prepared to serve in whatever office, or ministry, to which the congregation, or relevant superior, appoints one, while having a preference for "low and humble offices"; and there is similarity in abhorring the values of the world and in seeking, instead, "whatever Christ our Lord loved and embraced", even to desiring affronts and injuries in order to be more like him, provided these were without sin on the part of one's neighbour. Both emphasise esteem for the pursuit of solid virtues, recognising that it is from strong interior dispositions that energy flows to accomplish the end of one's vocation; and where the vows are concerned, there is a proximation, even in wording, on the spirit of poverty, on chastity, and with regard to the vow of obedience.[20]

In 1825, Fr "Daddy" Dunn, the former Jesuit, wrote to Kenney about an "establishment for lay monks in Preston". He had been urging foundations in Manchester as well. He also wrote to Fr Aylmer, and to Bishops Murray, Curtis and Doyle. On 24 June 1825, Edmund Rice accepted his invitation, but emphasised the Brothers' position on their vow of poverty and free schooling. As regards weekly money paid by the children for the purpose of providing the school with books, paper etc, they should prefer, he observed, that the money come from some other source, but were not opposed to some small sum being received for these and other school expenses. But, he went on, "from the nature of our vows we cannot conscientiously accept of any part of the money received from the children towards our own subsistence".[21]

Two years later, problems arose at Preston. The school management committee had difficulty providing the annual stipend for the brothers. They decided on a levy of three pence to six pence per week on each pupil, which would produce a yearly income of about £200.[22] In Ireland, a voluntary contribution of ½ penny a week had been the norm. The superior, Br Dunphy, uneasy about the decision, decided to refer the matter to the superior general. The latter and his council were of the view that the proposed arrangement conflicted with their understanding of the obligations of the vow of gratuitous instruction. Requests for permission to accept fees had been refused on previous occasions by the Holy See. Br Dunphy submitted a statement of the situation to Kenney for advice on 11 September, 1827. His reply on 13 September lacked his usual blend of clarity and applicability, and can scarcely have been of much practical assistance.

"The question proposed," he remarked, was "whether Mr Rice can, with safe conscience, suffer such payments as 3d or 6d per week to be exacted by the managing committee of the schools committed to your charge? I think that he can. The vow of the institute I conceive to be perfectly fulfilled when its members give their time and labour to the poor without their exacting payment for such instruction, or receiving from them anything that might be given by the children as a recompense for such service."

He went on to say, however, that though the vow was not violated by such arrangements, the arrangements, nevertheless, were objectionable "on the ground of expediency and edification", and should only be adopted when "absolutely necessary". It was not expedient to have many deprived of education because they could not pay; and it was not edifying, when the Brothers were the masters, that privation be inflicted for inability to pay.[23] He suggested that the Brothers, or Mr Rice, manifest their opinion as unfavourable to the measure, and obtain, if possible, a reduction of the higher charge unless the parents were clearly able to pay. The experiment of a charge would be particularly unwelcome if there were a *completely free school* in the neighbourhood of another persuasion. All that being said, he further remarked: "whatever remonstrances Mr Rice might advise to be made, I should not like that anything would lead to any interruption of the connection which you have formed in Preston."[24]

A little over a year later his advice was sought once more. This time the occasion was the threat of penal clauses against religious congregations in the forthcoming Emancipation Act. There was much menacing talk at public meetings, and the Duke of Wellington himself contributed to the anxiety experienced amongst Catholics by a statement in the House of Lords on 2 April 1829, that "there is no man more convinced than I am of the absolute necessity of carrying into execution that part of the present measure which has for its object the extinction of monastic orders in the country".[25] Some Brothers were so fearful for the future of their institute that they generated a demand for a special general chapter of the congregation.

Br Rice, advised, doubtless, by Daniel O'Connell, did not take the public threats too seriously. He was opposed to holding a special chapter, as there was one due in two or three years to elect a superior general and assistants. He brought the matter to Kenney. The latter counselled against the chapter. Under pressure, however, Br Rice gave way. It was a fateful decision. The chapter met at Mount Sion on 13 April, the day the Act of Emancipation received the unwilling assent of King George IV and became law. The chapter's progress, and many of its proposals and decrees, so upset Edmund Rice that he resigned his office on 1 May. On the assembly refusing his resignation, he agreed to stay on. The chapter dissolved on 4 May.[26]

Five months later, on 26 October, he wrote to the superior general of the De La Salle congregation in Paris, for advice with regard to matters arising from the chapter. In doing so, he mentioned Kenney's role on this and other occasions.

"My consent for calling this chapter was rather extorted from me than otherwise," he announced. He saw no need for it, "but the matter being still urged on me, I consulted Revd Mr Kenney, superior of the Jesuits, a gentleman who is deeply interested in everything that regards the welfare of our institute, and one on whom we are always in the habit of consulting on our affairs, and his opinion was against having this chapter called. Notwithstanding all this, through the workings of a few individuals,[27] the rest of the professed brothers got rather clamorous so that I was obliged to submit, and I am sorry to say that, in my opinion, the chapter produced not good but on the contrary." Seeds of independence subversive of religious discipline were sown. Young brothers were encouraged to come forward to make complaints of their directors, by which their authority, and that of those who would succeed them, was much lessened. And he went on: "hitherto the quantity and quality of our food and beverage were both wholesome and sufficient, but in this chapter a rule was made to increase the quantity by the addition of a supper, not before taken, as our dinner hour is about half past three in the evening"![28]

Given that the brothers had their breakfast at 8.00 a.m., and that their second and final meal was at 3.30 p.m.,[29] and that they were men who worked hard, its scarcely surprising that many were "clamerous" and insisted on having some evening meal! Whatever the merits and balance of Br Rice's complaints, the chapter, as he feared, did introduce a period of questioning, division and even intrigue within the congregation. Edmund Rice's actions and authority were to be called in question, and Kenney, as will appear in a later chapter, was to be called on for judgement in that very unhappy situation. Whatever the pressures on him from other people and circumstances, he remained, as the historian and archivist, Br M.C. Normoyle, observed, "always available for advice and consultation on the many problems that naturally arose in the young congregation of Edmund Rice".[30] That availability had extended to providing practical guidance on the length and practices of the noviceship,[31] and on many aspects of the institute.

His departure for Rome, and then the United States, in 1829, was a serious blow. Frs Bracken and Esmonde stood in, and advised and assisted as best they could. But they did not have the background and rapport with the congregation that Kenney had. Rice longed for his return, and feared that he might be lost for good to Ireland. A fear that Kenney could do little to dispel when he wrote to him from Baltimore in 1832: "About my return ... I know no more when it may occur or whether it will ever occur, than I did when I left Dublin."[32]

Meantime, however, and, as it might have seemed, his last positive contribution to the development of this cherished institute of lay religious men, he approached, while at Rome, the secretary of the Sacred Congregation de Propaganda Fide, Castruccius Castracane, to have extended to the Brothers all the indulgences enjoyed by the Freres des Ecoles Chretiennes. Castracane, as he observed in the subsequent rescript, referred the "humble suit of the Revd Father Peter Kenney of the Society of Jesus, and vicar-provincial of Ireland" to Pope Pius VIII, who "kindly granted" all and each of the indulgences and favours requested on 13 October 1829.[33]

The availability, and generosity with advice and time, remarked on by Br Normoyle, was also evident in his dealings with the body of religious women founded by Mary Aikenhead, which took the name Sisters of Charity

THE IRISH SISTERS OF CHARITY

Shortly after his return from Sicily, he acquired, as noticed earlier, a reputation as an orator. Part of what attracted crowds to his sermons at Mary's Lane chapel was, as will be recalled, a style which avoided the sensational and grandiloquent characteristics of the period and was, by contrast, calm, well reasoned, and persuasive; yet not without vigour and directness, and a blend of fire, pathos, and tenderness, as the occasion demanded.[34]

Because of his reputation, he was asked in 1812 to preach a charity sermon in support of a place of refuge for poor girls of good character. The house in Ash Street, near the Coombe, was run by Mrs John O'Brien, assisted by a Cork friend, Mary Aikenhead. The sermon raised the sum of £72.

Mary Aikenhead, that same year, was prevailed on by Bishop Murray to found a congregation of women to serve the poor. In preparation, she and a friend, Alice Walsh, went on 6 June 1812, to a convent of the Institute of the Blessed Virgin Mary, at Micklegate Bar, York, where the nuns had no vows of enclosure and went out to visit the sick. A few days later, in a letter to her, Dr Murray formulated the aim of their sojourn there, namely, "to acquire an interior spirit, and a total disengagement from the world". She was impressed by the rule followed in the convent. It was, in effect, the rule of Ignatius Loyola adapted, two centuries previously, to suit religious women. At the end of the year, she asked for a further year there.[36]

In 1815, after considering possible links with other congregations, Dr

Murray decided to establish a separate institute, suited expressly to Irish needs. Aikenhead and Walsh left York on 18 August 1815. They made the Spiritual Exercises retreat of St Ignatius before leaving. On 1 September they took religious vows for one year, in the presence of Bishop Murray. The latter asked Peter Kenney to be spiritual adviser to the young institute. Two days later, the first postulants for the new congregation arrived. On 7 September, Murray returned to Rome at the bishops' request to convey their reaction to the views of Roman authorities regarding the Veto. He left the emerging community at Summerhill, North William Street, in Kenney's care.

At this stage the bishop was still uncertain about a rule for the new body. Mary Aikenhead clung to the York rule. Kenney agreed with her as to its suitability, but they jointly envisaged adding to it a fourth vow – to devote one's life to the service of the poor. She wrote to Dr Murray, who was making use of his spare time in Rome to further the cause of the new foundation. He replied on 6 December 1815. After receiving her letter, he proceeded, he said, with more courage. The fact that she, and Mother Catherine (Alice Walsh), as well as Fr Kenney, seemed to approve so highly of the Rule of York, led him to perceive "that the simplest and easiest way of proceeding would be to obtain for the Archbishop of Dublin power from the Holy See to erect a congregation of Sisters of Charity, to live, under his jurisdiction, according to the rules of the Convent of York, approved by Clement XI, with the addition of a fourth vow" which expressed their commitment to "devoting their lives to the service of the poor".[38] The name of the body was still undecided.

On 6 January 1816, Archbishop Troy received from Pius VII a rescript imparting the permission sought. In March, Dr Murray returned. He sought Kenney's detailed advice with regard to the adoption of the York rule, and also his thoughts as to which of the feasts of the Blessed Virgin ought be adopted as the special feast of the institute. This, in preparation for the formal erection of the congregation under the jurisdiction of Dr Troy.[39]

Rule, titular feast, and name

Kenney gave a great deal of consideration to the request, and when he sat down to write on 18 July the letter ran into the following day. In typed form, the response covers almost eight quarto pages of single spacing. His closely reasoned presentation carried remarkable assurance and authority for a man so recently ordained.

He recommended that the York rule be immediately proposed to the observance of the community as the one given them by the Holy See, but suggested the introduction of some words which would perfect the rule by "a declaration of the specific object of this institution", such as "consecrating our lives to the service of our indigent fellow creatures and more particularly that of the sick poor". In accordance with "the constant practice in all religious orders", he went on to recommend that the rule be the sole consideration for some time, in order that experience be gained before the constitutions were finalised. The rule, since it was established by the bull of confirmation, was on a firm basis.

On the second matter, namely, which feast of the Blessed Virgin should be the special feast of the new institute, he concluded that since the rule express- ly constituted the Blessed Virgin as patroness under the title "Most Glorious Queen of Heaven", it would be appropriate to have the feast of the Assumption as the titular feast of the congregation. In support of the appro- priateness, he suggested that as the assumption was a reward for the Blessed Virgin's co-operation during her life, it presented a source of help and conso- lation for the sisters in their work. Again, as it marked a happy liberation from a life of suffering, it was an appropriate form of devotion for those who laboured to lessen the ills and solace the woes of others; and as it commemo- rated her most happy death, her special position in heaven, and her power of intercession, it represented the Blessed Virgin as someone whom the dying could invoke with confidence.

On the question of a name for the congregation, he declared that as well as a formal canonical title he would allow 'Sisters of Charity', which had already gone abroad, to be "their vulgar and common name". It was shorter and equally impressive, if not more so, of their object than any other English term that could well be given them, and, besides, popular denomination was a fre- quent occurrence in the history of the church.

After further detailed comments on the vows and other matters, he suggest- ed that the two older candidates (Srs Augustine and Catherine – Aikenhead and Walsh) make their vows in the new congregation on 15 August, after a retreat made by them and the whole community. He would have the Act erecting the congregation dated from that day; and as there were rumours that the house (at North William Street) was not a permanent one, he would have the vows pub- licly made there at high mass, sung if possible by the archbishop, who would thus, as it were, publicly announce the erection of a new congregation under his immediate jurisdiction. He suggested that Dr Murray preach. Finally, he recommended that to the rule and authenticated Act there be prefixed the title: "Rule of the Pius Congregation (which is usually called the Sisters of Charity) under the patronage of the most glorious Queen of Heaven, instituted by Apostolic Authority for the perpetual service of the poor, 1816."[40]

In practice, Mrs Aikenhead deferred the special mass to the octave day of the Assumption, 22 August, because of the difficulty of having certain invited clergy present on such a busy feastday. Moreover, she and Alice Walsh did not take their vows then, nor in the public manner Kenney had suggested. Dr Murray was chary at this period about drawing attention to the congregation. On 1 September, however, he had them renew their simple vows at a private mass.[41]

The canonical erection of the community into a congregation, by formal

deed, did not occur 'till the close of the year. It was arranged for another popular feast of the Blessed Virgin, that of the Immaculate Conception, on 8
December. The foundress and Mother Catherine received notice to prepare for
their perpetual vows on that date; and as part of the preparation were asked to
enter on a retreat commencing on 29 November. Kenney came from
Clongowes to conduct the Spiritual Exercises. On 8 December 1816, or the
following day, Dr Murray received the perpetual vows of the two women at a
private mass in the chapel at North William Street. Only two outsiders were
present, both of them guests of Dr Murray: namely, the vicar-general of the
diocese, and Miss Denis, whose generous contribution had been mainly
responsible for the building of the chapel.[42]

Looking back on this time, some 37 years later, Mary Aikenhead recalled
an hour they had spent with Fr Kenney, during which she learned for the first
time of the "Second Method of Prayer" of St Ignatius Loyola which came to
mean so much to her during her life.

The second method of prayer and Mary Aikenhead

Introducing this method of prayer, Ignatius Loyola had said: "I must," as in
all prayer, "recollect myself for a while before entering on the prayer, and,
either seated or walking up and down, as may seem better, I will consider
where I am going, and for what purpose." Then a "preparatory prayer" is
made asking for what one seeks. After this, the person praying might find it
helpful, to use the following method in saying the Our Father.

Taking up a posture which "suits one's disposition and is ... conducive to
devotion, one keeps one's eyes closed, or fixed in one position, not permitting
them to roam about. Then one should say, 'Father', and reflect upon this
word as long as one finds meanings, comparisons, relish and consolation in the
consideration of it. One should then continue the same method with each
word of the *Our Father*, or of any other prayer that one may wish to contem-
plate in this manner."

He envisaged the prayer lasting one hour, when said this way during a
retreat. But he insisted that if during the contemplation on the *Our Father* one
found in one or two words "good matter for thought, relish and consolation,
one should not be anxious to pass on, even though one spend the entire hour
on what one has found. When the hour is over, the rest of the *Our Father* is
said in the usual way."[43]

Writing to one of her religious sisters on 11 August 1842, Mrs Aikenhead
stressed that a frequent practice of St Ignatius' second method of prayer was
of great importance. "I fear," she continued, "and I have reason to fear, that
this holy practice is much neglected by many of our elders. Whilst you live,
keep on the alert to encourage everyone to have recourse to it." Sloth, and a
sort of contemptuous idea annexed to what was called second, as if it were

second rate, sometimes kept people from using this means towards high virtue. "The first time I *ever heard* of such a thing as St Ignatius's second method," she continued, "was when about a month from York, just after our holy vows were offered, venerated Fr Kenney spent an hour, as it were making his prayer aloud, half the hour rather explaining; and from him I learned, what I own to you experience daily proves, that it is in regard to the generality of religious persons, the best method; the only one some can ever deduce practical results from."[44]

Delay on the constitutions, and a celebrated sermon

In 1817 the members of the congregation assumed religious dress, at Dr Murray's suggestion, though in public they were still called by their family names. Thus, the foundress was always "Revd Mother" in community life, but outside the convent she was "Mrs Aikenhead". Meanwhile, Bishop Murray had left to Kenney the preparation of the constitutions.[45]

It was a considerable imposition at a time when he was putting down roots at Clongowes and facing criticism, and was also negotiating with Mrs O'Brien for the purchase of a house and land for a noviciate at Rahan, near Tullamore.[46] In April, Murray, as noted in an earlier chapter, complained, in a heavily jocose manner, of his travelling "about the world" while "your own little family at Summerhill is left in a state of confusion and disorder, uncertain as to what is to be the result of this unexpected delay". He asked him to take up his pen in earnest so that he would be in a position "to present the new constitutions to the sisters at Whitsuntide".[47] His letter had little effect. Kenney was too tired, too much under stress to face the detailed study, examination, and reflection required to construct new constitutions; and, besides, as he had indicated in his letter of 18 July, he did not approve of formulating constitutions so soon.

His delay in responding, obliged him to please the bishop by agreeing, in September 1817, to his request for a special sermon to grace a public ceremony marking the reception of the religious habit by two candidates. Dr Murray had decided the time had come to draw public attention to the new congregation. Kenney chose for his text, the words of St Paul: *Caritas Christi urget nos* (the love of Christ impels us; 2 Cor. v. 14). It was to prove an influential event.

The sermon was one of his most effective discourses. Some excerpts offer a glimpse of the content, and an indication of his style of preaching on such an occasion. Oratory, as all know, is quickly dated. And although he made little use of "the ornaments of eloquence" and "of rhetoric" compared to many of his contemporaries, his language to the modern reader seems diffuse and high-flown, and some of the religious terminology desiccated and obsolete. But, then, the written word has seldom done justice to the live sermon: so much depends on the personality, conviction, presence of the speaker. Despite his ornate language, and stylized constructions, it is possible from the artistic structure, the creative imagery, and his use of contrasts, to envisage the impact on the original audience; and the vigour and directness with which he juxtaposes the self-denying lives of the young Sisters with the indolent existence of many of their contemporaries, still has power to arrest attention.

In the presence of about sixty people, some of whom were prominent in Dublin society, he outlined the aim and scope of the institute recently established by Apostolic Authority; and taking the words – *"Greater love than this no man has than to lay down his life for his friends"*, he reminded his well-to-do listeners that those who vowed their lives to the service of the poor were virtually "martyrs of charity", and he challenged them to contrast these lives with their own.

> Look at these religious now assembled before you ... Compare your lives with that which they this day begin ... Mean is their attire, frugal their repast, they repose for seven hours each day, they labour, pray, and speak the things that are of God. Their visits to the poor ended, they return to offer them at the foot of the cross, and the archangel who stands at the right hand of the altar of incense bears to heaven the odour of their daily sacrifices.

And turning expressly to the lay women present, he continued:

> Indolent slumbers waste the morning of your day; the sun hath made half a world's course, before you have offered one moment to reason and to religion. From toilets you roll to entertainments, assemblies, balls, concerts, theatres, suppers, and when the morning, alas! proclaims the glory of the heavens to the coming day, you sink insensible to nature's voice, whilst from her you seek the strength to recommence the dissipation of another day. This is your life; that is theirs; until at the same moment death marks you both. Gracious heavens, what a contrast!

And addressing finally, in apostrophe, those being "clothed" and about to enter the novitiate, he exclaimed:

> Be your noviceship to you what the retreat in the upper chamber [upper room of the Last Supper] was to the apostles, a preparation to receive the grace that is to guide, and the power that is to strengthen you ... Aspire to this hidden life, which can only be obtained by a total separation from the world. In quiet solitude and silence alone you can learn, increase and perfect the spirit of your state, and the love of Him who, when exalted above the earth, drew all things to himself.

Many are the eyes this day fixed on you. Various the comments of
the votaries of the world. One answer I give to all its questions, to all
its arguments – these short words of the apostle, simple, sweet, divinely
energetic: *caritas Christi urget nos.*[48]

From that day, the theme of his sermon – "*Caritas Christi urget nos*" (The
love of Christ impels us) – became the motto of the congregation. Thus, his
close involvement with them, gave rise to the mottoes adopted by both the
Irish Christian Brothers and the Irish Sisters of Charity.

Handing over

In the weeks after his homily, he faced the Visitation of Fr Grivel, which was,
as has been seen, a time of hurt and humiliation. Replaced by Fr Aylmer, he
welcomed the pastoral work connected with the small church at Hardwicke
Street, and was always to feel grateful to Mother Catherine and her community at North William Street for their support during his time at the church.

In 1818 his work as confessor to the Sisters took on a sad dimension, when
two of the recently professed died of fever and consumption respectively. He
and Dr Murray visited them frequently during their illness.[50] Mother
Aikenhead's constant attendance, on top of so many other demands, led her to
the verge of breakdown. Her physicians counselled a long rest and change of
air. Mrs O'Brien's country house, Rahan Lodge, a virtual rest-home for
Bishop Murray, was made available to her. So, on a July morning, 1818, she
availed of the favoured form of transport between Dublin and Rahan: boarding
a covered barge at Portobello harbour, near Rathmines. The slow canal journey
was preferable to the dusty, cramped and jolting ordeal by stage coach. One
could walk on deck, enjoy fresh air and scenery, and not have to stop for
meals, which were served on board.

At Rahan, near Tullamore, she had time for rest and reflection. There were
also opportunities of meeting with Kenney, who had been moved to the new
Jesuit foundation, a few miles away, which had been bought from Mrs
O'Brien. As her energy returned, she began to think about formulating the
constitutions. She had hoped for Kenney's help, but he was laden with commitments for retreats, including one at Maynooth to the Dublin clergy.
Instead, he introduced her to Fr Robert St Leger, rector of the community
and of the newly established Jesuit College of St Stanislaus, at Tuallabeg,
Rahan. Dr Murray, then staying at Rahan Lodge, asked St Leger to give her
every assistance. He was to prove generous with his time and interest.

St Leger, in effect, took over Kenney's role in relation to the congregation.
He guided Mrs Aikenhead spiritually, giving her inspiration and spiritual
energy. She returned to Dublin, in September 1818, renewed in health and
braced in spirit. Under his direction, according to a biographer of Mrs

Aikenhead, "the keynote of her life" became "a childlike confidence in God, allied to a dauntless courage".[51]

Interrupted contacts and some tension

In November, Kenney gave the community retreat in North William Street. Some lay friends of the institute were permitted to attend the instructions, and all, apparently, had never before heard such discourses as he delivered during this retreat. The following February, he preached there for the benefit of the orphans being looked after by the Sisters. Mother Catherine (Alice Walsh), his friend and admirer, noted in her diary that the sermon was worthy of the subject and the preacher; "and oh!" she added, "may the lord in his mercy preserve this holy and matchless man!" There was great regret a few days later when they heard that the "matchless man", who had been confessor and friend to the community for nearly three years, was shortly to sail for America.[52]

In May 1821, when he arrived back in Ireland, "his return", according to Mary Aikenhead's first biographer, "was a joy to rich and poor, priests and people; a great blessing to the Sisters of Charity; and a source of real consolation to the William Street community. He soon visited Mother Catherine, gave the convent a precious relic of the true cross, and resumed his office of confessor."[53]

His closeness to the congregation was indicated in March 1823, when he was once more superior of the Irish mission and was concerned at its financial state. He obtained a loan of £300 from Mrs Aikenhead. On 26 September, he was happy to be able to return the sum, enlarged by £8.15 as "the amount of interest due from 1 March to 1st October".[54]

In the subsequent years of the 1820s there is little extant evidence of contact with the foundress. The one surviving letter, however, reflects an occasion of tension. He had brought back to Ireland from Sicily a set of meditations covering the thirty days retreat which he had made under Fr Plowden. These made such an impression when he used them that his words were taken down, transcribed, and passed around. They gradually underwent alterations which made them almost unrecognisable to him. They also became confused in people's minds with his meditations at Maynooth, which, as has been seen, were also eagerly transcribed. Mrs Aikenhead had a copy which he considered the nearest he had seen to the original. She cherished it jealously.

In 1826, the jubilee year, when he was in continuous demand for sermons, retreats, and conferences, he came across a number of incorrect versions. In talking to Mrs Ball, foundress of the Irish branch of the Sisters of Loreto, and to the Ursuline Sisters, he mentioned that the only correct copy was with Mrs Aikenhead, and they also understood that the meditations were expressly compiled for nuns. This led to requests to Mary Aikenhead, which she resented; and she made her feelings known to Kenney. He replied on 8 July 1826, in a civil but less than warm manner, providing something of a convoluted history of the meditations, and a form of apology for his action which carried a reproof with it.

In talking with Mrs Ball about the Spiritual Exercises, he had mentioned, he acknowledged, the set of meditations, but she was mistaken in thinking that he had compiled them, and that they were compiled for nuns. Her mistake may have arisen because he had made use of the meditations, and those who transcribed them, nuns and ecclesiastical students, sometimes sent them about under his own name; and though they were originally compiled for Jesuits, some transcribers made changes to render them suitable to their respective states in life. So many transcriptions had now been made, he went on, that the meditations had become "common property"; and as she, Mrs Aikenhead, had the only correct copy he had seen for a long time, he "thought it only charity" to put Mrs Ball and the Ursulines "in the right direction". Since, however, this did not meet with her approbation, he would not in future "take such a liberty". And he concluded:

> I was very grateful for the loan of them last March, and I shall not endanger the favour of again seeing them by an incautious disclosure of the spot where they may be found. You will believe me, I am sure, that the idea of attempting to compile a retreat for nuns never once entered my head. Had I leisure, I should not refuse to do so much for the bene-fit of coachmen or coal porters; but I would wait a very strong indica-tion of the Divine Will, before I should choose such a favoured class of God's servants as the objects of such labour.
>
> Most Sincerely,
> Yours,
> P. Kenney.[55]

None of the usual final salutations, request for prayers, and so forth!

From then, until his return from his second Visitation in the United States, his contacts with the congregation appear to have been confined to one or two convents. It was only on his arrival back in Ireland in the 1830s, and in the absence of Fr St Leger in India, that he found himself drawn again into the central affairs of the foundress and the institute; and that experience, as in the case of the Christian Brothers, was to prove difficult and distressful. The middle years of the 1830s were a time of uncertainty and division in the con-gregation.

A congregation at risk

From 1831 Mrs Aikenhead was invalided with a painful spinal complaint. She continued to rule the congregation from a recumbent position. Her struggle with the disability intensified both her will power and her sense of dependence on God. A favourite prayer in times of despondency was the "Take and Receive"[56] of Ignatius Loyola, and she constantly struggled to achieve the detachment, or balance, associated with the saint. In this Robert St Leger was a shrewd mentor.[57]

Her health and many preoccupations led her, in 1834, to hand over the role of mistress of novices to a very talented and articulate young English woman, who had already published a book before entering. She was Sister M. Ignatius. As well as mistress of novices, she also appointed her rectress of the Stanhope Street convent. Mary Aikenhead herself moved from there, first to a house in Sandymount, then to the congregation's St Vincent's hospital at Stephen's Green, Dublin. It marked the beginning of a period of tension and disruption which nearly wrecked the institute.

A definitive account of those years has never been written. The versions that have been published, have been written entirely from the perspective of Mother Aikenhead. At this stage, as a result, it is difficult to visualise another version. Within such limitations, the outline of events seems to have been somewhat as follows.

Sr M. Ignatius, coming from a particularly well-to-do family background, was more sophisticated and socially secure, more educated and articulate, than virtually all the other sisters in the congregation, and, moreover, she was widely read and well versed in spiritual matters, and had considerable charm and empathy. She is said to have come to question the body's almost exclusive emphasis on service of the poor and sick, and to have felt that the talents of many able young women were being neglected. The severe illness and invalided condition of the foundress raised questions for her, and other sisters, about her ability to continue as head of the organisation; and when Mary Aikenhead seemed to ignore the very constitutions, approved by Rome in August 1833, and did not have an election for superior-general as required, but continued to rule regardless, Sr M. Ignatius protested about the illegal behaviour and talked to others about it, though in reality she seems to have been moved more by ambition than concern for legality.

The first inkling Mrs Aikenhead had of any problems seems to have been in May 1835. Hearing of very splendid plans to celebrate the novices' reception of the habit on 10 May, she came to Stanhope Street and cancelled the ceremony. She soon perceived, it is said, the spirit of disaffection in the house. Sr M. Ignatius's role as superior, as well as mistress of novices, had placed her in a position of considerable influence; and she had also cultivated many people outside the community. Recognising the weakness of her own position, and also recognising that there could not be an immediate election to bolster it because she had not put anyone forward for the degree of *formed sister*, and the constitutions stipulated that the latter were to be the electors, Mrs Aikenhead approached Bishop Murray, who, as initiator of the body, had, like herself, a special interest in preserving the original ethos of the congregation. They decided to appeal to Rome to adjust the difficulty.

On 3 August 1835, the bishop informed her that Pope Gregory XVI had on 5 July supplied the deficiency by a special rescript appointing her superior general of the congregation, and authorising her to hold that office, from that date, for the term prescribed by the constitutions. Dr Murray then instructed her to "proceed with as little delay as may be consistent with your conscience, to admit to the degree of formed sister such members of the congregation as may be duly qualified for that distinction, and to arrange the whole system in the manner which the constitutions point out."[58]

Fortified in her office, she deposed Sr M. Ignatius from novice mistress and superior and sent her to the convent at Sandymount. She discovered, it appears, that arrangements had been secretly in train to open a convent at Hastings, England, and that M. Ignatius planned to bring thither the more intellectual of her novices.[59] At Sandymount, Sr Ignatius continued to make her case and won over some members of the community, including the very devout Sr Francis Teresa, a member of the influential More O'Ferrall family, who had contributed £3,000 towards the setting up of St Vincent's hospital. From Sandymount, M. Ignatius had written to Kenney giving her version of the affair and appealing for his help. The annals of the congregation state baldly that "he espoused her cause".[60]

Meantime, he had been consulted by Mary Aikenhead. Despite a very busy schedule, he was still spiritual adviser and "extraordinary confessor" to some of the convents, including, it would appear, Sandymount and the noviceship;[61] and his enthusiasm for the congregation had encouraged English Jesuits at Preston, at the start of 1835, to ask the Sisters to come thither to run a day school for poor children.[62]

In the light of his role as confessor, and also knowing Dr Murray's special interest in the congregation, he was very loath to get involved in its internal disputes. When Mrs Aikenhead consulted him, therefore, as to whether, in the light of the constitutions, it was in order to conduct an election for the to the superior general, he was slow to reply, and then quite circumspect in what he said. He excused his delay on the grounds of being much away from home, and certainly he was under considerable pressure in the summer and autumn of 1835, as will later appear, but it was also probably due to reluctance to be involved. When he did reply on 4 September, he confined himself strictly to the question.

He thought that in the present circumstances, he would have preferred that the names of the three or four assistants had been sent to Rome at the same time as that of the superior general, so that for this one occasion all had been made at the same time by the same authority. As there were now, presumably, a number of *formed sisters*, the election could take place; though there might be insidious remarks to the effect that the constitutions required the same electors for the general and the assistants. After further observations and suggestions, he went on mildly to warn against any further carelessness with regard to regulations: pointing out that the constitutions designated the qualifications which the assistants should have, and that it was important that the sisters to be chosen possess those qualification in a degree that would secure the confidence of the community. He concluded with a pious request, and a counsel which, perhaps, invited Mrs Aikenhead to reflect on the implications of her serious disability: "I hope that you and your Sisters will give me a share in your prayers. We should often ask for each other of our Lord that our infirmities may not impede the progress of his own divine work."[63]

He had great respect for her, and for the aims and work of the congregation, as has been seen; but once the constitutions had been approved by the pope he expected them to be followed with care, otherwise the very purpose of the congregation could be lost sight of. This attitude was also to be manifested in his dealings with the Christian Brothers. In this context, he sympathised with Sr M. Ignatius's case. Technically, Mary Aikenhead's authority had no legal foundation from the approval of the constitutions in May 1833 to July 1835. And as no formed sisters had been created, there was no real curb on her authority; and she could be formidably authoritative, as he had experienced as well as Sr Ignatius! His own reaction to that manifestation, helped him, no doubt, to empathise with M. Ignatius. And there was also the fact that Sr Francis Teresa's family was well known to him and had access to him, since Fr O'Ferrall of Gardiner Street, who died just the previous year (1834), was her brother. As the tension mounted and the disruption spread, therefore, and he, despite a multiplicity of other commitments, found himself drawn in, he sought to be scrupulously fair to both sides.

For a while it seemed that the congregation could not survive. Thirteen novices out of twenty-two left Stanhope Street. Two young professed sisters also withdrew.[64] The whole issue became public property, and was fanned by members of Sr Ignatius's family, and by those of Sr Francis Teresa (More O'Ferrall) whom Mrs Aikenhead had transferred from Sandymount to Stanhope Street to remove her from Ignatius's influence. Reports and distortions abounded; and the outside discussions and divisions made their way back into the convents. Kenney's attempt to be fair to both contestants and not appear partisan, led the eventual winning side to present him as espousing the enemy's cause, while he also experienced misinterpretation from members of the other camp. It was a time of particular stress for the principal protagonists, and more particularly, perhaps, for Mary Aikenhead, who saw what she had built up being rent apart, her character and judgement called in question, and her motives impugned.

Dismissal, reaction, and denouement

She determined that Sr M. Ignatius would have to leave. Already, by January 1836, she had proposed the matter to the archbishop. He shied away from the difficulty. So, articulate and well connected a person was likely to create a great stir. So, events dragged on, and Sr Ignatius continued to campaign from Sandymount, virtually dominating the community there. Eventually, in May 1837, Mrs Aikenhead, with her assistants in council, decided on the final step. They sent a very strongly worded request to Dr Murray. He replied on 2 June 1837, accepting their reasons why Sr M. Ignatius should cease to be a member of the institute. "I authorise you," he wrote, "to release her from every tie of obedience by which she bound herself to it."[65] It was left to the cowed superior at Sandymount to read out the decision to Sr M. Ignatius. She was said to have been amazed; and taken aback that it gave her no face-saving exit to smooth her entrance to any other religious community. Her supporter and friend, Sr Francis Teresa, took it on herself to leave.[66]

The problems, however, did not immediately cease. Sr Ignatius continued to carry on from Sandymount what Mrs Aikenhead called her "underhand correspondence".[67] Her brother, who had earlier supported her in her complaints, now, apparently, refused to receive her home. Kenney, concerned for her, wrote in very strong terms to Mary Aikenhead requesting that she be not required to leave until she was promised admittance to another congregation.[68] Meanwhile, the dismissal was discussed in the public arena and hard things were said again about the congregation and its foundress, and Kenney himself, as indicated, did not go unscathed. Sr Francis Teresa's brother, the prominent politician, Richard More O'Ferrall MP, who had become Lord of the Treasury in the Melbourne administration in 1835, wrote a censorious letter to him, and was reputed to have said to others, "We may thank such a person for that."[69] The grievance of the influential More O'Ferrall family added to the flood of fabrications and wild reports.

In July 1837, the Revd Dr Nicholson, voluble friend of O'Connell, of members of the English nobility, and of influential Roman cardinals, and a future archbishop of Corfu, entered the lists. He had formerly been chaplain to the More O'Ferralls in their County Kildare seat, so his main concern was with "Mrs O'Ferrall", as he termed Sr Francis Teresa, and with assailing Mrs Aikenhead. For the latter and her congregation he had an unveiled dislike, going back, perhaps, to his years as superior at Clarendon Street, Dublin, when he was embroiled with a number of people and most notably with his Carmelite brethren.[70]

On 7 July he sent a long, repetitious letter to Dr Murray from Frascati, Italy. Mrs O'Ferrall, he declared, had been badly treated by the Sisters of Charity. One well known priest, indeed, had said to some of the laity that "Mrs Aikenhead took her away *like a robber* from Sandymount to Stanhope Street." He wished Archbishop Murray to declare that there was nothing against her being accepted into another religious congregation, so that she might obtain approval at Rome to enter another order. As regards her brother's letter to Fr Kenney, too much should not be made of it: for More O'Ferrall, as he knew personally all too well, was very impetuous, and often regretted writing a letter immediately after he sent it! (An unlikely practice in a Lord of the Treasury, and future governor of Malta!?) His heart, however, was in the right place, and he spoke very highly of his Grace, speaking of him as a "very jewel". Mrs Aikenhead, on the other hand, had spoken most imprudently about Mrs More O'Ferrall, and had been opposed to that family for many years. She was, indeed, frequently critical and independent in her remarks; and "has not spared even your Grace and priests of your diocese". And so on, for several pages. Not without cause did historian and archivist, Mary Purcell, term him – "a meddler, who wrapped up his schemes in pious paragraphs"; and Cardinal Cullen perceive him as – "a busy, poor little body, thinking to do good but making mischief".[71]

The dismissal, as Mrs Aikenhead had feared, provided opportunities for such opponents of the congregation to rake up "much odium and scandal".[72] Eventually, "that poor unhappy person", as she described Sr. Ignatius, left Sandymount for England on 8 August 1837. Her brother came for her.[73] From England she went to a convent in Normandy. This appears to have been by Kenney's arrangement. She left it after his death. At Tours, she became a chanoinesse of the Royal Chapter of St Anne of Munich, with the honorary title of countess. From there, in 1847, she wrote to Dr Murray asking to be relieved of her vows and asking forgiveness for "every displeasure and every uneasiness" she had caused him. He granted her request, and she lived out her life as a lay person at Tours.[74]

The family name of Sr M. Ignatius does not appear in references to her in biographies of Mary Aikenhead. She is always referred to by her name in religion or as "Miss X". A clue was provided, in a postscript, as it were, to her story by the English historian of the Scotch, English and Irish Jesuits, Dr Oliver. Writing to Kenney on 10 December 1837, he remarked, almost in passing:

> Until I received your dear friend *Miss Bodenham's* letter on 22 October, I was not aware that she had exchanged the Society of the Sisters of Charity at Sandymount for the Visitation convent at Le Mans. I trust she will be happy.[75]

The reference to her being a "dear friend" indicates that Kenney must have found himself in a very difficult position, indeed, between her claims and those of the revered Mrs Aikenhead. Further investigation demonstrates how difficult that position was, for Eliza Mary Bodenham was the grand-daughter of Thomas Weld of Lulworth Castle who had presented Stonyhurst to the English Jesuits, the niece of Cardinal Thomas Weld, and of John Weld, Kenney's close friend, who had died in 1816 as rector of Stonyhurst.

He managed to maintain good relations with both women until near the very end. Even on 2 June 1837, the day on which the archbishop granted permission to dismiss Sr Ignatius, he joined Mrs Aikenhead and her Sisters at recreation to present her with "an anonymous gift of £525" to be disposed, as she judged, between the House of Refuge and St Vincent's Hospital.[76] His insistence, however, that Sr Ignatius not be sent away from Sandymount till an acceptance had been obtained from another religious body, appears to have caused a palpable coolness between himself and the foundress;[77] though their deep esteem for each other remained undiluted.

Associated with Mary Aikenhead and Mrs John O'Brien, in the apostolate of teaching and assisting the poor in Dublin, was another woman, Miss Fanny Ball, who founded the Irish branch of the Sisters of Loreto. She, too, was to benefit in a special way from Kenney's guidance in the early days of her institute.

SISTERS OF LORETO

Frances Mary Ball, sister of Mrs John O'Brien, was born in 1794. Her father, who had acquired considerable wealth in the silk trade, sent her at the age of nine to a celebrated convent school run by the Ladies of Loreto, or the Institute of the Blessed Virgin Mary. This was the Micklegate Bar convent, York, to which Mary Aikenhead and Alice Walsh were to go in preparation for their Irish undertaking. It was the first convent opened in England (1686) after the Reformation. The institute had originally been founded by Mother Mary Ward for the instruction of youth.

With her father's death in 1808, Frances suspended her education and came home to be a companion to her mother. She was a young woman of considerable charm, gentleness and piety. Dr Murray's friendship with members of her family, led to him becoming her spiritual adviser. She came to believe that she had a call to religious life. She was already familiar with the Loreto way of life in York; while Dr Murray was eager to introduce the Institute of the Blessed Virgin Mary into Ireland to provide quality education for Irish girls. He saw in her desires a means of combining her wishes and his hopes. He arranged for her to enter the novitiate at York, and undergo training and preparation. On 8 September 1814, she received the habit at the Bar convent, taking Teresa as her name in religion. There followed seven years of testing preparation which included, in the ethos of the time, much in the way of humiliations, and in trials of obedience, as a grounding in sanctity.[78]

Mother Teresa Ball returned to Ireland with two novices in 1821. They stayed for a while with the Sisters of Charity; and then moved to the former country seat of Mr Grierson, the "king's printer", in Rathfarnham, outside Dublin.[79] Their new establishment was called Loreto House. After Mother Teresa's return, she was, in the words of one of her biographers, "introduced by Dr Murray to the famous Jesuit, Father Peter Kenney", who "became a staunch friend" and "gave her invaluable help in the organization of the religious life of the new foundation".[80]

Further particulars regarding his "invaluable help" have been given in an earlier chapter.[81] With his second, extended Visitation to the United States, however, his contact with the administration of the Loreto Sisters seems to have greatly declined. While he was away, indeed, the congregation began to expand rapidly, opening boarding, day and free schools; and in 1841 Mother Teresa was to send sisters to India to found the first Loreto foreign mission. Despite their reduced opportunities of contact, she, as indicated in the earlier chapter, continued to look on him to the end of her days as one of her "unequalled friends".[82]

THOSE "CARDINAL POINTS OF SPIRITUAL LIFE"

From the start of his ministry of retreats, tridua, and spiritual conferences, to members of the foregoing congregations, and to the Presentation Sisters, the Ursulines, and others, Kenney, as has been noted previously, placed emphasis on what he termed "the Four Cardinal Points of Spiritual Life". In his elaboration of these, he pointed firmly, in the spiritual theology of the period, towards the goal of spiritual perfection. Such emphasis and direction constituted part of his considerable contribution to the life of religious congregations in Ireland in the first half of the nineteenth century.

"All the rules of interior direction prescribed by ascetics," he declared, "are intended to create and preserve in us *the vita abscondita Christi* [a life hidden in Christ]. And they may be briefly reduced to four points." These, as indicated earlier, were: Recollection, Generosity towards God, the Exercise of the Presence of God, and Purity of Intention. Of the first of these, he wrote:

> Without recollection no progress is made in virtue because it is impossible to pray ... It is the main secret of the spiritual life, to know how to control our thoughts and affections by habits of recollection.[83]

Much of Peter Kenney's career was marked by an effort to preserve "the habit of self-recollection". It was easier to live in that ambience in relative islands of quiet like Bohemia, St Inigoes, and even St Joseph's, Philadelphia; and in returning reluctantly to Ireland he had hoped for something similar, as part of a life devoted to the spiritual and pastoral work for which he always yearned, and which now was also more suited to his asthmatic state and declining agility. Within a short time of his return, however, he found himself, as observed in the previous chapter, saddled once more with overall authority and responsibility, so much so, indeed, that the renewed pressures of administration and the demands of pastoral service combined to burthen his days from early morning to late at night.

XIII

"The modern apostle of Dublin ... and Ireland at large": Confessor, orator and preacher – Censure and esteem

> Mary's prerogative was to bear Christ; so
> 'Tis preachers to convey Him, for they do,
> As angels out of clouds, from pulpits speak,
> And bless the poor beneath, the lame, the weak.
> E. Gosse, "Lines to a Mr Tilman" in *Life of John Donne*

The difficult transition

There was a sharp contrast between that sense of an expanding missionary church in a vast country, where priests were few and the people appreciative of their service, which Kenney experienced in the United States, and the reality of life on his return to Dublin, where his days of busy church work were filled with minutiae and routine amongst a demanding public with a relatively wide choice of priests and churches. Yet, his very commitment to that public, in the confessional and pulpit, together with what were termed his "wise counsels and saintly example" to clergy from far and near, earned him the subsequent ascription – "the modern apostle of Dublin ... and, indeed, to an incalculable extent of Ireland at large".[1]

Immediately following his return, he had sought wider horizons again, as has been seen, but was burthened instead with a further reluctant spell as vice-provincial, a position which the General, on 19 April 1834, trusted he would fill, as was his wont, "with great heartedness and a willing spirit", and that he would find consolation, like himself, in the thought that he occupied "the office of superior out of obedience". Additional grounds for misgiving on Kenney's part were conveyed later in his Paternity's letter when the latter declared that he had learned that Fr St Leger had previously spoken to Fr Aylmer about "his excessive style of living, his dining out till late at night and so on" but without success, and that consequently he required Kenney to "apply an effective rememdy *as soon as possible*" and suggested that as well as being vice-provincial he act as superior of the Dublin residence, in Aylmer's place, or at least make his ordinary residence there. It was a combination of roles which proved incompatible and altogether too onerous at that period in Kenney's life.

The General also directed him towards a critical examination of Clongowes where attention to prayer, the pursuit of perfection and charity, were said to be deficient, and where the rector had changed many things instituted by Kenney and had been careless in the administration of temporal affairs, especially the farm. He concluded his letter with the weighty expectation: "We hope to see, under your direction, the vice-province grow, and become stronger in numbers and spirit."[2]

The prospect of attempting to face down once more his old critics, Aylmer and Esmonde, was far from welcome. Kenney sought, however, to enter on his responsibilities in as detached and relaxed a manner as possible. "I do not wish to decline any share of responsibility that fairly belongs to my office," he informed Esmonde on 19 May, "but neither do I wish to assume any share of that which belongs to another."[3]

His endeavour to calmly mesh together the requirements of the office of vice-provincial and those of superior of a hard-pressed community serving a busy church, were soon upset, however, by imperative requests and disturbing happenings.

Imperative requests – Desolation at happenings

One of the imperative requests came from Dr Michael Slattery, recently consecrated archbishop of Cashel. Early in June 1834, his Grace requested him "as a favour" to give a retreat to the clergy of his diocese about the middle of July, and if that time did not suit him, he would arrange to meet his wishes in every way possible. He realised, Dr Slattery continued, that he was asking "a great deal" in making this request, but he considered that the future success of his ministry in the diocese, and the advancement of religion, would depend on the impression made on the clergy at this retreat, and he applied to Kenney "as the person best calculated to make this first impression". And he concluded with words difficult to resist: "Many of the clergy of this diocese were under your direction at Maynooth, the others know and respect your character, and all would feel inexpressible delight at receiving spiritual instruction from you." There had never been a retreat in the diocese before, the archbishop added, and this one conducted by Kenney would "establish a model" by which future retreats in the diocese would be regulated.[4]

The disturbing happenings came in sad array that summer and autumn, adding their weight to the already depressing load he carried. In June there occurred the decease, after a prolonged illness, of Bishop Doyle. Kenney joined the host of priests and five bishops who participated at the solemn office and high mass at Carlow Cathedral on 19 June, and was one of the three readers of the Lessons.[5] Then on 3 August came the shock of the sudden death in his own community of Fr John Shine, an able and competent young man who was in charge of the Hardwicke Street school. He was struck down by cholera.[6] It seemed like the crowning blow in a distressing year. He gave vent to feelings of deep desolation to John McElroy three days after Shine's death.

"God in his awful and ever blessed providence", he exclaimed, "has touched us to the very core ... with Fr Shine's ... sudden awful death!" Since he came back to Dublin, Kenney continued, he had not been a month without "some serious annoyance, affliction". In January he had learned of the destination of the St Legers. He strove to prevent it, but the General was "inexorable and displeased" with his opposition, and the Almighty allowed his Paternity place the painful burden of authority on his shoulders. Now the very prop of the college planned for Dublin had been taken away and there was no one to replace him from the vice-province's small numbers. But it was not just conditions in the Irish province that weighed him down. He wept, he declared, over what he saw and foresaw in Europe. Fifteen Jesuits, the flower of the Spanish province, had been murdered in the Jesuit college of St Isidore, Madrid; the rest had been dispersed, seeking asylum where they could find it. The Portuguese-French Jesuits had been banished from Portugal. In London, Bishop Brampston had refused permission to the English Jesuits to serve a church presented to them; while, in Dublin, the ultimate grief, it seemed to him that despite "prosperous exterior appearances", the archbishop, hitherto a "sincere, warm friend" was "now only an enemy".

And in this black mood, the litany of gloom was endless: the debt from the church was an incubus upon them; the gentry everyday got poorer, the extent of the beggary on the streets showed forth a frightful mendicity; there were reports of the cruelty of landlords and the resistance of tenants; and a weak government was supported by ultra Whigs, who had no care for religion, and by radical reformers who, apart from O'Connell and his followers, were infidels. "Such is our position," he concluded. "How often have I been tempted to wish that I had not left you. Shall I ever forgive Mr McSherry, whom I so much love, for letting me be sent back!" He, perhaps, thought that he, Kenney, would not have liked to be just a "humble missionary", whereas in St Joseph's of Philadelphia, or at Bohemia, or between both, he would have been the most happy of men. At this point he had the good grace to stop and exclaim – "See what I have written *currente calamo* [a continuous complaint]."[7]

That was the end of the depressing news to McElroy, but it was far from the end of the year's "disturbing happenings". The very next day, Fr Robert O'Ferrall, died unexpectedly, also from cholera. Shortly thereafter, Kenney himself suffered a slight bowel complaint which made the long hours in the confessional on Saturday, and the late masses on Sunday, an additional ordeal and contributed to "the image of death which seemed everywhere around" him.[8] The trials continued. On 4 September, an English Jesuit friend, Fr Pains died. Twelve days later, Fr Gahan, on the Isle of Man, broke his arm. And during the month there was also the news of the death of Fr Stone, of the

English province, and the illness from overwork of Fr Dubuisson at Philadelphia.[9]

The deaths in the community left the church understaffed. More and more work and responsibility fell to him. In October, in response to complaints at his not writing to Rome for a long time, he exclaimed to Thomas Glover: "If they knew that the hour before midnight is often the only one in the 24 left me for the recitation of my office, they would be a little more indulgent." He surely, he continued in what was to become a not infrequent complaint, was not to blame for that "union of such incompatible duties" as resulted from his post in the Society and his station as "a Dublin missionary".

The combined pressures of the "incompatible duties" prevented him visiting Clongowes before Christmas.[10] The demands of the church ministry on his time and attention coming up to, and including Christmas day, brought a very trying year to a close. Not surprisingly, when he wrote on 2 January 1835, to Fr Haly to sympathise with him on the death of his mother, he added: "What trials God has been pleased to reserve for us in the late year, 1834! It was the most melancholy that I have ever passed ... Most sincerely I wish you a more happy year. To me, I assure you, it is a relief not to write anymore, 1834."[11]

Neglect of Roman correspondence; and pastoral pressures

Three days after this, he availed of a relatively quiet time to write once more to Glover. Because of his negligence in writing to the General, he declared, the arrival of a letter from his Paternity on 20 December 1834, occasioned some trepidation. "Before I opened it," he added, with a revealing disclosure of his reverence for the office of General, "I knelt down to ask of God the grace to bear the reproof with becoming humility and patience." After this preparation, he was relieved and much affected by the mild tone of Fr Roothaan's letter, and its evidence of "indulgence and patience".

He then proceeded to emphasise again the incompatibility of the burthen of vice-provincial and the pressures of "missionary labour" in Gardiner Street. The fact that he viewed the church work as "missionary", testified to the importance he attached to it and the zeal with which he approached it. By comparison the writing of official reports in Latin seemed a relatively unimportant drudgery, and yet he was conscious that by the rules of his office and also by virtue of the General's personal request he had an obligation under obedience to write to Rome at specified times. The result was a nagging sense of guilt, which together with the high expectations of Fr Roothaan, his own concern and care for the vice-province in that year of death, illness and overwork, and the exhaustion of his church ministry, combined to produce the inner weariness and despondency mirrored in his letter to McElroy, something not dissimilar to "burn out", or, in the words of a spiritual leader a century later, Brother Roger of Taizé, he was enduring the frightening experience that in giving one's "whole existence for other people" one is "at risk of losing all of oneself".[12] And he was at a loss how to convey his situation.

Consequently, he informed Glover almost despairingly: "Many have been my unquiet moments that I have not kept my rule" regarding letters to Fr Roothaan, "but really, dear Father, it is almost impossible to get anyone living at a distance, and in all situations, to conceive how we are here everlastingly employed." He had so much to write both to Glover and the General that the "miserable half-hour" that he might have free from other duties appeared too short a space of time to begin the task, with the result that with "duty succeeding duty" he was left for months without a day free from missionary labour.

And trying to explain how this could be, he pointed out that because it was the General's own wish that he stop in Dublin this had meant that "all Sundays, and all Saturdays even to midnight, is occupied in the church". He had "to preach oftener than anyone else". And these sermons were long, as was the practice, and required much preparation. "I preached the last Sunday of the year, for instance, in our own church yesterday, and a charity sermon in another church, and tomorrow again in our church of St Francis. But the great labour of day and night is in the confessional. Often, often have I to begin the whole office of the day at 11.00 p.m." As the Christmas labours were now nearly over, he went on, he hoped to be more disengaged and to be regular in his correspondence with the General, and with many others both in Europe, America, and Asia who wrote to him, and with whom he wished earnestly to keep up a correspondence. In the meantime, he prayed his Paternity "to continue his great indulgence". It would not be abused.

And forestalling an obvious objection, he added: "Let it not be said – how did Mr St Leger write so regularly? He had all his time at his own command. He had not even the care of little Tullabeg, since he got his brother made rector. He had no duties of the ministry to perform except a few confessions weekly, and once in the month when a good number came to the *Bona Mors* (sodality).[13] He was in a remote situation free from all incursions from without. "I am the very contrary of all this," he continued "nor is it with nuns, or pious ladies," a reference to St Leger's apostolate, "that my time is spent. *Except on Saturday, I seldom hear an ordinary confession.* The other days are chiefly spent in hearing the general confessions[14] of men, who have either not received the blessed sacrament at all, or have been long absent. I do not look for those people, but when they come on me I have a scruple to refuse them. When I see that with all the opportunities they did not go, how can I hope they will seek another when mortified by my refusal." The death of Mr Shine, and the removal of Mr Curtis, to become rector of Tullabeg, had contributed, he went on, "to the increase of our labours".

He concluded his references to his intensive church work with the words; "It is unpleasant to say so much for oneself, but the necessity of an apology obliges me to state the fact. If the General still wishes me to reside in Dublin, I wish he would order me to spend some weeks, or even months, of the year", besides the time spent on visitation as vice-provincial, "either in Clongowes Wood or Tullabeg. My health and my office of vice-provincial would require this arrangement", which, without the General's order, "I could not so easily carry into effect".[15]

His susceptibility to colds and asthmatic attacks was in evidence a week or so later. Because of a cold, he informed Fr Ferley on 13 January 1835, he would not risk going to Clongowes before the weather became mild and settled. Besides he could not leave Gardiner Street for some time without causing inconvenience to many.[16] This last referred, most likely, to the special preparations for the ceremonies surrounding the blessing of the church.

Recording that important occasion in the history of the restored Irish Jesuits, the *Catholic Penny Magazine* reported that: "On Thursday, 12 February, his Grace, the Most Revd Dr Murray (assisted by almost all the bishops of Ireland then in town) solemnly blessed the elegant new church of St Francis Xavier, Upper Gardiner Street. After the ceremony, the Revd Peter Kenney delivered a most powerful discourse, in which he detailed the labours of the calumniated Society of Jesus, and passed an high eulogium on the late and present archbishops of Dublin, for the patronage they have bestowed upon it."[17]

Little more than a week later again, Lent commenced with its strict fast and limited use of flesh-meat, and its emphasis on the duties of prayer, penance, and works of mercy to the poor.[18] This brought increased work in the confessional; but it also meant, in accordance with the traditional Lenten programme, that at Gardiner Street church "the Revd Dr Kenney, Revd Messrs Aylmer and Haly" preached "every evening (Saturdays excepted) at seven o'clock".[19] Saturdays were excepted because through the day and into the night, the three men were likely to be kept busy in the confessional.

The constant reference to the work of the confessional testified to the strong sense of sin in nineteenth-century Catholicism, a sense which persisted into the late fifties of the twentieth century. Many of the saintly figures of the era, including the Curé d'Ars, devoted endless hours to hearing confessions, and in so doing saw themselves as continuing the healing and consoling work of Jesus Christ and fulfilling his instructions. Kenney was very much in that tradition, and as a Jesuit, or "companion of Jesus", felt himself called in a special way to this ministry; and his sensitivity to, and compassion for others, joined to clear, decisive judgement, made him an eminently popular confessor. Habitually reserved with women, he was indefatigable in his availability to men, especially those beset with difficulties. Numerous priests came to him privately; and in the public church it was said "that men of the highest rank were seen coming out of his confessional weeping, yet joyous; while there was frequently a large number of labouring men, sailors, and police men waiting their turn to enter".[20]

The Lenten months, February and March, were very severe that year. They took their inevitable toll on Kenney at a time of much added pressure at Gardiner Street because of the immensely popular Novena of Grace in honour of St Francis Xavier. He had to admit on 12 March, in a letter to Esmonde: "For the last fortnight a heavy cold has irritated my asthma so much that I did not like to go out to St Francis [novena] at night. I hear that considering the very severe weather, it is well attended. Messrs Aylmer and Haly take it in turns ..." He had been invited, he added, to preach on the 14 May at the consecration of the new abbot of Mount Mellary. He asked Esmonde to take his place.[21]

This last indisposition, however, enabled him to catch up on some outstanding business. In the same letter to Esmonde, he dealt clearly with disciplinary difficulties which had arisen in Clongowes.

Problems with Clongowes and Esmonde

The first of these difficulties regarded the fall off in the attendance of masters at litanies on Saturday; and the second, a matter of "far greater importance", which involved the good reputation of the order, was the practice of card-playing. At the last diocesan retreat, Dr Murray had expressed to him, he declared, his concern at the practice of some of the diocesan clergy playing until late in their own rooms and in the houses of lay people "to the great injury of that good name" which was "so requisite for the success of their ministry". What would he say, Kenney asked, if he knew that the same scenes were realised in Jesuit houses? He had heard many stories, he continued firmly, "but what mode has the provincial of ascertaining these facts but through the local superiors, and if they are so much afraid of making inquiry, as you state yourself to be, how can the statements be brought home to the individuals? I fear that you are too timid on these matters".[22]

A few days later, the General also was writing about Clongowes, and other houses in the province, bringing to his attention what was being reported in consultors' letters.

There was said to be, he observed, a need for an inspiring spiritual father at Clongowes, who would give talks on spiritual matters on a regular basis. The government of the superior was described as lacking in urbanity, partly because he was by temperament pernickety even about trivial matters, and partly because there were so few meetings with the consultors of the house. Again, the poor management of economic affairs, and especially of the farm, was mentioned. In Dublin, the General continued, the heavy debt on the house was unlikely to be removed for a long time, given the domestic economy being followed there. Above all, he wished to bring to his notice the frequent complaint that the vice-province was not being governed according to the rules of the Society in that meetings with consultors were not taking place; and as a result of this, rectors were ruling without reference to their consultors, and with a loss of "that courtesy and pleasantness in government so highly commended by the institute" and, indeed, with a loss of stability and order.[23]

In subsequent months, with the advent of milder weather, Kenney undertook his visitation of Clongowes and Tullabeg. At the former, he found much to criticise in the life style of the community. This was linked to Esmonde's poor judgement and overall ineffectiveness as rector. While Kenney was in America, he had almost stunned the vice-provincial with a proposal for the dissolution of the college! Robert St Leger, fortunately, responded with considerable vigour. The General, he stated, would not think of acceding to such a proposal "until it was clear that every means of supporting it had been adopted, and in vain adopted". And this was not the situation. Much had to be done that had not yet been attempted. And he went on to state very bluntly some of the things that had to be done by Esmonde and the Clongowes Jesuits.

"Your community must lay aside their lordly ideas, and assume ideas more becoming men whose profession is poverty, and who *are actually poor.*" He went on to make specific recommendations involving the disposal of all horses except those needed for agriculture, a reduction in kitchen and house staff, a cut-back in the number of milch cows, the virtual abandonment of large dinner parties, and the employment of a good carver in the scholars refectory which would save many pounds of meat daily. And as for Esmonde himself, he had more than once admired, he declared, the facility with which he could find £10 or £14 for a stove that could be dispensed with, when, at the same time he was deploring most pathetically his poverty. These were a few of his reflections, St Leger concluded, "think of them to God's greater glory". It was the kind of direct talk that Esmonde understood, and that Kenney could seldom use; though it is not clear that it produced any marked change in Esmonde's style of government.

Kenney, on his return from the stringency of mission life in North America, was taken aback, as has been indicated, by the absence of poverty in the life-style of many of his brethren. On his visitation of Clongowes now, in 1835, he found it necessary to criticise aspects of the community's way of life, and to lay down definite regulations to be followed. These also, however, do not appear to have been taken seriously. On 11 June 1835, he was moved to write censoriously to the rector.

He understood, he said, that Mr H. Rorke, when in Dublin some time ago, "went to a private ball. I can hardly believe it." And what of the "disedifying folly" on Monday night last in preparing a meat supper after an extra dinner at 6 o'clock. In face of actions of this kind, he went on, "to what purpose are regulations, or visitations?" In the light of the many abuses, he was now determined to hold fast to his views against having a villa, or vacation, away from

Clongowes. It was Esmonde's own creation, he continued, he might do with it what he liked. He, Kenney, would not interfere in his area of authority, but no power under the General would get him to approve. He could not do otherwise, as all reports indicated that this villa was "little less than an annual scandal".

With improved health, he tended once more to over extend himself. At the start of July, he conducted a retreat at Maynooth; and kept working through that month, and through August and September, without any break. Indeed, on 10 December he was to remark that he had not had time to make his own retreat, let alone take a holiday.[26] Inevitably, with the approach of winter, illness returned. On 12 November, Haly writing to Aylmer in the Isle of Man, observed that "our provincial has been confined to his bed with a heavy cold, which he caught by going bareheaded the other day into the vaults of Clarendon Street chapel" at an internment. Yet prior to that, he seems to have been alert and effective. For Haly also commented: "Fr Kenney's sermon on Sunday last (on purgatory) was *beyond the beyonds*. I certainly never heard a sermon of his I liked so well, and this seemed to be the general feeling. It made a powerful impression."[27]

The fact that Haly was writing to Aylmer in the Isle of Man, pointed to developments in that area which added considerably to Kenney's concerns during 1835 and 1836. The tensions between the English vicars apostolic and the English Jesuits had spilled over to the Irish Jesuits on the Manx mission.

In December 1835, he travelled thither himself, experiencing severe sea sickness on the journey.[28] Some weeks later he provided a summary of the mission – its origins and recent occurrences – in a letter to the rector of Stonyhurst college.

The mission to the Isle of Man: beginning and end

More than ten years ago, Kenney declared, Fr Gahan had yielded to the entreaties of the Catholics in the Isle of Man and settled amongst them as a resident missioner. He was the first such for a generation. So completely had the people been left to themselves, that the vicar apostolic for the region gave faculties to the archbishop of Dublin for any priest who would go to visit them. This induced some priests to go in the summer for a month or so. By one of them a chapel was built in a quarry a mile from Douglas and a small house for the missioner. Gahan, by means of funds collected in Ireland, purchased a theatre in Douglas to be transformed into a chapel, and he built from the ground a smaller chapel at Castletown. He assured the then Jesuit vice-provincial that the then vicar-apostolic, Dr Penzwick, had given him leave to open the chapels and had acknowledged them to be the property of the Society of Jesus.

When Gahan fell ill and returned to Ireland, Kenney sent Aylmer in his place in November 1834. He decided to open the new church at Douglas right away. Kenney, being assured by Gahan that he had leave from the former vicar apostolic to open it, gave his consent. Before Aylmer could open it, however, Dr Thompson, representing the vicar apostolic, wrote to prevent him doing so.

Subsequently the vicar-apostolic himself, Dr Briggs, stated that the chapel could be opened provided three conditions were fulfilled. These required, Kenney stated, that he and the incumbent sign a statement agreeing that a trustee be appointed by the bishop; that the bishop retain his right to nominate the missioner, when he chose to exercise it; and that the Society of Jesus would not claim or receive more than it had laid out on the premises.

Kenney wrote to Dr Briggs requesting that "the opening now daily expected" not be delayed, but that it be allowed to take place on "a solemn promise that no advantage would be taken by the concession" to support any right of the Society which he did not recognise. The bishop refused and rigorously demanded that the conditions be signed before the chapel could be opened. "This I will not do," Kenney continued, "so that I fear that our mission there is at an end." He would be most happy to make over all the property in it to Stonyhurst, if Mr Norris, the provincial, would take charge of the mission and make an accommodation with the bishop.[29]

Fr John Bird, the rector of Stonyhurst, replied on 3 February 1836, to say that they had discussed his letter at length and regretted that he had not got approval of the establishments in writing from the previous vicar apostolic. As matters stood, they were of the opinion that he should give up the property to the bishop immediately, requiring that he pay what was expended in the purchase and in the building, and also for the maintenance of Fr Gahan, or else requiring a legal instrument which might bind his lordship to this payment when called on. "Be assured," Bird warned, "that if you rely on verbal promises you will never be repaid." Dr Briggs, he concluded, was opposed to the religious orders making any increase in their establishments.[30]

It was not left to Kenney to finalise negotiations regarding the Manx mission. His protracted neglect of his official letters had worn thin the patience of the General. Bird's letter, indeed, contained an ominous reminder. While at Rome recently, he had done all he could to appease Fr General, he declared, who was much hurt at Kenney's long silence. Fr Roothaan, Bird cautioned, was "very particular on the subject of constant communication" that he might "be perfectly acquainted with everything, good and bad". He was also "suffering much from sciatica".[31]

The warning went unheeded. Kenney, shortly after hearing from Bird, was fully occupied, together with the priests of his community – Frs Aylmer, Ferguson, Haly, McDonnell and Meagher with the demands of the Lenten season, and with the special novenas in March to St Francis Xavier and St Patrick, and then with the Holy Week sermons, ceremonies and confessions, culminating in expansive celebrations on Easter Sunday. During that week, incidentally, the church choir and the now well publicised organ came into their own. The organ had been built originally for a great musical festival in Westminster Abbey at a cost of 1000 guineas, and, according to the *Irish Catholic Directory*, 1836, was "purchased by the Revd Gentlemen of the church for £800".[32] In the midst of all this activity, communication with Rome was yet again neglected.

His Paternity's long-suffering forbearance had not been helped by his sciatica. The feast of St Patrick served to focus his frustration at the absence of information from his Irish vice-provincial. Conscious of Kenney's performance in America, he could not understand how he could not combine his church work with care of a vice-province which numbered at most sixty men: some 25 priests, 15 brothers, and 15-20 scholastics, many of whom were studying abroad. Clearly disappointed, he addressed him on 17 March 1836, in a manner Kenney had never before experienced from a General of the Society. His letter was both a severe reproof and an attempt to re-stimulate Kenney's wide vision of the role of the Irish church in the English speaking world.

Stinging reprimand, and ultimatum

"I wrote to your Reverence," the General stated, "on 31 October last year and the 21 January this year. The last by 'express mail'. And now, after two months, I am still waiting. Be assured how this state of affairs must end. I've had three meetings with the assistants regarding your vice-province and your inexplicable silence. At this stage, I've been considering the appointment of another vice-provincial, and the dispatching of letters patent to Fr Curtis to publish them ... Since, however, there is rooted in my mind the memory of your services to the Society, and I greatly desire to maintain your authority, and since such an unwonted mode of acting is repugnant to me ... I delay the completion and dispatch of that letter to Fr Curtis for a short while, hoping that this ultimatum will provide a remedy." He went on to say that he had in mind to designate Fr Bracken, vice-provincial, but would desist from doing so if he heard from Kenney within a month and a half of this day of his patron saint.

He then proceeded to put matters even more starkly; hinting at amalgamation with the English province if matters did not improve greatly in Ireland. The Irish mission was erected into a vice-province at Kenney's request in 1829, and the hope was that within a short time it would be declared a province. But since then, there was not progress but deterioration. "Good Lord!" he continued, "at a time when there is so great a hope of extending the Society in those provinces in which English is the native language, and from them recruiting men to spread the divine glory in oriental and American missions, in Ireland not only is the Society not enlarged but is rushed to ruin by some of its sons. What a great loss of souls; what a neglect of the glory of God! ... Can we, who must give a very strict account of our administration, view this situation in silence?"

Kenney must respond to his requirements without delay, Roothaan concluded. If he wished to be relieved of his burden, he would be entirely freed. But he wished him to be liberated in the customary manner of the Society, without loss of honour, and protecting his reputation and authority. If, however, he persisted in his silence, he would post that letter on 3 May. "Whatever upset and embarrassments arise from that, your Reverence must ascribe to yourself. May the Lord judge between you and me."[33]

The General evidently had reports from consultors, and perhaps other members of the vice-province, which made him very concerned about aspects of religious life among Irish Jesuits. What precisely these concerns were is not clear, apart from his earlier references to life style and abuses of poverty. It also seemed that Kenney had made little or no effort to prevent the "deterioration", and, of course, had not even bothered to write about the problems or provide any clarification on the state of affairs. Not surprisingly, Roothaan felt he had no option but to remove his good friend, if he did not soon hear from him.

Allowing for Kenney's commitments at Gardiner Street, and the General's hunger for details which made long letters in Latin a considerable ordeal, his *protracted* neglect of his obligation to write remains something of a mystery. He did reply this time, as will appear, though the letter does not seem to have survived. Because of this, it is not clear what impact the General's letter had. A fortnight later, writing to Mulledy at Georgetown, 4 April 1836, Kenney mentioned that Rome was still quite dissatisfied with his level of communication, but he did not seem unduly upset about it.

He who had always been so sensitive to any criticism from the General, now had reached a point, it seemed, where almost any change was welcome from what he saw as an intolerable situation. He could not fulfil both the roles assigned him by Fr Roothaan. The Gardiner Street position was more than a full time occupation, but it appealed to him; the overall responsibility for Clongowes, Tullabeg, Hardwicke Street, the Isle of Man, as well as Gardiner Street, was more than he could accomplish at this stage in his career, and he partly recoiled from it. So, having requested that he be released from one or the other, without success, he appears to have largely concentrated on the task which was more immediately apostolic and congenial. And in this context, the continuous failure to write the official letters appears almost like a request, however unconscious, for removal from the burden of vice-provincial; though he persisted in ascribing his silence to the great demands of work at Gardiner Street – demands, indeed, which were linked to the national reputation he had personally acquired as a spiritual director and confessor.

It has to be added, however, that it was not just correspondence with the General that was neglected. In the same letter to Mulledy, he apologised for his long silence and gave the demands of his church work as the excuse. In the process, he provided further details on the intensity of his work life at this time, as well as some information on the wider concerns of the vice-province.

"My silence is not a special neglect of duty towards my friends at Georgetown," he wrote. "It is my misfortune at this moment to have almost every friend I have in Europe, Asia, and America complaining of me: and none more *bitterly*, than those whom I ought most respect in Italy!" The fault lay with daily increasing and urgent duties. And he continued: "You can have no idea of our constant occupations here; and they are the more unavoidable, because they arise from the position which we have taken with the public, which considers every member of the Society as their own servant, and they are literally disedified if they are not every moment at (their) command. My office in the Society is a mere name in their eyes; and limited as is the sphere of its duties in this country, I have no time to think even of them: so completely am I occupied with the duties of *missionarius urbanus* [an urban missionary]. Saturdays and Sundays are totally devoted to the church; and the rest of the week, confessions, either in the church or house, keep us occupied many hours in the forenoon; and during Lent from dinner to near midnight. And these confessions, I assure you, *non sono quelle delle monache – basta* [are not like those of nuns – enough!]." The demands of the church, he concluded, together with those of the Hardwicke Street school, would require ten men, not just six as at present.[34]

Further information about his relations with the General, and the "mystery" of his not complying with his Paternity's requests, were indicated in a letter to Aylmer on 1 May 1836. The latter had gone to Clongowes, it seems, to help out in the absence of Esmonde, who was in London for medical treatment, and of Dinan, who was ill, and also for reasons of his own health.

Having expressed his pleasure that "country air and exercise" was having such a good effect on him, Kenney referred to a letter which Esmonde in England had received from the General, and which contained "a complaint against me and you". His Paternity termed his, Kenney's, silence an "*explicabile mysterium*". Kenney continued:

> I wrote to him at length by Fr Bird. I wrote the beginning of the present month,[35] but he is not satisfied with either because these letters do not contain the particulars which he wants. And part of the *mysterium* is that I am silent *because I do not know them myself*, and I am waiting until I can obtain them in a satisfactory way. Then, the everlasting and ever increasing duties that are connected with this church leave me, I confess, less time than I ought to give to the affairs of the vice-province, and I find it impracticable to liberate myself from these occupations. If I constantly deny myself, some one is sure to be offended, or some person sent away that ought to be admitted; and if I see those

who come, in nine cases out of ten it is not possible to refuse to assist the poor applicant.

His Paternity, he went on, required as many letters as if he was quietly seated in Tullabeg without a visitor or a call. He feared that Fr Roothaan might now go so far as to send a Visitor, or maybe a vice-provincial from England.[36]

Happily demoted

On 19 May, the General appointed the rector at Tullabeg, Fr Patrick Bracken, as vice-provincial. He instructed him to ensure the accurate observance of the rules of the Society, and required him to brief him "accurately each month on the state of affairs".[37] More than four months later, 3 October, Fr Roothaan was to write him to complain that he had not heard from him since July! Monthly reports were intolerably frequent by Irish standards, it would seem.[38]

Roothaan was careful to avoid any suggestion of public censure on Kenney in making the new appointment. He made him one of the four consultors to Fr Bracken;[39] and subsequently, he made it clear that he wished him to stay on as superior of the Gardiner Street community.[40] On 22 June, Kenney wrote to express his gratitude to him for "liberating" him from the burden of governing the vice-province, and to convey how much he valued his new freedom.[41]

Occupation and health

More work, however, rushed in to fill whatever space was vacated. On 2 July he wrote to Fr Bracken regretting that he would not be able to visit him at Tullabeg on 30 July as he had intended. He was obliged to give a retreat at Thurles (his response to Dr Slattery), and was also "unhappily pledged to Dr MacHale" to preach at the consecration of his new cathedral at Tuam during August. He had to refuse a late request for a personal retreat from Dr Murphy of Cork. He added that he felt his health really declining "under the labours of the confessional, particularly those at night", yet one could only do one's duty "to the middle or lower classes" by being there in the evening.[42]

This reference to "middle or lower classes" seems to be his only express reference to class distinctions. His letters in these years, indeed, are, if possible, even more sparing than earlier letters regarding secular matters. The literary, social and political life of Dublin and the country might not have existed, so far as his extant correspondence is concerned. One would never have guessed that the sound and excitement of the railway age had commenced just a few streets away, with the opening of the line from Dublin to Kingstown (Dun Laoghaire) in December 1834, and that that very summer of 1836, from May to August, some 520,000 people were conveyed on it.[43] It is only from the frequent references to the pressure of work and the importunity of people that one gets an inkling of the effect of the expansion of Dublin's population: an increase of 50,000 in the years between 1820 and 1840.[44] But there is nothing about the squalor of huddled humanity in the north west quarter of the city, not all that far from Gardiner Street and its adjoining squares housing the merchant and official classes, nor of the oppressive aspects of work in the confessional – the sour, noisome odours, and the physical discomfort of long hours of concentrated attention in a cramped space in an unheated church.

Corresponding again

The removal of the onus of official letters, however, seems to have provided scope for re-establishing contacts with distant friends. Thus, during August, he sent a letter to Fr James McCarthy, at St Joseph's church, Philadelphia, by means of a returning resident of that city; and straightway asked for tidings of Fr Dubuisson, of Georgetown, Frederick, and the new diocese of Pittsburgh. Of Ireland, the only news, he remarked, concerned church building: "the only proof of amendment we see in the conduct of Irish Catholics"! Among the buildings particularly mentioned were the cathedral of Meath, and the opening of the "grand cathedral of Tuam" by Dr McHale.[45]

He also wrote to William McSherry, who replied with a variety of information and spoke of a policy "of opening schools or colleges in preference to missions"; and, reflecting his own burdens as superior, remarked that he envied Kenney's "present happiness".[46] The latter also found time to compile a report for the archbishop of Cashel on the state of religion in the new state of Mississippi, for which his Grace had received a request for priests.[47] And in November 1836, he got around to the laborious, but to him important task of replying to the English secular priest, Dr George Oliver, mentioned earlier, a former classmate of his at Stonyhurst, who was actively engaged in his Collections towards illustrating the *Biography of the Scotch, English, and Irish members, SJ* (1838), and depended on him for much of his Irish material.

Writing from Clongowes, on 13 November 1836, and attributing his delay to the long hours of work in Dublin, and an accumulation of letters to be answered "from the four quarters of the globe",[48] he was at pains to explain why he found great difficulty in giving exact answers to Oliver's queries.

> It will surprise you to know that we are wholly destitute of documents in any regular shape concerning my predecessors in the Irish mission. No catalogues, lists, notes etc. If any were kept by members of the ancient Society, they have all been nearly lost The caution which the penal statutes, and the jealous activity of our enemies, had inspired, seems to have made them dread to keep any memorandum of their former association.

He then proceeded to give such information as he had garnered himself concerning the members of the old Society, as well as information on current members.[49]

Some years later, the same Dr Oliver was to speak of Kenney as "a preacher of the highest order", and to single out his performance this year, at the dedication of Tuam cathedral, 18 August 1836, as an occasion when he had particularly "delighted and edified" people of different religious denominations, and had his great ability "justly celebrated".[50]

That ability has been touched on in treating of different periods of his life – in his youth, as a young priest and in relation to the Sisters of Charity, subsequently in the United States, and in the 1820s in Ireland when he occupied the pulpit on many of the notable occasions: the panegyric on Dr Troy in 1823, the consecration sermon of Dr Crolly of Down and Connor in 1825, the first appeal for the Propagation of the Faith ever preached in Dublin, and, of course, during the great Jubilee of 1826. His preaching was such an essential part of his influence and ministry, and won so much acclaim, that it evokes questions as to his style and comparative stature; and these may best be addressed at this point in his story, since the one or two people who spoke most at length of him as preacher and orator first heard him during the 1830s.

THE ORATOR AND PREACHER

By the 1830s the scrawny young clergymen, whom Grattan and other connoisseurs of public speaking came to hear, had become, in the stilted grandiloquent language of Dr Robert ffrench Whitehead, vice-president of Maynooth, 1835–72, a "large, though not corpulent figure" who had a fine voice and "spoke slowly and deliberately like a man who had been used to rule society".[51] At that stage he was "one of the greatest celebrities of Ireland ... a man of noble mien" who "had the bearing of a great man", and was "generally called ... the great Father Kenney".[52]

Another Maynooth man, possibly its most distinguished professor of theology in the nineteenth century, Dr Patrick Murray, provided, in the late 1850s, a far more informative and penetrating commentary on Kenney in the course of an essay, which was published posthumously in the *Irish Ecclesiastical Record* (1891) under the title – "Some Recollections of Father Peter Kenney, SJ, as a Preacher".[53]

"Although nearly twenty years have passed away," he wrote, "since I saw or heard Fr Kenney, I have a very distinct recollection of him." The "first trace of his luminous and powerful mind" he had encountered was in the second or third year of his course at Maynooth, which he had entered in August 1829, when, as noted earlier, he came across some of his manuscript meditations. Kenney conducted the September retreat towards the end of his course, and subsequently he heard him several times when conducting the July retreat for priests in the college. "The last time I ever heard him," he stated, "was in Gardiner Street, two or three years before his death, on the feast of St Francis Xavier."

He greatly surpassed the best of pulpit orators he, Murray, had heard. "His eloquence was not only superior in degree; it was of a different order." In writing down his memories of him, he sought to revive and relive the past as carefully as he could, Murray continued, and was not conscious of using the language of exaggeration.

Orator: "The O'Connell of the pulpit"

"The only other orator whom I ever thought of comparing him to," Murray went on, "was Daniel O'Connell." While both were yet living, he remarked to a very intelligent friend on Fr Kenney's great powers, that he was "the O'Connell of the pulpit". The friend agreed, expressing his surprise that the resemblance had never occurred to him. The reason, Murray thought, was that ordinarily men "set off pulpit orators against pulpit orators" and "do not think of searching for comparisons out of the species".

He then continued:

> Overwhelming strength and allsubduing pathos, were the leading, as they were the common, characteristics of these two extraordinary men. I say nothing of clearness, precision, and those other conditions ... without which all seeming, or so-called eloquence is mere hurdy-gurdy chattering. Also, I say nothing of O'Connell's inimitable and irresistible humour. There are, undoubtedly, certain occasions on which this talent may be exercised in the pulpit; but Fr Kenney, if he possessed it, never in the least degree displayed it. I never saw a more serious countenance than his on every occasion of my hearing him. Not solemn, not severe, but serious, and attractively and winningly so.
>
> There he stood – or sat, as the case might be – as if he had a special commission direct from heaven, on the due discharge of which might depend his own salvation, and that of every soul present. Indeed, so deeply did he seem to be penetrated with the importance of his sacred theme; so entirely did the persuasion of that importance display itself in his whole manner, that his discourses appeared to be the simple utterances of what his heart and soul had learned, or digested, in a long and absorbing meditation before the crucifix. That they often were, in fact, such utterances, I have no doubt whatever; one instance of this I once, by mere accident, happened to witness with my own eyes.

The significance of this last is not clear. It may refer to Kenney's spontaneous, or apparently spontaneous, outpouring of direct prayer in the course of some of his sermons. One elderly prelate used recall "the overmastering tenderness and vehemence of his apostrophies to the crucifix, which he delivered with streaming eyes on some occasions".[54]

"In another point," Murray continued, "he also strikingly resembled O'Connell. He never indulged in those poetic flights of fancy which delight only, or mainly, for their own sake"; and which, in fact, were not to be found in Demosthenes or Cicero, in Chrysostom or Bourdaloue. "Imagination he, of course, had, and of a high order, too; otherwise, he could never have been a true orator. But it was imagination subservient, not dominant, penetrating the main idea as a kindly spark of life, not glittering idly round about it." He also, of course, "had great felicity of diction, ... using the very words and phrases which above all others exactly suited the thought, and set it off in the best light; so that the substitution of any words would be at once felt as an injury ..."

"Real eloquence," Murray judged, had to be "the offspring of genius, but of genius well cultivated and tutored." And even men of exalted piety were obliged to cultivate their natural powers, and work as earnestly and assiduously in doing so as if success depended entirely on their own exertions – and then calmly leave the whole issue in the hands of God, as if all depended entirely on him. To some, the labour was protracted and severe, but to the really gifted it was, he surmised, a labour of love. However that might be, Kenney had, like O'Connell, "attained that highest perfection of his art", which consisted in "so appearing that no one dreams of any culture, or art, having been used".

"Fr Kenney, like O'Connell, used hardly any gesture," Murray went on. "His voice was powerful, and at the same time pleasing; but I do not remember to have ever heard from him any of those soft, pathetic tones sometimes used by O'Connell ... the sound of which, even at this distant period, seems still to vibrate in my ears."

Preacher

Turning more particularly to Kenney as a preacher, rather than orator, he paid a striking tribute:

> Fr Kenney was eminently a theological preacher, and this too without the slightest tinge of that pedantry and affectation always so offensive to good taste, but peculiarly so in the pulpit. Indeed, he was the only preacher I ever heard who possessed the marvellous power of fusing the hardest and most abstruse scholasticisms into forms that at once imparted to them clearness and simplicity, without in the least degree lessening their weight and dignity.

He presented this characteristic of him partly from what he witnessed himself, and partly from what he heard from others. Thus, for example, he heard a very competent judge speak many years ago of a sermon of this kind preached by Kenney on the mystery of the Trinity in, he thought, Gardiner Street. Again, "a sermon which he preached in Belfast, at the consecration of the late Archbishop Crolly as bishop of Down and Connor (1825), was one of his most successful efforts. It was on "The Triumphs of the Church"; and so powerful was the impression made by it, that for many years afterwards the substance of it used to be recounted by some who had not heard it themselves, but received the report from those who had. I myself once heard one of those outlines from the lips of a friend, who was too young to be present on the occasion, or to comprehend the subject fully if he had been present."

And concluding, rather wistfully, Murray wrote:

> It was only in their declining years – within the last ten years of their lives – that I heard either of these two great men, O'Connell and Father Kenney. If the Odyssey of the life of each shone with such brightness, what must have been the glowing splendour of its Iliad?[55]

There was some quality in Kenney as a preacher that evoked enthusiastic high flown responses, whether from sophisticated hearers like Murray, or Vincent Fitzpatrick, of Eccles Street, a devoted O'Connellite, who was wont to say – "to hear Fr Kenney, when prepared, is the greatest treat the human understanding can enjoy",[56] or from the earthier audience at Rahan, Co. Offaly, who judged that "he flogged the world for a preacher!"[57] And even the once critical Right Hon. R. More O'Ferrall, at the end of his days spoke of him as "a most approachable man; very strong minded, steady and gentle", who was noted for "very well structured sermons, powerfully presented".[58]

In Vincent Fitzpatrick's eulogy, there was an implication – "when prepared" – which others have echoed, namely, that when obliged to speak without due preparation he was not particularly impressive.[59] As against that, Fr Robert St Leger remarked on a splendid discourse to the boys at Clongowes with only a few minutes reflection; and he was said to cope so well with impromptu discussions when dining out, that local clergy were reputed to set genial traps in order to hear him speak on some difficult topics.[60]

Whatever about relatively poor performances as a preacher at times, and with his demanding schedule, especially in the 1830s, there had to be some such, there is no denying the impressive standard of attainment over nearly thirty years, and no denying his capacity to move people deeply. He had a strong awareness that the way to reach a congregation was through the heart; and that was "commonly reached", as John Henry Newman would later say, "not through the reason, but through the imagination, by means of direct impressions, by the testimony of facts and events, by history, by description".[61] Hence, as Murray put it, compared to other pulpit orators of his day, "his eloquence was not only superior in degree; it was of a different order".[62]

In August 1836, then, Kenney's performance at the dedication of Tuam cathedral was yet another milestone in the long procession of memorable sermons to grace special occasions; only, according to Dr Oliver's report, it evoked even more glowing, not to say fulsome, responses than usual.

Tributes at Tuam

Oliver's brief account was written with gusto: "As a preacher of the highest order, Fr Kenney is justly celebrated. At the dedication of Tuam Cathedral, 18 August 1836 ... he preached before the Archbishops of Armagh, Tuam and Cashel, the Bishops of Raphoe, Meath, Kildare and Leighlin, Kilmore, Killaloe, Galway, Killala, Elphin, Down, and Ardagh, and an immense confluence of clergy, and an overflowing audience of distinguished Catholic and Protestant laymen.

"At the public dinner after the ceremony, his Grace of Tuam, Dr MacHale, in proposing the health of the illustrious preacher, who had delighted and edified an auditory composed of every class of Christians, was pleased to add; 'the pathos with which the truths of religion had been delivered that day, showed they were the outpouring of the spirit which almost appeared under divine inspiration'. His Grace descanted on the profound humility of the preacher, resembling that of John the Baptist, and observed that in the long and useful career of this humble Father, he had always been careful to throw the oil of charity over the troubled waters of society, and ever most strenuous in recommending that all denominations of Christianity should unite in promoting peace and goodwill amongst their fellowmen."[63]

Amidst the hyperbole, expected on such occasions, and especially in that era, the reference to charity and humility was not unexpected. Kenney was known for his care in avoiding offence to others, and his dislike of uncharitable remarks; and, as is patently obvious by now, he held authority reluctantly, and carried unobtrusively and unassumingly such power and influence as he had.[64] The express reference to fostering unity across Christian denominations, however, was new; though scarcely surprising given his success with diverse acquaintances in the United States, and his closeness to Archbishop Murray, who displayed a readiness to work with all shades of opinion, and every government department, to achieve betterment for Catholics.

The really remarkable thing at first sight was such a glowing testimonial from a bishop known as the "Lion of the West", with a reputation for pugnacity and rudeness, even to fellow prelates, and who viewed with suspicion, rather than "peace and goodwill", all the intentions and efforts of English Protestant governments. Once again, it said much for Kenney's capacity to relate to, and befriend, very different people, and for the manner in which he had persistently sought to apply Ignatius Loyola's advice to always endeavour to put the best interpretation on what the other person said, and, if drawn into an argument, to so participate "that the truth may appear, and not to get the upper hand". But the testimonial was also a reminder of McHale's capacity for personal warmth – he had happy memories of Kenney's gracious welcome to Clongowes in earlier days – and of his potential for flexibility, even in theology, which, just a few years previously, won the admiration of the three renowned Catholic liberals, Lamennais, Lacordaire, and Montalembert, when he met them in Rome in 1832, and the admiration of the celebrated theologian Ignaz von Doellinger, whom he visited at Munich on the way home.[65]

From the triumph at Tuam, it was back once more to the daily grind and expanding work at Gardiner Street, and to the mounting tensions within the Sisters of Charity which, as has been seen, spilled over into the next year.

FOCUSED VISION AND PRESSURE OF WORK

The release from provincial authority which increased his correspondence, brought no increase in his references to political and public events. The decision of the Great Orange Lodge of Ireland to dissolve in 1836; the death of O'Connell's wife, Mary, whom he had known; and the excitement generated by the succession of the eighteen-year-old Victoria; all went unmentioned. This seemingly exaggerated remove from public affairs, was related directly to the increased volume of church work he was carrying. The withdrawal of Aylmer to the Isle of Man, and of Fr Haly to be rector of Clongowes, removed two of the main props of St Francis Xavier church. The result, where Kenney was concerned, was that as well as having care of the community and finances, as superior, he had, in addition to his usual ministry, an increased number of sermons, and the overall responsibility for the church – including the organising of rotas for masses, sermons and hours of confession – which had formerly fallen to Aylmer.

Not surprisingly, then, when he received a letter on 8 February 1837, asking for his views on a debate in the House of Commons the previous day, during which a Mr Sergeant Jackson MP, according to a report in the *Times*, stated that a friend of his had been told by "the head of Clongowes College" that the Catholic bishops hoped and expected that the Roman Catholic religion would become the established religion of both England and Ireland, he replied that his duties did not allow him "to give much attention, or time, to political matters", and often many days passed without his reading a single article in any newspaper. He, then, as might be expected, went on to say that if he were the supposed "head of Clongowes College", the statement was utterly destitute of truth. He never uttered such a sentiment, and never entertained such a hope or expectation, and he was sure that the same could be said of any other head of Clongowes. Besides, to implicate the Catholic bishops on a supposed sentiment of the head of Clongowes was quite ridiculous: Were the bishops to be implicated "in every folly that might chance to occupy the head of Clongowes College"?[66]

The Isle of Man and sad partings

Some days after this, there came sad news from the Isle of Man. The previous year, one of his two companions in restarting the Irish mission, William Dinan, had died at Clongowes. Now, a letter from Fr Aylmer announced that the other companion, for whom he had a special fondness, Matthew Gahan, had died.[67] The death had caused much upset on the island, where the members of the Catholic population resented the offhand treatment he had received from the bishop, and the latter's total disregard of his work and zeal. The obituary in the Manx newspaper was embarrassingly accusatory, remarking of Gahan that "he had the pain and sorrow of seeing his pious endeavours frustrated, his labours unappreciated, and himself unrewarded by those who say they are of Christ, but are of the synagogue of Satan".[68]

Kenney himself was deeply upset, and when the vice-provincial, Fr Bracken, wrote to tell him of his exchange of letters with the bishop, Dr Briggs, after Gahan's death, he replied that he was glad that Bracken had said so much of "good Fr Gahan"; and added – "I should like much that the bishop knew the strong reasons which lead us to fear that his severity ... and his indifference to the good man's labours have precipitated him into the grave." His Lordship, as he had admitted to Bracken, was indeed "guilty of an error of judgement in proposing his conditions, and of a greater (one) in making the opening of the chapel dependent on them, even after an express declaration that no advantage should be taken of that concession". Kenney considered it desirable to part with his lordship in peace and unity, particularly as the General's instructions did not permit contesting anything with him; but he would send Dr Briggs an account, as exact and well attested as possible, "of all Fr Gahan expended on the old chapel and in the erection of the new ones". And, after a great deal more advice, much of which Fr Bracken followed, he concluded with the recommendation that since they were to give up the property, the sooner they did so the better.[69]

His last gesture to his old friend and early companion was to give him a place in history. Dr Oliver, after receiving his account of Matthew Gahan's life, wrote to thank him for his valuable information, the substance of which he had embodied in his articles. He went on: "This good Father deserves the title of the Apostle of the Isle of Man; and how providential it was that, in his last illness" he had Fr Aylmer visit him.[70]

Fall-off at Gardiner Street

Oliver's letter was written in December 1837. For Kenney the year had brought not only additional work at Gardiner Street, but also falling attendances and falling income, and this was of serious concern because of the church's debt. Even the celebrated Novena of Grace was down. The numbers were much less than on many other occasions, he observed, and the collections produced little more than a fourth of what had been obtained in 1834. And he had never seen so few present in the church on St Patrick's day.[71] Because of the shortage of eloquent, established preachers, the provincial made Haly available from Clongowes to preach the three hours agony sermon on Good Friday. There was a good crowd, Kenney reported, but still down on other years, partly due to the severe weather and the malignant fever that was prevalent.[72] He, as usual, was affected by the severe weather. On 18 April, he wrote that the piercingly cold east and north-east wind had "teased" his asthma and caused stomach upset. But, he continued positively, his stamina was sound, and rest and warmth speedily restored him and banished, or at least mitigated, all his illnesses. Today, he added wonderingly, "Dr Murray closes his 69th year, and last night looked as well as if he were only 50. He lays the first stone today of an additional building to the diocesan seminary, Castleknock." It was a lean time generally for collecting money, he consoled himself. Easter collections were down, the archbishop obtained little response to his appeal to reduce the debts on the pro-cathedral, and there had been many financial failures in the city.[73]

Tidings from abroad

And as well as the letters he wrote to friends nearer home and in far flung parts of the English speaking world, he was also, wonderful to relate, writing regularly to the General as a consultor. Fr Roothaan, in a letter to Bracken, added a footnote in his own hand: "I wish to express my thanks to the father consultors, and particularly Fr Kenney." The same letter contained an explicit reminder, on a matter concerning which the General said he had often spoken previously, and on which Kenney had frequently laid empohasis, namely, that – "the Brothers", were to be *truly* regarded as *brothers*, not just as domestic servants". When Brothers sometimes behaved less well, Roothaan observed, the fault often lay with the superior who neglected their spiritual development, and so when they saw that they themselves and their religious state were not esteemed, they did not live up to that state.[74]

And the year drew to a close with Dr Oliver's letter which spoke of Gahan, and then requested further information on some twelve Irish Jesuits of the old Society.[75]

Pastoral assessment

And so another year ran out; and despite erratic health, concern about finances, and pressure of ministry, he was content. Writing of this period later, his colleague from time to time, Robert Haly, remarked:

> In the discharge of his sacred duty he made himself all to all, but he was particularly devoted to the poor. He was constantly looking out for servant men and car-drivers and labourers, and perpetually engaged in hearing their confessions. Engaged as he was in so many works of zeal, piety, and charity; his sermons and retreats extolled to the skies by all who heard them; possessing the esteem and confidence of the prelacy of Ireland; visited and consulted by the highest in rank, lay and clerical; he was never once, during the entire period of his lengthened labours, heard to say one single word in reference to anything he had done or undertaken to do, or to breathe the name of anyone of the distinguished personages who had visited him, or reposed their confidence in him, or asked his opinion or advice.[76]

Such laudable traits make life difficult for historians! So many intimations, so few precise details and concrete examples.

A further intimation was provided by one who qualified as a "distinguished personage", Bishop Ullathorne, who many years later recalled his acquaintances in Dublin during his visit there from Australia between the years 1836 and 1838.

> Another acquaintance in Dublin whom I recall with great respect was Father Kenney, the Jesuit, then in advanced years. He was a man who said but little, but was endowed with an eminent wisdom and prudence as well as sanctity. He was consulted by bishops as well as by many priests, and was a singularly wise and solid director. I have known several persons placed in distracting, secular positions in life who always ascribed their fidelity to their religion to the early guidance of Father Kenney.[77]

By the end of 1837, then, Kenney was held in high and revered standing, not just as an eminent preacher, but pre-eminently as a wise and prudent spiritual guide who was, evidently, an attentive and empathetic listener. He also, however, appeared to be "in advanced years", though he was still in his fifties. Asthma had rounded his shoulders and, allied to his long sedentary hours in the confessional, had lessened his opportunities for exercise and increased his corpulence. Reminders of mortality, moreover, had been forcefully conveyed by the deaths of his two earliest companions, William Dinan and Matthew Gahan. Nevertheless, there was no marked diminution in his work rate, and no indication that he had only four years to live.

XIV

A conciliating voice: As bishops dispute and brothers dissent, 1837–41

> To ride two horses at once, a foot on each
>
> ...
>
> That people are lovable is a strange discovery
> And there are many conflicting allegiances.
>
> Louis MacNeice, "Ode"

Tidings of some joy

The year 1838 brought two unexpected voices from the past. The first came on 27 April in a letter from a Fr Michael Fitzgerald of Ballingarry, Co. Limerick. Kenney had written him to seek information about one of his parishioners, and had queried if he had not been a student at Maynooth when he was vice-president there. Fitzgerald not only gave the required information, but, in words which must have warmed and moved Kenney, had added that he participated sincerely and deeply in "those sentiments of grateful and affectionate veneration" with which Kenney could not fail to be recollected by everyone who had, as Fitzgerald had, "the invaluable opportunity of profiting by his eloquent instruction, and still more eloquent example". He felt great pleasure in hearing from him and in complying with his request; indeed, he added, there were "few (if any) ecclesiastics in Ireland by whom the slightest intimation" of his wishes "would not be considered a law".[1]

Later, at the beginning of August, there came another unexpected letter. It was from "an old Sicilian correspondent", the army sergeant of those days, Richard Mulcahy. Recently, his brother, James Mulcahy, parish priest of the parishes of Castletownend and Myross, Co. Cork, had attended, he said, a retreat with a large body of clergy from the city and county of Cork, and when he spoke afterwards of the "extraordinary endowment of the distinguished individual divine", he, Richard, recognised of whom he was speaking. "It was the same religious zeal, which occasioned you about 30 years ago to forego all the comforts and ease of a collegiate life for a time, and to undergo all the privations of a long and tedious journey from Palermo to Melazzo in Sicily", in order to attend "to the spiritual destitution of the Catholic military engaged in the British service and stationed on that island; notwithstanding the blind prejudice and anti-Catholic fatuity of their military commanders".

As Kenney had always expressed an interest not only in his spiritual but also in his temporal concerns, he wished to inform him, he declared, that after

397

Kenney had left Sicily, he had been promoted in the army and, on leaving the service, had gone into business. He married the daughter of a "respectable" shopkeeper. One of her family, indeed, was Fr Patrick McSweeney, "at present chief of the Irish College, Paris". He, himself, now had two grocery establishments, and was also engaged in the iron trade. He requested Kenney to send him a letter. It "would be a most precious gift ... a spiritual nosegay", as all his former letters had been to him. And he recalled how often Kenney had directed him to turn his "affectionate heart to Him from whom emanated all love". That, and a thousand more of his instructions would never be effaced from his memory.[2]

Physical decline

Such appreciative letters came as a particular comfort in a year when Kenney's general health underwent obvious decline. The heavy demands of the Lenten season had been added to during March by four novenas in close succession, each requiring additional sermons, ceremonies, and confessional duties.[3] In June, the General in a letter to Bracken remarked that he was "very sorry to hear that Fr Kenney begins to suffer a deterioration in strength".[4] Although Kenney may not yet have been aware of it, his heart was registering the years of strain from asthma, extensive travel, the pressures of office, the nature of his church work, and the absence of exercise; though this last may have partly arisen from lack of energy as a result of the heart complaint, since in that health-conscious world, he was very aware of the need for fresh air and exercise.

The rather tremulous state of health, joined to a sense of the demands of the church ministry and that he was neglecting necessary exercise, had all come together in a letter to Bracken that March, just after the Novena of Grace in honour of St Francis Xavier. "In one way or another," he wrote, "we have finished our spoiled novena. Fr Meagher volunteered for two nights, and I gave him the last two; and the relief was most opportune to me, for on Sunday I felt very ill, but rest, and a good portion of medicine, made me feel much better yesterday. I walked as far as the canal bridge[5] before dinner; and little as it was, it was of use." In the previous forty days, he remarked, he had ventured out in the open air only about ten times. It was little wonder, therefore, that his limbs had "become torpid". Henceforth, he promised, he would endeavour "to get at least a run for an hour every day", and that he might not fail to do so that day he would end by saying "that all are well here".[6]

Whatever about the physical health at Gardiner Street, the spiritual health of the vice-province as a whole seemed very weak from the viewpoint of Rome. Aylmer, there for the procurators' conference, reported that everything seemed to flourish "in every part of the Society except in our vice-province" which had "no novices joining, no higher scholastics".[7]

As against that negative view, the vice-provincial was to report to Fr Roothaan from Clongowes at the start of the next year, that he found all in a healthy state spiritually; and that the Jesuits in Ireland generally, so far as he could judge, were "good, pious, hardworking, obedient, and dedicated to their vocation". Like Kenney at an earlier time, however, he sought to bring to his Paternity's attention that: "it's possible to lead the Irish, but they cannot be compelled ... Hence, the way to act with them is gently, paternally, and with much love ..."[8]

Despite Kenney's poor state of health, the General on 8 December appointed him again as one of the four consultors to the vice-provincial.[9]

The year, then, had been busy, but otherwise largely uneventful. Two important outside developments of an ecclesiastical nature came to the fore, however, which subsequently were to seriously engage his attention, namely: 1. The retirement from the position of superior general of the Christian Brothers of Edmund Ignatius Rice, and the controversy under his successor which threatened the very existence of the congregation; and 2. An open clash between Archbishops MacHale and Murray which occasioned some scandal and much embarrassment to the Catholic community.

Both controversies continued over some years. Kenney found himself drawn into the Brothers dispute as a result of requests from the new superior general, Br Riordan, and Archbishop Murray; while his more peripheral links with the other issue arose from his contacts with the archbishop and his empathy for the latter's position, and because his friend Thomas Glover, in Rome, had, to some extend, been put in an adjudicating posture between the two prelates. That issue, which turned on the government's system of undenominational elementary education, was relatively straightforward compared to the Brothers' problems.

DISCORD AMONG BISHOPS AND THE NATIONAL EDUCATION SYSTEM

Background

Complaints about proselytism by means of schools, especially in the 1820s, encouraged the Whig government to establish in 1831 a National Board of Education to administer a centralised system of undenominational elementary education.

The main religious denominations were to be represented in a board of seven commissioners. The Catholics were to have two representatives. Schools in receipt of subsidies from the board were to be run by mixed local committees. The board would give assistance to the local committees in building schools, in providing published texts; and in making the main contribution towards teachers' salaries. To avoid "any suspicion of proselytism", the curriculum was to be secular in content, though provision was made for separate religious instruction at special stated times by members of the different denominations. Denominational control over the appointment of teachers was not permitted, nor over school books, and no religious emblems were to be allowed.

The system met with a hostile reception from the members of the Established Church. "The exclusion of the scriptures and the admission of the priest" into the schools to give religious instruction, was unacceptable to them, as was the state's interference with their duty to proselytise. They accused the government of "establishing popery". So, the Established Church largely stood apart from the national schools. The Presbyterians, too, were highly critical at first, but later participated actively once their demands were met.[10] The Catholic bishops, for the most part, were convinced that, though far from ideal, the system was as good as could be expected in the circumstances. Archbishop Murray indicated the general acceptance when, along with A.R. Blake, the Catholic chief remembrancer of the treasury, he agreed to join the board of commissioners. Dr Doyle (J.K.L.), who had been the most vocal opponent of proselytism in education, supported the new system. He encouraged his friend, Fr Slattery, a parish priest in Co. Tipperary, to avail of it with regard to schools for the poor in his parish.[11] And he added, prophetically: "the Protestant clergy are standing aloof, they have abandoned the field entirely to us and will have the effect of throwing the education of the Catholic youth of the country into our hands ..."[12]

MacHale's opposition

Within a few years, however, opposition to the system was expressed by some of the hierarchy, notably Archbishop MacHale of Tuam and Dr Higgins of Ardagh. Both men had strong nationalist views, and were deeply suspicious of the motives of the government in introducing the schools. They suspected that they were to be a new vehicle of proselytism. In 1837, changes in the curriculum, which broke down the original strict barrier between religious and secular teaching, were perceived as confirming their suspicions, MacHale came out publicly and vigorously against the system. He pointed specifically to the composition of the board – only two Catholics though four-fifths of the population were Catholic, to the text books being used, and to the fact that the bishops had no direct authority over the schools. He addressed a series of open letters on these grounds to the prime minister, Lord John Russell;[13] attacked the schools at the bishops' meeting; and on 24 February sent a letter to Pope Gregory XVI requesting his protection against a system of education aimed at the extinction of the Catholic faith in Ireland.

On 2 May, the pope gave a non-committal reply, and asked the Congregation of Propaganda to write to Drs Murray and MacHale requesting each of them to submit to the Congregation a detailed account of the national school system together with their opinions in its regard. This the Congregation did on 15 May 1838.[14]

Dr Murray replied on 11 June. He pointed out that out of 27 bishops only four opposed the national schools; and in Dr MacHale's own province only he and the bishop of Elphin were opposed. Murray's own chief reason for favouring the system and accepting a place on the board was, he said, because of his concern that, if he did not, government funds would all go again to the Protestant schools; and he expressed his opinion that with sufficient vigilance on the part of the clergy, the national system could be safely operated.[15]

Towards condemnation?

Dr MacHale kept up a vigorous campaign, drawing particular attention to the school texts, especially those authored by two active members of the board: James Carlile, a Presbyterian, who had compiled a book of *Scripture Extracts*, and Dr Whately, Church of Ireland archbishop of Dublin, who had produced a text entitled *Introductory Lessons on the Truth of Christianity*. He sent a number of the school books to Dr Cullen, the rector of the Irish College, for transmission to Propaganda, where he knew Cullen was highly regarded. The rector of the Irish College, and his vice-rector, Tobias Kirby, were, he was aware, strong supporters of his position. Cullen decided, perhaps after consulting Propaganda, to bring the texts first of all to Thomas Glover, assistant to the Jesuit General, for examination and comment. Glover gave a verbal comment unfavourable to the texts to Cullen, who, then, it would seem, approached Propaganda, which, in turn, formally sought Glover's judgement on the books.[17] He gave his response in Italian in a fairly lengthy report. The subsequent document issued by Propaganda declared that it was difficult to perceive "how, in reason and conscience, such a system for the education of Catholics could be approved or even tolerated"; and, in a further progression from the particular to the general, went so far as to apparently quote him – "the whole national schools system in Ireland seems to me to be the most subtle and insidious plan ever thought out to overthrow the Catholic faith in that island".[18]

Meantime, at the general meeting of the Irish hierarchy in January 1839, the schools question was discussed, without an agreement being reached. MacHale now had the support of nine bishops. They petitioned the pope to declare against the schools. Dr Crolly, archbishop of Armagh, wrote on behalf of the other 16 bishops in favour of the system. The split was formalised. The disagreement between Drs Murray and MacHale spilled over into the public press and occasioned disquiet, division, and embarrassment among Catholics.

Propaganda submitted Glover's judgement to Dr Murray in February, without revealing his identity. Murray replied to Propaganda on 25 February and 12 March answering Glover's objections, though not always to Propaganda's satisfaction, and intimating that he would continue to favour the national schools unless they were definitely condemned.

Propaganda then placed the whole matter before another Jesuit, John Perrone, professor of theology at the Jesuit Roman College, and one of their consultors. He took a more lenient view than Glover. He thought both sides had been extreme in their protestations, and pointed out that the application of the system obviously varied from place to place, and that this accounted for differences among bishops. He judged that it should be neither positively approved nor positively condemned, but that certain modifications should be made. His report was submitted to Propaganda in April 1839.

With all the opinions before it, Propaganda decided on 15 July for *condemnation*. The decision was never promulgated. Hearing from friends in Rome that a condemnation was imminent, Dr Murray wrote to the pope on 8 July urgently requesting that before Rome came to a final decision on such a serious matter, either a legate should be sent to Ireland to examine the schools on the spot, or that one or more Irish bishops should be permitted to go to Rome to state their case there. The primate, William Crolly, wrote on similar lines. The pope was sufficiently impressed to postpone his approval of the censure. He referred Murray's letter to Propaganda.

Kenney's involvement

At this stage, although Glover's part in the whole process was meant to be strictly confidential, Kenney got word of it. It was an occasion of some embarrassment with the archbishop; but, more seriously, it held prospects of misunderstanding with the government. He knew well, from his own experience, how prone outsiders could be, even those well acquainted with the individualism of many Jesuits, to ascribe the comments of individuals to the Society as a whole. Hence, when he first heard that reports were in circulation that an English Jesuit, Glover, was criticising and interfering in British government policy on education in Ireland, and that as a result there might be a papal condemnation of the government's educational system, he felt it necessary to bring the matter to the attention of the English Jesuits. Strangely, he did not write to the provincial, but to Fr Randall Lythgoe, the energetic and influential vice-rector of St Ignatius College, London, destined to be a future provincial. He alerted him to the allegations that the Jesuits were interfering with the government's education system.

He wrote on 2 August 1839. Lythgoe did not reply till 13 November. Apologising for the long delay, he related that he had been on the continent until September; but on receiving his letter had immediately communicated its contents to the provincial, Fr Bird, who sent a letter to the Chief Secretary of Ireland, Viscount Morpeth, to explain that the English Jesuits had in no way interfered with the government's scheme of education. The only way, indeed, in which the Society might be considered implicated, as he understood it, was that "Fr Glover was desired by Propaganda to read over certain school books ... and to report upon them. This he declined to do, until compelled by superior authority. When he had read them, he pointed out certain passages which he considered exceptionable, and thus the matter ended." Commenting further on the dispute, Lythgoe informed Kenney that he had been assured that "an intimation of disapproval on the part of Rome" either had been, or would be "communicated to Dr Murray", and that this was not the work of "an Englishman or Jesuit, but may be considered the result of solicitations made by two Irish clergymen resident in Rome."[19]

The role being played by the "two Irish clergymen", Cullen and Kirby, had already raised the ire of the majority party of bishops as the threat of condemnation loomed. Firm warnings to Cullen from archbishops Crolly and Murray, and the threat of withdrawal of the Irish bishops' agency from him,[20] were not to be without effect. Modificiation in Cullen's advocacy over some months was gradually to ease the climate of conflict, and help towards a solution.

Meantime, Murray's proposal in July that members of the hierarchy come to Rome to present the arguments for and against, was watered down by Propaganda to a request that the main parties, Murray and MacHale, each send a priest as representative. Fr John Ennis, parish priest of Booterstown, Dublin, was chosen as the deputy for the majority party, and, cleverly, Fr William Meagher, also of Dublin, was sent as secretary. This, in effect, provided two deputies, both of them fluent in Italian. They reached Rome on 15 November. The representative of the other bishops, Fr John Loftus of Tuam diocese, who did not speak Italian, did not arrive till January 1840. The Dublin pair brought with them, or had already despatched to Rome, reports on the state of education in *each diocese*. The volume of material was considerable.

As he had done so often in the past, Dr Murray appears to have consulted Kenney in making the case in favour of the schools. Certainly, the latter had studied a copy of Glover's judgements, which, presumably, he received from the archbishop; and he had written to Esmonde at Rome, and had encouraged him to support as best he could Dr Murray's pro-school position. He himself sat down to study the education act and its practical operation, and then, on 30 January 1840, wrote directly to Glover. His letter expressed criticism of Glover's judgements, and then went on to to provide a benign interpretation of the operation of national education which, he hoped, would persuade his friend to change his mind and become a supporter of the pro-schools side. As usual, when he set out to persuade, he produced a thorough document as the basis for his strong advocacy.[21]

Letter to Glover

He was writing, he declared, in connection with certain "*animadversions*" on the school system and on the scripture lessons drawn up for the schools,

which were sent from Rome in the early part of 1839, and were said to have
been written by him. He made no excuse for troubling him about the matter,
he continued, because of their long and intimate acquaintance, their common
life and interest, and because he knew that what Glover expressed arose from
a sincere conviction of mind.

Having thus introduced the subject, he went on quite bluntly: "But, if you
really be the author of the *animadversions*, you were greatly in error when you
wrote of the national system – '*ubi nullum symbolum fidei, nullus catechismus,
nulla pietatis exercitia communis*' (a system 'where there is no symbol of belief,
no catechism, no common exercise of piety'). You were in error when you said
that the board nominated the masters of all these schools, prescribed books,
governed and directed everything. The board has nothing to do with the
choice or dismissal of the masters of the schools; nor does it force any books
on them. The regimen of each school lies with the patrons, who frequently are
the parish priests. All the concern of the board with these schools is to secure
that nothing be done in the hours of school at which all are bound to attend,
that would lead to suspicion of proselytism or injury to any of the various
sects of which the scholars are composed. These leading features of the system
the *animadversions* distort, omit, and in some instances substitute the very contrary in their stead."

He then went on to point out that the board did not force a school on any
locality, it merely granted aid to build or maintain one. And when the board
members granted aid to build, they did not seek possession, but merely
required that the house be not appropriated to any other purpose; and to this
end they required the patrons – "the influential inhabitants of the place, clergy
or laity, or both" – to choose trustees who are pledged to preserve the school
according to "the liberal principles of the present system" and are "empowered
to close the door against the intrusion of any proselytising or exclusive system,
so that the high church party, or others, cannot ever make these schools subservient to their bigoted purposes."

Further information, he declared, might be obtained from Dr Murray's
response to the *animadversions*, which, doubtless, Glover would have seen by
this. He then proceeded to explain his own position more clearly, and to
appeal for a change of view. He was not an advocate for the system, he had no
personal interest in it except as a matter of public good. Indeed, he was so
greatly occupied in his own duties that until recently he had never read the
constitution of the board or one of their texts. The Scripture Lessons he had
looked at and disliked "the form, language, tone and tendency", but he considered that Glover had given an erroneous sense to many passages "where error
was not asserted or meant". In any event, as the Lessons were not part of the
system, discussion about them was of less importance. His object in writing
would be gained", he announced, if he could induce him to review his opinion
with a view to revoking or modifying what he deemed right to so change. For

"proofs" on the entire issue, he referred him to Archbishop Murray's replies to the cardinal prefect on 28 February and 19 August, and to Messrs Ennis and Meagher who were in Rome in connection with the business. He concluded with a reminder which was to come much to the fore as the dispute drew near to settlement:

> Do not forget that the whole system must be kept in view: the part considered in relation to the whole. The question is not *de optimo* but *de meliore* (not about what is best, but what is better). Is not this system better than the one which preceded it and persecuted our children and annoyed our pastors for years? Is it not *better* than any other which *we could now obtain*? If the great majority of bishops, clergy, and laity, who have felt the past and know the present, say Yes, and say it decidedly, is not their *ability, piety, experience*, grand vouchers for the accuracy of their judgement?

The "Messrs Ennis and Meagher" to whom he referred had done trojan work from the moment of their arrival, and used to advantage their early start over MacHale's deputy. Ennis wrote home, however, to say that their most formidable adversary in Rome was Cullen.[22] That he had been a prime mover from early on was made clear, indeed, in Glover's reply to Kenney on 15 February 1840.

Glover's reply

"Many thanks for your kind letter," he wrote. "God help me! I have been dragged deeply into the mire, and then abandoned to get out of it as well as I may. It is hard to be called upon to give an account of a confidential communication, in which it ought never to have been known that I had been concerned; it is still harder to bear all the blame, which ought more justly to be laid on the shoulders of others."

"Many months ago," he continued, "Dr Cullen called upon me with five school books, requesting me, on the part of Propaganda, to look over them and give my opinion on them." Up to that point he had known nothing about such texts, nor about "a contest in Ireland, either about them, or about the schools in which they were used". He went on: "I read the books, and I found many passages marked with ink, a sign that somebody before had read them, and thus expressed his disapprobation ... When Dr Cullen called again ... I ... gave him a verbal answer, that there were several passages, particularly amongst those which were marked, that I could not approve; and I particularly remarked that much of the phraseology had more a Protestant than a Catholic turn; and although a Catholic interpretation might be given, it might be easily twisted into a Protestant sense. I complained also that there was in no part a clear exposition of doctrines peculiarly Catholic. Therefore, on account of these inaccuracies and deficiencies, I could not approve of these books for the Catholic education of Ireland." "And to speak frankly," he added, "I have not yet heard any reasons to make me change my opinion."

That was that, he thought, but two or three weeks afterwards he received again the books, and a sheaf of papers, from the Propaganda, with a request to make a report theron. This request amounted to a command. He read all the documents sent from Ireland with attention, and, he believed, without prejudice. Indeed, if anything his prejudice was towards Dr Murray for whose orthodoxy, zeal, piety and experience he had ever entertained the greatest respect, as distinct from Dr MacHale about whom "many things had been reported in Rome" which, if true, he could never approve. "Notwithstanding this," he continued, "it appeared to me that the arguments on the part of Dr MacHale outweighed the reasons of the opposite party. I formed my judgement from the documents before me. If I have erred, or have been led into error, I have nothing more to say than '*homo sum, nihil humanum alienum a me puto*'."23

That was "the beginning, middle, and end" of all his doings in this unpleasant affair, he declared. He advanced nothing which was not in the documents before him. "The *animadversions* sent to Ireland", he had never seen! They were "collected from more opinions than mine," he added; "for it should always be kept in mind that I was not the only one consulted."

In any event, he could not see how the *animadversions* could give mortal offence. They were not authoritative. Nothing could be fairer than to send them to Dr Murray to allow him to answer them. He understood that he had sent an answer. How far it would satisfy the Sacred Congregation, he could not say. It was no business of his, and so he had never enquired.

He then concluded with a pragmatic observation based on his experience of Rome.

> The greatest mistake, in my opinion, has been committed at home. The bishops ought to have settled the business among themselves, privately, and never have brought it before the public; above all they never ought to have brought it to Rome. Rome might easily have tolerated a lesser evil in face of a greater; but to try to force Rome to approve the lesser evil, to sanction in any form the system of mixed education, which has done and is still doing much mischief in Germany, was highly imprudent, to say the least. These are my own views of the matter, for I do not know what resolution Propaganda may come to.24

Ironically, by the time Glover wrote to Kenney, Dr Cullen had trimmed his sails and was giving Dr MacHale the kind of practical advice which Glover wished the Irish bishops had followed.

Towards a solution

Propaganda were anxious, Cullen wrote, that the question "be withdrawn from the eyes of the public" and that all be conducted "with the greatest calmness possible ... and without any breach of charity". He was now almost convinced that no decision would be reached at Rome.[25]

The drift of thinking among the cardinals was also clear to Meagher and Ennis, and in March they came up with a simple down-to-earth proposal which suited their Eminences and was almost identical to the eventual solution. They suggested that "for the present it be permitted to each bishop ... to approve or disapprove of the system for his own diocese, according as the Holy Spirit inspires him to judge that it is for the well-being of his flock"; and "that orders be given to all prelates that they and their clergy must not write on this subject in the public press, but must content themselves with transmitting to the S. Congregation [of Propaganda] any information which they think it necessary to send."[26]

Some time later, all the relevant documents were passed to the Belgian Jesuit, Cornelius Van-Everbrock, professor of Church History in the Roman College of the Jesuits, and a consultor of the Holy Office and of Propaganda. He examined the whole matter with great care, consulted with Fr Perrone at the pope's request, and then worked through the August heat of Rome to produce a magisterial report of 13 chapters.[27]

Also during that summer, while Van-Everbrock was labouring in Rome, Cullen was back in Ireland for the first time in six years, and sending reports to Cardinal Fransoni, Prefect of Propaganda, which were favourable to the pro-school side. "In the dioceses of Dublin and Kildare I have seen a good number of schools," he wrote on 7 August, "and I have noticed they could not be more Catholic than they are ... I do not think there is any danger to the Faith."[28]

The ground had been well prepared, therefore, when Van-Everbrock came up with his report. He boiled the whole issue down to two questions – whether the defects of the national system were such that Catholics could not accept it? and whether there was any reasonable hope of anything better being obtained? – and answered both negatively. The matter, in consequence, was virtually settled. He recommended a solution very similar to that of Ennis and Meagher.[29] On 22 December 1840, Propaganda went back on its former condemnation, and adopted the solution proposed by its consultor; and on 16 January 1842, Pope Gregory XVI issued a rescript to the four archbishops of Ireland leaving the decision to each bishop, and ordering prelates and ecclesiastics to refrain from controversy in the press on the question of the national schools.[30]

Thus, after very thorough investigation the case was settled, and the 1841 rescript became the basis of ecclesiastical legislation on primary education in

Ireland for the next fifty years and shaped its course. The controversy, however, was in many ways a prototype for even more serious controversies some years later: relating to the Charitable Bequests Act, and to the question of the Queen's Colleges and university education. Again, Drs Murray and MacHale were to be the leaders of the opposing parties. Not surprisingly, the consultor preparing a report on the university issue for Propaganda in 1846 commenced with a brief summary of the national schools dispute, and described it as "the first seed of discord among the bishops in Ireland" which, though happily settled, "left ... in the minds of the prelates a disposition to renew the contest every time a similar occasion arose".[31]

By then, however, Kenney was not in a position to become involved, even in the peripheral manner in which he engaged himself to safeguard, as he understood it, the reputation of the order and assist his long-time friend and prelate, Daniel Murray.

The other major area into which he was drawn by the archbishop, and by his long association with the Christian Brothers, was the internecine conflict among the latter in the years from 1838 to 1841. The tangled and dense story of those years, has been researched with painstaking thoroughness by the archivist and specialist historian, the late Br M.C. Normoyle, in his privately published *A Tree is Planted* and its two companion works of correspondence.[32] Kenney's important consultancy role can only be appreciated, alas, by entering into the complicated context.

CRISIS AND THE NEW SUPERIOR GENERAL OF THE CHRISTIAN BROTHERS

In 1838 the editor of the *Irish Catholic Directory* wrote of the Brothers of the Christian Schools: "Amongst the charitable establishments of this country, which may be said to demonstrate the providence of God, this noble institute stands preeminent."[33] The well earned recognition came, ironically, at a time of severe internal difficulties for the Brothers.

That they should have been experiencing strain and internal tension was not surprising. Something similar had happened with the early Jesuits and Redemptorists, and was likely to happen with any active apostolic body which grew quickly and was in great demand. In such a situation there was danger of over-stretching, and, in the process, of not giving sufficient time and attention to spiritual formation, so that very earthy considerations and ambitions might creep into the lives of men who had set out with the highest ideals.

The Brothers experienced a crisis of this nature in the second decade after Peter Kenney had brought the papal brief to them. They had grown very rapidly. They were sought not only throughout Ireland, but in Britain and in the United States. By the mid 1830s they had 18 different houses and schools.

Life was poor and hard. Pressures were such at times that even the novices were pressed into teaching.

Vocations were drawn from various parts of Ireland; but in the early years a very high proportion came from Cork, and they became a very powerful voice in the congregation. Provincial and county rivalries entered into problems, and the influential Cork members sought a voice in the central administration. By the end of the 1820s, indeed, there was evidence, on the part of some, of a desire to make the founder a mere figurehead,[34] and one of the latter's assistants, Joseph Leonard, one of two able Cork brothers, was a sick, obsessive man who nursed a deep antipathy to Edmund Rice.[35]

Not surprisingly, then, when Br Rice, against Kenney's advice, as will be recalled, gave way to demands and called a general chapter in 1829, it proved a turbulent and painful experience. In December 1831, when the normal time for a general chapter fell due, his term as superior general was at an end. He resigned his office; but, under pressure from the assembly, agreed to take it up again. Leading up to, and again after that chapter, opposition to him and his assistants, Brs Ellis and Austin Dunphy, was orchestrated from North Monastery School, Cork, by the two brothers, Baptist and Joseph Leonard, and Br Michael Paul Riordan, who were termed *"trio in uno"*.[36]

When, therefore, at the general chapter in July 1838, Edmund Ignatius Rice retired as superior general on the grounds of "advancing years and increasing bodily infirmity",[37] the election of a successor proved a discordant business. The eventual choice of Michael Paul Riordan, by a narrow margin over Austin Dunphy, was not calculated to satisfy those who viewed him as an agitator against the founder; and the fact that there had been so much confusion about procedures, and so many errors made, encouraged them to question the validity of his election.

In the acrimonious debate which followed, it was eventually proposed that a petition be sent to the pope for a *sanatio*, or healing, of all defects, and confirmation of the election. This was agreed by 17 votes to 2; and a memorial was drawn up by Austin Dunphy, the defeated candidate, and sent to Rome. On 9 September 1838, Gregory XVI, "having weighed all matters set forth in the memorial", confirmed, by Apostolic Authority, "the election lately made of Michael Paul Riordan as superior general ... thereby healing all defects whatsoever – all things whatsoever to the contrary notwithstanding".[38] As Peter Kenney would later remark, Br Riordan was appointed superior general as firmly as if he had received a papal brief nominating him.[39]

Much of the disharmony so much in evidence during the chapter, was carried over, unfortunately, into the reign of the new superior general; and where in the past a trio had provided opposition to the ageing founder and his assistants, now Edmund Rice and his close associates, Austin and his brother Bernard Dunphy, both, incidentally, from Edmund's native town of Callan, Co. Kilkenny, together with Brs Patrick Ellis and Myles Ignatius Kelly, seemed to form a rallying-point against Michael Paul Riordan; and he, while openly disagreeing with them and even ordering them under obedience, did not feel strong enough to face them down to the point of dismissal, and, consequently, appears to have resorted to deliberate subterfuge at times. Sadly, straightforwardness, charity and obedience, fell victim on both sides in the struggle.

The first issues on which Kenney was consulted were very different from each other, but were interconnected by the people involved. They concerned the question of pay-schools and the vow of poverty, and a matter of a will, property, and obedience. The former became a burning issue at the chapter; the latter went further back.

Richmond Street property: legal problems, and cross purposes

Richmond Street school had been built with the assistance of £1,000 from a benefactor, Mr Bolger. In return he received a bond signed by Br Rice, and two other brothers. In 1834, Bolger died and left the greater part of his property to the archbishop and the Brothers for the education of poor boys, appointing Brs Rice, Bernard Dunphy, and Ignatius Kelly as executors. Bolger's relations contested the will. The Brothers were instructed by their lawyer that the only means of securing the position of the executors and providing for the legal claims of the legatees was to effect a mortgage on the property.[40] The superior general, Michael P. Riordan, however, ordered the four of them "under their vow of obedience" not to effect a mortgage on the property, and refused to provide any other security for the bond.

In this serious predicament, Edmund Rice sought the advice of a theologian, the prior of the Carmelite monastery, Whitefriars Street, Dublin, Fr Colgan, who declared that no one could be obliged to obey a superior commanding something sinful, and to refuse to pay one's lawful debts was sinful, hence Br Riordan's prohibition against paying back the £1,000 due to the Bolger estate was contrary to justice.[41] Thus confirmed, Rice and Austin Dunphy took it on themselves on 7 July 1840, to sign a mortgage on the North Richmond property.

In August, at a meeting involving the general council and a number of other brothers, the superior general read out his own lawyer's advice on the mortgage issue, and charged Rice, Austin Dunphy and Ellis, with formal disobedience, although Rice was not present to offer an explanation.[42] The three men, nevertheless, defiantly entered the mortgage at the registry of deeds, Dublin, on 4 September 1840.[43]

Br Riordan, now adroitly decided to seek theological advice from someone of high integrity, who knew the congregation well, and who was a life long friend of both its founder and the archbishop of Dublin. He approached Kenney, and presented him with an incomplete and *ex parte* statement of the problem, in the form of questions so weighted as to ensure an answer in support of his own case.[44] The background information he supplied was also shown subsequently to have been inaccurate.[45]

Kenney found for him in that he judged that Riordan was within his rights in commanding under obedience in the circumstances of the case as presented to him; but even then he suggested that he had not exercised his authority prudently, and went on to make a general recommendation and appeal. "Let all attempts at carrying on such business independently of the superior be abandoned," he wrote, "and on the part of the superior let oblivion of the past prevent reproof or any act of severity. The faults that have been committed are the faults of misconception, not of malice, and are, therefore, entitled to charitable indulgence." He concluded unhappily: "I would give all the money at stake in this business to have prevented one of the obligors from signing the mortgage. I feel too strongly the influence of that act on the high reputation of him to whom you are all so much indebted."[46]

Edmund Rice, for his part, seemed to feel he had done the correct thing in following Fr Colgan's advice; and, confidently submitted that advice to Archbishop Murray.[47] Harmony might have been restored, if Kenney's recommendations had been accepted, but too many cross purposes rendered acceptance virtually impossible.

The next example of such cross purposes, was all too familiar to him: whether the institute could permit "pay-schools"? The issue had occasioned controversy and deep division at the chapter, and was also linked to the leadership struggle.

The issue of pay-schools: dispute, defiance, detraction

By "pay-schools", in the Brothers' debate, was understood – "having in each school (or some schools) a separate room for children in easy circumstances and receiving some moderate remuneration from them for the tuition."[48]

The obstacle to such was the very brief of Pius VII which established the congregation. It laid down that the brothers principal duty was "the teaching of male children particularly the poor", and while this did not entirely exclude better off children, any financial benefit from such pupils was excluded by a further article which laid down that all teaching was to be gratuitous. But schools catering for the really poor, as at North Richmond Street, Hanover Street, and Mill Street, Dublin, had no reliable source of income and could only hope to survive, in the experience of Edmund Rice and his associates, if some paying pupils were admitted. He put forward a proposal at chapter in support of such an arrangement.

Opponents of the proposal declared it contrary to the papal brief and the spirit of the institute, and also expressed the fear that it would lead to the better teachers being moved to pay-schools. Eventually, it was agreed by a large majority, to allow two of the three schools, namely Hanover Street and Mill Street, "to receive from the children of easy circumstances such sums as they may feel disposed to give in order to enable the brothers to uphold these establishments". In the schools in question, Edmund Rice's two close associates, Bernard Dunphy and M. Ignatius Kelly, were the directors. The chapter insisted, however, that it did not agree in principle to having pay schools, that the two were excepted out of necessity, and that the sanction of the Holy See should be sought for the two schools.[49] Later in the year, Fr Colgan was asked for his views as a theologian on their decision. He did not see any conflict, it would seem, between the establishment of pay-schools and the vow of poverty; indeed he encouraged such schools, and saw no need for any prior permission from the Holy See.[50]

After the chapter, Brs B. Dunphy and Kelly, as directors at Hanover Street and Mill Street, began preparing a room for paying pupils. Br Riordan, who had opposed the chapter's decision, intervened to suspend the preparations. He then brought the problem to Kenney for advice.

When the latter was asked if "it was lawful for them to keep such schools, he replied that it was not: that the chapter in allowing them [the two schools] had exceeded its powers, because the gratuitous education of the poor was among what are termed *substantialia instituti* (essential parts of the institute) in which chapters or superiors had no authority; and also because it was with them (the Brothers) an express object of vow, with which the chapter could not dispense." He quoted from the institute of the congregation in support of his statement; and then added: "that since the chapter had done it, the superior general was not responsible; and, therefore, he might allow the schools to go on until the next chapter when the pay schools might be abandoned, or a brief obtained to authorise them".[51]

The superior general allowed the schools to open in September 1838; but he made no move to contact Rome until July 1839. Then he did so in a manner which invited a negative response: using some of the content of Kenney's judgement to bolster his presentation. He stated that the majority of brothers were opposed to pay-schools, that "the chapter usurped authority it did not possess" in giving permission to establish them, and that he deemed the measure contrary to the spirit and authority of the institute.[52] On 13 August 1839, the pope agreed – emphasising the need for the brothers "to teach the children gratis; never accepting anything as a reward or retribution, either from them or their parents".[53] Despite this, Br Riordan did not close the pay-schools; but appears to have made clear his disapproval of the venture, and of the brothers involved in it.

It was, undoubtedly, very difficult for the new superior general to maintain the spirit of the institute, as he understood it, in opposition to the very founder and those who sheltered behind him. He may well have felt that others, particularly the Dunphy brothers, were manipulating Edmund Rice to their own ends. The founder's condition was noticeably feeble by the end of the 1830s, but there is scarcely sufficient evidence to support Riordan's comment to Dr Cullen on 15 November 1842, that "the ex-superior ... has been labouring under imbecility of mind for some time before he went out of office and he has been so ever since".[54] If Bernard Dunphy was to be believed, on the other hand, Br Riordan's hostility to Edmund Rice and the Dunphies extended even to the refusal of a loan of spare beds from his North Richmond Street residence to the Hanover Street house where they were staying.[55]

While they were in Dublin, Brs Rice and A. Dunphy became convinced, probably prompted by Bernard Dunphy, that the superior general was effectively working towards removing the pay-schools. Br Kelly had been replaced the previous month, June 1840, as director at Mill Street, by Br O'Flaherty, a determined opponent of such schools.[56] In July, without any prior consultation with their superior general, they prepared a memorial of protest for transmission to Cardinal Fransoni, Prefect of Propaganda. It was signed by Edmund Ignatius Rice, Bernard Dunphy, Myles Ignatius Kelly, and five other Brothers from the teaching staff of one of the two Dublin pay-schools.

The document pointed out that out of 18 houses, only five had a sure fund for maintenance. The only source of revenue was daily questing, which did not fit in with the brothers duties of constant daily teaching and studying. The general chapter, as a result, had supported pay schools for the upkeep of those houses that had no funds (no mention of the chapter not approving in principle, and only supporting two as exceptions) in order that the brothers could keep the schools open to serve the poor. Despite this, and the expressed approbation and desire of his Grace, the Archbishop of Dublin: "Michael P. Riordan, the person now holding office as superior general", openly discouraged these schools. Hence, they, "the founder and brethren of these very poor houses", considered themselves bound to lay this humble petition before his Eminence, requesting that he afford them protection by addressing a brief to his Grace, the archbishop, making it lawful for them "to have these pay schools ... as means ... to carry on ... the gratuitous education of the poor". The memorial carried a postscript with an "earnest recommendation" from Dr Murray.[57]

It is not clear that the document was ever sent to Rome, because, as will appear, a more extreme memorial was being contemplated and was subsequently sent. Dr Murray, however, believed it had been sent, and kept pressing its case with the Holy See. If not sent, it seemed to have been designed to obtain the archbishop's intervention on behalf of the pay schools against the wishes of Br Riordan, and in this it succeeded. Pope Gregory XVI sent a rescript granting the request on 7 February 1841. Dr Murray, receiving it in March, had an authenticated translation sent to the superior general. The latter, naturally, was greatly surprised and embarrassed. In a letter to his Grace, he expressed his regret "that this rescript had not been obtained with the consent of the body and those entrusted with its government, but rather without their knowledge".[58] But this is to run ahead. Already in the summer of 1840 there were more serious happenings in train.

By July and August of that year, the intransigence and suspicion on both sides was palpable. The matter of the beds, and the surreptitious memorial to Cardinal Fransoni, reflected the disharmony. Edmund Rice had earlier added further to it by making Brs Kelly and Bernard Dunphy executors of his will: giving into their hands a sum to pay off all his debts and borrowings on behalf of the congregation, and instructing them to apply the trust funds as they judged fit "without the control or interference of any person or persons whatsoever"![59] No permission appears to have been sought from the superior general.

Riordan, for his part, had acted heavy-handedly with two brothers of the Mill Street community. In 1839 he had received a report that they had come home drunk one evening. He did nothing at the time; but in August 1840, after he had installed a new director at Mill Street, he conducted a "trial" of the two men in the presence of the general council and six other brothers. It lasted over eight days! The charges were refuted. There were also charges brought forward, moreover, that Br Bernard Dunphy and some others in Hanover Street sought to bring about changes in the constitution and had sought to place themselves under the authority of bishops. These, too, were unsubstantiated. The week of "trial" produced nothing but resentment and did nothing to assert Br Riordan's authority. Already, indeed, the dissidents had taken the drastic step of formally writing to Rome for his dismissal

A momentous memorial to the Holy See

The memorial calling for his dismissal, and the appointment in his place of Br Austin Dunphy, was sent on 30 July 1840. It represented that once Br Rice went out of office "peace, concord and brotherly charity departed with him, for the spirit of intrigue and ambition, which manifested itself in opposition to the re-election of the founder in 1832, was now wielded successfully by the same party to have him, Michael Paul Riordan, unfairly and uncanonically elected general". The memorial also represented the application to the Holy See for a *sanatio* of the election as the work of a minority of the chapter. In addition, specific charges were made against the administration of Br Riordan:

1. The decrees of the chapter had been disregarded and the arbitrary will of Paul Riordan, and Leonard, his assistant, substituted in their stead.
2. There had been precept of obedience following precept of obedience commanding things contrary to prudence, justice, charity, and the laws of the state.
3. Brothers, who had long laboured in the institute, were deposed from

their office as directors, and replaced by brothers who applauded the misdeeds of M.P. Riordan.

4. The superior-general betrayed his trust by introducing a discussion as to putting the institute entirely under the control of the bishops.

The signatures appended to this document were "Edmund Rice, the humble instrument under divine providence in founding this Society, John J. Keane, Michl. B. Dunphy, Myles Ign. Kelly, R.F. Ryan, James L. Knowd, Mark T. Anthony, L.P. Naghten".[60] In short, the very same group of people who had signed the other memorial!

When the prefect of Propaganda received the document, he wrote to Dr Murray for further information and advice.[61] The matter took the archbishop by surprise. Surmising that Bernard Dunphy was likely to be a moving force in constructing the memorial, Dr Murray applied to him for a copy, and invited him to make any observations he might wish to make. Dunphy sent the copy on 23 November, and three days later a long letter giving the reasons for the appeal, with some additional comments.

He stated that Brs Riordan and Leonard disregarded the other assistant, Br Thornton, who was close to Br Rice's group, and acted as they liked. He recounted the harsh conduct shown to the founder, "charging him with being guilty of disobedience for having executed the mortgage, and in refusing him a bed to lie on out of the many vacant ones they had in the house". The August "trial" was mentioned, when the accused were never granted an acquittal though innocent; as was the necessity of pay schools, since only five of the 17 houses in the congregation "had ample funds for their support".[62] And there seemed to be no hope of redress at the next chapter, the writer went on, because Riordan and Leonard had appointed so many of their friends as directors of principal houses within the last two years, and these would be members of the approaching chapter by virtue of their office, and would "enable them to carry any measures they please".

Dunphy concluded by commenting that the only means of avoiding "our approaching break-up is an immediate appointment of a new superior and assistants by our Holy Father, Gregory XVI, and a rescript authorising us to have pay schools where we have not funds for our support". He added: "No one of our brothers, nor anyone else, knows a word of the above. I should not like the Jesuits should know anything about it, for Mr Kenney has been committed to Mr P. Riordan from the beginning."[63] Ironically, some years earlier one of the brothers Leonard, of the Cork trio, had complained of Kenney being too supportive of Edmund Rice and his assistants.[64]

Dr Murray, despite Dunphy's request, submitted the memorial and letter to Kenney for his examination, comment and advice. The latter, though very tired and anxious to get away for a break, addressed himself to the problem with considerable care and acumen, and despatched two long letters to the archbishop, on 31 December 1840, and 21 January 1841. He was clearly upset and saddened by what had taken place.

Advisory letters for the archbishop

"The subject," he observed on New Year's eve, 1840, "may be adequately divided into the following parts: the election in 1838; the *'sanatorium'*; the unfitness of the general superior; the memorial sent to Rome in August last."

"*The Election.* The entire course of this proceeding was a sequel of acts either absolutely invalid, or so-grossly irregular as to render the application to Rome quite necessary." Having mentioned some of these, he went on: "with all these, and other objections, I should hesitate, however, to pronounce what the memorial to the Holy Father so easily declares, that the election of the superior general was *evidently* null and void. Though there were no such evidence of nullity, the *sanitorium* might be quite necessary. On this point, I shall only further remark, that the papers sent furnish no proof, though they abound in insinuation that errors committed in the election were the result of party intrigue, or ... the fruit of malicious intention."

"*The Sanatorium.* In my judgement this is a valid and fully effective document so that, notwithstanding all the errors of the election, Br Michael Paul Riordan is made by it the superior general of the congregation, and not less so than if he had received a brief appointing him by name. The objections made to this document are in my mind most futile." He pointed out that 17 out of 19 members of the chapter favoured sending a memorial to Rome. In formulating it, Kenney continued, the superior general called around him "a few selected from both sides of the chapter. Dunphy, who was put in nomination with him, was the man who drew out the memorial. It is taken to the vicar general of the diocese, who adopts it as *his own*. It is received by the Congregation [Fide] under this title, and presented to the pope, who, in his affection for the Christian Brothers and at the prayer of the said v. general of Waterford, supplies *all defects whatsoever*; and, after a lapse of two years, are we to listen to such objections against an apostolic mandate."

"The third subject proposed for consideration," he continued, "is the *Unfitness of Br M.P. Riordan*[65] for the office of superior general in which he was confirmed by the sanatorium." Here, he observed, it was necessary "to separate the facts adduced in proof, from the insinuations which abound in almost every page of these documents". The facts stated were – 1. His breach of faith with the chapter with regard to pay schools; 2. His precept of obedience on the mortgage case; 3. His abuse of power in changing the directors (of schools); 4. His discussion on changing the government of the institute and placing the houses under the bishops as their religious superiors; 5. His trial of certain brothers at Mill Street house, and charges against some others.

Kenney's response to "these asserted facts" was, first, that even if "they were quite true, and quite free from all misrepresentation and from all exaggeration, they would not, either separately or collectively, amount to a canonical cause of deposition". The institute and the papal brief restricted the deposition of the superior general to "heresy, murder", and "cases of such enormity".

As to the individual facts, the information was "as yet *ex-parte*" and required that the superior be given an opportunity of exculpation or explanation. The alleged "trial", he found an enigma; but he suspected that there was much suppression in the narrative. "An observation," he added, that "is more or less applicable to all the facts here adduced."

The Memorial. "The last subject of these papers," he added, is "the memorial to the Holy See for his deposition. From what I have said it is manifest that my opinion must be that your Grace cannot sanction this memorial." He expressed the opinion the more confidently because it was formed solely on the cause shown by the memoralists themselves. They provided indications of unfitness which, even if true, were insufficient to justify deposition. They did so, moreover, "with a baldness of assertion, that makes suspicion a fact, and imputes crime where there is no proof of malice or vicious intention" ... "I shall now only add this one word, I know not if I ever felt for anything not done by myself, as I do feel to see the name of B. Rice to that unworthy document."[66]

Some wider comments and criticisms

After further reflection, he wrote again on 21 January 1841. He had become more deeply critical of the memorial. To depose the general superior in this instance, he announced, would be to do an injustice not only to an individual but to a whole congregation. What an example it would be if the pope "deposed the general superior, not at the instance of the chapter, not at the prayer of the assistants, whose duty it would be to prepare such a measure if requisite, but on a memorial got up by eight individuals, who ... assume the office of providing another head of the society, not according to the mode prescribed in the rules or constitutions, but by the absolute power of the pope, which should never be invoked to remedy the evils of a religious body, if there remained any constitutional means of attaining the said object." Such a deposition might cause a schism that would dissolve the congregation. "This is the honour that the seven brothers would procure for their Founder! I have finished with the memorial."

Having "finished with the memorial", he then went on to examine further the specific charges against the superior, and then, he moved on to more general, almost exasperated, observations.

The various matters in dispute had led him to believe, he wrote, that some of these good Christian Brothers did not sufficiently respect in their general

superior that immunity from domestic control which the constitutions attached
to his office. What, he asked, was the point of having assistants to the general
superior as a guarantee against the abuse of authority, and with power to call a
general chapter to depose a superior, if a faction of six or eight might get
together in secret and sign a memorial "to invoke the supreme power of the
Holy See to depose the superior unheard and untried?" In all this, there was a
desire "to make the head dependent on the members, instead of the members
dependent on the head".

He had often lamented to observe in the congregation, he continued, the
haste with which they adopted changes that seem extreme and inconsistent.
Thus, "in good Mr Rice's time, despite all his wishes, they gave up their connection with the Education Board on the principle of being more free to
attend to the religious education of the poor, and in the confidence of being
supported by the people if they took no money from the Board; now they say
that they cannot teach the poor gratuitously, unless they are allowed to teach
others for money, and thus cause a notable change in their institute!"[67]
Furthermore, "although it was directly opposed to the brief of Pius VII, and to
their own vow, to receive any compensation from the children or their parents,
they set up a pay school by way of a trial to see whether they would ask leave
or not!" Again, he added wickedly, because the election before last of the
superior general proved troublesome, they determined to have as few as possible, and got a rescript, or said they got such, declaring that all future elections
should be for life. They went ahead and elected a superior for life, "and two
years of his administration have scarcely passed, when eight of the society
petition the pope to depose him".

Having thus sweepingly expressed his frustration at what he perceived to
be blatant neglect of stability and good order, he went on to offer Dr Murray
some suggestions towards the healing of divisions in the congregation.

"Gentle advice" for peace and harmony

Before his Grace's reply went to Rome, he "would advise that all, or some, of
the eight who signed the memorial be called in and informed that your Grace
was required to examine the grounds" on which the memorial rested, and that,
as a result, it was clear that these did not justify so harsh and dangerous a
measure as deposition, and that, in consequence, there was no alternative but
submission to the authority under which they were placed, and accommodation of all their differences with the superior as peaceably as they could. As
their general chapter was to be held next Christmas, he felt that all unsettled
questions could be left till then.

He would also suggest, however, that the superior, assistants, and one or
more of the directors, be called in and informed that the Sacred Congregation
had been afflicted with reports, and particularly with the manner in which the

late chapter was conducted and the consequent dissension amongst its members, and that, therefore, it was up to the superiors "to do their utmost to conciliate the confidence of the whole body by abstaining from all harsh measures, and giving proofs of confidence to all according to their rank, merits and seniority in the society". It seemed to him, he added, that "this gentle advice would settle all things, particularly under the fear that further dissension would lead to greater changes than any of them might desire". It would also be the more speedy adjustment, without any further trouble to the Sacred Congregation.

Regret and conclusion

He concluded with an unhappy backward glance once again at the reputation of men whom he had greatly revered for so long, and with an assertion of his own absence of bias in what he had written.

"I cannot conclude without again assuring your Grace," he wrote, "that I have all through the consideration of these documents felt the greatest affliction, when I found that my conscientious conviction forced me to disapprove of the conduct of the very men, who were my own greatly revered friends and old acquaintances. I have been in close habits of sacred friendship with good Mr Rice for nine and thirty years, and the part he has taken with the memoralists is the only fault I had ever to complain of. With others of them I have also been long acquainted, and to some have been indebted for many attentions and services. There certainly could not be in me any predisposition to take an unfavourable view of their conduct. On the other hand, I know little or nothing of those who are called 'the Cork brothers'. I had not ever heard of Br Riordan until after the election." He had never been consulted by him on the subjects contained in the memorial, except with regard to the pay schools and the mortgage issues; and, to the best of his recollection. he "had been previously consulted on the same subjects by the brothers who are opposed to him", who received from him "the same answers". Consequently, he insisted, the judgement that he had formed, "be it erroneous or correct", was "certainly and truly unbiased".[68]

"Gentle advice" followed?

His "gentle advice" seems to have been transmitted; and the subsequent general chapter, held in July 1841, seemed at first sight to restore peace and harmony. With regard to the difference over the mortgage, both parties were judged to have acted conscientiously; and all were recommended "to bury the matter in oblivion". On pay-schools, it was agreed that only one be kept open in Dublin, that at Hanover Street. This was said to be as a gesture to placate Dr Murray, and as a test case to see if pay-schools would be expedient for the work of the institute. Concern and anger were expressed, however, regarding the rescript obtained from the Holy See as a result of a private memorial letter, and at the fact that papal approval for such schools was sought through the archbishop. The independence of the congregation was deemed to have been weakened, and the authority of the superior general undermined. The chapter decided not to accept the papal rescript! And then continued the Hanover Street pay-school! And it voted, moreover, by a large majority to delete from the minutes the paragraphs about the pay-schools!! Kenney, had he heard, must have smiled wearily.

After the assembly, the archbishop was informed that the vast majority of the brothers were working together in peace and harmony, that the superior "possessed the esteem, respect and confidence of the brothers", but that regretfully there were a few exceptions from the universal harmony which prevailed throughout the congregation. His Grace expressed his satisfaction that differences had been happily resolved, and advised charity towards all. All seemed well, but as the official historian, M.C. Normoyle, remarked: the statement to the archbishop "was more hopeful than the position warranted and the events proved".[69]

Postscripts: matters of fraudulent imitation

There are two significant postscripts which add to the confusion and piquancy of the overall scene, and reflect the byzantine politics of some members of the congregation at this period.

The first relates to the exclusion of Br Edmund Ignatius Rice from the general chapter of 1841.

The general chapter ten years earlier had requested the Holy See that an ex-superior general and ex-assistants who had resigned their offices be permitted to participate in the general chapter. A rescript was granted from Rome in 1833; but as the wording of the petition was not clear as to whether it applied to all future chapters or just to the one at which they went out of office, Br Riordan, it seems, put that question to Kenney with a view to the 1841 assembly. The alleged reply from Kenney in the general archives of the Christian Brothers, dated 9 February 1841, indicates that he was informed in the letter containing the query, that the previous general chapter had requested that these questions be put to him. His reply carried the question and response in a rather stilted form.

"Query – Whether the ex-superior and ex-assistants are entitled to assist and be members of all future chapters? And whether the assistants, who have not resigned until within a few days of the general chapter, are entitled to be members of it?

"You tell me *that the general chapter referred this question to me*,[70] but they arise from their own 48th decree. Who can tell the meaning of the law as well as the men who made it? I can only say what I take to be the meaning of their own words, and what I think they ought to have intended to do. I am then decidedly of the opinion that the privileges granted by the 48th decree to the ex-superior and ex-assistants is limited to the chapter at which they go out of office either by new elections or by resignation."[71]

On the basis of this, Br Riordan, it would appear, decided that the founder could not attend ex-officio. He put his name among the brothers on the general electoral list, but never told him he could not attend ex-officio. Other brothers presumed he would be present, and did not vote for him; and the old man himself turned up presuming a right to attend. A vote to coopt his attendance was not carried, probably because by this the assembly had become sensitised to the importance of keeping to procedures.

So far, the matter is not too complicated. Research in the Murray papers in the Dublin diocesan archives, however, turned up, accidentally, under the same date, a letter on the same subject matter, and signed with Kenney's name. It runs:

> At the last general chapter held in July 1838 ... it was resolved to make application to the Revd Dr Kenny to have his opinion whether the ex-superior and ex-assistants are entitled to assist at all future general chapters, and whether the assistants who have not resigned until that time expires, or within a few days of it, are entitled to be members of the chapter?
>
> Dr Kenny's reply – "I am then decidedly of opinion that the privilege granted by the 48th decree to the ex-superior and ex-assistants, is limited to the chapter at which they go out of office either by new elections or by resignation."
> Feb. 9 1841.
> P. Kenny.[72]

The first thing that catches the eye is that the name, "Kenny", is not spelled as Peter Kenney spelled it. Perhaps, however, it is just a paraphrase from another document, maybe from the one in the Christian Brothers archive, though that has some peculiarities of expression? But that is not all. There is an N.B. attached to this document, which has obviously been written by a member of the Christian Brothers congregation, and which runs:

> N.B. The above resolution is a mistake or a forgery – no such resolution was enacted at our last chapter as our written decrees prove.[73]

The word "forgery" is not a word that one uses easily.

What would have been the purpose? Not to have Edmund Rice present, even in his very weakened state, would have removed a possible problem for the Riordan camp. And their path was further smoothed by the non-election, possibly for reasons of health, of Bernard Dunphy.[74] But such reflections would scarcely merit attention, were it not for the second promised post-script.[75] This one concerns Edmund Ignatius Rice directly.

Brother M.C. Normoyle, the historian already referred to a number of times, was of the opinion that the style and contents of the memorial of 30 July did not quite correspond to what was known of Edmund Rice. Kenney's own reaction of surprise and upset corroborates such a view. Normoyle brought Rice's signature in the memorial, and a number of other signatures of his, to handwriting experts in Ireland and in Italy. Independently, these confirmed that the handwriting on the memorial, and on a number of other documents, was a forgery, while the Italian expert, Dr Paceri, spoke of it as *"falsa per imitatione"*, or a simulated forgery.[76]

Peter Kenney, however, went to his grave saddened and surprised by this "first fault" in thirty-nine years in a man he revered; and, of course, without the consolation of witnessing the extraordinary transformation worked by the commitment and skill of his Brothers on the educational life of Ireland. The distress occasioned by Edmund Rice almost coincided with the disappointment he experienced at Mary Aikenhead's handling of the Sr Ignatius case. Ask not for whom the cock crows. It seemed a sobering reminder of the fallibility and frailty even of the saints, and of the limitations, as well as the benefits, of sin-glemindednss.

This extended treatment of the major issues of the Bishops and National Education, and of the Brothers in their early critical years of strain and division, may convey the impression that these dominated Peter Kenney's life at the end of the 1830s and start of the forties. In point of fact, they were necessarily but a small, if important, part in his busy life of church work, consultations, meetings, and correspondence. Moreover, during 1839 physical exhaustion and declining health added to his preoccupations to the point of moving him, the following year, to seek permission to travel to a warm climate for a restorative period.

XV

"Towards the pebbled shore", 1839–41: Erosion of life – The final journey – Mortgaged to obedience – Mourning in Dublin, and appreciation

Like as the waves make towards the pebbled shore
So do our minutes hasten their end.

Shakespeare, Sonnet 60

When to go uphill is an ordeal
And a walk is something to dread

Yet the almond tree is in flower.

Ecclesiastes 12:5

EROSION OF ENERGY – THE SOLACE OF A SOUTHERN SKY

Variously occupied

Even by the standard of previous busy years, 1839 seemed incessant; and it appeared all the more so to Peter Kenney because of his waning energy and declining mobility. As if to symbolise the mounting pressure, the year opened with a natural phenomenon which left an indelible mark on Irish folk memory. The night of 6–7 January was "the night of the Big Wind". Some 38 houses, as well as "2,534 valuable trees", were said to have been knocked in Dublin, with a further 5,000 houses damaged. Two people were killed, and eighteen injured.[1] It is to be presumed that the church and residence at Gardiner Street suffered ill-effects; though these cannot have been serious since Kenney quickly made available to Clongowes, where there had been "considerable damage", the services of the Jesuit brother in the community who had a reputation as a capable handyman.[2]

That year was one of his busiest because, as earlier indicated, the consultations regarding the Sisters of Charity, and the beginning of his involvement in relation to the bishops' controversy and the Christian Brothers' dispute, were added to his combined care of church, community, and Hardwicke Street school, and to the regular outside requests for spiritual guidance and for clergy and convent retreats. And also, as always, there were the occasional, unusual queries or invitations from people of prominence which consumed time and attention. Examples of these in 1839, were the offer of premises for schools on the part of two bishops. Dr Browne of Galway visited Kenney on 20 January with a proposal for a day school in the city, and also for a small boarding school a few miles out of town;[3] Dr Murray of Dublin contacted him in June[4] with the offer of the Vincentian Fathers' school at Ussher's Quay, which the Fathers were relinquishing in order to release men for the work of popular missions throughout the country.[5] Both invitations were refused by the Jesuit provincial and his consultors because of shortage of men, but only after much deliberation.[6]

Incidentally, but also because of links with Kenney, there occurred during the year the possibility of two unusual entrants to the Jesuit order. A former student from Maynooth days, now a Fr McEnroe at Norfolk Island, to the east of Australia and north of New Zealand, wrote asking Kenney's advice and prayers with regard to his desire to enter the Society of Jesus;[7] while a rather depressed Daniel O'Connell, still grieving for his wife and feeling that he had "exhausted the bounty of the Irish people", wrote to his friend P.V. Fitzpatrick about giving up his income "and going, if I am received, to Clongowes, ... to spend the rest of my life there".[8] Kenney's advice to the first applicant is not extant, and there is no available evidence that McEnroe joined the Jesuits; and where O'Connell was concerned it is not clear that his words went beyond a velleity. He was in the habit of retiring for some days each year to make a retreat in the house of a religious order, and Clongowes, where he had always been made welcome by Kenney, had had his sons educated, and concerning which he had happy family recollections, was an obvious choice in his dejection. His resilient nature, however, soon reasserted itself, and the desire to spend his life in seclusion faded.

It was a measure of the range of Kenney's preoccupations during 1839, that in August the General was led to complain once again that he had not sent his reports as a province consultor, nor expressed his judgements regarding the forthcoming general congregation of the order.[9] Kenney remained preoccupied.

Then it was November with its additional church devotions; followed soon by the feast of the church's patron, Francis Xavier, and five days later by the December the 8th celebration of the Blessed Virgin, and then the hectic activity coming up to Christmas. With the New Year, church activity accelerated once more, and before long the church fathers were faced once again with the protracted, demanding Lenten season, with its numerous confessions and devotions and the many special novenas and sermons associated with the month of March. And although additional help had been provided, Kenney found that by the end of the Lenten season, 1840, he was deep in a trough of physical and psychological fatigue, which was increased by, and contributed to, his serious deterioration in general health. At last, he was obliged to face up to his need for a complete break from work. He had not had a proper holiday for years. And much as he disliked seeking any exemptions from common life for himself, he now acknowledged it necessary to do so, and felt freer in seeking permission because of the three recently ordained priests who had been made available for work in the church.

In the past, relief from asthma and a restoration of health and energy had come from sojourns in warm climates, so now he pinned his hopes on a year in Italy. During it, he might also perform his long deferred tertianship, that spiritual year of prayer and renewal which every Jesuit was supposed to undergo sometime after the completion of final studies, but which in his case had been put off again and again because of pressure of work. Hence, as he was also due out of office in 1840 in the normal course of events, he wrote eventually to Fr Roothaan to be not only relieved of superiorship, but also be permitted to spend a year in Italy for reasons of health and spiritual renewal.

Prelatical request and presentation

In the meantime, as he awaited a reply, he allowed himself be persuaded, despite exhaustion and shortage of breath, by the "most earnest and very humble request" of Dr John Cantwell, bishop of Meath, to conduct the spiritual retreat of prelate and clergy sometime between 20 July and 15 August. Again, it was very difficult to refuse, because of the personal nature of the request. His compliance would be seen "as the greatest blessing of heaven", and, Cantwell added, "words could not express how deeply grateful I shall feel for this fresh proof of your extreme kindness towards myself."[10]

The effect of the retreat has not been recorded, but that it took place was noted in the history of *The Diocese of Meath* for the year 1840: "the retreat of this year was conducted by the learned Dr Kenney, Jesuit, in the seminary of Navan, attended by 115 of the clergy of the diocese".[11]

Other episcopal friends and their clergy also expressed their esteem in a special way that benign summer, which marked the third centenary of the founding of the order.

His close links with diocesan priests extended across the country; but from early on he appears to have had a special affinity with the clergy of the dioceses of Cloyne and Cork, which, between them, covered almost all of Cork, city and county, and part of Co. Waterford. For twenty years prior to 1840, Dr Murphy, bishop of Cork, had come to Clongowes in June for the feast of St Aloysius, the young Jesuit saint of the Gonzaga family, who was the patron of the college. Almost invariably on these occasions, he was the chief celebrant at high mass. This year he brought a very special gift.

Writing to Dr Bartholemew Crotty, bishop of Cloyne, on 1 July 1840, to express his appreciation, Kenney remarked: that Dr Murphy, "in his own name and in that of your Lordship, and in the name of the clergy of both dioceses, with his usual grace and dignity, presented to me the magnificent chalice, which will for ever attest the unmerited kindness and munificent charity manifested to the Society of Jesus by the venerable, the bishops and clergy of

Cork and Cloyne in the year 1840, memorable as being the centennial anniversary of the institution of the same Society".

After further somewhat unctuous expressions of appreciation, which seem insincere today but were, as previously observed, part of the coinage of communication of the time, he asked his Lordship to express his most grateful and humble acknowledgements to his dear and respected clergy for this signal manifestation of their regard. And he added emotionally: "There is no hyperbole in the assurance that this gift bestows on me the greatest honour that I have ever received from man, an honour to me the more dear, because participated by all those who are to me the most dear amongst all mankind."[12]

The overflow of feeling suggested that in this centennial year, the personal presentation by the two prelates and their clergy was experienced by him as a confirmation of the success of his own early efforts in reintroducing the Society in Ireland, and an unspoken acknowledgement that he had fulfilled the high expectations raised by the reputation of the Jesuits of the old Society.

The Irish sense of world mission

His special standing was further indicated in these months by an invitation to preach at a much publicised commemoration, scheduled for 18 September 1840, to mark the first solemn anniversary of the establishment in Ireland of the Association for the Propagation of the Faith: a society founded to collect and distribute money for Catholic missions.

The invitation was not just a recognition of his position as spiritual guide to bishops, priests, and laity, nor of his distinction as a preacher for major occasions, but also, and perhaps mainly on this occasion, an acknowledgement of his first hand experience of overseas missions and his special interest in missionary activity across the world. His time in the United States as the Jesuit General's representative and as head of the Jesuit mission there, had accorded him an unique status in Ireland, and helped to make him, to some extent, an authority on the church in North America, and an adviser on missionary vocations.

Ireland by the 1830s had become mission oriented. A comparative survey, indeed, has indicated that the decade before the famine was one of the most active missionary periods of the century.[13] The country's six major Catholic seminaries, including Maynooth, were, between them, sending men to the United States, New Foundland, the maritime provinces of Canada, Australia, New Zealand, the Cape Province of South Africa, and vicariates in India, as well as to "the mission" in England and Scotland. Bishops seeking volunteers for their dioceses visited the country, and some of them, like Ullathorne, questing for Australia, called on Kenney or enquired after him.

The need to provide special training for the growing number of young diocesan clergy going overseas, had been raised in recent years by a Dublin parish priest, Fr John Hand. His proposal for "a foreign missionary seminary" had the support of Archbishop Murray and many of the clergy, including Kenney. Negotiations for approval of the proposal were commenced with the Congregation of Propaganda Fide at Rome. The Irish bishops, who were very conscious of their inability to provide financial support for the overseas jurisdictions where the Irish emigrants had settled, especially in the United States, greatly valued the financial support provided by a central source like the Association for the Propagation of the Faith. And this, together with their post-emancipation pride in being a chosen means of spreading the faith, encouraged them to make a big occasion of the first anniversary of the Association's establishment in Ireland.[14]

The choice of Kenney had a special appropriateness in that context. The Association had been founded by lay initiative at Lyons in 1822, with an initial focus on Bishop Du Bourg's missions in Louisiana; and in its first ten years 42 per cent of its total allocation of funds went to the United States.[15] Kenney knew Du Bourg, who, as noted previously, had recommended him for the see of New York,[16] and few in Ireland had Kenney's knowledge of the beneficial effects of the Association's allocations.

Additional appropriateness was provided by his position as superior of the Jesuit community at the church of St Francis Xavier – the "patron saint of the orient", hailed as the greatest missionary since St Paul. He could be relied on to bring all his celebrated oratorical skill and tact to bear on linking the universal zeal of the great missioner to the world-vision embraced by the Association, and encompassing in that vision the special historic mission of the Irish church of the nineteenth century in propagating the Catholic religion.

The sense of mission was tangible among a significant section of the population. The *Irish Catholic Directory*, which reflected an almost euphoric awareness of Ireland's historic role to extend "the kingdom of Christ in foreign lands", reported on the occasion of the solemn commemoration of the first anniversary that the ceremonies, which took place in the Metropolitan Church, Marlborough Street, Dublin, were presided over by Archbishop Murray, who "celebrated the pontifical high mass, assisted ... by about one hundred Catholic clergymen ... There was a splendid choir, and from 8,000 to 10,000 people attended."[17]

Of the specific impact of Kenney's sermon there appears to be no record. In his weakened condition it was unlikely to have been one of his more memorable performances; although, as against that, his strong will power often surmounted considerable difficulties. The overall occasion, in any event, was an undoubted success, and likely to be not unhelpful to the petition for a foreign missionary seminary. This last was approved by the Holy See in February 1842; and All Hallows College opened before the end of that year. The Congregation of Propaganda could scarcely avoid recognising the country's potential to assist it meet its pressing needs for administrators and priests in new vicariates across the English speaking world.

Permission to travel – New hopes and desires

The answer from the General for which he waited in some uncertainty, came at length on 27 September. It was favourable. Fr Roothaan suggested that he might spend the year based at a Jesuit house in Naples. He did not state, however, when he should set out, nor did he give any indication when his successor would be appointed. Two days later Kenney sent off an excited, almost ingenuous, and unconsciously poignant letter to Thomas Glover in Rome.

"I am quite delighted at the happy prospect of a year's rest in a healthy and warm climate," he declared, "and I am confident, with the divine blessing, that it may add ten years to my life. You know that it was my stay in Sicily that removed the debility both of my chest and my eyes, and enabled me to get through my studies and my labours ever since. If Naples cannot do so much for me in my sixty-first year as Palermo did in my 29th, it will not only lessen the evil of my habitual asthma, but totally remove symptoms of what I fear is the beginning of a complaint in the heart, which renders motion unpleasant and difficult, though it does not, when I am at rest, affect my voice or otherwise injure my general health."

He also prayed for this blessing of "a year under a southern sky" on another ground. He had been entitled to his third year's probation in the Society ever since he had completed his studies, but it had not been granted to him. "Since I left the school of theology in the year 1811," he continued, "I have been to this moment unceasingly occupied in the labours of missionary life, the turmoils of hasty travels, voyages, or the greater vexations of government. I have never had a month's vacation, and very seldom even one week's rest. Think how refreshing the quiet and ease of a religious house would be to me! How invigorating to every sense and feeling!"

A suggestion of presentiment appeared as he went on to speak of the "higher motive", for his request. "When I am well settled and rested, I would wish to make the month's retreat, and to spend the whole year in the full practice of our domestic discipline as a supplement for all the omissions of my spiritual duties caused by missionary duty or by my own sloth. I consider this a grand preparation for death, whenever it comes. Surely it will not be refused me!"

Lastly, he suggested that this year of rest could be of historical benefit to the Society and especially to the vice-province of Ireland. He did not need to point out, that he had been, from the beginning to the present, so much occupied in all the affairs of the revived Society in Ireland, that he was in possession of "many facts, circumstances, etc." which others did not know, which could not be mentioned in this letter, and which yet were necessary "to understand the causes of the rise, and the present depression of our affairs here". He went on: "I should at my leisure draw out a statement that would be a real chain of facts, and serve much to assist a future historian, though the statement itself never can be published as I shall write it."

All this, of course, was not merely written to share his excitement and hopes with his old friend. It was also meant to stimulate Glover to approach the General on the writer's behalf. So, he added, with the formality of the day which seldom used Christian names: "My dear Father Glover, I pray you to urge all these motives on the General to induce him to command that I should immediately set out. If he do not do this, delays will be created, and I shall not get what he is willing to allow me." He feared that his Paternity had not spoken in sufficiently positive terms to Fr Bracken about his departure, as the vice-provincial had as yet said nothing to him.[18]

In practice, he could not easily leave Gardiner Street until his successor was appointed; and, besides, he was almost certainly under pressure to defer his departure till after the tercentenary celebrations at the Gardiner Street church. On 15 October, the General wrote to Fr Bracken to say that he had appointed Fr Robert St Leger, recently back from Calcutta, to the rectorship of Clongowes, and this would release Fr Haly to succeed Fr Kenney.[19]

Tercentenary celebrations

The delay in the appointment of his successor, ensured his presence at the centenary ceremonies. The order had been established in October 1540, by Pope Paul III, so October was chosen as the appropriate month for commemoration.

The ceremonies took the form of a novena, or nine days retreat, based on the Spiritual Exercises of the founder. Kenney as the founding figure of the restored Society in Ireland, and its most distinguished preacher, found himself, as he feared, drawn into a central role in the celebration.

A historian of Dublin of the period, noted that "the Spiritual Exercises caused a spiritual sensation in Dublin. They were announced from the pulpits of the city parishes, and booklets were scattered far and wide to explain their meaning and object. The best Jesuit preachers were employed: Frs Kenney, Aylmer, Haly and Ferguson. Though the weather was inclement, and the distance to the church considerable for (many) people, yet, from the first mass at 6.30a.m. until 9 o'clock, the church was crowded";[20] and this despite the rival attraction, on at least one night, of a public repeal meeting at Capel Street, where Daniel O'Connell gave vent to his unhappy practice of vituperation of opponents and exaggerated praise of his supporters.[21] A contemporary report drew attention, moreover, to the practicality of the "Exercises of St Ignatius" which "were productive of the greatest possible good".[22] The lead up to the novena, and the vast crowds at it, added inevitably to Kenney's exhaustion, even though the work involved was exhilarating and satisfying.

October passed into the overcast gloom of November, as he waited for his successor, Robert Haly. The latter, for his part, was unable to leave Clongowes until after St Leger arrived there. The new rector reached the college on 7

November, and took some days settling in and receiving instruction from his predecessor. Eventually, Kenney was "released from the care of St Francis",[23] as he put it, on 24 November. It was too late in the year, however, to travel with any degree of comfort on the continent, so he set out instead for Clongowes, where he determined to spend the Christmas. While there he was to find himself drawn into examining and reporting on the Christian Brothers' memorial, and, also for Dr Murray, examining the national school system so as to assist the archbishop in his responses to Propaganda and Thomas Glover.

A gloomy Christmas

Among the Christmas cards he received was one from Esmonde, who by this had heard of his plans to go to Italy. He got around to replying on 26 December. If it were as easy to write in Latin as in English, he should at this time, he observed, be writing to the General to thank him for his charitable and kind indulgence in allowing him to spend the coming year in Naples. "I will, however, defer the pleasing duty a little longer," he continued ironically, "and give to you the gloomy hour which I am just now passing amidst the Xmas joys." He then outlined the grounds of his downheartedness: the trampling to death of six people at Francis Street church on Christmas morning, after a false report that the gallery was collapsing caused a stampede; and the failure of Wright's bank, as a result of which the English province was said to have "lost dreadfully", while the Irish Jesuits lost £120, for which, he declared, with a directness worthy of the recipient, "You, my dear Fr Esmonde, are the cause" in allowing "so much to lie idle there". The weather, he went on, was in accord with his narrative. "For three days not even a reflected ray of sun has been seen ... I can scarcely see what I am writing though I have my glasss on."

Then, standing back for a moment, he exclaimed: "What a gloomy letter! Well! if you have not yet heard what follows it will be better news. On the 7th of this month Mr Sylvester Young got possession for us of Belvedere House, opposite N. Great George Street. This will be worthy to be called a *collegium incohatum SJ*" (a secondary school).[24] It became, in fact, a "worthy", even famous, Dublin school.

Finally, he referred to his situation at Clongowes. He had been there with Fr St Leger "for the last month", and was greatly edified at the manner in which he bore "the awful burden" now placed on him. One consoling feature, however, was that "with more discipline" the community were "more united, more happy" than he had ever known them to be. As to his own plans, he added: "The floods in France, frost and snow in England etc. , have caused me to stop here. Fr St Leger's good care is making me strong for the journey. I shall not start now before the middle of January."[25]

As the previous chapter indicated, he certainly did not leave "before the middle of January". His second letter on the memorial was written on 21st of that month, and that to Glover regarding the national schools later again.

Inertia, delay, and superstition

The days and weeks passed, in fact, without his showing any determined sign of leaving for the continent. In the 1820s when given permission to go to France for a year, he had delayed and loitered once he had permission; now something similar seemed to be happening, only this time it was accentuated by his state of health. For though he left little information about his physical condition at this point, it is clear that he was now greatly over-weight and found activity distressing. Accordingly, the prospect of having a companion on the journey, if he delayed a few months, was attractive to him. This possibility had arisen by virtue of his being chosen by the members of the Irish vice-province to represent them at the Jesuit procurators' congregation at Rome in the coming October (1841) – a choice influenced, one suspects, by the expectation that he would be in Italy at the time. As there would be a representative going from the English province, there was the possibility of travelling with him.

And there was, perhaps, a further factor facilitating delay, a bizarre type of superstition which harked back to his novice master, mentor, and occasional disputant, Charles Plowden. During their presence in Rome at the general congregation of the Society in 1820-1, they went on a visit to St Peter's accompanied by Thomas Glover. After some hours there, as they stood under the porticoes, Kenney said: "I wonder shall we three ever see St Peter's again." Plowden replied to him: "You shall see it once more; I never again."[26]

Plowden died on the way home. Kenney had returned to Rome in 1829; and now wondered whether his forthcoming journey would fulfil Plowden's prophecy or prove it false. He could evade the issue by seeking a dispensation from the role of procurator on the grounds of ill health; but he did not wish to avoid the challenge by giving credence to a private prophecy and, besides, as his behaviour and words frequently demonstrated, he saw himself as a man under obedience and, in this instance, viewed his election as the Irish representative as part of God's plan. Hence, he determined to go in the coming autumn, even though he, and a number of fellow Jesuits, had doubts about his surviving the journey; but he wished to have a companion on the way.

Meantime, he continued to send letters to, and receive correspondence from, friends and acquaintances overseas, Jesuits, laity and secular clergy. Of the letters he received, however, those of most personal interest had to be the ones from North America; and in 1840-1 there was correspondence from the three regions of his work and interest while Visitor there.

Consoling letters from abroad

On 21 October 1840, Francis Vespre, procurator of the Maryland province, wrote from Georgetown College. He had never previously, he remarked, had the pleasure of writing to him, but knew well that he was no stranger to him either in acquaintance or affection. And, besides, he added: "I am fully persuaded that you will always welcome a letter from any of Ours, and particularly in this province which you have twice visited and directed, and *where remains so grateful a memory of Your Reverence.*"

Although he wrote primarily to ask Kenney's assistance in obtaining information from the English province with regard to documents relating to the first settlement at Maryland which had been requested a few years previously without reply, he devoted most of his letter to providing him with information about the American mission. He referred to almost every house in the province and the names of the men stationed in each. And with a touch of insight and empathy, added: "Young Mr Lowe studies law with Mr Edward Lynch, our former pupil, member of the Maryland legislature and prosecuting attorney of Frederick county."

Vespre then moved on to tell of happenings outside the Maryland province. Bishop Purcell of Cincinnati had with "a rare generosity" given to the vice-province of Missouri, his Athenaeum, seminary and church, considerable and valuable buildings, to establish a college for the city of Cincinnati. Fr Elet, former president of St Louis University, now held that position in the new college, and had with him, he understood, eight Jesuits from the said vice-province. He also mentioned, that Fr Murphy, nephew of the bishop of Cork, was president of St Mary's College, Kentucky.[27] Elet and Murphy were, indeed, to be Kenney's other correspondents from America.

Kenney had written to John Elet on 1 March seeking particular information, but also, presumably, to congratulate him and wish him well. The latter responded on 4 May 1841, from Cincinnati, still using stationery with the letterhead of St Louis University. He had clearly been moved by Kenney's thoughtfulness, and responded with much warmth.

> No letter, emanating from a different source could have afforded me the same gratification that I derived from yours. I gratefully remember all that Yr. Rev has done for the *right government of the now Missouri vice-province; and its present prosperity is the result of the wise regulations* which you have left, and *which are read in our monthly consultations.* We have *often wished* to have Yr. Rev for our 2nd Visitor, fully convinced that we could still greatly profit by your prudence and experience, and that the present state of all our houses *would be to Your Reverence a source of heartfelt pleasure.*

After this glowing introduction, he went on to report that St Louis University now numbered many distinguished graduates actually engaged in medical or law pursuits, and that many others had entered the Society of Jesus. "We have three stations among the Indians," he continued, the "1st at Sugar-Creek, 600 miles up the Missouri; (the) 2nd at Council Bluffs; (the) 3rd in the Rocky mountains among the Flat-Heads." Seven fathers and six brothers were employed in these stations. The 2nd numbered already 600 converts, imitating the fervour of the primitive Christians; while in the Rocky mountains, Fr De Smet baptised 600 in the course of last summer. And although manpower was greatly stretched, the future was bright. At the noviciate house of St Stanislaus, at Florissant, there were actually 32 novices, and there a fine burying-place for Jesuits had been made, in "one of the Indian mounds". The remains of Frs Van Lommel, Timmermans, Van Quickenborne and others, had been, or were about to be, transported thither. The fervent prayers of the good novices would be recited daily over their graves.

After further detailed information, he commented: "Truly, everything in the US connected with our holy religion is advancing at an *alarming* rate. Here in Cincinnati, where 16 years ago there were not 200 Catholics, we number at present between 15 and 16,000." The college was doing well considering it dated only from the 3rd of last November. The bishop and his worthy brother occupied a part of the building. Both had "Irish hearts as big as themselves".

Finally, having reported his failure to obtain any information on the subject of Kenney's enquiry, he concluded with the news that the Revd Jeanjean had died the previous April, and that the bishop and his clergy desired to be remembered to him.[28] It was an unwitting reminder that he could well have been the bishop of that thriving diocese.

It was unlikely, however, that Kenney, at this stage of his life, devoted much time to regrets at might-have-beens. In these his final years, he had received from all over Ireland, as well as from the extensive province of Maryland and the wide reaches of Missouri, a degree of appreciation and confirmation on his life's work given to few religious men.

The third correspondent, William Stack Murphy, was superior of the Kentucky mission, rector of St Mary's College, Lebanon, Kentucky, and was destined to be provincial-superior of the vice-province of Missouri. A Corkman, he was noted for a range of abilities, as well as for his wit and charm.[29] His acquaintanceship with Kenney appears to have been of long standing, and owed its origins, no doubt, to their mutual links with the bishop of Cork. His letters to Kenney, unfortunately, have not survived, but that they did exchange letters at this time is clearly indicated by him in a long, breezy communication to Fr Patrick Bracken on 5 May 1841, which touched on the discipline of young southern gentlemen, and the influence of Fr Mathew's temperance movement in the United States, and dismissed Daniel O'Connell's "invectives against slavery" as out of touch with reality. He wrote particularly, however, he declared, because he had learned from Fr Kenney that the books he had recently received had been sent by Bracken. And he went on to give further indications of communications with Kenney which, to judge by his references, must have made for cheerful reading.

He remarked that he had exchanged letters with him concerning an Irishman who had imposed on them in Kentucky. He had been accepted into the Society, but Murphy became suspicious and wrote to Kenney. Subsequently, the man was dismissed, but not without some money and a new suit of clothes. Later, however, "a ludicrous and nearly fatal mistake" made a sober man of him. Being intoxicated, and wishing for more liquor, he snatched up a bottle, and emptied it at one draught, without perceiving that he was swallowing a quart of castor oil. "My old acquaintance, Fr Mathew," Murphy continued, "might try this remedy on those hitherto incurable topers whom his exhortations have not reclaimed"! On par with this "ludicrous mistake" was one by Murphy himself: sending congratulations to Kenney on hearing, he knew not from what source, that he had been appointed "Rector of Palermo"! Kenney in writing to him had mentioned going to Naples, and Murphy wondered why he had not mentioned his preferment![30]

An uncertain traveller

Although he wrote to fellow Jesuits in distant Maryland, Missouri, and Kentucky, Kenney, strangely, did not write to one who had been close to him during his second American visitation, and was now stationed nearer home, namely Thomas Mulledy. He, it will be recalled, had been exiled to Europe following his disastrous handling of the sale of the slaves, and for the past year had been at Nice, where he served as unofficial chaplain to the English-speaking community. Whether Kenney felt awkward about writing to him in such unfortunate circumstances, or for whatever reason, he did not write. Now, as summer moved into autumn, and his departure for Rome loomed nearer, he stirred himself to communicate, though, as so often in the past, the immediate occasion was to seek assistance for a traveller from Ireland. He commended to his "kind and charitable attention" a friend of the community at Gardiner Street, "a great invalid", Mr James O'Shaughnessy, who planned to go to Nice that winter.

He then proceeded to speak about himself, displaying uncertainty and almost reluctance about his departure for the continent. "I *must* (if God will it) be in Rome before the 15 Nov. My hope is to be there early in October; but days I cannot mention until I have quit the land of Erin." He added that Mulledy's friend, Fr St Leger, was now vice-provincial, and it would give him great pleasure to see Mulledy in Ireland on his way to the United States.[31]

Kenney wrote that letter from Clongowes on 6 September 1841. At the end of the month, 29 September, when he had hoped he would be already on his way, he handed over to Fr Haly at Gardiner Street all balance of monies he had in hand from various fund raising efforts for a new altar, and for improvements to the chapel of the Madonna, and the portico.[32]

Such clearing of the decks, did not seem to reflect, at this stage, any special premonition; rather was it the action of one taking ordinary prudent steps: after all, his health was bad, his heart clearly affected, the journey long and arduous. A betting man would give long odds against a safe return.

THE HAZARDOUS FINAL JOURNEY

Under way

He eventually set out from Dublin on 1 October 1841. He planned to meet Fr George Connell, a native of Cork, in London. En route, however, he spent some days near Preston, where he visited the Irish Sisters of Charity, providing them with news from home. Subsequently, the superioress, Mary Ignatius Sweetman, "remarked that ... he departed from his usual reserve" in speaking to them. He called them "his beloved friends", and spoke thus "especially of Mrs Aikenhead, whose greatness of character and whose noble work he highly extolled".[33]

On 11 October, he and Connell left London on a "beautiful day" and reached Dover that night. Next day was very different. The sea was so agitated, they could not go to Boulogne as intended. Instead, they headed for Calais. "We went in the tail of a thunderstorm," he wrote, "the last peal of which was given as we cleared the harbour. In four trips across the Atlantic, I never suffered so much as I did in those wretched straits and a corkboat of a steamer". He had made the crossing in such weather to suit the inclination of his "more courageous companion", who had, however, shown great care of him and a personal amiability.

He wrote this account to Robert Haly, from Paris, on 14 October. They had a happy meeting there with Frs Dubuisson, procurator of Maryland, and Van de Velde, representing the vice-province of Missouri. They would accompany them to Rome. "Another great comfort," he continued, "was the meeting with Dr Rosati, bishop of St Louis", who was stopping with his brethren the Lazarites, on his way to America, through London and Liverpool.

Why he wrote first to Haly was made evident in the remainder of the letter. "So much for myself," he remarked, "now for my books." He wrote of them because of an unpleasant experience as he was leaving.

In his room at Gardiner Street there had been four volumes of a breviary. "Just as the packet was underway" he received a card with a few pencilled lines asking where the two other volumes of his breviary were to be found! In other words, the enquirer had already entered his room and taken two of the volumes. He would hope, he said, that for them, or any other books in his room, no application would be made as long as there was any hope of his return. He went on to give a detailed description of books and periodicals in the room. The only books of any account, however, he declared, were "a good and complete edition of Bourdaloue, which, with one or two smaller works of Bellarmine,[34] were given me by good Miss Bodenham" (formerly the Sister of Charity). "As the library had copies already," he had kept them for private use; the same applied to the *American Gazetteer*. There was also a regular series of American almanacs that he "should not wish to be disturbed or diminished".

In addition to the books, he drew attention to some other items he did not wish disturbed or purloined. These included some pictures and a crucifix, gifts of several persons for whose sake he would not like to lose them; particularly the "Ecce Homo", brought to him by good Fr McSherry from Rome in 1832, and the crucifix, sent him by a good young man now living in France. "This I missed out of my room the few days I was last there," he remarked. With that reminder, he concluded his letter.

Against rain, floods, and time

There was a postscript, however, two days later, 16 October. "The Saone and Rhone have overflowed their banks. The steamer from Chalons cannot ply. We must go all the way to Lyons in diligence on Tuesday, the 19th. God send that we may arrive safe in Rome." It had been a day of unceasing rain.[35] Despite the weather, the long distances, and the almost continuous physical discomfort, and uncertainty, there was no word of his own disability, or of any pains or aches. And the same applied, except for one indirect, revealing request, when he wrote to Thomas Glover from Lyons some days later.

With an almost cavalier attitude to distances and hardships, he informed him on 22 October:

> We arrived here last night. Tomorrow at 5.00 a.m. we go by steamer to Avignon, and thence to Marseilles. I left Dublin on the 1st, and I am afraid the month will be out before I get to Rome, though I have taken every railroad and steamer I could find in my way. This plaguey Saone has caused me to lose two days by rising so high that the steamer could not ply for about a week. Now, however, it is so far diminished that the boat, by taking down the funnels, can get under the arches.

He continued, with the only acknowledgement of any physical handicap. Before leaving London, he had written to Esmonde at Rome "to pray Fr Minister to give me a room, if possible, on the 1st piano [floor], that I may not have to mount more than two flights of stairs. So much is a great journey for me now-a-days!" He went on to say that he was pleased to meet at Lyons with Fr Chazelle, whom he had last encountered in Kentucky. He found "Frs Dubuisson and Chazelle looking poorly".[36] No doubt they could more readily return the compliment!

The fragments of a diary, and a letter soon after his arrival in Italy, provide the highlights of the rest of the troubled journey. In the diary, as well as to Glover, he spoke of the very warm welcome they received from the French Jesuits at Lyons on the night of 21 October. On the instructions of the provincial, they were made at home, given a meal, and "two bottles of better wine". He also had "an excellent room on the 1st piano" together with "breakfast in bed"and "leave to sleep to midday". The immediate concessions by the provincial suggest that he must have presented a distressing sight.

The frugal meals next day filled them with admiration for the community constantly living on such food. He visited the cathedral with Fr Chazelle. As a group, they planned to leave very early next morning, Saturday 23rd, by boat for Avignon. Their departure was deferred till Monday, however, by the sudden illness of Connell. "Three days in the diligence, and two days on such meagre food as we had, brought on an attack in the bowels." Stormy and cold weather, succeeded by continual rain and thunder, kept them indoors over the weekend. They were joined by a Fr O'Reilly from Pittsburgh, who planned to accompany them to Rome.

Their ill luck continued on Monday, as they set out at 5.00 a.m. in dense darkness and "in frightful and continuous showers".[37] Subsequently, he informed Miss Denis, the whole journey from Lyons to Marseilles lasted from 5.00 a.m. on Monday to 5.00 a.m. on Wednesday, and "was attended with much danger and great annoyance". Their steamer was held up at the bridge of Tournon, four hours out from Lyons, so that they were obliged to travel packed together, six of them, in a small conveyance called a Rotondo, from 10.00 a.m. Monday to 5.00 a.m. Wednesday, without ever emerging from their "little prison" except for a hasty dinner each evening. "There is no use in writing," he continued, "about torrents, broken bridges, fording afoot where it was possible, and getting up hills of sand and mud etc. It is all over now; but do not you ever let any friend go by the Rhone once the month of September has set in"![38] They arrived at Marseilles on 27 October, he noted in his diary, "most dreadfully tired and sick of the diligence; the dangers and difficulties of our route in continual and heavy rains scarcely at all interrupted by a moment of sunshine".[39]

From there, however, they took a steamer to Rome, and enjoyed a most favourable journey along the Mediterranean, spending a day and a night at Genoa, and 10 hours of another day at Leghorn.[40] They landed at Civita Vecchia on 2 November, which recalled memories, inevitably, of the occasion many years earlier when he waited off the port in a British naval vessel to effect the rescue of the pope.

Immediately on arrival, he wrote to Matilda Denis:

> This is to be posted in Rome; but I wished to have it in readiness that
> the first news of my safe arrival, in improved health, be despatched to
> you, whose kindness and charity have so amply contributed to supply
> the comforts, that can well be appreciated by a traveller, and whose
> prayers have followed me and contributed to obtain for me the happy
> termination of my journey and of my ardent wishes.

Then, having given his detailed account of the stormy and protracted itin-
erary, he observed that though "the wicked straits between Calais and Dover"
gave him more to suffer within three hours, in the way of sea-sickness, than
all his voyages across the Atlantic, there was scarcely any danger involved. In
France, it was otherwise, for, as he pithily put it, "though it looks like an Irish
saying, it is very true, that we suffered much more from water on land than
we did at sea".[41]

Arrival at Rome

They got to Rome at sunset on Wednesday 3 November. The resolution that
kept him going for a month was no longer required. His exhausted body react-
ed. The following day, his diary noted: "slept to a late hour. Did not go out,
and felt myself quite weak and unwell. Said mass in the chapel of St
Ignatius." His room was on the bright side of the house, but its appointments
were basic; a bare floor with some mats, a simple hardish bed, a table and
chair, a wardrobe, an armchair, some bookshelves, a jug of water and a basin
for washing, and a fire place – though it is not clear that there was a fire.

The note on how he felt, as it turned out, was an understatement. And the
remainder of his entries up to the final one on 11 November, were even less
revealing, chronicling mainly that he had said mass. Like many travellers from
Ireland to Rome, he had been requested to carry various parcels and messages
to people there. He brought a present of a case for Esmonde from Miss Denis,
pamphlets and cash from a Mr Cooper, a Dublin priest, for Dr Cullen at the
Irish College, and also for him a gift from Archbishop Murray. Despite feeling
"weak and unwell", he was restless until he fulfilled his obligations. So, the
next day, as he informed Miss Denis in a postscript to the letter, which was
delayed till 6 November, he made the journey on foot to the Irish College.

"I took the archbishop's map with me yesterday evening, and called at the
Irish College in the hope of having the pleasure of handing it to Dr Cullen,
but he was not at home. He called on me this morning to let me know that he
had got it, and felt very grateful to the archbishop for sending it, and to me
for bringing it." He was very sorry to see that Cullen was not quite well himself. "He caught a cold in Ireland and has ever since felt its effects." After

other items of news, and messages for home, he asked her to let Mr Cooper know that he had also handed "the pamphlets and cash", which he had entrusted to him, to Dr Cullen that day.[42]

Neither from this long letter with its detailed account of the exhausting and perilous road to Rome, nor from letters en route, nor, indeed, from his own diary, would the reader have reason to believe, apart from the reference to the first floor room, that the writer was disabled, a heavy, corpulent man in his sixties, with a strained heart, and tormented by deep-seated asthma. His references to the journey were purely factual. There was never a mention of his own personal discomfort, pain, or anxiety. No foothold was provided for self-pity or courting sympathy. It was left to Bartholemew Esmonde, in a long letter to Miss Denis shortly after his death, to reveal something of his determined efforts to carry on as normally as possible despite embarrassment and suffering. It conveys the story of his last days and hours with an humanity and detail seldom available to biographers, and is best given entirely in the author's words.

THE FINAL DAYS AND HOURS

On 22 November Esmonde commenced his letter, which was not completed and sent till the 29th. In the process he revealed his own deep affection for Kenney, which had so often been obscured by irritation and criticism arising partly from his own ill-health.

"Fr Haly has, of course, communicated to you," he remarked, "the painful news in mine to him of the fatal 19th and 20th inst. The present must be to you (particularly painful), for few knew better than you the worth of him whom it has pleased God to take from us. I hardly knew what I was writing the other day, and even now it all seems like a dream, except when I am asleep; for then it seems that I am by his bedside, talking to him of 50 things – but the dream soon vanishes, and I awake to the reality and pain of loneliness, and he is gone; and though I watched his last breath and accompanied him to the vault under our church, and remained there till all was over and all were gone, still I can hardly believe he is gone, and I seem still to dream while I write.

"He wrote to you a day or two after his arrival here, in company with Revd Fr Connel of Stonyhurst and two fathers from America. He was, of course, tired and jaded with the long journey, still I was delighted to see him so well and in good spirits. I found him, however, awfully fat and heavy, and, as I thought, an unhealthy over-red in the face, and his neck so short, that the Fathers here said they feared apoplexy. His room was ready on the sunny side of the house and on the 1st floor, which pleased him much – but even mounting to the 1st floor was to him a painful and tedious exertion, obliged to stop and rest frequently, almost every 2nd step, before reaching the last of the 40 steps leading to the 1st floor. The asthma was painful to himself, and to us all (to) see him so; and (it) seemed so confirmed," Esmonde added, that all "concluded he never could be actively employed again, or have comfortable health."

"However, after resting a day or so, his first visit was to St Peter's, in a carriage of course. Arrived in the great porch, he retold with much humour the circumstances of a former visit to St Peter's with good old Fr Plowden: that on coming out he had said to Fr Plowden – 'Well this, I suppose, is the last time I shall see St Peter's', on which the saintly old man added with a smile, 'No, you'll see St Peter's once more, but only once'; and having narrated this anecdote he added as a joke, 'Well, at all events I have fulfilled the first part of the prophecy, for I now see St Peter's again.' – He little thought that the 2nd part was to be so faithfully verified, he never saw St Peter's again." This version, it must be said, is difficult to accept, for as noted earlier, Plowden's prophecy had to be made in 1820–1, and Kenney had already been back to Rome in 1829. Hence, his presence at St Peter's in 1841 was a negation of the alleged prophecy, not a confirmation of it; and his humorous retailing of Fr Plowden's comments suggests that he was smiling because he had just *disproved* them.

Kenney's next visit, Esmonde continued, "was to the Irish College to deliver in person to Dr Cullen, a parcel, a map of Ireland, I think, from his Grace. Here we always go out two and two together, but as his Jesuit's gown was not ready, and he still wore his secular dress, he stole out by himself on foot (while he knew I was in the confessional) and laboured up the not trifling hill to the Irish College and back again. Next day he kept to his room, resting and battling with the asthma. Another trip was with Fr General and the assembled procurators to the country house. After this he remained quiet till the festival of St Stanislaus, Nov. 13, when he insisted on joining the other procurators to dine at the noviciate. Of course, he went in a carriage. I tried several times to dissuade him from going, as the fine weather had changed to cold and damp. But he would go, and came back not well, went to bed, and was never himself after. However, he said mass next day (Sunday), and this was his last mass. He went to bed early, and did not get up till Thursday for a few hours. During these days, fever was added to asthma. so he had an uneasy time of it. On Thursday, being somewhat relieved, he took a little broth and a bit of chicken, and wished to see good Mr Bacon's nephew, John Dwyer, a novice, with whom he conversed for some time. I induced him to go to bed early, and said all I could to persuade him not to think of attending next morning (Friday) at the concluding meeting of the procurators. But in vain.

"Next morning, when I went to my confessional about 6½ he was asleep. I stole away from it about 8 o'clock, and he was still asleep, so I left him undisturbed, consoling myself that it was now too late to get up (even if he awoke) and be in time for the meeting. But behold, while I was in the confessional, he awoke, got up, and was off to the place of meeting on the 2nd floor, like the first about 40 steps, a hard job for him.

"On my returning to his room, I found the bird flown; so I waited till the meeting was over in order to assist him down the stairs to his room. In descending, he had to sit down on a chair several times. We wanted to carry him in an armchair, but he would not hear of it. To my eye there appeared something vacant and strange in his looks, which much alarmed me, especially as his utterance became at times indistinct, as if his tongue was swollen, or something affecting it. We put him to bed, (he) took a little warm drink, and seemed more composed. They thought it nothing more than the extra fatigue of the stairs and that there was no cause of alarm, that quiet and rest would set all to rights. The doctor had been with him just before he went up to the meeting, and seemed to think there was nothing to make us uneasy.

"We were now (at) mid-day. He took a little broth, but did not seem refreshed. His looks alarmed me, so I went to the superior to state my fears and suggest to send again for the doctor, and also get a second with him, which was done accordingly. The ordinary attending physician had recommended bleeding (him) from the arm some days before, but did not insist on it, as Mr K. had great objections and said the physicians at home had forbid him ever to be bled. When the 2nd physician came, he lamented he had not been bled three or four days ago; and both ordered instant bleeding. I held the cup, and they took about 12 ounces from the right arm. It was unusually black, but came freely. When our father said he felt more comfortable, took a drink, and wished to doze, ... we left him with closed shutters. Occasionally I stole in, and found him calmly dozing, apparently asleep, and not wishing to be disturbed. At length, I thought his breathing different from his usual way, though not more oppressed. He awoke, but answered with such a thick and indistinct utterance that I was frightened, and opened the shutters. I thought there was something distorted in his mouth, and (his) voice still more indistinct. I immediately gave the alarm. It was evident he had had a slight apoplectic stroke.

"In a few minutes, they were bringing the viaticum, all the community in attendance. Having made his confession, mostly by signs, I gave him a drink. He swallowed with great difficulty a little ... It was evident he could not swallow the holy viaticum, so we did not try it ... He received Extreme Unction, I think conscious, but unable to speak. The distortion in his mouth became more apparent. He seemed to have another slight stroke.

"Fr General, and all of us, continued kneeling round his bed; I whispering a word in his ear now and then; the scene visibly and calmly drawing to a close. All the prayers, litanies ... being said, he received the last absolution and papal benediction, and after a few short breathings, lying calmly on his right side, he closed his lips and both eyes as if going to sleep. When, in a few moments, breathing seemed suspended, we continued to gaze, but his fine soul was gone. For a long time I could not believe that he was gone, he seemed to sleep so calmly. A slight drag of the whole upper lip from left to right remained, the effect of the slight apoplectic stroke (some think, and not without reason, that he had two). I don't remember ever to have seen anyone dying thus – to of himself close his eyes and lips completely, so that no one had to touch them after.

"Next morning he was laid out in our church before the altar of St Francis Xavier, whose right arm is there visible in a ... shrine as if blessing our dear Father. We all said the office ... around (the body). Our people here do these things in the simplest way, but the good Franciscans from St Isidore, thinking they might join in the office, came in a body, everyone of them and their superior at their head." Also attending were the Irish Augustinians, two priests of the Irish College, and representatives of the Carmelites and Dominicans. "The Misses O'Ferrall of Balyna attended as if they had lost a brother, and stunned by the suddenness of the thing, while the amiable youth, Christopher Bellew (a fine ... representative of the youth of Ireland) wept like a child over a parent". Mrs Henry and her daughter entering the church for mass were deeply shocked to see him there before the altar of St Francis Xavier, especially as he had sent word to them and the Misses O'Ferrall, just a few days previously, that he planned to call on them.

"By dying here, while the procurators from all parts were assembled," Esmonde continued, "he had several hundred masses more than if he had closed his days in Ireland, so he gained much on this score. Notice was immediately sent to all the houses in the Roman province for each priest to offer up their three first masses for him. I sent for a first rate painter to take his likeness in his Jesuit dress. The painter had never seen him alive, still I think it not unlike. Our Fathers here think it very like, but 'tis hard to give the eyes, for instance, which the painter had never seen. I tried to direct him. I'll send it, with the mask in plaster, taken to facilitate the painting. Judge how lonesome I felt, when all had retired, and I alone in the silent vault where they laid him on the gospel side of our high altar! There our dear Father Kenney rests in peace among many of our former fathers; and looking at their names and years our dear Father is the youngest.

Esmonde finished with the hope that Miss Denis could make out his cramped writing. "I began it," he wrote, "as the date says, above a week ago, but had no heart to finish it. God help you ..."[43]

Into thy hands ... mortgaged to obedience

The strikingly factual account of the events leading up to the death, requires elaboration with regard to one particular, namely the circumstances of the blood letting, shortly after which he died. The General's part in the decision was omitted, to prevent, perhaps, any sense of grievance on Miss Denis's part. The highly regarded minister of the house, however, who was also in charge of health, Fr Manfredini, later to become secretary to Fr Roothaan, told of the incident with a different emphasis: an emphasis intended, no doubt, to reflect favourably on Kenney as a "true Jesuit".

He stated that when the physician first proposed bleeding, Kenney considered it his duty to inform Manfredini, as minister and the prefect of health in the house, that his doctor in Ireland had warned that it would be fatal for him to be bled. Manfredini referred the matter to Roothaan, who, when Kenney repeated the statement, announced – "We shall call a second physician and what they both advise shall be done, for they understand best the climate and the present circumstances of the case."[44] Accordingly, it was decided that the patient should be bled.

Kenney was a man mortgaged to obedience. Hence, he could be expected to seek to accept the decision in the spirit and tradition of the Society's constitutions, which counselled obedience in time of illness "not only towards spiritual superiors ... but also with equal humility towards physicians"; adding, however, that if a patient perceived something to be harmful he ought represent it to the superior, and thereafter leave it entirely in his hands.[45] He was very conscious, indeed, that it had been a theme from the early days of the order, that Jesuits practised Christian self-denial "through the abnegation implied in obedience to superiors".[46]

The medieval image of his founder – being available in a superior's hands like a stick in those of an old man – was a theme in his own life, which he solidly sought to live up to, as has been seen – except when it came to writing Latin letters to Rome! And that obedience of "execution, will, and understanding" which was meant to be a hallmark of the Jesuit, was part of a spiritual heritage to which he aspired, and concerning which he animated others.[47] Already as a young priest, he had emphasised in a retreat to young Jesuits what he termed the "three classes of Religious" – distinguished by their ascending practice of religious perfection. The second class had already reached a high level: men who would on no account consciously commit a venial sin, and who consciously exercised detachment, or inner freedom – "one of the most necessary virtues for a religious" – towards all plans, employments and duties. The third, however, to which he exhorted his hearers, were those men who sought "to perform every action in obedience to God, wishing only to do his will". It was the road, he said, that had led the saints of the Society to eminent sanctity, and the way to imitate them was to make a formal election, or choice, of "the grand virtue and *principle of obedience* in its full extent, and to offer yourself to Jesus Christ to act upon it in all things without respect to yourself ... It is what you will wish to have done at the hour of your death, it is what you would advise others to do, were you consulted on the subject."[48]

Thus, he was prepared – so far as one can ever be in one's own case – for the General's disturbing decision; and, presumably, he sought to accept it with at least the basic peace and detachment of the second class of Religious, though Fr Manfredini, in fact, suggests more, saying that he "submitted cheerfully".[49] Within a matter of hours he was dead: praised as a model of obedience, and hastened on his way by an antiquated medicine credulously accepted.

MOURNING IN DUBLIN, AND APPRECIATION

News of his death only reached Ireland on 3 December, the feast of St Francis Xavier, patron of Gardiner Street church. Large crowds, who had often heard him preach the panegyric of the most famous of Jesuit missionaries, now came to the church to express their grief and regard.[50]

Archbishop Murray was particularly upset. His biographer, the Revd William Meagher, drew attention to it even though twelve years had passed. In his experience, the two men were very close and remarkably alike "interiorly". And so with evident admiration for both, though in an ornate, and at times selective manner, he declared that they exhibited – "the same humility – the same distaste for the world – the same unwearied pursuit of one absorbing object – the same generosity – the same noblemindedness – the same unselfish natures – the same gentle and warm hearts – flowers of different species, both equally beautiful, pendant on the same blooming bough ... It was delightful to observe how these two great men esteemed, respected, loved each other. The veneration of Dr Kenney for his archbishop was unbounded. His opinions he regarded with the most reverential deference ... and he approached his person, and addressed him, with the modesty and submission of a child. And all this esteem and confidence and veneration his Grace reciprocated supremely. His concern at the death of the good religious was extreme upon hearing of which he exclaimed with bitter despondency, 'Alas! he has not left his like behind!' "[51]

Dr Murray was due to dine with the Gardiner Street community that day, 3 December, in honour of their patron's feast, but could not bring himself to do so. He sent a note by hand to the superior, Fr Haly, to say: "The afflicting intelligence which I have just received of the death of our most honoured Friend in Rome, puts it out of my power to dine with you today. I need not say how sincerely I sympathise with you for the irreparable loss we have sustained. RIP."[52] Shortly afterwards, he ordered that a solemn public requiem should be celebrated for the repose of his friend's soul, both at this time and on the anniversary of his death. He, assisted by a large number of clergy, presided at these ceremonies, which were attended by large crowds. And at Maynooth, professors and students likewise assisted at a solemn requiem.[53]

Matilda Denis, too, as might be expected, was deeply affected by the death.

So much so, that her friend, Mrs Molloy, felt it necessary to write a mannered request to Fr Haly to come to visit her "and, if possible, to soften ... the irreparable loss she has sustained of her beloved friend, the late venerated Mr Kenney". "Though less exalted piety and virtues," she continued, "give well-grounded hope of his translation to *eternal happiness*, the grief of friendship must long endure and blend with *that* of the distinguished order revived under his auspices in Ireland ..."[54]

Another woman friend also left a record of her distress at the news from Rome. Despite some coolness in recent years, the strong-minded, indomitable Mary Aikenhead preserved a great fondness for him and sense of gratitude to him. She became physically upset when she heard of his death. On 3 December, on hearing the news, she wrote to Sr Francis McCarthy in Cork, to request her "pious suffrages and those of all our dear sisters" for Fr Peter Kenney, the "venerable and zealous son of St Ignatius". Her request was dictated, she said, "by grateful remembrance of a principal and most esteemed benefactor (in a spiritual sense) ... Most truly he has not left his like. I really did receive a painful shock."[55]

Some days later she was more explicit. Perceiving that Sr Mary Ignatius Sweetman, superior at Preston, had not heard of the death, she wrote her and reminded her "that this holy man has special claim for our fervent prayers and suffrages as one of our best benefactors"; adding – "never could there be a greater loss to Dublin than has been since his health prevented the accustomed zeal of this extraordinary missioner, and truly we see not one to take his place ... Our dear venerated archbishop is truly afflicted, few knew Mr K. as well as he did." She then indicated her own personal sense of loss and shock. She wrote from bed, she said. "I had been rising every day and was pretty well, when, on the feast of St F. Xavier, the hearing of inestimable Father Kenney's death occasioned a sudden and powerful emotion which brought on an attack on my poor weak bowels. I have still to submit to remedies for the effects which remain and are likely to do so."[56]

His memory remained with her, and in succeeding years she recalled how their motto was "so beautifully recommended by holy Fr Kenney", and how she had been introduced to the second method of prayer by him;[57] while a pleasant meeting with the English provincial, Fr Lythgoe, which she expected to be confrontational, recalled the ease of the earlier relationship – not "since the days of my discussions with poor Fr Kenney on points where I sought his advice, have I felt less embarrassed".[58] And eight years after his death, she was still recalling various contributions made by "the very saintly Fr Peter Kenney" or "the late revered Fr Peter Kenney".[59]

Although she kept his memory green, it seems to have faded quickly among the people of Dublin – crowded out by a succession of momentous events: by the mass meetings and excitement of O'Connell's movement for repeal of the union, by its failure and the horrors of the great famine, the death of O'Connell himself, and the publicity surrounding the insurrection of 1848. It was a changed country which faced into the second half of the nineteenth century. And as if symbolising further the passing of an era, Archbishop Murray died in 1852.

In celebrating his life, William Meagher remarked "how unjust has not Catholic Ireland shown herself to the memory of her great men", and especially to her "noble ecclesiastics"; and as "an illustration of this neglect" went out of his way to focus benignly on the memory of Peter Kenney and how "up to this hour, the slightest attempt has not been made, or seems likely to be made, to save the history and character of the great good man ... from perishing – a character", he continued in remarkable tribute, "abounding in rarest and most instructive, and most edifying traits – a history replete with facts of most absorbing interest to the illustrious Society which he adorned, and which was proud of him – and to the country on which heaven bestowed his transcendent abilities, and still more transcendent virtues: *the modern Apostle of Dublin, in no ordinary sense of the word; and, indeed, to an incalculable extent, of Ireland at large.* Whose impetuous and high-toned eloquence in the pulpit, and never tiring labours in the confessional, kindled up the coldest hearts, and purified the most abandoned; while his retreats and meditations, and wise counsels and saintly example, impelled the clergy far and near, in town and country, to loftiest conceptions of their celestial calling, and to burning zeal and steadfast fidelity in performance of its obligations."[60]

In the context of such an encomium, the present attempt "to save the history and character of the good man" could scarcely hope to win William Meagher's approval. For Kenney, thankfully, was far more complex in his person and appeal than he depicted him; a reminder, if needed, of the warning of another more celebrated contemporary – "All things human, even the best, have two faces. Whoever shows only one of them may be an artist, but assuredly he is not an historian."[61]

So, for all his esteem of obedience, Peter Kenney was frequently neglectful, as has been seen, of his obligation to write regularly to Rome, and often continued to put off doing so even after reminders from the General; and despite the Jesuit emphasis on detachment and inner freedom, he was easily upset by any indication of disapproval from significant others. Again, though he was regarded with warmth and great respect by bishops and secular clergy at home and abroad, and by fellow Jesuits overseas, he was often reserved and on his guard with a number of his Irish brethren, who were also less respectful of his authority, and less appreciative of his abilities, than were outsiders.

And Fr Meagher would clearly have found it difficult to understand that the very "reverential deference" and submissiveness, which he praised in Kenney's attitude towards prelates, would not appeal to later generations bred to democracy, or that the kind of "humility", which frequently complained of the burden of authority and voiced longing for a simple life of pastoral work, was more likely to engender impatience than admiration in later readers, sensitive to any suggestion of opting out and the use of outworn expressions of piety. His "reverential deference" towards the prelates of the church, however, came closer, it should be said, to Jonathan Swift's description than that of William Meagher:

> He kept with princes due decorum
> Yet never stood in awe before 'em.[62]

But whatever the perceived failings, and the differences of perception of much later generations, and despite the decline in his public memory, it seems evident that William Meagher was expressing the views of numerous people of all classes, from sailors and cabbies to bishops and gentry, and of friends and acquaintances across the world, when he remarked that he continued to "esteem his acquaintanceship with Father Peter Kenney as among the chief blessings for which he had to thank a bountiful providence".[63] Yet, Kenney's real significance transcended personal ties. It requires a longer and wider perspective.

Epilogue: Appraisal – In the long perspective

Introducing an overview

Those who spoke of Peter Kenney after his death – Esmonde, Dr Murray, William Meagher, Mary Aikenhead, or Mrs Molloy – had a sense of him not just as a wise and spiritual man, but also as a historical figure. They were conscious that the Society of Jesus had been revived in Ireland through him, and that such success as its foundations enjoyed had been largely due to him; but much further than that their vision did not extend. They had only the vaguest idea of his significance in the United States, or of the overall impact of his life. They were too close in location and time, their view foreshortened, their horizon limited. There was need of the *long and wide perspective*: wide, in encompassing his whole life; long, in terms of what has been sifted over more than 150 years – for time is the leveller, the master of perspective.

In this final part, then, there is an attempt to recapitulate, to view the picture whole, to see his life in terms of its overall contribution to wider society and to the benefit of the church he served.

Formative years

Born into fairly poor circumstances in Dublin of the last quarter of the eighteenth century, he grew up in a world of dramatic change. The American Revolution, Grattan's Parliament, the French Revolution, and the commencement of the industrial and technological revolutions, made it an exciting period compared to earlier times, and such developments brought in their wake an easing of the penal laws, the atrocities of 1798, and the Act of Union.

In that era when European and world affairs impinged more than previously, he received an immediate sense of Europe and the international church through his contacts with a local priest, the widely venerated Fr Betagh, and other former Jesuits. Through them he acquired his first academic education, and developed his oratorical gifts and powers of leadership; and when he sought to join the reviving Society of Jesus they paid for his education in Carlow, Stonyhurst, and then in Sicily. In the last named, particularly, he was brought into the mainstream of Jesuit training and theology, acquired a deep appreciation of the humanities and the classical languages, and a sense of being Irish *and* European; and this while experiencing the imminent threat of French invasion. And this period was further marked by his first active contact with the Irish diaspora – soldiers serving in the British army, whom he stubbornly sought to assist despite the opposition of their commanders, and by his involvement in the vain attempt to rescue the pope from French control.

What a resolute man can do

When he returned home, then, he was a man formed for the years ahead: able, energetic, confident, zealous, and very conscious of being both a Jesuit and Irish. All combined to enable him to take an immediate and far-reaching stand: asserting the independence of the Irish Jesuits from the control of the English province, and that of the bishops. At the same time, his reluctant participation in Maynooth proved one of the great benefits to his mission – giving him an *entree* to priests from all over the country, and assuring the bishops that the revived Society was continuing in the co-operative footsteps of its predecessor.

From his days at Maynooth began those clergy retreats and spiritual conferences which were a feature of much of the rest of his life, and which helped raise the spiritual standard of clerical life and prepared the ground for the future flowering of devotion in the Irish populace; and also operating in the same direction was his work for the new religious congregations, the Sisters of Charity – among the poor, in hospitals and schools; the Sisters of Loreto and the Christian Brothers in education. By means of assistance with their constitutions, by retreats, conferences, and counsel, he was, in their critical early years, a formative influence, and a supporter of the first steps of their extensive apostolates across the English speaking world.

The story of the establishment of Clongowes Wood College, in the face of opposition even in the House of Commons, is familiar. There followed in those years of confident zeal, the purchase of Hardwicke Street chapel and residence – a beginning in Dublin which led to Gardiner Street church, still continuing its long history of service, and to Belvedere College, which has vied with Clongowes in providing candidates for the professions and business, as well as men prominent in the arts, and in the service of church and state; and the purchase of a property in the midlands, meant for a noviceship, but soon destined to become a small school, and to play later in the century a conspicuous role in Catholic secondary and university education.

But such undertakings, it will be recalled, were not without their serious setbacks. During the years in Sicily his main difficulties came from his own younger colleagues. Then at Clongowes they resented what they deemed his spartan regime, reported him to a Visitor from the General, who took their part, and removed him from the position of rector. After some months of hurt and some humiliation – during which he added to his reputation as preacher and confessor at Hardwicke Street – he found himself appointed Visitor to North America. A second appointment followed ten years later.

Responding to the North American question

The development of the American Jesuit mission proved to be probably his greatest contribution to the church. His visitations constituted a watershed.

Through them he helped bring harmony where there was division, established solid links with the European roots of the order – sending to Rome for training the young men who became the leaders of the Maryland province. He helped set finances in Maryland and Missouri on a sounder basis, improved the economy of the farms, opened the possibility of a change from the slave economy, and emphasised commitment to the Indian missions. And while divided between the prior demands of mission stations and colleges, he nevertheless helped ensure the financial survival of Georgetown and St Louis universities in conjunction with Bishop Rosati, and assisted their academic futures by his emphasis on a high standard of education and scholarship, which later became part of a proud tradition.

During his visitations long distances were traversed. Each mission station was visited. Some of them a number of times. And he received back from the bishop the order's former church and residence of St Joseph, Philadelphia. It was an earnest of the overall good will he generated across the hierarchy, some of whom, indeed, proffered him the ultimate badge of approval by pressing for his appointment, at different periods, to the sees of Philadelphia and Cincinnati, and raising his name in connection with a number of other dioceses.

Most important in those years, however, were, perhaps, the imponderables: the example of his own spirituality, his suavity in government, his patient respect for others, his care of the sick; all backed up by the decision to commit to written rules and instructions details of the Jesuit way of life, which might not be changed except with the approval of the General, and which provided the solid rails on which the Society moved forward in the United States during the next hundred years. Indeed, it might be said that his contribution to the co-ordination and focusing of the order's apostolate had a far reaching and multiplier effect beyond anything he could have envisaged – as the Society's expanding work in the realms of education reached more and more people, and as its work among the American Indians attracted more and more young men to its ranks.

As he left America, at the end of the second visitation, Maryland had become a province of the order, and Missouri an independent mission. Not surprisingly, his memory was held in warm regard for generations in both regions; and his success of so many varied and daunting circumstances led a later historian of "The History of the Maryland – New York Province" to marvel at his courage, and to add: "Rarely, indeed, are such talents as were his united in one person."[64]

Years between and after

In the years after each American visitation, his life, as has been seen, was devoted to the responsibility of administration, and to the more satisfying, if exhausting, work of preaching, retreats, and administering the sacrament of penance.

In the 1820s pastoral activities brought him throughout the country, and they had their apex, perhaps, during the great jubilee ceremonies of 1825–6. His contacts with various religious congregations, including the three mentioned above, were particularly close in these years, and he also kept in touch with the leaders of the swelling movement for Catholic Emancipation. The Jesuit mission in Ireland appeared to be thriving, so he prepared and successfully presented a petition which resulted in its elevation to the status of a vice-province at the general congregation of 1829, at which Jan Roothaan was elected.

On his return from the second American visitation, a tired man, he was appointed vice-provincial, as well as superior and church father in Gardiner Street. It was too much. He neglected the epistolary duties of provincial, and was removed from office, though not it seems with any great sign of upset. He was happily involved in a deeply intensive period of work in pulpit and confessional. His capacity to be all to all, his compassion and empathy, the common touch that had moved the soldiers and sailors in Sicily – the last letter from one such arrived in Gardiner Street three years after his death – was in evidence now with sailors, cabbies, and labourers as well as with professional and commercial classes. His work at this time, above all, earned him the title "the modern apostle of Dublin". His appeal, inevitably, bore some of the lineaments of Donne's ideal pastor:

> Nor only in the pulpit dwelt his store,
> His words work'd much, but his example more,
> That preach't on working days ...[65]

His health noticeably declined under the continuous pressure, and he aged perceptibly. Bishop Ullathorne, it will be recalled, remembered him not just as a man of "eminent wisdom and prudence, as well as sanctity", who was consulted by bishops, priests, and "persons ... in distracting secular positions", but also as being, at that time already, "in advanced years",[66] though, in fact, he was still only in his fifties.

The decline in health led to the dream of obtaining a new lease of life from a sojourn in a warm climate, and the opportunity to write the history of the restoration of the Society in Ireland. Combining desire with attendance at the General Procurators Congregation at Rome, he embarked, as has just been described, on that long journey, under most arduous conditions, reached his destination, and died soon afterwards.

Mention of that journey brings to mind the amount of travel in his life: to various parts of Ireland, to Sicily and within it, to Malta, over and back to England and across it again and again, four crossings of the Atlantic in two visits to the United States, and the extensive travels while there by coach and steamer, and then the final ordeal through France when he was barely able to breathe and walk. The long journeys endured with little fuss, with scant reference to discomfort, or to the regular problems presented by his habitual asthma and proneness to chest infection, somehow make one take for granted what was really an on-going triumph of resolution over obstacles; as was, indeed, his capacity to preserve his equanimity and good spirits in trying circumstances.

Rome and home

When he died at Rome, after the exhausting final journey, Archbishop Murray is said to have remarked, almost melodramatically, that it was "the only spot worthy to be his death-place".[67]

The remark was appropriate in this, that it was an acknowledgement that he was very much a man of the universal Church, and that, in that regard, Rome was a fitting place for him to have died. Thus, his letters contained frequent references to the pope of the time, his health and pronouncements, the more frequently the farther he was from Rome, as when in the United States; every bishop was treated with the deference due to a successor of the apostles; and his international contacts including Jesuits, other clergy and laity, were to be found not just in Europe and America, but, as has been seen, in India and Australasia, indeed across the English speaking world; and they were usually Irish people, sometimes his former pupils, participating, as he saw it, in one of the great ironies of history, in that a powerful, persecuting, anti-Catholic power such as Britain had opened up vast areas of the world to Catholicism through the agency of the Irish, who had taken her language but kept their faith. His own personal response to the needs of these areas, apart from exhortations and teaching at home, was manifested in his wish to stay in the United States, and, that failing, his volunteering for the Indian mission.

Within the universal Church, however, he was very particularly a man of the world-wide Society of Jesus. He learned of it and worked for it in England, Sicily. Malta, Rome, and America, as well as Ireland; he followed its fortunes throughout the world – rejoicing at its progress, lamenting its sufferings and setbacks; he grounded himself thoroughly in its constitutions and in its Spiritual Exercises, guided his life by them, and imparted his knowledge and experience not only to Jesuits, but to members of other religious organizations, and to bishops, clergy, and laity; and he made significant contributions to the whole Society in two general congregations – with regard to scholastic theology, and the *ratio studiorum*, and in his report on North America.

In these contexts , then, there was an appropriateness in he dying in Rome, and in he having by his bedside the General of the order and representatives of the Society from across the world.

And for an Irish Catholic of that generation there was also something fitting about ending one's days in the "eternal city". It was the focal point. Daniel O'Connell would die on his way there, and, very symbolically, ask to have his heart transported thither. From Kenney's beginnings in the side-streets of penal Dublin to the vaults of the Gesu was a long and testing journey, but in a particular way it was a homecoming.

> Christ calls ... and I must go,
> Not as an exile, No,
> Nor as one deprived, but as one
> Moving to fulfilment, moving home
> Out of the ancestral mesh.[68]

NOTES

ABBREVIATIONS

IJA	Irish Jesuit Archives.
EPA	English Province Archives.
CWCA	Clongowes Wood College Archives
DDA	Dublin Diocesan Archives
SCA	Stonyhurst College Archives
MPA	Maryland Province Archives
JAR. Maryl.	Jesuit Archives Rome (relating to) Maryland.
JAR. Miss.	Jesuit Archives Rome (relating to) Missouri.
SLULA	St Louis University Library Archives
JPA. SL	Jesuit Province Archives, St Louis.
AA. St Louis	Archdiocesan Archives St Louis
GUA	Georgetown University Archives
AISC	Archives Irish Sisters of Charity
CBGA	Christian Brothers General Archives

GROWING UP IN DUBLIN, 1779–1801

1   T.S. Eliot, "Gerontion", in *Selected Poems* (London, 1961), p. 32.

2   The date of birth is given in W.J. Battersby, *The Jesuits in Dublin* (Dublin, 1854), p. 113, and variously in Irish Jesuit Archives. Drogheda Street is confirmed by the mss. of R. Burke Savage SJ. The ref. to the records of Knockbeg College, in *Knockbeg Centenary Book*, p. 35, gives Cook Street as his birthplace; but this was probably the family address after the dissolution of Drogheda Street – see *Reports of Wide Street Commission, 1789–90*, Dublin City Archives, pp. 4ff.

3   Certificate extracted from baptismal register, signed & dated 20 April 1801, stating that Peter Kenney, son of Peter Kenney and Ellen Molloy, was baptised on 10 July 1779, by Bartholomew Sherlock, a priest of St Catherine's, Meath Street.

4   William Yore to Peter Kenney, 26 April 1806: Irish Jesuit Archives (IJA), Kenney Letters 1806–41, inner file, 1806–14.

5   The register of profesions, Harold's Cross, records the entry of Anne Mary Clare Kenney as postulant on 12 August 1815, the religious profession, taking the name Sr Clare, "on 25 March 1818, in the 35th year of her age ..."

6   The Transactions of the Corporation of the Apothecaries' Hall, Dublin, vol. 1, minutes 1791–6.

7   Maurice Lenihan in *Limerick Reporter and Tipperary Vindicator*, 16 August 1869. He was a Waterford man, who had lived near to the Kenney's shop and residence at Broad Street.

8   English Province Archives (EPA), A 2, Varia 1706–1815, ff. 215–20.

9   In C. Maxwell, *Dublin under the Georges, 1714–1830* (Dublin, 1946), p. 48.

10 Charles Topham Bowden in *A Tour through Ireland* (1791), p. 5. quoted in Maxwell, p. 308, n. 19; and Henry Flood spoke of Grattan as "dressed in a rich wardrobe of words to delude the people", in Charles Phillips, *Recollections of Curran and Some of his Contemporaries* (London, 1822), pp. 106-7.

11 Milner, writing in 1807; quoted in Maxwell, pp. 264-5 .

12 Quoted by Young, in A.W. Hutton edition, London, 1892, vol. 1, p. 114. The work first appeared in 1780.

13 R.F. Foster, *Modern Ireland, 1600–1972* (London, 1988) p. 265.

14 Dr Plunkett, bishop of Meath, to Betagh, 29 January 1792, quoted by A. Cogan in *The Diocese of Meath*, iii (Dublin, 1870), p. 171.

15 Maxwell, *Dublin Under the Georges*, p. 36.

16 R.F. Foster, *Modern Ireland*, p. 280.

17 Dr. Troy's pastoral letter, 1798, quoted by A.C. Hepburn, *The Conflict of Nationality in Modern Ireland*, Docs. of Modern History (London, 1980), pp. 12-14.

18 Irish Jesuit Archives (IJA), "Suppression and Restoration of the Society of Jesus in Ireland", in a notebook with hand-written contributions to the history of the Irish province after 1800. Author and date not given.

19 A. Cogan, *The Diocese of Meath*, iii (Dublin, 1870), p. 138; see W.J. Battersby, *The Jesuits in Dublin*, p. 109, and under Austin and Betagh; also G.A. Little, *Revd John Austin sj*, (Dublin, 1910).

20 Battersby, p. 109; Little, *Revd John Austin sj*, lists various centres of education associated with Austin and Betagh.

21 "A Short History of the parish of SS. Michael and John's" in *Year Book*, 1957. Here reference is also made to the Derby Square school.

22 Battersby, p. 109; also Warburton, *History of the City of Dublin*, (1818), vol. II, p. 811.

23 Burke Savage ms.; Battersby, pp. 108-9; and *Year Book*, 1957, for Ss. Michael & John's.

24 *Mary Aikenhead, her Life, her Work, and her Friends*, by Mrs Sara Atkinson, is just attributed to "S.A." (Dublin, 1879), p. 132 f.n.

25 The account is given by the Revd E.I. Devitt sj in "History of the Marvland and New York Province", *The Woodstock Letters*, lxii, no 3, pp. 340-2.

26 W.J. Fitzpatrick, *Irish Wits and Worthies* (Dublin 1875), p. 144.

27 "History of Parish of SS. Michael & John's", *Year Book*, 1957.

28 Extract from old Minute Book of SS. Michael & John's: minutes for 11 March 1832, notes a resolution "on behalf of the institution founded nearly forty years ago by the Revd Peter Kenney sj, under the auspices of Dr. Betagh". Elsewhere, he is mentioned as among the "regulators, rectors, superiors" of the confraternity founded in 1799; see also Myles Ronan, *An Apostle of Catholic Dublin. Fr Henry Young* (Dublin, 1944), p. 158.

29 IJA. Gardiner Street papers; with transcripts from Stonyhurst Mss. made by Prof. Edmund Hogan at close of nineteenth century; portfolios 1, 2, 5, 8 no 1; see also *Knockbeg Centenary Book*, pp. 35ff. for records of Carlow College at that time.

30 Ibid.

31 Extracts from old minute books of SS. Michael & John's for 31 March 1833; IJA, Gardiner Street papers, file: Documents VI.

32 Some, like William Yore, had to leave the Society for reasons of health and

became secular priests; others left because they found the life was not for them; while others were sent away as unsuitable. In some instances, Fr Callaghan showed more zeal than judgement in accepting candidates.

33 Burke to Wm. Smith, Esq., Irish MP, January 1795, in *Edmund Burke and Irish Affairs*, ed. Arnold, pp. 324-5.

34 Ranke, *History of the Popes*, ii, p. 498.

35 Pastor, *History of the Popes*, vol. 39, p. 209.

36 Pastor, ibid., p. 179

37 The eleven working in Dublin accepted the brief from Dr Carpenter, archbishop of Dublin, on 7 February 1774; five others accepted it in Waterford, and the remaining one in Wexford: IJA, file 1744–74; "Subscriptiones Patrum Suppressae Societatis, Dublinii, 7 Februarii 1774", IJA, Suppression papers.

38 On the general history of the Irish Jesuit mission funds, see "Memoirs of the Suppression and Restoration of the Society of Jesus in Ireland" by Patrick Bracken SJ, in *Memorials of the Irish Province*, vol. 1, no iii, June 1900.

39 Bracken, p. 189.

40 Ibid., p. 148.

41 IJA, Callaghan to Strickland, 26 July 1802; also 7 October; and Callaghan to Stone, 8 October 1802; Gardiner Street papers, transcr. Stonyhurst Mss.

42 Callaghan to Strickland, 17 December 1802. Italics mine.

43 Dr Troy to Stone, 18 March 1803; copy IJA, ibid, envelope entitled "correspondence".

44 Strickland to Callaghan, 18 April 1803; IJA, Gardiner Street papers, transcr. by Hogan.

45 Ibid.; Troy to Stone, 18 March 1803; Hogan transcr; Stonyhurst Mss.

46 B. Basset, *The English Jesuits* (London, 1967), p. 366; Charles Plowden only rejoined after the restoration in Sicily in 1804.

47 EPA, A2, f. 294, quoted in Transcripts of Fr R. Burke Savage, IJA.

48 Cardinal Borgia to Troy, 24 February 1804; Propaganda to Troy, 17 March 1804; Dublin Diocesan Archives, Troy Papers, Green file 3:1804-5. 29/10, no. 23; Plunkett to Callaghan on 19 October 1804, EPA, A.2. f. 295; Burke Savage transcripts, IJA.

49 Strickland to Betagh, December 1803, no precise date given, IJA, Gardiner Street papers, transcripts Stonyhurst.

50 Carroll to Betagh, 22 October 1805, IJA, Betagh file.

51 EPA, *Syllabus Admissorum*;B. Savage transcr. IJA.

52 Callaghan to Strickland, 30 December 1803, IJA, Stonyhurst transcripts as above.

53 B. Basset, *The English Jesuits*, p. 370. It opened on 26 September 1803, with twelve novices under Fr Plowden (1743–1821) as novice master.

TOWARDS AN UNCERTAIN FUTURE

1 *Knockbeg Centenary Book*, pp. 35-9. In Clongowes Wood College Archives.

2 Much information on the early years of the college may be found in the reply of Bishop Delany, successor to Dr Keeffe, to queries addressed by the government to Irish bishops in 1800. See *Memoirs and Correspondence of Viscount Castlereagh*

(London, 1849), iv, pp. 143ff; also in M. Comerford, *Collections. Diocese of Kildare and Leighlin* (Dublin, 1883), pp. 165-6.

3 Edward Wakefield, *An Account of Ireland, Statistical and Political* (London, 1812), vol. 1, pp. 39-40. He visited Carlow in 1809, and also described the college.

4 Comerford, pp. 168ff.; and W.J. Fitzpatrick, *Life, Times and Correspondence of Dr Doyle* (Dublin, 1890), vol. 1, pp. 48-9.

5 Plowden to Callaghan, 30 August 1806, Stonyhurst College Archives, F. vi, 78a.

6 Plowden to Callaghan, 29 January 1806, Ibid.

7 Kenney to Stone, November 1814, Stonyhurst College Archives (SCA), F. vi, 78b.

8 *Knockbeg Centenary Book*, pp. 35-6, which provides a sketch of Monsignor Yore's work. He was termed the Vincent de Paul of Dublin.

9 Connolly, *Priests and People in Pre-Famine Ireland*, pp. 65-70, 50, 54; also Fitzpatrick, *Life, Times ... of Dr Doyle*, vol. 1, p. 104.

10 "Memoirs of Fr Kenney SJ" in *Memorials of the Irish Province*, vol. 1, no. 1, June 1898, p. 37 (private circulation).

11 Comerford, op. cit., pp. 175-6.

12 Callaghan to Marmaduke Stone, 25 March 1804, Irish Jesuit Archives; Hogan transcripts from Stonyhurst archives. For Borgia's letter, see also Propaganda-Troy, Dr Troy papers, Dublin Diocesan Archives, Green file 3 (1804-5), 29/10, no. 23, 17 March 1804.

13 Callaghan to Plowden, 27 May 1807, SCA, F. vi, 78a.

14 Callaghan to Stone, 25 March 1804, IJA.

15 Plunkett to Callaghan, 19 October 1804, English Province Archives, A.2, f. 295.

16 Stone to Callaghan, 31May 1804, IJA.

17 Strickland to Callaghan, 3 August, IJA; also Stone to Callaghan, 17 June.

18 Strickland to Callaghan, June 1804, ibid.

19 Stone to Callaghan, 31 May 1804, ibid: Callaghan to Strickland, 30 July, ibid; and Strickland to Callaghan, 3 August, ibid.

20 Callaghan to Stone, 25 March 1804, ibid.

21 Callaghan to Stone, 8 January 1805, ibid.

22 Callaghan to Stone, 25 March 1804, ibid.

23 Stone to Callaghan, 17 June 1804, ibid; Callaghan to Strickland, 30 July 1804, ibid; Callaghan to Stone, 6 August, ibid.

24 Callaghan to Stone, 11 September 1804, ibid.

25 See Basset, *The English Jesuits*, pp. 355, 360, 370; and *passim* in Plowden's letters.

26 Stonyhurst Archives. A. 2. 29. N. 17, ref. in Basset, p. 373.

27 See Grugger & Keating, *History of Stonyhurst College*, pp. 73-4; Basset, pp. 371-2.

28 Quoted in "Hodder, Noviciate and School" by H.C. in *The Stonyhurst Magazine*, April 1953, p. 186. One of Kenney's first letters to England from Palermo in 1808 was to Hughes: Kenney's journal for 24 May 1808, IJA.

29 Stone to Callaghan, 31 May 1804, IJA (Hogan transcr. Gardiner Street papers).

30 Plowden to Callaghan, 29 January 1806; SCA, F. vi, 78a.

31 "Fr Postlewhite's Reminiscenses" in *Letters & Notices*, II, 1864, pp. 109-10.

32 Basset, pp. 370ff. & reminiscences of Kenney's contemporary, Fr Postlewhite; ibid., pp. 102ff.

33 Refs. to Formula and Constitutions are from *Our Jesuit Life*, Anand, India, 1990.

34 Yore to Kenney, 26 April 1806, IJA, Kenney Letters, 1806-41.

35 Plowden to Callaghan, 29 January 1806, SCA, F. vi, 78a.

36 Stone Letters, ff. 71-2: Stone to Strickland, 28 October 1805, quoted in Holt, *William Strickland etc.*, p. 91.

37 Plowden to Callaghan, 29 January 1806, SCA, F. vi, 78a.

38 Plowden to Callaghan, 29 January 1806, SCA, F. vi, 78a.

39 Betagh to Callaghan, 12 July 1806, SCA, F. vi, 78a.

40 Plowden to Callaghan, 13 July 1806, SCA, F. vi, 78a; also see Plowden to Glover, 20 August 1806, note 79.

41 Betagh to Callaghan, 12 July 1806, SCA, F. vi, 78a; italics mine.

42 Callaghan to Plowden, 20 July 1806, SCA, F. vi, 78a.

43 Plowden to Callaghan, 8 August 1806, ibid.

44 Ibid., 30 August 1806.

45 Ibid., 12 September.

46 Copy in IJA, Kenney papers. Published in translation in "The Suppression and Restoration of the Society of Jesus in Ireland" in *Irish Jesuit Directory*, 1942, pp. 213-14.

47 Betagh to Stone, 24 August 1806, SCA, F. vi, 78a. Italics in text.

48 Sewall to W. Clifford, 28 August 1806, EPA, Letters 1805-18, pp. 58-9.

49 Plowden to Glover, 20 August 1806, ibid.

50 Yore to Kenney, 26 April 1806, IJA, Kenney Letters, 1806-14.

51 Plowden to Callaghan, 13 July 1806, SCA, F. vi, 78a. Italics mine.

52 Ibid., 14 August 1806.

53 Ibid., 4 October 1806.

54 See a grim account of life at the school given by Kenney's contemporary Fr Postlewhite: "Postlewhite's Reminiscences" in *Letters and Notices*, Jesuit archives, vol. 2, pp. 102ff.; also Grugger & Keating, op. cit. p. 55.

55 EPA, Letters 1805-18; nos 73, 74; Plowden to Glover, 10 March 1807.

56 Plowden to Callaghan, 10 January 1807, SCA, ibid.; also above to Glover.

57 Plowden to Glover, 17 March 1807, EPA, Letters 1805-18, nos 75, 76.

58 Ibid., Letters, nos. 73, 74.

59 IJA, Transcript with note by aged Postlewhite, dated 26 January 1866.

60 Basset, p. 373.

61 Stone to Callaghan, 29 April, SCA, F. vi, 78a.

62 Plowden to Glover, 30 April 1807, EPA, Letters 1805-18, nos. 84, 85. Italics mine.

63 Dublin Diocesan Archives (DDA), Green file, Dr Troy Papers, 1806-8, no 40, 29/11.

64. Ibid., Michael, Cardinal di Pietro, Prefect Propaganda, nos. 43, 44.

65 Ibid., Troy's Roman Corresp. AB 2/28/1, f. 355, no 273.

66 Stone to Strickland, 20 June 1807, IJA, Hogan transcr.

67 EPA, Letters 1805-18, no 92. Stone to Wright.

68 Ibid., 1 July 1807.

69 EPA, Letters. 1805-18, Sewall to Wright, 7 July 1807.

70 Ibid., nos 105, 98, Sewall to Wright, 18 July & 7 July 1807.

71 Although born in Maryland, Nicholas Sewall was sent to St Omers at an early age with his brother, Charles. Both joined the Society. Charles returned home. Nicholas never did. He became thoroughly anglicised.

72 IJA, Kenney Letters, 1806-41. Kenney to ... 22 July 1807.

73 Kenney's contemporaries were even then empathising with Sydney Smith's celebrated fancy – that the moment the name of Ireland was mentioned, "the English seem to bid adieu to common feeling ... and common sense ...". This appeared in "Peter Plymley's Letters", 1807.

74 The actual sum was £32,450 in securities, in the hands of Rt Hon. David La Touche and Company of Dublin, and was the property of the Revd Marmaduke Stone, the Revd Charles Wright, and the Revd Nicholas Sewall. The bonds were spread between government debentures and Grand Canal debentures; with a small number in Royal Canal, and one pipe water debenture. IJA, Hogan transcr, letter from Wright & Co., 11 August 1807.

75 DDA, Troy's Roman Corresp., AB. 2/28/1, f. 356-7, no. 274, Concannon to Troy, 14 July 1807.

76 IJA (Hogan transcr. from Stonyhurst archives) Betagh to Stone, 20 August 1807.

77 EPA, Irish mission corresp. So/5. Italics mine. Strickland to Stone, 7 September. Strickland, Plowden, Carroll, and a number of bishops, had been disillusioned at the way Propaganda, and various churchmen, plundered Jesuit property at the time of the expulsions from different countries and at the Suppression. See Basset, p. 352.

78 IJA, (Greene/Hogan transcr. in copy book) Dr Troy to Stone, 31 March 1808.

79 DDA, Green file, Dr Troy, 1806-8, no 116, Stone to Betagh, 9 July 1808.

80 See Holt, *William Strickland* ..., pp. 94-5.

81 DDA, Green file, Troy papers, 1806-8, no. 115, Stone to Troy, 22 April 1808.

82 EPA, Letters 1805-18, no. 159, Plowden to Glover, 5 May 1808.

83 DDA, Green file, Dr Troy, 1806-1807-1808, no. 116, Stone to Betagh, 9 July 1808.

84 Ibid., Roman Corresp., AB. 2/28/1, ff. 373-74, no. 285, Concannon to Troy, 3 January 1810.

85 IJA (Gardiner Street papers, Hogan transcr.), di Pietro to Stone, 7 October 1809.

86 Ibid. (Gardiner Street papers, "Correspondence", Hogan transcr.), Stone to di Pietro, 25 April 1810.

87 EPA, Foreign Corresp. 1776-1859, nos. 220-1, Plowden to Glover, 20 November 1809. Edward Grainger, who lived in Co. Meath and had been educated with the Jesuits at Bruges or Liege, was friendly with both the Irish bishops and English Jesuits.

88 Before the Commissioners of Irish education in 1826, Kenney stated that doubts about the aggregation of the English province to the Society in Russia, and consequently about the validity of his vows, had occasioned his going to Palermo in 1808; but this was, to some extent, a reading back into history. That it was his *sole* motive is not accurate, nor were the issues as clear before his departure as they became while in Sicily. See House of Commons, *Eight Report of the Commissioners of Irish Education Inquiry. Roman Catholic College of Maynooth, 1827*, "Examination of Revd Peter Kenney", 8 December 1826, appendix 50, p. 395.

89 IJA (Gardiner Street papers, Hogan transcr.), Betagh to Stone, 20 August 1807.

90 SCA, F. vi, 78b, Betagh to Stone, 8 February 1808.

91 EPA, Letters 1805-18; nos. 84, 85, Plowden to Glover, 30 April 1807.

92 EPA, ibid., no. 143, Plowden to Glover, 14 January 1808. Italics mine.

93 SCA, F. vi, 78b, Betagh to Stone, 24 September 1809.

94 SCA, F. vi. 78b, Betagh to Stone, 8 February 1808.

95 Betagh to Stone, 21 Noember 1808, SCA, F. vi, 78b.

96 SCA, F. vi, 78a, Plowden to Callaghan, 13 June 1807.

WHERE TWO SEAS MEET

1 English Province Archives, Varia 1706-1815, f. 299; Plunkett to Strickland, 12 October 1804, quoted in G. Holt, *William Strickland*, pp. 100-1.

2 EPA, Letters 1805-18, no 107, Plowden to Glover, 21 July 1807.

3 EPA, quoted in Holt, p. 101.

4 EPA, Letters 1805-18, no 126, Sewall to Glover, 29 October 1807.

5 Ibid, no 159, Plowden to Glover, 5 May 1808.

6 IJA (Hogan transcripts, Gardiner Street papers), Kenney to Stone, 18/19 February 1808.

7 DDA, green file, Dr Troy 1806-1807-1808, no 116, Stone to Betagh, 9 July 1808.

8 House of those Jesuit priests who in addition to the three vows taken by religious, take a fourth vow of obedience to the pope. The casa professa is the house occupied by such Jesuits. It subsists entirely on alms.

9 The custom in Jesuit houses of formation, was for Jesuits to have a socius or companion when appearing in public.

10 A procesion in which the sacred host is carried in a ciborium or monstrance, and which, affirms belief in the real presence of Jesus Christ in the consecrated host.

11 A further devotion honouring the sacrament of the eucharist. During a period of 40 continuous hours the Blessed Sacrament is left unveiled in a church and the public come to pray there so that at all times during the 40 hours there are some people praying before the altar,

12 Apart from an eight-day period of spiritual lectures and meditation, Jesuits during the period of training have two other periods during the year, each of three days duration, during which they attend talks on spiritual themes and give additional time to prayer.

13 Queen Caroline was a formidable personage about whom there have been conflicting views. On the French side she was spoken of as a libertine. Others treat of her as religious and fastidious. Independent, running her own spy service, and much disliked in Palermo, she was a far more complex person than Kenney's comment suggests.

14 EPA, Letter 1805-18, no 173, Glover to Sewall, 15 September 1808.

15 Ryan recovered and was to work as a curate in several parish churches in Dublin. Betagh informed Stone, 27 January 1810, that he was ordained on "Saturday of last quarter tense *titulo paupertatis in Societate Jesu* and is the first ever ordained here on that title, having made his vows in Sicily"; SCA, F. vi, 78b.

16 EPA, Letters 1805-18, no. 175, Glover to Stone, 15 September

17 *Annali Siculi*, vol. 1, by A. Narbone (Palermo, 1910), extract in IJA entitled "Anno IV Della Nuova Provincia-1808", pp. 45-6.

18 Glover on 15 September, this time to Fr Stone, remarked that it was generally agreed that Angiolini would not land because he was "too well known in Rome". EPA, Letter 1805-18, no 175.

19 Card. B. Pacca in *Memorie Storiche*, ref. in E.E. Hales, *Revolution and Papacy 1769-1846* (London, 1960), p. 188.

20 Hales, ibid., p. 188.

21 S. Atkinson, *Mary Aikenhead* ..., p. 133, fn.

22 Journal entry. Italics mine.

23 It was built in 1170 for William the Good by Gualtero Offamilla (Walter of the Mill), the English-born archbishop of Palermo. It has a chapel of the Hohenstaufens where vast sarcophagi contain the remains of King Roger 1, his daughter Constance, her husband Henry IV, and the emperor Frederick II – *stupor mundi* (the wonder of the world), who had Palermo as his capital.

24 EPA, Letters 1805-1818, nos 73, 74, Plowden to Glover, 10 March 1807.

25 EPA, Foreign Correspondence, 1776-1859, no 199.

26 EPA, A.2, Varia 1766-1815, ff. 215-20; copy in IJA, brown folder, "Correspondence", Hogan transcr., Kenney to Plowden, 8 February 1809.

26a Report. Appendix no. 50, pp. 395 ff.

27 EPA, Foreign Corresp. 1776-1859, no 190.

28 Ibid., nos 72-3, Glover to Stone, 6 August 1809.

29 "*In quibus vel maxime excellivit P. Kenney*" IJA, Hogan transcr., folder "Correspondence".

30 EPA, Irish mission correspondence with General, 1807-27, code So/5, in English; also in IJA, Hogan Transcr., "Correspondence", in Italian.

31 Ibid., 14 September 1809.

32 EPA, Foreign Corresp. 1776-1859, no 184, Plowden to Glover, 25 February 1809 (wrongly entered as 1808).

33 G. Holt, *William Strickland*, p. 69.

34 Ibid., p. 71.

35 IJA, Hogan Transcr., "Correspondence", brown folder.

36 EPA Foreign Correspondence, 1776-1859, nos 72-3, Glover to Stone, 6 August 1809.

37 Ibid., no. 74, Glover to Stone, 6 December 1809.

38 A volcanic crater on the island of Stromboly.

39 EPA, Foreign Corresp. no 74, as above.

40 EPA, Varia 1706-1815, no 220.

41 Ibid.

42 Journal, 14 October.

43 Ibid., 20 October.

44 EPA, Foreign Corresp. 1776-1859, no 74.

45 Catholic Committee Minute Book, 1773-91, resolution at general meeting, 11 July, 1782, *Archivium Hibernicum*, ix, p. 77.

46 Dr Moylan to E. Jerningham, 3 April 1810, DDA, Troy Letters: 1809-11, 29/12, green file 5.

47 IJA (Hogan Tanscr.), Esmonde folder, Plowden to Esmonde, 28 June 1810.

48 H.C. Papers, "Regulation of Catholics in Foreign Countries", appendix no. xxii, (E); miscel. papers, General Order no. 211, p. 541. Ordered to be published 28 May, 1812.

49 Journal, 6 September 1810. The catechisms were presumably either the English "penny catechism" or that of Archbishop Butler of Cashel (1774-91); the "Acts" refer to the longer prayers – the Acts of Contrition, Faith, Hope, Charity, also attributed to Butler. *The Poor Man's Catechism*, by J.A. Mannock OSB, has been

described as "a classic of prayerful instruction" (see M. Tynan, *Catholic Instruction in Ireland, 1720–1950*, Dublin, 1985). *The Grounds of the Catholic Doctrine* probably refers to a work by Bishop Challoner (1691–1781); and *Mayne's Conversion* seems to refer to an account of the Elizabethan martyr, Cuthbert Mayne. *The Spiritual Combat*, which was translated into most European languages, is attributed to the Italian priest Lorenzo Scupoli (1530–1610)

50 *Annuo vi della Nuova Provincia*, 1810, pp. 127-8, excerpt from A. Narbone, *Annali Siculi*, vol. 1, in IJA.

51 IJA (Hogan Transcr., folder "Correspondence"),

52 Ibid., 28 April 1810.

53 EPA, Foreign Corresp. 1776-1859, no. 76, Kenney to Glover, 20 October 1810.

54 Ibid., Plowden Letters, no. 206(211), Plowden to Stone, 21 April 1811

55 Ibid., Foreign Corresp., no. 76.

56 IJA (Hogan transcr., folder: Plowden to Kenney 1), Plowden to Cogan, 28 September 1809. "*Filii Resurectionis*" – sons of the Resurection.

57 Ibid., Kenney to Glover, 20 October 1810.

58 Ibid.

59 Ibid., Kenney to Glover, 20 October 1810.

60 IJA, Journal, September 14-17, 1810.

61 Ibid., under February 1811. Italics mine.

62 R.B. Savage SJ, "Fr. Peter Kenney SJ. A Modern Apostle of Dublin" in *The Irish Jesuits*, vol. 1 (private publication, 1962), p. 87.

63 EPA, Plowden Letters, no 207 (212), Plowden to Stone, May 1811.

64 IJA (Hogan, folder: Plowden–Kenney, 1), Plowden to Cogan, 28 September 1809.

65 Ibid., Esmonde folder, Plowde to Esmonde, 28 June 1810.

66 J.C. Jeaffreson, *The Queen of Naples and Lord Nelson*, vol. 11 (London, 1889), pp. 171 ff.

67 Despite Kenney's impression at the time, later information suggested that the invaders were Neapolitans, perhaps only 1600 men, while the French general, Grenier, in Calabria, refused to cross the straits with his French troops. (See Jeaffreson, ibid.)

68 IJA (Hogan, "Correspondence" folder), Kenney to Glover, 20 October 1810.

69 Betagh to Stone, 27 September 1810, SCA, F. vi, 78b.

70 Ibid., Kenney Letters, 1806-41.

71 Ibid.

72 IJA, Hogan "Correspondence", a folder relating to Ireland and Palermo, and with some letters of the General, 1807-22, Angiolini to Stone, 5 April 1811 :"*l'ottimo ed incomparabile P. Kenney*".

73 Ibid., Zuñiga to Stone, 26 March 1811. The Latin is nuanced.

74 EPA, Plowden Letters, no. 206 (211), quoted in Plowden to Stone, 21 April 1811.

75 IJA, Narbone, *Annali Siculi*, 1, p. 125.

76 Journal, 12 April 1809. Other references to the instruction of Mrs O'Higgins include 14 January, 13 & 14 March, 12 April.

77 Journal, 17 May 1809.

78 Plowden made a passing reference to a memorable visit to Syracuse in a letter to Aylmer, 7 April 1821, when hearing of Kenney's difficult homeward journey from Rome: "It seems my friend, Fr Kenney, suffered more in his late journey than in

his progress some years ago from Syracuse to Palermo." IJA (Hogan transcr., folder: Plowden to Aylmer).

79 *Memorials of the Irish Province. SJ*, vol. 1, no. iv, 1901, pp. 205-8.

80 Journal, March 1809.

81 EPA, Irl./USA, Kenney Corresp. 1808-41, SO/l, K. to Glover, 29 September 1840.

82 Kenney to Stone, 6 September 1811, SCA, F. vi, 78b. Longer italics mine, others as in text.

"ALL DEPENDED ON THE BEGINNING"

1 *Freeman's Journal*, 21/22 February 1811; see *Dublin Magazine*, March 1811; & V.J. Fitzpatrick, *Irish Wits and Worthies* (Dublin, 1873), pp. 144-6.

2 Plowden to St. Leger, 5 August 1811, IJA. transcripts, Gardiner Street papers, folder: Plowden–Kenney 1.

3 Kenney to Stone, 6 September 1811, SCA, F. vi, 78b.

4 Ibid.

5 Plowden to St. Leger, 31 October 1811, IJA. transcr. Gardiner Street papers, folder: Plowden to Kenney 1.

6 On Dr Moylan see Bolster, E. *A History of the Diocese of Cork, from the Penal Era to the Famine* (Cork, 1989); on his brother, Stephen, see Hennessy, M.N., *The Wild Geese. The Irish Soldier in Exile* (London, 1973), pp. 171ff.

7 Jerningham to Moylan, 28 March, 1810; Moylan to Jerningham, 3 April, DDA, Troy Letters, 1809-11, nos 51, 52.

8 Kenney's views on this were still doubtful as late as 1827. See Appendix to Eight Report of the Commissioners of Irish Education Inquiry, Maynooth College, pp. 395, 397.

9 EPA, Plowden Letters, no 206 (211), Plowden to Stone, 21 April 1811.

10 IJA, folder: Plowden–Kenney 1, Plowden to St Leger, 31 October 1811.

11 Kenney to Stone, 19 October 1811, EPA, Irish Mission Correspond., SO/5.

12 Haly to Fr. Greene, March 1876, IJA, Haly papers (1796-1882).

13 Plowden to Stone, 8 March 1833, EPA, Plowden Letters, no. 224.

14 Maurice Lenihan in *Limerick Reporter and Tipperary Vindicator*, 17 August 1869.

15 Kenney to Stone, 22 October 1811, SCA, F. vi, 78b.

16 Plowden to Kenney, 26 October 1811, IJA, folder: Plowden–Kenney 1.

17 Plowden to St Leger, 31 October 1811, ibid.

18 Zuñiga to Stone, 4 April 1812. He had received the request from Kenney the previous December and had sent on the letters. IJA, Brown envelope of transcripts 1807-22, mainly of letters relating to Ireland and Sicily, and some from the General.

19 EPA, Irish Mission Corresp. 1807-27, SO/5. A single page of excerpts from Kenney's letters, without a date, and not in Kenney's hand.

20 Kenney to Chas. Wright, from George's Hill, 17 July 1812, EPA, Irl./USA, Kenney Corresp. 1808-41, SO/l

21 Chas. Wright to Kenney, 29 February 1812, IJA, Gardiner Street papers, copy-book with copies of letters.

22 Kenney to Wright, 17 July 1812, EPA, Irl./USA, Kenney Corresp. 1808-41, SO/l.

23 Brzozowski to Kenney, and three other Irish priests, 6 March 1812, EPA, Irish Mission Corresp., SO/5
24 Brzozowski to Stone, 6 March 1812, Gardiner Street papers, transcr. from EPA, 1807-22 in IJA.
25 Jautard to General, 27 July 1812 (with a copy in French), EPA, Irish Miss. Corresp., SO/5
26 Brzozowski to Kenney, 30 September 1812, EPA, copy IJA, file "General to Provincials, 1806-69".
27 General to Stone, 30 September 1812, copy IJA, Kenney papers. Text is difficult to follow in parts.
28 Plowden to Stone, 12 November 1812, EPA, Plowden Letters, no 220.
29 Stone to Kenney, 4 December 1812, EPA, Irish Miss. Corresp, SO/5.
30 Stone to Kenney, 4 December 1812, transcr. in copy, IJA.
31 Brzozowski to Kenney, 7 April 1813 (arr. 7 May), IJA, file: General to Provincials, 1806-69.
32 Stone to Kenney, at George's Hill, 29 July 1813, IJA, copy in notebook.
33 Stone to Kenney, 20 August 1813, IJA, ibid.
34 EPA, Irish Miss. Corresp., SO/5, no date, though addressed to Stone and seems to be in Plowden's writing. Its ref. to sending Fr Young's Ms. suggests a date of November 1812.
35 Plowden to Kenney, 4 August 1813; transcr as above in IJA, folder: Plowden–Kenney 1.
36 General to Kenney, 10 July 1814, IJA, Generals to Provincials, 1806-69.
37 Kenney's letter is not extant and its content is gleaned from what Plowden wrote to Stone on 30 September 1813, which date should probably be 1814, since a letter to Kenney on the same theme is dated 30 September 1814 and mentions the restoration of the Society.
38 EPA, Ir. Mis. Corresp., SO/5, Plowden to Stone, 30 September 1813 (rightly 1814, see previous note).
39 Plowden to Stone, 17 June, 1814, EPA, Plowden Letters, no. 228 (233).
40 Plowden to Kenney, 30 September 1814, transcr. IJA, folder: Plowden to Kenney 1.
41 General to Provincial, 22 July 1813, EPA, Ir. Miss. Corresp., SO/5
42 Zuñiga to Stone(?), 26 March 1811, IJA. transcr. Excerpts from letters, envelope in Gardiner Street papers.
43 IJA, R. Burke Savage ms. ch. ii.
44 Kenney to Stone, 17 November 1811, SCA, F. vi, 78b.
45 Dr Donnelly, *Short Histories of the Dublin Parishes*, part xi, parish of St Michans (CTS, 1912), p. 62.
46 Kenney to Stone, 10 December 1813, SCA, F. vi, 78b.
47 IJA. Excerpt from *Watty Cox's Irish Magazine* (1807-14), p. 28. The fourth man from Palermo, John Connolly, is not mentioned. It is not clear that he ever worked in Ireland. He went to the Oxford mission in 1812, where he died. (*Records of English Province SJ*, vii (London, 1882), p. 158). Both Kenney and Plowden considered him unreliable.
48 S.A. *Mary Aikenhead ...*, p. 132; and see Kenney to Dr Murray, 31 October 1812, IJA, Kenney papers 1806-41

49 R. Burke Savage sj, "The Growth of Devotion to the Sacred Heart in Ireland", *Irish Ecclesiastical Record*, October-November 1968.

50 Plowden to Kenney, 2 and 4 August 1813, IJA, transcr. folder:

51 Donnelly, *Short Hist. Some Dublin Parishes*, part vi. sect. ii. p. 65.

52 Stone to Kenney, 7 September 1812, IJA, Kenney Letters, 1806-41.

53 Ibid.

54 Letter of Lord Lieutenant Rutland, 1 July 1812, approving election of Dr Murray as president on 26 June, DDA, Troy papers, green file 6, 30/1; also Dr Murray to Dr Bray of Cashel, 18 July 1812, on his intention of staying only one year, DDA, Troy papers, Corresp. AB 2, 30/1-3, green file 6, no 13.

55 Kenney to Archbishop, 31 October 1812, copy IJA, brown notebook.

56 Stone to Kenney, 7 September 1812, IJA, Kenney Letters, 1806-41.

57 Kenney to Stone, 29 August 1812, SCA, F. vi, 78b.

58 Kenney to Archbishop, 31 October 1812, IJA, Kenney Letters, also copy in brown notebook.

59 Trustee Returns, 1808, quoted in S.J. Connolly, *Priests and People in Pre-Famine Ireland, 1780-1845*, (Dublin, 1982), p. 39;

60 See Eugene Francis O'Beirne, *An Accurate Account of the Papal College of Maynoth* (Hereford, 1840), pp. 14-19. O'Beirne, a former student who subsequently joined the Established Church, provides an unfriendly, rather patronising account.

61 Dr John Healy, *Maynooth College, 1795-1895* (Dublin, 1895), p. 250.

62 Ibid., p. 231 ff.

63 Ibid., pp. 223, 226-7.

64 Ibid., pp. 228, 230.

65 Plowden to St Leger, 5 August 1811, IJA, folder: Plowden to Kenney 1, Gardiner Street papers .

66 Healy, p. 229.

67 Plowden to St Leger, 5 August 1811, IJA.

68 Troy to Delahogue, 10 November 1793, and 3 September 1803, Clogher Diocesan Archives, D 10(RC) 1/1, no 18A and no 27.

69 See P.J. Corish, "Gallicanism at Maynooth ..." in *Studies in Irish History*, presented to R. Dudley Edwards (Dublin, 1979), p. 183.

70 Hippesley to Delahogue, 23 June 1817, Clogher Diocesan Archives as above, No. 39A. There were three letters where he queried whether Delahogue upheld ultramontane principles. Kenney's own position does not appear to have differed much from that of Delahogue to judge by his responses to the Commisioners' Inquiry into Maynooth College, 1826-7.

71 Healy, p. 284.

72 On rigorism see *Sacramentum Mundi. An Encyclopaedia of Theology*, iv (London, 1969), pp. 130-1.

73 Appendix to the Report, no 25, p. 181.

74 The judgement on Antoine is that of St Alphonsus Liguori and the Jesuit theologian, Jean Pierre Gury. For information on this I am indebted to Prof. P.J. Corish, Maynooth.

75 Kenney to Stone, November 1814, SCA, vi, 78b; House of Commons Report from Committee on Regulation of Catholics in Foreign Countries. Appendix N, xxii (D), Letter of the Revd Daniel Murray, President of Royal College, Maynooth, 23 April 1813, pp. 540-41.

76 P.J. Corish in "Gallicanism at Maynooth" in *Studies in Irish History*, op. cit., p. 183 f.n.

77 "Lough Derg" in Penguin book of *Irish Verse*, ed. B. Kennelly, pp. 360, 345.

78 Evidence before Commissioners of Education, 8 December 1826, Appendix no. 50, p. 398.

79 Ibid., Appendix no. 25, p. 182.

80 "Some Recollections of Fr Peter Kenney SJ, as a Preacher" in *Irish Ecclesiastical Record*, xii, 1891, pp. 794-5; from ms. found in Dr Murray's possessions and written about 1868 or 1869. Italics mine.

81 Appendi no 40, p. 334

82 Healy, p. 231.

83 Ibid., p. 264.

84 *Notices of Life and Character of ... Most Rev. Daniel Murray* (Dublin, 1853), pp. 90-1. Italics mine.

85 Appendix no. 51, 20 December 1825, p. 411. Italics mine.

86 P.J. Plunkett to Kenney, Maynooth, 25 Januart 1813, in A. Cogan, *Diocese of Meath*, iii, pp. 402-4.

87 DDA, Green file 6, 30/1, no 41, Troy papers. Milner to Troy on 27 June 1812, refers to speech of Hippesley of 24 April.

88 Ibid., no 38, Milner to Troy, 17 May 1812.

89 Kenney to Stone, 19 July 1813, EPA Irish Mission Corresp., SO/5.

90 Stone to Kenney, at George's Hill, 29 July 1812, IJA, transcr. in a copybook in Gardiner Street papers.

91 Certificate signed by Stone and witnessed, 20 August;, IJA, ibid.

92 T. Corcoran, *The Clongowes Record, 1814-1932* (Dublin, 1932), pp. 44-5.

93 Denys Scully to Kenney, 19 December 1812, IJA, Kenney papers.

94 Stone to St Leger, 30 September 1813, IJA, St Leger file in Gardiner Street papers.

95 A further 96 acres was later to be leased for £2,753. Converting the building for school use cost £3,820; while fitting out both college and farm cost £2,750. P. Costelloe, *Clongowes Wood*(Dublin, 1989), p. 20.

96 T. Corcoran, *The Clongowes Record*, p. 52.

97 Ibid.

98 Stone to St Leger, 30 September 1813, EPA, Irish Miss. Corresp., SO/5. Hippesley had first voiced suspicions about the remission of Jesuit funds to Ireland when he spoke in the House of Commons, 11 May 1813: *Hansard* xxvi, 15; and see B. McDermott ed., *The Catholic Question in England and Ireland, 1798-1822. The Papers of Denys Scully* (Dublin, 1988), p. 497, f.n. 3.

99 Kenney to Stone, 17 February 1814, EPA, Irish Miss. Corresp., SO/5.

100 Kenney to Plowden, 25 April 1814. ibid.

101 Robt. Peel to Hippesley, 24 February 1814; typed document in IJA, Kenney papers, 1806-1841, 24 February 1814.

102 Cit. by T. Corcoran, *Clongowes Record*, p. 53. The source is not given, and no extant account by Kenney appears to be available in Irish or English Jesuit archives.

103 *Diaries of Lord Colchester; Abbot* (London, 1861), vol. 2, pp. 498-9. Kenney only made his solemn profession of four vows on 16 June 1819.

104 Peel to Hippesley, 24 February in Kenney papers, IJA. There is typed and hand-written version, the latter having one line additional to the typed version.

105 R.B. Savage ms. in IJA.

106 The document no longer seems to be extant.

107 Plowden to Kenney, 15 March 1814, IJA, folder: Plowden–Kenney.

108 Peel to Kenney, 15 March, IJA, Kenney papers 1806–41. He makes the appointment for "next Friday" in response to Kenney's letter of 10 March, rough draft ibid., undated.

109 Kenney to Plowden, 20 March 1814, SCA, F. v, 78b. Italics in text.

110 Kenney to Plowden, 29 March, EPA, Irish Miss. Corresp., SO/5; and ditto, 26 April 1814, SCA, F. vi, 78b.

111 Power to Kenney, 28 March, and J. Tristram to Kenney, same date, IJA, Kenney papers 1808–41.

112 Kenney to Plowden, 29 March, EPA, Irish Miss. Corresp., SO/5.

113 Kenney to Lord Donoughmore, 30 March 1814, IJA, Kenney papers.

114 Plowden to Kenney, 30 March 1814, IJA, Gardiner Street papers, Folder: Plowden to Kenney 1.

115 Kenney to Stone, 21 April 1814, EPA, Irish Miss. Corresp., SO/5. n.b. Milner informed Troy, 10 April, about the forthcoming rescript, saying Stone wished to keep it secret for fear of Hippesley and other enemies (DDA, Troy Foreign Corresp. AB 2/28/l, no 323, f. 428); also in Plowden to Kenney, 13 April (IJA, folder: Plowden to Kenney 1).

116 Kenney to Plowden, 25 April 1814, EPA, Irish Miss. Corresp., SO/5.

117 R.B. Savage, "Clongowes 1814–17" in *Clongownian*, 1982,
pp. 7-11.

118 Donoughmore to Kenney, 28 April 1814, IJA, Kenney papers.

119 Ignatius Rice to Kenney, 13 May 1814, IJA, Kenney papers.

120 They had been presented to the House on 21 July of the previous session of parliament: see *Hansard*, Parliamentary Debates, vol. 27, May 1814, p. 934.

121 *Hansard*, ibid., 27 May, pp. 1028, 932, 939.

122 Ibid., p. 936.

123 Ibid., p. 935.

124 Ibid., pp. 937-8.

135 Ibid., p. 938.

126 Plowden to Kenney, 26 May 1814, IJA, Folder: Plowden–Kenney 1.

127 Kenney to Stone, 2 June 1814, EPA. Irish Miss. Corresp., SO/5.

128 Referred to in Plowden to Stone, 17 June, EPA, Plowden Letters, no 228 (233).

129 *Scully Papers*, op. cit., 3 June 1814, no 481, pp. 515ff.

130 Plowden to Stone, 17 June 1814, EPA, Plowden Letters, no 228 (233).

131 Kenney to Scully, 19 June 1814, *Scully Papers*, pp. 522-3.

132 Plowden to Kenney, 2 July 1814, IJA, Folder: Plowden–Kenney 1.

133 *Scully Papers*, p. 523, f.n. 1; report of an informer transmitted to Peel, 24 June 1814.

134 Fentan Aylmer to Peel, 28 December 1815, Irish State Paper Office, 435/32 in IJA, Kenney papers.

135 Peel dining at Lulworth Castle with Mr Weld is said to have expressed to him his high opinion of Kenney's abilities, IJA, R. Burke Savage papers.

136 Kenney to Scully, 19 June 1814, IJA, Kenney papers; also in the *Scully Papers*, pp. 522-3.

137 Kenney to Scully, 12 February 1815, IJA, Kenney papers.

138 Scully to Kenney, 15 February 1815, IJA, Kenney papers.

139 Ibid., 27 February 1814.

140 Copy of printed page, June 1814, IJA, Kenney papers.

141 IJA, Kenney papers, Ig. Rice to Kenney, 13 May 1814; Jeremiah Collins, Dean of Cork to Kenney, 14 August 1814; Bishop Plunkett to Kenney, 30 September 1814, *Scully Papers*, p. 511, no. 479B. Scully to Kenney, 13 May 1814, gives a list of people interested in sending pupils to the college from Cork, Tipperary, Limerick.

142 Kenney to Stone, 21 April 1814, EPA, Irish Miss. Corresp., SO/5. In IJA there is a handwritten chronology, seemingly by Prof. Edmund Hogan, for the years 1801-19, which shows John Shine, John Connor, William Shea, T. McGuire, Chas. Frazer, and James Mullen leaving Stonyhurst for Clongowes during May. In November Patrick Moran followed. All had done extra studies in humanities or mathematics.

143 Burke Savage, "Clongowes 1814-1817" in *Clongownian*, no 82, 1982, pp. 7-11.

144 Bangert, *Hist. of Soc. of Jesus*, p. 429.

145 Aylmer to Plowden, 8 August 1814, IJA, Kenney papers, which has a typed copy from Stonyhurst Archives, II. 21. doc. 49.

146 Plowden to Kenney, 3 September 1814, IJA, folder.

147 Aylmer to Plowden, 8 August 1814, IJA, Aylmer papers.

148 Troy to Murray, 6 September 1814, DDA, Troy papers, green file 7, 30/2, no 26

149 Power to Kenney, 12 November 1814, IJA, Kenney papers.

150 Plowden to Kenney, 13 April 1814, IJA, folder.

151 General to Kenney, 19 November 1814, IJA, General to Provincials file. A note attached in Kenney's hand mentions the date of arrival,

152 Kenney to Plowden, 25 April 1814, EPA, Irish Miss. Corresp., SO/5.

153 A. Cogan, *Diocese of Meath*, iii, pp. 407-8: Kenney to Bp. Patrick J. Plunkett, 27 September 1814.

154 Plowden to Kenney, 2 July, 1814, IJA, folder,

155 Dr Troy to Kenney, 29 November 1814, IJA, Kenney papers.

156 Litta to Troy, 24 January 1815, DDA, Troy papers, green file 7, 30/2, no 50

157 Aylmer in his letter to Plowden of 8 August 1814 (copy IJA, from SCA, II, 21, Doc. 49) mentions that he had written about it in an earlier letter to Plowden, Kenney and Stone. Plowden did not receive it, so its not clear that Kenney did, in which case he only heard of it from Alymer's letter of 8 August to Plowden.

158 Referred to by Plowden in his letter of 17 November 1814 to Kenney, IJA, folder,

159 Kenney to General in Italian, to Aylmer in English, 13 October 1814, IJA, Kenney papers, Rough drafts of letter.

160 General to Kenney, 3 September 1814, IJA, File: General to Provincials, 1806-69.

161 Plowden to Kenney, 17 November 1814, IJA, Folder: Plowden to Kenney

162 Kenney to Archbishop, 6 December 1813, IJA, Kenney papers. The cost was £400.

163 IJA, R. Burke Savage papers.

"WHAT AN INTELLIGENT MAN CAN ACHIEVE"

1 The two published books are: *The Clongowes Record, 1814-1932*, by T. Corcoran SJ (Dublin, 1932), pp. 291; and *Clongowes Wood. A History of Clonqowes Wood College, 1814-1989*, by P. Costello (Dublin, 1989), pp. 273. There are many valuable articles by the resident historian and authority on the college, R. Burke Savage SJ. A number of these have appeared in issues of *The Clongownian*, e.g. for 1982, "Clongowes, 1814-1817"; and in the 1984 issue, "Clongowes, 1815-1830".

2 Daniel O'Connell to Kenney, 4 January 1815; quoted by Corcoran, p. 86.

3 Op. cit. in *Meagher of the Sword*, ed. A. Griffith (Dublin, 1917) p. 272.

4 R.B. Savage, "Clongowes 1815-30" in *Clongownian*, 1984, p. 13.

5 "Two schools of Rhetoric" is an abbreviation for a school of Humanity (Poetry) and one of Rhetoric.

6 IJA, Kenney papers. Typed copy of a draft, no date, but evidently October 1815.

7 IJA, Memorials of the Irish Province SJ, vol. II, no. ii, June 1899, pp. 114-17.

8 R. Burke Savage, "Clongowes 1815-30", *Clongownian*, 1984, p. 13.

9 Eight Report of Commissioners of Irish Education Inquiry, on Roman Catholic College of Maynooth, House of Commons, 2 June 1827, Appendix no. 60, pp. 434-9.

10 An indication of the astonishing range of material for examination may be seen in the Academy Bill of 1820; cf. R. Burke Savage, "Clongowes 1815-30" in *Clongownian*, 1984, p. 17.

11 Op. cit. Corcoran, *Clongowes Record*, p. iii; also R.B. Savage, p. 13ff.

12 IJA, large copybook of Reports (transcribed) from Clongowes archives. The first 69 pages cover the years 1816 to 1821. The references above are to pp. 1-11, esp. pp. 1-3, 6, 10-11.

13 John M. Daley, *Georgetown University: Origin and Early Years*, Washington DC, 1957, p. 214.

14 IJA, Kenney Letters, 1816. Aylmer's Diary, 3 December 1816 , noted that the number of students on the roll was 201.

15 William O'Brien SJ, Clongowes, to Fr Grivel, 28 October 1819.; IJA, Gardiner Street papers; transcript from Jesuit Archives, Paris.

16 *The Correspondence of Daniel O'Connell*, vol. II, 1792-1814, ed. Maurice R. O'Connell, Irish University Press, 1972, pp. 92-3, no. 264; Mary O'Connell, Dublin to Daniel, in Cork, 1 April, 1816.

17 See 2 June 1815, O'Connell writing to his son Maurice, in W.F. Fitzpatrick, *Correspondence of Daniel O'Connell*, vol. 1 (London, 1988), p. 47; and also *The Correspondence ...*, II, ed. M. O'Connell, pp.94-5, and 104-6, 110-11.

18 Ibid., vol. II, Mary O'Connell to Daniel, 11 August 1817, p. 162, no. 717.

19 Recollections of Sir John Nugent, who entered Clongowes in 1816, quoted by Corcoran, op cit, p. 111. See earlier description of Stonyhurst uniform.

20 IJA, Kenney papers, 1806-41, N. Sewall to Kenney, 2 December 1815; and Stone, from Bristol, to Kenney, 20 January 1816.

21 IJA, Gardiner Street Papers, folder: Plowden to Kenney II, 12 October 1816. Bold print mine.

22 IJA, Gardiner Street Papers, folder: Plowden to Kenney II, 24/25 March 1820.

23 IJA, Kenney Letters, Plowden to Kenney, 25 September 1815.

24 IJA, Gardiner Street Papers, correspondence of the Visitation, transcribed from French Jesuit Archives, Paris. On 15 August 1818 he informed Fr Grivel, the Visitor, that the theologians at Clongowes "had need of his (Kenney's) severe hand".

25 Stonyhurst Archives, A11, 28 Doc. 27a; copy in IJA, Kenney Papers: Kenney to Weld, 17 February 1816.

26 IJA, folder: Plowden–Kenney. Plowden wrote to Kenney on Good Friday, 8 April 1816, and mentioned that John Weld had "expired last night at half-past ten". At the foot of the same letter is an attached note by Fr John Greene, a collector of historical material, relating the story of Kenney and the alleged appearance.

27 IJA, Kenney Leter, 1806-41. Dean Collins was very well disposed to the order and hoped to have a Jesuit college in Cork: Collins to Kenney, 14 August 1814. On 2 February 1816, he made it clear that his committee still wished to have him, despite his earlier refusal.

28 IJA, ibid, Tuohy to Kenney, 13 March 1817.

29 IJA, Diary in Aylmer file. The chapel & residence were bought for £400.

30 *Memorials of the Irish Province*: "Brief Chronological Notes", 1803-1914, p. 12.

31 IJA, Kenney Letters, Plunkett to Maria O'Brien, 8 January 1815.

32 Ibid., M. O'Brien to Kenney, 12 September 1815.

33 Ibidem, Gahan to Kenney, 18 October 1816.

34 IJA, Aylmer file. Diary entry for 13 November 1816, regarding the availability of communion for all the feasts of Jesuit saints. The principle was the same – how one starts is important; it sets the trend.

35 IJA, Kenney Papers, Murray to Kenney, 15 April 1817.

36 Ibid., O'Brien to Kenney, 23 April 1817.

37 IJA, File: "General to Provincials, 1806-69", Brzozowski to Kenney, 9 July,1917. It is not clear who had applied directly to the General.

38 IJA, Gardiner Street papers. Transcripts from papers on Grivel's visitation, Jesuit Archives, Paris, Brzozowski to Grivel, 23 July 1817.

39 IJA, Ibid., Transcr. from Jesuit archives, Paris, in Latin, Kenney to Grivel, 4 August 1817, Gardiner Street papers.

40 Ibid., Esmonde, from Clongowes, to Grivel, at Stonyhurst, 15 August 1817.

41 IJA, Excerpt from a letter of General Brzozowski to Fr Kohlman, in United States America, dated 23 April 1820, but Brzozowski died in February 1820!

42 In a letter on 12 October 1817, after his visitation was over, Grivel mentioned to Aylmer that the General's approval for the visitation had just arrived, and there is also mention of the letter signed by Aylmer and the four consultors. IJA, Aylmer papers.

43 IJA, Gardiner Street papers. Transcript. of Visitor's correspondence, Jesuit archives, Paris, Kenney to Grivel, 28 October 1818. Grivel read "for reasons of impurity" instead of "impunity" or without sufficient care.

44 Ibid, Kenney to Grivel, 15 July 1818.

45 IJA, Kenney papers. Interview of Robert Haly by Fr John Greene, 22 March 187-. The precise year in 1870s is missing.

46 IJA, visitation of Fr Grivel, ms. Fr Burke Savage from CWC archives.

47 IJA, Aylmer file, transcript. Visitation Corresp, Paris archives, Grivel to Aylmer, 12 October 1817.

48 Ibid., transcripts of papers of Visitation, Paris archives, Gardiner Street papers, Kenney to Grivel, 22 June 1818.

49 Ibid., Aylmer to Grivel, 28 December 1817.

50 IJA, Kenney papers, Aylmer to Kenney, 30 April 1818.

51 IJA, Transcr. visitation, Paris archives, Gardiner Street papers Kenney to Grivel, 15 July 1818.

52 Ibid., Esmonde to Grivel, 15 August 1818.

53 Ibid., Butler to Grivel, 26 September 1818. Among his complaints was that Kenney permitted "the reading of the famous historian and deist, Hume" on the grounds that "it was the lesser of two evils to permit the reading of these books at this stage when they can be guided by their instructors…"

54 IJA, Gardiner Street papers, transcript papers of Visitation, Paris archives, Kenney to Grivel, 26 October 1818.

55 Ibid., Grivel to Aylmer, 3 December 1818.

56 Ibid., Grivel to Aylmer, 12 November 1818.

57 Ibid., Aylmer to Grivel, 23 December 1818.

58 Ibid., Esmonde to Grivel, 19 February 1819.

59 Italics mine.

60 It may have been at this time, rather than earlier, that Henry Grattan's attendance to hear him preach took place.

61 IJA, Gardner Street papers, transcript Paris archives, Esmonde to Grivel, no date, 1819.

62 IJA, "General to Provincials, 1806–69", Brzozowski to Aylmer, 23 April 1819.

63 IJA, Kenney papers, copy from Jesuit archives USA, Maryland, 2. III. 1. R.182.

64 IJA, Kenney papers, Plowden to Kenney, 12 June 1819. Giovanni Grassi was a native of Bologna, and was made rector of the college at Polotsk at 29 years of age, and later at Georgetown raised its standing by means of an ordered curriculum, discipline, and motivation.

65 IJA, Papers of Visitation, transcript Paris archives, Aylmer to Grivel, 7 August 1819.

66 IJA, Gardiner Street papers, Aylmer folder: Plowden to Aylmer, 15 July 1819.

67 IJA, Kenney papers, Kenney to Roger Therry Esq., 31 July 1819, – "from the mouth of the Mersey".

68 M.P. Harney, *The Jesuits in History* (NY, 1941), p. 107.

69 On the medical advice, see R. Burke Savage, "Clongowes 1815–30", op. cit., pp. 14–15; and on misleading symptoms and faulty medical diagnosis see Plowden to Kenney, 19 May 1819, IJA, Gardiner Street papers, folder: Plowden to Kenney, 1; and the third year theologian William O'Brien to Grivel, 28 October 1819, IJA, transcr. from Paris archives: "England/2/Several F.F./ to R.F./Grivel".

70 IJA, Kenney papers 1806–41, Aylmer to Kenney, 20 November 1819.

71 O'Brien to Grivel, 28 October 1819.

72 O'Brien gives few details. The charges are general. It may be significant that following his death, after a long life, the obituary provided by near contemporary, John Curtis, described him as "an edifying religious, though somewhat peculiar and rather severe". (*Memorial of the Irish Province*, I, no. ii, June 1899, p. 101.)

73 IJA, Esmonde folder, Aylmer to Esmonde, 10 January 1821.

74 IJA, Folder: Plowden to Kenney II. Writing to Kenney at Georgetown on 24/25 March 1820, refers to the letter of Rosaven, written 3 January: "The General, or

rather Fr Rosaven in his last, 3 January ..." etc.

75 Kenney to Chas. Wright, 16 February 1816, Stonyhurst College Archives, ms. C. v. i, Bruges, Liege, Stonyhurst Letters etc. 1808-1820, a bound book or ledger.

76 Carroll to Plowden, 24 February 1790, ms. Woodstock archives, 202, B. 26, quoted in J.M. Daley, *Georgetown University* ..., p. 58.

77 The cash-book kept by Kenney at Clongowes, 1814-17, followed these simple headings; and, as appears from his Report to the General on Temporal Administration on the American Jesuit Mission, he introduced it there.

78 Troy to Bp. Milner in SCA, Stonyhurst Mss. B.1. 17, f.n. p. 226.

79 IJA, Gardiner Street papers, folder: Plowden to Aylmer, 23 May 1819; folder: Plowden to Kenney II, 27 May 1819.

80 Ibid., folder: Plowden to Aylmer, 5 August 1819.

81 IJA, Kenney papers, Kenney to Esmonde, 6 August 1819. In the letter he sent his regards to Mrs Denis Dillon, Miss Brennan, and mentions that he had written to James Bacon and Roger Therry.

A MAN SENT

1 In the seventeenth and eighteenth centuries some 320 French Jesuits and 144 members of the English province, had served in North America. T. Hughes, *Hist. Soc. Jesus in N. America*, Text, vol. II, pp. 704, 598-9.

2 Bangert, *A History of the Society of Jesus*, p. 407. Bp. Carroll, 13 July 1802, writing to the Revd Jn. Rossiter, pointed out that the Jesuit property was vested in an individual, as required by law, with a view to passing it on to successors having "the care of souls" since "in those times congregations were not called on for the support of their pastors"; quoted by Hughes, vol. I, Docs., part 1, p. 243.

3 Bangert, ibid.

4 Bangert, ibid., pp. 407-8; and Ed. B. Bunn SJ (ed.), *"Georgetown" First College Charter from the US Congress* (1789-1954); Newcomer Society publication (NY, 1954), p. 15.

5 Lester Cappon (ed.), *The Adams–Jefferson Letters*, II, pp. 474, 484, 494; quoted by Bangert, p. 479.

6 Carroll to Plowden, 24 February 1790; quoted by Jn. M. Daley, *Georgetown University: Origin and Early Years* (Washington, 1957), p. 58.

7 Kenney to Dr De Barth, 7 January 1820, Maryland Prov. Archives (MPA), 205, K.2, copy in IJA.

8 Carroll to Plowden, 25 June 1815; Stonyhurst transcr., quoted by Daley, *Georgetown University...*, p. 149.

9 *Archivium Historicum SJ*, January to June 1992, review by T.H. Clancy of *American Catholic Preaching & Piety in the Time of John Carroll*, ed. R.J. Kupke, Univ. America Press, 1991, p. 259.

10 See, too, Roothaan to Dubuisson, 1 May 1830, JAR, Register 1.

11 "Account of the State of the Jesuit Mission in America given to General Congregation at Professed House, Rome, by P. Kenney", October 1820, English translation, IJA, Kenney Papers.

12 Kenney to McElroy, 28 June 1822, MPA, 206, W, 9a, copy in IJA. For a more

favourable view of Dzierozynski, see "Francis Dzierozynski and the Jesuit Restoration in the United States" by A.J. Kuzniewski SJ, *Catholic Historical Review*, January 1992, p. 56, n. 20.

13 Curran, p. 89.

14 Daley, p. 179.

15 Kenney to General, 4 March 1820, JAR Maryl., 2, vii, 5, copy IJA.

16 Kenney to General, 2 December 1819, from Georgetown, JAR Maryl., 2, ii, copy IJA, no ref. number.

17 Quoted by Daley, p. 190.

18 Hughes, *Hist. SJ in N. America*, Documents, vol. 1, part 1, p. 572, n. 50.

19 See Dr Marechal to Grassi, 31 October 1819; JAR Maryl., 2, iii, 4. Roll 182 in St Louis U.A.; and letter to General, 20 November 1819; JAR Maryl., 2, iii, 2, Roll 182. Curran, *Bicentennial History of Georgetown*, p. 83, mentions the fund-raising aim.

20 Woodstock Letters, vol. 72: "Neale and the Restoration", pp. 125-8.

21 Ibid., p. l26.

22 E.E. Curran, "From Mission to Province, 1805-1833" in *The Maryland Jesuits, 1634-1833*, Maryl. Prov. public., 1976, pp. 53-4.

23 Curran, *Bicentennial History ...*, vol. 1, p. 84.

24 Ibid., p. 88.

25 Chas. Neale to Brzozowski, from Port Tobacco, 20 June 1818, JAR M.D., 215; quoted by Curran, p. 88.

26 Curran, ibid., pp. 84-5.

27 Plowden to Grassi, 11 June 1819, JAR. Angl. 1011, V.2; quoted by Curran, p. 88.

28 Curran, ibid., p. 89.

29 Brzozowski to Kenney, 23 April 1819, *Archivium Romanum SJ* (Jesuit Archives Rome = JAR) Maryl. 2, iii, 1; in micro film, St. Louis Univ. Archiv. in Pius XII Library, Roll 182.

30 IJA, folder: Plowden to Kenney II, 28 November 1819. Plowden pointed out that Kenney's letter for the General of 5 October took seven weeks to reach Stonyhurst, and from there it would take 40 days to St Petersburgh. In reverse there would be 40 days to Stonyhurst, and at least 45 days from there to Georgetown. Hence, a total of six months.

31 Ibid., Plowden to Kenney, 23 November 1819.

32 Kenney's report to the general congregation at Rome, October 1820: "Relatio de Statu Missionis S. J. in Statis Americae Foederatae".

33 1 Tim. 4: vv, 12, 14, 16; 5:1.

34 Kenney to Aylmer, 5 October 1819; IJA, Kenney papers.

35 Georgetown U.A, 62. ii. quoted by Daley, p. 219.

36 Plowden to Aylmer, 5 October 1819, speaks of Kenney bringing the gift, IJA, folder: Plowden–Aylmer.

37 Plowden to Aylmer, 14 October 1819, ibid.

38 Plowden to Kenney, 28 August 1919, IJA, Folder: Plowden–Kenney II.

39 Aylmer to Kenney, 20 November 1819; also in Ms. book including "Testimonials to Fr Kenney" with transcripts of letters from Dr Sughrue to Aylmer, 26 August and 24 November 1819, IJA, Kenney papers.

40 Plowden to Kenney, 24 September 1819. It is noted on the letter that it arrived on 5 Octobre, IJA, Folder: Plowden to Kenney II.

41 Marechal's report to Cardinal Litta, prefect of the Congreg. of Propaganda Fide, 16 October 1818, in J. Tracy Ellis (ed.), *Documents of American Catholic History* (Milwaukee, 1956) p. 208.

42 Ibid., p. 211.

43 Kenney to Aylmer, 5 October 1819, IJA, Kenney papers; also MPA, 205, M.6a.

44 Aylmer's delays in writing to the General led to sharp complaints, and the General felt obliged to write to Plowden for information, IJA, folder: Plowden to Aylmer, 22 November 1819.

45 Aylmer to Kenney, 20 November 1819 (arr. 10 February), IJA, Kenney papers.

46 T. Hughes, Docs. vol. 1, part 1, pp. 272 et alibi.

47 IJA, Typed copy in Kenney papers, from Maryl. archives.

48 Plowden to Kenney, 23 November 1819 (arr. 29 December), IJA, folder: Plowden to Kenney II.

49 General Brzozowski to Kenney, 3 January 1820, IJA, file: "General to Provincials".

50 Marechal to Grassi, 31 October 1819, JAR Maryl., 2, iii, 4. Roll 182, SLUA.

51 Marechal to Brozozowski, 20 November 1819; ibid., 2, iii, 2, Roll 182. ibid.

52 Plowden to Aylmer, 29 November 1819, folder II, IJA.

53 Plowden to Kenney, 28 November 1819, folder II, IJA.

54. "Rules of Fr Kenney", Doc. in MPA, 2, vi, 3, Roll. 182. St. L.U.A.

55 De Barth to Adam Marshall, 26 September 1820; quoted by T. Hughes, vol. 1, part 1, p. 358.

56 Kenney to General, 4 March 1820, JAR Maryl., 2, iii, 5.

57 Baxter was said to be unduly fond of wine, unduly relaxed in behaviour, and unduly republican in sentiment. Curran, *Bicentennial Hist.*, vol. 1, p. 93.

58 See *"Motiva quibus P. Renney statuit visitationem ... finem imponere ..."*: Motives why Fr Kenney decided to terminate his visitation and return to Europe; motive no. 2, JAR Maryl., 2, iii, 12; Roll 182. St. L.U.A., 27 October 1820.

59 Kenney to General, 2 December 1819, from Georgetown, JAR Maryl., 2, ii, copy IJA.

60 Kohlmann to Grassi, 7 December 1819, JAR Maryl., 2, i, 14. Roll 181.

61 Plowden to Kenney, 20 December 1819 (arr. mid February), IJA, folder II.

62 Report to Card. Litta, 16 October 1818, *Docs. Am. Catholic Hist.*, p. 214.

63 T.E. Wangler, *Catholic Historical Review*, July 1992, p. 472, reviewing *Living Stones: The History and Structure of Catholic Spiritual Life in the United States*, by J.P. Chinnici (NY, 1989).

64 T.H. Clancy, review in *Archivium Historicum SJ*, January-June 1992, pp. 258ff, of *American Catholic Preaching & Piety in the time of John Carroll*, ed. R.J. Kupke; and see R.E. Curran, *American Jesuit Spirituality* (1988), on preaching in English, 1750-1800, most of which was done by Jesuits or ex-Jesuits.

65 Kenney to M. Gahan, 3 and 6 April 1820, describing the "inconstancy of this climate", MPA, 205, H.O.; copy IJA.

66 Within three months of consecration, a new archbishop was required to apply to the pope for the pallium. It had arrived eventually in North America, and 19 December was fixed as the day of presentation, with a special sermon to mark the occasion.

67 Kohlmann to Grassi, 24 December 1819, JAR Maryl., 2, iii, 3, Roll 182.

68 C.P. Maes, *Life of Rev. Charles Nerinckx* (Cincinnati, 1880), p. 428; mentioned

in diary of John McElroy, 24 March 1820 – see Woodstock Letters, vol. XXXIII, no. 1, p. 10.

69 Kohlmann to Grassi, 24 December 1819.

70 Kenney to Gahan, 3 and 6 April, MPA, 205, H.O., copy IJA.

71 Daley, *Georgetown Univ* ..., p. 213, no. 70. The diary entry was for 4 January 1820.

72 "The Substance of some General Principles ... proposed for Adoption by Fr Visitor ... " in *Classical Journal of Georgetown College*, p. 25, in G.U. Arch., quoted by Daley, p. 214, n. 75.

73 Daley, p. 214

74 Ibid., pp. 225-6.

75 McElroy diary for 4 January 1820, quoted by Daley, p. 213, n. 70.

76 Kohlmann to Grassi, 24 December 1819, JAR Maryl., 2, iii, 3, Roll 182.

77 Kenney to Gahan, 3 and 6 April 1820, outlining weather since he arrived in America, MPA, 205, H.O., copy in IJA.

78 Ref. in Kenney to Bescheter, 17 February 1820, MPA, 205, K.5.

79 Ref. by Plowden, 24/25 March, to a letter of Kenney from Newtown on 2 February, IJA, folder: Plowden to Kenney II.

80 Ref. to visit in undated document on Jesuit farms, entitled "Opinion", copy in IJA, Kenney papers.

81 Kenney to Francis Neale, 24 February 1820, MPA, 205, K.7.

82 Kenney to E. Fenwick, 19 February 1820, copy IJA, Kenney papers.

83 Kenney to Maleve, 21 February 1820, MPA, X, W.1, copy IJA.

84 Kenney clarified this in a letter to Grassi, 31 May, MPA, X, W.2.

85 Kenney to General, 4 March, JAR. Maryl., 2, vii, 5.

86 Kenney to Grassi, 31 May, JAR. Maryl., X, W.2.

87 Kenney to General, 4 March 1820, JAR. Maryl., 2, vii, 5.

88 Kenney to Gahan, 6 March 1820, MPA, 205, W.8a. Italics mine.

89 See R.E. Curran, " 'Splendid Poverty': Jesuit Slaveholding in Maryland, 1805-1838" in *Catholics in the Old South*, eds. R.M. Miller and J.L. Wakelyn (Macon, 1983), p. 128.

90 C. Davis (Crossroads, NY, 1990), p. 59.

91 Ibid., pp. 40-1.

92 Curran, pp. 133-4.

93 T. Hughes, *Hist. sj N. America*, Text, vol, II (1645-1773) p. 559.

94 P. Finn, "The Slaves of the Jesuits in Maryland", M.A. thesis Georgetown U., 1974, pp. 50-51, and ch. 2 generally; also Br Mobberly's diary, 1820, GUA, pp. 142-3; both quoted by R.E. Curran, article in book already mentioned pp. 130-1; see, too, Hughes, pp. 560f.

95 Curran, art, 131-2.

96 Beschter to Parain, 27 March 1829, quoted by Curran, art., pp. 132-3.

97 Marshall to General, 5 March 1821, with notes attached on individual farms, for dates 6 February and 5 March, JAR. Maryl., 2, ii, 5 in Roll 181, St. L.U.A.

98 Mobberly diary, l:43; GUA; op. cit. Curran, art., p. 133.

99 Finn, "The Slaves of the Jesuits ...", p. 81, quoted in Curran, ibid., n. 37.

100 Corporation Minutes, 20 April 1820, MPA, XTI, Kenney, "Temporalities", ref. Curran, ibid., p. 133. n. 37

101 Dzierozynski to General Fortis, from Georgetown, 29 January 1825, JAR, quoted by Curran, ibid., p. l31.
102 MPA, XTI., "Temporalities, 1820".
103 Marshall to Fortis, 6 February 1821, JAR. Maryl., 2, ii, 5, Roll 181.
104 JAR. Maryl., 2, ii, 4, Roll 181.
105 IJA, copy of undated document relating to Jesuit farms, without a reference and merely entitled "opinion".
106 Italics mine. Kenney's references to the critics of the system referred to the abolitionists in England and elsewhere, but also, perhaps, to criticism of the Jesuits in America as "lords of the land" and slaves. See Curran, op. cit. in *Catholics in the Old South*, pp. 125-6.
107 Statement of Visitor for the Consultors of the Mission, MPA, X.T.I., Kenney, "Statement ...", 1820. Copy IJA.
108 Kenney to De Barth, 24 April 1820, MPA, 205, H.3.
109 Curran, art and book, p. 130.
110 L. Edelen to General Fortis, from Georgetown, 22 June 1823 JAR. Maryl., 2, i, 63, Roll 181.
111 Curran, "Ministry to Slaves: USA" in forthcoming Jesuit Encyclopedia.
112 Plowden to Kenney, 24 February 1820, IJA, folder: Plowden–Kenney II.
113 Kenney to Grassi, 31 May 1820, JAR. Maryl., X. W.2; copy IJA.
114 In "Statement for Consultors of the Mission ...", 1820, MPA., X.T.I., end of April.
115 Kenney to Francis Neale, 24 April, MPA, 205, H.2.
116. Kenney to De Barth, 24 April 1820, MPA, 205, H.3; see also Kenney to Francis Neale, 24 April, ibid., 205, H.2.
117 "Statement ... for Consultors of the Mission ... Kenney, 1820, Religious Discipline", MPA., X.T.I.
118 Kenney to Esmonde, 20 March 1820, MPA, 205, K.16; also IJA.
119 Ibid.
120 Italics mine.
121 "Statement. . . Kenney 1820", MPA, X.T.I.
122 Kenney to Grassi, 31 May 1820, JAR. Maryl., X.W.2. Italics mine.
123 Kenney to Marechal, from Georgetown, 11 June 1820, Baltimore Cathedral Archives, 17, R.3; see also Daley, p. 212.
124 Kenney to Wallace, at Catholic Chapel, Charleston, S. Carolina, 30 July, 1820; MPA, X.W.4.
125 Edelen to Kenney, 27 July 1820, MPA, X.W.3.
126 Kohlmann to Kenney, 1 October 1820, JAR. Maryl., 2, i, 29, Roll. 181.
127 Curran, *Bicentennial History...*, p. 90
128 Kenney to Brzozowski, 2 December 1819, IJA, Kenney papers.
129 Kenney to Francis Neale, 24 April 1820, MPA, H.2.; also IJA.
130 Marechal to E. Fenwick, 23 July 1820, GUA, 4, 3. Quoted by Daley, p. 213.
131 Quoted by Daley, p. 213.
132 Baxter to Grassi, 4 June 1820, JAR. Maryl., 2, i, 24, Roll 181.
133 McElroy to Grassi, 7 June 1820, JAR. Maryl., 2, iii, 8, Roll 182.
134 Plowden to Kenney, 24/25 March, 1820, IJA, folder II.
135 Kenney to Grassi, 31 May 1820, JAR. Maryl, X.W.2.

136 Maleve to Grassi, 2 June, 1820, JAR. Maryl., 2, i, 21, Roll 181.

137 JAR. Maryl, 2, vii, 5. Roll 182; and see *Hughes. Hist. S J in N. America*, Docs. vol. i, part i, p. 561.

138 Kohlmann to Grassi, 2 June 1820, JAR. Maryl, 2, vii, 5, Roll 182.

139 Inferred in Plowden to Aylmer, 30 July, IJA, folder: Plowden–Aylmer.

140 Kenney to Chas. and Francis Neale, 6 June 1820, MPA, 205, H.8.

141 McElroy to Grassi, 7 June, JAR. Maryl., 2, iii, 8, Roll 182.

142 Kohlmann to Vicar-General Petrucci, 8 June 1820, JAR. Maryl., 2, iii, 9, Roll 182.

143 Plowden to Aylmer, 30 July: "Kenney at his last date to me, 7 June, was in doubt what to do, whether to stay or return", IJA, folder: Plowden–Aylmer.

144 Baltimore Cathed. Arch. Ms. 17. R.3; quoted by Daley, p. 212.

145 "Motiva", document giving reasons why Kenney decided to return to Europe, JAR. Maryl., 2, iii, 12, Roll 182.

146 Du Bourg to Plessis, 26 August 1820, Quebec archdiocesan archives; cited by Garraghan, *The Jesuits of the Middle United States* (NY, 1938), vol. i, pp. 312-13.

147 "Motiva" Doc., as above.

148 McElroy to Grassi, 7 June 1820, JAR. Maryl., 2, iii, 8, Roll 182; also Edelen to Kenney, 27 July, MPA, X.W.3.

149 Kenney to Gahan, 6 March 1820, MPA, 205, M.8a; also in IJA.

150 Kenney to Gahan, 26 April 1820, IJA. Italics as in text.

151 on Marshal's negative view of the plantations, see letter to Enoch Fenwick, on 14 August 1820, MPA, 205, G.6.

152 Plowden to Kenney, 20 July 1820, IJA, Kenney papers.

153 Petrucci to Kenney, 7 September 1820, JAR. Maryl., 2, iii, 10, Roll 182.

154 Plowden to Aylmer, 20 September 1820, IJA, folder: Plowden to Aylmer.

155 Kohlmann to Petrucci, 30 August 1820, JAR. Maryl., 2, i, 28, Roll 181.

156 E. Fenwick to Francis Neale, 6 September 1820, Woodstock College Archives, 205. G. H., quoted by Daley, p. 215.

157 Daley, pp. 250-1.

158 Curran, *Bicent. Hist.*, vol. i, p. 107.

159 Kenney to McElroy, ibid.

160 Kenney to Ryder, 27 August 1821, MPA, 205, B.1.

161 Kenney to McElroy at Georgetown, 20 June 1822, MPA, 206, W.9a; and copy in IJA.

162 Kenney to Gahan, 3 to 6 April 1820, MPA, 205, H.O., copy in IJA.

163 Tristram to Aylmer, 12 October 1820, IJA, Aylmer folder.

164 Kenney to Esmonde, from Dover, 16 September 1820, IJA, from CWC archives.

165 Tristram to Aylmer, 12 October 1820, IJA, Aylmer file.

166 Kenney to Esmonde, 16 September 1820, from Dover, IJA, CWC archives.

167 Wylmer to Esmonde, 7 October 1820, IJA, Esmonde folder.

168 Aylmer to Esmonde, 11 November 1820, IJA, CWCA.

169 Two had come over previously with Grassi.

170 "Relatio de Statu Missionis SJ in America Foederata facta Congregationi Generali in Domo Professorum Romae", October 1820, JAR. Maryl., 2, iii, 12, Roll 182. Typed copy in IJA.

171 IJA, Kenney papers contain a time-table for a retreat, dated 5 November 1820. The day began at 5.00 a.m.

172 Aylmer to Esmonde, 11 November 1820, IJA, CWCA.

173 Aylmer to ? (Esmonde ?), 29 November 1820, IJA, Aylmer folder.

174 Joint letter of Plowden & Aylmer to Esmonde, 6 & 10 January 1821, IJA, Esmonde folder.

175 Aylmer to Fortis, 22 January 1821, IJA, Kenney papers, typed copy.

176 Card. Argenti to Dr Troy, 24 February 1821, DDA, Troy's Roman Correspondence, AB2/28/1, no. 133, f. 162.

177 Plowden to Aylmer, 7 April 1821, IJA, folder: Plowden to Aylmer.

178 Aylmer to General, 24 April 1821, IJA, Kenney papers.

179. Kenney to Dunn, 11 April 1821, EPA, Dunn papers, 1819-23, letters of Kenney to Dunn, 1819-23.

180 Aylmer to General, 24 April 1821, IJA, CWCA.

181 Kenney to James Ryder, 6 June 1821, MPA, 205, C.16a, copy IJA.

182 Aylmer to General, 18 October 1821, IJA, Kenney papers.

183 Kenney to McElroy, 29 June 1821, MPA, 209. 7. 17. At this point Kenney mistakenly reported that Plowden died "at Joigny on the road from Auxerre to Paris".

184 *Le Journal des Jougnards*, September 1936, "Decouverte Interessante", in Stonyhurst College Archives, courtesy Fr Turner, Librarian.

185 Kenney to Dunn, 15 August 1822, EPA, Dunn papers, no. 13.

186 Following a visit to the cemetry on 29 October 1991, the mayor and officials decreed that a number of neglected and ancient graves be removed. Among them was that of Plowden. Members of his family agreed to receive back the remains, and the inscribed grave stone recording in Latin the death and merits of the deceased. (Information still posted at cemetry, 1993; and see also *Le Journal des Jougnards*.)

A TIME OF AGITATION, RENEWAL AND EMANCIPATION

1 Kenney to McElroy, 30 March 1822, Maryland Province Archives, 206, 2, 10a; copy in IJA. Italics mine.

2 Ibid., 20 April, 1822, MPA, 206, 2, 15; copy IJA.

3 Kenney to McElroy, 29 August 1822, MPA, 206. 7. 8a.

4 Aylmer to Plowden, 24 April 1821, mentions a retreat to the Dublin clergy, copy in IJA, Aylmer file, Hib.1C, g; Aylmer to General, 18 October 1821, spoke of a retreat to the clergy of Meath, and also that the clergy of Cashel wished to have him as archbishop. Copy IJA, Aylmer file, Hib. 1, IC, ii; his retreat to the Christian Brothers at the start of the new year, following which Edmund Ignatius Rice was elected superior general, is referred to in *Tipperary Vindicator*, 4 September 1844, and in a letter Br M.C. Normoyle to the Revd R. Burke Savage sj, 6 March 1978, IJA.

5 Kenney to McElroy, 30 March 1822, MPA, 206, 2, 10a, copy in IJA.

6 Kenney to Edward Scott, 30 October 1822, copy in IJA, from EPA, Irish mission correspondence, SO/5.

7 In H.J. Coleridge, *The Life of Mother Frances Mary Teresa Ball* (Dublin, 1881), pp. 88-95.

8 *Joyful Mother of Children*, by "A Loreto Sister" (Dublin, 1961), p. 131.

9 Kenney to Doyle, 6 March 1823, Kildare Leighlin diocesan archives, 1823/12.

10 Curtis to Kenney, 6 March 1823, IJA.

11 Kenney to McElroy, 4 September 1823, MPA, 206. R. 11a. The reference to the archbishop of Baltimore is to Dr Marechal who was laying claim to all the lands of the Jesuit corporation on the grounds that they were originally given in trust to the whole church.

12 Fr McMahon was parish priest at Clane; James Colgan was a pupil at Clongowes.

13 Curtis to Kenney, 6 March 1823, IJA.

14 *Letters on the State of Ireland*, letter iii, by J.K.L. (Dublin, 1825), pp. 55-6.

15 It is not clear when the friendship started, but already in April 1821, he was acting as adviser to Dr Doyle.

16 See Fitzpatrick, *The Life, Times, and Correspondence of Dr Doyle*, vol. 1 (Dublin, 1890), p. 244.

17 Ibid., p. 244.

18 Ibid.

19 Dr Doyle to Mrs Teresa Brenan, Presentation Convent, Clane, 6 May, 1823, copy in IJA, Kenney file. On this letter the date, 6 May 1820, seems to be a mistake since Dr Doyle refers to Kenney as present. He was in the United States 1819-21. Fitzpatrick, who gives much of the letter, though with inaccuracies, including to whom it was addressed, gives the more likely date of 1823.

20 John Lynch, 1796-1867, was ordained priest at Clongowes, 20 May 1826, and served there for many years as master and prefect. Hence, he would have known Kenney well. There is no extant "memoir" by him, but there is by a Henry Lynch who, however, does not include this incident in his anecdotes.

21 Fitzpatrick, *Life ... Dr Doyle*, vol. 1, p. 245. On Dr Doyle's manner, see DNB, xv.

22 McMahon to Kenney, 21 February 1823, IJA, Kenney papers.

23 Doyle to Esmonde, 5 April 1824, CWC archives, but copy IJA.

24 Ibid. The originals at CWCA have copies usually in IJA.

25 Fitzpatrick, vol. 1, p. 142.

26 McGrath thesis, p. 210.

27 Nolan to Kenney, 15 March 1824, CWC archives.

28 Esmonde to Doyle, 2 June 1824, CWCA.

29 Typed copy of 8-day retreat, the "Consideration on Holy Communion", IJA, Kenney files on Meditations.

30 Bound copy of the meditations given to students of Maynooth College; talk for the first week of Advent – "I will not the death of the sinner"; also pp. 3-4, IJA, ibid.; also retreat to convent Georges Hill, day five, Meditation on the Prodigal Son, IJA, ibid.

31 Quoted by Fitzpatrick, p. 143.

32 Ibid.

33 Ibid.

34 Doyle to Esmonde, 5 April 1824, CWCA.

35 Esmonde to Doyle, undated, but almost certainly April or early May 1824, CWCA.

36 Doyle to Esmonde, 23 May 1824, CWCA.

37 Esmonde to Doyle, 2 June 1824, CWCA but now missing; ref. Fitzpatrick, p. 143; and McGrath thesis, pp. 213-14.

38 Esmonde to Doyle, no date, but clearly July 1824, CWCA.

39 Doyle to Esmonde, 30 July, CWCA.

40 Kenney to Esmonde, 12 August, CWCA.

41 Doyle to Esmonde, 7 August 1824, CWCA.

42 Notes by Esmonde, 1824, CWCA.

43 *Irish Monthly*, 1890, vol. 18, p. 10. A somewhat similar story is given in "Reminiscences of Fr Henry Lynch sj", IJA, Kenney papers, only he places the confrontation at a large clerical gathering in Dublin.

44 "Reminiscences of Kenney" by Henry Lynch, IJA, Kenney papers; transcribed by Jesuit historian, Professor Edmund Hogan, during an interview in Lynch's later years.

45 Kenney to Doyle, 6 March 1823, IJA.

46 Fitzpatrick, vol. 1, p. 407.

47 *Parliamentary Papers*, 1825, viii, Report from House of Lords Committee "On the State of Ireland", Examination 18 March 1825, p. 203.

48 Ibid., ix, p. 113.

49 Letter of Fr McDonnell, referred to in R. Burke Savage's notes on Kenney as an orator, CWCA.

50 Fitzpatrick, pp. 432-3.

51 Sheil in *New Monthly Magazine*, March 1829, quoted by J.K.L. in *Essay on Education in Ireland*, first published 1880, with notes, by Fitzpatrick, p. 22, f. n.

52 Fitzpatrick, *Life ... Dr. Doyle*, vol. 1. p. 414, 434

53 Ibid., p. 434.

54 Ibid., p. 401.

55 Kenney's Journal, *c.*August 1825, IJA.

56 Curtis to Kenney, 25 April 1825, IJA, Kenney papers.

57 A. Macaulay, *William Crolly. Archbishop of Armagh, 1835-49* (Dublin 1994), p. 41.

58 He maintained that the frequent directing of one's thoughts and affections to God would produce an habitual state in which one would be always inclined to think of God.

59 In Kenney files on Meditations, IJA. The frequent reference to the "glory of God" in Jesuit writing, as in the Society's motto "To the Greater Glory of God", may be taken as – promoting the manifestation of God's presence, his shining forth.

60 "Henry Lynch Reminiscences", Kenney papers, IJA.

61 Kenney to Scott, 12 August 1825, English Province Archives, Irish Mission correspondence, So/5.

62 Kenney to Fortis, 22 December 1825, JAR, Hib. 1, 1b, 24, in R. Burke Savage Ms. notes.

63 Ibid., JAR. Hib. 1, 1b, 21. Year not clear. Maybe 1829.

64 Journal, 1 January, 23 January, IJA.

65 Fortis to Kenney, 23 February 1826, IJA, file: "General/Provincial Letters".

66 Myles V. Ronan, *An Apostle of Catholic Dublin, Fr Henry Young* (Dublin, 1944), p. 207.

67 Rt. Hon. R. More O'Ferrall recalling Kenney as a preacher in interview with Ed. Hogan, IJA, Kenney papers.

68 Based on interview of Hogan with Henry Lynch, part of docs. collected by Fr.

Rabbitte SJ, also cited by M. Lenihan in *Limk. Reporter & Tipperary Vindicator*, 17 August 1869, IJA, Kenney papers.

69 Wm. Meagher, *Notice of the Life and Character of Most Rev Daniel Murray* (Dublin 1853), pp. 106-7.

70 Ibid., p. 107.

71 Kenney to McElroy, at Frederickstown, 2 July 1826, MPA. 207. H.1a.

72 *Dublin Evening Mail*, 15 March.

73 Ibid., 20 March.

74 Kenney to McElroy, 2 July 1826, MPA, 207. H.1a.

75 Kenney to Dubuisson, 2 July 1826; cit. *Woodstock Letters*, vol. 35, pp. 400ff.

76 Kenney to Fortis, 29 April 1828, JAR. Hib. 1001. 1b. 21.

77 Kenney to Daniel O'Connell, 16 December 1823, in *Correspondence of Daniel O'Connell*, ii, no. 1067, ed. M.R. O'Connell, Irish Univ. Press, 1972.

78 Ibid., iv, no. 1882, p. 409. O'Connell to his wife, Mary, 3 April 1832

79 Alexis de Tocqueville's *Journey in Ireland*, July-August 1835, trans. & ed. E. Larkin (Dublin, 1990), pp. 10-11.

80 Kenney to Haly, 30 September 1828, IJA, Haly papers. Two different letters, with different handwriting, seem to have been run together.

81 See Curtis to Doyle, 26 December 1828, KLDA, 1828/62; The Duke's reply was published on 23 December 1828.

82 Kenney to Fortis, 3 February 1829, JAR. Hib. 1b, 23; copy IJA.

83 Fr J.L. Rozaven to Kenney, 29 January 1829, IJA.

84 Text of "Catholic Emancipation Act in Great Britain and Ireland", April 1829, esp. clauses 28, 29-38, in Ehler & Morrall, *Church and State Through the Centuries* (London 1954), pp. 267-70.

85 Kenney to Murray, 3 April 1829, DDA, Murray papers, 31/1-2. "ordinary" 1829; also R. Burke Savage. "Clongowes, 1815-1830" in *Clongownian*, 1984, pp. 20-2.

86 Kenney to Vicar General, 30 May 1829, JAR. Hib., i-iii, 8; and Kenney to R. Haly, 31 May, from Lyons, IJA. Kenney papers.

87 "Documents vi" printed copy entitled "Remarks on the Case of the Jesuits", IJA, Gardiner Street papers. The quote from Kenney is from Eighth Report of Commissioners of Education, p. 391.

88 Kenney to Murray, 3 April 1825, DDA, Murray papers, 31/1-2, "ordinary", 1829.

89 Portion of an undated letter from Kenney to an unknown author, IJA, 1829.

90 Excerpts from the letters to his wife and E. Dwyer, 6 March 1829, are taken from *Irish Historical Documents*, ed. A. O'Day & J. Stevenson (Dublin, 1992), pp. 39-40.

91 The Act, ibid., p. 43.

92 T.D. Williams, "O'Connell's Impact on Europe" in Thomas Davis Lectures, *Daniel O'Connell. Portrait of a Radical*, ed. K.B. Nowlan & M.R. O'Connell (Belfast 1984), p. 100-3. Balzac died in 1850 aged 51. Cuvier was a celebrated French biologist, naturalist, and author.

93 Cited by D.L. Kelleher, *Great Days with O'Connell*, p. 118.

94 *Recollections of Aubrey de Vere* (London 1897), p. 21.

95 *O'Connell Correspondence*, iv, p. 96, 11 September 1829; and see O. McDonagh, *Hereditary Bondsman. Daniel O'Connell, 1775-1829* (London, 1988), p. 269.

96 Kenney to McElroy, from Liverpool, 11 September 1830, MPA, 209, k.2; IJA.
97 Kenney to Haly at Fribourg, 31 May 1829, IJA, Kenney papers.

IMPACT AT 21ST GENERAL CONGREGATION

1 Jesuit Archives Rome , Hib. 1, iii, 5: "A.M.D.G. Acta in Consultatione Speciali de Presenti Statu Missionis Soc. Jesu in Hibernia, habita 6 & 7 Maii, 1829". Copy IJA.

2 St Leger to Kenney in America, on 19 June 1831: "Dr Murray just the same as when I last wrote, no smile of benignity yet on St Fra. (Church of St. Francis Xavier) from his sweet face, and his Lady as hostile, I believe, as ever". IJA, copy in Kenney papers. "His Lady" refers presumably to the celebrated Mrs O'Brien.

3 Arianism – a fourth-century doctrine which denied the divinity of Jesus Christ and hence the doctrine of the Trinity; Socianism – a seventeenth-century form of rationalism which viewed Christ as a mere man and the Holy Spirit as an impersonal divine force and not a person. Deism – admitted creation by God but denied all subsequent intervention by Him in created things.

4 Dr Murray's testimonial is in bound notebook, IJA, containing "testimonials to Fr. Kenney". The account of his journey is in letter to Esmonde, 17 June 1829, from the Gesu, IJA.

5 "Fragmentum Diarii P. Patris Kenney", IJA, Kenney papers, "Original Letters".

6 Kenney to McElroy, 1 September 1829, MPA, 209, R.O. copy IJA.

7 Kenney to Haly, from Gesu, 25 July 1829, IJA.

8 Kenney to McElroy, 1 September 1829, MPA, 209, R.O. copy IJA.

9 Kenney to Haly, 25 July 1829, IJA.

10 "Reminiscences of Dr Whitehead of Maynooth", recorded by Ed. Hogan, IJA, Kenney papers.

11 Pietro Pirri, *P. Giovanni Roothaan* (Rome, 1930), ch. xiii, p. 306.

12 Kenney to Haly, 25 July 1829, IJA, Kenney papers.

13 Kenney to Esmonde, 1 September 1829, IJA, Kenney papers.

14 JAR. Hib. 1001, III, 9.: "Brevis Notitia etc.", copy IJA.

15 Aylmer to Kenney, from Hardwick St. , 24 July, 1829. IJA.

16 Kenney to Esmonde, 1 September 1829, IJA, Kenney papers.

17 J. Janssen to Vice Province of Ireland, 11 October 1829. It was handed to Kenney before he left, IJA.

18 IJA, Kenney papers, in 1830 file; copy, 2 pages.

19 Kenney to McElroy, 1 September 1829, MPA, 209, R.O. Italics mine.

20 Kenney to Glover, 13 October 1829, EPA, Ireland/USA, P. Kenney Correspondence, 1808-1841, SO/1.

21 Kenney to Glover, 31 October 1829, EPA, ibid.

22 Ibid.

23 Kenney to Roothaan, 29 June 1830, JAR. Hib, 2.i.7; copy IJA.

24 Kenney to Glover, 1 January 1830, EPA, Ireland/USA, Kenney Corresp. 1808-41, SO/1.

25 Kenney to Roothaan, 29 June 1830, JAR, as above.

26 Kenney to Glover, 1 January 1830, EPA, as above.

27 Kenney to Roothaan, 29 June, 1830, as above.
28 E. Curran, *Hist. of Georgetown University*, vol. 1, pp. 109 f., provides a sketch of Mulledy as president.
29 Kenney to McElroy, 11 September 1830, MPA, 209, k.2.
30 Bart. Esmonde's Journal, 1830, CWC Archives, copy IJA.
31 Contemporary Irish Jesuit catalogue.
32 Unknown to him, Moran had died suddenly on 30 April, IJA, Catalogue, 1831.
33 Kenney to Roothaan, 29 June 1830, JAR. Hib. 2.I.7.
34 Esmonde Journal, as above.
35 Kenney to Glover, 16 August 1830, EPA, Ireland/USA, Kenney Corresp. 1808-41, SO/1.
36 Journal, 10 June, 1830, copy in IJA.
37 Journal. Italics as in text.
38 Kenney to Esmonde, N.Y., 3 November 1830, MPA, x.2.4.
39 Kenney to R. Haly, Dublin, 17 September 1830, from Stonyhurst, IJA.
40 Kenney to Ryder, 14 September 1830, MPA, 209, k.1.
41 Kenney to McElroy, date not clear, probably between 12 and 17 September 1830, MPA, 209, k.2.
42 Kenney to Haly, from Liverpool, 24 September 1830; IJA.
43 R. St Leger to Kenney, 19 June 1831, Maryland, no ref. number. Copy in IJA.
44. Roothaan to Kenney, 24 July 1830, JAR, Reg. Prov. Hib. vol. 1, pp. 4-5. Frazer disappears from Irish Jesuit records after 1830, apart from a brief note that he died at Aberdeen in 1835, IJA, unprinted catalogue. He was born in Scotland. There is no reference to him in the diocesan archives of Kildare and Leighlin, Doyle papers (Letter from Bishop Laurence Ryan, 24 August 1993) ; and there appears to have been no reference in the public press of the day.
45 Curran, *Hist. of Georgetown* ..., p. 117.
46 Kenney to Roothaan, Liverpool, 24 September 1830, JAR. Hib., 2.ii.2.
47 Ryder to McSherry, 16 September 1828, *Woodstock Letters*, vol. 44, p. 323.
48 Curran, *Hist. Georgetown Univ* ..., vol. 1, p. 113.
49 O. MacDonagh, *The Hereditary Bondsman*. Life of Daniel O'Connell, vol. 1 (London 1988), p. 280.

MARYLAND REVISITED

1 Kenney to Esmonde, 3 November 1830, from N.Y., CWC Archives, and MPA, x, 2.4; & Journal in IJA, Kenney Journals, and MPA, x.2.3(?).
2 Kenney to Esmonde, 3 November, ibid.
3 Kenney to Dzierozynski, 3 November 1830, MPA, 209, h.2; also Journal of voyage, copy IJA.
4 Journal of voyage.
5 Kenney to Esmonde, 3 November, as above.
6 Ryder to Kohlmann, 30 September 1831, Rome F.G. vii, Epist. Collectio, No. 718.16/Kohlmann.
7 Kenney to Dzierozynski, 3 November 1830, MPA, 209, h.2
8 Kenney to McElroy, from Frederick, 12 November, MPA, 209, h.6.
9 Curran, *History Georgetown University*, vol. 1, pp. 93-4.

10 Roothaan to Kenney, from Rome, 3 July 1830, MPA, 500, 61.

11 Roothaan to Dzierozynski, 1 May 1830, JAR. Register 1; and see Curran, p. 113, and p. 361 n. 31.

12 "Consultations" between Kenney and his consultors, 1830-31; copy in IJA.

13 Kenney to General, 15 November 1830, JAR. Maryl. x.R.1.

14 Kenney to Fairclough, copy in IJA, no code number.

15 IJA, "Scattered Notes taken in the Visitation of the Mission of the Society of Jesus in the United States of North America, from November 1830 to 1832"; in Kenney's handwriting, no ref. number; also copy in IJA of Kenney's own Day Book of Charge and Discharge, 1830-31.

16 Kenney to Mulledy, Conewago, 11 March 1831, MPA, no ref. number.

17 Journal, 5 December 1830, MPA, copy in IJA.

18 Kenney to McElroy, Georgetown, 23 November 1830, MPA, 209, h.12.

19 Journal, 6-9 December 1830.

20 Ibid., 11 December, "Consultations" November 1830-31.

21 Kenney to McElroy, 14 December 1830, MPA, 209, h.14.

22 "Consultations", 21 December.

23 Kenney to Glover, 1 February 1831, EPA, Ireland/USA, Kenney Corresp. 1808-41, SO/1.

24 Kenney to Glover, 1 February 1831, ibid.

25 "Consultations", 21 December 1830; copy IJA.

26 Kenney to Glover, 1 February 1831.

27 Dzierozynski to Roothaan, 28 July 1830; JAR. Maryl., 3.iv.26.

28 Kenney to General, 10 January 1831, JAR. Maryl., 4.I.3., Roll 182.

29 Ibid.

30 Kenney Journal, 25 December 1830.

31 Kenney to Mulledy, 29 December 1830, MPA, Kenney to McElroy, 27 December; MPA, 209, h.15.

32 Journal.

33 "Peter Kenney's own Day Book", IJA, entry, 22 January 1831.

34 Kenney to Glover, 10 February 1831, EPA, Stonyhurst, Ireland/USA, Kenney Corresp. 1808-41; SO/1.

35 Kenney to Haly, 1 February 1831, IJA, Kenney papers.

36 Dubuisson to General, 24 March 1831, JAR. Maryl., 4.i.10. (R. 182)

37 Kenney to Glover, 1 February 1831, EPA, Ireland/USA, Kenney Corresp. 1808-41; SO/1.

38 Kenney to Glover, 10 February 1831, ibid. The letter appears not to have ben posted till 19 February.

39 E. Curran, *The Maryland Jesuits, 1634-1833*, p. 59.

40 "Death of Fr John McElroy", *Woodstock Letters*, VI, 1877, pp. 178 ff.

41 Kenney to Dzierozynski, 14 January 1831, MPA, 110.z.3; copy IJA.

42 Kenney to Glover, 10 February 1831, EPA.

43 Ibid.

44 Kenney to Haly, 16 February 1831, IJA.

45 Grivel to Roothaan, 26 January 1831, JAR. Maryl. 4.ii.1 (R. 182).

46 Dzierozynski to Roothaan, 28 January 1831; JAR. Maryl., 4.i.5 (R. 182).

47 Mulledy to General, 28 January 1831, JAR. Maryl. 4.iii.3. (R. 182).

48 Ryder to General, 29 January 1831, JAR. Marl. 4.iii.4 (R. 182).

49 Dubuisson to General, 24 March 1831, JAR. Maryl. 4.iii.10. (R. 182).

50 Kenney to Haly, 16 February 1831, IJA.

51 Kenney to Roothaan, 10 March 1831 (completed 26 April), JAR. Maryl. 4.i.9 (R. 182)

52 *Memoriale* for White Marsh, MPA; copy in IJA. no re. no.

53 "Notes Taken in the Visitation of the Mission of the Society of Jesus in the U.S. of North America, 1830, 1831" in Kenney papers, IJA. On the subsequent history of the boys'school, see *Woodstock Letters*, V (187), p. 108.

54 *Memoriale*, MPA, 573:8; copy IJA.

55 Hughes, *Hist. Soc. Jesus in N. America*, vol. 1, p. 379.

56 Kenney's Journal.

57 Kenney to McElroy, 3 March 1831, MPA, 210.z.12; copy IJA.

58 Kenney to Mulledy, 14 March 1831; MPA, no code ref.; copy IJA.

59 Kenney to McElroy, 19 March 1831, MPA, 210.z.11.

60 Dubuisson to Roothaan, 24 March 1831, JAR. Maryl. 4.i.10 (R. 182)

61 Kenney to McElroy, 19 March, as above.

62 The missionary contact seems to have gone back to 1742; *Catholic Encyclopaedia*, vol. 6, p. 932.

63 "Scattered Notes on Visitation of Mission of Soc. Jesus ... 1830-1831-1832" in IJA.

64 Kenney to McElroy, 12 March 1831, MPA. 210.z.9.

65 The reasons he gave for McElroy's unsuitability were that though he had a good brain and sound judgement, he had not the knowledge and experience for matters concerning estates and such like; also it would be very difficult to call him from Frederick where he was working with such fruit. The unstated reason may have been his recognition that the strong individualistic personality of his friend McElroy would not have been comfortable to work with.

66 Kenney to Roothaan, 10 March 1831 (28 April), JAR. Maryl. 4.i.9. (R. 182).

67 Ibid.

68 Kenney to Mulledy, 14 March 1831, MPA, no ref. no.; copy IJA. Kenney to Francis Dzierozynski, 14 March, 1831, MPA, 210.z.9a.

69 Kenney to Mulledy, 5 April 1831, MPA. no ref. number; copy IJA.

70 Kenney to Mrs Dillon, Ireland, no date but written in early summer 1831, while on circuit. Copy, unfinished, IJA;no further ref.

71 Kenney to Roothaan, JAR. Maryl, 4.i.9. (R. 182)

72 Kenney Journal, April-October 1831, IJA.

73 "Memorial or Memoranda written by The Revd Peter Kenney, Superior and Visitor, in the Visitation of this Residence of the Sacred Heart of Jesus in Conewago, anno Domini 1831", written 8 May 1831 , MPA, no call no.; copy IJA.

74 Kenney to Mulledy, Conewago, 8 May 1831, MPA, no call or ref. no.

75 See Hughes, vol. 1, pp. 379, 350.

76 Kenney's own note in Diary of the Residence, 25 May 1833, typed extract, IJA.

77 Copy of *Memoriale* in Latin in IJA: "Memoriale relictum anno 1831 a R. P. Petro Kenney in Visitatione mense Maio facta"; no source ref. given.

78 "The Catholic Religion in the United States in 1818", in *Woodstock Letters*, 11, 1882, 238-9; quoted by Curran in *The Maryland Jesuits, 1634-1833*, Maryland Jesuit Province publication 1976, p. 60.

79 Kenney to Mulledy, 19 June 1831, MPA, no ref. no.

80 "Fr. Kenney's own Day Book of Charges and Discharges, 1830-1832"; incomplete entries, CWCA; copy IJA.

81 Kenney to Mulledy, from Bohemia, 7 June 1831, MPA, no ref. no.; and Kenney's retreat order of time, 8 June 1831, in IJA.

82 Kenney to Mulledy, 7 June.

83 Kenney to Mulledy, 19 June 1831, MPA, Georgetown Univ. Archives, no call no. It is not clear what "exhibition" was in question, whether one apart from the college or one of the many events and celebrations introduced by Mulledy to raise the image of the college.

84 Province Catalogue, 1833, MPA; and Robt. K. Judge, "Foundation and First Administration of the Maryland Province", *Woodstock Letters*, vol. 88, 1959, p. 385; and Hughes, vol. 1, p. 379.

85 Curran, *Hist. Georgetown*, vol. 1, p. 119.

86 "The Jesuit Farms in Maryland" in *Woodstock Letters*, vol. XLII. no. 1, p. 277.

87 Robt. Judge art. in *Woodstock Letters*, vol. 88, pp. 393, 396.

88 Kenney to Mulledy, 19 June 1831, Georgetown U.A., no call no.; in a postscript he mentioned he would go to Mr Hardy's place on Monday, 26 June.

89 Hughes, vol. 1, p. 379. Fr. Dzierozynski's tables.

90 "Jesuit Farms in Maryland", *Woodstock Letters*, XLII. no. 1, p. 278.

91 Dr P. Mulligan, "Dr James Donnelly: The Early Years", in *Clogher Record*, XI, 1984, pp. 365-67: Donnelly on a visit to the United States in 1851 spoke of 4th July as – "Anniversary of America's greatest diaster … Independence, America's greatest curse", and remarked "God will blast this godless nation".

92 Dzierozynski's tables of property, when he was superior, 1824-1830; in Hughes, vol. 1, p. 379.

93 Grivel to Nicholas Sewall, 30 May 1832, in *Woodstock Letters*, X, pp. 246ff., MPA, 4-5-6. (R. 138); EPA, Maryland vol. no. 132.

94 *Memoriale*, White Marsh 1831, MPA, no ref. no.; copy IJA.

95 "Jesuit Farms in Maryland", *Woodstock Letters*, XLII, p. 279

96 Roothaan to Dubuisson, October 1830, 18, JAR. Register 1. Dzierozynski to Roothaan, 28 January 1831, JAR. Maryl. 4.I.5; Grivel to Roothaan, 26 January 1831, JAR. Maryl. 4.ii.1 (Roll 182).

97 James Ryder to Kohlmann, 30 September 1831; F. G. vii. Epist. Collectio, No. 718.16/Kohlmann (Roll. 217.SLULA.).

98 Curran, *Georgetown Univ.* 1, p. 119.

99 The Bill of 1833. *The Correspondence of Daniel O'Connell*, vol. V, no. 1976a; ed. M. O'Connell for Irish Mss Commission.

100 In *Supremo Apostolatus Fastigio*, 1839; quoted by Cyprian Davis in *The History of Black Catholics in the United States* (Crossroads, N.Y., 1990), pp. 39-40.

101 Dzierozynski to Roothaan, from Georgetown, 28 January 1831, JAR. Maryl. 4.i.5.

102 Grivel to Roothaan, 26 January 1831, JAR. Maryl. 4.II.1 (Roll. 182).

103 Ryder to Kohlmann, 30 September 1831, F. G. vii, Epist. Collectio, No. 718, 16/Kohlmann.

104 Curran in *Georgetown Univ.*, 1, p. 119.

105 Kenney to Dubuisson, from Georgetown, 20 July 1831, MPA, 210.t.4; italics mine.

106 Roothaan to Kenney, 25 October 1831, JAR. Maryl. 500:65a.

107 Curran, *Georgetown Univ.*, 1, p. 119.

108 Ibid., p. 120; and R.K. Judge, art., p. 398; C. Davis, *History of Black Catholics ...*, pp. 36-7.

109 Davis, ibid., pp. 37, 39-40, 65-66. Gregory XVI, who had a very conservative reputation, was yet a prominent defender of the rights of oppressed peoples such as the Indians and Negroes: see *In Supremo Apostolatus Fastigio*, and Davis, pp. 39-40.

110 Glover to Kenney, Rome, 7 May 1831; received 22 July; JAR. Maryl. no call no.; copy IJA.

111 Name of writer partly obliterated, but appears to be James Ryder to Kohlmann, Georgetown, 30 September 1831; F. G. vii. Epist. Collectio No. 718, 16/Kohlmann Roll 217, SLULA.

112 MPA? No source attached; copy in IJA.

113 Ryder to Kohlmann, 30 September 1831; F. G. vii. Epist. Collectio No. 718. 16/Kohlmann R. 217, SLULA.

114 Kenney to Roothaan, 14 September 1831, from Georgetown, JAR. Maryl. 4.i.14, R. 182.

115 Kenney to Sr Mary Clare, from Philadelphia, 1 September 1831, MPA. S.Z.X.

116 Diary, October 1831.

117 Dubuisson to Roothaan, 9 December 1831, JAR. Maryl. 4.i.16 R. 182. SLULA.

WESTWARD TO ST LOUIS

1 "Letters of Fr James O. Van de Velde" (he kept his diary in the form of letters), in *Woodstock Letters*, x, pp. 53-132; trans. from original French.

2 This was not an unusual experience or reaction. See P. Mulligan, "Dr James Donnelly: the Early Years"in *Clogher Record*, 1984, p. 369.

3 "Letters ... Van de Velde", p. 60.

4 Ibid., "Letters ... ", or Diary, de Velde, p. 124.

5 Ibid., p. 127.

6 Ibid., p. 131.

7 Ibid., p. 130.

8 *Mrs Royall's Southern Tour, 1830-31* (Washington: Royall, 1830/31), p. 155; quoted by Faherty, *Better the Dream ...*, p. 29.

9 Faherty, pp. 29, 25.

10 IJA, Kenney's Diaries & Journals, April-October 1831.

11 Van de Velde to George Fenwick, St Louis, 16 November 1831, MPA, op. cit. Garraghan, vol. 1, p. 295.

12 The French traders were led by Pierre de la Clede, who had great hopes for his foundation according to his secretary, August Chouteau, who left an evocative "Narrative of the Founding of St Louis".

13 Kenney to Glover, St Louis, 25 April 1832, E.P.A. Ireland/USA, Kenney Corresp. 1808-41, SO/1.

14 J.N. Primm, *Lion of the Valley. St Louis, Missouri* (Colorado, 1981), pp. 102-3, 111-112.

15 The first newspaper, the *Missouri Gazette*, was produced by Joseph Charless, an Irish emigrant, in 1808: W.B. Faherty, *St Louis. A Concise History* (St Louis, 1990), p. 15.

16 Primm, *Lion of the Valley*, pp. 138-9.

17 T. Flint. Account in "Readings" displayed in the History Museum, the Old Courthouse, St Louis.

18 Primm, p. 136.

19 Ibid., p. 161; see too Faherty, *St Louis. A Concise Hist.*, chs. 2 and 3.

20 Kenney to Glover, 25 April 1832, EPA.

21 Faherty, *St Louis ...*, p. 21.

22 Primm, pp. 98-9.

23 Kenney to Grivel, 25 April, 1832, EPA, Ireland/USA, Kenney Corresp. 1808-41, SO/1.

24 Primm, pp. 98-9.

25 Cited by Primm, p. 99.

26 Copy of concordat, 19 March 1823, between "L. Wm. Du Bourg, Bishop of New Orleans, and Charles Neale, Superior of the Mission of the Society of Jesus in the United States of America" in Archdiocesan Archives St Louis; text also in G. J. Garraghan, *The Jesuits of the Middle United States*, vol. 1, pp. 61-4; also in JAR. Mis. 1.ii.7, in R.184, SLULA.

27 Garraghan, pp. 79ff; and Faherty, "Father Van Quickenborne: Religious Pioneer", *Jesuit Bulletin*, October 1965, p. 3.

28 Kenney to McElroy, from Dublin, 4 September 1823, MPA, 206, R. 11a; see Garraghan, p. 72.

29 *Life, Letters, & Travels of Fr Pierre Jean De Smet SJ*, (N.Y., 1905), ed. H.M. Chittenden & A.T. Richardson, vol. 1, p. 5.

30 Kenney to General, 4 March 1820, JAR. Maryl. 2.iii.5. R. 182.

31 *The Life of Mother Duchesne*, by Abbe Baunard, trans. Lady G. Fullerton (1879), pp. 258-9.

32 Cit. Annabelle M. Melville in *Louis William Du Bourg*, vol. II, *Bishop in Two Worlds, 1818-1833* (L.U.P. Chicago), p. 738.

33 W.B. Faherty, "Father Van Quickenborne" in *Jesuit Bulletin*, October 1965 (St Louis), pp. 3-5.

34 Faherty, "Father Van Quickenborne ...". ibid.

35 Elet to Dzierozynski, 29 August 1830, from Florrissant, MPA, 3M.11; cited by Faherty, *Dream by the River ...*, p. 220.

36 Kenney to Roothaan, 27 January 1832, JAR. Miss. 2.ii.2. R. 184, SLULA.

37 Rosati Diary, 24 October 1831, Arch. Archdiocese St Louis.

38 Kenney to Miss Denis, 24 February 1832, IJA.

39 Cited by Garraghan, p. 101.

40 Ibid., p. 319.

41 Jesuit Archives Missouri, Catalogue of Missouri Mission, II.59.

42 IJA, typed copy of the reasons.

43 McSherry to General, 23 January 1832; JAR. Miss. 2, R. 184, SLULA.

44 Kenney to Roothaan, 27 January 1832; JAR. Miss. 2.ii.2; R. 184, SLULA.

45 Garraghan, vol. 1, p. 320.

46 Kenney to Roothaan, 27 January 1832; JAR. Miss. 2.ii.2; R. 184, SLULA.

47 Smedts to Roothaan, 12 January 1832; JAR. Miss. 2.i.17; R. 184, SLULA

48 McSherry to Roothaan, 23 January 1832,JAR. Miss. 2; R. 184, SLULA.
49 Elet to Roothaan, 15 September 1842, 29 April 1844, and pen picture by a former novice, Fr Boudreaux, 5 September 1881; cited by Garraghan, 1, pp. 483-7.
50 Quoted by Walter Hill sj in "Historical Sketches of the Missouri Mission", vol. 2, 23, p. 53, Jesuit Province Archives, St Louis.
51 Kenney to General, 27 January 1832, JAR. Miss. ii.2; R. 184, SLULA.
52 Rieselman to General, 1 January 1832, JAR. Miss. 2.i.3; R. 184, SLULA.
53 Ref. in Kenney Diary for 11 April 1832; IJA.
54 Kenney to Roothaan, 22 February 1832; JAR. Miss. 2.ii; R. 184, SLULA.
55 Kenney Diary, 11 April 1832, IJA.
56 Italics as in text.
57 Kenney to Glover, 2 January 1832, EPA, Ireland/USA, Kenney Corresp. 1808-41, SO/1.
58 Kenney to McElroy, 9 February 1832, MPA, 210, R.6a. "Examen ad Gradum" refers to the final examination in theology for Jesuits. The examiners were four senior Jesuits, who had to testify to the examinee's worthiness in theology to receive the special grade of fourth vow.
59 Roothaan to Kenney, 12 May 1832, JAR, quoted by Garraghan, 1, p. 483.
60 Kenney to Roothaan, 22 February 1832; JAR. Miss. 2.ii; R. 184, SLULA.
61 Kenney to Miss Denis, 24 February 1832, IJA.
62 Kenney to McElroy, 9 February 1832, MPA, 210, R.6a.
63 Kenney to Glover, 25 April 1832, EPA, Ireland/USA, Kenney Corresp. 1808-41; SO/1.
64 Kenney Diary, IJA.
65 Van Quickenborne to Dzierozynski, 13 November 1829; quoted by Garraghan, vol. 1, pp. 220.
66 Ibid. p. 221.
67 Fr Van Assche to De Nef, 1 September 1825, MPA. quoted by Garraghan, 1, p. 221.
68 Van Assche to De Nef, 4 September 1828; ibid., p. 223.
69 Kenney Diary, 11, 12, 15 April, IJA.
70 Flaget to Kenney, 8 October 1831; copy IJA.
71 Roothan to Kenney, 20 December 1831, MPA, 500:65b;copy IJA.
72 Kenney to Glover, 1 March 1832, EPA, Ireland/USA, Kenney Corresp. 1808-41, SO/1.
73 Diary, March 1832.
74 Quoted by Faherty, *Better the Dream* ..., pp. 29-30
75 W. Hill, "Historical Sketches of St Louis University", p. 41, Jesuit Archives St Louis; and see Faherty, p. 26.
76 Kenney to McElroy, 9 February 1832; MPA, 210; R.6a; copy IJA.
77 Kenney to Roothaan, 25 April, 1832; JAR. Miss. 2.iii; R. 184, SLULA.
78 Verhaegen to Roothaan, 15 January 1831, JAR. Cited by Garraghan, 1, p. 300.
79 Verhaegen to Kenney, 2 February 1832; copy IJA; italics in text.
80 Kenney to McSherry, 14 February 1833; Maryl. 5(?). i.2; R. 182, SLULA.
81 Verhaegen to Roothaan, 25 August 1832; JAR. Miss. 2.iii.4; R. 184, SLULA.
82 Roothaan to Kenney, 23 October 1832; IJA,
83 Kenney to McSherry, 14 February 1833; JAR. Maryl. 5.i.2, R. 182 ibid.
84 Kenney to General, 12 June 1833, JAR. Maryl. 5(?).v.2; R. 182; copy IJA.

85 Verhaegen to McSherry, 17 August 1833; MPA, quoted by Garraghan, 1, p. 301.

86 Roothaan to Van de Velde, 18 June 1833; quoted by Garraghan, 1, p. 301.

87 Kenney to Roothaan, 25 April 1832; JAR. Miss. 2. iii; R. 184, SLULA. The General later declared that the Society was "bound in justice" in this matter (Roothaan to Kenney, 28 October 1832; cited by Garraghan, 1, p. 145).

88 Quoted in Garraghan, 1, p. 325.

89 Kenney to Roothaan, 25 April 1832; JAR. Miss. 2.iii; R. 184, SLULA.

90 Roothaan to Verhaegen, 25 October 1832; quoted by Garraghan, 1, p. 325.

91 Roothaan to Kenney, 23 October 1832; JAR, no code no.; copy IJA.

92 In the *Memoriale* he also gave as a reason for abandoning the Salt River residence that it was not included in the area assigned originally by Du Bourg.

93 Rosati Diary, October 1831-November 1833, in Souvay Papers, Archives St Marys of the Barrens, Perryville, Missouri.

94 *Rules of the Society of Jesus* (Roehampton, England, 1863), p. 11.

95 Kenney to Roothaan, 25 April 1832, JAR. Miss. 2.iii; R. 184, SLULA.

96 Quoted by Garraghan, 1, pp. 324-5.

97 Verhaegen to Roothaan, 4 February 1833; quoted by Garraghan 1, p. 306.

98 "Suggestions for Consideration by Consultors, Missouri, and Responses"; copy IJA.

99 1 March, 1832: covering note in abstract of correspondence, Archives St Louis Diocesan Chancery, Bk. 8, no. 49; in Souvay Papers, St Mary of the Barrens, Perryville, Missouri.

100 Kenney's Diary, 25 February 1832.

101 Rosati to Cardinal Pedicini, 13 May 1832, St Louis Archdiocesan Archives; quoted in Faherty, *Dream by the River* ..., p. 41.

102 "Instructions Given by Rev Fr Kenney, Superior of the US Mission, to Rev Fr McSherry, Procurator of the Same Mission", September 4 1832, MPA, X.M.2.

103 For the General's instructions on putting the papal concession into effect, dated 1 February 1833, see Garraghan, 1, pp. 307-8, based on Roothaan's directions in his *ordinatio de Minervali*.

104 Kenney to McElroy, 14 April 1833, MPA, 210, H.9; quoting McSherry's letter. Commenting on this news, Kenney observed that "with regard to Ireland, the old privilege has never been withdrawn, and of its existence in the old Society I gave abundant proof to the General in 1829; and the school in Dublin has been receiving 12 guineas or 60 dollars ever since it has been opened. I am persuaded," he added, "that America, that is the portion that formerly belonged to the English province, had the same privilege until General Fortis took it away." "The school in Dublin" referred presumably to the one opened in 1832 in the former chapel at Hardwicke Street, which transferred nine years later to Belvedere House.

105 Roothaan to De Theux, 22 January 1833, JAR; quoted by Garraghan, 1, p. 307.

106 Roothaan to Rosati, 21 February 1833; quoted by Garaghan, ibid.

107 Rosati to Kenney, 16 May 1833, responding to a letter of Kenney of 30 April; copy IJA.

108 Kenney to McElroy, 14 April 1833, MPA, 210, h.9.

109 Bill of Incorporation, 28 December 1832; copy IJA.

110 Kenney to McElroy, 6 February 1833; MPA, 210, k.4.

111 Kenney to McSherry, 14 February 1833; MPA, 5.i.2; R. 182, SLULA.

112 Verhaegen to Kenney, 21 March, 1832; copy IJA.

113 Italics in text.

114 Memoriale of Fr Peter Kenney, 8 May 1832, Jesuit Missouri Province Archives – Varia vii, Visitations, Memorials.

115 Verhaegen to Dzierozynski, 8 May 1832; MPA; quoted by Garraghan, 1, p. 327.

116 Verhaegen to Roothaan, 25 August 1832; JAR. Miss. 2.iii.4; R. 184, SLULA.

117 Faherty, *Better the Dream* ..., p. 37.

118 Kenney to Rosati; quoted by Garraghan, 1, p. 327.

119 Kenney to Roothaan, 28 August, 9 September 1832; JAR; quoted by Garraghan, 1, p. 328; italics mine.

120 Roothaan to Kenney, 23 October 1832, IJA.

121 Kenney to McSherry, from Liverpool, 13 September 1833, MPA, 210, d.2.

122 Kenney to Dzierozynski, 5 November 1832, MPA, 210, m.1.

123 Kenney to McSherry, 13 September 1833, MPA, 210, d.2.

124 Van Quickenborne to General, 17 August 1833, JAR. Miss. 2.i.29; R. 184, SLULA.

125 Kenney to McSherry, 14 January 1833, JAR. Maryl. 4.i.22; R. 182, SLULA.

126 Grivel to N. Sewall, 30 May 1832, R. 138, SLULA; and see *Woodstock Letters*, x, pp. 246ff.

127 Flaget to Kenney, 26 March 1832, bound journal of extracts, IJA.

128 M.J. Spalding, *Sketches of Life and Times of Rt. Rev. Benedict Joseph Flaget, First Bishop of Louisville* (Louisville, 1852), p. 71.

129 Dr Donnelly's journal, 1851; quoted in "Dr James Donnelly: the Early Years" by P. Mulligan, *Clogher Record*, 1984, p. 387.

130 Flaget to Kenney, 25 July 1832, MPA; copy IJA.

131 Kenney to Haly, 13 July 1832, MPA, 210, p.4a; copy IJA.

132 *The Life, Letters and Travels of Fr Pierre Jean De Smet, SJ*, by H.M. Chittenden & A.T. Richardson eds., N.Y., reprint 1969; p. 115; quoted in W.B. Faherty in *Jesuit Roots and Pioneer Heroes of the Middle West*, Jesuit Historical Museum (Florissant, Mo., 1988), p. 69.

133 Fr Wm. Murphy, vice-provincial, to Fr. General Beckx, 15 April, 1861, JAR. quoted by Garraghan, vol. iii, pp. 99-100.

134 Kenney to Roothaan, 5 May 1832, JAR. Miss. 2, vi, 1, R. 184, SLULA.

135 Kenney's Journal, August 1832-March 1833; "Giornale de Governo", 14 March, 1833.

136 Garraghan, 1, pp. 351-3

137 Verhaegen to Kenney, 21 March 1832; copy IJA.

138 Roothaan to Kenney, 23 October 1832; IJA.

139 Quoted by Garraghan, 1, p. 506: On 1 July, 1846, the quotas for the various countries represented among the Missouri Jesuits were as follows: Ireland 45; Belgium 42; Holland 16; United States 16; Germany 13; Italy 11; France 9; Spain 2. As all but five of the 45 Irish were coadjutor brothers, the dominant element remained Belgian for many years.

MARYLAND, FROM MISSION TO PROVINCE

1 Kenney to Haly, 13 July 1832, Bohemia, MPA, 210, P.4a; copy IJA.

2 Ibid.

3 Journal, 1 July 1832; IJA.

4 Ibid., 4 July.

5 Kenney to McElroy, 6 July 1832, Georgetown; MPA, 210, r. 2.

6 Kenney to Haly, 13 July.

7 Esmonde to Kenney, 8 July 1832; CWC Archiv.; copy IJA.

8 Haly to Kenney, 18 August 1832, IJA.

9 Kenney to Mulledy, 16 July 1832; GUA, no number; copy IJA.

10 Journal, 17-18 July 1832.

11 R. K. Judge, "Foundation and First Administration of the Maryland Province" in *Maryland Province*, p. 385.

12 Journal, 19 July 1832.

13 Kenney to Mulledy, 25 July 1832, GUA, no number; copy IJA.

14 *"Giornale de Governo"*, August 1832-March 1833, 506; Copy IJA.

15 Ibid.

16 Kenney to McElroy, 19 August 1832; MPA, 210, P.9.

17 "Measures Proposed and Discussed in a Special Consultation with the Consultors both of the Mission and of the College of Georgetown, and by them Recommended to the Superior to be by him Submitted to the Consideration of Most Rev. Fr General", 28 August 1832; MPA, i.w.x.; copy IJA.

18 Journal, 5 September

19 "Instructions Given by Revd Fr Kenney ... to Revd Fr McSherry, Procurator of the Same Mission", 4 September 1832, MPA, x.m.2; copy IJA.

20 Kenney to General, 8 September 1832, JAR. Maryl. 4.1.26, in SLULA, R. 182.

21 Kenney to Glover, 18 September 1832, Georgetown; EPA, Irl./USA, Kenney Corresp. 1808-41, SO/1.

22 Dzierozynski to Roothaan, 6 September 1832; JAR. Maryl. 4.1.24, SLULA, R. 182.

23 Dubuisson to Roothaan, 6 September 1832, Georgetown; JAR. Maryl. 4.iii.18, SLULA, R. 182.

24 Kenney to Francis Neale, 10 September 1832, MPA, 210, n. 1; copy IJA.

25 *"Giornale de Governo"*, entries 29 September, 10 October; IJA.

26 Kenney to McElroy, MPA, 210. n.5; copy IJA.

27 Kenney to Archbishop Whitfield, 10 December 1832, no ref.; copy IJA.

28 E. Fenwick to Rosati, 23 August 1832, St Louis Archdiocesan Archives, R.G.1.B.4.3A; see too *St Louis Catholic Historical Review*, v, April-July 1923, pp. 175-7. Dr. Fenwick's diocesan jurisdiction extended over Michigan, Wisconsin and Ohio.

29 Rosati to Pedicini, 5 September 1832, Kenrick Seminary Archives; quoted by Garraghan, vol. 1, p. 329.

30 Diary, 4 December 1832.

31 Kenney to Mulledy, 12 December 1832, GUA, no ref. no.; copy IJA.

32 Kenney to Whitfield, 10 December 1832; no source ref., copy IJA. In a subsequent letter to McSherry, 14 January 1833 (JAR. Maryl. 4.i.22, SLULA, R. 182) he summarised the arguments made to the archbishop and made clear his comment concerning French: "Now though I know the language for my own satisfaction above 30 years, yet I have never had an opportunity of speaking it so as to

acquire any facility in it, or any correctness in pronunciation."

33 James, Archbishop of Baltimore, to Kenney, 17 December 1832, no ref. number; copy in IJA.

34 Kenney to McSherry, 14 January 1833, JAR. Maryl. 4.i.22, SLULA, R. 182.

35 William Matthews, administrator of the diocese of Philadelphia, wrote to Fr Kohlmann, in Rome, on 2 July 1828, regarding a meeting with the new archbishop – "He is an enemy of the Jesuits, at least as much as his predecessor defunct." See Hughes, *Hist. of Soc. of Jesus in North America*, vol. 1, part ii, pp. 1110, 1134-5.

36 Bp James Whitfield to Bp Rosati, 12 December 1832, Archives Archdioc. St Louis. RG.1.B4 3A.

37 McSherry to Kenney, 29 December 1832; MPA, no ref. no.; copy IJA. Italics in text.

38 Jn. England to Rosati, 14 January 1833; A.A. St Louis. RG.1 B4 3A.

39 Roothaan to Kenney, 28 February 1833; no ref. number; copy IJA.

46 Kenney to McSherry, 14 January 1833; JAR. Maryl. 4.i.22, SLULA, R. 182.

40 Rosati to Kenney, 16 May 1833; no ref. no.; copy IJA. Italics as in text.

41 Kenney to McSherry, 14 January 1833; JAR. Maryl. 4.1.22, SLULA, R. 182.

42 Whitfield to Rosati, l9 March 1833, MPA; quoted by Garraghan, 1, p. 329, n. 34.

43 Kenney to McSherry, 20 July 1833, MPA, 210, F.6; copy IJA.

44 Ibid.

45 Kenney to Dubuisson, 22 July 1833, MPA, 210, F.1. Dubuisson was conscious of his own unsuitability for authority. He reminded the General, with regard to the bishopric, of his almost "complete breakdown" as rector of Georgetown. "To put me in government ... is to lay me open to a sort of anxiety ... dangerous for my poor head", Dubuisson to Roothaan, 18 July 1833, Baltimore; JAR. Maryl. 5.v.9, SLULA, R. 182.

46 Kenney to McSherry, 9 August 1833; MPA, 210, f.11.

47 Journal, November 1832.

48 Kenney to Mulledy, 2 November 1832; GUA, no ref. no.; copy IJA.

49 There are normally considered to be three orders of Greek classical architecture, Doric, Ionic, Corinthian; three derived orders, Tuscan, Doric Roman, Composite. See A. White & B. Robertson, *Architecture and Ornament* (London, 1990), p. 10.

50 Kenney to McElroy, 12 November 1832; MPA, 210.m.4. On "Grecian orders" see previous note.

51 Kenney to Mulledy, 15 November 1832; GUA. no ref. no.; copy IJA.

52 Kenney to Ryder, 16 November 1832; MPA, 210.m.4a.

53 Kennedy to Ryder, 3 December 1832, MPA, 210.m.8b.

54 Kenney to Dzierozynski, 3 December 1832, MPA, 210.m.8a.

55 Kenney to McElroy, 23 November 1832, MPA, 210.m.5.

56 Journal, 4 December on, 1832; IJA.

57 "*Giornale De Governo*", August 1832-March 1833.

58 McSherry to Kenney, 29 December; MPA; copy IJA.

59 Kenney to Haly, 18 January 1833, MPA, x.z.6.

60 M.C. Normoyle, *A Companion to a Tree is Planted*, letter No. 177, Generalite Archives Irish Christian Brothers, pp. 421-4. The Grace family were natives of Callan, Co. Kilkenny, as was Ed. Ignatius Rice. William Auburn Grace was one of ten children, of whom only two emigrated. William died 8 March 1840.

61 Ibid. Italics as in text.
62 Kenney to McElroy, 6 February 1833; MPA. 210.k.4.
63 Kenney to McSherry, 14 February 1833, JAR. Maryl. 5.1.2, SLULA, R. 182.
64 Kenney to McSherry, 20 February 1833, MPA, 210.k.5.
65 Roothaan to Kenney, 20 January 1833, MPA, 500:68.
66 Bp Kenrick to Kenney, 16 April 1833; copy IJA.
67 Dubuisson to Roothaan, 16 April 1833, MPA, 210.h.10.
68 Roothaan to Kenney, 28 February 1833; JAR. no ref. no.; copy IJA.
69 Kenney to Dzierozynski, 9 May; MPA, 210.g.2.
70 Journal, May 1833.
71 *Woodstock Letters*, vol. 60, pp. 250-1, quoting Kenney's entry in Goshenhoppen house-diary, 25 May 1833. Kenney signed himself "Peter Kenney, the Visitor Superior of the Mission in the United States". He was there from 13 May – letter to McSherry, 29 May, 1833; MPA, 210.g.41.
72 Kenney to McSherry, 29 May 1833; MPA, 210.g.41.
73 Kenney to McSherry, 30 May 1833; MPA, 210.g.5.
74 Journal, June (typed section).
75 Ibid.
76 Kenney to Esmonde, 7 June 1832; MPA, 210.f.1a.
77 Kenney to Roothaan, 12 June 1833; JAR. Maryl. 5.v.2, SLULA, R. 182.
78 Kenney to Mulledy, 22 June 1833; GCA; copy IJA. The "Yankee part" of Ireland was presumably the northern part , whence McElroy came.
79 Kenney to George Fenwick, 23 June 1833; MPA, 210.g.13.
80 *Woodstock Letters*, vol. 12, pp. 208-9.
81 Ibid.
82 Grivel to N. Sewall, 9 July 1833, White Marsh; MPA, 4-5-6, Grivel Letters, no. 134, SLULA, R. 138; and see *Woodstock Letters*, vol. 10, pp. 246 ff.
83 Kenney to Francis Neale, MPA, 210.f.2.
84 *Woodstock Letters*, vol. 12, "The Jubilee of the Province", p. 207.
85 Edward J. Devitt, "History of the Maryland-New York Province. IX. The Province in the Year, 1833" in *Woodstock Letters*, vol. lxii, no. 3.
86 Kenney to McSherry, 12 July 1833; MPA, 210.f.3.
87 Journal/Diary, 14-15 July (typed section).
88 Journal.
89 Kenney to McSherry, 16 July 1833, MPA, 210.f.4.
90 Kenney to McElroy, 19 July, St Joseph's, MPA, 210.f.5.
91 *Clongownian*, June 1904, vol. iii, no. 3, p. 55.
92 Francis Vepre to Kenney, 21 October 1840, Georgetown, IJA.
93 *Clongownian*, already quoted pp. 55-6.
94 Legal document, and deed witnessed by notary public, 9 August 1833; MPA ... z.64; copy IJA.
95 Fr. Bracken to Gahan, 6 November 1836, from Tullabeg, Gahan file, IJA.
96 Dubuisson to Roothaan, 25 July 1833; JAR. Maryl. 5.v.9, SLULA, R. 182.
97 Kenney to McSherry, 29(?) July 1833, N.Y., MPA, 210.f.8.
98 Kenney to Miss Denis, 27 July 1833, N.Y.; no call no. typed copy, IJA.
99 Kenney to Dubuisson, 28 October 1833, Hardwick Street, MPA, 210.d.21.
100 Kenney to McSherry, 9 August 1833, MPA, 210.f.11.

101 "Memoranda ...", IJA.

102 Kenny to McElroy, 13 September 1833, Liverpool; MPA, 210.d.4.

103 Ibid.

104 Kenney to McSherry, 13 September 1833, Liverpool; MPA, 210.d.2.

105 Kenney to McElroy, 13 September.

106 Kenney to Dubuisson, 28 October 1833; MPA, 210.d.21.

107 Kenney to Roothaan, 20 October 1833; JAR. Hib. 2.ii.5; copy IJA.

108 "Memoranda ..."; also Kenney to Roothaan, 20 October 1833.

109 Roothaan to Kenney, 21 September 1833, General to Provincials file, IJA.

110 Kenney to Roothaan, 20 October 1833; JAR. Hib. 2.ii.25; copy IJA.

111 Kenney to Richard Norris, provincial, 12 December 1833; EPA, Kenney Letters, No. 103, in vol. India, 1802-1911.

112 Kenney's special memorandum, 13 November 1833; IJA, re. St Leger's disclosure to him of the General's wishes and St Leger's unease about going to India.

113 Roothaan to Kenney, 10 December 1833, General to Provincials file, 1806-1869, IJA.

114 Kenney to Esmonde, 31 December 1833, IJA, typed copy: gives account of his letter to the General.

115 Roothaan to Kenney, 19 April 1834, General to Provincials file, 1806-69, IJA.

CONFIDANT AND ADVISOR TO NEW RELIGIOUS CONGREGATIONS

1 Kenny to E. Rice, 18 July/8 September 1832, from Barnum's Hotel, Baltimore, Generalate archives, Irish Christian Brothers, given by M.C. Normoyle in *A Companion to A Tree is Planted* (Dublin, 1977) private circulation, the Correspondence of Edmund Rice and his Assistants, 1810-42, no. 170, pp. 405ff.; italics mine.

2 Whitfield to Rice, 25 October 1828; ibid no. 97, pp. 208ff.

3 Br Ellis to Whitfield, 16 January 1829, ibid., pp. 224-5.

4 *A Tree is Planted*, by M.C. Normoyle, (Dublin, 1976) private circulation, p. 237.

5 Ibid., p. 136.

6 J.D. Fitzpatrick, *Edmund Rice* (Dublin 1945), pp. 125-6.

7 Kenney to Dr Murray, 21 January 1841; DDA, Murray Papers, file 33/35, "Christian Brothers 1823-1843".

8 Rice to Knowd, 2 November 1813, in *A Companion ...*, no. 4, p. 12.

9 Rice to Kenney, 11 May 1814; Arch. CWC; quoted in *A Companion ...*, pp. 17-20.

10 Normoyle in *A Tree is Planted*, pp. 156-8; and Br J.D. Burke's *The History of the Institute*, vol. 1, p. 32.

11 Br P.J. Leonard to Kenney, 17 January 1817, from North Monastary School re. Kenney's forthcoming arrival there; IJA, Gardiner Street papers, Christian Brothers file.

12 *A Tree is Planted*, p. 125.

13 Ibid., p. 136.

14 Ibid., p. 139.

15 Ibid., p. 480; and Burke's *History of the Institute*, vol. 1, p. 55.

16 *Hist. of Institute*, vol. 1, p. 54; *A Tree is Planted*, p. 143; "Facere et Docere" = To Do (make) and to Teach.

17 *Hist. Instit.*, ibid., p. 55.

18 Ibid., p. 57.

19 *A Tree is Planted*, p. 144.

20 *A Companion ...*, pp. 561-70.

21 Ibid., p. 117.

22 *A Tree is Planted*, p. 195.

23 Italics mine.

24 Dunphy to Kenney, 11 September 1827; Kenney to Dunphy, 13 September 1827, in *A Companion ...*, no. 87, pp. 181 ff.

25 *Hansard*, House of Lords, 2 April 1829, p. 56, quoted by Normoyle in *A Tree is Planted*, p. 228.

26 *A Companion ...*, no. 107, pp. 237-8.

27 Notably, Br Joseph Leonard, North Monastery, Cork, and associates, who attributed to Rice mental instability, eccentricity, and neglect of consultation.

28 De La Salle Archives, Rome, cited in *A Companion ...*, no. 119, pp. 272-3.

29 *A Tree is Planted*, p. 230.

30 Br M.C. Normoyle to Revd R. Burke Savage SJ, undated letter, IJA.

31 Kenney to E. Rice, 31 January 1826, in *A Companion ...*, no. 62, pp. 129-31.

32 Kenney to Rice, 18 July/8 September 1832; ibid., no. 170, pp. 405ff.

33 In *A Companion ...*, no. 117, p. 265.

34 A conflation of the description of his preaching given by S.A. (Sarah Atkinson) in *Mary Aikenhead, Her Life, Her Work, and Her Friends* (Dublin, 1879), p. 132; and *Life and Work of Mary Aikenhead, by a Sister of the Congregation* (London, 1925), pp. 23 to 4.

35 Mary Aikenhead to Sr M. Ignatius (Sweetman), 29 January 1849, Archives Ir. Srs. Charity (AISC), Dublin, letter no. 427.

36 *Life and Work of Mary Aikenhead*, p. 36.

37 Ibid., pp. 36-8.

38 Dr Murray to Aikenhead, 6 December 1815; ibid., p. 39.

39 S.A., *Mary Aikenhead ...*, p. 158.

40 Kenney to Dr Murray, 18/19 July, 1816, AISC 1/B/38; also IJA.

41 *Life and Work ...*, p. 44.

42 Ibid., p. 45; S. A., *Mary Aikenhead ...*, p. 163.

43 Excerpts on Second Method of Prayer from *The Spiritual Exercises of St Ignatius*, trans. L.J. Puhl (Maryland, 1960); and another translation by A. Mattola (Image Books, N.Y., 1963).

44 Aikenhead to M.C. (Mother Mary de Chantal), 11 August 1842, AISC., letter no. 105; also in *Letters of Mary Aikenhead* (Dublin, 1914), pp. 141-2.

45 *Life and Work...*, pp. 45-6.

46 Mrs O'Brien to Kenney, 23 April 1817; and 29 April, 1817, IJA, Kenney Papers.

47 Murray to Kenney, 15 April 1817, from London; IJA, ibid.

48 Text AISC, 1/C/40: "Sermon Preached by Father Kenney SJ, On the Occasion of the First Clothing Ceremony of the Religious Sisters of Charity", 24/9/1817.

49 Kenney to Aikenhead, 9 October 1822, AISC, 1/B/40.

50 *Life and Work ...*, p. 47; S.A., *M. Aikenhead ...*, p. 166.

51 *Life and Work ...*, pp. 50-51.

52 S.A., *M. Aikenhead ...*, p. 179.

53 Ibid., p. 180.

54 Kenney to Aikenhead, 26 September 1823, AISC, 1/B/41; also IJA.

55 Kenney to Aikenhead, 8 July 1826, AISC, 1/B/42; also IJA, Kenney Papers, file on Mrs Aikenhead and Irish Srs of Charity.

56 "Take and Receive" refers to a well known prayer in *The Spiritual Exercises of St Ignatius* at a point of great trust, generosity, and renunciation on the part of the retreatant: "Take, Lord, and receive all my liberty, my memory, my understanding and my entire will, all that I have and possess. You have given all to me; to you, Lord, I return it. All is yours; do with it what you will. Give me only your love and your grace, that is enough for me."

57 See *Life and Work ...*, p. 125.

58 Ibid., pp. 181-2.

59 Ibid., p. 182.

60 Ibid., p. 190.

61 Kenney to Aikenhead, 20 December 1836, to say the archbishop had appointed him "extra-ordinary confessor" of Stanhope Street and Sandymount in preparation for "the approaching renovation of vows". He planned to be at Stanhope Street on 30 December 1836; and at Sandymount on 4 January 1837. IJA, Kenney papers, file on Irish Sisters of Charity.

62 Correspondence of Kenney and Francis West SJ, ref. nos. 102, 103, 153 in vol. on "College of St Aloysius. St Ignatius, Preston, 1832-1903", English Prov. Archives; see too Kenney to Aikenhead, undated, AISC, 1/13/43.

63 Kenney to Aikenhead, 4 September 1835, AISC, 1/B/44. Italics in text.

64 *Life and Work ... Aikenhead*, p. 182.

65 Ibid., op. cit. p. 184.

66 See DDA, Nicholson file, letter to Dr Murray, 17 July 1837.

67 Aikenhead to Mother Mary de Chantal, 21 June 1837, in *Letters of Mary Aikenhead*, p. 79.

68 *Life and Work ... Aikenhead*, p. 188. The letter no longer seems to be extant.

69 Nicholson to Murray, 17 July 1837, DDA, Nicholson file.

70 DDA, Nicholson file. Summary profile by Mary Purcell.

71 Ibid.

72 Aikenhead to de Chantal, 2 June 1837, *Letters of Mary Aikenhead*, p. 75.

73 Ibid., 9 August 1837, p. 82.

74 *Life and Works ...*, p. 189.

75 Dr Oliver to Kenney, 10 December 1837, IJA, Kenney Papers; italics mine.

76 *Letters of M. Aikenhead*, p. 76.

77 *Life and Work ...*, p. 190.

78 *Joyful Mother of Children*, by a Loreto Sister (Dublin, 1961), pp. 64-68; and Henry J. Coleridge, *Life of Mother Frances Mary Teresa Ball* (Dublin, 1881), pp. 28-9, 35 and elsewhere.

79 S.A., *Mary Aikenhead ...*, p. 181.

80 *Joyful Mother of Children*, p. 127; Coleridge, pp. 88-95.

81 See ch. vii: the years after his first Visitation of American Jesuits.

82 *Joyful Mother. . . ,* p. 131.

83 Typed sheets in IJA entitled: "Consideration of Four Cardinal Points of Spiritual

Life", with handwritten note "Fr Kenney Retreat 1815". Kenney Papers, file on religious congregations; italics mine.

"THE MODERN APOSTLE OF DUBIN"

1 Revd W. Meagher, *Life of Archbishop Murray*, p. 90.
2 Roothaan to Kenney, 19 April, 1834, at 5 Hardwick Place, arr. 5 May; IJA, General to Provincials file op. cit.
3 Kenney to Esmonde, 19 May 1834, IJA, copy from CWCA.
4 Dr M. Slattery to Kenney, c/o Esmonde, Clongowes, 3 June 1834; IJA, Kenney papers: Bishops letters.
5 *Catholic Penny Magazine*, 12 July 1834, vol. 1, p. 227.
6 Kenney to Esmonde, 4 August 1834; IJA, Kenney papers.
7 Kenney to McElroy, 7 August 1834; MPA, 211.t.7.
8 Kenney to Esmonde, 11 August 1834; IJA, Kenney papers.
9 Kenney to Glover, 9 October 1834; transcr. IJA.; EPA. Irl./USA, Kenney Corresp. 1808-41, SO/1.
10 Kenney to Esmonde, 14 December 1834; IJA, copybook in Kenney papers.
11 Kenney to R. Haly, 2 January 1835; IJA, Kenney papers, typed copy.
12 Br Roger of Taizé, *Struggle and Contemplation. Journal 1970-72* (Oxford, 1983), p. 32.
13 *Bona Mors* or "Happy Death": a confraternity of people who meet regularly to pray for a happy death – i.e. a death where one feels prepared to meet one's God.
14 A "general confession" referred to the confession of the sins of one's whole life in a summary way: usually after many years away from the sacrament, the priest assisting the penitent's memory by reference to adherhence to the ten commandments etc.
15 Kenney to Glover, 5 January 1835; EPA, Irl./USA, Kenney Corresp. SO/1. Italics mine.
16 Kenney to P. Ferley, 13 January 1835, IJA, Kenney papers, copy.
17 *The Catholic Penny Magazine*, from 15 February 1834 to 25 April 1835, p. 127.
18 Ibid., from Pastoral Letter of Dr Murray, 20 February 1835, pp. 112-3.
19 Ibid., p. 114.
20 Ms. notes in IJA.
21 Kenney to Esmonde, 12 March 1835, IJA, copy from CWC archives.
22 Ibid.
23 Roothaan to Kenney, 21 March 1835, IJA, General-Provincials, 1806-69; copy in Kenney papers.
24 St Leger to Esmonde, 13 September 1832; CWC archives.
25 Kenney to Esmonde, 11 June 1835; IJA, Kenney papers.
26 Kenney to Bracken, 10 December 1835; IJA.
27 Haly to Aylmer, 12 November 1835, IJA; copy in Kenney papers.
28 Bishop Jn. Bigs to Kenney, 13 December 1835; IJA, Kenney papers, Bishops letters.
29 Kenney to Bird or Parker(?), 26 January 1836; EPA, Kenney Corresp., SO/1.
30 Bird to Kenney, 3 February 1836; IJA.

31 Ibid.

32 *Irish Catholic Directory*, 1836, p. 80.

33 Roothaan to Kenney, 17 March 1836; IJA, Generals' Letters.

34 Kenney to Mulledy, 4 April 1836; MPA, 211.k.9. A letter sent through Mrs Ferrelly going to visit her son at Georgetown.

35 This must refer to April, as he was writing on 1 May.

36 Kenney to Aylmer, 1 May 1836; IJA.

37 Roothaan to Bracken, 19 May 1836; IJA, Bracken papers; copy in Kenney papers.

38 Ibid., 3 October 1836; IJA, File: Generai-Provincials, 1806-1869; copy in Kenney papers.

39 Ibid., 19 May

40 Roothaan to Bracken, 18 November 1836, ibid.

41 Kenney to Roothaan, 22 June, 1836; JAR. Hib. 2.iii.6.

42 Kenney to Bracken, 2 July, 1836; IJA.

43 *Lewis's Topographical Dictionary of Ireland*, vol. 1, p. 532 (London, 1837).

44 M. Craig, *Dublin 1660-1860* (Dublin, 1969 ed.), graph of Dublin population, p. 341.

45 Kenney to James McCarthy, 8 August 1836; MPA, 211.h.4.

46 McSherry to Kenney, 27 September 1836; IJA.

47 Kenney to Abp. Slattery, 18 November 1836, Papers Abp. Michael Slattery, Cashel, at Abp's House, Thurles, NLI, microfilm no. 6001-2.

48 He exchanged letters with friends, acquaintances, past students, or fellow Jesuits in, among other places, North America, Australia, India, Italy, France, and Britain.

49 Kenney to Dr Oliver, 13 November 1836; IJA. See Appendix.

50 Dr Oliver. A special interleaved edition in Stonyhurst archives of *Collections Towards Illustrating The Biography of the Scotch, English, and Irish Members, sj*, (1838), with an account of Kenney's career, obviously written later, interleaved between pp. 236-37.

51 The slow and deliberate delivery may have been related to his asthma: part of an attempt to pace, control, his breathing.

52 IJA, Reminiscences of Kenney by Dr Whitehead, in Ed. Hogan's handwriting. Whitehead was born 1807, and died 1879. Walter McDonald, DD, a student under him, in his *Reminiscences of a Maynooth Professor* (London, *c*.1921), pp. 33-34, spoke of his stilted speech and formality of manner.

53 The essay was found among Murray's papers, and in the Ms. he noted himself that it was written between 1863 and 1869, but if, as he said, it was not 20 years since he saw Kenney it must have been written before 1861.

54 R. Burke Savage, "Fr. Peter Kenney, 1779-1841" in *The Irish Jesuits* (collection of articles, 1962 for private circulation), p. 96.

55 *Irish Ecclesiastical Record*, xii, 1891, pp. 794-99.

56 IJA, typed Ms. notes by R. Burke Savage.

57 Ibid.

58 Interview conducted by Ed. Hogan after O'Ferrall had retired from being governor of Malta. IJA, Kenney papers.

59 J. Greene sj, "A Contribution towards a History of the Irish Province sj" in *Memorials of the Irish Province*, vol. 1, January 1903, p. 313.

60 IJA, Burke Savage typed notes in Kenney papers; also Greene passim in *Memorials of Irish Jesuit Province.*

61 J.H. Newman, *Grammar of Assent* (N.Y., 1959), pp. 89-90.

62 *I.E.R.*, xii, 1891, Murray, p. 704.

63 Dr Oliver, *Collections towards Illustrating etc*, interleaved edition, Stonyhurst archives, between pp. 236-7.

64 Greene, "Further Testimonials to Fr Peter Kenney, SJ" in *Memorials of the Irish Province*, vol. I, pp. 300ff; and see Meagher, *Life of Archb. Murray*, pp. 90-93.

65 L. McRedmond, *Thrown Among Strangers. John Henry Newman in Ireland* (Dublin, 1990), pp. 129-30.

66 Kenney to ?, 13 February 1837; IJA, Kenney papers; recipient's name and address not given.

67 Alymer to Kenney, 24 February 1837; IJA.

68 Bracken to Kenney, 3 March 1837, Bracken file; copy in Kenney papers.

69 Kenney to Bracken, 20 March, 1837; Bracken folder, IJA; copy in Kenney papers.

70 Dr Oliver to Kenney, 10 December 1837; IJA, Kenney papers. Italics mine.

71 Kenney to Bracken, 20 March, 1837; IJA, Bracken file.

72 Kenney to Aylmer, 6 April 1837; ibid.

73 Kenney to Aylmer, 18 April 1837; IJA, Aylmer folder.

74 Roothaan to Bracken, 15 July 1837; IJA, Bracken file; copy in Kenney papers.

75 Dr Oliver to Kenney, 10 December 1837, from Exeter; IJA.

76 Robert Haly to Fr John Greene, 22 March 187?, typed copy in Kenney papers, IJA.

77 Autobiography of Archbishop Ullathorne, *From Cabin Boy to Archbishop* (London, 1941), p. 103.

A CONCILIATING VOICE

1 Fitzgerald to Kenney, 27 April, 1838, IJA, Kenney Papers. Italics mine.

2 Richard Mulcahy to Kenney, 1 August 1838, ibid.

3 *Irish Catholic Directory*, 1838, p. 18.

4 Roothaan to Bracken, 19 June 1838, IJA, Generals to Provincials file.

5 The canal bridge was about ¼ mile away.

6 Kenney to Bracken, 13 March 1838; IJA, Bracken papers.

7 Aylmer to Kenney, 30 November 1838; IJA, Aylmer papers.

8 Bracken to Roothaan, 27 January 1839; JAR. Hib. 2.iv.21; copy IJA.

9 Roothaan to Bracken, 8 December 1838; IJA, Generals to Provincials.

10 P.J. Dowling, *A History of Irish Education* (Cork, 1971), pp. 118-19.

11 See McGrath, T., "Archbishop Slattery and the Episcopal Controversy on Irish National Education, 1838-1841" in *Archivium Hibernicum*, xxxix, 1984, p. 18; also Dowling, pp. 117-18.

12 Slattery to unnamed clergyman, March 1841, Cashel Diocesan Archives 184/9; quoted by McGrath, p. 19.

13 J. McCaffrey, *Hist. of Catholic Church in the Nineteenth Century*, 1789-1908, vol. II (Dublin, 1910), pp. 223-4

14 P.C. Barry, "The Holy See and the Irish National Schools" in *Irish Ecclesiastical Record*, xcii, 1939, pp. 91-2.

15 P.C. Barry, pp. 92-3.

16 Ibid., p. 93.

17 Glover to Kenney, 15 February 1840; IJA, Kenney papers.

18 Acta S. Congregationis de Prop. Fide, 1839, f. 216v-219v; quoted by Barry, p. 94.

19 R. Lythgoe to Kenney, 13 November 1839; IJA, typed copy Kenney papers.

20 Crolly to Murray, 4 August 1839, DDA, Murray papers, 31/7.1839. Murray to Cullen, 13 March 1839 and 24 February 1840; quoted by E. Larkin, "The Quarrel Among the Roman Catholic Hierarchy over the National System of Education in Ireland, 1838-41". Publication in *The Humanities*, Number 68, MIT, 1965, p. 131.

21 Kenney to Glover, 30 January 1840; EPA, Irl/USA, Kenney Corresp. 1808-41, SO/1; copy IJA. Italics as in text save for "animadversions".

22 P. Mac Suibhne, *Paul Cullen and His Contemporaries*, vol. 1 (Naas, 1961), p. 227.

23 "I am a human being, and nothing human is foreign to me."

24 T. Glover to Kenney, 15 February 1840, IJA. Italics in text save for final paragraph.

25 Cullen to McHale, 12 January 1840, in *Paul Cullen and His Contemp.*, vol. 1, pp. 226-7.

26 Acta SCPF. 1840, f. 420; quoted by Barry, p. 98.

27 Barry, pp. 98-9.

28 Cullen to Fransoni, 7 August 1840, in MacSuibhne, *Paul Cullen and His Contemporaries*, vol. 1, p. 230.

29 Acta SCPF. 1840, f. 419v, f. 472v-3; quoted by Barry, pp. 100-1.

30 Acta SCPF. 1841, f. 150; quoted by Barry, p. 103.

31 Acta SCPF. 1846, f. 265; quoted by Barry, p. 104.

32 M. C. Normoyle, *A Tree is Planted*, 1976 ed.; and the works of correspondence: *A Companion to a Tree is Planted*, (1977); and *The Roman Correspondence, 1803-44* (1978).

33 *Irish Catholic Directory*, 1838, p. 298.

34 Normoyle, *A Tree is Planted*, p. 227.

35 Ibid., p. 243.

36 Ibid., p. 319.

37 Ibid., p. 314.

38 Ibid., p. 317.

39 Kenney to Dr. Murray, 31 December 1840, DDA, Murray papers, 33/5. File on Christian Brothers.

40 Normoyle, op. cit. pp. 345-6: opinion of Dickson, 15 August 1839, from C.B., General Archive.

41 Normoyle, p. 349.

42 Bernard Dunphy to Murray, 26 November 1840, DDA; quoted by Normoyle, p. 350.

43 Normoyle, p. 350.

44 Br Riordan to Kenney, undated, CBGA; quoted by Normoyle, pp. 350-51.

45 Normoyle, pp. 351-2; opinion of Dickson, 9 October 1839.

46 Kenney's reply, undated, CBGA; quoted by Normoyle, p. 352. Italics mine.

47 Ed. Rice to Dr. Murray, 14 September 1840; DDA; quoted by Normoyle, pp. 352-3.

48 Memoirs of Br T.J. Hearn, CBGA; quoted by Normoyle, p. 319.

49 Normoyle, pp. 321-2.

50 Ibid., Appendix XVIII, pp. 462-4.

51 Kenney in the course of his letter to Dr Murray, 21 January 1841, DDA, Murray papers 33/5, file on Christian Brs 1823-43.

52 Normoyle, pp. 330-31.

53 Ibid., p. 331.

54 Riordan to Cullen, 15 November 1842, Arch. Ir. College Rome, Cullen Corresp. no. 754; quoted by Normoyle, p. 470.

55 B. Dunphy to Murray, 26 November 1840, DDA, C.B.'s file; quoted by Normoyle, p. 333.

56 Normoyle, pp. 333-4.

57 In DDA, 23 July 1840; quoted by Normoyle, pp. 334-5.

58 Normoyle, p. 337.

59 Ibid., p. 338.

60 Ibid., pp. 354-5.

61 Letters and Decrees of Sacred Congreg., 1840, vol. 324, f. 877, 7 September 1840; ref. Normoyle, p. 355.

62 Normoyle, p. 356. The number had fallen to 17, as Ennis school had closed for want of funds.

63 Br B. Dunphy to Dr Murray, 26 November 1840, DDA, Murray papers, Christian Brs. file; quoted by Normoyle, p. 356.

64 Normoyle, pp. 243-4. Joseph Leonard seemed to have lost any reverence for the person and position of his superior. He spoke of the superior general and assistants as "Rice and Co.", and rejoiced at scoring at their expense, 1830. On Kenney's recent return, he commented: "Our taskmasters are in high spirits since his arrival."

65 Italics mine.

66 Kenney to Murray, 31 December 1840; DDA, Murray papers, 33/5, C.Brs file.

67 One of the eight might well remind him, had they known, of his own efforts to obtain exemptions in order to have Jesuit pay schools!

68 Kenney to Dr Murray, 21 January 1841; DDA, Murray papers, C.Brs file, 33/5.

69 Normoyle. pp. 366ff., 372.

70 Italics mine.

71 Letter of Kenney? 9 February 1841; CB Gen. Arch.; quoted by Normoyle, p. 362.

72 Letter of Kenney? 9 February 1841, DDA, Murray papers, 33/5, in Christ. Brs. file.

73 Doc. in DDA, Murray papers 33/5.

74 Normoyle, p. 363, who notes that B. Dunphy was suffering from cancer.

75 Italics mine.

76 Normoyle, pp. 358, 465-6.

"...TOWARDS THE PEBBLED SHORE"

1 *Irish Catholic Directory*, 1840, p. 342.

2 Haly to Bracken, 7 January 1839; Bracken folder, IJA.

3 Kenney to Bracken, 20 January 1839; IJA, Bracken folder

4 Bracken to General, 31 August 1839; JAR. Hib. 2.iv.27.

5 Kenney to Bracken, 11 July, 1839; IJA, Bracken folder.

6 Bracken to General, 31 August 1839.

7 McEnroe to Kenney, 17 August 1839; Kenney Papers, IJA.

8 O'Connell to P.V. Fitzpatrick, 8 August 1839, from London, in *Correspondence of Daniel O'Connell*, vol. 1, ed. W.J. Fitzpatrick (London, 1888), pp. 194-5.

9 Roothaan to Bracken, 22 August 1839, IJA, File: General-Provincials.

10 Bp Cantwell to Kenney, 6 June 1840, Kenney papers, IJA.

11 A. Cogan, *History of the Diocese of Meath*, vol. III, p. 432.

12 Kenney to Dr Crotty, 1 July 1840, CWCA; copy IJA.

13 See Hogan, E.M., *The Irish Missionary Movement. A Historical Survey, 1830-1980,* (Dublin/Washington D.C., 1990), pp. 13-16; and Condon, K., *The Missionary College of All Hallows, 1842-91* (Dublin, 1988), p. 26.

14 *Irish Catholic Directory*, 1840, pp. 355, 229; and Hogan.

15 *New Catholic Encyclopedia*, xi (Washington D.C., 1967), pp. 844-6.

16 Du Bourg to Bp Plessis, Quebec, 26 August 1820; quoted by Garraghan, *The Jesuits of the Middle United States*, vol. 1, pp. 312-13.

17 *Irish Catholic Directory*, 1840, pp. 229, 355; 1841, p. 194.

18 Kenney to Glover, 29 September 1840; EPA. Irl/USA, Kenney Corresp. 1808-41, SO/1.

19 Roothaan to Bracken, 5 December 1840, refers to the letter of 15 October, IJA, General to Provincials file.

20 Myles V. Ronan, *An Apostle of Catholic Dublin, Father Henry Young* (Dublin, 1944), p. 242.

21 *Freeman's Journal*, 24 October 1840.

22 *Irish Catholic Directory*, 1841, p. 279.

23 Kenney to Esmonde, 26 December 1840; IJA. Kenney papers.

24 Belvedere House, according to Kenney's letter, was bought , through F. Charles Young, from a son of Lady Belvedere, who had inherited the property.

25 Kenney to Esmonde, 26 December 1840; IJA, Kenney/Bracken papers.

26 R. Haly to Fr John Greene, 22 March 187?; IJA, Kenney papers.

27 Vespre to Kenney, 21 October 1840; typed copy in IJA. Italics in text.

28 Elet to Kenney, 4 May 1841, from St Francis Xavier's College; IJA, Kenney papers. Italics as in text.

29 Garraghan, *The Jesuits of the Middle United States*, vol. iii, pp. 558-60.

30 W.S. Murphy to Bracken, 5 May 1841, IJA, Bracken folder. Italics as in text.

31 Kenney to T. Mulledy, at Jesuit College, Nizza (Nice), 6 September 1841; copy IJA.

32 Notes in Kenney's hand relating to Gardiner Street, from 1832-41, in marble coloured copybook containing accounts and some letters, IJA. Kenney papers.

33 The date of his departure is given in Kenney to Glover, 22 October 1841; EPA, Ireland/USA, Kenney Corresp. 1808-41, SO/1; the refs. to his visit to the Sisters of Charity are in *Mary Aikenhead, Her Life, Work and Friends*, by S.A., p. 303; and in *The Life and Work of Hary Aikenhead*, p. 243.

34 Louis Bourdaloue was one of the most celebrated Jesuit preachers of seventeenth century France; Robert Bellarmine was a famous sixteenth/seventeenth-century Jesuit theologian, who was made a cardinal, and declared a saint and doctor of the Church.

35 Kenney to Haly, 14 October 1841; IJA, Kenney papers, typed copy. Italics as in text.

36 Kenney to Glover, 22 October 1841, from Lyons; EPA, Irl./USA, Kenney Corresp. 1808-'41, So/1; copy IJA.

37 From "Fragmentum Diarii, P. Kenney, 21-28 October 1841", typed copy, IJA, Kenney papers.

38 Kenney to Matilda Denis, 2 November 1841; IJA, typed copy. It was not completed till some days later.

39 Fragment of Diary.

40 Kenney to Denis,

41 Ibid.

42 Ibid.

43 Esmonde to Miss Denis, from the Gesu, Rome, 22 November 1841, not sent till 29th; IJA, Esmonde papers; copy Kenney papers.

44 John Greene, "A Contribution Towards a History of the Irish Province of the Society of Jesus" in *Memorials of the Irish Province*, vol. 1, no. vi, January 1903, f.n. p. 314; also in R.Burke Savage sj, "A Modern Apostle of Dublin, Fr Peter Kenney" in *The Irish Jesuits*, vol. 1, p. 100 (private circulation, Dublin).

45 *The Constitutions of the Society of Jesus*, trans. & comment. by G.E. Ganns sj (St Louis 1970) "The General Examination and its Declaration", ch. 4; "Some Observances within the Society", p. 103 (84); & see f.n. 17; also part III, ch. 2. on "The Preservation of the Body", p. 167.

46 John W. O'Malley, *First Jesuits* (Harvard, 1993), p. 352, & cf. pp. 350-3

47 Ibid., p. 351.

48 IJA, Kenney papers, bound copybook entitled: "Points of Meditation for Religious" addressed to young Jesuits in a consideration on "The Three Classes of Religious and Election" in seeking the grace to choose and pursue the greatest perfection of your state of life", pp. 37ff. The scripture ref. for the talk was Mt. 16:24.

49 Ref. in Greene, "Towards a Hist. of the Irish Prov ...".

50 R. Burke Savage in *The Irish Jesuits*, p. 100.

51 Wm. Meagher, *Life of Most Rev Daniel Murray*, p. 92.

52 Murray to Haly, 3 December 1841,IJA, Haly papers; copy Kenney papers.

53 R. Burke Savage, ibid.

54 Mrs Molloy to Haly, 3 December 1841, from Belvedere Place; IJA, Haly papers.

55 M. Aikenhead to Mother Francis Magdalen (McCarthy), 3 December 1841, *Letters of Mary Aikenhead* (Dublin, 1914), p. 329

56 Aikenhead to Mother Mary Ignatius (Sweetman), 12 December 1841, in Archives of Ir. Srs. Charity, Letter no. 390.

57 Aikenhead to Mother De Chantal, 4 May, 11 August 1842, *Letters of Mary Aikenhead*, pp. 136, 141.

58 Aikenhead to Mother McCarthy, 4 July 1843, ibid., p. 330.

59 Aikenhead to Mother Sweetman, 29 January 1849, ibid., p. 424; and to De Chantal, 30 January 1849, p. 206.

60 Wm. Meagher, Life Dr Murray, pp. 89-90. Italics mine.

61 Lamennais , quoted by A.R. Vidler, *Prophecy and Papacy* (London, 1954), p. 284.

62 Jonathan Swift, "Verses on the Death of Dr Swift" in *50 Great Poets*, ed. Milton Crane (N.Y., 1961), p. 241.

63 Wm. Meagher, *Life of Dr Murray*, p. 93.

EPILOGUE

64 E.I. Devitt in *The Woodstock Letters*, lxii, no. 3, p. 342.

65 *The Poems of John Donne*, ed. Sir Herbert Grierson (Oxford, 1960 ed.), p. 350.

66 W.B. Ullathorne, *From Cabin Boy to Archbishop* (London, 1941), p. 103. He was visiting Ireland from Australia at the time. In 1850 he became the first bishop of Birmingham.

67 Stated in S.A., Mary Aikenhead, *Her Life, Her Work, Friends*, p. 304.

68 J.R. Clemo, From Epilogue to "The Wintry Priesthood" in *Penguin Poets 1951*, p. 184.

BIBLIOGRAPHY

PRIMARY SOURCES

SOCIETY OF JESUS

Archivum Romanum Societatis Jesu: Jesuit Archives Rome (JAR).

English Province Archives (EPA).

Stonyhurst Mss./Stonyhurst College Archives (SCA).

French Jesuit Archives, Paris: Grivel Papers. Transcripts.

Irish Jesuit Archives (IJA): Kenney Papers. Also Papers of Revds Aylmer, Bracken, Esmonde, Haly, St Leger; and a mixed collection, not fully catalogued at time of writing, termed Gardiner Street Papers from their location at the former provincialate there. Also collection entitled: Letters of Generals to Provincials; and part of the Burke Savage papers.

Clongowes Wood College Archives (CWCA): Letters, journals, diaries, brochures, various programmes, house histories.

Maryland Province Archives (MPA): Transcripts.

Georgetown University Archives (GUA): Transcripts.

St Louis University Library Archives (SLULA): Vatican Film Library: collection of Jesuit material from Jesuit Archives Rome in micro-film, esp. rolls 182, 184, 185; also on micro-film, the Maryland Province Archives.

Jesuit Archives, Missouri Province: Kenney's Memoriale, rules and customs, catalogues, annual letters, histories of the mission, miscellaneous papers, including the Helias papers, and "Historical Sketches of St Louis University" by Hill, W.

Archives, St Stanislaus Seminary/and Museum, Florissant, Missouri.

DIOCESAN ARCHIVES

Clogher Diocesan Archives (CDA): Anglade, Delahogue, McNally Papers.

Dublin Diocesan Archives (DDA): Troy, Murray, Hamil

Kildare and Leighlin Diocesan Archives (KLDA): Dr Doyle Papers.

Papers of Archbishop Slattery of Cashel: Microfilm in National Library of Ireland.

St Louis Archdiocesan Archives: Mainly Bishop Rosati papers, and part of his diary.

St Mary of the Barrens Archives, Perryville, Missouri: Souvay Papers, with further part of Rosati diary.

OTHER ARCHIVES

Archives George's Hill Convent, Dublin.

Archives Irish Sisters of Charity (AISC).

Dublin City Archives: Reports of the Wide Street Commission 1789-1790.

Transactions of the Corporation of Apothecaries (Ireland): Transactions 1747–95; Minutes 1791–96.

PRINTED SOURCES

RELIGIOUS CONGREGATIONS

Annali Siculi, vol. 1 (Annals of Sicilian Province SJ) ed. Narbone, A.

Christian Brothers, Archives of Generalate (CBGA): "The Correspondence of Edmund Rice and his Assistants, 1810–42" in *A Companion to a Tree is Planted* (Dublin, 1977), private circulation, and *Roman Correspondence, 1803-1844* (Dublin, 1978), private circulation, both edited by Normoyle, M.C.

Records of the English Province SJ, vii, by Foley, H. (London, 1882).

Letters and Notices of English Province SJ, vol. 2, 1864.

Memeorials of the Irish Province SJ, vol. 1 (Dublin, 1903).

The History of the Society of Jesus in North America: Documents, vols. 1 & 2, 1605-1838; ed. Hughes, T. (London/N.Y., 1908, 1910).

Letters of Mary Aikenhead (Dublin, 1914).

Life, Letters and Travels of Fr Pierre Jean de Smet, SJ, vol. 1, ed. Chittenden, H.M., and Richardson, A.T. (N.Y., 1905)

Oliver, Dr G., *Collections towards Illustrating the Biography of the Scotch, English, and Irish members SJ* (Exeter, 1838), interleaved edition, Stonyhurst Archives.

The Woodstock Letters – "A Record of Current Events and Historical Notes connected with the Colleges and Missions of the Society of Jesus", published at Jesuit Theological College, Woodstock, USA, vols. 5, 6,10-14, 16, 32, 33, 42, 58, 60, 62, 72, 88.

DIOCESAN SOURCES

Comerford, M., *Collections from Diocese of Kildare and Leighlin*, (Dublin, 1883).

Paul Cullen and His Contemporaries, with their Letters from 1820–1902, ed. Mac Suibhne, P. in 6 vols. (Naas, from 1961).

OTHER PRINTED PRIMARY MATERIAL

Correspondence of Daniel O'Connell, vols. 1-6 (Irish Univ. Press, from 1972), ed. O'Connell, M.

Correspondence of Daniel O'Connell, vol. 1 (London, 1888), ed. Fitzpatrick, W.J.

Diaries of Lord Colchester: Abbot, vol. 2 (London, 1861).

Documents of American Catholic History, ed. Ellis, J. Tracy (Milwaukee, 1956).

Documents of Church and State through the Centuries, ed. Ehler, S.Z. and Morrall, J.B. (London, 1954).

Irish Historical Documents, 1800–1990, ed. O'Day, A. and Stevenson, J. (Dublin, 1992).

Letters on the State of Ireland, no. III, by J.K.L. (Dublin, 1825).

Memoirs and Correspondence of Viscount Castlereagh (London, 1849).

The Catholic Question in England and Ireland, 1798–1822. The Papers of Denys Scully, ed. McDermot, B. (Dublin, 1988).

PARLIAMENTARY PUBLICATIONS

Hansard's Parliamentary Debates, May 1813, vol. 26; and ibid. May 1814, vol. 27.

Report from Select Committee on Laws in Foreign States respecting the Regulations of Roman Catholic Subjects in Ecclesiastical Matters, H.C., 25 June 1816, esp. Appendix no. XXII.

Report from House of Lords Committee "On the State of Ireland", Parliamentary Papers, 1825, viii.

Eight Report of Commissioners of Irish Education Inquiry. Roman Catholic College of Maynooth, H.C., 1827.

Sixth Report of Commissioners of National Education, 1839, H.C., 1840, vol. 28.

PUBLISHED MEMOIRS AND OTHER PUBLICATIONS CONTAINING RELEVANT
CONTEMPORARY DOCUMENTS

Arnold, M., *Edmund Burke on Irish Affairs* (London, 1881).

Battersby, W.J., *The Jesuits in Dublin* (Dublin, 1854).

Burke, Ed., *Burke's Works* (London, 1869).

Corcoran, T., *The Clongowes Record, 1814–1931* (Dublin, *c.*1932).

Curran, R.E., *The Bicentennial History of Georgetown University*, vol. 1, 1789–1889 (GUP, Washington D.C., 1993).

De Tocqueville, A., *Journey in Ireland*, trans. & edited by Larkin, E. (London/ Washington D.C., 1990).

Donnelly, Dr N., *A Short History of Some Dublin Parishes*, Pamphlet series, CTS (Dublin, 1909–13).

Faherty, W.B., *Better the Dream*, St Louis University and Community, 1818–1968 (St Louis Univ., 1968); *Dream By the River, Two Centuries of St Louis Catholicism, 1766–1967* (St Louis, 1973).

Fitzpatrick, W.J., *The Life, Times, and Correspondence of the Right Rev Dr Doyle*, vols. 1 & 2 (Dublin, 1890 ed.).

Garraghan, G.J., *The Jesuits of the Middle United States*, 3 vols., esp. vol. 1 (N.Y., 1938)

Gilbert, Lady (ed.), *Calendar of Ancient Records of Dublin*, xiv (Dublin, 1909)

Gruggen, G. & Keating, J., *History of Stonyhurst College* (London, 1901).

Healy, Dr J., *Maynooth College 1795–1895* (Dublin, 1895).

Hepburn, A.C., *The Conflict of Nationality in Modern Ireland. Documents of Modern History* (London, 1980).

Hill, B.W. (ed.), *Edmund Burke on Government, Politics and Society* (London, 1975).

Holt, G., *The English Jesuits 1650–1829. A Biographical Dictionary* (CRS Publication, 1984); and *William Strickland and the Suppressed Jesuits* (London, 1988).

MacDowell, R.B., *Irish Public Opinion 1750–1800* (London, 1944).

Maxwell, C., *Dublin under the Georges 1714–1830* (Dublin, 1946); and *Country and Town in Ireland under the Georges* (London, 1940).

Meagher, Wm., *Notice of the Life and Character of His Grace Most Revd Daniel Murray* (Dublin, 1853).

Phillips, C., *Recollections of Curran and Some of his Contemporaries* (London, 1822).

O'Beirne, F., *An Accurate Account of the Papal College of Maynooth* (Hereford, 1840)

Stevenson, J. (ed.), *The Irish Jesuits: Collection of Essays* (Private publication, 1952).

Tone, Wolfe, *Autobiography of ...*, ed. O'Faolain, S. (London, 1937)

Ullathorne, W.B., *From Cabin Boy to Archbishop* (London, 1941).

Wakefield, E., *An Account of Ireland, Statistical and Political*, vol. 1 (London, 1812).

Wall, M., "The Catholic Merchants, Manufacturers, and Trades of Dublin, 1778–82", based on Index to the Catholic Qualification Rolls, Irish Public Records Office, in *Reportorium Novum*, vol. 2 (Dublin, 1959–60)

The Year Book of the Parish of SS Michael and John's (1957).

Young, A., *A Tour of Ireland 1776–78*, vol. 1, ed. Hutton, A.W. (London 1892).

NEWSPAPER, PERIODICALS, AND SCHOLARLY JOURNALS: CONTEMPORARY OR DEALING WITH CONTEMPORARY ISSUES

Archivium Hibernicum, vols. 9, 31, 32, 36-39, 43, 47.

Archivum Historicum Societatis Jesu, lxi, January-June 1992 (Rome).

Catholic Historical Review, October 1988, January 1990, January 1992, July 1992 (CUAP, Washington D.C.).

Catholic Penny Magazine (weekly), esp. 12 July 1834 and 20 February 1835 (Dublin).

Clogher Record (Journal of the Clogher Historical Society), 1986, 1989.

Clongownian, esp. 1904, 1982, 1984.

Collectanea Hibernica (Sources for Irish History), nos. 21, 22 (1979, 1980), no. 30 (1988), and 33 (1991).

Watty Cox's Irish Magazine (1807-14), excerpts.

Dublin Evening Mail, 15 March 1826.

Dublin Magazine, March 1811.

Freeman's Journal, 21, 22 February 1811, 24 October 1840.

Hibernian Magazine, March 1811.

Irish Catholic Directory, 1836, 1838, 1840, 1841.

Irish Ecclesiastical Record (IER), xii, 1891, xcii, 1939, and October-November 1968.

Irish Jesuit Directory, 1942.

Irish Monthly, June 1874, vol. 18, 1890.

Irish Times, 12 May 1992.

Jesuit Bulletin, St Louis, October 1965.

Le Journal des Jougnards: "Decouverte Interessante", September 1836.

Knockbeg Centenary Book, (1893), Centenary of St Patrick's College, Carlow.

Limerick Reporter and Tipperary Vindicator, 4 September 1844, 16 November 1866, 16, 17 August 1869.

Reportorium Novum (Dublin Diocesan Historical Record), vol. 1 (1955), vol. 2 (1959-60).

St Louis Catholic Historical Review, vol. 5, April-July 1923.

Seanchas Ard Mhacha, 1982 (Journal of the Armagh Diocesan Historical Society).

Stonyhurst Magazine, April 1953.

Studies (Dublin), Winter 1993.

Waterford News, 23 September 1930, "Story of St Patrick's Church".

SECONDARY SOURCES

Anonymous, *A Glimpse of the Great Society* – "that the Jesuits are the secret and sworn enemies of all law and order ..." (London, 1825).

Anon., *A Roll of Honour*. Irish Prelates and Priests of the Last Century (Dublin, 1905).

Anon., *Life and Work of Mary Aikenhead, by a Sister of the Congregation* (London 1925).

Atkinson, S. (S.A.), *Mary Aikenhead: Her Life, Her Work, Her Friends* (Dublin, 1879)

Bannon, J.F., *The Missouri Province, SJ. A Mini-History* (St Louis, 1977).

Barry, P.C., "The Holy See and the Irish National Schools", *IER*, xcii, 1939.

Bartlett, T., *The Fall and Rise of the Irish Nation. The Catholic Question, 1690–1830* (Dublin, 1992); and "The Origins and Progress of the Catholic Question in Ireland, 1690-1830" in *Endurance and Emergence, Catholics in Ireland in the Eighteenth Century*, ed. Power, T.P. and Whelan, K. (Dublin, 1990).

Bascom, M., *Rose Philippine Duchesne* (N.Y., n.d.).

Basset, B., *The English Jesuits* (London, 1967).

Baunard, Abbé, *The Life of Mother Duchesne*, trans. Fullerton, G. (Roehampton, 1879).

Biever, A.H., *The Jesuits in New Orleans and the Mississippi Valley* (New Orleans, 1924).

Birch, P., *Saint Kieran's College, Kilkenny* (Dublin, 1951).

Bolster, E. "The Last Will and Testament of Archbishop Daniel Murray (*d.*1852)" in *Collectanea Hibernica*, combined nos. 21 and 22, 1979–80; and *A History of the Diocese of Cork. From the Penal Era to the Famine* (Cork, 1989).

Broderick, J., *The Holy See and the Irish Movement for the Repeal of the Union with England, 1829–1847* (Rome, 1951).

Bunn, E.B. (ed.), *"Georgetown." First College Charter from the US Congress, 1789–1954* (N.Y., 1954).

Burke, N., "A Hidden Church? The Structure of Catholic Dublin in the mid-Eighteenth Century", *Archivium Hibernicum*, xxxii, 1974.

Burke Savage, R., *A Valiant Dublin Woman* (Dublin, 1940); *Catherine McAuley* (Dublin, 1949); and "Fr Peter Kenney, SJ. A Modern Apostle of Dublin" in *The Irish Jesuits*, vol. 1 (Private publication, Dublin, 1962); "The Growth of Devotion to the Sacred Heart in Ireland" in *Irish Ecclesiastical Record*, October–November 1968; also "Clongowes 1814–17" in *Clongownian*, 1982, and "Clongowes 1815–1830" in *Clongownian*, 1984.

Callan, L., *Philippine Duchesne. Frontier Missionary of the Sacred Heart, 1769–1852* (Westminister, Maryland, 1965).

Chadwick, O., *The Victorian Church, 1829–1859* (London, 1987 ed.).

Clancy, T.H., *Review of American Catholic Preaching and Piety in the Time of John Carrol*, ed. Kupke, R.J. (Washington D.C., 1991), in *Archivium Historicum Societatus Jesu*, vol lxi (Rome).

Clemo, J.R., "The Wintry Priesthood" in *Penguin Poets*, 1951.

Coakley, P., "Most Rev James Doyle OSA, Bishop of Kildare and Leighlin, 1786–1834" in *A Roll of Honour* (Dublin, 1905).

Coldrey, B., *Faith and Fatherland. The Christian Brothers and the Development of Irish Nationalism, 1838–1921* (Dublin, 1988).

Coleridge, H.J., *The Life of Mother Frances Mary Teresa Ball* (Dublin, 1881).

Comerford, R.V., Cullen, M., Hill, J., Lennon, C., *Religion, Conflict and Coexistence in Ireland. Essays presented to Monsignor Patrick J. Corish* (Dublin, 1990).

Connolly, SJ, *Priests and People in Pre-Famine Ireland, 1780–1845* (N.Y., 1982); and *Religion and Society in Nineteenth Century Ireland* (Dublin, 1985).

Corcoran, T., *The Story of Clongowes Wood, 1450–1900* (Dublin, n.d.)

Corish, P.J., "Gallicanism at Maynooth" in *Studies in Irish History* (Dublin, 1979); *The Catholic Community in the Seventeenth and Eighteenth Centuries* (Dublin, 1981); "The Catholic Community in the Nineteenth Century" in *Archivium Hibernicum*, vol. 38, 1983; *The Irish Catholic Experience* (Dublin, 1985).

Costelloe, P., *Clongowes Wood. A History of Clongowes Wood College, 1814–1989* (Dublin, 1989).

Craig, M., *Dublin 1660–1860* (Dublin, 1969 ed.).

Crane, M.(ed.), *50 Great Poets* (N.Y., 1961).

Cullen, L.M., *An Economic History of Ireland since 1660* (London, 1976 ed.); and

"Catholic Social Classes under the Penal Laws" in *Endurance and Emergence*, ed. Power, T.P., Whelan, K. (Dublin, 1990).

Curran, R.E., "From Mission to Province, 1805–1833" in *The Maryland Jesuits 1634–1833* (Maryl. Prov. publicat., 1976), ed. Curran, R.E., Durken, J.T., Fogarty, G.P.; and " 'Splendid Poverty': Jesuit Slaveholding in Maryland, 1805–1838" in *Catholics in the Old South*, ed. Miller, R.M. and Wakelyn, J.L. (Macon, USA, 1983); and *Georgetown University, 1789-1889*, vol. 1 (Georgetown, 1993).

Daley, Jn. M., *Georgetown University: Origin and Early Years* (Washington D.C., 1957).

Daly, M.E., *Dublin. The Deposed Capital* (Cork, 1984).

Davis, Cyprian, *The History of Black Catholics in the United States* (N.Y, 1990).

Devitt, E.J., "History of the Maryland and New York Province" in *Woodstock Letters*, lxii.

de Vere, A., *Recollections of Aubrey de Vere* (London, 1897); and *English Misrule and Irish Misdeeds*, 2nd ed. (n.d.).

Donne, Jn., *Poems of …*, ed. Grierson, Sir H. (Oxford, 1960 ed.).

Dowling, P.J., *A History of Irish Education* (Cork, 1971).

Doyle, D.N., *Ireland, Irishmen and Revolutionary America, 1760–1820* (Dublin, 1981).

Edwards, F., *The Jesuits in England* (London, 1985); and "Expulsions and Suppressions of the Jesuits in the 18th Century as an European and Colonial Problem", paper read at Institute of Historical Research, London University, June 1991.

Eliot, T.S., *Selected Poems* (London, 1961).

Fagan, P., *Cornelius Nary, 1658–1738. Dublin's Turbulent Priest* (Dublin, 1991).

Faherty, W.B., *St Louis. A Concise History* (St Louis, 1990); also "Father Van Quickenborne: Religious Pioneer" in *Jesuit Bulletin* (St Louis), October 1965; *Jesuit Roots in Mid-America* (Florissant, 1980); *Jesuit Roots and Pioneer Heroes of the Middle West* (Florissant 1988).

Fitzpatrick, D., *Irish Emigration 1801–1921* (Dublin, 1984).

Fitzpatrick, J.D., *Edmund Rice* (Dublin, 1945).

Fitzpatrick, W.J., *Irish Wits and Worthies* (Dublin, 1875).

Giblin, C., "Papers of Richard Joachim Hayes, OFM, 1810–24, in Franciscan Library, Killiney: Part 1, 1810–15", in *Collectanea Hibernica*, nos. 21 & 22, 1979–80.

Greene, J. "Further Testimonies to Fr Peter Kenney SJ" in *Memorials of the Irish Province*, vol. 1, pp. 300 ff.; and "A Contribution Towards a History of the Irish Province SJ", ibid. p. 313.

Griffith, A. (ed.), *Meagher of the Sword* (Dublin 1917).

Guilday, P., *Life and Times of John England, 1786–1842* (N.Y., 1927).

Haile, M. and Bonney, E., *Life and Letters of John Lingard, 1771-1851* (London, 1911).

Hales, E.E.Y., *Revolution and Papacy, 1769–1846* (London, 1960).

Harney, M.P., *The Jesuits in History* (N.Y., 1941).

Hart, H.M., *Pioneer Forts of the West* (N.Y., 1981).

Harvey, K.J., "The Family Experience: The Bellews of Mount Bellew" in *Endurance and Emergence*, ed. Power and Whelan (Dublin, 1990).

Hempton, D.N., "The Methodist Crusade in Ireland, 1795–1845" in *Irish Historical Studies*, xxii, 1980–81.

Hennessy, M.N., *The Wild Geese. The Irish Soldier in Exile* (London, 1973).

Hogan, E.M., *The Irish Missionary Movement. A Historical Survey, 1830–1980* (Dublin, 1990).

Hutton, Edwd., *Cities of Sicily* (London, 1926).

Jeaffreson, J.C., *The Queen of Naples and Lord Nelson*, vol. 2 (London, 1889).

Jone, H., *Moral Theology* (Maryland, 1959).

Judge, R.K., "Foundation and First Administration of the Maryland Province" in *Woodstock Letters*, vol. 88, 1959.

Keenan, D., *The Catholic Church in Nineteenth Century Ireland. A Sociological Study* (Dublin, 1988).

Kelly, J., "The Parliamentary Reform Movement of the 1780s and the Catholic Question" in *Archiv. Hibernicum*, xliii, 1988.

Kelly, M.T., "Most Rev John MacHale, Archbishop of Tuam, 1791-1881" in *A Roll of Honour* (Dublin, 1905).

Kerr, D., "Charles MacNally, Maynooth Professor and Bishop of Clogher", *Clogher Record*, 1981; "Peel and the Political Involvement of the Priests" in *Archiv. Hibernicum*, xxxvi, 1981; "Charles MacNally: O'Connelite Bishop and Reforming Pastor", ibid., xxxvii, 1982.

Kuzniewski, A.J., "Francis Dzierozynski and the Jesuit Restoration in the United States" in *Catholic Historical Review* (January 1992).

Larkin, E., *The Historical Dimensions of Irish Catholicism* (N.Y., 1976); and *Alexis de Tocqueville's Journey in Ireland* (Dublin, 1990); "The Quarrel Among the Roman Catholic Hierarchy over the National System of Education in Ireland, 1838–41", in *The Humanities*, no. 68, MIT, 1965.

Laveille, E., *The Life of Father De Smet SJ, 1801–1873*, trans. Lindsay, M. (N.Y., 1915).

Leavitt, M., *A Short History of New Orleans* (San Fancisco, 1982).

Lecky, W.E.H., *History of Ireland in the Eighteenth Century*, vol. 2 (London, 1913).

Lighthart, C.J., *The Return of the Jesuits*, trans. from Dutch by Slijkerman, Jan J. (London, 1978).

Little, Dr G.A., *Rev John Austin SJ* (Dublin, 1960).

A Loreto Sister, *Joyful Mother of Children* (Dublin, 1961).

Macauley, A., "The Appointments of Patrick Curtis and Thomas Kelly as Archbishop and Coadjutor Archbishop of Armagh", *Seanchas Ard Mhacha*, 1982; *William Crolly. Archbishop of Armagh, 1835–49* (Dublin, 1994).

Maes, C.P., *Life of Rev Charles Nerinckx* (Cincinnati, 1880).

Melville, A.M., *Louis William Du Bourg*, vol. 2; *Bishop in Two Worlds, 1818–1833* (Chicago, 1986); and "John Carroll of Baltimore: A Bicentennial Retrospect" in *Catholic Historical Review*, lxxvi, January 1990.

Miller, K.A., *Emigrants and Exiles* (Oxford 1985); also Miller, K.A., Boling, B., Doyle, D.A., "Emigrants and Exiles: Irish Cultures and Irish Emigration to North America, 1790–1922" in *Irish Historical Studies*, xxii, 1980–81.

Miller, R.M. and Wakelyn, J.L. (ed.), *Catholics in the Old South* (Macon, USA, 1983).

Mulligan, P., "Dr James Donnelly: the Early Years" in *Clogher Record*, 1984.

Murphy, Ignatius, *The Diocese of Killaloe, 1800–1850* (Dublin, 1992).

Murray, Patrick, "Some Recollections of Fr Peter Kenney, SJ, as a Preacher" in *IER*, xii, 1891.

Newman, J.H., *Grammar of Assent* (N.Y., 1959 ed.).

Nolan, K.B. and O'Connell, M.R., *Daniel O'Connell, Portrait of a Radical* (Belfast, 1984).

Normoyle, M.C., *A Tree is Planted. The Life and Times of Edmund Rice* (private circulation, Dublin 1976).

North, R.G., *The General Who Rebuilt the Jesuits* (Milwaukee, 1944).

O'Brien, G., "Robert Peel and the Pursuit of Catholic Emancipation, 1813–17" in *Archiv. Hib.*, xliii, 1988.

O'Donoghue, P., "The Holy See and Ireland 1780–1803" in *Archiv. Hib.*, xxxiv, 1976–7.

O'Dufaigh, S., "James Murphy, Bishop of Clogher, 1801–1824" in *Clogher Record*, 1986.

O'Flaherty, E., "Ecclesiastical Politics and the Dismantling of the Penal Laws in Ireland, 1774-82" in *Irish Historical Studies*, xxvi, 1938.

O'Malley, J., *The First Jesuits* (Harvard, 1993).

O'Neill, T.P., "The Catholic Church and Relief of the Poor, 1815–1845" in *Archiv. Hib.*, vol. 31, 1973.

O'Tuathaigh, G., *Ireland before the Famine, 1798–1848* (Dublin, 1987).

Pare, G., *The Catholic Church in Detroit, 1701–1888* (Detroit, 1951).

Pastor, L. von, *History of the Popes*, vols. 37-9 (London, 1950–2).

Pirri, Pietro, *P. Giovanni Roothaan* (Rome, 1930).

Plowden, Francis, *The History of Ireland from its Union with Great Britain in January 1801 to October 1810* (Dublin, 1811).

Power, T.P., "Converts" in *Endurance and Emergence*, ed. Power, T.P. and Whelan, K. (Dublin, 1990).

Primm, J.N., *Lion of the Valley. St Louis, Missouri* (Colorado, 1981).

Purcell, M., "Sidelights on the Dublin Diocesan Archives" in *Archiv. Hib.*, xxxvi, 1981; and "Dublin Diocesan Archives: Murray Papers" in *Archiv. Hib.*, xxxix, l984; "Dublin Diocesan Archives: Hamilton Papers (2)", ibid., xlv, 1990; and "Hamilton Papers (4)", ibid., xlvii, 1993.

Ranke, L. von, *History of the Popes*, vol. 2 (London, 1907).

Roger, Br, *Struggle and Contemplation. Journal 1970–72* (Oxford, 1983).

Ronan, Myles, *An Apostle of Catholic Dublin. Fr Henry Young* (Dublin, 1944).

Russell, W.E., *Sydney Smith* (London, 1905).

Schauinger, H.J., *Cathedrals in the Wilderness* (Milwaukee, n.d.).

Sigourney, L.H., "The Return of Napoleon from St Helena" in *An American Anthology*, ed. Stedman, E.C. (N.Y., 1900).

Spalding, M.J., *Sketches of Life and Times of Rt Rev Benedict Joseph Flaget, First Bishop of Louisville* (Louisville, 1852).

Stanford, W.B., "Undertone" in *Penguin Book of Irish Verse*, ed. Kennelly, B. (London, 1981).

Swift, Jonathan, "Verses on the Death of Dr Swift" in *50 Great Poets*, ed. Crane, M. (N.Y., 1961).

Thackeray, W.M., *The Irish Sketch Book...* (London, 1879 ed.).

Twain, Mark, *The Way West*.

Tynan, M., *Catholic Instruction in Ireland, 1720–1950* (Dublin, 1985).

Veale, J., Review article on *The First Jesuits in Studies*, winter, 1993.

Vidler, A.R., *Prophecy and Papacy. A Study of Lamennais* (London, 1954); and *The Church in an Age of Revolution* (Pelican, 1977 ed.).

Wall, M., *The Penal Laws, 1691–1760* (Dundalk, 1976).

Wall, T., "Archbishop John Carpenter and the Catholic Revival, 1770–1786" in *Reportorium Novum*, vol. 1, no. 1, 1955.

Wangler, T.E., Review of *Living Stones: The History and Structure of Catholic Spiritual Life in the United States*, by Chinnici, J.P. (N.Y., 1989), in *Catholic Historical Review*, July 1992.

Warburton, Whitelaw, and Walsh, *History of the City of Dublin*, vol. 2 (London, 1818).

Ward, M., *Young Mr Newman* (London, 1948).

White, A. and Robertson, B., *Architecture and Ornament* (London, 1990).

Williams, M., *The Society of the Sacred Heart, 1800–1975* (London, 1978).

Williams, T.D., "O'Connell's Impact on Europe" in *Daniel O'Connell. Portrait of a Radical*, ed. Nolan, K.B. and O'Connell, M.R. (Belfast, 1984).

WORKS OF MORE GENERAL REFERENCE AND BACKGROUND

Bangert, W.V., *A History of the Society of Jesus* (St Louis ,1972).

McRedmond, L., *To the Greater Glory: A History of the Irish Jesuits* (Dublin, 1991).

The Constitutions of the Society of Jesus, trans. Ganss, G.E. (St Louis, 1970).

Rules of the Society of Jesus (Roehampton ed., England, 1865).

The Spiritual Exercises of St Ignatius Loyola, trans. Puhl, L.J. (Westminister, Maryland, 1960).

The New Catholic Encyclopedia, vol. 6 (Washington D.C., 1967).

Sacramentum Mundi. An Encyclopedia of Theology, vol. 4 (London, 1969).

Jedin, H. (ed.), *History of the Church*, vols. 6-8 (London, 1981).

D'Arcy, F. and Hannigan, K., *Workers in Union. Documents on Irish Labour* (Dublin, 1988).

A New History of Ireland, vols. 5 and 7 (Oxford 1989, 1982).

Foster, R.F., *Modern Ireland, 1600–1972* (London, 1988).

Lewis's Topographical Dictionary of Ireland, vol. 1 (London, 1837).

Miller, Wm., *A New History of the United States* (N.Y., 1969 ed.).

INDEX

De Neckere, Leo, bishop of New Orleans
296, 297, 326
Denis, Miss Matilda 127, 120, 289, 317,
341f, 360, 437-8, 442 443-44
Dens, Pierre, theologian 283

De Smet SJ, Peter 279, 282, 297, 311f, 433;
ills. 20, 21
De Theux, John Theodore, Jesuit superior
in Missouri 259, 280, 282; consultor to K
as Visitor 282; intractable and inflexible
283f, 288, 291, 294, 301; trustee of St
Louis University 302; his 'odious suspi-
cion' of K 307, 308; neglectful of De
Smet (q.v.) 312, 331de Tocqueville,
Alexis 215
de Vere, Aubrey 218
Dinan (Dynan) SJ, William 25, 51, 67, 69,
77, 88f, 112, 194, 385, 394, 396
Dixon, Revd. T.W. 96
Donahue, pastor at St Joseph's, Philadelphia
334
Donoughmore, earl of 105, 106, 109
Douglas, Isle of Man 381, 382
Doyle, James Warren, bishop of Kildare and
Leighlin ('J.K.L.') 15, 194, 195, 196ff,
204, 230, 264, 354, 374, 400
Drogheda town 194
Dublin in late 18th century 4f
Du Bourg, Louis, bishop of St Louis 177,
277, 298, 311, 427
Dubuisson, Stephen, French emigré, president of Georgetown College 146, 214;
proposed by K as assistant during his
American visit 232; appointed a consultor
by General 238, 249, 251, 254; opposed
to sale of farms 263; regarded by K as
neurotic 265; praises K 270; a possible
bishop 326f; helps K at Philadelphia
334f, 340; taken ill 376; now procurator
of Maryland, he meets K in Paris 435,
437
Duchesne, St Rose Philippe 157, 278, 279f;
ill. 14
Dunboyne Castle 90
Dunn, Fr, "Daddy", former Jesuit 183, 184,
354
Dunphy, Austin, Irish Christian Brother
355, 409, 412, 415
Dunphy, Bernard, Irish Christian Brother
409-16 *passim*, 422
Dwyer, secretary of Catholic Association
217

Dwyer, John, Jesuit novice 440
Dzierozynski SJ, Francis, new (1819) superi-
or of American mission, recently come
from Russia 142; his kindness to K at
Bologna 214; a consultor during K's
second American visit 237 (when K
acted as superior) 238; attitude to day
scholars and tuition fees 243; his piety
and care 244, 245; 249; his view of K
251, 320, 259; saw Jesuit plantations as 'a
perpetual good' 264; too indulgent
towards novices 269, 280

Easton, Penn. 258, 261
Eccleston, Samuel, archbishop of Baltimore
266
Edelen SJ, Leonard 145, 151, 156, 162, 169,
174
Edgeworth, Maria 122
Elet SJ, John 279, 280, 282, 432
Ellis, Patrick, Irish Christian Brother 353f,
409
Emigrant, SS 272
Emmetsburg, Penn. 254
England, John, bishop of Charleston 15,
165, 268, 325, 335, 351
Ennis, John, parish priest of Booterstown,
Dublin 403, 405, 407
Erskine, Cardinal 46
Esmonde SJ, Bartholomew, comfortable
background 66; his father, Dr John
Esmonde, was executed in Dublin (1798)
101; as a young priest, present at restora-
tion of Jesuits (Rome, 1814) 112; ships
three tons of books to Ireland 120; due
to ill health, stayed with his brother Sir
Thomas in Waterford 125f; K ready to
send him to England 125; returns to
Clongowes and is appointed consultor
127; complains about K to Visitor and
General 130; unhappy with K's lifestyle
and 'broad views 132f; 136; argues with
Bishop Doyle re restriction of faculties
198ff; rector of Clongowes 211, 224;
preaches jubilee in Clare 213; K runs
gauntlet of Esmonde's criticism 228ff,
374; reassures K re cholera 216; receives
credit for Gardiner Street Church 345;
ineffective rector of Clongowes 380f, 385,
403, 430; his poignant account of K's last
days 439, 448
Esmonde, Sir Thomas 125